B U S I N E

BUSINESS
PRINCIPLES, GUIDELINES, AND PRACTICES

John M. Ivancevich
*Hugh Roy and Lillie Cranz Cullen Profressor
of Organizational Behavior and Management,
University of Houston*

Thomas N. Duening
*Director, Center for Entrepreneurship and
Visiting Assistant Professor of Management,
University of Houston–Downtown*

ATOMICdogPUBLISHING

Cincinnati, Ohio
www.atomicdog.com

Library of Congress Control Number: 2003105480

ISBN 1-59260-043-3

Printed in the United States of America by Atomic Dog Publishing,
1148 Main Street, Third Floor, Cincinnati, OH 45202-7236.

10 9 8 7 6 5 4 3 2 1

Brief Contents

Contents

Focus Boxes

Preface

Business as a field of interest and study has and continues to make a dramatic impact throughout the developed and developing world. Today and into the foreseeable future, many college students will continue to either major in a business discipline or take courses in the business school or in some other professional unit that offers introductory business courses. *Business: Principles, Guidelines, and Practices* originated with the view that conducting business is exciting, challenging, and globally oriented. The excitement of starting your own business, investing in a company, or negotiating a new car deal are part of the daily menu of how business is conducted in New York, Madrid, Tokyo, Lima, Hong Kong, or Sydney.

The challenges of learning about and conducting business are interesting and rewarding. Most people believe that they have common business sense. People also believe they know how business is transacted and understand the laws that pertain to business, which are bandied about in informal conversation. As this book clearly shows, business transactions are sometimes simple and sometimes very complex. Commonly accepted business practices in one country are considered unethical or even illegal in another country. Business is not mysterious, but as you will learn, it is not always based on simple common sense.

The global, technological, and consumer orientation of business is a part of every reader's daily life. Clothing, food, transportation, entertainment, electronics, and service industries are booming around the globe. Countries that are thousands of miles from the United States are providing products and services that have become household names. Sony, Nestle, Mercedes, and Heineken are just a few of the common foreign brands. Although the United States is a powerful market-system-oriented country, there are a growing number of countries such as Germany, Canada, China, South Korea, India, Singapore, and Japan that are competing head-on with the United States for customers, market share, and resources.

As we move further into the twenty-first century, the business world will become more global. New markets are opening in Latin America, Africa, Eastern Europe, and the Pacific Rim. The American economy is becoming more dominated by service businesses, and *quality* is the initiative of many firms. Even though business scandals occur, social responsibility and ethical practices are emphasized as the way business must be conducted. Demographic and lifestyle shifts are changing the way we shop, where we work, and how we live. Students who understand the business environment and the changes occurring will be more likely to succeed than those who do not. This book uses principles, guidelines, and practices to illustrate and frame how business impacts our lives every single day as employees, consumers, and owners.

ORGANIZATION OF THE BOOK

Business: Principles, Guidelines, and Practices is organized into six parts that provide students with an integrated and practical approach to understanding business. Every chapter fits logically into this integrated approach and is relevant and timely. Part 1 provides an overview of the foundation of business, the business enterprise, discussing the economics, global transactions, forms of business ownership, small business, entrepreneurship, franchising, the law, and ethics. Part 2 focuses on managing the business and on the management of production and operations. Part 3 examines the management of human resources, as well as human relations. Part 4 covers marketing strategy, including product, price distribution, and promotion decisions. Part 5 is devoted to accounting and information systems. Part 6 explores the financial management of business firms.

FEATURES OF THE BOOK

The book has several features that add an action orientation and are challenging to teach. The book is purposefully written to provoke critical thinking about business principles, guidelines, and practices. Students can use the following learning tools to help them understand and use the material to critically analyze business principles, guidelines, and practices.

- **Learning objectives.**   Each chapter begins with several clear, attainable learning objectives; questions in the test bank are keyed to these objectives.

- **Illustrations.**   Numerous charts, graphs, diagrams, and photos reinforce and explain concepts in the text.

- **Marginal notes.**   Definitions of key terms are placed in the margins next to where the terms are introduced to facilitate learning.

1 ☞
- **Suggested websites.**   Company URLs are provided at the end of most chapters. An icon and number appears in the margin next to the company names, which are highlighted within the text.

- **Summary of learning objectives.**   The chapter summary is concise yet complete. Each item in the summary is tied to the corresponding chapter opening learning objective to provide a cohesive, integrated chapter review.

- **Key terms.**   A list of key terms at each chapter's end helps students identify and review important concepts.

- **Questions for discussion and review.**   Students can use these questions to evaluate their understanding of the chapter.

- **Glossary.**   Key terms and their definitions may be quickly located in the comprehensive end-of-book glossary.

- **Name, subject, and company indexes.**   Topics in the book can be easily located with the name, subject, and company indexes.

This textbook also offers several application elements that will engage students so that they can relate the text material to their own experiences and apply the concepts in the text to the real world of business.

- **Opening Vignettes.**   The text of each chapter begins with a current news story that introduces students to the chapter's topics.

- **Business Applications.**   Each chapter features a story that focuses on recognizable firms and contemporary topics, extending the concepts discussed in the text.

- **Assessments.**   A number of the chapters feature a short self-assessment quiz that helps students evaluate their attitudes, orientations, and values as they pertain to business.

- **Focus elements.**   Each chapter uses a number of focus elements to emphasize technology, diversity, ethics, the future, small business, or some other relevant area of business. These are company-, industry-, or person-specific focus stories.

- **Real world examples.**   Current examples of practices in large, medium, and small organizations and how business issues impact people are used throughout each chapter to relate the text to the real world.

- **Cases.**   One current, realistic case at the end of each chapter helps students put business concepts into practice.

- **Internet Exercises.**   Each chapter includes a "to do" Internet experience so that students can search, find, and analyze data, knowledge, and information. The experience will help students become more comfortable with business sites and databases.

- **Experiential Exercises.**   Each chapter contains what we refer to as "hands-on" individual and/or group projects. Working alone or with others on relevant topics will help each reader view business from a more personal perspective.

Online and in Print

Business: Principles, Guidelines, and Practices is available online as well as in print. The online chapters demonstrate how the interactive media components of the text enhance presentation and understanding. For example,

- Animated illustrations help to clarify concepts.
- *QuickCheck* interactive questions and chapter quizzes test your knowledge of various topics and provide immediate feedback.
- Clickable glossary terms provide immediate definitions of key concepts.
- Highlighting capabilities allow you to emphasize main ideas. You can also add personal notes in the margin.
- The search function allows you to quickly locate discussions of specific topics throughout the text.

You may choose to use just the online version of the text, or both the online and print versions together. This gives you the flexibility to choose which combination of resources works best for you. To assist those who use the online and print versions together, the primary heads and subheads in each chapter are numbered the same. For example, the first primary head in Chapter 1 is labeled 1-1, the second primary head in this chapter is labeled 1-2, and so on. The subheads build from the designation of their corresponding primary head: 1-1a, 1-1b, etc. This numbering system is designed to make moving between the online and print versions as seamless as possible.

Finally, next to a number of exhibits in the print version of the text, you will see an icon similar to the one on the right. This icon indicates that this exhibit in the online version of the text is interactive in a way that applies, illustrates, or reinforces the concept.

ANCILLARY MATERIALS

Instructor's Manual

John Bowen and Hal Babson, Columbus State Community College, created a complete instructor's manual. The instructor's manual provides a master plan for implementing the various instructional tools provided with this textbook. Each chapter of the instructor's manual includes: (1) chapter overview, (2) list of resources, (3) learning objectives, (4) lecture outline, (5) answers to questions for discussion and review, (6) list of key terms with definitions, (7) case notes, and (8) exercise notes.

PowerPoint® Presentations

Four hundred PowerPoint® presentations available for classroom use of text materials were created by Rick Bartlett and Hal Babson, Columbus State Community College.

Test Bank

Murray Brunton and Hal Babson, Columbus State Community College, created a test item file that is available in the ExamView® Pro format. ExamView® Pro enables instructors to quickly create printed tests using either a Windows or Macintosh computer. Instructors can enter their own questions and customize the appearance of the tests they create. The test bank contains 2,100 questions.

ACKNOWLEDGMENTS

We are grateful to Steve Scoble, Dan Jones, Vickie Putman, Laurie McGee, Alex Von Rosenberg, and the entire Atomic Dog Publishing team. They each have, because of their professionalism, made this book's preparation and delivery a pleasant and enjoyable experience.

Peggy Adams of Applied Management Sciences Institute served as the coordinator, manager, and preparer of the book. Her ability to manage and lead the two authors has been exceptional. Schedules, reviews, and changes were ably handled by Peggy. We thank her for everything.

We would like to thank the following colleagues for reviewing *Business: Principles, Guidelines, and Practices*. We appreciate their contributions.

Imad Samarah, *Southern Illinois University–Carbondale*
Steve Norman, *The University of Colorado–Colorado Springs*
Dennis Foster, *Northern Arizona University*
Edward Fritz, *Nassau Community College*

John M. Ivancevich

Thomas N. Duening

DEDICATION

This book is dedicated to our families, starting with the very top managers and leaders, Pegi Ivancevich and Charlene Duening.

About the Authors

Dr. John M. Ivancevich is currently the Hugh Roy and Lillie Cranz Cullen Chair in Management at the University of Houston. As a part of a continuing academic career as distinguished professor, dean, provost and recognized authority in management, John (Jack) Ivancevich is currently working on teaching, textbooks, professional books, field research, and developing Web-enabled courseware products and services.

As Dean of the College of Business Administration 1988–1995 and Provost 1995–1997, Jack was recognized for his leadership in academic program building, fund raising, curriculum reform, the development of innovative programs in entrepreneurship, dispute resolution and environmental concerns, and initiating international exchange and degree programs with institutions in Europe and the Far East.

Jack joined the UH faculty in 1974 as professor in the College of Business Administration. Previously, he taught at the University of Maryland and the University of Kentucky. In 1975, he became Chair of the Department of Organizational Behavior and Management and was named Associate Dean for Research in 1976, where he was responsible for stimulating research activities and the creation of the school's first information technology support center. In 1979 Jack was awarded the Hugh Roy and Lillie Cranz Cullen Chair of Organizational Behavior and Management.

Jack has a B.S. in Industrial Management from Purdue University, an MBA in Organizational Behavior from the University of Maryland, and a DBA (Doctor of Business Administration) in Administrative Behavior and Organizational Analysis, also from the University of Maryland.

He is the author or co-author of over 60 textbooks and 150 refereed articles in management, human resource management, and organizational behavior and an increasing library of Web-enabled courseware on management and organizational behavior, which are used by educational and corporate institutions around the world. Jack serves on a number of boards of business associations and organizations and is a reviewer and member of editorial boards for a number of academic journals. He has conducted research, training and consulting in over 100 firms of all sizes.

He is the recipient of numerous awards, among them the Esther Farfel Award, UH's highest faculty award; The Academy of Management's Hall of Fame, as one of the first 33 charter members for recognition of research and productivity; the Presidential Service Award from the UH Alumni Organization; the University of Houston Law Alumni Association Faculty Award. He is listed in the *Who's Who Registry of Global Business Leaders*.

Dr. Thomas N. Duening is the director of the Center for Entrepreneurship at the University of Houston–Downtown and visiting assistant professor of management. He formerly served as assistant dean of the C.T. Bauer College of Business, from 1991–2000. Tom is an active author, having written both management and business trade books as well as management textbooks. His trade publications include *Managing Einsteins: Leading High Tech Workers in the Digital Age* (Chicago: McGraw-Hill, September 2001), and *Always Think Big: Mattress Mac's Principles of Management and Marketing* (Chicago: Dearborn, May 2002). Tom is also the author or co-author of several management and organizational behavior college-level textbooks: *Management 2.0: Managing in the 21st Century* (Cincinnati: Pinnaflex, 2000) and *Managing Organizations: Principles and Guidelines* (Cincinnati: Atomic Dog, 2002). Tom has published numerous articles in business journals, magazines, and newspapers, and popular media often seeks his views on management, business trends, and other issues. Tom also consults broadly with firms of all sizes in business development and strategy. Dr. Duening has MA and PhD degrees from the University of Minnesota.

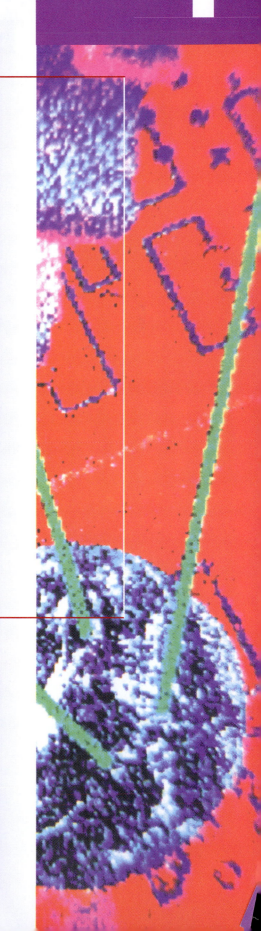

part 1

Foundations of Business

1

Business and Economics

Photo: comstock.com

Chapter Objectives

After completing this chapter, you should be able to:

1   **Comment** on the study and importance of business and define business in your own terms.

2   **Explain** why people are the key to any business.

3   **Identify** the four main objectives of business.

4   **Explain** why profit is important to the owners of a business.

5   **Describe** and compare the three types of economic resources.

6   **Distinguish** between planned and mixed market economic systems.

7   **Determine** how gross domestic product (GDP) is calculated.

American Business Influence

In the past twenty years U.S. companies have aggressively expanded their business overseas. One sees McDonald's arches, Coca-Cola signs, and Dell computers all over the globe. Foreign companies have quietly adopted many American business practices. The number of foreign companies listed on the New York Stock Exchange (NYSE) increased from 96 in 1990 to 434 in 2001.

Will the trend to Americanize continue even after the September 11, 2001, terrorist attack? Although some companies are pushing back against the American way of transacting business, the rules of global business have spread too far and too wide. Paola Fresco, Fiat's chairman in Turin, Italy, states, "The only durable business model that works is American." John Viney, European chairman of the executive search firm of Hiedrick & Struggles, proposes that "America is the only country in the world that has a business culture. Most other countries struggle. But Americans have no great strain about whether they are doing the right thing about making money. . . ."

The dominance of American business took hold after World War II, when companies such as IBM, Kellogg, Ford, Pfizer, General Foods, and Alcoa began expanding overseas. This growth introduced millions of foreigners to American business practices.

In former communist countries, bankers and consultants who preached about privatization and entrepreneurship pushed the conversion to American business methods. The communist populations were starved for new methods and new ideas as well as for more Western consumer goods.

Juergen Schrempp of Germany's Daimler Chrysler set off a revolution in the non-American corporate establishment by listing Daimler on the NYSE in 1993. Although many non-American CEOs warned him that the Securities and Exchange Commission rules governing the NYSE were too restrictive and cumbersome, Schrempp wanted to plant his feet right in the middle of the U.S. financial establishment to learn firsthand how to compete for financial resources.

Many other non-American CEOs have followed Schrempp's lead and are doing many things the American way. At India's Tata Steel, the CEO has instituted bonuses based on performance. Royal Dutch/Shell has reconfigured its entire office work flow area with glass walls to make executives more accessible and has promoted more women to encourage a diversity of views in decision making.

Of course there are critics of doing business like Americans. There have been rejections of the supremacy of shareholder opinions, participative management, and rigorous quarterly reporting systems. Some consider these American standards to be too general, unproven in terms of improving effectiveness, and contrary to the authority of executive-level managers.

Sources: Janet Guyton, "The American Way," *Fortune.com*, November 26, 2001; Brian O'Keefe, "Global Brands," *Fortune.com*, November 26, 2001; and David K. Carr, Kelvin J. Harx, and William J. Trahant, *Managing the Change Process* (New York: McGraw-Hill, 1996).

1-1 INTRODUCTION

A full analysis of the geopolitical, social, and economic effects of the destructive and fatal September 11, 2001, terrorist attacks on the New York World Trade Center and the Pentagon will take years to unfold. Certainly these attacks will have an impact on business, business transactions, and business contacts. This book is about business, economics, and worldwide markets in a world that is exciting, challenging, and intent on upgrading the lives of billions of people in developing nations. A safe estimate is that despite a new era of terrorism economic transactions will still occur across borders and across oceans. The world is so interconnected in terms of telecommunications, markets, and business transactions that understanding how business is conducted will remain a top priority.

Each day business is conducted within and between countries. Even a devastating terrorist act or wars cannot stop business transactions from occurring. During the intense bombing attacks in December 2001 around Kandahar, Afghanistan, street merchants continued to market their products. Bombs, bullets, bandits, soldiers, and many citizens with weapons did not stop consumers from coming to the market to purchase food, blankets, water, or whatever meager inventory the Afghani street merchants had to sell.

The future of business is impossible to predict with certainty. Instead of using projections, it is more accurate to understand the forces that are reshaping how business is conducted in the world. The fundamental forces, which are discussed again and again throughout this book, are technology, globalization, demographics, freedom, and education.

Within these five fundamental forces lie the elements of how business is transacted. For example, technological changes extend human capacity, while the spread of freedom multiplies the choices people have in selecting goods, services, and careers.

As the opening vignette suggests, the United States is considered a land of business opportunities from New York to Chicago to Houston to Los Angeles to Honolulu. There are problems, deficiencies, serious questions and issues, and many challenges facing Americans and their institutions. However, as this book illustrates clearly, there is a lot of vitality and growth left in American businesses and the U.S economic system.[1] We believe enough evidence shows that the United States will continue to be a major economic power, certainly one of the top four countries in the world in terms of productivity, standard of living, quality of life, and job opportunities.

As of 2003 about 134 million Americans were in the workforce. This workforce has significant buying power that influences how business is transacted. However, not only Americans have buying power that influences trends in business. A number of trends that likely will extend through the first decade of the twenty-first century include the following:

- The average business firm will become smaller than today's enterprise, employing fewer people.
- The changes in American and worldwide consumer tastes and needs will continue to place a special emphasis on the quality of goods and services.
- Technicians, ranging from computer repair specialists to radiation therapists, will replace manufacturing technicians as the worker elite.
- The key role of business will continue to shift from making a product to providing a service.
- Work itself will require continuous relearning, more high-order thinking, and less routine or working a nine-to-five job.
- An increasing amount of training, education, and recertification will be done through e-learning; that is, instead of relying solely on traditional instruction, employees will upgrade and improve by using e-learning.
- Different races, ethnic groups, cultures, and languages will be more valued in more culturally diverse countries.
- The information superhighway (the national information infrastructure) will grow in importance each day, with managers, entrepreneurs, and workers learning how to use the information it makes available.

Resources, knowledge, and talent fueled the world's economic growth in the twentieth century. It is likely that we have only begun to see what technology, globalization, demographics, freedom, and education can accomplish. These five forces have the potential to improve the standard of living and the quality of life for more people than ever before in the history of human beings. A key concept is the word *potential*. Unless the world's resources and business acumen are used effectively, the gap between the world's advantaged and less-advantaged citizens will grow. A growing gap will likely lead to more poverty, unrest, uncertainty, and turmoil. The world's political leaders and policymakers need to harness resources, knowledge, and business talents so that more people can benefit from what business can provide.

U.S. business will need to develop workers, technology, and markets to remain a powerful force in the global marketplace. Reinventing and renewing the way business is transacted across oceans, telecommunications networks, or negotiating tables will

---

1. Michael Hammer, *The Agenda* (New York: Crown Business, 2002).

require new ideas, new ways of performing work, and new workers.[2] Students should openly consider the tremendous range of opportunities available to them. They should ask themselves: What skills will I need to become a productive contributor to the business opportunities that are available? What do I have to learn in order to work for an employer in a global business or to operate my own business?

The way Americans conduct, negotiate, and transact business has been copied, vilified, praised, misunderstood, and debated. Without question, the American way of business can be improved; however, to borrow from the words of Mark Twain, rumors of its death have been greatly exaggerated. Actually, it works exceptionally well compared with other systems around the world. U.S. business has helped provide Americans with a relatively high standard of living in both *goods*, such as homes, cars, and clothing, and *quality of life*, such as a free public education system and clean environment. The freedoms enjoyed by U.S. businesses and consumers are typically not appreciated until they are compared with the lack of such freedoms in Cuba, North Korea, Libya, and Iraq.[3]

This chapter begins with a discussion of why the study of business is important. We explain how people—owners, managers, employees, and consumers—form the core of business. Next we discuss the business objectives of survival, growth, social responsibility, and profit. The discussion of profit leads to a description of economics and economic systems. We also present some challenges and issues that must be addressed both today and in the future to ensure the continuing success of U.S. business. The final section of the chapter explains how the organization and structure of the book will guide the student through the study of business.

1-2 YOUR CURRENT BUSINESS IQ— BEST IN CLASS

The world's largest, most powerful, and most influential economy is the U.S. economy. Much of what is known about it, however, is not fully understood or is based on conventional judgment. This is not for lack of information. Daily newspapers, television programs, movies, books, and trade publications bombard the public with business data, information, and stories. Unfortunately, the bits and pieces of information are not coherently organized and are difficult to interpret. Studying business and how it is conducted can be more informative and coherent if the field of business is presented in an accurate, straightforward, and dynamic manner.

Before we start to present the world of business, it is important to determine how much the bits and pieces of information have influenced your thoughts and thinking. Try the quiz in the Focus on Business box, "Check Your Business IQ," to obtain feedback regarding your current knowledge of business. By the end of the book we will have succeeded as authors—and you as students—if your knowledge about business has increased.

Everyone in society should have at least some knowledge of business. You have probably determined that there is a lot to learn about business. The course and this book will help you build up your business knowledge. Are you ready now to start the journey toward becoming business intelligent? Why do you need to learn about business and how it is conducted around the world?

1-3 WHY LEARN ABOUT BUSINESS?

A liberal arts major, an engineer, and a business major will all eventually end up working in a business, owning a share of a business, or transacting business with an enterprise. It doesn't matter what course of study a person undertakes or which college degree or diploma a person earns; eventually, he or she will be engaged in some form of business

2. Yves Doz, Jose Santos, and Peter Williamson, *From Global to Metanational* (Cambridge, MA: Harvard Business School Press, 2001).

3. Robert E. Litan, Paul Masson, and Michael Domerleano, *Open Doors* (Washington, DC: The Brookings Institution, 2001).

FOCUS ON BUSINESS

Check Your Business IQ

Directions

It is interesting to trace your progress as you learn about a subject. This quiz is designed to help you measure your business knowledge as you start the course.

Answer the questions; then turn to the Feedback section. Score one point for each correct answer.

1. What does the gross domestic product (GDP) measure?
2. In the United States, which industry spends the most on advertising?
3. The United States annually imports more goods and services than it exports. By what amount do imports exceed exports?
4. What does liquidity mean?
5. The consumer price index (CPI) calculates inflation. What would $1 in 1913 value buy at the supermarket today?
6. What is a flextime work schedule?
7. What does the term ESOP mean?
8. What is a *direct* channel of product distribution?
9. What is the most powerful American brand name in the world?
10. Where is the European Union (EU) headquarters?

Feedback

How do you think you did on the quiz? The questions were not tricky, but you had to be knowledgeable about current events to score a perfect 10. Here are the answers:

1. Gross domestic product (GDP) measures the market value of all final goods and services produced by resources located within the United States.

---

activity. The person may be a worker in a business or provide consulting expertise to a firm or purchase an automobile from a dealer that provides the best price.

A **business** is any activity that attempts to earn a profit by providing goods and services to others. The person who is aware of and knowledgeable about and who understands business can function better in a society built on business enterprises than an individual who is not educated about businesses and business transactions. Learning about business through education, training, attending seminars, self-improvement, and observation can improve a person's ability to live and work in society.

Business The exchange of goods, services, or money for mutual benefit or profit.

1-3a Protecting and Improving Our Standard of Living

One reason to study business is to protect our way of life. Americans, Europeans, Canadians, and most people in the world take great pride in being free and independent. Because of the independence, hard work, and values embodied in business institutions, citizens enjoy a comfortable standard of living. Exhibit 1-1 presents a sampling of a few standard of living indicators across four countries. The United States leads in all indicators except life expectancy, which presents an interesting dilemma to policymakers. Are Americans getting soft because they possess more goods, eat too many McDonald's french fries, or do not engage in enough physical work and exercise?

2. The automotive industry spends the most at about $1.7 billion annually.

3. U.S. imports exceed exports by more than $300 billion. This is referred to as a trade deficit.

4. Liquidity is a measure of how quickly any item, such as a car, can be converted into cash.

5. You could purchase about $17.95 worth of 2002 merchandise with a 1913 dollar.

6. A flextime work schedule allows workers to vary their starting and quitting times. It is used by one in eight full-time workers.

7. The acronym ESOP stands for Employee Stock Option Plan. Nearly 10 million employees own ESOPs, which means they own part of their companies.

8. It is the movement of goods directly from the producer to the consumer. An example would be a farmer selling produce at a roadside stand.

9. Coca-Cola. It is found all over the world.

10. The EU headquarters is in Brussels, Belgium.

How did you do?

0–5 You are not yet familiar with some business concepts or issues, but that's why we're here. There is some work to be done.

6–8 Not a bad beginning. With some work, you can be really knowledgeable.

9 Outstanding. Not perfect, but really a great beginning.

10 Wow, you might be one in a thousand. Don't get too excited, because a lot of areas were not included in the quiz. Take a bow, but it is time to go to work and learn more.

EXHIBIT 1-1

Standard of Living Indicators

	Life Expectancy	Schooling Mean Years	Number of People Per:			
			Doctor	TV	Telephone	McDonald's
U.S.	75.9	12.3	404	1.2	1.3	28,000
China	70.1	4.8	724	37.5	76.9	384,000,000
Japan	78.6	10.7	609	1.6	1.9	130,000
Hong Kong	77.3	7.0	933	4.0	1.6	95,000

We need to understand the contributions of business and also to learn how to maintain an acceptable standard of living for future generations. **Standard of living** describes the amount of goods, services, and quality of life that an average family or individual can achieve with its income. The standard of living of each generation of Americans has been better than the previous generation. How has this happened? We believe that a minimal amount of government interference and a free market business system have been the major reasons for perpetuating a high standard of living. This free market system, called **free enterprise,** means that private businesses are able to organize and conduct business activities competitively with minimal government regulation. As a result of this system, the productive activities of people have been as free as possible.

Standard of Living A measure of how well a person or family is doing in terms of satisfying needs and wants with goods and services.

Free Enterprise A system in which private businesses are able to start and do business competitively to earn profits, with a minimal degree of government regulation.

The Heritage Foundation has found that the freedom found in a nation is a critical factor in its relative wealth.[4] The Foundation has calculated an "index of economic freedom" for 101 nations. Just 43 nations (e.g., Hong Kong, Singapore, Bahrain, U.S., Japan) were found to have "free" ratings. The index, the first comparative analysis of its kind, measures the degree of economic freedom each country allows on such areas as trade policy, taxation policy, property rights, regulations, and foreign investment. A few of the most economically repressed countries (eight were identified) were Sudan, Mozambique, Cuba, and North Korea. The index provides some evidence that countries with the highest level of economic freedom also have the highest living standards.

1-3b Coping with Change

Business is dynamic—always changing. Coping with both predictable and unpredictable events can be easier, more efficient, and less traumatic if we understand business. Prices increase or decrease, products are added, needs change, services are created to meet needs, laws are passed, and unexpected events occur—for example, stock market crashes, rapid growth of Wal-Mart, the stunning demise of Enron, new digital technology, and the elimination of layers of management hierarchy. Changes are occurring at a rapid rate, and the need to cope with them is becoming increasingly important in conducting business intelligently.

1-3c Understanding Mutual Dependence

Over the years, people have become more and more dependent on one another. This book is about understanding mutual dependence, using the business system effectively, and being a part of business. As stated earlier, *business* is the exchange of goods, services, or money for mutual benefit or profit. Years ago, our ancestors discovered that producing everything one needs occasionally requires doing some undesirable work. They also discovered that individuals have various traits, needs, and skills. If a person specialized in a particular job, such as making shoes or growing corn, the surpluses produced could be traded for other desirable goods. Today, the business conducted in and among the United States, Canada, Great Britain, Germany, Japan, and other countries is more complicated than trading shoes for corn.

Few people today produce everything they need or use; a complex division of labor has encouraged us to not be self-sufficient. For example, you buy food at the local supermarket. You drive a car manufactured in Dearborn, Michigan. You use fuel pumped from oil wells in west Texas. You go to schools built by carpenters, bricklayers, ironworkers, and cement workers. You watch news programs produced in Atlanta, Georgia. You wear clothing designed in Milan, Italy. You pitch baseballs manufactured in Haiti.

4. Jeff Wurorio, CNBC *Guide to Money and Markets: Everything You Need to Know About Your Finances and Investment* (New York: John Wiley, 2001).

1-3d Realizing Global Opportunities

The new era of business performance in the global marketplace requires leaders who know how to start, operate, and sustain businesses. Business negotiations, joint ventures between companies in different countries, travel across borders, investment across geographical boundaries, and working for foreign-owned enterprises are becoming commonplace. To function in such a world, each of us must understand the principles of business.

1-3e Preventing Misconceptions

Understanding business also prevents accepting misconceptions, misinformation, and inaccurate data as truths. Many people still believe that Japan has the number one economy, that the average U.S. business earns 15 percent profit, that most new jobs are created by large business, and that most Japanese managers have guaranteed jobs for life. Each of these assumptions is inaccurate.

1-4 PEOPLE: THE KEY TO BUSINESS

The human element is the key to any business. Business needs people as owners, managers, employees, and consumers. People need business for the production of goods and services and the creation of jobs. Whether business is transacted in Africa, Canada, or China does not matter. Businesses may be operated differently and the objectives of businesses may differ, but the universal element in all business activities is people (see the Focus on Diversity box, "People, Standards, and Activity Forecasts").

1-4a Owners

People who directly own a business, as well as those who invest money in one, do so because they expect to earn a profit. Most of the giant corporations, such as General Motors, Eastman Kodak, Dow Chemical, Du Pont, and Exxon, are owned by large numbers of people. General Motors has over 1.2 million shareholders (owners) and 388,000 employees.[5] When making decisions, the professional managers in business organizations need to consider the owners and what they expect from the business.

1-4b Managers

The person responsible for operating the business may be the owner (an owner-manager, also called an *entrepreneur*) or a professional manager employed by the owner. Both types of managers seek to achieve survival, profit, growth, and social responsibility.

---

5. Mirjam Schiffer and Beatrice Weder, *Firm Size and the Business Environment: Worldwide Survey Result* (Washington, DC: World Bank, 2001).

FOCUS ON DIVERSITY

People, Standards, and Activity Forecasts

The look of the U.S. workforce and other subjects in the years to come will be different than it is today. It will be different in terms of age distribution, gender mix, culture diversity, people with disabilities, the mix of attitudes, standards, and economic activity. Here are a few forecasts:

- As the population ages, younger persons will manage older persons to a greater extent than ever before.
- Nontraditional workers, such as people with disabilities, retirees, immigrants, and women who are not currently in the workforce, will be in demand.
- Leave policies will be revamped. There will be increasing pressure for both parents to be on leave for childbirth, child-related emergencies, and elder care.
- It will be increasingly common for men to be working for women.
- Companies will establish rewards that are valued by different cultural groups and will be flexible about holidays, time off, and leaves.

An increasing number of organizations will adopt SA8000 (Social Accountability), a global, verifiable standard for managing, auditing, and certifying compliance with workplace issues. The certification covers a range of issues: child labor, health and safety, the right to collective bargaining, working hours, and disciplinary practices.

The owner-manager sets his or her own objectives, whereas a professional manager attempts to achieve objectives set by others. The professional manager is accountable to the owners of the business who judge the manager's performance by how well their objectives have been accomplished over a period of time.

Entrepreneurs   People who take the risks necessary to organize and manage a business and receive the financial profits and nonmonetary rewards.

Many business owners are **entrepreneurs,** people who take the risks necessary to organize and manage a business and receive the financial profits and nonmonetary rewards. In Chapter 3, a more thorough discussion of entrepreneurs will be presented. Today's entrepreneurs are expected to be innovative, practical, and strong willed. This view was actually established years ago by noted Austrian economist Joseph Schumpeter. He stated:

> The function of entrepreneurs is to reform or revolutionize the pattern of production by exploiting an invention or, more generally, an untried technological possibility for producing a new commodity or producing an old one in a new way, opening a new source of supply of materials or a new outlet for products, by organizing a new industry.[6]

The owner-managers who fit Schumpeter's description are too numerous to list, but they would include people such as Bill Ford Jr. (Ford), Jean Marie Messier (Vivendi Universal), Fred Smith (Federal Express), Bob Reis (Final Technology, Inc.), Frank Perdue (Perdue Chickens), Debbie Fields (Mrs. Field's Cookies), John McCormick (Visible Changes), Bill McGovern (MCI Communications), Elizabeth Fettinger (Beacon Metal Fabricators), and Barbara LaMont (WCCL-TV). Each of these entrepreneurs practices what Schumpeter described. They personify the term *entrepreneur*.

---

6. Joseph A. Schumpeter, *The Theory of Economic Development* (Cambridge, MA: Harvard University Press, 1934), p. 74.

1-4c Employees

Employees supply the skills and abilities needed to produce the goods or services the business sells to earn a profit. Most employees expect to receive an equitable wage or salary and to be given gradual increases in the amount they are paid for the use of their skills and abilities. To compete with other businesses, a business enterprise needs a committed and effective team of employees. Today's portrait of diversity will be broadened in U.S. businesses. The need to effectively use and develop the skills and competencies of an increasingly diverse workforce will become a major responsibility of anyone in a leadership position in a business enterprise.

1-4d Consumers

In the global marketplace, from Bangkok to Lima to Seattle to Budapest, the target of business activity is the consumer. A **consumer** is a business or a person who purchases a good or service for personal or organizational use. Consumers everywhere want more and better goods and services. They want better automobiles, better homes, more luxuries, and better leisure equipment, and they want to pay a fair price.

> **Consumer** A person who purchases a good or service for personal use.

Business attempts to satisfy consumer demands in order to earn a profit. To do so, businesses must determine what those consumer demands are. Because consumers continually want more and better things, new businesses are formed and existing businesses make adjustments to accommodate the demand. When a demand for products or services exists, a business can earn a profit by supplying it promptly, efficiently, and cost-effectively. The uncertainty and risk involved in assessing consumer demands pose a challenge to business decision makers.

1-5 BUSINESS OBJECTIVES

Businesses must achieve their objectives to remain in operation. Business objectives include such factors as profit, survival, growth, and social responsibility.

1-5a Survival, Growth, and Social Responsibility

Survival is an obvious objective. Other objectives can be accomplished only if the business enterprise survives.

Growth is an objective because business cannot stand still. Increased market share, personal and individual development, and increased productivity are important growth objectives. The growth of Exxon and Wal-Mart to multibillion-dollar enterprises is often used as an example of business success accomplished through growth.

In recent years, many businesses have recognized meeting social responsibilities as an important objective. Businesses, like each person in society, must accept their responsibilities in areas such as pollution control, eliminating discriminatory practices, and energy conservation.[7]

1-5b Profit

Although survival, growth, and social responsibility are important objectives, the profit objective plays a major role in business. Profit, however, means different things to different people because of their values, attitudes, and perceptions.

Typically, a businessperson calculates profit by subtracting all the costs, including taxes, from the revenue received for selling a product or services in the market. The difference is referred to as **profit.** For example, the franchise owner of a Wendy's fast-food restaurant subtracts all expenses (for supplies, staff wages, property, advertising, etc.) from all income to determine the business profit.

> **Profit** The difference between business income (revenue) and business expenses (costs); the selling price of a product minus all costs of making and selling it, including taxes.

7. Edward O. Wilson, *The Future of Life* (New York: Knopf, 2002).

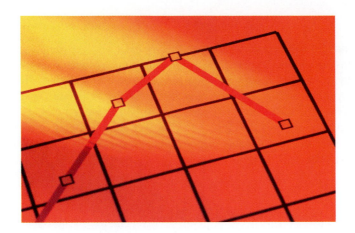

Successful business organizations earn a profit because their goods and services effectively meet customers' needs and demands. Basically, profits reward a business enterprise for effectively conducting a number of activities. The business may earn a profit when it takes risks by entering a new market or by competing head-on with another business. For example, Honda invested millions of dollars in promoting and selling small cars in the United States. This Japanese corporation has become one of the top five sellers in the U.S. market.

Business organizations that evaluate consumer demand and then move efficiently into a market can earn substantial profits. Xerox in the photoreproduction industry, Dell Computer in personal computers, and Papa John's in the pizza business are examples of companies whose accurate assessments of consumer demands resulted in good profits.

Efficient planning, organizing, controlling, directing, and staffing can help ensure satisfactory profits. Some of the most profitable enterprises (e.g., Monster.com, Yahoo, AOL, Marriott, and Ryder Systems) are also known as well-managed businesses. Such well-managed enterprises earn, on the average, 5 percent profit a year on total sales. Of course, business profit rates vary greatly by industry, size and location of the business, as well as managerial effectiveness. A major cause of business failure is improper or inadequate management of people, technology, materials, and capital.

1-6 ECONOMICS: THE FOUNDATION OF BUSINESS

Economics The study of how a society chooses to use scarce resources to produce goods and services and to distribute them to people for consumption.

Microeconomics Involves the study of household decision making on what to buy, business pricing decisions, and how markets allocate resources among alternatives.

Macroeconomics The study of inflation, unemployment, business cycles, and growth focusing on the aggregate relationships in a society.

Understanding economics is essential to understanding business.[8] **Economics** is the study of how a society chooses to use scarce resources to produce goods and services and to distribute them to people for consumption. Economic theory is divided into two branches: microeconomics and macroeconomics. **Microeconomics** is the study of individual choice and how choice is influenced by economic forces. It considers economics from the viewpoint of individuals and firms. Microeconomics involves the study of household decision making on what to buy, business-pricing decisions, and how markets allocate resources among alternatives.

Macroeconomics is the study of inflation, unemployment, business cycles, and growth focusing on the aggregate relationships in a society. Micro and macro analysis of an economy are related, and both need to be used to better understand how a country functions economically. Three issues are key to understanding economics: (1) resources, (2) goods and services, and (3) allocation of both resources and products.

8. Thomas Sowell, *Basic Economics: A Citizen's Guide to the Economy* (New York: Basic Books, 2000).

1-6a Resources

A nation's resources consist of three broad areas: natural, capital, and labor. **Natural resources** are provided by nature in limited amounts; they include crude oil, natural gas, minerals, timber, and water. Natural resources must be processed to become a product or to be used to produce other goods or services. For example, trees must be processed into lumber before they can be used to build homes, shopping malls, and schools.

    Capital resources are goods produced to make other types of goods and services. Some capital resources, called *current assets*, have a short life and are used up in the production process. These resources include fuel, raw materials, and paper. Long-lived capital resources, which can be used repeatedly in the production process, are called *fixed capital*. Examples include factory buildings, personal computers, and railroad cars.

    Labor resources represent the human talent of a nation. To have value in the labor force, individuals must be trained to perform either skilled or semiskilled work. For example, the job of physicist requires extensive training, whereas only minimal training is needed to operate a service station's gas pumps. This collection of human talent is the most valuable national resource. Without human resources, no productive use of either natural or capital resources is possible.

1-6b Goods and Services

A nation's resources are used to produce goods and services that will meet people's wants. Wants are things people would like to have but do not absolutely need for survival. Such items as food, clothing, shelter, and medical care are *needs*; video recorders, cassettes, fashionable clothes, and luxury vacations are *wants*.[9]

    A person's wants can be unlimited: As soon as one want is satisfied, another is created. Even wealthy people tend to have unlimited wants. Henry Ford was once asked how much money it would take before a person would stop wanting more. He reportedly answered, "Just a little bit more."

1-6c Allocation

All countries face the age-old economic problem of limited resources and unlimited wants. We all know, for example, that the supply of oil and natural gas in the United States is a limited natural resource.

Resource Allocation

Because we live in a world in which the quantity of all resources is limited, we must make choices about allocation—how these scarce resources are to be used. To make these choices, we have to answer three fundamental questions:

1. What goods and services will be produced, and in what quantities? What industrial goods and what consumer goods will be produced? Apartments or new houses? Railroad cars or large trucks?
2. How will goods and services be produced, and by whom? For instance, will energy be produced from coal, natural gas, or nuclear power?
3. Who will use the goods and services? When the goods and services are divided, who is to benefit from their use? Rich or poor? Families or single people? Old or young?

    Once these questions are answered, we have a basis for choosing how our resources will be used; that is, how they will be allocated to best satisfy consumers' wants and needs. In a market economy, allocation of resources also involves other issues. Should the need for business prosperity and success be a consideration? What priority should be given to

---

Natural Resources Resources that nature provides in limited amounts, including crude oil, natural gas, minerals, timber, and water.

Capital Resources Goods produced for the purpose of making other types of goods and services; includes current assets (short-lived) and fixed capital (long-lived).

Labor Resources The human talent, skills, and competence available in a nation.

---

9. Brian O'Connell and Bill Griffeth, *CNBC Creating Wealth: An Investor's Guide to Decoding the Market* (New York: John Wiley, 2001).

government's need for resources? In our economy, allocating resources—especially scarce resources—involves all these questions. Allocation can be very complicated, indeed.

Product Distribution

The issue of allocation is not limited to scarce resources. It also involves the distribution of goods and services to the consumer. In this context, allocation involves an exchange (e.g., money, goods, time, services) between a business and a consumer (e.g., client, customer, patron). In an ideal pattern of distribution in a market economy, the business earns a profit and the customer is satisfied with the good or service; the exchange provides mutual benefit. That is important in a market economy. A tailor able to earn a profit is likely to continue to work hard at the job. Likewise, a customer who likes the price and quality of the tailor's services will continue to use that tailor. When goods and services get to the customers who want or need them and mutual satisfaction occurs, both resources and products have been well allocated.

1-7 ECONOMIC SYSTEMS

> **Economic System**
> The accepted process by which labor, capital, and natural resources are organized to produce and distribute goods and services in a society.

An **economic system** is an accepted way of organizing production, establishing the rights and freedom of ownership, using productive resources, and governing business transactions in a society. There are three basic types of systems: (1) the government can produce almost all the goods and services (a planned economy); (2) private enterprise can produce almost everything (a pure market economy, found only in textbook examples); and (3) there can be some government production and some private production (a mixed economy).

No economy is entirely privately owned, but a few (e.g., North Korea and Cuba) are almost entirely government owned. The United States is a mixed economy, with about 90 percent of production provided by the private sector.

1-7a Planned Economies: Socialism and Communism

Modern socialism has much of its roots in the ideas of Karl Marx (1818–1883), published in 1867 in *Das Kapital*. Marx believed that workers were being exploited by owners (capitalists) and forced to work for wages that barely allowed them to survive. Capitalists, who owned the means of production, were viewed as a separate, distinct class. According to Marx, capitalists made profits by paying workers less than the value of their production.

Socialism

Socialism is a system based on government ownership. Government planning, rather than the market, is relied on to coordinate economic activity.

> **Planned Economy**
> An economy in which the government owns the productive resources, financial enterprises, retail stores, and banks.

Prior to major changes in 1989 and 1990, countries such as East Germany (now part of Germany), Romania, Bulgaria, and the former Soviet Union had planned economies. The governments owned productive resources, financial enterprises, retail stores, and banks. In a **planned economy,** the government is the owner because it speaks for the people. Personal property, such as automobiles, clothing, and furniture, is owned by private citizens; however, government owns almost all housing and the means of production. In a planned economy, politically appointed committees plan production, set prices, and manage the economy. Each factory receives detailed instructions on how many goods to produce.

Before 1990, socialist economic systems used administrative controls or central planning to answer the questions of what, how, and for whom. Recent reforms in countries such as China have reduced the central planner's power and role and increased the market's role.

Communism

Communism is a form of autocratic state socialism. A small group of nonelected officials decides what society's needs and goals are. In a pure communist economic system, the state owns most resources, including labor. Workers under pure communism have no claim to any of their work earnings. They provide their labor in service to the government.

FOCUS ON GLOBALIZATION

China Awakens Economically

China joined the World Trade Organization (WTO) in 2002. Its 1.2 billion people will be purchasing more foreign goods because entry into the WTO brought down many trade barriers. In 2008 China will be a showcase country as the host of the Summer Olympics. Although the full extent of opening up the large Chinese market will not be known for five or more years after WTO entry, the business challenges will be significant.

China's growth and progress economically depend on the need for foreign direct investment. They also depend on foreign trade. If there is a global recession it will be felt by all nations but will have an especially strong impact on China. Slowing growth would mean few jobs for the growing number of unemployed in China. In 2002, more than 12 million Chinese were unemployed.

China's plans to become the second-largest economy, behind the United States only, are centered on it becoming a major world-class manufacturing center. It has an abundant pool of young, educated workers, with millions more entering the workforce each year. Even India, which has the world's lowest wages, can't compete with the Chinese in productivity. Shops in Bombay and Calcutta are flooded with Chinese products.

China is a sleeping business giant that is just beginning to make an impact on world business and trade. Changing its infrastructure and methods of transacting business will take time and hard work. Economic and business activity reforms for a nation as vast as China will be difficult. China's long-term growth will only come when foreigners are convinced that China is willing to conduct business by following acceptable business practices rules.

Sources: James Kynge, "China Goes for the Gold," *The World in 2002: The Economist,* January 2002, pp. 34–35; and Peter Engardio, "Asia's Future: China," *Business Week,* October 29, 2001, pp. 48–52.

Resentment of autocratic control in the former Soviet Union, East Germany, Hungary, and other countries led to demands for democracy in the late 1980s. The pure communist system has never actually existed, but it was the stated goal of many socialist countries until their demise. Today, many previously Communist Party–controlled countries hold elections and use multiparty political groups to change their political orientations.

The People's Republic of China was established as a communist state in 1949. China's famous five-year economic plans emphasized heavy industry, defense, and self-sufficiency. Wage differentials were frowned on as a way to motivate workers. In the late 1970s China opened its doors to international trade, foreign investment, and communication. Worker incentives were improved through installing bonus systems, and private enterprise was encouraged in agriculture and consumer goods. The Chinese have even developed a stock market. The People's Republic of China is moving away ever so slowly from a planned communist-controlled state. There is still a high degree of central planning, but there are more market incentives. Today's business world illustrates that China has the potential to become the world's biggest economy, as the Chinese are fast becoming very knowledgeable about business, trade, and competition (see the Focus on Globalization box, "China Awakens Economically"). Profit making, which was once a dirty word, has become acceptable and encouraged.[10]

10. Caroline Liou, Marie Cambon, Alexander English, Thomas Huhte, and Bradley Wong, *Lonely Planet China* (New York: Dimensions, 2000).

1-7b Mixed Market Economy

Capitalism A type of economic system characterized by private ownership of capital, competition among businesses seeking a profit, and consumer's freedom of choice.

Capitalism is an economic system based on private ownership of property and the market in which individuals decide how, what, and for whom to produce. Under a pure capitalist system, individuals are encouraged to follow their own self-interest, while market forces of supply and demand are relied on to coordinate economic activity. Markets work through a system of rewards and payments. If you work, you get paid for that work; if you want a product or service, you pay the owner or provider for it. In a capitalist economy, individuals are free to do whatever they want as long as it's legal. The market is relied on to see that what people want to get and want to do is consistent with what is available. Under capitalism, fluctuations in prices coordinate individuals' wants.

The United States is not a pure capitalist nation. It is instead a mix of free markets plus government ownership and involvement. A pure capitalist nation would have no government control or ownership of markets. In a **mixed economy,** both the government and private business enterprises produce and distribute goods and services (see Exhibit 1-2). The government usually plays a role in supplying defense, roads, education, pensions, and some medical care.

Mixed Economy An economy in which both the government and private business enterprises produce and distribute goods and services.

A mixed market economy allows the freedom to start a business.[11] *Freedom of enterprise* means that businesses and individuals with the capital may enter essentially any legal business venture they wish. This important feature of the market economy permits individuals to seek out profit-making business opportunities. Under the market economy, any business or individual can earn a profit by producing a useful good or service. However, businesses and individuals do not have an automatic right to profit.

Profit is a reward to a business for using scarce economic resources efficiently. Consumers must consider a good or service reasonable in price, quality, and value before a profit can be made.

Competition is yet another important part of a market economy. In general, *competition* refers to the rivalry among businesses for consumer dollars. Because of competition for consumer dollars, businesses have to be aware of what consumers want to buy. If they ignore consumer wishes, they are likely to lose sales, which directly affect the level of profit. A business that consistently loses money and makes no profit will fail. Consequently, competition among businesses generally provides consumers with lower prices, more services, and improved products. The continual fare wars in the airline industry illustrate how fierce competition among businesses can become.

Exhibit 1-2 summarizes some key characteristics under the different types of economic systems.

Over time, companies can lose their stature or competitive position. Fearsome, larger megacorporations have vanished like dinosaurs, but in a much shorter time period. Poor decision making, improper business practices, lazy responses to competitors' actions, poor selection of top executives, inadequate training of the workforce, and ignoring signals of problems have all contributed to the fading of many business enterprises.

In two decades, IBM, General Motors, and Sears Roebuck have lost their leadership positions on the world stage. These three seemingly invincible giants are today fighting for their lives against global competitors. In this short time period, Wal-Mart has shot to the number two position in terms of revenues generated and number of employees, as shown in Exhibit 1-3.

Each of the fading U.S. giants appears to have miscalculated the competition. In a mixed market economy, competitors are likely to seek out the most vulnerable areas of a firm. Dell, Honda, and Wal-Mart were not frightened by the three "kings of the mountain." As Exhibit 1-3 illustrates, a business shouldn't be impressed with its market position, profits, or wealth. Everything can change in a few years.

The U.S. economic system became mixed when government established operating guidelines and laws for businesses to follow. For example, one important federal law requires a variety of safety rules to be followed on construction jobs. An economic system

11. Emma Rothschild, *Economic Sentiments: Adams Smith, Condorcet, and the Enlightenment* (Cambridge, MA: 2001).

EXHIBIT 1-2 Comparison of Three Economic Systems

System Features	Mixed Socialism	Communism	Market Economy
Ownership of enterprises	Basic industries are owned by government, but small-scale enterprises can be privately owned.	The government owns the means of production with few exceptions, like small plots of land.	A strong private sector exists along with public enterprises in a mixed economy. The private sector is larger than that under socialism.
What is produced	What planners believe is socially beneficial.	What central planners decide the citizens need.	What producers believe people want and will make the firm a profit.
Rights to profits	Profits officially exist only in the private sector of socialist economies.	Profits are not acceptable under communism.	Entrepreneurs and investors are entitled to private-sector profits. State enterprises are also typically expected to break even or provide a return to the government.
Management of enterprises	Significant degree of government planning exists.	Centralized management of all state enterprises is a traditional feature. Management is subject to centralized plans (five-year plans). Planning is now being decentralized.	Managed by owners or people who represent the owners.
Rights of employees	Workers have the right to choose their occupations and to join labor unions. However, the government influences many career decisions.	Employee rights were traditionally limited in exchange for a promise of no unemployment.	Workers have the right to job choice and labor union membership.
Worker incentives	Incentives are usually limited in state enterprises, but do exist in the private sector.	Incentives are emerging in communist economies (e.g., Vietnam and China).	Incentives exist in the private sector. Incentives in the public sector are more limited.

EXHIBIT 1-3 Global 500

Revenue ($millions)			Number of Employees			
Global 500 Rank	Company	Revenues	Rank	Company	Global Rank Revenues	# of Employees (2000)
1	Exxon Mobil	$210,392.0	1	China Petroleum	83	1,292,558
2	Wal-Mart Stores	193,295.0	2	Wal-Mart Stores	2	1,244,000
3	General Motors	184,632.0	3	Sinopec	68	1,173,901
4	Ford Motor	180,598.0	4	State Power Corp.	77	1,137,025
5	Daimler Chrysler	150,069.7	5	U.S. Postal Service	33	901,238
6	Royal Dutch/ Shell Group	149,146.0	6	China Telecommunications	228	588,882
			7	Agricultural Bank of China	448	500,000
7	BP	148,062.0	8	Industrial & Commercial Bank of China	213	471,123
8	General Electric	129,853.0				
9	Mitsubishi	126,579.4	9	Siemens	23	447,000
10	Toyota Motor	121,416.2	10	China Construction Bank	411	420,000

Sources: Fortune, July 23, 2001 and *www.fortune.com* (Global 500).

Flow of Money and Products in the U.S. Economy

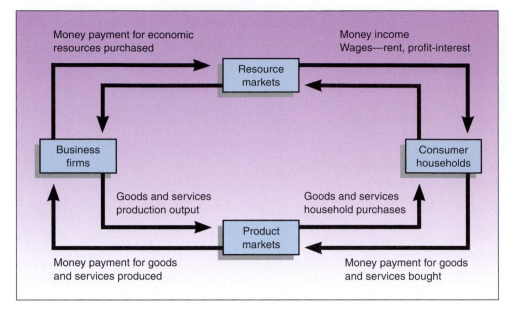

also becomes mixed when government competes directly with business. This often happens in such areas as medical research, electric power generation, and communication. The U.S. Postal Service is an example of a government-subsidized business that competes with private businesses such as Federal Express.

1-7c The U.S. Economic System

The United States has developed the world's largest economic system. The basic parts of the U.S. economy are illustrated in Exhibit 1-4. This model, a simplification of our mixed economic system, includes only the broadest parts of the economy; it does not include the government. If there's not enough of something to go around (excess demand), its price goes up. If something isn't wanted (excess supply), its price goes down.

Note the differences between resource markets and product markets in the exhibit. *Resource markets* are places where economic resources—natural, labor, and capital—are bought and sold. The New York Stock Exchange, where money is invested in companies, is a financial capital resource market. The employment section in local newspapers is a resource market where labor is bought and sold. *Product markets* are the thousands of markets in the United States where business outputs (goods and services) are sold to consumers (the government can be viewed as a consumer in some cases). Consumers pay for goods and services with money. This type of consumer expenditure is called *retail sales*. The money businesses receive from retail sales is *revenue*.

Where do consumers get money to spend for goods and services? Exhibit 1-4 shows that consumer households supply economic resources to the resource markets. In return for money, people provide labor through work, invest in businesses (capital), and sell natural resources to businesses. The money received in payment for these economic resources is then used to purchase goods and services. Of course, businesses view money paid to suppliers of goods and services as an expense.

Two distinct types of economic resource flows are illustrated in Exhibit 1-4. The flow of economic resources and products is shown by the inner loop. It flows counterclockwise, showing that economic resources move from consumers to businesses and then return to consumers as finished goods and services. Money flow, on the other hand, is shown by the outer loop. This clockwise flow of money begins when firms pay consumers for the economic resource they purchase. Consumers use their money to purchase the goods and services produced by businesses. These two economic flows take place continuously and at the same time. As long as consumers spend all their money, the flow of money into and out of consumer households is equal. However, some money is diverted into savings, and the government needs to intervene to bring about a balance in the flows.

1-7d What Economic System Is Best?

The most appropriate economic system for a nation depends on several things, including cultural factors and the availability of economic resources. For example, the free market system is unlikely to be appropriate for a nation that creates hurdles for individuals who want to organize their own businesses. The right of business owners to use economic resources for whatever purpose they want is the backbone of the free market system. The free market system normally works best with people who are willing and able to make their own economic decisions. In fact, the free market system encourages people to take the initiative to become better educated and to make their own decisions.

1-7e How Is the U.S. Mixed Market Economy Doing?

A business generally measures how much market it has, how much profit it earns, and how much it produces or the volume of service it provides. To discuss how well an economic system is doing, a concept called **gross domestic product (GDP)** is used. GDP is the total market value of all goods and services produced in a one-year period within the boundaries of a nation. Thus, GDP excludes what products or services U.S. firms produce overseas but includes products and services produced by foreign companies operating in the United States.

GDP figures are used to make comparisons between countries, and this enables each nation to learn how it matches up with others. Per capita GDP is another measure used to make comparisons. To arrive at per capita GDP, a nation's GDP is simply divided by its total population. This gives a sense of the relative standard of living of the people in a country. Bangladesh has a per capita GDP of about $200, compared with U.S. per capita GDP of over $29,000.[12] However, remember that GDP is a measure that values activities at the market price in a society. Renting an apartment in downtown Chicago for $2,500 a month would provide you with a one-bedroom space. In a poorer country such as Bangladesh, $2,500 a month would be exceptional.

To avoid the problem in comparing per capita GDP, a **purchasing power parity (PPP)** measure is used. This is done by comparing the cost of a market basket of goods in one country to the same basket in another country.

Gross Domestic Product (GDP)
A measure of the economic activity within the physical borders of a country.

Purchasing Power Parity (PPP)
The adjustment of relative prices. A relative market basket of consumer goods is compared to the same market basket in terms of the currencies of the two countries.

1-7f Economic, Social, and Technological Trends

We live in a period of extraordinary changes. An important theme in this text is that it is important for each person to be knowledgeable about the business world and how business is transacted. Although no one can predict exactly what will occur in the future, individuals will have to respond to some noticeable trends. There is no step-by-step prescription for responding, but some driving forces exist that are discussed throughout the remainder of the text. Identifying and learning about these forces can be helpful in dealing with the future instead of being overwhelmed or controlled by what is happening in the business environment.

1-7g Demographic Trends

In 2002, 285 million Americans lived in a world of about 6.2 billion people. Forecasts indicate that by the year 2050 there will be 385 million Americans; the country will then be about 13 percent African American, 25 percent Hispanic, 7 percent Asian, 52 percent white non-Hispanic, and about 3 percent other.

The average American is getting older. In 1820 the median age of the population was only 16.7 years. Today the median age is about 32. An older population is not bad for business, but changes must be made in what products and services are produced. The aging of the U.S. population also benefits those who will grow up and begin their business careers

---

12. Edmond Malenvaud, *Management Development Strategy and Management of the Market Economy* (New York: Oxford Press, 2001).

in future decades. With fewer young workers available to produce goods and services, wages and salaries are expected to rise. The downside is the cost of caring for an aging population. With fewer workers bearing the tax burden to support programs for the care of the elderly, some difficult political decisions must be made. Social security and pension funds will have to be carefully managed to withstand the drain.

The increasing number of older workers means that motivations for working will change. What is motivational and stimulating to 20-year-olds may not be for 40- and 50-year-olds. Older workers may also be less willing to relocate. In addition, there will be an increased emphasis on health care and wellness.

1-7h Diversity in the United States

The United States has always been a country of minorities, a nation of immigrants and refugees. In 1920, of 105 million Americans, 14 million were foreign born and 10.5 million were African American. In 2002, of 285 million Americans, over 29 million were foreign born. As the number of minorities and immigrants increases, they will play a more significant role in the U.S. economy and workplace.

Like other Americans, minorities seek entrepreneurial opportunities. The number of nonwhite, self-employed persons increased by over 50 percent in the 1990s—faster than white self-employment, which grew by over 40 percent during the same period. African-American entrepreneurs have made inroads in all industries including entertainment and media, led by long-established, black-owned firms such as Motown (entertainment) and Johnson Publishing (*Ebony* magazine).

Hispanic businesses has grown significantly in recent years; the Hispanic population is expanding at four times the national rate. As Hispanics begin to gain more affluence, they draw the attention of businesses. Hispanic-owned businesses such as Goya Foods, Inc., Banco Popular de Puerto Rico, E&G Trading, and Sedano's Supermarkets are already producing goods and services geared to the needs and wants of Hispanics.

1-7i Growth of the Marketplace

In past centuries, heads of state were all-important because the relationships between countries were primarily political. Nations are now linked by telecommunications and trade. Americans made overseas calls totaling over 5 billion minutes in 1990, up from 580 million in 1970. A fiber optic cable across the Pacific went into service in April 1989, linking the United States and Japan. North America, Europe, Asia, and Australia are being strung with fiber optic cable. In 2002, more than 50 million miles of fiber optic cable were in place, tripling the volume of calls that could be placed simultaneously in the 1980s.[13]

Telecommunications will continue to link nations, people, and businesses. Just as we are becoming a global marketplace, we are moving toward a single worldwide information network. Businesses will soon have the capacity to communicate anything to anyone, anywhere in the world, by any form—voice, data, text, or image—at the speed of sound. Business students need the skills to work with computers and communications systems because the world of business will require these skills.

Developing economies will expand the global marketplace. Five hundred years ago, the world's trade center began moving from the Mediterranean to the Atlantic. It is now moving from the Atlantic toward the Pacific. Los Angeles, Tokyo, Sydney, and Hong Kong are major centers of business. In 2002, Asia had two-thirds of the world's population, while Europe had only 6 percent and the United States about 4.8 percent. Asia is a $5 trillion market growing at a rate of $4 billion a week.

The Pacific Rim stretches from the west coast of South America northward across the Bering Strait to Russia, southward to Australia. It includes all countries touched by the Pacific Ocean. The lifeblood of Japan, a tiny group of islands that is far from self-sufficient, is trade with the United States, Europe, and other countries. Although Japan

---

13.   Bob Boiko, *Content Management Bible* (San Francisco: Hungry Minds, 2001).

is the Pacific Rim's economic power today, South Korea, Taiwan, Hong Kong, and Singapore (called the "Four Tigers") are also major business centers.

Eastern Europe, Russia, Chile, and a growing number of developing nations have begun to move toward democracy. The democratizing of these nations will have a significant impact on how business is conducted. To clean up the chaos and poor economies of Eastern Europe, more private ownership and free enterprise is still needed. Hungarians, Poles, Russians, Czechs, and Slovaks want more, better, and reliable goods and services. The opportunities for U.S. businesspeople in democratizing countries are constrained only by limits to their creativity.

1-7j Growth of the Service Sector

Overall, employment was about 134 million in 2002, according to the U.S. Labor Department. The service sector is creating more jobs (20 million) than any other part of the economy.[14] *Services* are intangible products (e.g., insurance, airline travel, tax preparation advice) that are not physically possessed and that involve a performance or an effort. Examples of service industries include banking, transportation, retail trade, and entertainment.

Already about 70 percent of the GDP is being provided by the service sector of the economy. It is the dominant sector in terms of jobs, opportunities, and new business start-ups. The American economy is depending more and more on the service sector for growth, jobs, and expansion into global markets.

1-7k The Explosion of Information Technology

The total amount of information in the world is doubling every eighteen months. The microprocessor is making everything in the developed economies of the world move faster. Computing power is now increasing at a rate of 4,000 times per decade for a given unit of cost. That means that a personal computer bought in the year 2012 will be 4,000 times more powerful than one purchased in 2002.[15]

One of the most significant trends is the rapid interconnection of individual computers. Global networks of millions of personal computers, connected by fiber optic and satellite links, will eventually allow almost instantaneous around-the-clock communication to anyone else, anywhere in the world. The Internet ("the network of networks") started in 1968. The Internet is a combination of software, print, video, audio, and phone systems that can be used twenty-four hours a day, seven days a week. Today, over 100 million Americans are connected through the Internet. People can interchange mail, documents, books, pictures, voice and music, and films on the Internet. Users can access databases from around the world.

---

14. Eric Schlosser, *Fast Food Nation* (Boston: Houghton Mifflin, 2001).

15. Neal Plotnick, *The IT Survival Guide* (New York: McGraw-Hill, 1999).

The boom in information technology has led some futurists such as Alvin Toffler to speak of future economic systems as being "knowledge based." As information becomes more important in the success of businesses, the most significant resource then becomes the base of knowledge that has been acquired about the business.

The information technology explosion suggests that businesses will need to be fast since speed is increasingly being used to mean value. Information availability is what allows speech. Faster production, faster delivery, and faster service are becoming important indicators of whether a business is successful or not.

1-7l Business in All Sizes

A steady stream of warnings about the dwindling concentrations of economic power in big business has been popularized by the media. Big businesses are not as dominant as they were in the 1960s and 1970s, but they are still around and are likely to be a major source of jobs and economic influence far into the future. Big businesses are still very dominant in services, where commercial banks, diversified financial companies, and retailers have done very well in the past ten years.

The United States rediscovered small businesses and entrepreneurs in the early 1980s. Like big business, small business is here to stay, and it will continue to provide opportunities for individuals. People can select how to invest, where to work, and how to live in a society that is likely to be based on big and small businesses. One size doesn't fit every individual. Fortunately, in the mixed market economy in which we live each of us can decide whether our careers and future rest in working for a large or a small enterprise. Small business is the place for some, and large business is the place for others. Trends indicate that businesses of all sizes should prosper if leaders understand and conduct business effectively.

1-7m Environmental Responsibilities

Worldwide, the momentum of the environmental movement has created a shift in how business operates. There is a growing awareness and concern about global environmental issues. Television has shown us the effects of the Valdez oil spill, complete with oil-drenched wildlife and blackened landscapes. The thick gray-black air in Kuwait resulting from hundreds of burning oil fires was seen around the world on television. Reports about illness years after the Chernobyl nuclear accident frighten everyone.

As the public becomes more aware of and concerned about the environment, business leaders pay more attention. If a company's environmental reputation affects people's buying decisions, then business attention may be focused on survival of the enterprise. Business leaders in the early 2000s will have to make environmental considerations (e.g., pollution, waste, recycling) a part of product decision making. Businesses will have to do the right things routinely and by choice, not because some group or law forces them to do so. Chapter 6 discusses the environment further.

Changes in business concerns about the environment appear daily. At Wal-Mart, environmentalism is a cause; suppliers are asked to provide recycled or recyclable products. The London-based Body Shop, with fourteen U.S. outlets, puts the environment at the center of its business. Its skin and hair care stores display literature on ozone depletion next to sunscreens and fill their display windows with information on issues like global warming. Each employee must spend half a day each week on activist work. Customers get discounts if they bring their old bottles back for recycling. Sales are skyrocketing, the company gets frequent positive publicity, and the environmental theme excites Body Shop employees. They love to work for a responsible firm.

EXHIBIT 1-5
Organization of the Book

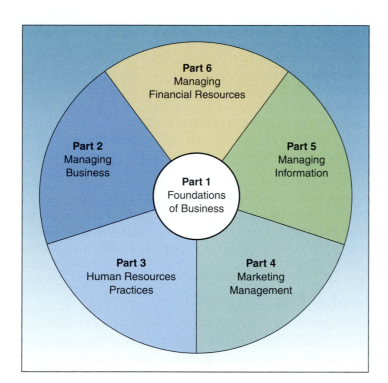

1-8   THE THEMES OF THIS BOOK

The excitement, challenges, trends, and opportunities in business are what this text intends to portray to students. The book is organized into six parts (see Exhibit 1-5). Each of the parts projects five themes that business leaders and employees will face in making decisions and in performing their respective jobs.

1-8a   Technology

The applications of science and engineering skills and knowledge to improve productivity and to solve problems must be managed and applied appropriately. Technology is being used to create, sustain, and accomplish change. The use and management of technology is presented, debated, and analyzed.

1-8b   Global Markets

The U.S. consumer is richer, more educated, and more demanding of quality than ever. But the United States is not alone. The average consumer in every industrial country fits the same profile—having more discretionary spending power, more education, and more purchasing discrimination. The emerging world middle class wants a world of easy access to products and services unhindered by any national geographical boundaries. The businesses that are filling these demands are presented throughout the text. As will become apparent, some are doing better than others in the global marketplace.

1-8c Small Business

For decades, large corporations like IBM, Sears, Wards (out of business), and U.S. Steel (out of business) dominated markets. Today, however, about 96 percent of the over 7 million businesses in the United States have payrolls with fewer than 100 employees. Autonomy, personal satisfaction, control, and a faster route to success are reasons why more people are starting their own businesses than at any time in history.

1-8d Careers

Since individuals change jobs frequently, managing and controlling changes and other career decision making is becoming more of an individual factor. How to manage one's career effectively is important so that heartbreaking downsizing, termination, and job loss doesn't result in giving up, emotional problems, or premature physical disorders. We pay attention to career management, improvement, and analysis in various elements and content.

1-8e The Skill Mix: Best in Class

The information and technology revolution has created a host of opportunities for those skilled in using a host of technologies. The worldwide shift to more market-based economies, increased educational levels, and increased technical training have produced a global workforce skilled to work in high-technology-oriented jobs. The changing skill mix is a theme that is illustrated in every chapter in this text. Global competition for the higher-skilled jobs is increasing.

In addition to high-tech-type skills, employers are interested in hiring individuals who have communication, interpersonal, teamwork, leadership, problem-solving, and flexibility skills. Also in demand are workers who are responsible, hardworking, and comfortable with diversity.

Jobs are not reserved for Americans, Italians, Canadians, or people only in a developed society. Jobs are likely to be held by anyone from any location around the globe who can perform the best. The skill mix needed to be successful in business should become evident to each person using this text.

SUMMARY OF LEARNING OBJECTIVES

1. *Comment on the study and importance of business and define it in your own terms.* We need to study business because (a) we have become so interdependent on others, both individually and as a nation, (b) increasing globalization of business will bring many opportunities, (c) we strive to maintain and improve our standard of living, (d) coping with unforeseen events will be easier and less traumatic, and (e) we will be able to separate fact from fiction in business issues. Business involves the exchange of goods, services, or money for mutual benefit.

2. *Explain why people are the key to business.* Business needs people as owners, managers, employees, and consumers. Businesses may be operated differently, and the objectives of business may differ, but the universal element in all business activities is people.

3. *Identify the four main objectives of business.* A business must first *survive* if other objectives are to be accomplished. *Growth* is an objective because business does not stand still. Businesses must accept *social responsibility* in areas such as the environment and protection from discrimination. The *profit* objective plays a major role in business. Profits reward a business enterprise for effectively or efficiently conducting a number of activities.

4. *Explain why profit is important to the owners of a business.* Profit is calculated by subtracting all costs, including taxes, from the revenue received from selling a product or service in the marketplace. Profit represents the owners' reward for conducting business. Profit is a motivational force that serves to attract people to own or invest in businesses.

5. *Describe and compare the three types of economic resources.* Economics is the study of how a society chooses to use scarce resources to produce goods and services and then distribute them to people for consumption. *Natural resources* are provided by nature in limited amounts (e.g., coal, oil, natural gas); *capital resources* are goods produced to make other goods and services (e.g., fuel, money, factories); *labor resources* are the nation's human talent, the most valuable national resource. Each of these resources must be managed properly and coordinated to achieve goals.

6. *Distinguish between planned and mixed market economic systems.* In *planned economies*, such as those in Cuba, North Korea, and Vietnam, the government owns the means of production, financial enterprises, retail stores, and banks. Prior to 1988 in what was then the Soviet Union, politically appointed committees planned production (by telling factories how much of which goods to produce), set prices, and managed the economy. This is now slowly changing. In a *mixed economy* both the government and business enterprises produce and distribute goods and services. The government provides defense, roads, education, pensions, and some medical care. Markets are free and competitive.

7. *Determine how gross domestic product (GDP) is calculated.* GDP is the total market value of all final goods and services produced in an economy in a one-year period. The market value of millions of different products (e.g., cars, personal computers) and services (e.g., financial advice, airplane trips) is calculated to arrive at a total.

KEY TERMS

business (p. 6)
capital resources (p. 13)
capitalism (p. 16)
consumer (p. 11)
economic system (p. 14)
economics (p. 12)

entrepreneurs (p. 10)
free enterprise (p. 7)
gross domestic product (GDP) (p. 19)
labor resources (p. 13)
macroeconomics (p. 12)
microeconomics (p. 12)

mixed economy (p. 16)
natural resources (p. 13)
planned economy (p. 14)
profit (p. 11)
purchasing power parity (PPP) (p. 19)
standard of living (p. 7)

QUESTIONS FOR DISCUSSION AND REVIEW

1. In a free enterprise system, should a limit be placed on the amount of profit a business owner can earn? Explain.
2. When calculating GDP, why is the market value of the product or service calculated?
3. In considering the skill mix needed for global businesses, how can a student interested in working in a large business prepare for a career?
4. How would the incentive to produce high-quality goods be affected by a centrally planned (government) approach to quality control.
5. Should the U.S. government become more of an owner of businesses such as an airline? The airline industry has been impacted by the September 11 terrorist attacks. Is it time for the government to take over? Why?
6. How do you currently use the Internet? Do you expect to increase your use of the Internet? Why?
7. You are asked to prepare a speech on how a more diverse workforce must be managed. Provide some examples of key points in your speech.
8. The service sector of the economy has grown beyond the product sector. What implications does this have for job opportunities in the next two decades?
9. How do you plan to improve your business IQ? Why is it necessary to have a business IQ in a mixed market society?
10. What type of government intervention occurs in the United States, Japan, China, and North Korea manufacturing industries? Search out information in your library and compare it with what is shown in Exhibit 1-2 on page 17.

END-OF-CHAPTER QUESTIONS

1. The United States leads in all standards-of-living indicators except life expectancy.   **T** or **F**
2. Business functions best when it is static and unchanging. **T** or **F**
3. According to Karl Marx, capitalists made profits by paying workers less than the value of their production.   **T** or **F**
4. An economic system becomes mixed when government competes directly with private businesses.   **T** or **F**
5. The average American is getting younger.   **T** or **F**
6. Big businesses are more dominant than they were in the 1960s and 1970s.   **T** or **F**
7. The U.S. consumer is richer, more educated, and more demanding of quality than ever before.   **T** or **F**
8. In former communist countries, the conversion to American business methods was pushed by _____, who preached about privatization and entrepreneurship.
   a. American businesses   b. government officials
   c. bankers and consultants   d. consumers
9. Which of the following is not a primary business objective?
   a. Profit   b. Survival
   c. Growth   d. None of the above
10. Secondary objectives can only be achieved if the business enterprise.
    a. expands   b. diversifies
    c. survives   d. reorganizes
11. If there is not enough of something to meet demand (excess demand), its price _____.
    a. goes up   b. goes down   c. stays the same
12. Who among the following is not considered a service industry employee?
    a. Banker   b. Cab driver
    c. Retail clerk   d. Baker
13. Approximately how many people are in the U.S. workforce?
    a. 10 million   b. 57 million
    c. 78 million   d. 134 million
14. The study of inflation, unemployment, business cycles, and growth, and focusing on the aggregate relationships in a society, is called _____.
    a. economics   b. microeconomics   c. macroeconomics
15. An economic system based on private ownership of property and a market in which individuals decide how, what, and for whom to produce is called _____.
    a. socialism   b. communism   c. capitalism

INTERNET EXERCISE

Use Google or Northern Light as your search engine and use as keywords: "China Economy" and "Internet Growth."

Prepare a short descriptive report (500 words) on what you find for "China Economy." Where would you search to find the best, most accurate, up-to-date information and historical perspective on the economic system and plans of the People's Republic of China?

Do the same type of report for the second phrase, "Internet Growth."

EXPERIENTIAL EXERCISE

Finding Business Data

Activity

This exercise will familiarize the student with the materials available to improve a person's knowledge about business. The time required to complete the project is two to three hours.

The project is designed to have the student identify places to find relevant business information and data. If the information is not available in the city, the student will have to go outside the area or access computer databases to complete the project.

Directions

1. Identify three separate sources (location) of materials and data that address the following topics:
   Economics
   Business Performance (e.g., stock market valuation)
   The Great Depression
   Globalization
   Workforce Diversity
   Free Enterprise
   Business Technology
2. Select three topics and find three different sources of information in your city or town. Prepare a one-page report on each of the topics from the available sources.
3. How do you rate the sources of information in terms of currentness, ease of accessing, and completeness?

BUSINESS APPLICATION

A Values Exercise

How Does Everyone View the Business World?

"You can't judge a book by its cover" is an old saying that is becoming very important in the determination to use the talents of every single citizen to improve a country's standard of living. An older person doesn't necessarily have traditional values. A college graduate doesn't necessarily lack the background to operate a business. Today's workforce is, and tomorrow's will be, characterized by a mix of values, backgrounds, and attitudes. Values and attitudes change with significant life experiences or simply with age. Backgrounds remain fixed.

Although values and attitudes vary greatly, it is important for people with differing values to work effectively with each other. Participants in surveys indicate that a number of values are extremely important to men, women, old people, young people, African Americans, Hispanics, Caucasians, Asians, Southerners, Northerners, and every possible mix of the diverse demographic landscape of the United States. The most important common values include:

1. Recognition for competence and accomplishments
2. Respect and dignity
3. Personal choice and freedom
4. Pride in one's work
5. Lifestyle quality
6. Financial security
7. Self-development
8. Health and wellness

Questions for Discussion

1. Form into groups of four or more students and discuss the preceding eight values. Are they the most important values among the group members?
2. In operating a business, would a manager need to know the values of his or her employees? What does the group think? Why?
3. In this chapter various countries were mentioned, such as China, the former Soviet Union, Iraq, and Japan. In the group, discuss the eight values as they pertain to these four countries. Would different values emerge as the most important in other countries? Why?
4. Does the increasing diversity of the U.S. workforce mean that U.S. managers/leaders will have a more difficult time learning about the values of workers than managers/leaders in India? Think about the diversity of India and of the United States. What does the group think?

Case

Google Extends Its Reach

Larry Page and Sergey Brin, both in their midtwenties, started Google, a search-engine firm, in 1998. They worked for three years as graduate students at Stanford on their business model and concept. Their business plan was so compelling they pulled in Sun Microsystems as an investor. Stanford also put money into Google.

In just a few years, despite spending nothing on marketing, Google has become the fifteenth most-visited website in the United States, handling about 120 million web searches every day. Google's technology ranks web search results on the quality of links. Brin and Page keep Google free of any clutter—advertisements. The result is high ratings from users because of usefulness, user satisfaction, and speed.

Google has reached a point where it must now manage its success, growing size (over 250 employees), and paying customers (over $50 million in annual revenue). Eric Schmidt, the former CEO of Novell has been brought in to become Google's top executive. His objective is to capitalize on Google's search technology by entering new markets. Now the business model becomes more difficult as Schmidt attempts to sell search technology to corporations for use on their in-house networks.

Google is also extending its global reach by expanding the number of languages (e.g., Spanish, Russian, Arabic, Hebrew) it can deal with. It now can do the job in sixty-six languages. The closest rival is Alta Vista, which performs searches in twenty-five languages.

The key to Google's growth plan is to crack the corporate market. Alta Vista has more than a thousand corporate customers, while Google's paltry list totals only about ten, including Procter & Gamble and Cisco. By improving technology, entering more corporate networks, and going more global Google believes that business will only get better.

To accomplish the kind of growth that Google's executives desire, the firm must keep innovating its technology. Page and Brin put together a staff of over 100 engineers who excel at finding new and better ways to search the Web. These engineers concentrate on fast and accurate searches. This is what users want. Finding and keeping new customers flows from having the best technology and how Google plans, organizes, and executes business.

To grow at the rate it desires, Google will likely have to raise money by going public. However, before it goes public the executive team that Google and Schmidt needs must be recruited and hired and become aligned with the firm's culture. These are parts of doing business that managers in any type of business must pay attention to and perform effectively. Even though Page and Brin's business concept and original technology were superb, they cannot sit back and rest while competitors attempt to outdo, replicate, or overwhelm them.

Questions for Discussion

1. What characteristics in the U.S. economic system encourage the work, effort, and risk taking displayed by Google's Larry Page and Sergey Brin to start their business?
2. What has been Google's competitive advantage? How can it maintain its competitive advantage?
3. Why does Google need to continue expanding outside of the United States?

Sources: Ben Elgin, Jim Kerstetter, and Linda Himelstein, "Why They're Agog Over Google," *Business Week*, September 24, 2001, pp. 83–86; and Mark Durham, "Google: We're Down with ODP," March 24, 2000, www.salon.com/tech/feature/2000/3/24/google-odp.

Global Business

Photo: comstock.com

Chapter Objectives

After completing this chapter, you should be able to

1 **Discuss** the meaning and scope of global business.

2 **Explain** why firms become involved in global business.

3 **Define** the basic concepts of global business.

4 **List** the various barriers to global business.

5 **Identify** the ways in which global business is regulated.

6 **Describe** the different approaches firms take to conduct business globally.

7 **Determine** how a firm can adapt to foreign markets.

The "Euro" Is Launched

The **euro** (EUR), the new currency of the European Union (EU), has been years in the making. The name "euro" was chosen by the European heads of state at a meeting in Madrid in December 1995. There are now seven euro notes and eight euro coins. Notes come in denominations of 500, 200, 100, 50, 20, 10, and 5. The coins come in amounts of 2 euro, 1 euro, 50 euro cent, 20 euro cent, 10 euro cent, 5 euro cent, and 1 euro cent.

The separate currencies of all fifteen EU nations are now transformed into a single currency. The theory of a single currency is that each nation will now have more buying power, better efficiency for paying for goods and services, and more economic stability. The euro provides a psychological boost to EU citizens, as it is now something that can be seen and actually held in the hands of a consumer.

The euro's performance in domestic and global business transactions will rest on the strength of the EU's economy. In 2002, about 20 percent of the world's GDP and over 360 million people were in the EU.

The euro provides the type of single currency used by the United States (the dollar) that is attractive around the world. Now that people, services, capital, and goods can move freely within the fifteen EU nations, the Treaty of Rome (1937) objectives of creating a closer union among the people of Europe is completed.

Sources: David Fairlamb, "A Real Currency with Real Impact," *Business Week Online*, January 2, 2002, pp. 1–3; "Questions and Answers on the Euro and European Economic and Monetary Union," *European Commission*, August 8, 2002, pp. 1–8; and "History of the Euro," *European Central Bank*, January 19, 2002, pp. 1–2.

2-1 THE IMPORTANCE OF GLOBAL BUSINESS

In the global economy, products have to compete with similar products made anywhere else. Cars made in Tennessee compete with cars made in Japan, Europe, and South Korea. Flowers grown in Florida compete with flowers grown in Columbia; wine bottled in California competes with wine bottled in France. The question facing firms throughout the world isn't whether they should compete with foreign firms, but how they can survive and grow in the global economy.

The answer to this question, of course, is complex. We know that customers are demanding better products, improved service, and lower prices, and the way to compete is through quality, convenience, and fair prices for the value received. Global competition means that consumers have a better choice of products and lower prices; management's common goal must be customer satisfaction. There is around the world a concerted movement to trade liberalization. By opening markets, nations and people become more bound together through the exchange of goods and services. Trade liberalization provides the greatest opportunity for developing nations. It will provide for more investment, increased number of joint ventures, and eventually an increase in the standard of living.[1]

2-1a Defining Global Business

Global business is the performance of business activities across national boundaries. Every nation in the world participates in global business to some extent. Involvement in global business has increased steadily since World War II, and it's expected to continue growing. More than $4.25 trillion is spent annually on trade among nations.[2] Worldwide employment will increase for many U.S. firms. This growth will be due in part to the global boom and new business opportunities throughout the world.

Today Japan is one of the world's largest economic powers. About fifty-seven years ago the country was left devastated by American bombing raids during World War II. Tokyo was burned to the ground; atomic bombs leveled Hiroshima and Nagasaki. When

> **Euro** The new currency of the European Union (EU).

> **Global Business** The performance of business activities across national boundaries.

---

1. Michael Arndt, Pete Engardio, and Joshua Goodman, "Smart Globalization," *Business Week*, August 27, 2001, pp. 132–138.

2. Constantine Michalopoulos, *Developing Countries in the WTO* (New York: Palgrave, 2002).

EXHIBIT 2-1

Opinions about Global Business

Directions: For each statement, circle the number that shows your level of agreement.

	Strongly Disagree					Strongly Agree
Foreign individuals and firms should be restricted from purchasing assets, such as banks, farmland, and hotels, in the United States.	1	2	3	4	5	6
Americans should purchase American-made products whenever possible.	1	2	3	4	5	6
The United States should limit the amount of foreign goods it imports.	1	2	3	4	5	6
Foreign companies should not be allowed to build factories in American cities.	1	2	3	4	5	6
The United States should put a high tax on all foreign goods entering the country.	1	2	3	4	5	6

Feedback: Americans often have strong feelings about foreign companies selling products in our country and competing with U.S. firms. If you strongly disagreed with most of the statements, you favor foreign firms being able to do business in the United States. If you strongly agreed with the statements, you tend to be against such business. You may echo a popular phrase of the last several years, "Buy American!"

Some Americans fear foreign competitors because they do not fully understand them—in language, culture, or social values. Some American companies have been hurt by foreign competition; you may know people who lost jobs after U.S. firms closed or moved operations overseas. Conversely, some Americans have few qualms about foreign companies conducting business on U.S. soil. They, and you, may think that international business is exciting and that competition from all manufacturers of product, regardless of country of origin is fair to businesses and beneficial to consumers. Regardless of your position on this issue, you as a student of business have already realized that international business will continue to expand in the United States and throughout the world.

the war ended, Japan's economy no longer existed. But Japan learned from the disaster. Ever since, the Japanese have invested in people. Trade liberalization across Asia, Africa, and North and South America also suggests a global environment in which market power becomes more important each year. Learning how to manage organizations in a global business environment is critical to firms throughout the world.

As more and more firms conduct business with foreign countries, the importance of global business increases. The values and attitudes quiz in Exhibit 2-1 will help you assess your thoughts about foreign firms doing business in the United States.

2-1b Global Opportunities

The global boom has resulted in a customer-driven world economy. Harvard University professor Rosabeth Moss Kanter says that information, the computer, and transportation advances have caused the global market. She contends that many of the changes taking place in the EU today are because people wanted more choices. Through the World Wide Web, TV, and other mass media, people can learn about lifestyles in the rest of the world.
1, 2 ☞ It's interesting to think that Levi Strauss and Bon Jovi—not only U.S. military strength—helped cause the Soviet bloc's breakup.[3]

A customer-driven economy means new opportunities throughout the world. For example, Russians know that their standard of living is lower than that of citizens in the

3. Catherine Belton Starobin and Stan Crook, "Putin's Russia," *Business Week,* November 12, 2001, pp. 66–72.

FOCUS ON TECHNOLOGY

The Hybrid Vehicle Is Coming

The U.S. Congress is working on mandates to toughen fuel economy standards. The hybrid car, one that combines a conventional gasoline engine with a battery-powered electric motor, is on the verge of going mainstream.

Global competitors such as Honda and Toyota are surging ahead of America's big three automakers with the hybrid technology. Honda has the Insight and Toyota has the Prius. The eye-popping miles per gallon are getting everyone's attention: 68 miles per gallon for the Insight and 52 for the Prius.

Honda will be placing the hybrid powertrain into its Civic compact to gain more market share. By the mid-2000s hundreds of thousands of hybrids will be driven in the United States. Ford's new Escape sports utility, a hybrid, is forecasting 40 mpg in city driving. General Motors will have hybrid powertrains in its pickups, the Chevrolet Silverado, and GMC Sierra.

The price for a hybrid will increase the sticker prices by between $1,500 and $3,000. To stay competitive, car manufacturers will have to address customer responses to the hybrids and price increases. The car world is changing because customers want more value, cleaner emissions, and more miles per gallon.

Sources: Jim Motavalli, *Forward Drive: The Race to Build the Car of the Future* (San Francisco: Sierra, 2000); and Michael H. Westbrook, *The Electric Car: Development and Future of Battery, Hybrid and Fuel Cell Cars* (New York: Inspec/IEE, 2001).

West. As Russia's economy changes, consumers are demanding all types of products—food, clothing, appliances, leisure items, medical care, and so on. Countless new opportunities will arise for firms to offer goods and services that meet these demands. In short, the global economy means global opportunities for firms that simply need the vision to act upon them. Russia has undergone one of the fastest processes of privatization. The state-owned factories, railroads, telephones, and television and radio stations have been privatized. Inflation has dropped from 2,000 percent in 1990 to about 16 percent in 2001.[4] Foreign investors, including EU, Japanese, and U.S. firms—such as Motorola, AT&T, Chrysler, IBM, and Apple—are flocking to China to invest in that country's double-digit growth.[5] Western firms also are finding new business opportunities in India, the world's fifth-largest economy, with a middle class of approximately 300 million people eager for new products.[6]

3, 4, 5, 6, 7

Taking advantage of global opportunities won't be easy. Firms throughout the world are poised to offer products to emerging markets (see the Focus on Technology box entitled "The Hybrid Vehicle Is Coming"). More competition means more choices, which drives the need for quality even higher. In 1980 there were seven primary competitors in the luxury car market. By 2003 the number was over twenty, including companies in the United States, Japan, Germany, South Korea, and several other European countries. Competition in other industries is following the same pattern. The increased globalization of markets has led to greater competition among corporations throughout the world and

4. Robert C. Stuart and Paul R. Gregory, *The Russian Economy: Past, Present, and Future* (Reading, MA: Addison-Wesley, 1998); and *Russian Economy: Trends and Perspective* (Moscow: Institute for the Economy in Transition, 2001).

5. Nicholas R. Lardy, *Integrating China into the Global Economy* (Washington, DC: The Brookings Institution, 2001).

6. Peter Nolan, *China and the Global Economy: National Champions, Industrial Policy, and the Big Business Revolution* (New York: St. Martin's, 2001).

Absolute Advantage   When a country can produce a product more efficiently than any other nation.

Comparative Advantage   When a country can produce one product more efficiently and at a lower cost than other products, in comparison to other nations.

erosion in the world dominance of U.S. firms—a trend that's expected to continue.[7] Firms that supply high-quality products will be in the best position to survive and prosper in the global economy.

2-1c Why Firms Conduct Global Business

Scarcity of resources is perhaps the major reason why nations trade with each other.[8] A country with a surplus of some product may decide to sell this surplus to other nations. Such sales enable the country to purchase other products that it may not have the ability to produce.

No nation has every raw material or resource; no nation can produce everything it needs. Most nations specialize in producing particular goods or services. The United States, for example, has developed a specialty in producing agricultural products efficiently; thus, it sells food to many nations of the world. But the United States purchases much of its oil from other countries, such as Saudi Arabia, Venezuela, and Nigeria, that specialize in the production of crude oil.

A nation has an **absolute advantage** if it can produce a product more efficiently (using fewer resources) than any other nation. South Africa has an absolute advantage in the production of diamonds. Absolute advantages are rare because usually at least two countries can efficiently supply a specific product.

A country has a **comparative advantage** if it can produce one product more efficiently than other products in comparison to other nations. For instance, countries with low labor costs, such as China and South American countries, have a comparative advantage in producing labor-intensive products such as shoes and clothing. Many nations become involved in international business because they have a comparative advantage. Firms sell those goods for which they have the greatest comparative advantage over other countries. The United States has its greatest comparative advantage in food products, engineering, medical technology, software, aircraft, and coal.

Comparative advantages shift frequently. For many years, the United States held a comparative advantage in manufacturing a variety of products, such as automobiles, television sets, and appliances. Today many of these products are made in Japan, Germany, and South Korea. The United States, for instance, experienced a dramatic loss of comparative advantage in manufacturing televisions. One reason for shifts in comparative advantages is competition.

Some nations want to become self-sufficient and thus do not specialize in the production and sale of particular products. The choice of specialization or self-sufficiency is generally a political and economic issue. For instance, communist nations traditionally have strived for self-sufficiency because they feared economic dependency on other countries. Some nations also view self-sufficiency as necessary for achieving military supremacy. Of course, no country is completely self-sufficient.

In an increasingly globalized world, countries trade goods, services, art culture, medical know-how, and labor with each other. The English economist David Ricardo in 1809 suggested that a nation's competitive advantage would provide the basis of economic and other forms of exchange.[9]

2-2 BASIC CONCEPTS OF INTERNATIONAL BUSINESS

Several basic concepts are important for an understanding of global business. In this section, we discuss the concepts of exporting and importing, balance of trade, balance of payments, and exchange rates.

7. "The Global 1,000," *Business Week*, July 10, 2000, pp. 107–138.

8. Morgan W. McCall, Sr. and George P. Hollenbeck, *Developing Global Executives* (Cambridge, MA: Harvard Business School Press, 2002).

9. Paul R. Krugman, *International Economics: Theory and Policy* (Reading, MA: Addison-Wesley, 2000).

2-2a Exporting and Importing

The United States is one of the world's largest exporters and importers. In 2000, the United States exported about $1.10 trillion and imported about $1.45 trillion worth of goods and services.[10] **Exporting** is selling domestic-made goods and services in another country. **Importing** is purchasing goods and services made in another country. Most of the video recorders purchased in the United States are imported from Japan.

The United States imports a wide variety of products: food, oil, automobiles, electronic equipment, clothing and shoes, iron and steel, and paper products, to name a few. But U.S. exports are on the rise, up 121 percent since 1978.[11] The major growth is in exports to Canada, Japan, Mexico, Taiwan, Korea, and Germany. The fastest-growing U.S. exports are music, video, and computer tapes; cigarettes and tobacco products; meat; pulp and wastepaper; and synthetic resins, rubber, and plastics.

2-2b Balance of Trade

A country's **balance of trade** is the result of importing and exporting. In 2000, the United States had a trade deficit (more imports than exports) of $364 billion. The United States' balance of trade is the difference (in monetary terms) between the amount it exports and the amount it imports. The United States has shown a deficit for many years. Some nations export more than they import and maintain a favorable balance of trade, or a *trade surplus*. Japan and Taiwan have a favorable balance of trade. In the late 1990s, countries such as Japan, Russia, and Great Britain were in a recession. America's relatively strong economic health attracted more exports from these flagging economies at a time that the demand of U.S. products and services decreased. The result was U.S. balance of trade deficits of $236 billion in 1998, $290 billion in 1999, and $364 billion in 2000.[12]

2-2c Balance of Payments

A country's **balance of payments** is the total flow of money into and out of the country. The balance of payments is determined by a country's balance of trade, foreign aid, foreign investments, military spending, and money spent by tourists in other countries. A country has a favorable balance of payments if more money is flowing in than is flowing out; an unfavorable balance of payments exists when more money is flowing out of the country than in. For many years, the United States enjoyed a favorable balance of payments. But in recent years, more money has been leaving the country than has been flowing in. Exhibit 2-2 shows the balance of payment deficit the United States has with its largest global trading partners.

2-2d Exchange Rates

The rate at which one country's currency can be exchanged for that of another country is called the **exchange rate.** For instance, on April 2, 2003, one U.S. dollar exchanged for 1.469 Canadian dollars, for .930 euro, and for 119.011 Japanese yen. If a country's currency depreciates in value, more of the currency is needed to buy the other country's currency.

The appreciation and depreciation have an effect on the prices of a country's goods and services. Suppose a red Ferrari is wanted and it costs 90,000 euros. Assume the U.S. dollar, which has been equal to .88 euros, depreciates. That is, the dollar is now worth only .98 euros. At the new exchange rate the desired red Ferrari priced at 90,000 euros would cost $88,200 (90,000 euros × .98) instead of $79,200 (90,000 × .88). As the dollar depreciates, the prices of EU country goods will increase for U.S. consumers, so they will

Exporting Selling domestic-made goods in another country.

Importing Purchasing goods made in another country.

Balance of Trade The difference (in dollars) between the amount a country exports and the amount it imports.

Balance of Payments The total flow of money into and out of a country.

Exchange Rate The rate at which one country's currency can be exchanged for that of another country.

10. "The World in 2002," *The Economist,* January 2002.

11. U.S. Department of Commerce, Bureau of Economic Analysis, June 22, 2001.

12. Ibid.

U.S. Balance of Payments Eight Largest Trade Partners ($Billions)

	2000		
	Exports	**Imports**	**Trade Balance**
Canada	$178.9	$230.9	–$52.0
Mexico	111.3	136.0	–24.7
Japan	64.9	146.5	–81.6
China	16.2	100.0	–83.8
Germany	29.4	58.6	–29.2
United Kingdom	41.6	43.3	–1.7
South Korea	27.8	40.3	–12.5
Taiwan	24.4	40.6	–16.2

Source: U.S. Commerce Department, June 21, 2001.

likely reduce their purchases. This will result in a decrease in EU country imports. Likewise, as the dollar depreciates relative to the euro, the euro appreciates in value relative to the U.S. dollar. The result is that Europeans would purchase more U.S. goods and services, which means that U.S. exports will increase.

Governments and market conditions determine exchange rates. *Devaluation* by a government reduces the value of a nation's currency in relation to currencies of other nations. If the United States were to devalue its currency, for example, the cost of American goods in foreign countries would decrease. *Revaluation* increases the value of a country's currency in relation to that of other countries. Revaluation of the dollar would increase the cost of American goods purchased in foreign countries.

After World War II, during a meeting held at Bretton Woods, New Hampshire, the major industrialized nations of the world established a **fixed exchange rate.** Known as the Bretton Woods Accord, this agreement mandated that a nation pay its debts by transferring gold reserves to the reserves of creditor nations. As the U.S. balance of payments deficit began to exceed its gold reserves, President Richard Nixon took the United States off the gold standard. Today this has led to a **floating exchange rate,** which allows the exchange rate to fluctuate with market conditions. For instance, when Americans spend U.S. dollars to buy automobiles and other products from Japan, the value of the dollars relative to the Japanese yen goes down. Today, many nations use a floating exchange rate.

Fixed Exchange Rate
An unvarying exchange rate set by government policy.

Floating Exchange Rate
An exchange rate that fluctuates with market conditions.

2-3 BARRIERS TO INTERNATIONAL BUSINESS

Trading between businesses and governments occurs as long as there are no barriers created. Unfortunately, firms and governments desiring to enter global business face several obstacles, some much more severe than others. In this section, we examine the most common barriers to effective international business: culture, social, and political barriers, and tariffs and trade restrictions.

2-3a Cultural and Social Barriers

Understanding differences in cultures and social forces is a basic requirement for successful international business.[13] *Culture* consists of a country's general concepts and values and tangible items such as food, clothing, and buildings. *Social forces* include family, education, religion, and customs. Selling products from one country to another is sometimes difficult when the cultures of the two countries differ significantly.

Cultural diversity refers to the differences that exist both within and among cultures.[14] Meanings attached to body language, time, greetings, spatial patterns, and other symbols

13. Lee Gardenswartz and Anita Rowe, "Cross Cultural Awareness," *HR Magazine,* March 2001, pp. 139–142.

14. Mark A. Williams, Mark W. Williams, and Donald O. Clifton, *The 10 Lenses: Your Guide to Living and Working in a Multicultural World* (New York: Capital Books, 2001).

differ significantly across cultures. When products are introduced into one nation from another, acceptance is far more likely if differences between cultures are recognized and accommodated. For example, managers of McDonald's realized that when they opened restaurants in Japan, they would have to adapt to Japanese culture. The first McDonald's restaurant was therefore located in a prestigious area in Tokyo to impress the Japanese. Had the restaurant been opened in the suburbs, the Japanese would have considered it a second-class enterprise. Understanding how Japanese consumers view locations helped McDonald's succeed in Japan. Conversely, Yokohama Rubber Company, based in Tokyo, recalled auto tires with a tread pattern that resembled the Arabic word for Allah, discontinued the tires, and replaced them free of charge in Islamic nations.[15]

Some countries also have different values about spending. The Japanese have long been a people who believe in paying cash for the products they buy, although the use of credit cards has soared in Japan over the last few years. The more the Japanese borrow and spend, the more they import—meaning increased trade for countries such as the United States. Yet the Japanese as a nation still save nearly 20 percent of individual income, compared with about 4 percent saved by people in the United States.[16]

Social forces can create obstacles to international trade. In China, for instance, a firm cannot claim in its advertisements to be number one, since the moral system there holds that everyone is equal. In some countries, religion can influence purchasing items as basic as food and clothing. In many nations, individuals do not have the choices in food, clothing, and health care that we do in the United States. And some societies simply do not value material possessions to the same degree that Americans do.

Most firms know the importance of understanding the cultural and social differences between selling and buying countries. However, managers still make costly mistakes when conducting business internationally simply because they do not understand such differences. For instance, a business deal in Japan can fall through if a foreign executive refuses a cup of green tea during a visit to a native Japanese firm, or if a Japanese businessperson is put in a position where he or she must admit failure.

An important potential barrier in some countries is the role that women play. As women move up the management hierarchy they are beginning to play larger roles. The Focus on Diversity box, "Global Power Group," illustrates the importance of four women in global business.

2-3b Political Barriers

The political climate of a country can have a major impact on global business. Nations experiencing intense political unrest may change their attitude toward foreign firms at any time; this instability creates an unfavorable atmosphere for global trade. The greatest risk for international firms is in politically unstable areas of the world such as Africa and the Middle East.

Nationalism, or a sense of national awareness and consciousness that promotes the values, culture, and interests of one county over others, can discourage global transactions. For example, in France the government requires that pop music stations play at least 40 percent of their songs in French. This law was passed because the youth of France love American music and artists. Without this nationalistic barrier American music sales would literally swamp anything else in the French market.[17]

Nationalism   A sense of national awareness and consciousness that promotes the values, culture, and interests of one county over others.

2-3c Tariffs and Trade Restrictions

Tariffs and trade restrictions are also barriers to international business. A nation can restrict trade through import tariffs, quotas and embargoes, and exchange controls.

---

15. "Tires Recalled So They Don't Tread on Allah," *Lexington Herald Leader*, July 25, 1992, p. A3.

16. Makoto Ito and Makoto Itoh, *The Japanese Economy Reconsidered* (New York: St. Martin's Press, 2000).

17. Christine White, "An Encore for French Cinema," *Business Week*, September 10, 2001, p. 61.

FOCUS ON DIVERSITY

Global Power Group

Women are starting to work their way into key positions in global business. The climb has been slow, but each year an increasing list of global businesses are now being led by creative, powerful, and knowledgeable women. A few of these powerful global superstars are as follows:

Marjorie Scardino: CEO of Pearson, a British firm. She has turned a hodgepodge firm into a focused media and entertainment powerhouse. She has proposed a significant set of growth goals.

Eiko Kono: President of Recruit, a Japanese firm. The company is the largest (sales of $3 billion a year) company in Japan headed by a woman. The company's classified advertising magazine seems to be on every newsstand and in every convenience store, offering jobs, used cars, and apartments.

Patricia Barbizet: CEO of Artemis, a French firm. She administers an eclectic array of investments for this private holding company. Artemis holdings run the gamut from timber to Christie's auction house.

Abigail Johnson: President of Fidelity Management and Research, an American firm. This largest mutual fund company in the United States is responsible for $1 trillion in assets. Abigail Johnson is the owner of almost 25 percent of the company.

Source: Patricia Sellers, "Patient But Not Passive," *Fortune*, October 15, 2001, pp. 200–204.

Import Tariffs

Import Tariff A duty, or tax, levied against goods brought into a country.

A duty, or tax, levied against goods brought into a country is an **import tariff.** Tariffs can be used to discourage foreign competitors from entering a domestic market. Some Americans have called for high tariffs on Japanese products such as cars and stereos. The risk in imposing tariffs is that the other country could take the same action against U.S. products.

Quotas and Embargoes

Quota A limit on the amount of a product that can leave or enter a country.

A **quota** is a limit on the amount of a product that can leave or enter a country. The United States protects its dwindling textile industry with quotas. China sells over $7 billion of textiles to the United States annually while the United States ships only about $70 million of textiles annually to China.[18] This significant imbalance was addressed by the U.S. government, which threatened to impose a fine on China. The Chinese government countered by threatening to place quotas on American food products being exported to China. The U.S. government backed down and imposed no fines on China's exporting of textiles to the United States.

Embargo A total ban on specific imports and exports from and to a country.

An **embargo** is a total ban on certain imports and exports. Many embargoes are politically motivated, such as the United Nations' embargo of goods to Iraq after that nation invaded Kuwait in 1990. The United States prohibits the importing of Cuban cigars that some aficionados claim are the best in the world. Often, if a country places an embargo on products imported from or exported to another country, the second country retaliates with an embargo. In recent years, American firms found that doors that once were closed in Vietnam soon became wide open when American and Vietnamese business leaders applied pressure on their governments to permit previously embargoed products to be traded.[19]

18. John Wong, Mia Yinhua, and Luo Qi, *Sino-U.S. Trade Accord and China's Accession to the WTO* (New York: World Scientific Publishing, 2000).

19. Evangelos O. Simos, "International Economic Outlook: The World Economy in 2009," *The Journal of Business Forecasting Methods and Systems*, Fall 2000, pp. 31–35.

Law	Purpose
Webb-Pomerene Export (1918)	Exempts U.S. firms from Trade Act antitrust laws if they are acting together to develop international trade
Foreign Corrupt Practices Act (1977)	Makes bribing foreign officials to obtain sales illegal for American firms
Export Trading Companies Act (1982)	Encourages the formation of export trading companies by eliminating antitrust barriers and allowing banks to participate in such ventures

EXHIBIT 2-3

U.S. Laws Affecting International Business

Exchange Controls

Restrictions on the amount of a certain currency that can be bought or sold are called **exchange controls.** A government can use exchange controls to limit the amount of products that importers can purchase with a particular currency. This type of restriction requires a firm receiving foreign currency from its exports to sell the money to a central bank; for example, a French wine maker selling 42,000 bottles of wine to a U.S. distributor for $200,000 (U.S. dollars). If France had exchange controls, the wine maker would have to sell its U.S. dollars to a French central bank and would receive euros.[20]

> **Exchange Controls**
> Restrictions on the amount of a certain currency that can be bought or sold in a nation.

2-4 REGULATION OF INTERNATIONAL BUSINESS

As business between nations has grown, so has the number of laws and organizations involved in the regulation of international trade. In this section, we look at major legislation and organizations that have been developed to regulate international business.

2-4a Legislation

The major U.S. laws affecting American firms engaged in international business are summarized in Exhibit 2-3. The *Webb-Pomerene Export Trade Act* of 1918 exempts U.S. firms from certain antitrust laws if they are working together to develop export markets. The Webb-Pomerene Act does not allow companies to reduce competition in the United States or to use unfair methods of competition. The *Foreign Corrupt Practices Act*, passed in 1977, prohibits American firms from making bribes to foreign officials. This law spells out the penalties for companies and individuals who are in violation: Companies may be fined up to $1 million, and individuals may receive a fine up to $10,000 and a prison sentence of up to five years. The *Export Trading Companies Act* of 1982 eliminates some antitrust barriers and allows banks to participate in joint ventures. An export trading company is an organization that attempts to create exports.

Unfortunately, many firms can take advantage of weak regulation in foreign countries. For example, products that are regulated in the United States, such as dangerous pesticides and drugs, may not be regulated in other countries, so firms look to those foreign markets to sell dangerous products. Third World nations are often the target of dangerous products because they have the weakest regulation.

2-4b Organizations That Facilitate Global Business

Several organizations exist to facilitate world trade. Some of the major ones are summarized in Exhibit 2-4.

GATT

Signed in 1947, the **General Agreement on Tariffs and Trade (GATT)** formed an international organization of twenty-three nations, including the United States. GATT works

> **General Agreement on Tariffs and Trade (GATT)**
> An international organization formed to reduce or eliminate tariffs and other barriers to international trade.

---

20. William Erikson, Frederick Balfour, Kerry Capell, Linda Himelstein, and Gerry Khermouch, "Wine War," *Business Week,* September 3, 2001, pp. 54–60.

Organizations that Facilitate Global Business

General Agreement on Tariffs and Trade (GATT)
Formed in 1947 by 23 nations to reduce or eliminate tariffs and other barriers to international trade.
Members: 134 countries, including the United States, Russia, China, Taiwan, and India.

European Union (EU)
Founded in 1957 to reduce barriers among members.
Members: Austria, Belgium, Denmark, Finland, France, Germany, Greece, Ireland, Italy, Luxembourg, the Netherlands, Portugal, Spain, Sweden, and the United Kingdom.

Latin American Free Trade Association (LAFTA)
Founded in 1960 to develop free trade among member nations.
Members: Argentina, Brazil, Chile, Columbia, Ecuador, Mexico, Paraguay, Peru, and Uruguay.

European Free Trade Association (EFTA)
Founded in 1960 to eliminate trade restrictions among members and develop common trade policies.
Members: Austria, Iceland, Norway, Portugal, Sweden, Switzerland, and Finland (associate member).

Organization of Petroleum Exporting Countries (OPEC)
Established in 1960 to provide oil-producing nations control over prices and reduce the oversupply of oil.
Members: Algeria, Ecuador, Gabon, Indonesia, Iran, Kuwait, Libya, Nigeria, Qatar, Saudi Arabia, United Arab Emirates, and Venezuela.

International Monetary Fund (IMF)
Founded in 1944 to promote trade among member nations by eliminating trade barriers and increasing cooperation on financial issues.
Members: 149 industrial and developing countries.

World Bank
Founded in 1946 to lend money to underdeveloped and developing countries for a variety of projects.
Members: 149 industrial and developing countries.

World Trade Organization (WTO) Headquartered in Geneva, Switzerland, created by the GATT to mediate and resolve trade disputes.

Economic Community An organization that facilitates the movement of products among member nations through the creation of common economic policies.

to reduce or eliminate tariffs and other barriers to international trade. Today over 120 countries agree to the guidelines established by GATT.[21]

Since it was organized GATT has sponsored several rounds of negotiations to reduce trade barriers. President John F. Kennedy, through authority granted by the Trade Expansion Act of 1962, called for the reduction of tariffs through GATT. The Kennedy Round, which began in 1964, led to a nearly 40 percent reduction in tariffs. The Tokyo Round, held from 1973 to 1979, led to a reduction of over 30 percent. Other nontariff restrictions, such as import quotas and unnecessary red tape in customs procedures, were also removed. In 1986, the Uruguay Round of GATT convened to deal with the renegotiation of trade agreements. After eight years of debate and negotiations, a new GATT accord adopted by 124 nations, including the United States, reduced tariffs worldwide by an average of 38 percent.[22]

On January 1, 1995, the **World Trade Organization (WTO),** headquartered in Geneva, Switzerland, was created by the GATT to mediate and resolve trade disputes. The WTO has over 130 member nations who comply with the decisions reached in disputes. It is a global mediation and service resource.

Economic Communities

An organization formed to facilitate the movement of products among member nations through the creation of common economic policies is called an **economic community.**

21. Terence P. Stewart, ed., *The GATT Uruguay Round: A Negotiating History* (New York: Kluwer, 1999).
22. Ibid.

One of the largest, the fifteen-nation EU, created by the Treaty of Rome in 1957, called for eliminating most trade barriers between its original members (Germany, France, Italy, the United Kingdom, Spain, and Netherlands, Belgium, Denmark, Greece, Portugal, Ireland, and Luxembourg). Historically the member nations have primarily been separate markets, unable to compete with the giant resources of Japan and the United States. With the barriers dissolved, however, competitive European companies now tap into a unified European market. With over 340 million consumers, unified Europe is one of the largest markets in the world.[23] The elimination of trade barriers has meant gains for Europe in several industries, including airlines, telecommunications, and financial services. The launching of the euro in 2002 as the official currency of the EU is a historic milestone.

Another economic community, the Latin American Free Trade Association (LAFTA), was organized in 1960. Its purpose is to develop free trade among members, a goal yet to be achieved. The European Free Trade Association (EFTA), organized in 1960 in response to the European Community (EC), has eliminated many trade barriers among members. Two original members of EFTA, the United Kingdom and Denmark, dropped out to join the EU. Another well-known economic community is the Organization of Petroleum Exporting Countries (OPEC). Established in 1960, OPEC exists to give oil-producing nations some control over the price and supply of oil. OPEC has been fairly successful in controlling both.

The United States and Canada signed the *Free Trade Agreement (FTA)* in 1989, providing for the eventual elimination of tariffs and other trade barriers. The agreement essentially merged the U.S. and Canadian markets and made them the largest free trade zone in the world. Trade between the United States and Canada was nearly $170 billion annually before the FTA was signed. Even greater commercial activity is expected as barriers to trade are further removed.

Even more far reaching is the *North American Free Trade Agreement (NAFTA)*, a three-nation alliance of the United States, Canada, and Mexico signed on August 12, 1992. The United States receives resources and a source of new labor, Canada is resource-rich but small in population, and Mexico has an abundance of oil and workers but desperately needed to increase exports to fuel its economy. The three nations combined comprise a $7 trillion market of nearly 370 million consumers.[24] Trade among the three nations, $237 billion a year before NAFTA, has increased dramatically since trade barriers were removed to annual trade of over $1 trillion.[25] There were fears that the agreement would mean more U.S. jobs lost to Mexico, where wages are about 10 percent of those in the United States. Many economists argue, however, that lower labor costs should put U.S. firms in a better position to take on global competitors and thus should provide a long-range benefit to the economy.

IMF and World Bank

Two international organizations have been established to help finance international trade. The **International Monetary Fund (IMF)** was founded in 1944 to promote cooperation among member nations by eliminating trade barriers. The IMF lends money to countries that need short-term loans to conduct international trade. The **World Bank** was formed in 1946 to lend money to underdeveloped and developing countries for various projects. The World Bank loans most of its money to poorer member nations to fund the development of roads, factories, and medical facilities. In 2002 and 2003 the World Bank was criticized by environmentalists who contended that World Bank–supported projects have damaged ecosystems. In addition, AIDS activists have complained that the Bank isn't aggressive enough in getting low-cost AIDS drugs to poorer nations.

International Monetary Fund (IMF)   An international financial organization that lends money to countries to conduct international trade.

World Bank   An international organization that lends money to underdeveloped and developing countries for development.

23. Gabriel Tondl, *Convergence After Divergence? Regional Growth in Europe,* (New York: Springer Verlag, 2001).

24. See U.S. Department of Commerce by using www.ita.doc.gov/td/industry/otea/usfth/aggregate.

25. U.S. International Trade, Department of Commerce, June 21, 2001.

2-5 APPROACHES TO INTERNATIONAL BUSINESS

A firm that decides to enter international trade must select an approach. There are several choices, some requiring relatively low levels of commitment and others requiring much higher levels. Approaches to international business include exporting, licensing, joint ventures, strategic alliances, trading companies, countertrading, direct ownership, and multinational corporations.

2-5a Exporting

The simplest way to enter international business is through exporting—selling domestic goods to a foreign country. It requires the lowest level of resources and commitment. The U.S. government has created Export Assistance Centers in seventeen U.S. cities to assist in conducting export business. More than half of the U.S. firms involved in global trade do so through exporting.[26] In many cases, a firm can locate an exporting firm that can provide assistance in selling products to foreign countries, thereby making significant upfront investments.[27]

The United States is one of the world's largest exporters ($1.1 trillion in 2000) and importers ($1.45 trillion) in the world. Products (e.g., manufacturing, agriculture, computer chips) and services (e.g., transportation, consulting, license fees) have increased each year, especially since the 1970s, to a point where it is difficult to determine in what country products and services originated.

2-5b Licensing

> **Licensing**   An agreement in which one firm allows another firm to sell its product and use its brand name in return for a commission or royalty.

In a **licensing** agreement, one firm (the licensor) agrees to allow another firm (the licensee) to sell the licensor's product and use its brand name. In return, the licensee pays the licensor a commission or royalty. For example, a beverage company such as PepsiCo might enter into a licensing agreement with a firm in Taiwan. The Taiwanese firm would have the right to sell Pepsi products in Taiwan and would pay PepsiCo a specified percentage of the income from sales of Pepsi products.

Licensing offers advantages for both licensor and licensee. The licensor can become involved in international trade with little financial risk. The licensee gains products and technology that may otherwise be too costly to produce. For the licensor, the agreement usually results in a payoff of only about 5 percent of sales. Some American executives and managers believe that licensing agreements merely give away trade secrets for a meager 5 percent of sales; after the agreement expires (usually in less than ten years), the licensee may continue to market the product without paying the licensor.

2-5c International Joint Ventures

> **Joint Venture**   A special type of partnership established to carry out a special project or to operate for a specific time period.

Firms may also conduct international business through a **joint venture,** in this case a partnership between a domestic firm and a firm in a foreign country. Because of government restrictions on foreign ownership of corporations, joint ventures are often the only way a firm can purchase facilities in another country. For instance, after years of negotiations, McDonald's of Canada opened a restaurant in the Soviet Union. The Moscow City Council's Food Service will own 51 percent of the enterprise, a requirement under Soviet joint venture laws.

In 2001, Walt Disney and its Japanese strategic partner, Oriental Land, opened the gates to DisneySea, a $2.8 billion marine-themed attraction built next door to Tokyo Disneyland, which opened in 1983. Disney and Oriental have joined together to attract customers and receipts. The partners are hoping that a combined 25 million visitors a year will visit both Japanese parks (about 17 million visit Tokyo Disneyland annually). The

26. Ibid.
27. Ibid.

DisneySea park is estimated to generate $15 billion a year in related business in the area malls, gasoline stations, and support services.[28]

One major drawback to international joint ventures is that organizations may lose control of their operations. For example, because India does not allow foreign companies to own industries, Coca-Cola once entered into a joint venture with the Indian government. Despite the huge soft drink market in India, Coca-Cola pulled out of the agreement rather than risk giving up majority control and its secret formula.

2-5d Strategic Alliances

A recent strategy for entering foreign markets is a strategic alliance. A **strategic alliance** occurs when two firms combine their resources in a partnership that goes beyond the limits of a joint venture. Strategic alliances have been growing in the highly competitive global marketplace at an annual rate of 20 percent since 1895.[29] IBM alone has established more than 400 strategic alliances with U.S. and foreign firms. Trust is the major requirement for an effective partnership. If a firm can't trust its prospective partners, it shouldn't enter into a strategic alliance with them. Trust generally evolves over time, so firms must give strategic alliances adequate time to prosper. Ford and Mazda formed a strategic alliance nearly fifteen years ago to cooperate on new vehicles and exchange expertise. Ford is now the best-selling foreign auto in Japan; building trust over the years was a major factor in its success.[30]

> **Strategic Alliance** An agreement in which two firms combine their resources in a partnership that goes beyond a joint venture.

2-5e Trading Companies

Another approach to international business is to use or form a trading company to provide a link between buyers and sellers in different countries. A **trading company** buys products in one country and sells them in another without being involved in manufacturing. Trading companies take title to products and move them from one country to another. Trading companies can simplify entrance into foreign markets because they are usually favored by the foreign governments. Many major corporations such as General Electric and Sears, Roebuck have developed trading companies.

Some countries—Brazil, for one—give trading companies tax advantages. In the United States, the 1982 *Export Trading Company Act* encourages the efficient operation of trading companies, helps finance international trade, and provides limited protection from antitrust laws when conducting export activities. After the act was passed, many major companies (such as General Electric, Kmart, and Sears, Roebuck) developed their own export trading companies.

> **Trading Company** A firm that buys products in one country and sells in another without being involved in manufacturing.

2-5f Countertrading

Countertrading involves complex bartering agreements between two or more countries. (*Bartering* refers to the exchange of merchandise between countries.) Countertrading allows a nation with limited cash to participate in international trade. The country wishing to trade requires the exporting country to purchase products from it before allowing its products to be sold there. Agreements like this account for an estimated 20 percent of U.S. exports, or $210 billion; the use of countertrade agreements is expected to grow. Countertrading provides an established trading vehicle for companies such as General Electric, Caterpillar, Pepsi, Boeing, Sears, and General Motors. For example, GM's trading section employs twenty-five people and does about $200 million annually in trade. Boeing has sold billions of dollars worth of 747 aircraft to Saudi Arabia in exchange for oil.

> **Countertrading** Bartering agreements between two or more countries.

---

28. Chester Dawson, "Will Tokyo Embrace Another Mouse?" *Business Week,* September 21, 2001, p. 65.

29. Ed Rysbee, *Developing Strategic Alliances* (New York: Crisp, 2000).

30. Yves Doz, Jose Santos, and Peter Williamson, *From Global to Multinational: How Companies Win in the Knowledge Economy* (Boston: Harvard Business School Press, 2001).

Countertrading has several drawbacks. First, it's often difficult to determine the true value of goods offered in a countertrade agreement. Second, it may be difficult to dispose of bartered goods after they're accepted. These problems can be reduced or eliminated through market analysis and negotiation. Companies have been developed to assist firms in handling countertrade agreements. Despite these drawbacks, companies that choose not to countertrade may miss significant opportunities.

2-5g   Direct Ownership

Direct Ownership
The purchase of one or more business operations in a foreign country.

A much more involved approach to international business is **direct ownership**—purchasing one or more business operations in a foreign country. Direct ownership requires a large investment in production facilities, research, personnel, and marketing activities. Many large companies, such as Ford, Polaroid, and 3M, own facilities outside the United States. Some well-known firms operating in the United States are actually subsidiaries owned by foreign firms. Magnavox, Pillsbury, Saks Fifth Avenue, and Baskin-Robbins are wholly owned subsidiaries of foreign multinational companies. Nonprofit organizations (such as the Red Cross) and the U.S. Army also own foreign subsidiaries or divisions.

Firms invest in foreign subsidiaries for a number of reasons. Direct ownership can reduce manufacturing costs because of lower labor and operating costs. Direct ownership also enables a firm to avoid paying tariffs and other costs associated with exporting. Additionally, by paying taxes in the host country and providing employment for local residents, a foreign country can build good relations with the host government. The greatest danger of direct ownership is that a firm may lose a sizable investment because of market failure or nationalization of its interest by a foreign government. When problems arise in a foreign country, it's often very difficult and expensive to move operations out of the country.

2-5h   Multinational Corporations

Global Market   The entire world is considered to be a potential consumer of a firm's products or services.

Multinational Corporations
A firm that operates on a global basis, committing assets to operations or subsidiaries in foreign countries.

Some corporations operate as if the world were a single **global market**.[31] This approach represents a total commitment to international business and is used by **multinational corporations** who have assets committed to operations or subsidiaries in foreign countries. Large organizations such as Exxon, General Motors, IBM, Grand Metropolitan (a British company), and Nestle (a Swiss company) are multinational corporations. Exhibit 2-5 lists the world's largest multinational corporations in terms of annual revenue.

Products most suitable for this approach include airlines, automobiles, heavy equipment, machine tools, computers, petroleum, cosmetics, and soft drinks. KLM Royal Dutch Airliner's strategy is to use global alliances to serve airline passengers around the world.[32]

2-6   ADAPTING TO GLOBAL MARKETS

Because of differences from country to country, a firm engaged in global trade must generally adapt to foreign markets. In this section, we examine how a firm gears its product offerings, prices, distribution systems, and methods of promotion to foreign countries.

2-6a   Product

In some cases, the same product developed for the U.S. market can be sold in a foreign country. Coca-Cola and PepsiCo have successfully taken their soft drinks to foreign markets without changing them. But usually products have to be altered to meet conditions in a foreign market. General Electric faced problems selling refrigerators in Japan because they were too large to fit into most Japanese homes.

---

31. J. De la Torre, Y. Doz, and T. Devinney, *Managing the Global Corporation* (New York: McGraw-Hill, 2000).

32. Doz, Santos, and Williamson, *From Global to Multinational.*

Global 500 Rank	Company	Country	Revenue ($millions)
1	Exxon Mobil	U.S.	$210,392.0
2	Wal-Mart Stores	U.S.	193,295.0
3	General Motors	U.S.	184,632.0
4	Ford Motor	U.S.	180,598.0
5	Daimler Chrysler	Germany	150,069.7
6	Royal Dutch/Shell Group	Netherlands	149,146.0
7	BP	Britain	148,062.0
8	General Electric	U.S.	129,853.0
9	Mitsubishi	Japan	126,579.4
10	Toyota Motor	Japan	121,416.2
11	Mitsui	Japan	118,013.7
12	Citigroup	U.S.	111,826.0
13	Itochu	Japan	109,756.5
14	Total Fina Elf	France	105,869.6
15	Nippon Telegraph & Telephone	Japan	103,234.7
16	Enron	U.S.	100,789.0
17	AXA	France	92,781.6
18	Sumitomo	Japan	91,168.4
19	International Business Machines	U.S.	88,396.0
20	Marubeni U.S.	Japan	85,351.0

EXHIBIT 2-5

World's Twenty Largest Global Organizations

Source: "Global 500," *Fortune*, July 23, 2001.

In some cases, companies cannot modify existing products to fit the needs of a foreign country. They then can either develop a new product for that country or try to sell the current product in other countries. Developing new products is a costly alternative, but many provide a large payoff. Colgate-Palmolive, for example, developed Axion, a dishwashing paste packaged in a plastic cup, for consumers in South America who traditionally used leftover soap chips kept in a bowl to wash their dishes.

2-6b Price

The price of a product is usually different in domestic and foreign markets. The costs of foreign trade, such as taxes, tariffs, and transportation, often result in higher prices in the foreign country. Exchange rates can also influence the price of foreign goods.

In some instances, firms intentionally establish lower prices in foreign markets. The practice of selling surplus products in a foreign country at a lower price than that in the country of origin is called **dumping.** Japanese companies have been accused of dumping computer chips, television sets, steel, and automobiles on the American market while charging Japanese customers high prices that include all research and development expenses. China has been accused of dumping bicycles on the U.S. market. The United States has laws that require products sold in the United States to include a 10 percent overhead cost plus at least an 8 percent profit margin.

2-6c Distribution

The task of providing products in foreign nations often presents challenges and problems. Many international business firms attempt to move and sell goods and provide services through existing transportation systems, stores, and suppliers. In some countries, however, adequate distribution systems do not exist. Then a firm must develop ways to get its products to the customers. In China, for example, manufacturers typically do not make deliveries to stores and other outlets. Both Coca-Cola and PepsiCo have invested heavily in trucks and refrigeration for storeowners to use to obtain and sell Coke and Pepsi products in China.[33]

Dumping Selling surplus products in a foreign country at a lower price than in the country of origin.

33. Dean Forest and Gerry Khermouch, "Shaking Up the Coke Bottle," *Business Week*, December 3, 2001, pp. 74–75; and Gerry Khermouch, "Whoa, Cool Shirt, Yeah It's a Pepsi," *Business Week*, September 10, 2001, p. 84.

2-6d Promotion

Many companies use the same message worldwide to inform customers about products and persuade them to buy. Uniform promotion, including advertising and publicity, enables firms to gain recognition throughout the world. But promotion often must be modified because language, laws, and culture differ from country to country. For instance, Japanese advertisements commonly use ideas that people elsewhere would consider sexist. Household appliances have been promoted with the phrase "So simple a woman can operate it." Japanese companies have issued wall calendars featuring nude women. In many countries, such promotional methods would not be acceptable.

Decisions concerning which media to use for advertising or publicity must also be adapted to different countries. Some nations do not have commercial television. Others do not have advertising space in newspapers. The circulation of magazines and newspapers also varies greatly from one country to another. In nations with a low literacy rate, radio and television advertising, if available, is more effective than print media.

SUGGESTED WEBSITES

Note: These websites were functional when we went to press. Please access the online text for the most up-to-date URLs.

1. www.levi.com
2. www.bonjovi.com
3. www.motorola.com
4. www.att.com
5. www.daimlerchrysler.com
6. www.ibm.com
7. www.apple.com
8. www.wto.org

SUMMARY OF LEARNING OBJECTIVES

1. *Discuss the meaning and scope of global business.*   Global business is the performance of business activities across national boundaries. Involvement in global business is increasing, with growth expected to continue.

2. *Explain why firms become involved in global business.*   Countries cannot produce everything for themselves. Most nations specialize in the production of certain goods and services and sell any surplus to other nations. A country has an absolute advantage if it can produce a product more efficiently than any other nation. A country that can produce one product more efficiently than other products, in comparison to other nations, has a comparative advantage.

3. *Define the basic concepts of global business.*   *Exporting* is selling domestic goods to a foreign country; *importing* is purchasing goods from another country. A country's *balance of trade* is the difference between the amount it exports and the amount it imports. The total flow of money in and out of a country is the *balance of payments.* The *exchange rate* is the rate at which one country's currency can be exchanged for another's currency.

4. *List the various barriers to global business.*   A nation's culture and social forces can create obstacles to international trade. The political climate of a country also influences international trade. A nation can also restrict trade through import tariffs, quotas and embargoes, and exchange controls.

5. *Identify the ways in which global business is regulated.*   Several laws affect American firms doing business in foreign countries. These laws generally exempt U.S. firms from certain antitrust laws, prohibit bribing of foreign officials, and allow banks to participate in joint ventures. Several organizations also exist to facilitate world trade, including the General Agreement on Tariffs and Trade (GATT), the World Trade Organization (WTO), the International Monetary Fund (IMF), the World Bank, and economic communities such as the European Union (EU) and the Organization of Petroleum Exporting Countries (OPEC).

6. *Describe the different approaches firms take to conduct business globally.*   A firm can take several approaches to international trade. Some require little commitment on the part of the firm, while others require a great deal of involvement. The approaches to global business are exporting, licensing, joint ventures, trading companies, countertrading, direct ownership, and multinational corporations.

7. *Determine how a firm can adapt to foreign markets.*   A firm engaged in global business must generally adapt to foreign markets. Some products have to be changed to be suitable to another country. Prices of products may be set differently in various countries. In some cases, products can be distributed through existing systems, but if appropriate distribution systems do not exist, firms must develop them. Advertising and publicity often must be modified because of differences in language, laws, and culture.

KEY TERMS

absolute advantage (p. 34)
balance of payments (p. 35)
balance of trade (p. 35)
comparative advantage (p. 34)
countertrading (p. 43)
direct ownership (p. 44)
dumping (p. 45)
economic community (p. 40)
embargo (p. 38)
euro (p. 31)
exchange controls (p. 39)

exchange rate (p. 35)
exporting (p. 35)
fixed exchange rate (p. 36)
floating exchange rate (p. 36)
General Agreement on Tariffs and Trade
  (GATT) (p. 39)
global business (p. 31)
global market (p. 44)
import tariff (p. 38)
importing (p. 35)

International Monetary Fund (IMF) (p. 41)
joint venture (p. 42)
licensing (p. 42)
multinational corporations (p. 44)
nationalism (p. 37)
quota (p. 38)
strategic alliance (p. 43)
trading company (p. 43)
World Bank (p. 41)
World Trade Organization (WTO) (p. 40)

QUESTIONS FOR DISCUSSION AND REVIEW

1. Why do firms become involved in global business? What is the result of global competition? Can firms avoid competing with foreign firms?
2. In what product and service areas does the United States have a comparative advantage? Would you expect this to change in the future?
3. Explain the difference between exporting and importing. Give examples of products that the United States exports and those it imports.
4. Why is the United States' balance of trade considered unfavorable? What must be done to make it favorable? Is this possible?
5. What impact has NAFTA had on the economies of the United States, Canada, and Mexico?
6. What will need to be done by U.S., Canadian, and French businesses to attract a larger share of business from China and India?
7. Why is the European Union (EU) excited and optimistic about having a single currency, the euro, for all fifteen member nations?
8. Name and explain three different approaches to conducting global business. Under what conditions should each of these approaches be used?
9. How are trade disputes between nations settled?
10. What is dumping? Give an example of a product that has been dumped in the United States and explain why this practice is illegal in many countries.

END-OF-CHAPTER QUESTIONS

1. Russia has undergone one of the fastest processes of privatization.   **T** or **F**
2. Absolute advantages shift frequently.   **T** or **F**
3. In China, a firm cannot claim in its advertisements to be number one because the moral system there holds that everyone is equal.   **T** or **F**
4. A *tariff* is a limit on the amount of a product that can leave or enter a country.   **T** or **F**
5. The *Foreign Corrupt Practices Act* prohibits American firms from making bribes to foreign officials.   **T** or **F**
6. The Free Trade Agreement (FTA) essentially merged the U.S. and Canadian markets and made them the largest free trade zone in the world.   **T** or **F**
7. The World Bank lends money to countries that need short-term loans to conduct international trade.   **T** or **F**
8. By opening more _____, nations and people become more bound together through the exchange of goods and services.
   a. telephone lines   c. schools and universities
   b. markets   d. banks
9. Approximately how much money is spent annually on trade between nations?
   a. $4.25 million   b. $4.25 billion   c. $4.25 trillion
10. If offered a cup of green tea during a business meeting at a native Japanese firm, you should _____.
    a. politely refuse it   b. accept it
11. When two firms combine their resources in a partnership that goes beyond the limits of a joint venture, it is called a _____.
    a. licensing agreement   c. strategic alliance
    b. modified joint venture   d. partnership
12. Boeing has delivered billions of dollars worth of 747 aircraft to Saudi Arabia in exchange for _____.
    a. money   c. reduced taxes
    b. reduced labor rates d. oil
13. Baskin-Robbins, Pillsbury, Magnavox, and Saks Fifth Avenue are all subsidiaries of _____ firms.
    a. foreign   b. United States
14. General Electric faced problems selling refrigerators in Japan because they _____.
    a. opened on the wrong side c. were too large
    b. were the wrong color   d. were over-priced
15. The practice of selling surplus products in a foreign country at a lower price than in the country of origin is called _____.
    a. choking   c. dumping
    b. trashing   d. looting

INTERNET EXERCISE

8 ☞ The World Trade Organization (WTO) website provides data, statistics, news, discussions, documents, and resources. Examine each of the sections displayed on the site and provide an analysis of what is available on goods, services, intellectual property, and dispute resolution. What kind of dispute settlement cases does the WTO present?

How would you use this site to examine the global business conducted by a particular country?

What other sites can you find that provide the wealth of information on global business?

EXPERIENTIAL EXERCISE

Deciding on International Operations

Activity

This activity is designed for small group and classroom discussions on the issues a company might confront when considering a change in operations.

Directions

1. Divide the class into groups of four to seven members and ask each group to appoint a recorder/spokesperson.
2. Explain the scenario: The students are to be a manufacturing plant owner contemplating whether to close a textile mill in North Carolina and open up a replacement in Mexico. The owner believes the move may be needed to keep labor costs under control.
3. Ask each group to identify the advantages and disadvantages of moving the plant out of the United States in general and the North Carolina community in particular. What problems might surface in North Carolina when the move is announced?
4. Ask each group to identify the advantages and disadvantages of setting up the manufacturing plant in Mexico. Have each group conclude by deciding whether to move the operations from North Carolina to Mexico.
5. Ask each spokesperson to share the group's conclusions with the class and to explain the reasons for the decision on moving the plant.

BUSINESS APPLICATION

Protecting American Executives in Foreign Countries

Because of the increasing concern over terrorism in foreign countries and a growing anti-American sentiment from many terrorist organizations, American companies have had to reexamine their policies and practices related to American executives traveling in foreign countries. Terrorist groups know that a kidnapped U.S. citizen held for political or criminal gains will bring tremendous publicity and, they hope, more leverage in negotiations. If a terrorist group is able to extract a $2 million ransom from an American company in exchange for the release of an American captive, then U.S. companies need to carefully think through their policies.

Assume that you are the president of an American corporation who must decide how the company will respond to the threat of executive kidnappings. Respond to the following scenarios:

1. One of your executives has been kidnapped by a terrorist group demanding a ransom of $2 million dollars for the executive's release.
2. Would you pay the ransom?
3. If yes, what might be the repercussions to your company?
4. If not, what might be the repercussions?
5. One of your executives refuses an assignment to travel in a country known to tolerate terrorists.
6. Would you insist that the executive travel despite the resistance?
7. Would you consider not doing business in that country, rather than pressuring executives to enter into potentially dangerous situations?

Case

Chiquita's Fall from the Top

Chiquita banana plantations dot the landscape in Bocas, Panama. Chiquita Brands International (originally named the United Fruit Company) grows and markets over $2.3 billion of bananas each year. In the past decade the profitability of Chiquita has been only an unachievable goal. Chiquita has lost more than $700 million. The company with a brand recognized around the world and that has about a third of the global market is having difficulty surviving.

The management of Chiquita claims that its image and profits began to suffer in 1993 when the EU imposed a restrictive quota system. Overnight, Chiquita's share of the EU market was cut in half. For eight years now, Chiquita has engaged in an expensive trade dispute with the EU. Finally, in the summer of 2001 the dispute was resolved in Chiquita's favor. However, it may be too late to save the company from bankruptcy.

The full story of Chiquita's crippling decade may be more than just the impact of the EU's quota actions. A newspaper story in the *Cincinnati Enquirer* in 1998 charged the company with perpetrating political, environmental, and human rights abuses in Central America. The story's lead reporter had illegally hacked into Chiquita's voice mail system. The newspaper issued a front-page apology, fired the reporter, and agreed to pay Chiquita $14 million in damages.

Throughout its history Chiquita has been referred to as the "octopus" for its broad reach and influence. The octopus was happy to talk about the illegal acts used by the reporter, but never denied most of the charges. The term the "banana republic" was coined because of Chiquita and its impact on Central America, South America, and the American corporate establishment. As the firm's power and market share grew it imposed systems to control its workers. It built entire villages with homes, schools, and medical facilities for Chiquita workers.

Chiquita is still a widely known brand, but its problems with the EU and its past oppressive control of workers have damaged the firm's image. Nevertheless, the global markets for bananas continue to expand. It is a food that people around the world like and consume when it is available.

Questions for Discussion

1. Could an eight-year trade dispute result in the global image and market losses faced by Chiquita?
2. In the future, how can Chiquita avoid the past missteps it is accused of committing?
3. How would you improve Chiquita's image in exploding markets in Asia?
4. Why is the EU an important global market for Chiquita?

Sources: Nicholas Stein, "Chiquita Has No Profits," *Fortune*, November 26, 2001, pp. 182–196; and www.chiquita.com/discover/oshistory.asp for a historical snapshot of the company.

3

Forms of Business Ownership

Chapter Objectives

After completing this chapter, you should be able to

1 **Discuss** the advantages and disadvantages of sole proprietorships.

2 **Discuss** the advantages and disadvantages of partnerships.

3 **Identify** the features that should be included in a written partnership agreement.

4 **Explain** the advantages and disadvantages of corporations.

5 **Discuss** the advantages and disadvantages of limited liability companies.

6 **Identify** other incorporated forms of business.

7 **Define** the term *merger* and identify three types of mergers.

Edible Arrangements Make Fruity Gift Baskets

When the occasion calls for something lighter than chocolates but tastier than tulips, Tariq Farid has just the gift: a bouquet, not of flowers but of fruit. It's fruit artfully arranged: sculpted pineapple and cantaloupe shaped into daisy look-alikes, skewered grapes that resemble willow branches, and a whole array of other succulent produce fitted into a floralesque design.

This is not a business plan gone bananas, contends Farid, founder and CEO of Edible Arrangements, based in East Haven, CT. Americans love fresh fruit. And as Farid points out, their love, fueled by a health-crazy mindset, is growing. In 1999, Americans consumed, on average, 102 pounds of fruit per person, the third highest level in two decades. Add that to a $55 billion gift-giving industry and Farid thinks he's got the makings of a bountiful national franchise. "We want to become the Domino's of edible fruit bouquets," he says.

Farid is no rookie in the bouquet business. As a 17-year-old, he borrowed $6,000 from his parents and bought his own flower business in East Haven after working part-time in another shop. Four years later he had two shops and was pulling in 15 times what the former business had grossed.

He launched Edible Arrangements after spotting a fruit bouquet in a photo that a friend had brought back from a Bahaman cruise. The idea intrigued him, but he believed he could do it better. So in late 1997 he turned the flower shops over to his family and began test-marketing his own fruit designs out of his home. Two years later he opened his first Edible store in East Haven, and a second followed the next year in nearby Norwalk. By 2001 the stores were pulling in combined revenues of $1.2 million.

Convinced he has a winning concept, Farid is now on a mission to bring fruit bouquets to the rest of the country. During 2002 he sold his first two franchises, in Boston and Atlanta, and is aiming to open four more company stores and some 30 franchises in the next five years.

All the outlets will sell a range of nine bouquets, priced from $29 to $179 and targeted at various market segments. Because the products are so perishable (the company prides itself on using no preservatives), stores can provide only local service. So Farid is avoiding any nationwide branding efforts until he has more reach, instead pushing his slogan, "It's a bouquet, it's a banquet," through direct mail and local media outlets.

Farid is seeking his first round of outside financing to bankroll the expansion. In the meantime he's relying on word of mouth and his website to sell franchises, which cost $60,000 to $120,000 depending on their location. Franchisees pay a $25,000 fee and a 4% royalty, which Farid plans to kick up to 6% once things get rolling.

Source: Adapted from Tahl Raz, 60-Second Business Plan: Berries Jubilee, *Inc.*, September 1, 2002.

3-1 INTRODUCTION

You do not have to be an experienced corporate titan to start your own business. As the opening story illustrates, all it takes to be successful in business is a good idea that repackages existing resources. Tariq Farid's Edible Arrangements business simply combines gift-giving with changing American diets. All he did was identify the opportunity and bring together the resources to exploit it. The U.S. legal and political systems are generally very favorable to new business creation, enabling people from a variety of backgrounds, ethnic groups, income brackets, and age groups to start their own business. For example, at the age of 15, Erica Gluck started a business selling pasta. Erica went to the local pasta shop that her family frequented and asked the owners if she could sell their pasta at a San Diego farmer's market. The first week, she bought 120 packages for $1.25 each, hoping to sell them for twice that amount. Erica reasoned, "At worst, we would be eating pasta at home for a few weeks." Her family didn't have to; the pasta sold out fast and Erica's Pasta Company was born.[1]

Eighteen-year-old Panjak Arora is a self-employed computer consultant. He began writing software when he was 12, moved on to building computers, and now owns his own company, paWare, that "provides complete solutions for business." Panjak charges up to   ☞ 2

---

1. Janet Bodnar and Courtney McGrath, "No Kidding," *Kiplinger's Personal Finance Magazine*, September 2001, pp. 110–113.

$300/hour for his consulting services. He intends to use the money he's earning to pay for college at the University of Minnesota.[2]

In 1996, 5-year-old Devon Green recycled a bag of aluminum cans and changed her world. Now, at the age of 10, she's out to change everyone else's, with Devon's "Heal the World" Recycling Company. Each week she and her dad make the rounds of businesses in the Stuart, Florida, area, collecting aluminum, brass, copper, and stainless steel, for which she is paid 32 cents to 38 cents a pound at the local recycling center. To line up customers, Devon made cold calls to businesses, which, unlike households, don't have on-site recycling pickup. "She's in charge of marketing," says her dad, Michael Green. "It's impossible to say no to her." Starting with two customers, Devon has built her clientele to more than eighty. She and her dad start their rounds every Thursday morning and pick up again after school. Using a trailer donated by the local recycling center—in which they invested elbow grease to clean off the rust—they usually collect seventy to a hundred pounds of recyclables a week, mainly cans.

In an average week Devon earns about $32. She puts $50 a month in Citizens Core Growth fund, which invests in environmentally friendly companies, and gives 30 percent to charity, notably the Humane Society. Her parents match all of her charitable contributions. Two local chambers of commerce have given her complimentary memberships.[3]

As you read this chapter, think about Erica Gluck, Panjak Arora, Devon Green, and others who have decided to start their own businesses. The environment in our mixed economy permits people to form their own businesses, start partnerships, or work in other people's businesses. You, too, can make decisions about the type of business you want to be in, where you want to work, and how you want to spend your time.

Throughout this chapter, we discuss the guidelines that can help you make a decision about which type of business ownership is best for you. We present the basic legal forms of business organizations and discuss the advantages and disadvantages of each. We begin with sole proprietorships, followed by partnerships (general, limited, and joint ventures) and other unincorporated forms of business (syndicates and business trusts). We then discuss corporations and mergers. We conclude by examining other incorporated forms of business (S corporations, nonprofit corporations, cooperatives, and professional service organizations).

3-2 SMALL-BUSINESS STATISTICS

4 ☞   The most recently available data from the U.S. Small Business Administration indicate that *the number of businesses in the United States has increased steadily over the past decade.* Employer firms (firms with at least one nonowner employee) have made up most of this increase, growing 15.5 percent in ten years or 1.5 percent annually.[4] Interestingly, firms with fewer than twenty employees make up nearly 86 percent of all businesses in the United States. Exhibit 3-1 lists the top ten small businesses by number of independent enterprises in the United States and the percentage of each that is profitable.

The number of employer firms has increased in forty-six states and the District of Columbia. Utah had the largest increase in the number of employer firms (5.8 percent) followed by Nevada (4.2 percent). Alabama had the largest decline (–1.3 percent), while Indiana and Hawaii had declines of less than 1 percent. The number of firms in all three states is still well above the levels in the early to mid-1990s. California had the highest number of employer firms (906,092 or 15.6 percent of all employer firms); the rest of the top five were New York (462,473), Texas (383,148), Florida (374,867), and Illinois (277,313). These five states combined accounted for more than one-third of all U.S. employer firms.

---

2. Ibid.

3. Ibid.

4. U.S. Small Business Economic Indicators for 2001, U.S. Small Business Administration, Office of Advocacy, Washington, D.C., February 2003.

Type of Firm	Number of Firms	Percentage That Are Profitable (%)
Special trade contractors	1,763,890	88.2
Administrative and support services	1,433,426	84.6
Personal and laundry services	1,104,628	81.5
Nonstore retailers— includes multilevel marketing	1,075,154	48.8
Artists, entertainers, and related industries	876,286	57.6
Offices of real estate agents, managers, and appraisers	673,734	79.6
Child day care services	606,038	85.0
Management, scientific, and technical consulting services	589,950	73.6
Miscellaneous store retailers	422,688	50.7
Professional and consulting services not classified elsewhere	368,420	70.2

EXHIBIT 3-1

Type and Number of New Business Starts

Source: BizStats.com

Self-employment as a primary occupation declined by 2.1 percent nationwide according to the most recent data. Kentucky had the highest increase (18.7 percent). New Hampshire, Georgia, Connecticut, and North Carolina also posted double-digit increases. Arkansas, Missouri, and West Virginia had decreases of just over 15 percent. California had the highest state total, representing about 15 percent of all self-employed in the United States.

The self-employment rate declined in the 1960s and early 1970s as the economy moved from an agricultural base toward an industrial base. But from the late 1970s to the early 1980s, the rate increased, surprising analysts who had expected the decline to continue, signaling the demise of small business. The rate has fluctuated at around 8 percent since then, demonstrating the acceptance and viability of self-employment as an alternative to working for an employer.

3-3 STARTING A BUSINESS

Every day in the United States someone is opening a new business for the first time. Restaurants, consulting firms, e-businesses, nonprofit organizations, and other business types are appearing each day. Behind every one of these new enterprises resides a person with a dream—a dream of making a living by owning and operating his or her own company.

For a select few of these individuals, that dream will result in tremendous success. Houston entrepreneur Jim "Mattress Mac" McIngvale opened his Gallery Furniture store in 1980. In the early days, he didn't have much cash, and he certainly didn't have time to worry. Jim and his wife, Linda, worked backbreaking twenty-hour days to pay the bills and grow the business. Today, twenty years after the firm was founded, Gallery Furniture is the most productive retail space in the world, selling over $180 million worth of furniture annually from a single site in Houston, Texas. Gallery bills itself as "The World's Furniture Store" and now sponsors special sporting events, a major men's tennis tournament, and other civic and national causes.[5]

Starting a company is a risky proposition for anyone. There are no guarantees. In fact, most new businesses end in failure. Not everyone is cut out to be an entrepreneur. A person thinking about owning a business should examine the following factors:

- *Capital requirements*—the amount of funds necessary to finance the operation
- *Risk*—the amount of personal property a person is willing to lose by starting the business
- *Control*—the amount of authority the owner exercises

5. Jim McIngvale with Tom Duening and John Ivancevich, *Always Think Big* (Chicago: Dearborn Trade, 2002).

FOCUS ON CAREERS

Are You Ready to Go It Alone?

Self-employment is about being in control of your life. You're the boss. You get all the benefits of your hard work. When you work for someone else, your economic and personal potential is usually limited. That ceiling goes away once you're on your own. Most people who become wealthy are self-employed. And today self-employed individuals can work from virtually anywhere.

It's also true, however, that most people who are self-employed don't get rich. In fact, many of the self-employed are unable to match the earnings potential of their counterparts who work for someone else, but most consider this a fair trade for having more control over their time and their work. Health insurance is more expensive and, for some people, virtually unavailable. While there are tax benefits to being self-employed, small businesses often bear an unfair tax burden. In addition, self-employed people have to deal with rules and regulations, government policies, legal issues, and other matters on their own.

Source: Adapted from Paul Edwards and Sarah Edwards, "What Are the Pros and Cons of Working for Yourself?," *Inc.com*, March 7, 2000.

- *Managerial abilities*—the skills needed to plan, organize, and control the business
- *Time requirements*—the time needed to operate the business and provide guidance to the employees
- *Tax liability*—what taxes a business must pay to various governments on earnings of the business

Each of these factors should be considered along with your own personal values and philosophy. Do you have the character, work ethic, and style to succeed? Many entrepreneurs prefer to work for someone else for a while to learn how an industry operates or to learn how to manage other people. Other entrepreneurs jump right in with both feet and learn as they go. The latter type of business owner will often find that they must cycle through several start-ups before they hit upon the recipe for success.

All entrepreneurs will face the issue of the type of legal form to use for the structural basis of their company. In essence, aspiring business owners have four business forms to choose among:

1. Sole Proprietorship
2. Partnership
3. Corporation
4. Limited Liability Company

The situation is actually more complicated, because each of these business forms has multiple varieties. In the sections that follow, we look at each business legal form and its relative advantages and disadvantages. First, look at the Focus on Careers box, "Are You Ready to Go It Alone?," to determine if you have what it takes to be an entrepreneur.

3-4 SOLE PROPRIETORSHIPS

The oldest, most common form of private business ownership in the United States is the sole proprietorship. A **sole proprietorship** is a business owned and managed by one individual. That person may receive help from others in operating the business, but he or she is the only boss; the sole proprietor is the company. *Sole proprietorships are an extremely pop-*

Sole Proprietorship   A business owned and managed by one individual.

ular form of business, comprising 72 percent of total businesses and nearly $1 trillion in total revenue. There are about 17.5 million sole proprietorships in the United States.[6]

Typically the sole proprietor owns a small service or retail operation, such as a roadside produce stand, hardware store, bakery, or restaurant, which frequently caters to a group of regular customers. The owner normally provides the capital (money) needed to start and operate the business through personal savings or borrowed money.

The sole proprietor is usually an active manager, employing only a few people and working in the business every day. He or she controls the operations, supervises the staff, and makes the decisions. The managerial ability of the owner usually accounts for the success or failure of the business.

3-4a Advantages of a Sole Proprietorship

Many people desire to be their own boss. A sole proprietorship accomplishes this goal and takes it a step further. In the eyes of the U.S. Internal Revenue Service, the owner of a sole proprietorship *is* the business. If something should happen to the owner, the business immediately ceases to exist. From a tax perspective, the owner pays taxes on all earnings from the sole proprietorship at the personal income tax rate. The advantages of a sole proprietorship go beyond being your own boss. They also include the following:

Ease of Starting   A sole proprietorship is the easiest way to start a business. It involves a minimum number of forms and legal paperwork. For example, 33-year-old Kimberly Testa was a programmer who had worked for a high-flying dot-com company in Silicon Valley. When the firm went bust along with many others during the stock market collapse of 2000–2001, she was out of work and disillusioned. To insulate herself from being laid off again, Kimberly decided to open her own business—one that she would control herself. She decided to open a company called "The Doggie Dentist." She did so by filing a DBA ("doing business as") form with her local county clerk for about $15. Within a day, she was in business as a sole proprietor.[7]

Control   Kimberly has sole control of her business. That means she's in charge of marketing, sales, doggy dentistry, customer relations, and maintenance. She is the sole owner of the firm so she doesn't have to have board meetings or meet with shareholders to make changes to her business plan.

Sole Participation in Profits and Losses   Because she has no outside investors, Kimberly is the only one to participate in the profits and losses of the business.

Use of Owner's Abilities   Kimberly has the satisfaction of running her business and making as much money as her abilities will allow. The limits of her personal income are bounded by her own skills and business savvy.

Tax Breaks   A major advantage of the proprietorship is that the business itself pays no income tax. By way of contrast, a corporation pays taxes on profits; its owners, the shareholders, also pay taxes on their dividends. This is known as *double taxation*. Sole proprietorships, in contrast, are taxed only once. Kimberly keeps everything the business makes and pays taxes on that income at the individual income tax rate (which is normally less than the corporate tax rate). If the business loses money, that shows up as a net loss on Kimberly's personal income tax filing.

Secrecy   Since there are no shareholders in a sole proprietorship other than the owner, there is no need for disclosure of business information. Companies with more than one shareholder are required to disclose financial performance, governance decisions, and information about financing and shareholder rights.

Ease of Dissolving   If Kimberly Testa were to decide to dissolve her business for any reason, there would be no legal complications. As long as she had paid all the outstanding bills, her decision would be all that was needed to close the company.

6. BizStats.com.

7. Andrew Raskin, "Letter from Silicon Valley," *Inc.*, November 30, 2001, pp. 72–74.

3-4b Disadvantages of a Sole Proprietorship

If the sole proprietorship had only advantages, a person organizing a business would have little to consider. But the realities of business are never so simple or certain. Sole proprietorships also have a number of disadvantages:

Unlimited Liability Obligation of investors to use personal assets, when necessary, to pay off debts to business creditors; a disadvantage of sole proprietorships and partnerships.

Unlimited Liability   The law provides that Kim Testa's total wealth may be used to satisfy claims against her sole proprietorship. This is called **unlimited liability.** For Testa, this means almost everything she owns could be sold to pay any debts or legal claims against the business. For example, if the business failed, she might have to sell her personal jewelry or automobile to pay business debts that couldn't be paid by the liquidation or sale of business assets.

Difficulty in Raising Capital   Testa's investment in The Doggie Dentist was limited to her personal wealth. The amount she could borrow to operate the business was also limited by her personal wealth; if she had a large estate, she would have little problem borrowing money. Generally, however, businesses requiring large amounts of capital are not formed as sole proprietorships.

The U.S. government, through the Small Business Administration (SBA), does have a loan program for people like Testa who desire to start their own small business. However, such programs generally require a great deal of financial and other reports, and they can limit the decision-making authority of the business owner through restrictive covenants written into the loan. For example, the SBA may require that the business owner retain a certain percentage of the profits within the business, restricting the owner from using the money for personal expenses.

Limitations in Managerial Ability   Kimberly Testa must have or must obtain all the know-how needed to manage her business. Operating a business requires planning, organizing, controlling, marketing, financial, motivational, and customer relations skills. Rarely does an individual have this range of needed expertise. However, many of these skills can be bought. For example, Kimberly could hire an accountant to keep the books and an advertising consultant to help promote her services.

Lack of Stability   Death, illness, bankruptcy, or retirement of the owner terminates the proprietorship. Testa's business could be sold to others, but The Doggie Dentist, as organized, would cease to exist.

Demands on Time   Although Testa loves to take walks with her own dogs, she will have trouble finding the time. The Doggie Dentist has to be open all day to develop a customer base. Owners such as Testa often work sixty to eighty hours a week, especially when the business is new.

Difficulty in Hiring and Keeping Highly Motivated Employees   The sole proprietor is the business. Where can a self-motivated, high-energy employee go in the business? Workers with their own visions and goals and a high drive to succeed often have to quit the sole proprietorship to find opportunities for personal growth.

3-5 PARTNERSHIPS

Partnership law in the United States has been derived from only one source—the Uniform Partnership Act (UPA), originally promulgated in 1914 by the National Conference of Commissioners on Uniform State Laws, and subsequently enacted in forty-nine states. The more recent Revised Uniform Partnership Act (RUPA) was approved by the Conference in 1994, bringing the law of partnerships in line with modern business practices and trends while retaining many of the valuable provisions in the original act. It was amended in 1997 to provide limited liability for partners in a limited liability partnership.

Adopted with the newest amendments in twenty-one states, the District of Columbia, Puerto Rico, and the U.S. Virgin Islands, and without the limited liability partnership amendments in four additional states, RUPA is the only revision since the original was promulgated. It governs the relations among general partners and between the partners and the partnerships.

Section 6 of the Uniform Partnership Act defines **partnership** as "an association of two or more persons to carry on as co-owners of a business for profit." The law regards individuals as partners when they act in such a way as to make people believe they operate a business together. A partnership can be based on a written contract or a voluntary and legal oral agreement. Other than the difference in the number of owners, a partnership is similar in many respects to a sole proprietorship. In a partnership the co-owners share everything, including the risk, hard work, assets, and profits. Some of today's large corporations, including Sears, Procter & Gamble, and Lever Brothers, began as partnerships. Partnerships account for 8 percent of U.S. businesses and 6 percent of the total revenue. There are about 2 million partnerships in the United States[8]

> **Partnership**   A business owned by two or more people.

3-5a Types of Partnerships

About 1.8 million partnerships of various types exist in the United States.[9] The three major types are general partnerships, limited partnerships, and joint ventures. A **general partnership** is a business with at least one *general partner* who has unlimited liability for the debts of the business. A **limited partnership** has at least one general partner and one or more *limited partners*. Finally, the **joint venture** is a special type of partnership established to carry out a special project or to operate for a specific time period. Let's look at each type separately.

> **General Partnership** A partnership in which at least one partner has unlimited liability; a general partner has authority to act and make binding decisions as an owner.
>
> **Limited Partnership** A partnership with at least one general partner, and one or more limited partners who are liable for loss only up to the amount of their investment.
>
> **Joint Venture** A special type of partnership established to carry out a special project or to operate for a specific time period.

General Partnership

Regardless of the percentage of the business they own, general partners have authority to act and make binding decisions as owners of the business. Each general partner is liable for all the debts of the business. Partners generally share profits and losses according to a plan specified by a partnership between or among them (see below).

Limited Partnership

All partnerships must have at least one general partner. A limited partnership includes one or more general partners and one or more limited partners. The general partners arrange and run the business, while the limited partners are investors only. The limited partner investors receive special tax advantages and protection from liability. Limited partners legally may have no say in managing the business. If this requirement is violated, the limited partnership status is dissolved.

Limited partnerships are usually found in service industries or in professional firms such as real estate and dentistry. They are also used extensively to enable various international arrangements. In some states, a special notice must be filed in the county or district where the limited partnership has its offices.

A limited partner has limited liability, being liable for loss only up to the amount of capital invested. Thus, a limited partner who invests $30,000 in the business is liable for only that amount. In contrast, general partners have unlimited liability in the partnership.

The **master limited partnership (MLP),** used since 1981, is a partnership that sells units traded on a recognized stock exchange. The MLP has been popular in real estate and oil. It has many of the advantages of a corporation, such as unlimited life, limited liability, and transferable ownership. However, MLPs do not pay corporate taxes, because earnings are passed directly to unit holders.

> **Master Limited Partnership (MLP)** A partnership that sells units traded on a recognized stock exchange.

Joint Venture

Sometimes a number of individuals and businesses join together to accomplish a specific purpose or objective or to complete a single transaction. For example, they may wish to purchase a building in downtown Boston and resell it for a profit. This would be called a joint venture.

8. BizStats.com.

9. Ibid.

A joint venture in the United States or abroad is something less than the ordinary partnership, which continues as a business. There is some confusion among the courts as to whether a joint venture is a partnership. We think there are enough similarities to categorize it as such. For instance, one of the joint venture partners acting within the scope of his or her authority may bind the other partner(s) in the joint venture. Also, the liabilities of the parties to a joint venture are similar to the liabilities of the partnership.

3-5b The Partnership Agreement

Partnership Agreement
A written or signed agreement between partners that can prevent or lessen misunderstandings at a later time.

Sound business practice dictates that a partnership agreement be written and signed, although that is not a legal requirement. *A written* **partnership agreement** *can prevent or lessen misunderstandings at a later date.* Oral partnership agreements, though quite legal, tend to be hard to re-create and are open to misunderstandings. Written articles of partnership provide proof of an agreement.

A written partnership agreement includes the following main features:

- Name of the business partnership
- Type of business
- Location of the business
- Expected life of the partnership
- Names of the partners and the amount of each one's investment
- Procedures for distributing profits and covering losses
- Amounts that partners will withdraw for services
- Procedure for withdrawal of funds
- Duties of each partner
- Procedures for dissolving the partnership

Like the sole proprietorship, the partnership has both advantages and disadvantages. Any person considering a partnership should carefully weigh each of the following advantages and disadvantages before closing the deal. Do some of the pluses outweigh the minuses?

3-5c Advantages of a Partnership

The partnership form of business ownership has a number of distinct advantages that include:

Greater Access to Capital   In the sole proprietorship, the amount of capital available to the new enterprise is limited to the personal wealth and credit of the owner. In a partnership, the amount of capital may increase significantly. A person with a good idea but little capital can look for partners with the capital and/or credit standing to develop and market the idea.

Combined Managerial Skills   In a partnership, people with different talents and skills may join together. One partner may be good at marketing, the other may be expert at accouning and financial matters. Combining these skills could provide a greater chance of success.

6 ☞   Outback Steakhouse, founded in 1987, is a company that generates nearly $1 billion in annual sales and is operated as a partnership.[10] Exhibit 3-2 on pages 60–61 illustrates how the partnership was formed. Three businessmen, Basham, Sullivan, and Gannon, used different experiences, backgrounds, and goals; combined them with strong work ethics; and started a successful business.

10. Jay Finegan, "Unconventional Wisdom," *Business Week,* September 12, 1994, pp. 30–38.

Ease of Starting   Because it involves a private contractual arrangement, a partnership is fairly easy to start. It is nearly as free from government regulation as a sole proprietorship. The cost of starting a partnership is low; it usually involves only a modest legal fee for drawing up a written agreement among the partners, which is not necessary but highly desirable.

Clear Legal Status   Over the years, legal precedents for partnerships have been established through court cases. The questions of rights, responsibilities, liabilities, and partner duties have been covered. Thus the legal status of the partnership is clearly understood: Lawyers can provide sound legal advice about partnership issues.

Tax Advantages   The partnership has some potential tax advantages over a corporation. In a partnership, as in a sole proprietorship, the owners pay individual taxes on their business earnings, but the partnership, as a business, does not pay income tax.

3-5d Disadvantages of a Partnership

Although a popular form of structuring a business, the partnership form has a number of disadvantages. Some of these are listed below:

Unlimited Liability   Each general partner is liable for a partnership's debts. Suppose Jack and Jill's partnership fails with outstanding bills of $25,000. This amount must be paid by someone. If Jack lacks the personal assets to pay his share of the debt, Jill would be called on to make up the difference. This is one reason for choosing partners carefully.

Potential Disagreements   Decisions made by several people (partners) are often better than those made by one. However, having two or more people deciding on some aspects of the business can be dangerous. Power and authority are divided, and the partners will not always agree with each other. As a result, poor decisions may be made. Also, decision making becomes more time-consuming because agreement must be reached before action can be taken.

Investment Withdrawal Difficulty   A person who invests money in a partnership may have a hard time withdrawing the investment. It is much easier to invest in a partnership than to withdraw. The money, typically considered a "frozen investment," is tied up in the operation of the business. The partnership agreement generally specifies how or when partners may be able to recover their investments. In general, the criteria for getting money back out are stringent since cash is a precious resource to a new enterprise.

Limited Capital Availability   The partnership may have an advantage over the sole proprietorship in the availability of capital, but it does not compare to a corporation in ability to raise capital. In most cases, partners have a limited capability and cannot compete in business requiring large outlays. The amount of financial capital a partnership can raise depends on the personal wealth of the partners and their credit ratings. It also depends on how much they are willing to invest.

Instability   If a partner dies or withdraws from the business, the partnership is dissolved. A new partnership or some other form of business organization must be legally established.

3-6 OTHER UNINCORPORATED FORMS OF BUSINESS

Besides proprietorships and partnerships, several other forms of ownership do not require incorporation. These forms are used by people who want to join together to accomplish various objectives without going to the trouble of forming a corporation.

There is one similarity between LLCs and partnerships, however. They both offer "pass-through" taxation, which means that the owners report business income or losses on their individual tax returns; the partnership or LLC itself does not pay taxes.

3-8a Advantages of a Limited Liability Company

There are many advantages to an LLC. Combining the best features of both partnerships and corporations, the main advantages of an LLC include the following:

Limited Liability   The investors in an LLC enjoy limited liability for the commitments and actions of the company. Thus, their personal assets are not at risk as long as the company does not engage in fraudulent business practices.

Pass-Through Taxation   As with sole proprietorships, partnerships, and S corporations, the LLC is not separately taxed. Profits and losses of the LLC "flow through" to the owners and are taxed according to the individual income tax rate.

Investors Can Manage   Unlike a limited partnership, which does not allow limited partners to manage, the LLC allows any shareholder to also be a manager without risking limited liability status. This advantage is significant, especially to the founders of a company who want to contribute funds and be part of the active management team.

Unlimited Membership   The LLC has no restrictions regarding the number of individuals who may participate as shareholders. In most states, the S corporation restricts the number of investors to thirty-five individuals. An LLC can have as many "members" as necessary.

Ease of Organizing   Organizing an LLC is usually a simple matter, requiring only the filing of articles of organization with the appropriate state secretary of state. Usually, LLC owners can file this paperwork without the aid of an attorney for less than $500.

3-8b Disadvantages of a Limited Liability Company

The disadvantages of an LLC are due primarily to its relatively recent adoption by state legislatures. With the LLC form now less than a decade old, many people still don't understand it well, and courts have only begun to form a record of common law. The latter is important because well-established common law makes for a more predictable legal environment. For example, most cases involving small corporations are settled out of court because the attorneys can determine from common law the likely outcome of an expensive trial. With the LLC and its limited history of common law the outcome of legal disputes is less certain.

Other disadvantages of the LLC form of business include the following:

Difficult to Raise Money   The LLC does not allow for the issuance of stock shares. Rather, individuals who invest in an LLC are known as "members." Many seasoned and savvy investors are less comfortable with this form of investment, preferring to have actual stock certificates on file with their attorneys.

No Continuity of Life   An LLC does not have a reliable continuity of existence. The articles of organization must specify the date on which the LLC's existence will terminate. Unless otherwise provided in the articles of organization or a written operating agreement, an LLC is dissolved at the death, withdrawal, resignation, expulsion, or bankruptcy of a member (unless within ninety days a majority in both the profits and capital interests vote to continue the LLC).

Transferability   No one can become a member of an LLC (either by transfer of an existing membership or the issuance of a new one) without the consent of members having a majority in interest (excluding the person acquiring the membership interest) unless the articles of organization provide otherwise.

See Exhibit 3-6 for a listing of state websites that provide information to help in choosing a business structure.

EXHIBIT 3-6   Small Business Basics Secretary of State Websites

Find the information you need to choose your business structure at the following state websites:

Alabama (www.sos.state.al.us)	Louisiana (www.sec.state.la.us)	Oklahoma (www.sos.state.ok.us)
Alaska Division of Banking, Securities and Corporations (www.dced.state.ak.us/bsc)	Maine (www.state.me.us/sos)	Oregon (www.sos.state.or.us)
	Maryland (www.sos.state.md.us)	Pennsylvania (www.dos.state.pa.us/DOS/site/default.asp)
Arizona (www.sosaz.com)	Massachusetts (www.state.ma.us/sec)	Rhode Island (www.state.ri.us)
Arkansas (www.sosweb.state.ar.us)	Michigan (www.michigan.gov/sos)	South Carolina (www.scsos.com)
California (www.ss.ca.gov)	Minnesota (www.sos.state.mn.us)	South Dakota (www.state.sd.us/sos/sos.htm)
Colorado (www.sos.state.co.us)	Mississippi (www.sos.state.ms.us)	
Connecticut (www.sots.state.ct.us)	Missouri (www.sos.state.mo.us)	Tennessee (www.state.tn.us/sos)
Delaware (www.state.de.us/sos)	Montana (www.sos.state.mt.us/css/index.asp)	Texas (www.sos.state.tx.us)
Florida (www.dos.state.fl.us)	Nebraska (www.sos.state.ne.us)	Utah Department of Commerce (www.commerce.state.ut.us)
Georgia (www.sos.state.ga.us/default1024.asp)	Nevada (www.sos.state.nv.us)	Vermont (www.sec.state.vt.us)
	New Hampshire (www.state.nh.us/sos)	Virginia (www.soc.state.va.us)
Hawaii Division of Business Registration (www.state.hi.us/dcca/bregseu/index.html)	New Jersey (www.state.nj.us/state)	Washington (www.secstate.wa.gov)
	New Mexico (www.sos.state.nm.us)	West Virginia (www.wvsos.com)
Idaho (www.idsos.state.id.us)	New York (www.dos.state.ny.us)	Wisconsin (www.state.wi.us/agencies/sos)
Illinois (www.sos.state.il.us)	North Carolina (www.secstate.state.nc.us)	
Indiana (www.state.in.us/sos)	North Dakota (www.state.nd.us/sec)	Wyoming (www.soswy.state.wy.us/index_1.htm)
Iowa (www.sos.state.ia.us)	Ohio (www.state.oh.us/sos)	
Kansas (www.kssos.org)		
Kentucky (www.sos.state.ky.us)		

3-9 NONPROFIT ORGANIZATIONS

There are more than 1.1 million nonprofit organizations that employ about 12 million people in the United States. Many organizations are **nonprofit corporations;** that is, they are not profit-seeking enterprises. The nonprofit sector includes universities and other schools, charities, churches, volunteer organizations, credit unions, country clubs, government organizations, cooperatives, and a number of other organizations. The nonprofit enterprise is prohibited by law from distributing any earnings (paying dividends) to owners. It exists because the founders believe that the firm provides something of value (e.g., help to the homeless, research, education) that is not being provided well or at all by other enterprises. Donations, dues, and the sale of goods or services provide the funds to pay employees and finance operations.

An organization in which a group of people (members/customers) collectively own and operate all or part of the business is a **cooperative (co-op).** The member/customer owners pay an annual membership fee. The first formal co-op, the Philadelphia Contributorship, was organized by Benjamin Franklin in 1752 and is still in business today. Co-ops are often found where a large number of small producers can band together to become more competitive. Such well-known brands as OceanSpray juice, Sunkist oranges, and Sun-Maid raisins are the property of food producer cooperatives that formed to market the products grown by many members.

More than 5,500 producer co-ops do business in the United States, with annual sales of over $16 billion. In addition, approximately 7,500 farmer-owned buying co-ops purchase machinery, fertilizer, seeds, materials, and so on, spending over $4 billion annually. Farm co-ops have increased their annual revenues from $25 billion in 1970 to over $60 billion today. Farmland Industries, Inc., an agricultural food marketing and manufacturing co-op headquartered in Kansas City, Missouri, is the largest farmer-owned cooperative association in the United States. Other billion-dollar co-ops are

> **Nonprofit Corporation**
> An enterprise (e.g., university, charity, church) that is not driven by a profit-seeking motive.
>
> **Cooperative (Co-op)**
> An organization in which people collectively own and operate a business in order to compete with bigger competitors.

✍ 13

✍ 14, 15
✍ 16

✍ 17

18, 19 ☞ Associated Milk Producers, Grain Terminal Association, and Land O' Lakes. Most farm co-ops are generally unknown to the public.

Dividends are paid to co-op members in proportion to the amount of goods that each member has bought or sold through the cooperative. These patronage dividends are considered a refund of overpayment rather than a distribution of profits.

A disadvantage of co-ops is that as they grow larger they become more visible to the public. And if the public questions their market power, they may lose their special status under the law.

3-10 SUMMARY OF BUSINESS LEGAL FORMS

Exhibit 3-7 summarizes the main advantages and disadvantages of each of the business legal forms discussed in this chapter.

3-11 MERGERS AND ACQUISITIONS

> **Merger**   Combining two or more business enterprises into a single entity.
>
> **Acquisition**   The process in which one firm buys the assets and assumes the obligations of another company.

Over the past century, surges in merger and acquisition (M&A) activity have occurred at various times. In 2001, more than 8,000 M&A deals were transacted in the United States for a net value of more than $800 billion.[13] **Merger** refers to the joining together of two corporations to become a single corporation. An **acquisition** refers to the process in which one firm buys the assets and assumes the obligations of another company. The federal government is concerned with M&As if there is a reduction in competition. Mergers that reduce market competition can result in government action under the Celler-Kefauver Act and review by the Justice Department and the Federal Trade Commission (FTC). Exhibit 3-8 on page 72 presents a ten-year summary of the number of mergers that occurred in the United States between 1991 and 2001.[14]

20, 21 ☞

Within and across borders M&As are continuing, but at a slower rate and for lesser amounts of money. Economic, political, and attitudinal differences at various times largely determine the attractiveness of M&A activity within a country and across borders.[15]

A **horizontal merger** occurs when competitive firms in the same market merge into a single firm. For example, in early 1995 aerospace/defense companies Lockheed Corp. and Martin Marietta Corp. merged to form Lockheed Martin Corp. A firm's merger with a supplier or distributor is called a **vertical merger.** In late 1993 the large pharmaceutical firm Merck merged with Medco Containment Services, Inc., a pharmacy benefits management company. A **conglomerate merger** joins firms selling goods in unrelated markets. Many conglomerate mergers occurred during the early 1980s, but few have taken place in more recent years.

22 ☞

23 ☞

> **Horizontal Merger**   A merger involving competitive firms in the same market.
>
> **Vertical Merger**   A merger in which a firm joins with its supplier.
>
> **Conglomerate Merger**   A merger involving firms selling goods in unrelated markets.

In general, the government allows mergers when the market share of the largest firms in the industry is relatively low or when new firms can enter the market easily. Government also has intervened less when mergers seem needed to meet foreign competition. Some people believe mergers bring cost and productivity advantages that can help reduce prices, making U.S. products cheaper and more competitive on the world markets. Exhibit 3-9 on page 72 highlights the top ten M&A deals consummated in the United States in 2001.

According to an August 2001 report by The Conference Board, M&As tend to increase jobs, worker wages, and productivity.[16] However, the study also found that most employees in acquired firms experience job losses (the average acquired plant lost about 10% of its jobs), slower wage growth, and increased stress.

13. MergerStat.com.

14. Ibid.

15. Ann K. B. Buchholtz and Barbara A. Ribbens, "Role of Chief Executive Officers in Takeover Resistance: Effects of CEO Incentives and Individual Characteristics," *Academy of Management Journal*, June 1994, pp. 554–579.

16. The Conference Board, "Why All the Uncertainty, Fear, and Doubt? Are Mergers and Acquisitions Bad for Workers?," Report #1295-01-RR, August 2001.

 **Advantages and Disadvantages of Legal Form Options**

Type of Entity	Main Advantages	Main Disadvantages
Sole Proprietorship	Simple and inexpensive to create and operate. Owner reports profit or loss on his or her personal tax return.	Owner personally liable for business debts.
General Partnership	Simple and inexpensive to create and operate. Owners (partners) report their share of profit or loss on their personal tax returns.	Owners (partners) personally liable for business debts.
Limited Partnership	Limited partners have limited personal liability for business debts as long as they don't participate in management. General partners can raise cash without involving outside investors in management of business.	General partners personally liable for business debts. More expensive to create than general partnership. Suitable mainly for companies that invest in real estate.
Regular Corporation	Owners have limited personal liability for business debts. Fringe benefits can be deducted as business expense. Owners can split corporate profit among owners and corporation, paying lower overall tax rate.	More expensive to create than partnership or sole proprietorship. Paperwork can seem burdensome to some owners. Separate taxable entity.
S Corporation	Owners have limited personal liability for business debts. Owners report their share of corporate profit or loss on their personal tax returns. Owners can use corporate loss to offset income from other sources.	More expensive to create than partnership or sole proprietorship. More paperwork than for a limited liability company, which offers similar advantages. Income must be allocated to owners according to their ownership interests. Fringe benefits limited for owners who own more than 2% of shares.
Nonprofit Corporation	Corporation doesn't pay income taxes. Contributions to charitable corporation are tax deductible. Fringe benefits can be deducted as business expense.	Full tax advantages available only to groups organized for charitable, scientific, educational, literary, or religious purposes. Property transferred to corporation stays there; if corporation ends, property must go to another nonprofit.
Limited Liability Company	Owners have limited personal liability for business debts even if they participate in management. Profit and loss can be allocated differently than ownership interests. IRS rules now allow LLCs to choose between being taxed as partnership or corporation.	More expensive to create than partnership or sole proprietorship. State laws for creating LLCs may not reflect latest federal tax changes.
Limited Liability Partnership	Mostly of interest to partners in old-line professions such as law, medicine, and accounting. Owners (partners) aren't personally liable for the malpractice of other partners. Owners report their share of profit or loss on their personal tax returns.	Unlike a limited liability company or a professional limited liability company, owners (partners) remain personally liable for many types of obligations owed to business creditors, lenders, and landlords. Not available in all states. Often limited to a short list of professions.

**M&A Transactions
Over the Past Decade**

Source: U.S. Department of Commerce

	M&A Transactions	Total Deal Value
2001	8,267	$704.0
2000	9,566	$1,325.7
1999	9,278	$1,425.9
1998	7,809	$1,192.9
1997	7,800	$657.1
1996	5,848	$495.0
1995	3,510	$356.0
1994	2,997	$226.7
1993	2,663	$176.4
1992	2,574	$96.7
1991	1,877	$71.2

**U.S. Transactions:
Top Ten Deals of 2001**

Source U.S. Department of Commerce

Rank	Seller	Unit Sold	Buyer	Value ($mm)
1	AT&T Corp	AT&T Broadband & Internet Services	Comcast Corp	$44,047.13
2	General Motors Corp	Hughes Electronics Corp	EchoStar Communications Corp	$29,658.45
3	Compaq Computer Corp		Hewlett-Packard Co	$25,734.61
4	American General Corp		American International Group Inc	$22,378.33
5	Immunex Corp		Amgen Inc	$15,877.69
6	Conoco Inc		Phillips Petroleum Co	$15,159.24
7	Wachovia Corp		First Union Corp	$13,996.74
8	ALZA Corp		Johnson & Johnson	$12,415.72
9	Grupo Financiero Banamex Accival SA De CV		Citigroup Inc	$12,284.52
10	CIT Group Inc (The)		Tyco International Ltd	$10,416.22

The overwhelming evidence indicates that M&As improve company efficiency. "Synergistic" mergers take well-performing plants and make them better, while "managerial discipline" mergers involve improvements to poor performers. So, aside from mistakes and the small likelihood (given antitrust enforcement) of anticompetitive consequences, M&As are good for the economy and good for business.

For the worker involved in a merger or acquisition, the bottom line depends heavily on the size of the plant undergoing ownership change. For a significant fraction of M&As—mostly of larger plants—improvements in performance come from restructuring and eliminating jobs. Restructuring and layoffs tend to intensify performance pressures for workers continuously employed in these businesses. So, although M&As provide broad benefits to the economy in terms of jobs, wages, and performance, they create significant stresses for workers directly involved.

There is some good news for employees in plants that were acquired, as noted in The Conference Board's report. The level of wages at acquired plants was higher, even after accounting for the effects of plant size on wages in both 1977 and 1987. So while acquisitions slowed wage growth for workers in the largest plants, wages remained above average for these workers. In addition, M&As also improve the probability that a worker's plant, particularly a large, poorly performing one, remains open.

SUGGESTED WEBSITES

Note: These websites were functional when we went to press. Please access the online text for the most up-to-date URLs.

1. www.ediblearrangements.com
2. www.paware.com
3. www.devonshealthworld.com
4. www.sba.gov
5. www.galleryfurniture.com
6. www.outback.com
7. www.fortune.com
8. www.microsoft.com
9. www.att.com
10. www.gm.com
11. www.ibm.com
12. www.supremecourtus.gov

13. www.ushistory.org/tour/tour_contrib.htm
14. www.oceanspray.com
15. www.sunkist.com
16. www.sun-maid.com
17. www.farmland.com
18. www.ampi.com
19. www.landolakes.com
20. www.usdoj.gov
21. www.ftc.gov
22. www.lockheedmartin.com
23. www.merck.com
24. ww.conseva.com

SUMMARY OF LEARNING OBJECTIVES

1. *Discuss the advantages and disadvantages of sole proprietorships.* The advantages are (a) ease of starting, (b) owner's control over daily operations and decisions, (c) owner's sole right to profits, (d) use of owner's abilities, (e) secrecy about business information, (f) tax breaks, and (g) ease of dissolving. The disadvantages are (a) owner's unlimited liability, (b) difficulty in raising capital, (c) limitations of owner's abilities, (d) lack of stability, (e) demands on time, and (f) difficulty in hiring and keeping self-motivated employees.

2. *Discuss the advantages and disadvantages of partnerships.* Advantages include (a) more available capital, (b) combined managerial skills of the partners, (c) ease of starting, (d) clear legal status, and (e) tax advantages. Disadvantages include (a) general partners' unlimited liability, (b) potential for disagreements, (c) investment withdrawal difficulty, (d) more capital than the sole proprietorship but less than that available to corporations, and (e) instability.

3. *Identify the features that should be included in a written partnership agreement.* The main features of a written partnership agreement include the name of the business partnership, type of business, location of the business, expected life of the partnership, names of the partners and the amount of each one's investment, procedures for distributing profits and covering losses, amounts that partners will withdraw for services, procedure for withdrawal of funds, each partner's duties, and procedures for dissolving the partnership.

4. *Explain the advantages and disadvantages of corporations.* Advantages include (a) limitation of owners' liability to the amount of their investments, (b) use of skilled management team to run the corporation, (c) easy transfer of ownership, (d) greater availability of capital, (e) stability, and (f) status as legal entity. Disadvantages include (a) difficulty and expense in starting, (b) individual owner's lack of control, (c) double taxation, (d) government involvement, (e) lack of secrecy, (f) managers' possible lack of personal interest in the corporation's success, and (g) credit limitations.

5. *Discuss the advantages and disadvantages of limited liability companies.* Limited liability companies combine the advantages of partnerships and corporations into a relatively new business legal form. LLCs enjoy the benefits of limited liability for all owner-members, while at the same time receiving pass-through taxation. LLCs are easy to organize and register, and they are not restricted to a limited number of owners. On the other hand, disadvantages of the LLC form include a less well established body of common law and less acceptance among the investor community than other business forms such as partnerships and corporations.

6. *Identify other incorporated forms of business.* The corporation is not the only incorporated form of business. Four other widely used incorporated forms of business are S corporations, nonprofit corporations, cooperatives, and professional service associations.

7. *Define the term* merger *and identify three types of mergers.* A merger takes place when two or more businesses combine to form a single enterprise. There are three types of mergers: horizontal, vertical, and conglomerate.

KEY TERMS

acquisition (p. 70)
business trust (p. 61)
conglomerate merger (p. 70)
cooperative (co-op) (p. 69)
corporate charter (p. 63)
corporation (p. 62)
domestic corporation (p. 63)
double taxation (p. 67)
foreign corporation (p. 63)
general partnership (p. 57)

horizontal merger (p. 70)
joint venture (p. 57)
limited liability company (LLC) (p. 67)
limited liability partnerships (LLPs) (p. 62)
limited partnership (p. 57)
master limited partnership (MLP) (p. 57)
merger (p. 70)
nonprofit corporations (p. 69)
operating agreement (p. 67)
partnership (p. 57)

partnership agreement (p. 58)
professional service organizations (p. 62)
proxy (p. 64)
S corporation (p. 62)
sole proprietorship (p. 54)
syndicate (p. 60)
unlimited liability (p. 56)
vertical merger (p. 70)

QUESTIONS FOR DISCUSSION AND REVIEW

1. Describe some of the advantages and disadvantages of a sole proprietorship, partnership, and corporation.
2. What are the requirements for a nonprofit organization? Can a nonprofit organization make money?
3. Why would a person want to start their own business? What are the benefits of having your own business? What are the risks?
4. What are the major differences between an S corporation and an LLC? Why would a new business choose one form over the other?
5. What factors would a manager consider in deciding whether to attempt to acquire another firm through a merger?

6. What characteristics of the sole proprietorship make it the most popular form of business ownership?
7. Why would a person be attracted to join a cooperative?
8. Why does double taxation irritate stockholders in a company?
9. Why have joint ventures between American and non-American partners become so popular?
10. What factors should you consider when deciding whether to team up with someone in a partnership form of business?

END-OF-CHAPTER QUESTIONS

1. Firms with fewer than twenty employees make up the majority of all businesses in the United States.   **T** or **F**
2. Texas had the highest number of employer firms in the early to mid-1990s.   **T** or **F**
3. Gallery Furniture in Houston, Texas, is the most productive retail space in the world.   **T** or **F**
4. The amount of personal property that a person can lose by starting a business is called a capital requirement.   **T** or **F**
5. Partnerships comprise 72 percent of the businesses in the United States.   **T** or **F**
6. A sole proprietorship is the hardest way to start a business.   **T** or **F**
7. Partnership law in the United States has been derived from only one source, the Uniform Partnership Act (UPA).   **T** or **F**
8. A partnership can be based on either a written contract or an oral agreement.   **T** or **F**
9. Limited partners legally may have no say in managing the business.   **T** or **F**
10. A written partnership agreement must include a procedure for dissolving the partnership.   **T** or **F**

11. A person who invests money in a partnership may have a hard time withdrawing the investment.   **T** or **F**
12. A business trust prohibits the transfer of legal title to a property of one person for the use and benefit of another.   **T** or **F**
13. A partnership is an incorporated form of business.   **T** or **F**
14. The primary advantage of an S corporation is that _____
    _____.
    a. it is easy to form
    b. it is easy to dissolve
    c. it allows shareholders to be corporations
    d. the shareholders' tax brackets can result in tax savings
15. A _____ is a special type of partnership established to carry out a special project or to operate for a specific time period.
    a. limited partnership
    b. general partnership
    c. joint venture

INTERNET EXERCISE

YoungBiz.com

"Ten years ago, many adults didn't know what an entrepreneur was," says Bonnie Drew, editor in chief of YoungBiz Media, which publishes magazines and educational material for young people interested in business. But today's kids, with Bill Gates and Michael Dell as role models, "understand and think in business terms. YoungBiz estimates that the top 100 young entrepreneurs in its annual survey earned a total profit of more than $7 million. While not all youth-run businesses make a lot of money, they all capitalize on simple ideas that appeal to their creators.

To learn more about young entrepreneurs and the kinds of businesses and nonprofit organizations they're starting, go to www.youngbiz.com. Explore the site, read about the young entrepreneurs, and learn the types of resources that are available to you.

EXPERIENTIAL EXERCISE

Importance of Small-Business Development

General Information

A review of the literature shows that after years of government control Eastern Europe is fascinated by Western-style small business (sole proprietorship and partnership). There is now little doubt that small businesses will play a large role in any turnaround of economies that have been stagnate for decades in Hungary, Russia, Poland, and the Czech and Slovak Republics. Exactly what model of small-business development each Eastern European nation will follow is not known at this time. The governments and citizens of each nation will have a lot to do with what happens in Eastern European economies.

Directions

Groups of four to six students will be formed by the instructor to examine the history and current progress of various Eastern European nations regarding small-business development. The nations to be studied are as follows:

Poland	Slovak Republic
Russia	Hungary
Ukraine	Rumania
Kazakhstan	Lithuania
Czech Republic	Latvia

Each group should go to the library (or contact the relevant embassy if possible) and examine historical facts, laws, government taxation policies, regulations, labor markets, and other data for each nation.

Each group should prepare a five- to ten-page report to be shared with other groups.

In a class discussion determine which of the nations studied has the best chance of succeeding in terms of small-business growth and economic impact. Also, decide which nation has the most similarities when compared with the United States.

BUSINESS APPLICATION

The Decision to Franchise: What Are the Concerns?

Activity

Students will analyze the concerns an entrepreneur or several entrepreneur partners may have when contemplating a move to franchise.

Directions

Divide the class into small groups of four to seven members, asking each group to appoint a recorder/spokesperson for the group.

Provide the class with the following background and ask them to consider pertinent concerns about a decision to franchise:

- The owner of a pizza shop has been running this successful business from five locations within the central Florida area for the past four years.

- Some potential investors have approached the owner about selling them a franchise to allow the investors to use the good name associated with the high quality of pizza and service.

- The amount of money the investors have offered is very attractive to the owner and will be difficult to turn down.

Before the owner signs an agreement to franchise, what should the owner ask the potential buyers to agree to do? Ask each group to come up with a list of conditions the potential franchise operators will have to pledge agreement to prior to letting the franchise begin.

Ask each group's spokesperson to tell the class about the group's list and to explain the rationale behind each item in the list.

Note: If the groups have trouble getting conversation started, the instructor might provide the class with one item for the list. For example, the owner might insist on having the pizza made from certain brand names of flour, tomato sauce, pepperoni, and so on.

Case

When Partnerships Go Bad
Don Weiss Picks Up the Pieces

One of the major challenges of a general partnership is going into business with someone you can rely on and trust. Business partners spend as much or more time together than spouses, and they are faced daily with difficult decisions that could determine the life or death of the business. In general partnerships, each partner has the ability to make commitments on behalf of the firm. Partners must be sure that they are in agreement with where the firm is going and how to get it there.

In the summer of 2001, Don Weiss found out how difficult it can be when a partnership dissolves. His computer-programming school, Conseva Learning Center of Kansas City, was coming off a spectacular run, with a five-year revenue-growth rate of 1,588 percent and a first-time recognition (#172) on the *Inc. Magazine* list of the 500 fastest-growing start-up ventures. The annual list recognizes the 500 fastest-growing privately held companies across the country, based on the percentage of growth in revenues during the preceding five-year period. Conseva ranked second of all Missouri-based companies in the 1996–2000 period. Don Weiss should have been out celebrating—or at least giving himself a good pat on the back.

Instead Weiss spent the summer in Conseva's Missouri headquarters worrying that the business might not last the year. In June, after four years of increasing friction, Weiss's longtime partner split. Alone, Weiss found himself in the middle of a costly national franchising plan. Enrollment in Conseva's programming schools had dropped off sharply in the middle of the technology slump, and there were few signs that demand for software training would ever come roaring back. The thirty-five-employee company's cash reserves were running dangerously low. "We were going to spend the year ramping up for phenomenal growth," Weiss said, sighing. Now his partner was gone, having sold Weiss his 49 percent stake in Conseva in a bitter breakup. And Weiss suddenly had to troubleshoot crisis after crisis entirely on his own. "It was a very scary time," he said. "Every mistake, every shortcoming, was on my shoulders."

Weiss was suffering through a classic case of post-business-breakup trauma. But partnership splits happen. Two colleagues with a few thousand in the bank and lofty dreams come together to build the next Ben & Jerry's or Hewlett-Packard. At first the union is happy. Then the honeymoon ends and problems arise.

One partner wants to expand from chocolate-chip cookies into espresso brownies. Another wants to kick back. Whatever the cause, sometimes the differences just can't be mended. One partner clears out, and the other is suddenly solo at the helm.

It's a panic-inducing prospect. For starters, there's the sticker shock entailed in valuing the exiting partner's cut of the business. Weiss, for instance, will shell out in excess of $1 million for his partner's stake over the next several years. In some cases, there may be emergency operations issues to face, especially if the outgoing partner brought a unique skill to the business. Then there's the very real danger that creditors will start putting the squeeze on and skittish clients and employees will bolt.

That's the bad news. Now for some good: The *Inc.* 500 list of 2001 was scattered with at least half a dozen companies that not only survived but thrived after a partnership split. For some, the booming economy in the late 1990s served as the perfect bandage to what otherwise might have been a fatal event. For others, surviving the divorce took some serious triage. But the partners who stayed on managed to remain focused—and they coddled customers and cheered up employees. And despite the anemic economy of the early 2000s, most are faring better than ever on their own.

Don Weiss is still getting used to that freedom. On one hand, he's finding it exhilarating. On the other, he knows what kind of economic climate the company is up against, and he admits to a certain amount of dread. "It's up to me now," he says. "There's nobody else to blame."

Questions for Discussion

1. What would happen in the event of a partnership breakup if a partnership agreement was not in place?
2. When a partnership breaks up, how should the partner(s) who stay(s) in the business handle the situation with customers?
3. What do you think are the most important things to look for when considering going into a business partnership with another person? List and explain.

Sources: Adapted from Krysten Crawford, "Suddenly Solo," *Inc.*, October 30, 2001, pp. 62–66; and Emily Banker, "Bust-Up's Outcome: More Start Ups," *Inc.*, October 17, 2000, p. 19.

4

Entrepreneurship and Business Start-ups

Photo: comstock.com

Chapter Objectives

After completing this chapter, you should be able to

1 **Define** the term *entrepreneurship*.

2 **Identify** the types of risks that an entrepreneur takes in starting a business.

3 **Identify** services the Small Business Administration offers to small-business owners.

4 **Explain** the concept of franchising.

5 **Compare** the advantages and disadvantages of becoming a franchisee.

EcoFish

How do you go about branding a product that, like meat, conjures up in the minds of consumers a distinctly generic picture: slabs of flesh displayed behind a spotless glass counter? If you're Henry Lovejoy, 37, you try a low-overhead pure marketing play. Your niche concept: Tap into a rising tide of concern over endangered fish populations by wholesaling only ecologically acceptable fare—that is, fish and shellfish harvested in sustainable fashion. Among the possible offerings: West Coast troll-caught albacore tuna, Oregon Dungeness crab, Ecuadorian long-lined mahi-mahi, and Prince Edward Island rope-grown blue mussels. "We believe we've got a very captive audience of at least 13 million," says Lovejoy, citing surveys of consumer responsiveness to environmental concerns.

With no fishing boats, no aquaculture operation, and no processing plant, the business, which is based in Portsmouth, New Hampshire, is banking on its first-ashore catchy name—
1 ☞ EcoFish Inc.—and a splashy five-color logo to establish it as a trusted supplier of only good-for-the-planet seafood. A Seattle-based company supplies and processes most of Lovejoy's fish; it vacuum-packs six-ounce frozen fillets for natural-food stores. EcoFish shrewdly downplays retail prices that are 10 to 20 percent higher than its competitors' by selling servings by the ounce, rather than by the pound. The company also overnights fresh fish to high-profile restaurants like New York City's Oceana and Philadelphia's White Dog Café. The hope is that ecologically concerned, trend-setting restaurants will provide ancillary marketing by educating their customers with "green" menu descriptions. Imagine "potato-encrusted wild Alaskan longlined salmon" rather than "grilled salmon in a potato crust."

Lovejoy expects some chefs will also cite EcoFish by name in the manner that many already credit their beef tenderloins and lamb chops to Niman Ranch. "The ultimate test," he says, "will be if we're branded on the menus, even if only on the back, where a lot of restaurants tell their story and mention their suppliers." The idea that became EcoFish was inspired by Ben & Jerry's, the Vermont ice cream maker that has been a pioneer in mass marketing with a conscience. Among its initiatives, Ben & Jerry's gives 7 percent of pretax profits to charity. Lovejoy's Portsmouth, New Hampshire–based company offers 25 percent to marine conservation efforts.

Before it even started, the business faced tough obstacles, namely credibility and research, Lovejoy said. Consumers need to know that EcoFish products live up to the company's mission, he said. And that requires significant and continuing research of fish stocks, harvesting methods, and consumer demand. Lovejoy came up with a solution to both problems: an advisory board made up of conservationists that would approve all contracts with fisheries.

So far, the board, which includes officers of the National Audubon Society and World Wildlife Fund, has approved contracts with ten fisheries. Though there are no national sales figures for sustainable seafood, sales of organic products have grown by 20 percent every year since 1990 and represent a roughly $7.8 billion industry, according to the Organic Trade Association, based in Greenfield, Massachusetts.

Sustainably harvested seafood does not come cheap. Lovejoy's catches cost as much as 20 percent more than traditional seafood. But the higher costs bring an unexpected benefit, Lovejoy said. Fishermen are paid more for using sustainable practices, and that helps conservation efforts.

Sources: Adapted from John Grossman, "High Concept: Sea Change," *Inc.* January 15, 2002; J. M. Hirsch, "Eco-Friendly Fishing Is Catching On," *Detroit Free Press,* July 31, 2001; and Margot Higgins, "EcoFish.com Is No Red Herring," *Environmental News Network,* January 30, 2000.

4-1 INTRODUCTION

Entrepreneurship often involves a great deal of risk and personal sacrifice, especially in the first couple years of operating a new business. No one should even think about going into business for themselves unless they are prepared to work long hours, endure hardships, and persevere based on a vision of future rewards. Running your own business requires an ability to deal with the unknown. It is well known that most business start-ups fail within their first five years. Entrepreneurs and small-business owners have nowhere to turn when failure occurs. They must rely on their own resolve and resourcefulness to pick themselves up and try again until they achieve success.

For example, ketchup king H. J. Heinz was all but washed up at the tender age of 31. In November 1875 he wrote that he was deeply in debt and had "not a penny to meet it with." Heinz's pickle company was bankrupt, and a newspaper tartly dubbed him and his partners a "Trio in a Pickle." The failure must have galled Heinz given that, except for cash flow, his company was booming. The cucumber harvest of 1875 had been a bumper crop, and sales were growing apace. Indeed, the reason Heinz couldn't pay his bills was that he had expanded capacity without first lining up enough financing. After the company imploded, Heinz ended up personally liable for at least $20,000. Undaunted, he launched a second food company the very next year. Adding a ketchup product line—and careful cash management—made the difference this time, propelling Heinz to entrepreneurial glory.[1]

This chapter discusses the entrepreneurial and small-business spirit. First, we examine entrepreneurship and the risks that entrepreneurs take. Then we examine small business. Finally, we examine franchising, looking at both the advantages and disadvantages of being in the franchise business.

4-2 ENTREPRENEURSHIP

The debate about what makes an entrepreneur continues. Years of scholarship to identify the essential ingredients of an entrepreneurial personality have yielded little consensus. Entrepreneurs, it turns out, come in all shapes and sizes: Some are young, others are old; some start out rich, others start out poor; and some are smart, others just work very hard.

Despite the lack of consensus on the essential *traits* of successful entrepreneurs, some characteristics of entrepreneurs and entrepreneurship are consistently portrayed and cited as important elements of entrepreneurial success.

4-2a The Individual Entrepreneur

The entrepreneur, according to French economist J. B. Say, "is a person who shifts economic resources out of an area of lower and into an area of higher productivity and yield."[2] But Say's definition does not tell us who this entrepreneur is. Some define the entrepreneur simply as one who starts his or her own new and small business. For our purposes, we define the **entrepreneur** as the person who organizes the resources, takes the risks, and who receives the financial profits and other nonmonetary rewards of starting a new enterprise. (Note that we use the word *enterprise* to denote that an entrepreneur can start a business, a nonprofit organization, or some other organized activity.)

> **Entrepreneurs** People who take the risks necessary to organize and manage a business and receive the financial profits and nonmonetary rewards.

The person who opens a small pizza restaurant is in business, but is he or she an entrepreneur? The individual took a risk and did something, but did he or she organize the resources to start the business? If the answer is yes, then the individual is considered an entrepreneur. Steve Case is an example of an entrepreneur because he founded and established America Online (AOL). His Internet access business was not a new concept, but he applied new techniques, unique content, and took advantage of his customers' desire to connect to one another through chat and instant messaging. This is what entrepreneurs do; this is what entrepreneurship means.[3] Furniture magnate Jim McIngvale now sells $180 million worth of furniture each year through Gallery Furniture, a single location store beside Highway 45 in Houston (see Chapter 3 for more on Gallery). How does he sell so much furniture? Simple; he promises people that he will deliver their furniture the same day they buy it. That simple change in the overall furniture buying process has provided McIngvale a significant and sustainable competitive advantage in his market.[4]

Over the past decade, many of the sharp contrasts between the entrepreneur and the professional have faded away. Formerly, professionals such as doctors, lawyers, dentists, and accountants were not supposed to be entrepreneurial, aggressive, or market oriented. They were "above" the market-driven world. Entrepreneurs, on the other hand, were the

1. Mike Hofman, "If at First You Don't Succeed," *Inc.*, January 1, 2002, archive.

2. Robert D. Hisrich and Michael P. Peters, *Entrepreneurship* (Homewood, IL: Richard D. Irwin, 1989), p. 9.

3. William D. Bygrave, "The Entrepreneurial Process," in *The Portable MBA in Entrepreneurship*, ed. William D. Bygrave (New York: John Wiley, 1994), pp. 1–23.

4. Jim McIngvale, Tom Duening, John Ivancevich, *Always Think Big* (Chicago: Dearborn Trade, April 2002).

mavericks of society. They were risk takers who aggressively sought to make something happen by responding to market opportunities. Long hours were about all the two worlds had in common. However, increased competition, saturated markets, and a more price-conscious public have changed the world of the professionals. Today even the most buttoned-down professionals need to market their skills, talents, and competencies: Lawyers advertise their services; doctors specialize in one or another form of surgery; accounting firms join with other businesses (e.g., consulting and law) to serve clients. These professionals have had to become entrepreneurial in order to survive. Many have crafted unique services—such as catering to specific markets—or have come up with some other innovation that differentiates them from their competitors.

4-2b The Entrepreneurial Personality

Entrepreneurs exhibit many different personality types; searching for a specific personality pattern is very difficult. Some entrepreneurs are quiet, introverted, and analytical. On the other hand, some are brash, extroverted, and very emotional.[5] As we have stated, there are probably as many personality varieties among entrepreneurs as there are entrepreneurs. However, all entrepreneurs exhibit one consistent trait: optimism. Across the different types of personality, researchers have found that entrepreneurs have an optimistic way of thinking that leads them to deal with failure and change differently than do pessimists. Whereas pessimists view failure as personal and long-lasting, optimists view failure as due to causes beyond their control and short-lived. Optimists see failure as an opportunity to grow, whereas pessimists see failure as a reflection of their own shortcomings.[6] Can you see how this personality trait is important to someone starting a business of his or her own?

Viewing change as the norm, entrepreneurs usually search for it, respond to it, and treat it as an opportunity. An entrepreneur such as Steve Case is able to take resources and shift them to meet a need. Making the decision to shift resources works better if a person is creative, experienced, and confident.

One example of how an entrepreneur exhibits boundless optimism and creativity is Doug Evans, the 35-year-old founder of Servador Inc., a print outsourcing provider in New York City. Evans didn't have any formal training when he started any of his three businesses (Servador being his third). With only a high school diploma to his name, Evans joined the army and became a paratrooper at 18. A graffiti artist in his youth, he decided to tap into his artistic background upon leaving the army. A business in graphic arts and printing fit his meticulous nature to a tee—but he knew nothing about the graphic arts business. "I knew I was going to become a great graphic designer," says Evans. "And I think the lesson there was having a mission."

5. John H. Christy, "The Americanization of Matthais Zahn," *Forbes*, March 13, 1995, pp. 123–124.

6. Martin Seligman, *Learned Optimism* (New York: Alfred A. Knopf, 1991).

FOCUS ON GLOBALIZATION

Entrepreneurship around the World

14 ☞

The **Global Entrepreneurship Monitor (GEM)** research program is an annual assessment of the national level of entrepreneurial activity. Initiated in 1999 with ten countries, expanded to twenty-one in the year 2000, with twenty-nine teams in 2001, it expects close to forty national teams in 2002. The research program, based on a harmonized assessment of the level of national entrepreneurial activity for all participating countries, involves exploration of the role of entrepreneurship in national economic growth. Systematic differences continue, with few highly entrepreneurial countries reflecting low economic growth. There is, further, a wealth of national features and characteristics associated with entrepreneurial activity. The key findings from the 2001 assessment are as follows:

Entrepreneurship is a global phenomenon with significant differences between countries. About 1.4 billion working-age individuals (20 to 64 years old) live in the twenty-nine GEM 2001 countries. Slightly less than 10 percent of these people are, at any point in time, in the process of creating and growing new businesses. Thus, in the GEM countries alone, almost 150 million people are engaged in some form of entrepreneurial activity!

Several national contextual factors influence the level of entrepreneurial activity. Both opportunity and necessity entrepreneurship were higher in countries where there was greater income inequality and where the adults expected the national economic situation to improve. Opportunity entrepreneurship was higher where there was (a) a reduced national emphasis in manufacturing, (b) less intrusive government regulations, (c) a higher prevalence of informal investors, and (d) a significant level of respect for entrepreneurial activity. Necessity entrepreneurship was higher in countries where (a) economic development was relatively low, (b) the economy was less dependent on international trade, (c) there was not an extensive social welfare system, and (d) women were less empowered in the economy.

Source: Adapted from Paul D. Reynolds, S. Michael Camp, William D. Bygrave, Erkko Autio, and Michael Hay, "Global Entrepreneurship Monitor 2001," November, 14, 2001.

tasted good; a restaurant owner named Colonel Sanders owned a small cafe that served "finger-lickin' good" chicken; and a salesperson named Ray Kroc discovered a tasty hamburger in California that he turned into the McDonald's burger. Today, entrepreneurs take a global view when crafting new business concepts and models, as discussed in the Focus on Globalization box, "Entrepreneurship around the World."

15 ☞

4-3a Characteristics

What characterizes small businesses? The Small Business Act of 1953 defines **small business** as "one which is independently owned and operated and not dominant in its field of operation." The act authorized the Small Business Administration (SBA) to use a number of yardsticks to identify a small business. For example, in lending money to small businesses, the SBA has established the following limits for qualifying:

Small Business One that is independently owned and operated and is not dominant in its field of operation.

- Represent more than 99% of all employers
- Employ 51% of private-sector workers, 51% of workers on public assistance, and 38% of workers in high-tech jobs
- Represent nearly all of the self-employed, which are 7% of the work force
- Provide two-thirds to three-fourths of the net new jobs
- Produce 51% of private-sector output
- Represent 96% of all exporters of goods
- Obtain 33.3% of federal prime and subcontractor dollars
- Are 53% home-based and 3% franchises

EXHIBIT 4-4

Basic Facts about Small Businesses in the U.S.

Sources: U.S. Department of Commerce, Bureau of the Census; U.S. Department of Labor, Bureau of Labor Statistics; Advocacy-funded study by Joel Popkin & Company; U.S. Department of Commerce, International Trade Administration; SBA Office of Government Contracting.

- *Retailing and service* The sales limit varies depending on the industry. In some industries, the maximum amount of sales is $3.5 million. In others, the maximum amount may be as high as $13.5 million.
- *Wholesaling* The maximum number of employees cannot exceed 500.
- *Manufacturing* The business must have 250 or fewer employees. If employment is more than 250 but less than 500, a size standard for a particular industry is used.
- *Special trade construction* The maximum amount of sales is $7 million, regardless of industry.

These criteria suggest that smallness depends on your point of view. Marshall Field's (a department store company that started in Chicago) might be considered small in comparison to Wal-Mart, but compared with many other department store companies, Marshall Field's is large. Therefore, a small business is one that is not dominant (does not control a large market share) in its industry and one that can be started with a moderate investment for that industry. Exhibit 4-4 provides some facts about small businesses.

16
17

4-3b Advantages and Disadvantages

Any business venture involves potential benefits and costs. For many people, one important benefit is the personal gratification gained from operating one's own business. Business owners can exercise all their talents and can do so with some degree of independence; some also can obtain power by operating their own business. Another benefit of starting a small business is financial gain. The financial return from a successful small business can be substantial.

On the other hand, potential and actual costs can be important. The initial investment may be lost. Some risks are out of the entrepreneur's control; fashion changes, government regulations, competition, and labor problems may threaten the business. Some businesses also tend to produce irregular income; during the first six months of many potentially profitable firms, the owner may receive zero profits. Being in business for yourself also means long hours, generally leaving less time for recreation and family. These important parts of life sometimes must be sacrificed to operate a business successfully.

4-3c The Small Business Administration (SBA)

The U.S. Small Business Administration (SBA), an independent agency of the federal government, was created in 1953 to protect the interests of small-business owners. Big-business interests are promoted in Congress by well-organized lobbies, which work to create an atmosphere favorable for big business. Small businesses did not have this type of lobby power; for this and other reasons, the SBA was created.

18

Small Business Administration (SBA) An independent agency of the federal government created in 1953 to protect the interests of small-business owners.

SBA Loans

The SBA enables its lending partners to provide financing to small businesses, when funding is otherwise unavailable, on reasonable terms by guaranteeing major portions of loans made to small businesses. The agency does not currently have funding for direct loans nor does it provide grants or low-interest rate loans for business start-up or expansion.

The eligibility requirements and credit criteria of the program are very broad in order to accommodate a wide range of financing needs. When a small business applies to a lending partner for a loan, the lender reviews the application and decides if it merits a loan on its own or if it requires additional support in the form of an SBA guaranty. The lender then requests SBA backing on the loan. In guaranteeing the loan, the SBA assures the lender that, in the event the borrower does not repay the loan, the government will reimburse the lending partner for a portion of its loss. By providing this guaranty, the SBA is able to help tens of thousands of small businesses every year get financing they would not otherwise obtain.

To qualify for an SBA guaranty, a small business must meet the SBA's criteria, and the lender must certify that it could not provide funding on reasonable terms without an SBA guaranty. The SBA can guarantee as much as 85 percent on loans of up to $150,000 and 75 percent on loans of more than $150,000. In most cases, the maximum guaranty is $1 million. There are higher loan limits for international trade, defense-dependent small firms affected by defense reductions, and Certified Development Company loans.

Business Information Centers

The SBA's business information centers (BICs) provide a one-stop location where current and future small-business owners can receive assistance and advice. BICs combine computer technology, hardware and software, an extensive small-business reference library of hard copy books and publications, and current management videotapes to help entrepreneurs plan their business, expand an existing business, or venture into new business areas. The use of software for a variety of business applications offers clients of all types a means for addressing diverse needs. In addition to the self-help hardware, software and reference

19 ☞ materials, BICs have on-site counseling provided by the Service Corps of Retired Executives (SCORE). These former businessmen and -women lend their expertise and knowledge to assist clients with problems and issues confronting those starting, managing, and growing a small business. Counseling provides the one-on-one interaction that helps small-business owners develop personalized plans of action leading to better choices for their businesses.

Small Business Development Centers

20 ☞ The SBA administers the Small Business Development Center (SBDC). Program to provide management assistance to current and prospective small-business owners. SBDCs offer one-stop assistance to small businesses by providing a wide variety of information and guidance in central and easily accessible branch locations. The program is a cooperative effort of the private sector; the educational community; and federal, state, and local governments. It enhances economic development by providing small businesses with management and technical assistance.

There are now fifty-eight SBDCs—one in every state (Texas has four), the District of Columbia, Guam, Puerto Rico, Samoa, and the U.S. Virgin Islands—with a network of more than 1,100 service locations. In each state there is a lead organization, which sponsors the SBDC and manages the program. The lead organization coordinates program services offered to small businesses through a network of subcenters and satellite locations in each state. Subcenters are located at colleges, universities, community colleges, vocational schools, chambers of commerce, and economic development corporations.

Women-Owned Small-Business Assistance

A growing number of women have decided that the "glass ceiling" in corporations or someone else's business has blocked their career progress. Other women desire the autonomy of heading their own business. The Women's Business Ownership Act of 1988 has helped many women secure loans to start their own businesses. Banks make loans of less than $50,000, and the SBA guarantees them. The SBA also has a microloan program granting from $50 to $15,000 to single mothers to start businesses.

Minority Business and the SBA

In the United States, which has about 50 million minority citizens, the number of African-American and Hispanic minority-owned businesses is disproportionately small. This may be due to lack of funds, inexperience, inability to obtain credit, or lack of interest in business. Minority small-business people tend to have a harder time finding investors.

The business community, government, and a large portion of society are promoting minority ownership. Large corporations are attempting to buy from and support minority-owned businesses. In cooperation with the U.S. Department of Commerce, the SBA has instituted programs that assist small businesses owned and managed by the socially or economically disadvantaged. The category includes but is not restricted to African Americans, Native Americans, Mexican Americans, Asian Americans, and Inuits (native Alaskans).

The Small Business Investment Act of 1958 allows small firms to more easily get needed long-term capital to finance their growth. This act authorized the SBA to license **small-business investment companies (SBICs),** privately owned and operated companies that furnish loans to small firms,

SBICs dedicated to assisting small firms owned and operated by minority-group members are called **minority-enterprise small-business investment companies (MESBICs).** A MESBIC is owned and operated by established industrial or financial concerns, private investors, or business-oriented economic development organizations. Minority owners can ask for financial and managerial support from a MESBIC.

The SBA does more than lend money. It offers a starter kit for owners, sponsors local college courses and workshops, puts clients in touch with volunteers, and helps owners secure contracts with the federal government.

4-3d Small-Business Opportunities

Three typical ways to become a small-business owner include taking over a family business by succession, buying an existing business, or starting a new business. Children of entrepreneurs often take over the family business. In many cases, the employees in small bakeries, barbershops, grocery stores, and butcher shops are the owners' children. They learn the business by working with their parents. Sometimes the children learn well and want to continue the business. In other cases, the parents force the business on the children, resulting in parent-child conflict and business failure.

Passing a business on to children is known as **succession.** Families that want to continue to run a business by passing on responsibilities need to begin succession planning while the business leader is in his or her 50s, and the children are in their mid-20s or early 30s. Small-business consultants estimate that the succession process can take ten to fifteen years.[14]

Some people **buy out** an established business. The buyer and seller agree on terms involving the inventory, equipment, and price. The details of this purchase agreement should be spelled out in a legal contract between the buyer and seller. Research suggests that before a buyout can occur three parties need to be satisfied. Managers in the firm must feel comfortable about who is buying the firm. Institutions doing business, such as suppliers and banks, need to be satisfied. Employees who are operating the business must feel comfortable about the buyer. A discussion with these parties could go a long way toward making the buying of an existing business an eventual success.[15]

The third method of becoming a small-business owner, *starting* a new business, requires hard work and careful planning. Without solid planning, a new owner is likely to be swamped by the first wave of problems. Because a new business has no previous customers or business records, as an established business does, getting all the information needed to do a good job will involve hard work. The new owner must study materials about products and markets, consult with professional and business experts, and perhaps attend seminars and workshops for a quick education about managing a small business.

Small-Business Investment Companies (SBICs) A privately owned and operated company licensed by the SBA to furnish loans to small firms.

Minority-Enterprise Small-Business Investment Companies (MESBICs) Minority-enterprise small-business investment company. Such a company is owned and operated by established industrial or financial concerns, private investors, or business-oriented economic development organizations.

Succession Passing a business on to children.

Buy out When a buyer and seller agree on terms involving the inventory, equipment, and price of an established business.

14. Sharon Nelton, "What I've Learned—Part Two," *Nation's Business,* May 1994, p. 74.

15. Stanley Kaplan, "The Staying Power of Leveraged Buy-outs," *Journal of Financial Economies,* Spring 1991, pp. 287–313.

FOCUS ON CAREERS

Are You Ready to Run Your Own Business?

Directions

Are you ready to run your own business? An important starting point in making a decision is determining your goals in life. Then you must match these goals with the benefits offered by the type of business you are considering. Other important questions to ask yourself include:

- Are you a self-starter?
- Do you like other people?
- Can you lead others?
- Are you well organized?
- Are you a decisive decision maker?
- Do you enjoy hard work and long hours?

- Do you stick with a project?
- Can you handle pressure?
- Can you communicate well?
- Do you understand planning, organizing, and controlling?
- Do you learn from past mistakes?
- Are you in excellent health?

Feedback

Operating a small business can be both challenging and rewarding. But owning or running a small business is not for everyone. A small business can be a lot of pressure, long hours, and a test of management and leadership skills. The reward is the satisfaction in running your own show and succeeding both personally and financially.

A score of at least nine yes responses indicates a strong interest in running your own business. If you answered no to four or more of these questions, you may want to think carefully before attempting to operate a small business. Of course, this is only a checklist of questions, and is only meant to help assess your own entrepreneurial potential. And even if you answered no, you can change—good communication skills can be developed, leadership skills can be acquired, and so on. If you answered yes to most of these questions, you seem to have what it takes to operate a small business.

Answering these types of questions requires honesty. Ask a few close friends or relatives how they would answer these questions about you. How does your view compare with how others see you?

The result of all the study and research is the business plan. As we've studied, the business plan is a formal document of what the entrepreneur intends to do to sell enough of the firm's products or services to make a satisfactory profit.

Many people imagine themselves running their own business, making the key decisions, and earning a profit. Becoming a small-business owner can provide these opportunities. The values and attitudes quiz in the Focus on Careers box, "Are You Ready to Run Your Own Business?," can help you decide whether you are ready to operate your own business.

Manufacturing

Small manufacturing businesses number in the thousands. In fact, about 30 percent of all manufacturing companies are considered small.[16] This category includes printing shops, steel fabricating shops, recreational equipment plants, clothing manufacturers, cabinet shops, furniture shops, and bakeries. The manufacturing business involves converting raw materials into products needed by society. Therefore the owner must understand production and marketing and how these business functions complement each other.

---

16. Carol Steinberg, "Turnaround," *Success*, January–February 1995, pp. 71–77.

Service

The service sector is a diverse field; there are hundreds of service business opportunities. About 60 percent of all private business jobs in the United States involve selling services to consumers. **Services** are intangible products that cannot be physically possessed and that involve performance or effort. Service businesses include:

- *Business services*—businesses that provide service to other business organizations include accounting firms, advertising agencies, software writers, computer programmers, systems analysts, blueprint service, tax consultants, collection agencies, and so on

- *Restaurant services*—include fast-food restaurants, franchised restaurants, and standard restaurants

- *Personal services*—include barber and beauty shops, baby-sitting agencies, piano teachers, laundries, and travel agencies

- *Repair services*—include automobile, jewelry, appliance, furniture, plumbing, and truck repair services

- *Entertainment and recreation services*—include racetracks, motion picture theaters, amusement parks, golf courses, and bowling alleys

- *Hotels and motels*—include the operation of hotels, motels, and recreational vehicle (RV) camps

With increased leisure time and consumer spending power, individuals, families, and other businesses are expected to increase their use of service firms.

> **Services** In business, intangible products that cannot be physically possessed and that involve performance or effort; examples include teaching, nursing, air travel, tailoring, accounting, and the opera. In employee compensation, indirect compensation in the form of programs, facilities, or activities supplied by employers for employees' use.

Wholesaling

Wholesaling involves selling to other sellers, such as retailers, other wholesalers, or industrial firms. Wholesale trade consists mainly of small businesses. Firms with fewer than 100 employees are responsible for more than 75 percent of the industry's employment. In fact, very small firms (those with fewer than twenty employees) have 41 percent of the total employment.

Retailing

Retailers are merchants who sell goods to consumers. The giants of retailing include Wal-Mart, Sears, Walgreen's, Home Depot, and Nieman Marcus. Small, local retail businesses sell many of the same products as these giant corporations. Corner drugstores, shoe stores, grocery stores, restaurants, jewelry stores, and hardware stores appear in almost every populated area in the United States.

Home-Based Businesses

Twenty-five percent of the total U.S. workforce now works at home, either full or part-time. At the end of 1994 over 33 million Americans were working out of their homes. The keys to succeeding in a **home-based business** are to (1) select a business you truly enjoy, (2) do your research on the business idea, (3) prepare a thorough business plan, (4) have enough start-up money, and (5) start on a part-time basis.

> **Home-Based Business** Business in which an individual works or conducts activities out of the home. About 22 percent of the total workforce now works out of the home.

> **Franchise** The right to use a specific business name (Pizza Hut, Subway, H&R Block, Blockbuster, Masterworks International) and sell its goods or services in a specific city, region, or country.

4-4 FRANCHISING

Today franchising is an international phenomenon. A **franchise** is a legal and commercial relationship between the owner of a trademark, service mark, trade name, or advertising symbol and an individual or group seeking the right to use that identification in a business. The franchise governs the method of conducting business between the two parties. Generally, a franchisee sells goods or services supplied by the franchisor or sells goods or services that meet the franchisor's quality standards. Franchising is based on mutual trust between the franchisor and franchisee. The franchisor provides the business expertise (i.e., marketing plans, management guidance, financing assistance, site location, training, etc.) that otherwise would not be available to the franchisee. The franchisee brings to the franchise operation the entrepreneurial spirit and drive necessary to make the franchise a success. Examples of franchise opportunities for entrepreneurs include Wendy's, Jiffy Lube, Mail Boxes, etc., and many others.

There are primarily two forms of franchising:

1. Product/trade name franchising
2. Business format franchising

In the simplest form, a franchisor owns the right to the name or trademark and sells that right to a franchisee. This is known as "product/trade name franchising." In the more complex form, "business format franchising," a broader and ongoing relationship exists between the two parties. Business format franchises often provide a full range of services, including site selection, training, product supply, marketing plans, and even assistance in obtaining financing. The International Franchise Association is a leading trade association in the franchise industry. Its website lists "hot" franchises.

4-4a Franchising: A Brief History

An attractive way to become involved with business is to invest in a franchise. Legislation mandates that three components must be present for a franchise to exist:

1. The utilization of a uniform trade name or service mark (e.g., Dairy Queen, Subway, Blockbuster)
2. A uniform system of operations
3. A fee of at least $500 during the first six months of business

With these components, a franchise relationship is established between the franchisor (the company) and the franchisee (the small-business owner). A new franchised business opens every fifteen minutes in the United States. Franchising is the fastest-growing method of doing business, but it is not really new. Some believe that franchising dates back to the Middle Ages (A.D. 476–1453), when it was common practice for governments to offer people a license or franchise granting them the right to do business or to establish and collect tax revenues.

The first contractual commercial franchise in the United States was Singer Sewing Machine Company in 1851. To solve the "sewing machine war," in which four manufacturers were suing one another, Isaac Singer and his attorney-partner, Edmund Clark, organized the Sewing Machine Combination. It became the first patent pool in the United States, dividing the distribution rights among the manufacturers. The franchisees were granted worldwide rights, territories, and exclusive rights to sell and service their machines.

Two other early franchise operations in the United States were Coca-Cola, which first supplied its syrup to franchised bottlers around 1900, and Rexall Drug Stores, which started around 1902. Other early franchise pioneers included automobile dealerships and gasoline stations. Oil companies had been operating their own stations until about 1930. A few of them began to license dealers, and the practice spread from 1930 to 1935 until it became the sole method employed to distribute gasoline. In the 1950s franchising spread across the United States. In fact, 90 percent of all franchise companies doing business today started in the early 1950s.

Obvious signs of franchising's popularity are the numerous fast-food outlets lining the highways and shopping malls. They serve everything from special flavors of ice cream to hot dogs. McDonald's has an international network of over 8,000 restaurants that sell a billion hamburgers every five months.

4-4b The Uniform Franchise Offering Circular

Franchising is governed primarily by laws that require franchisors to inform prospective franchisees about the system. This information is contained in a document called the Uniform Franchise Offering Circular, or simply the UFOC. Under the federal and state rules, a franchisor cannot offer a franchise until the franchisor has prepared a UFOC.

In a nutshell, the UFOC provides information on the franchisor, the company's key staff, management's experience in franchise management, the franchisor's bankruptcy and litigation history, and the initial and ongoing fees involved in opening and running a franchise. Also included is information on the required investment, purchases you will be required to make from the franchisor or approved suppliers, and territory rights you will be granted. You also find information about the legal responsibilities of the franchisee and franchisor.

In addition, the UFOC presents information about the company-owned locations and the franchisees in the system, including the number of franchises opened, the number closed and transferred, and, most important, a list of existing and former franchisees with their contact information.

It's important that you fully understand the **franchise agreement** and any other agreements you need to sign. If you don't understand what you're signing, you may find yourself locked into a business relationship that doesn't wear well for you.

4-4c The Ten-Day Rule

Included in the regulations governing the sale of franchises is a cooling-off period called the ten-day rule. Franchisors are required to wait a minimum of ten business days after giving a prospect the UFOC before allowing the franchisee to sign the franchise agreement. As a potential franchisee, you are also legally entitled to have the final franchise agreement—with all the blanks filled in—for at least five business days before you are allowed to sign it. This gives you time to review and consider the terms of the agreement.

The franchise agreement provided in the UFOC may contain some blanks to be filled in, including who the franchisee is, where the franchise will be located, the size of the protected territory (if there is one), and other matters specific to the franchisee. On occasion, the franchise agreement must be changed as a result of changes made during negotiations. The franchisee must be given a copy of the final agreement—with the changes—at least five business days prior to signing the agreement.

4-4d The Franchising Agreement

The franchise organization enters into a contractual agreement with each of its franchisees. These contracts may differ in a number of areas, such as capital needed, training provided, managerial assistance available, and size of the franchise territory. But most franchise contracts have points in common. The franchise buyer normally pays an initial fee to the company and agrees to pay the franchisor a monthly percentage of sales. In exchange, the franchisee has the right to sell a standard product or service.

In almost every franchise, the franchisee must invest some money. The amount can vary from a few thousand dollars to millions. Despite having to put money down, people still have to wait for certain franchises. Each year, more than 2,000 people apply for the approximately 150 franchises granted by McDonald's.

A McDonald's franchise can cost as much as $600,000. Although most of the fee can be borrowed from a bank, $66,000 would be the minimum cash down payment required. This payment covers landscaping and opening costs, license fee, site development fee, equipment down payment, signs, and security deposit. McDonald's Corporation does not lend money or guarantee loans. The company will provide a site, build the restaurant, and develop the parking lot. In return, the franchisee must pay 12 percent of gross sales to McDonald's and put at least 4 percent of gross sales annually into marketing and advertising.

Franchise purchasers enter the business to earn money; in fact, the owner and the company both want to earn money. Earnings are a measure of the franchise's success. To succeed, it must be well managed, provide good products or services, and obtain repeat customers.

The franchisor begins to earn money when the cash down payment is made. In some cases, a franchise fee must be paid before certain rights of operation are granted. The franchisor also requires some type of royalty payment on gross sales (e.g., the 12 percent franchisees pay to McDonald's). The amount of royalty, or share of the proceeds, paid to the

Franchise Aggreement
Contractual agreement between franchise organization and franchisees. Usually outlines, among other things, amount of capital needed, training provided, managerial assistance available, and size of the franchise territory.

franchisor differs from company to company. Typically, a franchisee pays a royalty of between 3 and 15 percent on gross sales (total sales revenue).

No matter what the percentage of royalty, franchisees often dislike paying profits to someone else. It is only human nature for people to feel pain when they see part of the fruits of their labor go to someone else. Paradoxically, this pain may become more intense as franchise operation becomes more successful. The franchisee may be making many thousands of dollars, but so is the franchisor.[17]

Being involved and working hard to make the franchise a success, then being required to share the earnings deflates the ego of some franchisees. If franchisees believe the sharing of profits is unfair, this perceived inequity is also a problem. The franchisee may believe that he or she does all the work and the franchisor takes too big a share of the earnings.

Many people who consider entering into a franchise contract assume they will be their own boss. This assumption is only partially accurate. The franchisor exercises a significant amount of control over the franchisee in such areas as (1) real estate ownership, (2) territorial restrictions, (3) cancellation provisions, and (4) required exclusive handling.

Some franchise companies own the real estate, select the site of the business location, and build the facility. These companies then lease the facility to a franchisee. Exxon, Shell, Gulf, and Texaco, for example, often select the location for a service station and build it according to their specifications.

The **cancellation provision** in a contract is a powerful control device. For instance, gasoline companies often issue operators of service stations a one-year franchise. If the company does not consider the operator successful, the franchise agreement can be canceled after that time. This provision can force operators to run the business as directed by the franchisor.

Exclusive handling means that the franchisee will only sell items, products, or services that are acceptable to the franchisor. This means that the franchisor has control over what is sold directly to customers or clients.

> **Cancellation Provision**
> The contract provision giving a franchisor the power to cancel an arrangement with a franchisee.

> **Exclusive Handling** A form of control in which a franchisor requires the franchisee to purchase only supplies approved by the franchisor.

4-4e Advantages of Owning a Franchise

Although owning a franchise business has its problems, there are reasons why it appeals to people. A person who has never owned or managed a business needs guidance to operate successfully. This guidance can be provided by a well-run franchise organization. Also, franchisors can provide a brand name, proven products or services, and financial assistance.

Guidance A glaring weakness in small businesses is lack of managerial ability. A person with limited managerial skills may be able to get by in a large organization because he or she is just one of many managers. But no one can cover up for or "carry" a franchise manager. Many franchisors try to overcome managerial deficiencies or inexperience by providing some form of training. For example, Kwik Kopy operates its own training school for improving management skills. The initial training focuses on managing a business rather than on operating a printing press. Subjects include financial management, marketing, advertising and much more. Kwik Kopy also offers Personal Development Workshops to sharpen the people skills of trainees. Continuing education through seminars and periodic conferences covers all aspects of center operations.

Brand Name The investor who signs a franchise agreement acquires the right to use a nationally or regionally promoted brand name. This identifies the local unit with a recognized product or service. Travelers recognize the Holiday Inn sign, the colors of a Pizza Hut building, and Century 21 real estate signs. National promotion brings these features and characteristics to the attention of potential consumers.

21 ☞

22 ☞
23, 24 ☞

---

17. Ibid.

Proven Product   The franchisor can offer the franchisee a proven product and method of operating the business. The product or service is known and accepted by the public: Customers will buy Baskin-Robbins ice cream, AAMCO transmissions, Athlete's Foot sneakers, and H&R Block income tax counseling.

☞ 25, 26, 27
☞ 28

Financial Assistance   By joining a franchise company, the individual investor may be able to secure financial assistance. Start-up costs of any business are often high, and the prospective investor usually has limited funds. The sole owner generally has a limited credit rating, making it difficult to borrow needed funds. In some cases, association with a well-established franchisor—through its reputation and its financial controls—may enhance the investor's credit rating with local banks.

4-4f Disadvantages of Owning a Franchise

As does any business venture, franchising has some disadvantages. Many were mentioned briefly earlier in this chapter. Some of the more pressing negative features include costs, lack of control, and inadequate training programs offered by some unscrupulous promoters.

Costs   As already mentioned, franchisees must pay franchise fees. In return, the franchisor can provide training, guidance, and other forms of support that would otherwise cost money. Thus the franchisee pays for the opportunity to share in these forms of support. If it were possible to earn the same income independent of the franchisor, the investor could save the amount of these fees.

External Control   A person who signs a franchise agreement loses some independence. The franchisor, in order to operate all of the franchise outlets as a business, must exercise some control over promotional activities, financial records, hiring, service procedures, and managerial development. Although useful, these controls are unpleasant to the person who seeks independence. In the best of circumstances, the franchisee is semi-independent. In a sole proprietorship, by contrast, the owner is totally independent.

Overdependence   Often new franchises become overdependent on the franchisor, and this can lead to an inability to make timely or even simple decisions without constantly checking and asking for advice. Franchisees need to use judgment and not rely on the franchisor to check every decision about the local market.

Poor Local Reputation Can Spread   In some communities where there are multiple franchise units with different franchisees, the performance and reputation of one can affect all the units. For example, Jack-in-the-Box restaurants were affected negatively nationwide because some franchises in the state of Washington improperly cooked food, allowing the spread of *E. coli* bacteria and resulting in the deaths of three young children.

4-4g Franchisor Disclosure

Because of the nature of franchising in the United States, evaluating an opportunity carefully before signing an agreement is important. The large number of franchise companies makes the task difficult. The Federal Trade Commission requires every franchisor to provide buyers with a full disclosure form. The form has twenty categories of information, including a financial statement, company history review, fees, investment requirements, and a litigation history. The best investment a prospective franchisee can make is to have an attorney and an accountant review the document and provide opinions.[18] Exhibit 4-5 presents a sample of the types of questions that need to be asked and answered before signing a franchise agreement.

---

18. Philip K. Howard, *The Death of Common Sense* (New York: Random House, 1995).

EXHIBIT 4-5

Questions to Address before Signing a Franchise Agreement

Since a franchise agreement can be a legally binding contract that defines the franchise relationship between the franchisor (company) and franchisee (small-business owner), it should be carefully reviewed.

1. What are the legal obligations of the franchisee? Of the franchisor?
2. Are there any legal suits currently pending or recently settled by the franchisor and other franchisees?
3. What is the financial history of the franchisor?
4. What amount of royalty must be paid to the franchisor? When?
5. Please provide me with a list of all current franchisees in my area.
6. What type of support services will the franchisor provide and how good are the services?
7. Does the franchise agreement conform to the requirements of the Federal Trade Commission?
8. Can the franchise agreement be terminated by either party? What are my (franchisee) obligations if the agreement is terminated by me? By the franchisor?

Legal guidelines are crucial to the continued success of franchising. Currently, thirty-five states have laws on franchising issues such as disclosure, registration, and franchise-relationship definitions. The most stringent state law is the Iowa Franchise Act of 1992. The Iowa law requires that franchisors disclose financial information to prospective buyers. It also stipulates that franchisors agree to pay fair market value for any franchise location they decide to close. Moreover, franchisors are barred from terminating, refusing to renew, or denying a transfer of a franchise to another owner except for "good cause."

4-5 CONCLUSION

Small business and entrepreneurship continue to be important forces for economic growth in the United States and around the world. A business education would hardly be complete without a thorough understanding of the role of entrepreneurship in the creation of wealth. This chapter has examined only a few of the important topics associated with small business and entrepreneurship. Whether or not you determine that your career will take you on an entrepreneurial path, you should be aware of the opportunities and challenges that small and start-up enterprises face. The next time you walk into that mom-and-pop grocery or hardware store, look for the proprietor and imagine yourself in his or her shoes. Do you have what it takes to be an entrepreneur?

SUGGESTED WEBSITES

Note: These websites were functional when we went to press. Please access the online text for the most up-to-date URLs.

1. www.ecofish.com
2. www.aol.com
3. www.galleryfurniture.com
4. www.ge.com
5. www.mmm.com
6. www.hp.com
7. www.merck.com
8. www.rubbermaid.com
9. www.elite.com
10. www.mayoclinic.org
11. www.menninger.edu
12. www.hp.com
13. www.coca-cola.com
14. www.gemconsortium.org
15. www.mcdonalds.com
16. www.walmart.com
17. www.marshallfields.com
18. www.sba.gov
19. www.score.org
20. www.sba.gov/sbdc
21. www.kwikkopy.com
22. www.holidayinn.com
23. www.pizzahut.com
24. www.century21.com
25. www.baskinrobbins.com
26. www.aamco.com
27. www.theathletesfoot.com
28. www.hrblock.com
29. www.segway.com

SUMMARY OF LEARNING OBJECTIVES

1. *Define the term* entrepreneurship   An entrepreneur is a person who takes the risks necessary to organize and manage a business and receives the financial profits and nonmonetary rewards.
2. *Identify the types of risks that an entrepreneur takes in starting a business*   An entrepreneur faces substantial risks, including personal risk of failure, financial risk, career risk, and family and social risks.
3. *Identify services the Small Business Administration offers to small-business owners*   The SBA was created in 1953 to help, support, and encourage small business through a variety of services. The SBA provides direct, participating, and guaranteed loans to entrepreneurs. The SBA's Office of Management Assistance sponsors management-training courses to aid people who want to develop their managerial skills. The SBA also helps small businesses owned and managed by the economically and socially disadvantaged. The SBA licenses small-business investment companies (SBICs) and minority-enterprise small-business investment companies (MESBICs), which provide financial and managerial support to small-business owners. It also offers a starter kit for owners, sponsors courses and workshops, and assists owners trying to secure government contracts.

4. *Explain the concept of franchising*   Franching is a system for the selective distribution of goods and services, under a brand name, through outlets, called franchises, owned by independent businesspeople. The franchisor (company) supplies the franchisee (person) with know-how and/or brand identification on a continuing basis; the franchisee enjoys the rights to profit and runs the risk of loss. The relationship between the franchisor and the franchisee is regulated by a contractual agreement.
5. *Compare the advantages and disadvantages of becoming a franchisee*   The advantages of owning a franchise include (a) managerial guidance from the franchisor, (b) the right to use a nationally promoted brand name, (c) use of a proven product and method of operating the business, and (d) financial assistance. The disadvantages of owning a franchise include (a) costs, in the form of franchise fees and also paying the franchisor a percentage of the franchise's profits; (b) loss of control over promotional activities, financial records, hiring, service procedures, and managerial development; and (c) the weak training programs offered by some franchisors.

KEY TERMS

business plan (p. 84)
buy out (p. 89)
cancellation provision (p. 94)
entrepreneur (p. 80)
exclusive handling (p. 94)
franchise (p. 91)

franchise agreement (p. 93)
home-based business (p. 91)
intrapreneur (p. 82)
minority-enterprise small-business investment
   companies (MESBICs) (p. 89)
need for achievement (p. 83)

services (p. 91)
small business (p. 86)
Small Business Administration (SBA) (p. 87)
small-business investment companies
   (SBICs) (p. 89)
succession (p. 89)

QUESTIONS FOR DISCUSSION AND REVIEW

1. Women have started over 40 percent of the new firms in the United States. Why would new business start-ups be attractive to women?
2. Why should a person hire a lawyer and an accountant to go over a franchise agreement?
3. How do entrepreneurs contribute to America's standard of living?
4. Why are international markets attractive to American franchisors such as McDonald's, Pizza Hut, and Marriott Hotels?
5. Do you believe that the large start-up costs of opening a McDonald's—about $600,000—discourage many potential franchisees?
6. If you were a franchise owner, would paying a royalty to the franchisor be a major issue and concern? Why or why not?

7. Does an organization have to be small to be considered entrepreneurial? Explain.
8. Entrepreneurs have been described in this chapter as risk takers. What risks are involved in running a business as an entrepreneur? What are the benefits of entrepreneurship?
9. There is an ongoing debate about whether people can learn to be entrepreneurs or whether they must be born with an "entrepreneurial spirit." Do you think people can learn to be entrepreneurs?
10. Why is a business plan important for new business ventures?

END-OF-CHAPTER QUESTIONS

1. Most business start-ups fail within their first five years.   **T** or **F**

2. Pessimists view failure as short-lived and due to causes beyond their control.   **T** or **F**

3. Two out of three new jobs in the economy are in small businesses.   **T** or **F**

4. The U.S. government publishes a report each year listing the specific reasons why thousands of businesses failed.   **T** or **F**

5. A stockholder is the person who organizes the resources, takes the risks, and receives the financial profits and other nonmonetary rewards of starting a new business.   **T** or **F**

6. Entrepreneurs face significant financial risk.   **T** or **F**

7. In the 1940s, an IBM executive estimated the worldwide market for computers at no more than five computers.   **T** or **F**

8. Passing a business on to *stockholders* is known as succession.   **T** or **F**

9. The first contractual commercial franchise in the United States was the Singer Sewing Machine Company.   **T** or **F**

10. Included in the regulations governing the sale of franchises, there is a cooling-off period called the thirty-day rule.   **T** or **F**

11. To qualify as a small business, a wholesaling firm can have up to _____.
    a. 1,000 employees   c. 250 employees
    b. 500 employees   d. 100 employees

12. The SBA has a microloan program granting loans from $50 to $15,000 to _____ to start businesses.
    a. Native Americans   c. college graduates
    b. displaced homemakers   d. single mothers

13. About _____ of all manufacturing companies are considered small.
    a. 10 percent   c. 50 percent
    b. 30 percent   d. 75 percent

14. Which of the following services is *not* considered a personal service?
    a. Baby-sitting   c. Automobile repair
    b. Piano lessons   d. Hair styling

15. What percent of the total U.S. workforce now works at home, either full- or part-time?
    a. 1 percent   c. 25 percent
    b. 5 percent   d. 50 percent

INTERNET EXERCISE

Franchise Opportunities: Knowing the Difference between Real and Scam

Introduction

The Internet has become a haven for get-rich-quick and scam artists of all types. Many of the latest scams surround business opportunities. Using the Internet to "troll" for likely targets, these unscrupulous "entrepreneurs" try to lure others into their get-rich-quick mentality. They set up phony business opportunities, and then turn on the hype machine. Students who are interested in franchising opportunities should be prepared to tell the *real* opportunities from the scams.

Directions

1. Each student in the class should visit the following website outside of class:
   http://www.wemarket4u.net/netops/index.html
   Be sure to click on to register for the "NetOpportunities Seminar" as requested. Don't worry, students won't have to provide any private information or give their credit card number.

2. Next, students should go to the following website:
   http://www.viocfranchise.com/
   Students should be sure the "vioc window" pops up. They should explore the information available about this franchise opportunity.

Discussion

After reviewing the information provided by these franchisors, compare what distinguishes a "viable" opportunity from a "scam." Students should record their thoughts on a sheet of paper and be prepared to discuss them in class. Discussion should focus on the differences between real opportunities and scams, as well as on the ethics of offering scams to an unwitting public.

EXPERIENTIAL EXERCISE

Portrait of an Entrepreneur

Activity

This activity is designed to enhance students' understanding of the entrepreneurial personality and the motivations, challenges, and rewards of entrepreneurship.

Directions

Each member of the class should complete the following assignment:

1. Each student should identify a successful entrepreneur in the community that they can interview. Students should concentrate on identifying a small business that is directed by its founder. The business section of recent issues of the community newspaper should be helpful in locating an entrepreneur.
2. After the entrepreneur has been identified, students should contact the person and arrange an interview.
3. Students should conduct a thirty- to sixty-minute interview, including the following questions:
   What motivated you to start your own business?
   How would you describe yourself to a stranger? Are you self-confident, energetic, independent? Are you an optimist, a realist, a pessimist?
   Which personality characteristics and abilities are essential for success as an entrepreneur?
   How would you describe your leadership style?
   Describe a typical workday.
   What aspects of your work do you find the most satisfying? The most frustrating?
   Which aspects of your work are the easiest for you? The most difficult?
   In which of your business's activities (operations, finance, marketing, and personnel) are you most involved?
   How much emphasis do you place on motivating employees?
   What important lessons have you learned from your experience in creating and running your own business?
   What advice would you offer to a young, prospective entrepreneur?
4. After completing the interview, students should prepare a short (one- to two-page synopsis).
5. Students should be asked to share and discuss their findings in class.

BUSINESS APPLICATION

The Decision to Franchise: What Are the Concerns?

Activity

Students will analyze the concerns an entrepreneur or several entrepreneur partners may have when contemplating a move to franchise.

Directions

1. Divide the class into small groups of four to seven members, asking each group to appoint a recorder/spokesperson for the group.
2. Provide the class with the following background and ask them to consider pertinent concerns about a decision to franchise:
   * The owner of a pizza shop has been running this successful business from five locations within the central Florida area for the past four years.
   * Some potential investors have approached the owner about selling them a franchise to allow the investors to use the good name associated with the high quality of pizza and service.
   * The amount of money the investors have offered is very attractive to the owner and will be difficult to turn down.
3. Before the owner signs an agreement to franchise, what should the owner ask the potential buyers to agree to do? Ask each group to come up with a list of conditions the potential franchise operators will have to pledge agreement to prior to letting the franchise begin.
4. Ask each group's spokesperson to tell the class about the group's list and to explain the rationale behind each item in the list.

Note: If the groups have trouble getting conversation started, the instructor might provide the class with one item for the list. For example, the owner might insist on having the pizza made from certain brand names of flour, tomato sauce, pepperoni, etc.

Case

Riding the Segway to Success

29 ☞ Segway LLC, the business founded by inventor and entrepreneur Dean Kamen to transform the way people work and live, recently announced the much-anticipated debut of the Segway™ Human Transporter (HT), the first self-balancing, electric-powered transportation machine. With dimensions no larger than the average adult body and the ability to emulate human balance, the Segway HT uses the same space as a pedestrian and can go wherever a person can walk. The Segway HT will allow people to go farther, move more quickly, and increase the amount they can carry anywhere they currently walk.

"The Segway HT is an enhancement to personal mobility that will allow people to make better use of their time," said Dean Kamen, Segway's chairman and CEO and the man with the technological vision behind the human transporter. "Ultimately, the Segway HT can make urban environments more livable by providing a solution to short-distance travel. If the Segway HT is widely adopted, it could help solve major urban problems, such as pollution, congestion and livability."

The company will produce three distinct models: The i-series optimizes range and speed across a variety of terrain; the e-series is designed for business applications where it is necessary to carry cargo—up to seventy-five pounds in addition to the rider; the p-series will be ideal for densely populated areas, both indoors and out. The Segway HT's footprint is narrower than the average adult's shoulders and its length is no greater than a large shoe. And it's quiet—designed to emit only a barely audible harmonic hum.

The most magical aspect of this unconventional battery-powered sidewalk cruiser is what engineers call the "man-machine interface." Using a Segway is so intuitive that it feels as though the thing has somehow been plugged into your central nervous system. To move forward, just think sincerely about moving forward; you'll instinctively lean forward a bit. A suite of miniature gyroscopes, tilt sensors, and other silicon smarts in the eighty-pound Segway's control system picks up on this and sends power to a pair of electric motors at the wheels. Arch your back a tad, and Segway slows to a halt. Lean back a bit more, and you'll begin gliding along in reverse.

The gyro stabilizing system, based on one that Kamen developed for his IBOT stair-climbing wheelchair, is another truly amazing feature. The Segway remains upright without a kickstand while the rider hops off for a moment, and the motors automatically make the necessary fore-and-aft corrections. Gyro stabilization lets users glide confidently up and down twenty-degree ramps in forward and reverse, and even traverse a bed of three-inch-diameter stones.

The only traditional control on this unconventional vehicle is a twist grip for steering that the engineers located on the left handgrip so that riders familiar with motorcycles wouldn't confuse it with a right-hand throttle. Like an army tank or a bulldozer, the Segway can turn within its own footprint, so that you can amuse yourself and others by spinning left and right without going anywhere at all.

Because Segway HT was developed far from the public eye, the people who were introduced to the product for the first time had a unique opportunity—the chance to try a never-before seen technology. Here are a few first impressions of the product:

"As someone who rides motorcycles, I wondered how something with two wheels parallel to each other would balance. But I was surprised at how easy it was. Most high tech products look like they'll be hard to learn, but using Segway HT was effortless." "The interesting thing was that I'd done a lot of research and was pretty close to guessing what it was, right down to the balancing aspect. But even knowing as much as I knew, I was completely blown away by how it felt. It's like flying in a way, not the height but the sensation of being able to move without any effort. Your body is completely still but at the same time it's controlling your speed."

U.S. Post Office to Give It a Try

Tampa Postmaster Rich Rome announced that the Tampa Post Office is the first United States Postal Service site to test feasibility of the Segway for use in mail delivery.

"The United States Postal Service has a long history of testing innovative modes of transportation," said Postmaster Rome. "As an organization dedicated to deploying technology that drives efficiency, we are proud to be selected as a test site and look forward to giving the Segway HT a thorough evaluation."

The Segway HT will be used on five "park and loop" residential delivery routes where a portion of deliveries is made by a letter carrier on foot. Each route has approximately 500 delivery addresses.

The Postal Service will be evaluating whether use of the Segway HT results in greater delivery efficiency. "To determine the potential for cost savings and increased efficiency, we'll be evaluating delivery time using the Segway HT compared to straight walking time, as well as safety and ergonomics," said Rome. With the Segway HT, up to thirty-five pounds of mail normally carried by the letter carrier can be transferred to satchels mounted on the human transporter.

Police Departments to Try Segway

The Boston and Manchester, New Hampshire, police departments will become two of Segway's first community policing test partners. Boston Police Commissioner Paul Evans said, "We are enthusiastic about putting a force on the Segway HTs. We believe this may enable our officers to have far-reaching contact and access to the residents of our neighborhoods, visitors in our historic tourist districts, and businesses in our city centers."

As the oldest police department in the country, the Boston Police Department is home to many firsts in law enforcement, including the first mounted patrol established in 1873 and the first motor patrol wagon placed in service in 1903.

The International Association of Chiefs of Police (IACP) will be asked to evaluate how implementation of the Segway HT can benefit urban police forces. Joe Estey, IACP third vice president, said, "The application of the Segway Human Transporter for police forces in urban environments has enormous potential for enhancing public safety and a greater sense of community."

Segway HT will first be introduced for commercial use. Initial applications include large-scale manufacturing plants and warehousing operations, travel and tourism, public safety, corporate and campus transportation, and mail, package, and product delivery. Consumer availability is planned for late 2002.

Questions for Discussion

1. What do you think are the challenges that Dean Kamen faces as the founder of Segway, LLC? Do you think his challenges are unique because of the high expectations that have developed around his product?
2. Do you think inventors, in general, should be the ones who own and operate the companies that market their inventions? Why or why not?
3. How would you bring the Segway to market? What other potential uses do you think this product will have?

Sources: Adapted from David Futurelle, "Ginger and Tonic," *Money*, February 2002, p. 26; F. Brown Stuart, "IT Surpasses My Wildest Dreams," *Fortune*, December 24, 2001, p. 38; and Jennifer Norton, "Police Forces to Evaluate Segway™ Human Transporter," *Manchester Times*, December 7, 2001.

Business, Law, and Government

Photo: comstock.com

After completing this chapter, you should be able to

1 **Identify** the sources from which laws are derived.

2 **Outline** the court system in the United States.

3 **Identify** the various categories of business law.

4 **Discuss** how government regulates business activities to encourage competition.

5 **Explain** the effects of deregulation on business.

6 **Define** the different types of taxes and their effects on business.

7 **Describe** how taxation supports the activities of government.

Microsoft's Monopoly

What are the legal rules of the road for a high-tech monopolist? That is the key policy question for Microsoft Corporation following the ruling of the U.S. Court of Appeals that overturned the November 2000 decision by District Judge Thomas P. Jackson to split Microsoft in two. The court severely reprimanded Judge Jackson for criticizing Microsoft in public and failing to hold a hearing on the breakup proposal. But the Appeals Court did unanimously support Jackson's finding that the Windows operating system holds a monopoly in the PC market and that Microsoft used its market clout to maintain that monopoly, thus violating the Sherman Antitrust Act.

Congress, which was concerned about concentrations of power, passed the Sherman Antitrust Act of 1890 by an almost unanimous vote. The first two articles declared: "Every contract, combination in the form of trust or otherwise, or conspiracy in restraint of trade or commerce among the several states, or with foreign nations is hereby declared to be illegal. . . . Every person who shall monopolize, or attempt to monopolize. . . any part of the trade or commerce among the several states, or with foreign nations, shall be deemed guilty of a misdemeanor. . . ." It is these provisions of a nineteenth-century law that Judge Jackson used to rule that one of the world's biggest technology companies needed to be broken up.

Microsoft's legal problems regarding its monopoly status are not just limited to the United States. Brazil's Ministry of Justice also accused the company of violating antitrust laws in its drive to obtain market leadership. The Ministry's secretary of economic rights (SDE) says Microsoft bundled its financial management software Money with its Office Suite of business applications. Paulo de Tarso Ramos Ribeiro, the secretary of the SDE, likened the practice to the bundling of Internet Explorer with Microsoft Windows—the tactic that triggered investigations by the U.S. government.

Since the development of Windows in the early 1990s Microsoft's core strategy has been to bundle new features into Windows, using its monopoly power to push into new markets. Consumers love the convenience of a standardized operating system that comes with applications. Rivals complain they get unfairly frozen out. Now that two courts have concluded that Microsoft is behaving in a monopolist way, it has to change. The years to come will determine what new forms this software and hardware colossus will take.

Sources: Adapted from Raymond Colitt, "Bundling Concerns," *Latin Trade,* September 2001, p. 18; "Microsoft: Time to Change," *Business Week,* July 16, 2001, p. 100; and Lewis J. Walker, "Microsoft and the Trustbusters," *On Wall Street,* June 2000, pp. 143–145.

5-1 INTRODUCTION

Litigation in the United States is a growth industry. As our economy continues to mature and the complexities of business relationships and transactions increase, the potential for intentional and unintentional legal missteps grows. Business activity is governed by legal rules of fair play that are constantly evolving, both formally by statute and court decision, and informally by practice. Entrepreneurs, managers, and small-business owners must abide by the legal rules of business, whether or not they are familiar with all of them. The opening vignette highlights the case of Microsoft. The software giant was besieged during much of 2001 and 2002 as it fought antitrust accusations from federal and state courts, as well as from its leading competitors.

Another good example of the complexity of today's business environment is reflected in the story of the collapse of Enron Corporation. During the halcyon days of the Internet's rapid rise, Enron transformed itself from a wells and pipes oil company to an international energy and commodities trading powerhouse. For shareholders, Enron was a ticket to wealth, as its stock price soared throughout the late 1980s and all through the 1990s. For employees, Enron was a source of retirement wealth created through 401(k) plans, and a source of esteem in society to be one of the chosen few lucky enough (and smart enough) to be employed there. For the city of Houston, Enron was a shining example of its diversified economy, transforming the once predominate oil town into a gleaming new-economy Mecca.

Enron, formed in 1985, grew into the nation's seventh-largest company in revenue by buying electricity from generators and selling it to consumers. It was admired on Wall Street as a technological innovator. But it used complex partnerships to keep some $500 million

☞ 1

☞ 2

in debt off its books and mask its financial problems so it could continue to get cash and credit to run its trading business. Enron officials acknowledged that the company had overstated its profits by more than $580 million since 1997.

In a six-week downward spiral that began in the fall of 2001, Enron disclosed a stunning $638 million third-quarter loss, the U.S. Securities and Exchange Commission opened an investigation into the partnerships, and the company's main rival, Dynegy, backed out of an $8.4 billion merger deal. Finally, Enron filed for protection from creditors on December 2, 2001, in the biggest corporate bankruptcy in U.S. history. Its stock, worth more than $80 a share in late 2000, tumbled to less than a dollar a share by January 2002. Enron's collapse left investors burned and thousands of employees out of work with lost retirement savings.[1]

Among the collapse's biggest casualties are the workers who lost jobs (about 5,600, including 1,100 in Europe) and had their retirement savings wiped out. Many were dangerously overinvested in the company's stock. About 58 percent of the assets of the company's 401(k) retirement plan were invested in Enron stock.[2]

The U.S. Department of Justice investigation into Enron's collapse will address a wide range of questions: Were Enron's partnerships with shell corporations designed to hide its liabilities and mislead investors? Was evidence intentionally or negligently destroyed? Did Enron executives know the company was sinking as they sold $1.1 billion in stock while encouraging employees and other investors to keep buying?[3] A report commissioned by the Enron board of directors and released on February 2, 2002, admitted: "Enron executives reaped millions of dollars from off-the-books partnerships while the energy giant violated basic rules of accounting and ethics."[4]

The Enron collapse shocked the financial and investing world. For people to feel comfortable about investing their money in business ventures, they must be assured that the people managing those ventures are acting according to business law. The free-market capitalism that has been the foundation of the tremendous wealth generated by the United States must be guided by the rule of law. Contracts must be respected, private property must not be violated, and information regarding transactions must be fully disclosed.

When businesses are found to have violated the law, consequences occur: Lawbreakers go to jail, and the reputation of the business suffers. In the wake of the Enron collapse, indictments are likely that will end up sending some former executives to jail. Meanwhile, Enron will attempt to leverage its remaining assets to emerge from bankruptcy with a sustainable business model. The Enron board appointed a new CEO, Stephen F. Cooper, to help turn the troubled company around.[5] Cooper is an experienced turnaround leader who has a monumental challenge to rebuild the confidence of investors, employees, creditors, vendors, and others who were hurt by the previous Enron leadership.

Although the Enron collapse was unique in both its depth and scope, violations of business law are not uncommon. Statistics compiled by the Administrative Office of the U.S. courts indicate that total cases commenced declined slightly between 1996 and 1999, but cases pending stayed roughly the same. Exhibit 5-1 illustrates the types of cases brought to state courts in the late 1990s, the last period for which reliable data are available.

In the rest of this chapter, we examine the important roles of law and government in business. First we discuss business law, the sources of law, and the court system. We describe the various types of laws and specific laws affecting business. Then we examine government regulation of business, with emphasis on the laws designed to encourage competition. Next we discuss the trend toward deregulation. Finally we explain how the government uses various taxes to support its activities.

1. "Enron Bankruptcy Explainer," *CNN.com*, http://www.cnn.com/2002/US/01/12/enron.qanda.focus/index.html

2. Robert J. Samuelson, "A Complicated Collapse," *Newsweek*, December 19, 2001.

3. Daniel Kadlec, "Enron: Who's Accountable?," *Time*, January 13, 2002.

4. "The Powers Report," February 2, 2002.

5. Albert B. Crenshaw and Carrie Johnson, "New CEO Is Upbeat on Enron," *Washington Post*, January 31, 2002, p. E03.

EXHIBIT 5-1   Cases Brought to State Courts in the Late 1990s

Type of Case	Cases Commenced				Cases Pending			
	1996	1997	1998	1999	1996	1997	1998	1999
Cases total[1]	272,661	265,151	261,262	261,511	243,703	259,536	269,119	246,920
Contract actions[1]	33,413	38,858	44,205	46,721	28,999	31,613	32,403	35,415
Recovery of overpayments[2]	3,583	8,070	15,188	18,822	2,301	3,881	6,129	9,733
Real property actions	6,276	6,761	5,655	5,787	4,486	3,951	3,971	3,931
Tort actions	67,029	52,710	52,218	39,785	65,823	72,250	84,073	63,683
Personal injury	63,222	48,266	48,356	35,962	62,087	68,154	80,114	59,999
Personal injury product liability[1]	38,170	23,294	28,325	17,196	34,096	36,621	50,838	31,927
Asbestos	6,760	8,184	9,718	7,413	2,037	2,438	1,576	1,686
Other personal injury	25,052	24,972	20,031	18,766	27,991	3,533	29,276	27,972
Personal property damage	3,807	4,444	3,862	3,823	3,736	4,096	3,959	3,784
Actions under statutes[1]	165,922	167,807	159,172	159,205	144,094	151,655	148,630	158,163
Civil rights[1]	40,476	43,166	42,750	41,453	42,545	46,096	46,718	45,348
Employment	22,150	23,707	23,804	22,948	24,212	26,669	27,097	26,043
Bankruptcy suits	4,737	4,217	3,905	3,875	3,938	3,648	2,921	2,597
Commerce (ICC rates, etc.)	1,622	483	528	650	760	504	510	486
Environmental matters	1,158	973	1,007	882	1,869	1,630	1,602	1,406
Prisoner petitions	69,352	64,262	55,120	56,037	50,353	50,392	44,905	42,302
Forfeiture and penalty	2,255	2,301	2,431	2,207	1,999	1,905	1,959	1,787
Labor laws	15,068	15,320	15,039	14,325	11,742	12,199	11,807	11,265
Protected property rights[3]	6,800	7,511	7,660	8,062	6,273	6,765	7,037	7,344
Securities commodities and exchanges	1,741	1,737	2,166	2,684	2,872	2,591	2,998	3,538
Social security laws	8,517	13,047	13,955	14,511	9,153	12,978	14,844	14,407
Tax suits	2,078	2,294	1,733	1,280	1,646	1,668	1,507	1,254
Freedom of information	465	400	436	360	496	435	416	386

1 Includes other types not shown separately.
2 Includes enforcement of judgments in student loan cases, and overpayments of veterans benefits.
3 Includes copyright, patent, and trademark rights.
Source: Administrative Office of the U.S. Courts. *Statistical Tables for the Federal Judiciary,* annual.

5-2 BUSINESS LAW

A **law** is a standard or rule established by a society to govern the behavior of its members. Federal, state, and local governments, constitutions, and treaties all establish laws. So do court decisions. Laws have a direct and substantial impact on how business firms conduct various activities. In this section, we discuss some of the basic concepts of law, including the sources of law, the U.S. court system, and laws affecting business.

Law A standard or rule established by a society to govern the behavior of its members.

5-2a Sources of Law

The United States Constitution specifies how the U.S. government must operate. It is also the foundation of U.S. law. Federal and state constitutions provide the framework for the various levels of government, which derive laws from three major sources: common law, statutory law, and administrative law.

Common Law

The body of law created by judges through their court decisions is known as **common law.** Based on custom, usage, and court rulings of early England, common law came to America when the first colonies were established and has become a major body of law in the United States. Judicial decisions establish **precedents,** or standards, that later are used to help decide similar cases. Lawyers are trained to research and use precedents in their litigation and prosecution functions, and judges use precedents to help guide their decisions.

Common Law The body of law created by judges through their court decisions.

Precedents Standards established by judicial systems that later are used to help decide similar cases.

11 ☞

courts of appeal or state supreme courts. The Supreme Court decides which cases it will hear; roughly 4 percent of all appeals are heard each year. Many Supreme Court decisions affect businesses. For example, the Court decided on January 15, 2002, that the Equal Employment Opportunity Commission may pursue employee discrimination claims against a company in court even though the company has an agreement with the employee to settle all disputes out of court (e.g., through binding arbitration).[6] This decision has implications for businesses of all sizes that attempt to avoid potentially costly EEOC litigation through clever employment contracts. The Supreme Court has ruled they can't shield themselves in this manner.

State Courts

Most state court systems have a structure similar to the federal system (see Exhibit 5-3). Cases originate in a circuit court; each county generally has a circuit court. Most states also have courts of appeals. Decisions of a court of appeals can be appealed to the state supreme court. Finally, decisions made by a state supreme court that involve a question of constitutional or federal law can be appealed to the U.S. Supreme Court.

Specialized Courts

12 ☞
13 ☞

Several types of specialized courts have been created to hear certain types of cases. For example, some states have small-claims courts to hear cases involving disputes over small amounts of money, usually below $1,500. States also commonly have divorce courts, juvenile courts, and traffic courts. At the federal level, specialized courts include the U.S. Tax Court (for tax cases) and the U.S. Court of Federal Claims (for claims against the government).

5-3 LAWS AFFECTING BUSINESS

Numerous and varied laws regulate the activities of all businesses and everyone involved in the business, from owner to manager to employee. In this section, we discuss the major business law categories, which involve torts, contracts, sales, agency, property, bankruptcy, and negotiable instruments.

5-3a The Law of Torts

> **Tort** A noncriminal (civil) injury to other persons or their property or reputation; results from intentional acts or negligence.
>
> **Intentional Torts** Deliberate acts by a person or business firm.
>
> **Negligence Tort** When one party fails to exercise reasonable care and causes injury to another.
>
> **Product Liability** Area of tort law that holds business firms responsible for negligence in design, manufacture, sale, and operation of their products.

Whereas criminal law deals with crime against society or the state, tort law is concerned with compensating the victims of noncriminal wrongs. Derived from the French word for wrong, a **tort** is a noncriminal (civil) injury to other persons or their property or reputation. Torts can be intentional or they may result from negligence. **Intentional torts** are deliberate acts by a person or business firm. For example, slander (spoken defamation of character) and libel (written defamation of character) are intentional torts. A tort results from negligence when one party fails to exercise reasonable care and causes injury to another. **Negligence torts** arise from carelessness rather than intentional behavior. A hotel, for example, may be held responsible for injuries to a guest who trips on loose or worn carpeting on the premises.

Product liability is an important part of tort law. Product liability involves the responsibility of business firms for negligence in design, manufacture, sale, and operation of their products. For example, workers sued keyboard makers for selling products that cause wrist injuries, and not warning users of the potential risks.[7] Public interest groups constantly seek to broaden the liability of business and manufacturers of such products as breast implants, automobiles, cigarettes, and guns.[8] Conversely, opponents to such reform

---

6. *EEOC v. Waffle House, Inc.*, 193 F.3d 805, reversed and remanded, January 15, 2002.

7. Linda Himelstein, "The Asbestos Case of the 1990s," *Business Week*, January 16, 1995 pp. 82–83.

8. Milo Geyelin, "Product-Liability Groups Take Up Arms," *The Wall Street Journal*, January 29, 1993, pp. B1, B3.

use every available means—emotional appeals from victims of crimes, powerful lobbies for gun and cigarette manufacturers, and connections to key lawmakers—to fight the passage of product liability laws.[9]

In certain instances, product liability laws have been expanded to include cases in which the producer or marketer of the product is not proved negligent. Under **strict product liability,** the business is responsible for any damages that may result regardless of the care it observes to guard against such damages. Strict liability is commonly applied to "ultrahazardous" business activities such as crop dusting, pile driving, and storing flammable liquids. No amount of care can prevent companies in ultrahazardous industries from liability if their businesses should cause harm to a third party.

> **Strict Product Liability** Legal concept that holds manufacturers responsible for injuries caused by products regardless of whether negligence was involved.

5-3b The Law of Contracts

A **contract** is a legally enforceable, voluntary agreement between two or more parties. A contract is like a private statute, in which the parties define the considerations they owe each other. To be regarded as a contract, an agreement between two or more parties must have three elements:

1. Offer
2. Acceptance
3. Consideration

> **Contract** A legally enforceable, voluntary agreement between two or more parties.

The **offer** is the exchange that will occur between the parties. It may include such things as labor, real estate, physical assets, or something else. An offer to provide labor services, for example, qualifies as the "offer" element of a contract.

The **acceptance** is the receiving party's assent to the terms of the offer. For example, if the offer to provide labor services was suitable, the party to receive the services would accept the terms.

Finally, no contract is said to exist between two parties without some form of **consideration.** In our example, no contract would exist if the offering party did not receive something of value (e.g., money) for the provision of labor services. By offering to pay for the labor services, the party receiving the services completes the contract. Nothing more is needed. With these three elements in place, any disputes between the parties can now be settled in court. Notice that if no consideration were provided, there wouldn't be anything for a court to decide. If you agree to provide labor for someone, and they accept it without any further agreement to compensate you, you are not obligated to provide that labor.

> **Offer** The exchange that will occur between the parties.

> **Acceptance** The ascent on the part of the receiving party to the terms of the offer.

> **Consideration** The item(s) of value that are exchanged between parties to a contract as payment for services rendered.

The UCC uniquely assists courts in determining provisions of contracts that are not explicitly spelled out between parties. If parties to a contract go to court to dispute something that was not explicitly spelled out in a written agreement, the court will rely on the UCC to fill in the missing details. The UCC provides the court with **gap fillers.** These are reasonable provisions that are derived from the UCC and that help complete a contract. For example, if a party agrees to provide labor for $100, it may not be spelled out in the contract that U.S. currency is preferred. If a dispute arises because the second party wants to pay in Turkish lira (a currency that devalues quickly), the first party may go to court, where the court will use gap fillers to determine the *intent* of the offer, acceptance, and consideration.

> **Gap Fillers** Reasonable provisions that are derived from the UCC to help complete a contract in case of a court-mediated dispute between contracting parties.

Contracts are generally part of most business transactions. They can be either express or implied. An **express contract** is one in which the words are actually put forth, either orally or in writing. Generally, oral contracts are just as legally enforceable as written contracts. (Some types of contracts must be in writing to be valid, such as for the sale of an interest in land.) But since the words used in an oral contract may be difficult to prove at a later time when parties are in dispute, the best policy for business firms to follow is to put all contracts in writing. An **implied contract** results from the actions of the

> **Express Contract** A contract that is put forth in writing, usually on paper.
>
> **Implied Contract** A contract that is assumed to exist by virtue of the way parties behave toward one another in the exchange of goods or services.

---

9. Catherine Young, "Snatching Defeat from the Jaws of Victory," *Business Week,* August, 1, 1994, pp. 76–77.

parties rather than from all explicit promises. For example, when a passenger boards a train, it is implied that the passenger will have a ticket when the agent collects them and that the train will provide safe transportation to the destination. Again, since actions can be misunderstood, the best policy in business situations is for the contract to be expressed in words and written down.

To be enforceable, a contract must meet several requirements:

- *Voluntary Agreement*   Both parties must accept the terms of the agreement voluntarily, free of correction, fraud, and the like.
- *Consideration*   Each party must provide something of value to the other, such as money, a product, or a promise to do or not do something.
- *Contractual Capacity*   Each party must have the legal ability to enter into a binding agreement. (Generally, minors, persons with mental handicaps, and intoxicated persons do not have contractual capacity.)
- *Legality*   A contract must not involve any unlawful act.

Breach of Contract   The failure of one party to live up to a contractual agreement.

The failure of one party to live up to a contractual agreement is called **breach of contract.** For example, failure to make payments on a car loan would be considered breach of contract. The bank or other lending institution could bring legal action against the breaking party—the car owner who signed the loan—and recover damages.

Today, many firms are seeking alternative methods for resolving inevitable disagreements surrounding contracts. Alternative dispute resolution or ADR is a growing phenomenon that can be learned and practiced without a law degree. The Focus on Careers box, "Alternative Dispute Resolution," discusses how to become an ADR practitioner.

5-3c The Law of Sales

Sales Law   Body of law involving the sale of products for money or on credit.

Sales law, which grew out of contract law, involves products sold for money or credit. Sales agreements are contracts subject to the requirements discussed in Section 5-3b. Article 2 of the UCC provides that some sales contracts are binding even if all the requirements for a contract are not met. For instance, a sales agreement is legally binding even if the selling price is left out of the agreement; the buyer must pay the reasonable value of the goods.

Express Warranty   Oral or written assurances made by the seller regarding a product.

Implied Warranty   Warranty legally imposed on the seller; ensures that the seller owns the products and that they will serve the purpose for which they are sold.

Article 2 also establishes the law of warranty for sales transactions. An **express warranty** is any statement of fact or promise made by the seller to the buyer relating to the products sold, and which becomes an important part of the sales agreement. A warranty is in the nature of a guarantee, although no formal words such as *warranty* or *guarantee* need be used. If the products in fact are not as represented by the seller, the seller can be held responsible either to make the products as warranted or to give the buyer the money back. The law also imposes an **implied warranty,** not specifically expressed by the parties, ensuring that the business firm has clear title of the products it sells and that the products will serve the purpose for which they are sold.

5-3d The Law of Agency

Agency   A legal relationship between two parties who agree that the agent will act on behalf of the principal.

An **agency** is a business relationship in which a *principal* (the person or business entity that wants a task performed) appoints an *agent* (the person or business entity that performs the task) to act on his or her behalf. The actions of the agent, authorized by the principal, are legally recognized as though the principal performed them. For example, a talent agent can enter into a contract for a client as though the client personally signed the contract. Agents are used in many diverse industries, including insurance, sports, entertainment, and real estate. Generally, agents are paid a fee or commission for their services.

FOCUS ON CAREERS

Alternative Dispute Resolution

The high cost of legal fees for small businesses has led many business owners to seek other ways of redressing disputes. Alternative dispute resolution, including mediation and arbitration, is a popular way of resolving issues that arise between business parties.

While many people who choose to become mediators are trained in the law, many others are not. Full-time mediation jobs are not common. There are such positions, just as there are lawyers who spend most of their time in the courtroom, but just as most lawyers spend most of their time alone at a desk, most people in conflict resolution careers have other responsibilities as well. Those who work for nonprofit organizations that use volunteer mediators spend most of their time making it possible for others to do mediation. Most employers in need of an employee with dispute resolution skills will look for the following in the individual's resume:

- *Academic and technical achievements:* A degree and related work experience or training in conflict resolution, mediation, or facilitation are assets.
- *Personal suitability:* A mediator needs a high level of self-awareness, including the ability to self-evaluate, recognize limitations, and change as the situation demands. Mediators also require interpersonal skills such as active listening, a variety of assessment skills and the ability to manage high-conflict situations. A mediator must also be impartial, neutral, and nonjudgmental.
- *Mediation experience:* As mediation is a skill-based practice learned "by doing," individuals may want to gain experience through mentoring or volunteer work.

Because the principal is bound by the agent's actions, it is important to put the agency agreement in writing. Generally, a legal document called a **power of attorney** is granted to authorize the agent to act on behalf of the principal. For instance, a person may grant an accountant power of attorney to act as his or her agent during a tax audit. It is the agent's duty to act in a professional manner and to exercise good judgment. The agency relationship can be terminated when the task is completed or by mutual agreement of the parties.

5-3e The Law of Property

Anything that can be owned is considered property. Property is something for which a person or business entity has unrestricted right of possession or use. There are several categories of property. **Real property** is real estate, land, and anything permanently attached to it, such as houses, buildings, and parking lots. **Tangible personal property** means physical items such as equipment, automobiles, and a store's inventory of goods. **Intangible personal property** includes property shown by documents or other written instruments, such as checks, money orders, receipts, stocks, and bonds.

Three forms of intangible personal property provide legal protection for individuals or business firms. A **trademark** is a name or symbol registered with the U.S. Patent and Trademark Office. It guarantees the owner exclusive rights to the name or symbol for

Power of Attorney A legal document authorizing an agent to act on behalf of the principal.

Real Property Real estate and anything permanently attached to it, such as houses, buildings, and parking lots.

Tangible Personal Property Physical items, such as goods and equipment.

Intangible Personal Property Property represented by a document or other written statement.

Trademark A name or symbol, registered with the U.S. Patent and Trademark Office, that guarantees the owner exclusive rights to its use.

✍ 14

FOCUS ON TECHNOLOGY

Legal Resources for Small-Business Owners

Small-business owners oftentimes must literally "take the law into their own hands" since they are hard-pressed to afford an attorney. Although this is not a recommended way to proceed through the thickets of business law, small-business owners often have little choice.

Thankfully, there are a number of online resources small-business owners can consult to help them deal with legal issues. In the United States, individual states usually provide significant online legal resources through the Secretary of State office. Typical resources found there include the business legal forms needed to incorporate or form a partnership, legal guides to contract law, and the Uniform Commercial Code. Other, private resources will provide assistance ranging from how to write contracts to how to deal with employee issues. Several legal resources websites are as follows:

http://legalissues.dewrsb.gov.au/
http://www.eeoc.gov/small/
http://businessweek.findlaw.com/index.htm
http://www.businesstown.com/legal/basic.asp

Patent The exclusive right of an inventor to make, use, or sell the registered product.

15 ☞

Copyright Protection of an individual's exclusive right to publish and sell original written materials.

Chapter 7 Bankruptcy The business firm is dissolved and the assets are sold to pay off debt.

Chapter 11 Bankruptcy Temporarily relieves a company from its debts while it reorganizes and works out a payment plan with its creditors.

Chapter 13 Bankruptcy Allows an individual to establish a plan for repaying debts within three to five years.

---

twenty years and can be renewed as many times as the owner wishes. **Patents,** granted by the U.S. Patent and Trademark Office, give inventors the exclusive right to make, use, or sell their products for seventeen years. Patents cannot be renewed. The number of patent suits initiated in U.S. courts has jumped significantly in recent years, many involving small investors suing large companies.[10] A **copyright,** filed with the U.S. Copyright Office gives the creator exclusive right to publish and sell an original written work. Copyrights last for the lifetime of the author plus fifty years. Recently, recording companies have claimed that while it is legal to resell a copyrighted product, resales cut into the sales of compact discs (CDs), diminish their value, and deprive artists of royalties. This has led to a major battle between some recording companies and stores selling CDs, one the recording companies are not likely to win.[11]

The legal rules that govern business can be complex and confusing for managers. Hiring lawyers to deal with the complexity can be expensive and time-consuming. Many small-business owners manage some of their legal work themselves. They can do so using online legal resources, such as those described in the Focus on Technology box, "Legal Resources for Small-Business Owners."

5-3f The Law of Bankruptcy

Bankruptcy is a legal procedure provided for individuals and firms that cannot pay their debts. By declaring bankruptcy, the individual or firm asks to be declared legally unable to satisfy creditors and to be released from financial obligations.

Three types of bankruptcy are possible: Chapter 7, Chapter 11, and Chapter 13. Under **Chapter 7 bankruptcy,** the business firm is dissolved and the assets are sold to pay off debt. Individuals filing Chapter 7 are allowed to keep a limited amount of assets, determined by federal or state law. **Chapter 11 bankruptcy** temporarily relieves a company from its debts while it reorganizes and works out a payment plan with its creditors. At the

---

10. Richard B. Schmidt, "Discoverers Call Patent Lawyers for Recoveries," *The Wall Street Journal*, April 22, 1993, pp. B1, B10.

11. Larry Armstrong, "What's Wrong with Selling Used CDs?" *Business Week*, July 26, 1993, p. 38.

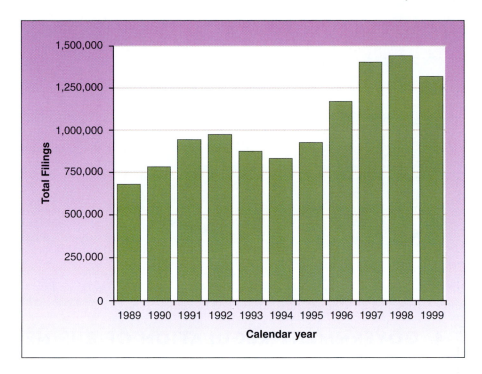

beginning of this chapter we reviewed the collapse of Enron Corporation. To protect its assets and try to rebuild, the company filed for Chapter 11 bankruptcy protection. **Chapter 13 bankruptcy** allows an individual to establish a plan for repaying debts within three to five years. Exhibit 5-4 shows bankruptcy filings in the U.S. between 1989 and 1999. Note that only about 10 percent of all bankruptcy filings are by businesses; the rest are by private individuals.

5-3g The Law of Negotiable Instruments

A **negotiable instrument** is a substitute for money. It is a written promise to pay a specified sum of money; it can be transferred from one person or business firm to another. Examples of negotiable instruments include checks, drafts, and certificates of deposit. The UCC specifies that negotiable instruments must meet the following requirements:

- They must be in writing and signed by the maker or drawer (the party who orders the payment of the money).
- They must contain an unconditional promise to pay a certain sum of money.
- They must be payable on demand or at a specific date.
- They must be payable to a specific person or business firm or to the bearer (the party who possesses the instrument).

The payee (the one to whom the instrument is written) must endorse a negotiable instrument before it can be transferred. An **endorsement** is a person's signature on the back of a negotiable instrument (see Exhibit 5-5). A **blank endorsement** is accomplished when the payee signs the back of the instrument. This type of endorsement can be unsafe because anyone can cash the instrument once it is endorsed. Restrictive and special endorsements protect the negotiable instrument should it be lost or stolen. Using the words *for deposit only* along with the signature constitutes a **restrictive endorsement;** it states what the instrument is for and is much safer than a blank endorsement. A **special endorsement** specifies to whom the instrument is payable by including the person's or firm's name on the back of the instrument along with the signature. Finally, a **qualified endorsement**—using the words *without recourse*—means the person who originally signed

Negotiable Instrument
A written promise to pay a specified sum of money; it can be transferred from one person or firm to another.

Endorsement   A person's signature on the back of a negotiable instrument, making it transferable.

Blank Endorsement
Accomplished when the payee signs the back of the instrument.

Restrictive Endorsement
An endorsement that uses the words *for deposit only* along with the signature; it states what the instrument is for and is much safer than a blank endorsement.

Special Endorsement
An endorsement that specifies to whom the instrument is payable by including the person's or firm's name on the back of the instrument along with the signature.

Qualified Endorsement
An endorsement in which the words *without recourse* are used—means the person who originally signed the instrument, not the endorser, is responsible for payment. The endorser does not guarantee payment if the instrument is not backed by sufficient funds.

EXHIBIT 5-5

Types of Endorsements

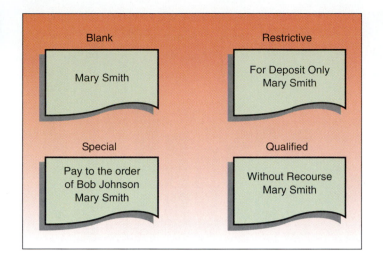

the instrument, not the endorser, is responsible for payment. The endorser does not guarantee payment if the instrument is not backed by sufficient funds.

5-4 GOVERNMENT REGULATION OF BUSINESS

The federal and state governments have enacted substantial legislation to encourage competition among business firms. Many laws, such as those outlawing monopolies, price fixing, and other practices that restrain trade, are intended to help ensure that consumers have a choice in the marketplace and that firms have the freedom to compete. For instance, the justice department recently launched an investigation of pricing in the cereal industry because prices are, according to them, way too high and controlled by four firms that dominate the industry and make huge profits. In this section, we discuss federal laws designed to regulate competition among American business firms. Exhibit 5-6 summarizes these laws.

5-4a Sherman Antitrust Act

Sherman Antitrust Act
One of the first laws passed to regulate competition, which declared that two or more business firms could not agree to the prices to be charged for goods; also prohibited business firms from dividing markets among themselves and from deciding not to sell or to buy from a particular company.

One of the first laws passed to regulate competition, the **Sherman Antitrust Act** (1890) declared that two or more business firms could not agree to the prices to be charged for goods. It also prohibited business firms from dividing markets among themselves and from deciding not to sell or to buy from a particular company.

The Sherman Antitrust Act was not used for more than a decade. But in the early 1900s, with Teddy Roosevelt in the White House, the act was used to break up J. P. Morgan's railroad monopoly, John D. Rockefeller's Standard Oil, and Buck Duke's tobacco trust. Today the Sherman Act is still the basis for legal action, as the opening vignette highlighted with respect to Microsoft. Major merger and acquisition activity in the United States is generally scrutinized by the Justice Department for compliance with the antitrust act. In 2001, Compaq and Hewlett-Packard announced their intention to merge. Prior to that transaction occurring, it had to be reviewed for antitrust compliance. The Compaq-HP merger eventually was approved, and the firms went ahead with the deal.

16, 17 ☞

5-4b Clayton Act

Clayton Act An act that regulates general practices that potentially may be detrimental to fair competition. Some of these general practices regulated by the Clayton Act are price discrimination; exclusive dealing contracts, tying agreements, or requirement contracts; mergers and acquisitions; and interlocking directorates.

Congress enacted the **Clayton Act** in 1914 to strengthen the Sherman Antitrust Act. Specifically, the Clayton Act outlawed the following four practices that reduce competition:

- *Price discrimination*—charging one firm (usually a large one) a lower price for goods than the price other (usually smaller) firms are charged
- *Tying agreements*—requiring a buyer to purchase unwanted products for the right to purchase desired products

Law	Purpose
Natural Gas Policy Act (1978)	Requires pipeline firms to transport natural gas owned by other companies
Airline Deregulation Act (1978)	Eliminates regulation of airline rates and schedules
Motor Carrier Act (1980)	Allows trucks to travel more freely and change prices more quickly
Staggers Rail Act (1980)	Gives railroads more flexibility to raise and lower rates without government approval
Depository Institutions Deregulatory Committee Act (1981) Depository Institutions Act (1982)	Permits financial institutions to complete on a more even basis for deposit accounts by paying higher interest rates and to broaden investments beyond homes and small commerical mortgages
Drug Price Competition and Patent Term Restoration Act (1984)	Allows generic drugs to reach the market sooner by awarding patents for shorter periods of time

EXHIBIT 5-6

Major Deregulation Laws

- *Binding contracts*—requiring a buyer to purchase products from a specific supplier
- *Community of interest*—a business buying stock in a competing firm to reduce competition between the two

5-4c Federal Trade Commission Act

The **Federal Trade Commission Act** (1914) established the Federal Trade Commission (FTC), a five-member committee empowered to investigate illegal trade practices. This act prohibits all unfair methods of competition. The **Wheeler-Lea Amendment** (1938) expanded the FTC's power to eliminate deceptive business practices, including those affecting consumers as well as competitors.

The FTC acts on its own accord to investigate a firm's business practices or on complaints made by other firms or individuals. Recent targets have included fly-by-night telemarketers who use television to help sell fraudulent products and advertisers who make unsubstantiated claims.[12]

5-4d Robinson-Patman Act

The **Robinson-Patman Act,** passed in 1936, outlaws price discrimination that substantially reduces competition. Price discounts are legal, however, if they are based on actual lower selling costs, such as discounts for large orders. The act also prohibits advertising and promotional allowances unless they are offered to all retailers regardless of size.

5-4e Celler-Kefauver Act

The **Celler-Kefauver Act** (1950) outlaws mergers through the purchase of assets, when the mergers tend to reduce competition. The act also makes it mandatory that the FTC and the Justice Department approve all mergers.

5-4f Antitrust Improvement Act

The **Antitrust Improvement Act** of 1976 strengthens previous antitrust laws. The act gives the FTC and the Justice Department a longer period of time to evaluate proposed mergers. It also allows state attorneys general to prosecute firms accused of price fixing.

18

Federal Trade Commission Act
An act that established the Federal Trade Commission (FTC), a five-member committee empowered to investigate illegal trade practices.

Wheeler-Lea Amendment
An amendment that expanded the FTC's power to eliminate deceptive business practices, including those affecting consumers as well as competitors.

Robinson-Patman Act
Passed in 1936, an act that outlaws price discrimination that substantially reduces competition.

Celler-Kefauver Act   An act that outlaws mergers through the purchase of assets, when the mergers tend to reduce competition.

Antitrust Improvement Act
An act that gives the FTC and the Justice Department a longer period of time to evaluate proposed mergers and allows state attorneys general to prosecute firms accused of price fixing.

12. Larry Armstrong and Maria Mallory, "The Diet Business Starts Sweating," *Business Week*, June 22, 1992, pp. 32–33.

Laws Designed to Preserve Competition

Law	Purpose
Sherman Antitrust Act (1890)	Prohibits contract or conspiracies that attempt to reduce competition
Clayton Act (1914)	Prohibits specific acts that reduce competition: price discrimination, tying agreements, binding contracts, and community of interest
Federal Trade Commission Act (1914)	Prohibits unfair trade practices and deceptive advertising
Robinson-Patman Act (1936)	Prohibits price discrimination that reduces competition
Celler-Kefauver Act (1950)	Prohibits mergers that reduce competition
Antitrust Improvement Act (1976)	Provides additional time for the Federal Trade Commission and the Justice Department to evaluate proposed mergers
Gramm-Rudman Act (1985)	Requires Congress to meet annual deficit targets and to balance the federal budget by 1993

5-5 DEREGULATION

Deregulation The process of reducing government involvement in the regulation of business, by eliminating legal restraints on competition.

Since the 1970s a trend toward deregulation of business has been evident. **Deregulation** is the process of reducing the involvement of government in the regulation of business by eliminating legal restraints on competition. The goal of deregulation is to make business regulations less complex and to lower the costs of complying with them. Laws that have been passed to preserve competition in major industries such as airlines, railroads, and banking are listed in Exhibit 5-7.

Deregulation of business results in several benefits for business firms and consumers. Regulation costs firms and consumers billions of dollars each year; deregulation eliminates or reduces some of the costs, and the savings can be passed on to consumers. Deregulation can also increase competition, resulting in lower prices for consumers. After the airline industry was deregulated, for example, airfares dropped to the lowest levels in many years. Increased competition can also lead to better service. Since the government deregulated the banking industry, many banks are providing more services, such as discount brokerages (for purchasing stocks, bonds, and other securities) and money market accounts.

Opponents of deregulation fear that this trend could actually reduce competition. For example, since the airline industry has been deregulated, many major carriers have gone out of business, while others continue to lose money. Many politicians and consumers believe that further deregulation will lead to some of the same problems that led to government regulation in the first place—pollution, poor working conditions, and low-quality products. The future of deregulation is uncertain, but it will depend to a large extent on the conduct of business organizations.

Do you think U.S. business needs more regulation or less? The values and attitude quiz in Exhibit 5-8 will help you determine your views about regulation.

5-6 GOVERNMENT TAXATION

Tax A payment for the support of government activities, required of organizations and individuals within the domain of the government.

Citizens of a country must pay for the services the government provides. This is accomplished through taxation. A **tax** is a payment for the support of government activities, required of organizations and individuals within the domain of the government. Revenues from taxes pay for national defense, roads, schools, social programs, medical care, regulation of business, and for government itself.

The U.S. government obtains about 95 percent of the money it needs to operate through taxes, including corporate and personal income taxes and other federal taxes. State and local governments are also financed through taxation. Taxation can be viewed

EXHIBIT 5-8

How Do You Feel about Regulation?

Directions: For each statement, circle the number that shows your level of agreement.

	Strongly Disagree					Strongly Agree
1. The government should let business regulate itself.	1	2	3	4	5	6
2. It is up to consumers to make sure the products they use are safe.	1	2	3	4	5	6
3. Firms should be able to advertise in the manner they desire.	1	2	3	4	5	6
4. Regulations and the paperwork they require cost businesses too much money.	1	2	3	4	5	6
5. The public and business firms, not the government, need to control pollution.	1	2	3	4	5	6

Feedback: Government regulation of business is a sensitive issue. It does indeed increase the amount of paperwork firms must do. It may limit business activities. Yet, without regulation, firms may not act in the interest of consumers or the public. In short, someone usually needs to police the activities of business firms, whether it be the government, business themselves, or another alternative.

Do you think government is the best source of regulation? If you circled 1 or 2 for most statements, you strongly think so. In which business sectors would you like to see more regulation? If you chose 3 or 4, you are neutral. Finally, if you circled 5 or 6, you strongly support less government regulation. In what realms of business should the government regulate less?

as another form of government regulation, because virtually all business firms and individuals pay taxes. In the United States, the primary agency in charge of collecting federal taxes is the Internal Revenue Service (IRS).

☞ 19

5-6a Corporate Income Tax

The first permanent corporate income tax was enacted in 1909, four years before the introduction of the modern personal income tax. The initial rate was 1 percent. As Exhibit 5-9 indicates, revenue increased steadily until 1943, when it peaked at 7.1 percent of gross domestic product (GDP).

But corporate income taxes have contributed a declining portion of federal revenue over the past fifty years. This portion has been made up by the increasing share of revenue from social insurance contributions, primarily the social security payroll tax. In 1943, corporate taxes comprised 39.8 percent of total federal revenues; social insurance contributions contributed 12.7 percent. By 1996, the situation was nearly reversed; social insurance contributions provided 35.1 percent of federal revenues, while corporate income taxes provided 11.8 percent. In 1994, corporate tax revenues amounted to just 2.5 percent of GDP.[13]

The **Tax Reform Act of 1986** eliminated many corporate tax preferences, including the investment tax credit enacted during the Kennedy administration. However, preferential tax treatment is still provided for expenditures on research and development.

Corporations are required to pay federal tax on their income, after deducting allowable business expenses. Corporations pay a **progressive tax,** meaning the percentage of

Tax Reform Act of 1986
A law with provisions that affect indirect compensation.

Progressive Tax   Form of taxation in which the percentage of income paid in taxes increases as income increases.

13. *Tax Reform: A Century Foundation Guide to the Issues* (New York: The Century Foundation Press, 1999).

EXHIBIT 5-9

Corporate Tax Revenues as a Percentage of Gross Domestic Product 1934–2002

Source: Office of Management and Budget, Budget of the United States Government, Fiscal Year 1998, Historical Tables, Table 2.3, p. 31.

income paid in taxes increases as income increases. In 2002, the federal tax rate for corporations was:

Taxable Income Over	Not Over	Tax Rate
$0	$50,000	15%
50,000	75,000	25%
75,000	100,000	34%
100,000	335,000	39%
335,000	10,000,000	24%
10,000,000	15,000,000	35%
15,000,000	18,333,333	38%
18,333,333	—	35%

Recall from the discussion in Chapter 3 that some corporate profits are actually taxed twice. The corporation must first pay a federal income tax on its profits. Then, if it distributes profits to shareholders by declaring dividends, the shareholders must pay a personal income tax on the dividends they receive.

5-6b Individual Income Tax

During America's first century, the federal government raised the bulk of its revenue from tariffs, excise taxes, and property taxes. (During the Civil War, an income tax was temporarily imposed in the North.) However, great industries had been established and great fortunes had been made by the end of the nineteenth century, and populist reformers were advocating for reform of the monopolies and trusts and for fairer treatment of citizens. These populist sentiments led Congress to enact a highly progressive income tax in 1894, but it was declared unconstitutional the following year. This led eventually to the passage of the Sixteenth Amendment, which empowered Congress to levy an income tax. Woodrow Wilson signed the modern personal income tax into law in October 1913.

This early personal income tax and today's version had many similarities—rates were graduated, home mortgage interest and tax payments to state and local governments were deductible, and interest on state and local bonds was excluded.

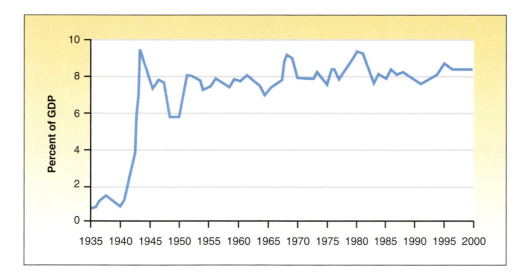

EXHIBIT 5-10

Individual Income Taxes as Percentage of GDP

Data for revenues are from Office of Management and Budget, Budget of the United States Government, Fiscal Year 1998, Historical Tables, Table 2.3, p. 31; data for tax rates are from Citizens for Tax Justice website (www.ctj.org/images/rates.gif).

Charitable contributions became deductible in 1917. Unlike today's tax, however, the original personal income tax applied only to the wealthiest Americans. Rates ranged from 1 percent to 7 percent, and well over 90 percent of the population was exempt from filing.

With the advent of World War II, the increased need for revenue required that rates be increased and exemptions lowered. As Exhibit 5-10 illustrates, personal income tax revenues, which had never exceeded 2 percent of GDP between 1913 and 1940, increased dramatically during the war. By the war's end, revenues stood at 8 percent of GDP.[14]

Despite the oft-heard claims about increasing income tax burdens in the postwar period, federal personal income tax revenues have remained close to 8 percent of GDP ever since World War II. At the same time, Exhibit 5-11 shows that federal tax rates have steadily declined since World War II and have only recently experienced a slight uptick.

Finally, there is an important distinction to be made between *average* (sometimes called *effective*) and *marginal* rates. For instance, in 1997 the top marginal rate of 39.6 percent applied to taxable income in excess of $271,050 for most taxpayers. A married couple filing jointly with taxable income of $300,000 thus would pay a marginal rate of 39.6 percent—but only on the last $28,950 ($300,000 – $271,050) of income. This is why the marginal rate is often referred to as the tax rate on the next dollar of income earned. The couple's average tax rate (tax liability expressed as a percentage of taxable income) would be significantly lower, about 30 percent, because lower rates are applied to income below $271,050. Average rates are useful for assessing the progressiveness of a tax, while marginal rates can reveal the incentive effects of a tax—that is, the additional tax someone would pay for behaving differently.

The most important changes to the personal tax code since the World War II rate increases were made during the Reagan administration in the 1980s. In 1981, the **Economic Recovery Tax Act (ERTA)** reduced the top rate by 20 percent—from 70 to 50 percent—and all other rates by approximately 23 percent over a three-year period. It also required that tax brackets be adjusted for inflation each year to address the "bracket creep" of the 1970s—the tax increases resulting from general price inflation that pushed taxpayers into higher tax brackets even though the purchasing power of their income may not have increased. Because tax revenues no longer automatically increase with inflation, Congress is now forced to enact tax increases when it needs to raise revenues. Moreover, because of the political obstacles to raising taxes, this change contributed to rising deficits in subsequent years.

Economic Recovery Tax Act (ERTA) An act that was enacted in 1981 during the Reagan administration to reduce taxes on corporate profits in hopes of stimulating a lagging economy.

14. Ibid.

EXHIBIT 5-11

Top Federal Tax Rates as Percentage of Income

Data for revenues are from Office of Management and Budget, Budget of the United States Government, Fiscal Year 1998, Historical Tables, Table 2.3, p. 31; data for tax rates are from Citizens for Tax Justice website (www.ctj.org/images/rates.gif).

1986 Tax Reform Act
Act passed during Ronald Reagan's second term as president that built on the corporate tax cuts from the 1981 Economic Recovery Tax Act.

The **1986 Tax Reform Act** further reduced tax rates (the top rate was reduced to 28 percent), but also broadened the tax base and simplified the tax code by eliminating many tax shelters and other preferences. Capital gains were now taxed at the same rate as ordinary income, interest on consumer loans and state and local sales taxes were no longer deductible, and the personal exemption and standard deduction were increased.

The top rate was increased during both the Bush and Clinton administrations, and today stands at 38.6 percent. Long-term capital gains (appreciation on assets held eighteen months or longer) regained preferential treatment, with a 28 percent tax cap on that form of income. Exhibit 5-12 provides the different individual tax rates and the estimated taxes on different income levels.

For employees, most income tax is withheld from paychecks by employers and paid to the IRS. Individuals whose income comes from ownership of a sole proprietorship or a partnership must pay their income taxes to the IRS in four quarterly payments.

Every individual subject to paying income taxes must file a return with the IRS on or before April 15 of each year (unless an extension is requested and granted). If too much money was withheld from an individual's paycheck, he or she is entitled to a refund. A person may owe additional taxes if insufficient taxes were withheld. Individuals also pay state and, in many cases, local (city) income taxes.

5-6c Other Taxes

Federal, state, and local governments use several taxes other than income taxes as sources of funds. The second-largest source of federal revenue is the social security and Medicare tax, which both employers and employees pay. This tax provides retirement, disability, hospital insurance, and death benefits for participants. In 1995 the social security tax rate was 12.40 percent of the first $61,200 earned; the employee pays half and the employer pays half. Medicare tax was 2.90 percent of all wages, also split between employee and employer. Employers also pay an annual unemployment tax of 6.2 percent of the first $7,000 of each employee's wages. This tax is used to fund benefits for unemployed workers.

| If Taxpayer's Income Is . . . | | Then Estimated Taxes Are . . . | | |
Between	But Not Over	Base Tax	+ Rate	Of the Amount Over
$0	$6,000	$0	10%	$0
$6000	$26,250	$600	15%	$6,000
$26,250	$63,550	$3,637.50	27%	$26,250
$63,550	$132,600	$13,708.50	30%	$63,550
$132,600	$288,350	$34,423.50	35%	$132,600
$288,350	—	$88,936.00	38.6%	$288,350

EXHIBIT 5-12

Personal Income Tax Rates

An **excise tax** is a tax on the manufacture or sale of a domestic product. The government uses excise taxes to help pay for services directed at those who use the products, and sometimes to discourage the use of potentially harmful products. For instance, Americans pay an excise tax on gasoline to help finance the construction of roads and bridges. The government has also set an excise tax on tobacco and alcohol products to discourage their use. The government also places an import tax on certain foreign products entering the United States.

The majority of states obtain most of their revenues through a **sales tax** on the merchandise consumers buy; some cities levy additional sales taxes on the same products. Some states have no sales tax, while others exempt certain items such as food from being taxed. Local governments raise the majority of their operating revenues through a **property tax** on residential and commercial property, such as houses, land, buildings, machinery, and automobiles.

Excise Tax   A tax on the manufacture or sale of a domestic product.

Sales Tax   Tax on the merchandise consumers buy.

Property Tax   Taxes on residential and commercial property, such as houses, land, buildings, machinery, and automobiles to help local governments' operating revenues.

5-7   CONCLUSION

Business law is a specialized area of study that cannot possibly be covered entirely in a single chapter of a textbook. Nonetheless, all managers, entrepreneurs, and business owners should have some familiarity with business law and its potential impact on business activities and transactions. Understanding a few of the fundamentals of business law and the structure of the courts can help managers who are faced with legal challenges or disputes. Going into a legal setting with no prior knowledge of procedures or possible outcomes can be unsettling for many managers. While studying business and the law can be useful to managers, most would be well advised to consult with an attorney when legal disputes arise.

SUGGESTED WEBSITES

Note: These websites were functional when we went to press. Please access the online text for the most up-to-date URLs.

1. www.microsoft.com
2. www.enron.com
3. www.sec.gov
4. www.dynegy.com
5. www.usdoj.gov
6. www.ftc.gov
7. www.cpsc.gov
8. www.fcc.gov
9. www.fda.gov
10. www.supremecourtus.gov
11. www.eeoc.gov
12. www.ustaxcourt.gov
13. www.uscfc.uscourts.gov
14. www.uspto.gov
15. www.loc.gov/copyright
16. www.compaq.com
17. www.hp.com
18. www.ftc.gov
19. www.irs.gov

SUMMARY OF LEARNING OBJECTIVES

1. *Identify the sources from which laws are derived.*   Laws have a substantial impact on how business firms conduct activities. The various levels of government derive laws from three sources: common law, created by judges through court decisions; statutory laws, passed by federal, state, and local legislatures; and administrative laws, enacted by federal and state administrative agencies.

2. *Outline the court system in the United States.*   The U.S. judicial system is charged with the application of law to settle disputes between parties. The United States has a dual court system. The federal court system includes district courts, courts of appeals, and the Supreme Court. The state court system includes circuit courts, courts of appeals, and state supreme courts. Specialized state courts include small-claims, divorce, juvenile, and traffic courts.

3. *Identify the various categories of business law.*   Several types of laws regulate business activities. These include tort law (which includes product liability) and laws governing contractual agreements, sales agreement, use of agents, property transactions, bankruptcy proceedings, and negotiable instruments.

4. *Discuss how government regulates business activities to encourage competition.*   The most important laws designed to preserve competition are the Sherman Antitrust Act (1890), which prohibits price fixing, firms dividing markets among themselves, and boycotting certain firms; the Clayton Act (1914), which prevents price discrimination, tying agreements, binding contracts, interlock-locking directorates, and community of interest; the Federal Trade Commission Act (1914), which prohibits all unfair methods of competition; the Robinson-Patman Act (1936), which outlaws price discrimination that reduces competition; the Celler-Kefauver Act (1950), which outlaws mergers through the purchase of assets; and the Antitrust Improvement Act (1976), which strengthens the previous laws.

5. *Explain the effects of deregulation on business.*   Since the 1970s the United States has experienced a trend toward deregulation, or reducing government involvement in the regulation of business. Deregulation can lower the costs of regulating business and can lead to increased competition, better service, and lower prices.

6. *Define the different types of taxes and their effects on business.* Corporations are subject to corporate income taxes that are defined as "progressive taxes." That means that the more money a business makes, the higher the rate of taxes it will pay on the next dollar earned. Other taxes on business include social security and Medicare taxes, which are meant to provide a fund for taking care of retirees and people without medical insurance. Excise taxes are taxes on the sale or manufacture of products, typically products that have an environmental or social impact that the government must expend funds to mitigate. State governments obtain most of their income through sales taxes and property taxes. Each of these taxes increases the cost of doing business, a cost that is reflected in the prices of goods that consumers must pay.

7. *Describe how taxation supports the activities of government.*   Citizens pay for the work of government through taxation. Corporations and individuals are subject to federal, state, and local taxes, including taxes on the income they earn, the property they own, and the products they purchase.

KEY TERMS

acceptance (p. 109)
administrative law (p. 106)
agency (p. 110)
Antitrust Improvement Act (p. 115)
blank endorsement (p. 113)
breach of contract (p. 110)
Celler-Kefauver Act (p. 115)
Chapter 7 bankruptcy (p. 112)
Chapter 11 bankruptcy (p. 112)
Chapter 13 bankruptcy (p. 112)
Clayton Act (p. 114)
common law (p. 105)
consideration (p. 109)
contract (p. 109)
copyright (p. 112)
deregulation (p. 116)
Economic Recovery Tax Act (ERTA) (p. 119)
endorsement (p. 113)
excise tax (p. 121)

express contract (p. 109)
express warranty (p. 110)
Federal Trade Commission Act (p. 115)
gap fillers (p. 109)
implied contract (p. 109)
implied warranty (p. 110)
intangible personal property (p. 111)
intentional torts (p. 108)
jurisdiction (p. 106)
law (p. 105)
negligence torts (p. 108)
negotiable instrument (p. 113)
1986 Tax Reform Act (p. 120)
offer (p. 109)
patent (p. 112)
power of attorney (p. 111)
precedents (p. 105)
product liability (p. 108)
progressive tax (p. 117)

property tax (p. 121)
qualified endorsement (p. 113)
real property (p. 111)
restrictive endorsement (p. 113)
Robinson-Patman Act (p. 115)
sales law (p. 110)
sales tax (p. 121)
Sherman Antitrust Act (p. 114)
special endorsement (p. 113)
statute (p. 106)
statutory law (p. 106)
strict product liability (p. 109)
tangible personal property (p. 111)
tax (p. 116)
Tax Reform Act of 1986 (p. 117)
tort (p. 108)
trademark (p. 111)
Uniform Commercial Code (UCC) (p. 106)
Wheeler-Lea Amendment (p. 115)

QUESTIONS FOR DISCUSSION AND REVIEW

1. Why are there three separate sources of law in U.S. government?
2. Outline the court system of the United States. Explain the relationship between the state court system and the federal court system.
3. Why is product liability a concern of business firms? To customers? To society?
4. What requirements must a contract meet to be enforceable? Have you ever entered into a contract? If so, explain why a contract was used.
5. What is the difference between an express warranty and an implied warranty? Give an example of each.
6. In a free enterprise system such as we have in the United States, why does government regulate business? Why should the government encourage competition, and how can regulation be used to preserve competition?
7. In our free enterprise system, why is it important to limit the size of an individual company? Is it fair to break up a large successful company like Microsoft or AT&T?
8. List the specific practices the Clayton Act outlaws and describe how each practice limits competition. Give an example of each based on real business situations.
9. What has the movement toward deregulation been intended to accomplish? Has it been successful?
10. How can government establish social policy through the use of taxes? Which do you expect to pay in the future?

END-OF-CHAPTER QUESTIONS

1. Litigation in the United States is a growth industry.   **T** or **F**
2. A law created by a federal, state, or local legislature, constitution, or treaty is called a *common law*.   **T** or **F**
3. A dual court system operates in the United States.   **T** or **F**
4. *Negligence torts* are deliberate acts by a person or business firm. **T** or **F**
5. An *offer* is a legally enforceable, voluntary agreement between two or more parties.   **T** or **F**
6. The court uses *gap fillers* to determine the intent of the offer, acceptance, and consideration.   **T** or **F**
7. An *implied warranty* is any statement of fact or promise made by the seller to the buyer relating to the products sold.   **T** or **F**
8. Real property means physical items, such as equipment, automobiles, or a store's inventory of goods.   **T** or **F**
9. The majority of all bankruptcy filings are by businesses; the rest are filed by private individuals.   **T** or **F**
10. The Sherman Antitrust Act declared that two or more business firms could not agree to the prices to be charged for goods. **T** or **F**

11. The highest court of the land, the U.S. Supreme Court, is composed of _____ justices, who are appointed by the president and confirmed by the Senate.
    a. six   c. twelve
    b. nine   d. fifteen
12. A _____ gives the creator the exclusive right to publish and sell an original written work.
    a. trademark   c. patent
    b. copyright   d. All of the above.
13. A _____ is accomplished when the payee signs the back of the instrument.
    a. blank endorsement   c. special endorsement
    b. restrictive endorsement d. qualified endorsement
14. The _____ outlaws price discrimination that substantially reduces competition.
    a. Robinson-Patman Act   c. Antitrust Improvement Act
    b. Celler-Kefauver Act   d. Wheeler-Lea Amendment
15. The U.S. government obtains about _____ of the money it needs to operate through taxes.
    a. 25 percent   c. 95 percent
    b. 70 percent   d. 100 percent

INTERNET EXERCISE

Searching for a Trademark

For this exercise, you will be searching the U.S. Patent and Trademark Office website to determine the availability of trademarks. The website is listed below:

http://tess2.uspto.gov/bin/gate.exe?f=tess&state=uioe77.1.1

1. At this site, click on the button labeled "New User Form Search." Your task is to search the site for trademarks for novel business names that you come up with on your own. For example, suppose you wanted to start a movie production business and name it "White Knight, Inc." What is the result of your trademark search? Try out a few names of businesses that you come up with. What

results do you get? Try to come up with a business name that has less than ten matches.
2. Once you have found a trademark with relatively few matches, you'll need to determine whether the URL (Internet address) is available. You can do that by visiting the following website:

www.alldomains.com

Is the name of your company available as a dot-com? As a dot-net?

By virtue of this exercise, you begin to get a sense of how difficult it is to find a novel business name that you can trademark and that has available the associated URL.

EXHIBIT 6-1

Social Responsibility Concerns of Business

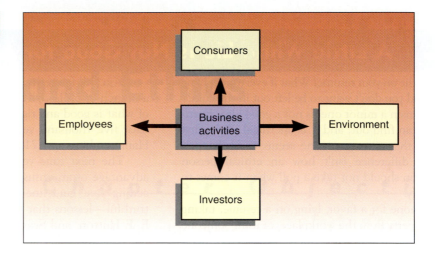

4 ☞ Newman's Own, a food company founded by actor Paul Newman, donates all profits (over $100 million since 1982) to charities in the United States. Working Assets Money Fund offers investors a chance to invest in a mutual fund according to their beliefs; it screens companies and excludes any with a history of environmental or discrimination violations, military contracts, or involvement in nuclear power plants.

5 ☞ J C Penney sponsors awards for outstanding community volunteers in many areas where its retail stores are located. McDonald's founded and supports Ronald McDonald House, which provides housing to families whose critically ill children require extended period medical care away from home.

Practicing social responsibility costs money. But failing to emphasize social responsibility also has its costs, whether in fines, increased regulation, negative publicity, public disfavor, or loss of customers. Consumers, special-interest groups, and the general public are aware of the impact of business on society and expect firms to do more than try to make profits. Most managers today regard the costs incurred in practicing social responsibility as a necessary part of doing business.[3]

Social responsibility raises many challenging questions for business firms. To whom are we responsible? How far should we go to satisfy our customers and achieve organizational objectives? Will our decisions affect any segments of society that we have not considered? Decision makers in every type and size of firm must address many such questions, which rarely have simple answers. Business activities have an impact on consumers, employees, the environment, and those investing in the firm, as Exhibit 6-1 shows. Socially responsible firms weigh the consequences of their decisions on these different concerns. To understand how firms try to achieve an acceptable balance, let's look more closely at each of these concerns.

6-2 RESPONSIBILITY TO CONSUMERS

When you make a purchase, you cast a vote for a product and indicate your approval of the product and the company providing it. If you are satisfied with the product, you will buy and use it again and maybe recommend it to your friends.

Firms trying to succeed provide products that satisfy the needs of their customers, since dissatisfied customers eventually take their business elsewhere. But a company also needs to consider how customers view the firm itself. Increasingly customers are looking beyond a firm's goods and services, evaluating its policies and actions, and taking action in the marketplace.

Pressure from consumers and special-interest groups has prompted many business firms to adopt socially responsible policies. For example, U.S. airlines banned smoking on

---

3. Simon Zadek, *The Civil Corporation: The New Economy of Corporate Citizenship* (New York: Earthscan, 2001).

domestic flights after hundreds of complaints flooded into executives' offices. **Consumerism** includes the activities of individuals, groups, and organizations aimed at protecting consumer rights. Consumer groups perform many activities, including testing and reporting on the safety and performance of products and service firms, informing the public and government officials of consumer issues, and advocating legislation.[4]

> **Consumerism** Activities of individuals, groups, and organizations aimed at protecting consumer rights.

Although many people think of the consumer movement as a 1960s phenomenon, consumerism actually originated with the Industrial Revolution. The rapid growth in the production of goods between 1870 and 1900 led to poor working conditions, the sale of harmful food and drugs, and false advertising. Shocking conditions in various industries were exposed in books such as Upton Sinclair's *The Jungle*, which chronicled dangerous working conditions and unhealthy practices in the meatpacking industry. Subsequently the Consumers' League was formed in New York City, followed by several other consumer groups.

The consumer movement gained momentum during the 1920s and 1930s. During the Great Depression, many consumers blamed business firms for joblessness and difficult economic times. Concern with product safety grew, and independent-testing groups such as Consumer Research formed. High school classes in home economics began to emphasize consumer rights.

Interest in consumerism peaked again in the 1960s and 1970s, when consumer advocates such as Ralph Nader called attention to abuses by business firms. Early in the 1960s, President John F. Kennedy established the consumer "bill of rights," which includes the right to safety, the right to be informed, the right to choose, and the right to be heard. These four rights still underlie many of the goals espoused by people and organizations active in consumerism today.

6-2a The Right to Safety

The most basic consumer right is the right to products that are safe to possess and use. To ensure safety of goods, manufacturers should test them and provide buyers with explicit directions for use. In 1972 the federal government created the Consumer Product Safety Commission (CPSC) to monitor the safety of thousands of products sold to consumers. Many state and local agencies also regulate product safety.[5]

Many companies around the world have made great strides in product safety, but more progress is needed. Products that are defective or dangerous damage public confidence in a company's ability to serve society. For instance, consumers have become concerned with electromagnetic fields and their possible link to cancer, reducing the public's confidence in utility companies and certain products such as cellular phones and electric blankets. Although the evidence linking electromagnetic fields to cancer is not conclusive, many industries have yet to address public fear in a convincing manner. The cellular phone industry has spent over $20 million on research, which has validated the findings of existing studies showing cellular phones to be safe.[6]

Automobiles, appliances, children's toys, and many other products are safer today than they once were. Product packages have also been made more tamper resistant. But instances of chemicals found in foods, such as apples treated with alar (a chemical linked to cancer) or bottled water with traces of benzene (a dangerous chemical used in cleaning fluids), illustrate that safety problems continue.

6-2b The Right to Be Informed

Consumers have the right to receive the information available about a product before they purchase it. Customers seeking a loan from a bank or other financial institution, for example, should be told of all costs and repayment terms associated with the loan.

4. Marjorie Kelly, *The Divine Right of Capital: Dethroning the Corporate Aristocracy* (San Francisco: Barrett-Koehler, 2002).

5. Frona M. Powell, *Law and the Environment* (Cincinnati, OH: West, 1998).

6. Richard Allen and Brenda Breslauer, "New Studies Call for More Research," *ABC News*, October 20, 1999.

Necessary information for foods includes ingredients and detailed instructions for use. To aid shoppers making decisions in the supermarket, FDA package labeling rules that went into effect in 1994 require food makers to adopt uniform labels for their products. The labels give consumers more information about nutrition content and limit health claims that can be made.

Consumers also have the right to know whether or not the product has any limitations or problems. In one case, regulators in Florida and a dozen other states are investigating whether Metropolitan Life Insurance Company agents sold life insurance to nurses while calling it a retirement plan. Failing to describe an insurance product as insurance is not only misleading, it is prohibited by state consumer protection laws. Another study found that many containers of milk sold at wholesale and retail contained less than the amount stated on the label. Although the individual shortages were small, the cumulative effect of short-filling was not acceptable.[7]

6-2c The Right to Choose

Consumers have the right to choose and make purchases from a variety of products at competitive prices. They also have the right to expect quality service at a fair price. Consumer demand for pesticide-free foods, for example, has resulted in a movement to grow vegetables and fruits without chemicals. Thousands of farmers are experimenting with different methods of crop rotation and greater use of natural materials to control insects and increase productivity. If the experiments are successful, consumers will have the choice they desire.

6-2d The Right to Be Heard

Consumers also have the right to have their opinions considered in the formation of government policies and in business firms' decisions that affect them. A number of large firms have established consumer affairs departments to address consumer concerns. Many, including Little Tikes (toys), General Electric (appliances), Nabisco (foods), and Smith Kline Beecham (toothpaste and other personal care products), provide toll-free telephone numbers as an easy way for consumers to ask questions, make comments, and register complaints. Small businesses may not have reason or resources to establish hot lines or hire personnel specifically for consumer relations. But small-business owners and managers can set up procedures and train employees to invite consumer comments, answer questions, and handle complaints.

6-3 RESPONSIBILITY TO EMPLOYEES

Like consumers, employees hold certain expectations of business firms. They expect safe working conditions, fair compensation, equal opportunities, and adequate benefits (e.g., health insurance, vacation, and time off to care for sick children). Employees also want to know what is going on in the company and want managers to be responsive to problems or complaints. Firms aware of their responsibility to the people who work for them make every effort to meet these expectations.

6-3a Safety in the Workplace

In 1970 Congress passed the Occupational Safety and Health Act, which created the **Occupational Safety and Health Administration (OSHA).** Charged with ensuring safe working conditions, OSHA has established many standards with which employers must comply. OSHA covers all employees except those working for government bodies and those covered by specific employment acts such as the Coal Mine Health and Safety Act.

Occupational Safety and Health Administration (OSHA) A federal agency with the primary purpose of ensuring safe working conditions.

7. See www.forums.treemedia.com/fb.

Under OSHA regulations, firms failing to protect the health of their employees can be held criminally liable.[8]

OSHA employs 1,000 field inspectors who make unannounced inspections of workplaces during normal working hours. Field inspectors concentrate their efforts in the most hazardous industries, such as construction and manufacturing. Firms with health or safety violations may be fined; the individuals responsible can receive prison terms. With more than 9 million workplaces to oversee, however, OSHA cannot identify every violation.

Many firms realize that responsibility for employee safety lies with them, not with a government agency; therefore, they adopt and carry out their own health and safety programs. Managers often face a balancing act to keep the workplace safe yet continually improve efficiency. At its Camry assembly plant in Georgetown, Kentucky, Toyota has been able to cut its injury and illness rate to half the national auto industry average.[9] The company emphasizes safety training to avoid repetitive-motion injuries, which result from performing the same stressful arm or hand motions over and over, and other injuries. Toyota matches workers to jobs physically so they do not work in areas for which they are too tall or too short. It has restructured workstations to eliminate awkward motions, improved job rotation so workers do not perform the same tasks all day, and analyzed every job in the plant to determine which ones are likely to produce injuries. Levi Strauss goes one step further, insisting that its contractors, regardless of where they are located, adhere to strict standards regarding minimum age of employees, plant safety, and healthy working conditions.

6-3b Equality in the Workplace

Individuals also expect to be treated equally in the workplace. The Civil Rights Act of 1964 guarantees equal employment opportunities for all people regardless of age, race, sex, religion, or national origin. This act established the **Equal Employment Opportunity Commission (EEOC),** a federal agency whose purpose is to increase job opportunities for females and minorities, who are defined by the EEOC as African Americans, Hispanics, Asian or Pacific Islanders, American Indians, or Alaskan natives. The EEOC can file legal charges against companies that discriminate in their hiring practices.

Nonetheless, some inequalities still exist. Although female and minority workers are being hired by some companies, they have generally been denied the needed experience to attain top-level positions. In some cases, females, minority workers, and people with disabilities earn less than white males, even when they perform the same work. In other cases, females and minorities continue to find it difficult to land certain jobs. For instance, female golfers find that many golf clubs hire only male pros. While women represent 22 percent of all U.S. golfers who play regularly, they account for only 6 percent of all accredited U.S. golf professionals.[10]

Equal Employment Opportunity Commission (EEOC)
A federal agency whose purpose is to increase job opportunities for women and minorities.

6-3c Sexual Harassment

Employers also have a responsibility to ensure a working atmosphere free of **sexual harassment,** defined by the EEOC as unwelcome advances and requests for sexual favors that affect a person's performance, and a hostile work environment in which employees are subjected to sexual comments, jokes, or materials. According to a Harris poll, 18 percent of all workers—31 percent of women and 7 percent of men—say they have experienced sexual harassment at work.[11] Examples of controversies that have placed sexual harassment in the limelight include the Tailhook incident in which male navy officers

Sexual Harassment
Unwelcome advances and requests for sexual favors that affect a person's performance, and a hostile work environment in which employees are subjected to sexual comments, jokes, or materials.

---

8. See www.osha.gov.

9. Shelley Reese, "Setting the Pace," *Business & Health*, August 1999, pp. 17–18.

10. Jane Horn, *Golf Is a Woman's Game* (New York: Adams Media, 1997).

11. See equal rights advocate summary data at www.equalrights.org/sexhar/work/workfact/htm.

FOCUS ON GLOBALIZATION

White Dog Café

Judy Wicks considers her restaurant, the White Dog Café in Philadelphia, as an experiment in bringing business, social responsibility, globalization, and community support together. Besides serving meals, Wicks works at raising consciousness and creating a sense of community. Everyone should share and have access to meals and other resources.

Wicks's business generates about $4.4 million annually. She gives more than 10 percent of this to nonprofit groups through food, labor, and cash donations. She organizes over 19,000 customers past and present around causes such as fair trade, global warming, and the School of the Americas. Some of her fervor comes from her experience as a VISTA volunteer in an indigenous community in Alaska.

In 1987 Wicks began the International Sister program, which she refers to as her "Eating with the Enemy" approach. She established relationships with socially conscious restaurants in countries that have a poor dialogue with the United States. Some of the countries she has toured with her customers are Vietnam, Thailand, and Nicaragua.

Wicks wants to be globally and locally connected in a network of socially responsible businesses. She leads through example and is an inspiration to other businesspeople in her community and around the world.

Source: Elizabeth Newberry, "Setting a Global Table," *Sojourners*, January–February 2000, p. 8.

Some firms enable employees to share their time and talent with their communities. IBM, for example, lends engineers to teach in schools.[28] Others provide company time, materials, or facilities for employees active in community organizations. Businesspeople also participate in the Rotary, Kiwanis, Junior Achievement, and other groups that raise money for local projects or help youngsters. Firms are major contributors to charities and encourage employees to donate to organizations such as the United Way, which distributes donations among many diverse social agencies operating in an area. Through such activities, the business sector makes a significant contribution to society (see the Focus on Globalization box, "White Dog Café").

6-6b Self-Regulation

The business community can also advance social responsibility by establishing standards of conduct and ensuring that firms follow them. One of the best-known self-regulatory agencies is the *Better Business Bureau*, a nationwide organization with local branches supported by local firms. The bureau's purpose is to help consumers settle problems with specific firms. Although the Better Business Bureau does not possess strong enforcement powers, it does maintain records of consumer complaints and warns consumers through local media when a firm is engaging in deceptive or questionable practices. More than 140 bureau branches operate today in the United States. Another active self-regulatory agency is called the *National Advertising Review Board* (NARB). NARB screens national advertisements for honesty and handles complaints about deceptive ads. If a firm refuses to comply with its directives, the NARB may publicize the incident or file a complaint with the Federal Trade Commission.

28. See IBM Grant Programs, www.ibm.com/ibmgives/grant.

- Companies should state clearly on bills what services a customer is receiving and how much they cost.
- Customers should be given a month's notice when a company is going to raise rates.
- Telephone calls should be answered within thirty seconds.
- A customer should receive a busy signal less than 3 percent of the time a cable company office is open.
- A company should respond to service interruptions within twenty-four hours in situations not beyond its control, within thirty-six hours otherwise.
- If an installer or technician is running late, an attempt must be made to contact the customer to set up a new appointment.

EXHIBIT 6-2

National Cable Television Association Standards

Source: National Cable Television Association

Many other industries, trade associations, and professional organizations establish self-regulatory programs. For example, the U.S. cable television industry, faced with complaints about service and prices, has established standards for cable companies to follow to guarantee better service. Exhibit 6-2 lists the standards set by the National Cable Television Association.

Standards

Businesspeople generally prefer self-regulation to that imposed by the government. The guidelines established within an industry are often more realistic than those established by the government. Self-regulatory programs usually cost less to put into place than does government regulation. The main drawback of self-regulatory programs is that sometimes they are difficult or impossible to enforce. Complying with standards is often voluntary (as is the case with the cable TV industry). When firms comply with the standards, self-regulation can be an effective way to foster social responsibility. When business behaves on the assumption that if it is not illegal then it is ethical, the government eventually responds with a host of laws and regulations.

6-6c The Social Audit

Some firms conduct a systematic review of their performance of social responsibility activities through a social audit. A **social audit** looks at the firm's short- and long-run contributions to society. Activities reviewed might include community involvement, product safety, and the impact of business practices on the environment.

With information from a social audit, managers can evaluate how effective the current programs are and decide whether they should initiate new courses of action. Some firms spend millions of dollars each year on social responsibility activities; they need to determine whether they are spending their money wisely. Although a social audit is more informal than an accounting audit, it can be a useful tool in accessing social responsibility.

Social Accountability **SA8000** is a global standard designed to make workplaces socially responsible. Based on conventions of the International Labor Organization, SA8000 has been adopted in twelve countries. The standard addresses issues such as discrimination, health and safety, child labor, and compensation. Some of the early adopters of the SA8000 approach are Dole Food Company, Cutter & Buck, Amana, Toys "R" Us, Avon, and Otto Versand. These firms believe that by complying with SA8000 they will benefit with improved productivity, quality, employee retention, and customer loyalty.[29]

SA8000 is now a voluntary code of conduct. By implementing SA8000, firms have enhanced their reputations for being responsible. To certify compliance with SA8000, qualified auditors visit facilities to observe, analyze, and study working hours, working conditions, safety, management, and human resource practices, freedom of association,

Social Audit   A systematic review of an organization's performance of social responsibility activities.

SA8000   Social accountability workplace standard that covers labor rights and certifies compliance through independent accredited auditors.

25, 26, 27, 28
29, 30

29. Deborah Leipziger, *SA8000: The Definitive Guide to the New Social Standard* (London: Person Education, 2001).

Avon SA8000 Selected Checklist for Suppliers

Health and Safety
- Company policy
- Schedule for health safety training
- Training procedure for first aid
- Protective gear policy
- Lighting, air, and water quality
- Toxic chemical handling procedures

Discrimination
- Policy on discrimination
- Policy on sexual harassment
- Analysis of pay and promotion by gender
- Complaint process

Disciplinary Practices
- Company disciplinary policy
- List of rules and actions if violated
- Appeal process
- Warning process

Working Hours
- Sick days
- Breaks
- Overtime policies
- Vacation time
- Workday length

---

the right to collective bargaining, disciplinary actions, and compensation. If the auditor identifies problems, they must be corrected.

Several costs are associated with SA8000:

- The cost of the audit
- The cost of preparing for an audit
- The cost of taking corrective action
- The cost of noncompliance

Avon has played a leadership role in developing and promoting SA8000. The company's goal is to have every single company factory compliant with SA8000 and all of its suppliers certified to SA8000. Each year, Avon buys $1 billion in goods; the company seeks to reinforce its value through its sourcing policy.

Exhibit 6-3 presents a checklist of a selected number of supplier compliance factors used by Avon to evaluate its suppliers.

By 2006, Avon and other adopters of SA8000 want it to have the same global stature and reach as ISO 9000. If this becomes true, SA8000 will help workplaces become more free, fair, open, and safe.

6-7 BUSINESS ETHICS

> **Ethics** The principles of behavior that distinguish between right and wrong.
>
> **Business Ethics** The evaluation of business activities and behavior as right or wrong.

Social responsibility requires individuals engaging in business endeavors to behave in an ethical manner. **Ethics** are principles of behavior that distinguish between right and wrong.[30] Ethical conduct conforms with what a group or society as a whole considers right behavior. People working in business frequently face ethical questions. **Business ethics** is the evaluation of business activities and behavior as right or wrong. Ethical standards in business are based on commonly accepted principles of behavior established by the expectations of society, the firm, the industry, and an individual's personal values.

With unethical business practices often receiving publicity, the public sometimes believes that people in business are less ethical than others in society. But ethical problems challenge all segments of our society, including government, churches, and higher education. For instance, college basketball players bring in millions of dollars every year for universities, coaches, television networks, and sports announcers, yet many of those athletes do not receive an education. Also, universities and professors have been accused of abandoning undergraduate students while professors pursue grants, conduct research, and participate in academic politics to further their careers and promote their universities. Such situations could destroy the trust society holds in higher education and may lead to close scrutiny of university policies and practices.

Most business leaders realize their firms cannot succeed without the trust of customers and the goodwill of society. A violation of ethics makes trust and goodwill difficult, if not

---

30. Natasha Tarpley, "Levi's Funds the Social Fabric," *Fortune*, July 10, 2000, p. 141.

impossible, to maintain, as firms such as Enron and Arthur Andersen have found out. In thousands of companies, executives and employees act according to the highest ethical standards. For example, over the years, Levi Strauss has created a culture that promotes to employees, customers, and suppliers that an organization should be an ethical creature capable of making profits and making the world a better place in which to live. Unfortunately, managers in some firms behave unethically, and these instances are often highly publicized. Fiat, Italy's largest company, became involved in a highly publicized scandal when top-level executives were implicated in making payments to leading Italian politicians and their parties. The company was already facing business problems, and its share of the Italian market slumped to a record low of 44 percent.[31] Human resource management executives say the major reason managers behave unethically is to obtain power and money. But significant costs result from unethical behavior, in the form of reduced sales and loss of goodwill.

6-7a Factors Influencing Ethical Behavior

To encourage ethical behavior, executives, managers, and owners of firms must understand what influences behavior in the first place. Exhibit 6-4 presents several factors that affect individuals' behavior in business: the business environment, organizational factors, and an individual's personal moral philosophy.

The Business Environment

Almost daily, business managers face ethical dilemmas resulting from the pressures of the business environment. They are challenged to meet sales quotas, cut costs, increase efficiency, or overtake competitors. Managers and employees may sometimes think the only way to survive in the competitive world of business is by deception or cheating. In some instances, an organization may use someone else's successful work without the permission of the owner or originator. Chase Manhattan, a large New York bank, sued advertising agency J. Walter Thompson for copying an advertisement. The suit charged that J. Walter Thompson got ideas when competing with other agencies for Chase's $35 million global campaign and used them to develop advertisements for Northwestern Mutual Life Insurance Co.[32]

Conflict of interest is another common ethical problem stemming from the business environment. Often an individual has a chance to further selfish interests rather than the interests of the organization or society. To gain favor with people who make purchasing decisions for their companies, a seller may offer special favors or gifts, ranging from a meal to clothing to trips. Some offer cash—a kickback—for putting through a contract or placing orders with a company. Others offer bribes. Such illegal conduct damages the organization in the long run. To limit unethical behavior, business firms must begin by expecting their employees to obey all laws and regulations.

---

31. John Rossant, "Fiat's Right Turn," *Business Week,* May 3, 1993, p. 38.

32. Laura Bird, "Thompson Is Named in Copycat Lawsuit," *The Wall Street Journal,* July 13, 1992, p. 83.

EXHIBIT 6-4

Factors Influencing Behavior in Business

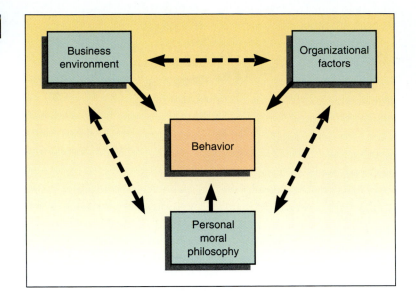

The global business environment presents further ethical dilemmas. Businesspeople and government officials in other countries and cultures often operate according to different standards than those held in the United States. Firms doing business internationally sometimes have separate ethical standards for domestic and international operations.

The Organization

The organization itself also influences behavior. Individuals often learn ethical or unethical behaviors by interacting with others in the organization. An employee who sees a superior or coworker behaving unethically may follow suit. In the Iran-Contra trial, Oliver North defended himself by saying that his actions (including shredding documents and withholding information from investigators), although unethical, were expected by his superiors. A simply stated directive from the person at the top can set the tone in an organization. In fact, an employee's perception of peers and superiors in an organization is often a stronger predictor of behavior than is the employee's own system of moral and ethical values.[33]

An organization can also use rewards to influence the behavior of its members. If an individual is rewarded or is not punished for behaving unethically, the behavior will probably be repeated. Likewise, the threat of punishment and the lack of reward for unethical activities encourage ethical behavior. The severity of punishment also sends a message to other individuals who might be considering similar activities. For example, the National Collegiate Athletic Association (NCAA) has placed member institutions such as Southern Methodist University, the University of Nevada at Las Vegas, the University of Alabama, and the University of Kentucky on probation for violating recruiting rules. Teams on probation have been barred from tournament games and from having games televised and have had limits placed on scholarships. These penalties should discourage other university athletic programs from violating NCAA rules.

The Individual

Moral Philosophy The set of principles that dictate acceptable behavior.

A person's own moral philosophy also influences his or her ethical behavior. A **moral philosophy** is the set of principles that dictate acceptable behavior. These principles are learned from family, friends, coworkers, and other social groups and through formal education. The values and attitudes quiz in Exhibit 6-5 will help you evaluate your moral philosophy.

33. Al Martin, *The Conspirators: Secrets of an Iran-Contra Insider* (Pray, MT: National Liberty Press, 2001).

EXHIBIT 6-5

Evaluating Ethical Behavior

Directions: Below are a number of statements that involve ethical decisions you may have to make when conducting business. Circle the number that represents your level of agreement with each statement.

	Strongly Disagree					Strongly Agree
1. It is OK to take supplies such as pencils and paper home from a company office.	1	2	3	4	5	6
2. I would break a company rule if my coworkers did.	1	2	3	4	5	6
3. If it meant getting ahead, I would take credit for some one else's work.	1	2	3	4	5	6
4. I would not turn in a fellow employee for breaking a company policy.	1	2	3	4	5	6
5. If I made a mistake that could hurt the company, I would cover it up to avoid being reprimanded.	1	2	3	4	5	6
6. I would not mind breaking a law to get a promotion, as long as I did not get caught.	1	2	3	4	5	6
7. I would be willing to provide customers false information to make a sale.	1	2	3	4	5	6
8. I see no problem with taking longer than necessary to do a job and then billing a client for the extra time.	1	2	3	4	5	6
9. It is OK to take care of personal business on company time.	1	2	3	4	5	6
10. I would call in sick to take a day off work.	1	2	3	4	5	6

Feedback: How are your ethical standards? Although the situations are hypothetical, they present typical business decisions. For item circled 1 or 2, you considered these behaviors unacceptable; 3 or 4 indicates you are uncertain or indifferent; and 5 or 6 suggests you believe these activities are acceptable.

Some people view the activities listed as common practices. Doesn't everyone take pens and paper home from the office? Yet many companies prohibit such actions. Some of the activities, such as misleading customers or covering up mistakes, can result in serious penalties. If you believe most of the activities are unacceptable, you have a solid ethical base from which to work. If you found most of these activities acceptable, think about them again. It may seem as though people must do such things to succeed in business. We hope that is not true.

In developing a moral philosophy, individuals can follow two approaches: humanistic and utilitarian. The **humanistic philosophy** focuses on individual rights and values. Individuals and organizations adopting this philosophy honor their moral duties to customers and workers. For example, if a product poses harm to workers or customers, it is taken off the market. Individuals and organizations following the **utilitarian philosophy** seek the greatest good for the largest number of people. Pharmaceutical manufacturers who make the vaccine for pertussis, the deadly disease of whooping cough, adhere to this philosophy. Some children react to the killed bacteria in the vaccine, which is administered three times in the first two years of life. Reactions include fevers, persistent crying, and temporary unresponsiveness. The vaccine has been blamed for severe brain damage

Humanistic Philosophy   A set of moral principles focusing on individual rights and values.

Utilitarian Philosophy   A set of moral principles focusing on the greatest good for the largest number of people.

in a few children, although several studies dispute this. Despite these problems, because so many children benefit from the vaccine, doctors continue to administer the current version while researchers work on new pertussis vaccines.[34]

6-7b Encouraging Ethical Behavior

Many organizations take positive steps to encourage ethical behavior. Some offer courses in ethics and include ethics in training programs. Most courses and training seminars focus on how to analyze ethical dilemmas. The emphasis is on understanding why individuals make the decisions they do rather than on teaching ethics or moral principles.

An organization can also encourage ethical behavior through a code of ethics.[35] A **code of ethics** is a statement specifying exactly what the organization considers ethical behavior. Many firms, as well as trade and professional associations, have established codes of ethics. For instance, the American Medical Association has its own code of ethics that limits the amount and types of advertising used by doctors. By enforcing codes of ethics, rewarding ethical behavior, and punishing unethical behavior, a firm limits opportunities to behave unethically. The Automotive Service Association (ASA) code of ethics is illustrated in Exhibit 6-6.

Employees of an organization can also encourage ethical behavior by reporting unethical practices. **Whistle-blowers** are employees who inform their superiors, the media, or a government regulatory agency about unethical behavior within their organization. Whistle-blowers often risk great professional and personal danger by reporting the unethical behavior of others. They may be harassed by coworkers or supervisors, passed up for promotions, fired, or even threatened with damage to their property or harm to themselves or their families. Nonetheless, some organizations have developed plans that encourage employees to report unethical conduct and that provide protection for whistle-blowers.

Enron vice president Sherron Watkins testified before a congressional committee on February 2002 about a "whistle-blowing" letter she wrote to then-CEO, Kenneth Lay, in August 2001. She explained in the letter her misgivings about Enron's accounting procedures, financial dealings, and partnerships. Watkins claimed that Lay was duped by other Enron executives who knowingly misrepresented Enron's financial situation.[36]

Roy Olofson, vice president of finance for Global Crossing, Ltd., the telecommunication firm that filed for bankruptcy in January 2002, wrote to the firm's general counsel alleging that some of the company's accounting practices inflated revenue. He was placed on paid administrative leave and fired a few months later.

Some claim that whistle-blowing is a life-changing event. Reprisals are almost routine. Karen Silkwood, the whistle-blower at a Kerr-McGee plutonium plant, died mysteriously in a car accident when she was gathering evidence of poor plant safety. Jeffrey Wigan, the Brown & Williamson Tobacco Corporation executive, was fired for revealing that the company deliberately had concealed potentially damaging research findings about the effects of smoking.[37] In the Watkins case at Enron, however, there appeared to not be any direct reprisal. It's not just the fear of reprisal or firing that makes whistle-blowing difficult, but also that the company culture turns cold. Colleagues often keep a distance because they do not want to be implicated with whistle-blowers.

Efforts to encourage ethical behavior will be effective only with the support of top-level management. Employees base their decisions on the guidelines and examples set by their superiors. Management must set the proper tone by never compromising ethical behavior in its dealings with customers, employees, and competitors.

Code of Ethics A statement spelling out what an organization considers ethical behavior for its employees.

Whistle-Blower An employee who informs superiors, the media, or a government regulatory agency about unethical behavior within an organization.

---

34. The Centers for Disease Control (www.cdc.com) examine pertussis vaccinations, February 16, 2002.

35. Archie B. Carroll and Ann K. Buckholtz, *Business and Society: Ethics and Stakeholder Management* (Cincinnati: South-Western, 1999).

36. Caroline E. Mayer and Amy Joyce, "Blowing the Whistle," *Washington Post*, February 10, 2002, p. H01.

37. Ibid.

The owners and managers of automotive service businesses that belong to the Automotive Service Association (ASA) agree to adhere to a code of ethics. ASA's code of ethics is the automotive service industry's standard for professional business practices.

EXHIBIT 6-6

Automotive Service Association Code of Ethics

- To perform high-quality repair service at a fair and just price.
- To use only proven merchandise of high quality distributed by reputable firms.
- To employ the best skilled technicians obtainable.
- To furnish an itemized invoice for fairly priced parts and services that clearly identifies any used or remanufactured parts. Replaced parts may be inspected upon request.
- To have a sense of personal obligation to each customer.
- To promote good will between the motorist and members of the association.
- To recommend corrective and maintenance services, explaining to the customer which of these are required to correct existing problems and which are for preventive maintenance.
- To offer the customer a price estimate for work to be performed.
- To furnish or post copies of any warranties covering parts or services.
- To obtain prior authorization for all work done, in writing, or by other means satisfactory to the customer.
- To notify the customer if appointments or completion promises cannot be kept.
- To maintain customer service records for one year or more.
- To exercise reasonable care for the customer's property while in our possession.
- To maintain a system for fair settlement of customer's complaints.
- To cooperate with established consumer complaint mediation activities.
- To uphold the high standards of our profession and always seek to correct any or all abuses within the automotive industry.
- To uphold the integrity of all members of the Automotive Service Association.

Source: asainfo@asahop.org. Copyright 2001 Automotive Service Association

SUGGESTED WEBSITES

Note: These websites were functional when we went to press. Please access the online text for the most up-to-date URLs.

1. www.pfizer.com
2. www.ford.com
3. www.lizclaiborne.com
4. www.newmansownorganics.com
5. www.jcpenney.com
6. www.littletikes.com
7. www.sb.com
8. www.toyota.com
9. www.levi.com
10. www.dupont.com
11. www.fedex.com
12. www.hudson.org
13. www.advantica-dine.com
14. www.fanniemae.com
15. www.mcdonalds.com
16. www.sce.com
17. www.sempra.com
18. www.xerox.com
19. www.chaparralsteel.com
20. www.att.com
21. www.apple.com
22. www.churchdwight.com
23. www.clorox.com
24. www.pg.com
25. www.dole.com
26. www.cutterbuck.com
27. www.amana.com
28. www.toysrus.com
29. www.avon.com
30. www.ottoversand.com

7-4b Departmental Objectives

The Northeast Insurance Company relies on its sales force to sell policies. In 2002 the sales team decided to set an objective of capturing at least 8 percent of the Chicago-Calumet regional market by 2006. The ambitious four-year objective means the sales department will have to increase its market share from 3.6 percent to 8 percent in only four years. An increase in market share means that someone else's business must be taken away, a hard task in the insurance industry.

7-4c Subunit Objectives

The operations department of Scott Manufacturing is divided into three teams. Each team or subunit includes technicians, operators, and material-handling personnel and has an informal leader and a team nickname—Wildcats, Pirates, and Copperheads. These teams compete to be the most productive group in the department without sacrificing product quality. Each team sets objectives for specific quantities and quality, and each outlines a plan for achieving the objectives and a set of target dates.

7-4d Individual Objectives

Dan Chubrich has been employed at Ford's Chicago assembly plant for twenty-five years. Chubrich's boss wants him to become certified as a quality control inspector. Chubrich wants to attend the quality control training program but has put it off for six years in a row. Whenever he planned to attend the program, some personal problem (such as too much unfinished work or a family crisis) prevented him from taking the course.

After one of his closest friends attended the program, Chubrich finally began to outline a set of objectives. He established July as the starting date to enroll in the program. He will have to help his boss find someone to operate his spot on the line while he attends the program. Chubrich's individual objectives are somewhat different from Ford's organizational objectives. However, they are just as important and challenging.

Objectives serve as targets for both managers at the top of an organization and those who work with operating employees. They are the specific guideposts around which the entire management group focuses. If the objectives are clear, challenging, meaningful, and measurable, the organization will have the standards to judge whether managers are efficiently performing the functions of management.

7-5 MANAGEMENT FUNCTIONS

Given our definition of management, exactly how do managers go about managing in an office, on a shop floor, or in a committee meeting? What do they do to help accomplish objectives? Management theorists (e.g., Henri Fayol, Mary Parker Follett, and Chester Barnard) have identified five primary functions of managers.[5] These functions (planning, organizing, staffing, directing, and controlling), first formally discussed more than eighty years ago, still characterize the activities of most managers. Although the amount of time spent on each varies, these five categories pinpoint the variety of work that managers perform.

7-5a Planning

Planning The management function of establishing objectives and developing plans to accomplish them.

Former U.S. president Dwight Eisenhower once said, "Plans are nothing, planning is everything." When managers plan, they project a course of action for the future. They will attempt to perform a systematic set of business actions aimed at achieving objectives. Thus, **planning** essentially means deciding in advance what is to be done. Of course, plans

---

5. Carol Ann Zulauf and Carol Zulauf, *The Big Picture: A Systems Thinking Story for Managers, Leaders, and Other Visionaries* (New York: Linkage Press, 2001).

alone do not bring about desired results; but without a plan and a set of objectives, managerial actions are likely to produce confusion. Planning is a task that managers must do every day.

The work of planning is basically mental. It requires thinking things through logically. Managers should think before acting and act in light of facts rather than best guesses.

One reason for the decline of Sears as one of the retailing giants of the decade is poor planning. For example, well into the 1980s Sears was still producing position papers that included no mention of Wal-Mart. Sears refused to consider Wal-Mart as a real competitor and was left behind as it blew right by.[6]

A manager must plan for many reasons. Planning helps provide the coordination needed to do the job. It helps ensure that things will get done; it can also show the manager when things may not get done and why they were not done right. Planning also aids the manager in determining who will do what job, how long the job will take, and what resources are needed to get the job done. Although planning takes time and energy and involves making complex decisions, firms must plan in order to keep their competitive edge in today's changing business environment.

7-5b Organizing

The **organizing** function of management consists of grouping people and assigning activities so that job tasks and the mission can be properly carried out. The establishment of the managerial hierarchy, which we discuss later, is the foundation of the organizing function. Specific details of organizing are discussed in Chapter 8.

> **Organizing** The management function of grouping people and assignments to carry out job tasks and the mission.

7-5c Staffing

Selection, placement, training, development, and compensation of subordinates make up the **staffing** function. A manager's staffing activities also include the evaluation and appraisal of performance. Specific details about this function are covered in Chapter 11.

> **Staffing** The management function of selecting, placing, training, developing, and compensating subordinates.

7-5d Directing

As the managerial function that initiates action, **directing** means issuing directives, assignments, and instructions. Directing also means building an effective group of subordinates who are motivated to perform. It means getting subordinates to work to accomplish objectives. Directing can be accomplished through *leadership*, the process of influencing the activities of an individual or group toward the accomplishment of an objective.

> **Directing** The management function of initiating action; issuing directives, assignments, and instructions.

The directing function is a part of any manager's job, but the time and effort managers spend in directing vary with their position in the managerial hierarchy, the number of assigned subordinates, and the type of job activities being performed. For example, the supervisor in a McKesson's distribution center in Milwaukee spends most of the day directing subordinates, whereas the president of McKesson's spends significantly greater time in more abstract and general activities.

Generally speaking, managers use many different directing styles. Three of the most common styles are referred to as autocratic, democratic, and laissez-faire leadership.

Autocratic leadership, a close style of supervision, means providing subordinates with detailed job instructions. The manager structures and specifies exactly what is to be done and when the work is due. Managers using this style delegate as little authority as possible. Autocratic managers assume they should do the planning and make the necessary decisions.

> **Autocratic Leadership** A type of close supervision in which the manager delegates as little authority as possible.

6. Bob Ortega, *In Sam We Trust: The Untold Story of Sam Walton and Wal-Mart, The World's Most Powerful Retailer* (New York: Time Books, 2000).

Some employees respond positively to the autocratic style. Others tend to lose interest and lack initiative when working for an autocratic manager. In some cases, individuals or even groups of subordinates may actively resist and develop hostilities toward the autocratic manager.

Under certain circumstances and with specific employees, autocratic direction may be necessary. Employees with skill deficiencies, lack of experience, or certain personality traits want firm and structured direction. For example, the new employee who is unsure of the job, his or her skills, and the manager's expectations would probably respond positively to an autocratic style.

Many managers are moving away from the old autocratic style of telling their employees what to do, how to do it, and when to do it. Instead they are focusing on involving their employees in the decision-making process. *Empowering* employees means granting them the authority and power to make a decision. Thus, the decision-making point is moved down to the lowest level where a competent decision can be made. **Empowerment** involves sharing information, providing the authority and power to make decisions, and encouraging people to go ahead and make the decision. These behaviors require an adjustment in traditional management practices. In traditional management "the manager" possesses the power, information, and authority.

An example of empowerment is found at W. L. Gore and Associates, which operates with no titles, hierarchy, or structure. The employees are empowered to make decisions and they are given the power to do so. Employees make hiring, discipline, and compensation decisions that were previously made by managers.[7]

The opposite of autocratically leading is **democratic leadership.** A manager using this style consults with subordinates about job activities, problems, and corrective actions. Managers using the general approach seek help and ideas. Democratic leadership does not lessen managers' formal authority; decision-making power still rests with them. With an experienced, skilled, and intelligent group of employees, a manager would likely benefit from using a democratic style that encourages participation.

Probably the best reason for considering the democratic style is that subordinates who participate in a job-related decision are apt to be more enthused about performing the job. Those allowed to take part in decision making generally support the final decisions enacted and try hard to make the decision a success.

With **laissez-faire leadership,** the supervisor avoids power and responsibility. He or she exists as a contact person who provides helpful information and guidance to accomplish objectives. The laissez-faire, or free-rein, supervisor may give task assignments and offer support when requested but stays out of the group's way. Such a style may be appropriate when, for example, a person is handling more than one job at once. Louis Lenzi, a general manager at PCA, is one such manager. While working on a team of employees who developed ProScan, a successful high-end line of televisions, he also had to handle his day-to-day job of managing thirty-seven people designing other RCA products. His trick for juggling both important duties was to show up only when he was crucially needed.[8]

7-5e Controlling

The managerial function of checking to determine whether employees are following plans and progress is being made, and of taking action to reduce discrepancies, is called **controlling.** The core idea of control is to modify behavior and performance when deviations from plans are discovered.

Planning, organizing, staffing, and directing are the initial steps for getting the job done. Controlling is concerned with making certain that plans are correctly implemented.

Empowerment   In a business environment, involves sharing information, providing the authority and power to make decisions, and encouraging people to go ahead and make the decision.

3 ☞

Democratic Leadership   A type of general supervision in which the manager consults with subordinates about job-related issues.

Laissez-Faire Leadership   A type of supervision in which the manager avoids power and responsibility by giving assignments and support but staying out of the group's way.

Controlling   The management function of checking to determine whether employees are following plans and progress is being made, and of taking action to reduce discrepancies.

---

7. Jay A. Conger and Robindra N. Kanungo, "The Empowerment Process: Integrating Theory and Practice," *Academy of Management Review,* August 1998, pp. 471–482.

8. "The Non-Managers Manager," *Fortune,* February 22, 1993, pp. 80–84.

FOCUS ON TECHNOLOGY

Technology Helps Siebel

Industry Week each year selects a top CEO. The 2001 winner was Thomas M. Siebel, CEO of Siebel Corporation. While many CEOs have founded a company or authored a book, Siebel has created an entire industry. Customer relationship management (CRM) was conceived and built by Siebel.

CRM allows companies to track customers, monitor revenue and expenses, and target marketing prospects. It enables sales managers to know exactly what point in the sales process a particular prospect or deal is at, so that decisions can be made to maximize revenues as well as customer service. The benefit to a company of using CRM is better management of sales, marketing, and customer service.

Siebel explains that technology is crucial to help accomplish CRM goals. CRM software is essential at Siebel for maintaining customer relationships. By 2005 the annual CRM software market is expected to be about $16 billion. Siebel, the market leader, has a 30 plus percent share. CRM software helps keep track of customer preferences, inquiries, and complaints, which provides firms with a system of control.

Other companies, such as Whirlpool, use CRM software. Whirlpool coordinates its interactions with customers and business partners over the Web. Call centers and the field service staff are coordinated with the help of CRM software. The technology that Siebel provides has become the key to making the customer the key focus.

As a CEO, Siebel practices what he preaches. Twice a year the company hires an outside firm to measure its own customer service level. Siebel ties its compensation and reward practices to customer satisfaction scores.

Source: Doug Bartholomew, "CEO of the Year—The King of Customer," *Industry Week,* February 1, 2002, pp. 51–55.

Supervisors who delegate their responsibility should also take care to control, because the ultimate responsibility for the delegated work is theirs. The process of control has four basic steps:

1. Set standards for time, quality, quantity, and so on.
2. Measure performance (results).
3. Compare performance with standards.
4. Make necessary modifications.

A standard indicates to employees what is expected. Ideally standards are measurable and easy to understand. For example, a management team may set a standard for producing two acceptable units a day or for achieving industrial sales of $50,000 a month. But how are standards set for an accountant or personnel manager? Standards in these and other staff areas often are somewhat fuzzy attempts to determine the important functions in the departments.

An important part of a manager's job is to monitor performance so that problems can be pinpointed. Once managers assess performance and compare it with the standards set earlier, they can begin a course of action. Of course, too much measurement can be expensive and can alienate the people being monitored. Each person involved in the control checks needs to understand his or her importance. An example of using technology to check on customer relationship service performance is provided in the Focus on Technology box, "Technology Helps Siebel."

EXHIBIT 7-2

Del Ray Electronics' Control Process

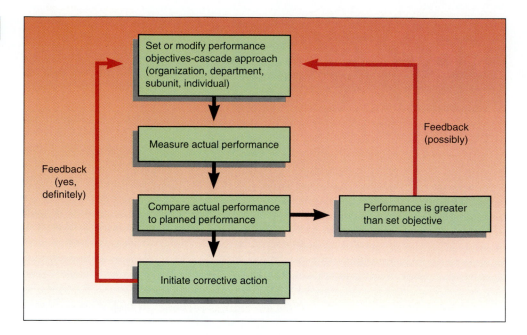

Managers often develop clear standards and monitor results, yet fail to make the necessary corrections. If standards are not being met, the manager must search for the problem, find it, and correct it. In the centralized planning systems now being dismantled in Eastern Europe, managers failed to search for problems and correct them. An old Soviet story associated with the five-year plans tells of the plant manager who needed an accountant. He asked each applicant for the position, "How much is two and two?" He gave the job to the applicant who answered, "How much do you need it to be, Comrade Manager?[9]

Adapting a result to fit the standards is the complete opposite of using control to improve performance. "Controlled flight into terrain" occurs when a competent crew flying an airplane flies it into the ground. This usually happens at night or in bad weather. The crew is unaware of the location or impending danger. Worldwide about six crashes a year are caused by this phenomenon. To control this serious problem the Federal Aviation Administration (FAA) began to install Minimum Safe-Altitude Warning Systems (MSAWS). Even with the MSAWS used to control flights there were still a few accidents, such as the crash of Korean Airlines Flight 801 into a hillside on Guam in 1997, killing all 228 people aboard.[10] Since the Guam tragedy, the FAA has improved MSAWS through a better control and monitoring system.

The control process at Del Ray Electronics (a small firm in Florida) is spelled out in Exhibit 7-2. An important phase of organizational control is the feedback that occurs. If performance is acceptable, no modification may be needed; if performance is unacceptable, objectives will not be met, so modifications are needed.

Sometimes the manager him- or herself may be the problem. Robert Allen, while CEO of AT&T, introduced a rather unique type of feedback into the company's organizational structure. After an employee survey reflected that only 19 percent of AT&T's workers thought top management's statements were believable, Allen decided to have subordinates evaluate their managers. He started by getting appraised himself, and then more than 800 executives were rated by their followers. This type of "upward feedback" still exists throughout AT&T.[11]

Planning, organizing, staffing, directing, and controlling—these five functions must be carried out in all firms, large or small, in the United States or elsewhere in the world, profit or nonprofit. Bank of Tokyo-Mitsubishi, Aurora Foods, Blue Bell Ice Cream, and

4, 5, 6 ☞

9. "Borderless Management," *Business Week*, May 23, 1994, pp. 24–26.

10. A. Lewin, "Without Warning," *USA Today*, October 18, 1999, p. A1ff.

11. "Could AT&T Rule the World?" *Fortune*, May 17, 1993, p. 64.

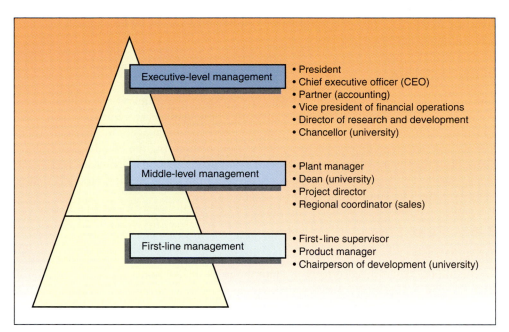

EXHIBIT 7-3

**Levels of Management:
The Managerial Hierarchy**

Tom's of Maine all have managers who plan, organize, staff, direct, and control. As firms grow in size, they tend to have layers, or levels, of managers. At each level, these functions are carried out to some degree.

7-6 LEVELS OF MANAGEMENT

As enterprises grow from an owner to a group to a corporation, a number of managerial levels or layers are created, and they begin to take on a shape. Three distinct levels of management—executive, middle, and first-line—are usually portrayed as a **managerial hierarchy.** This hierarchy depicts what is called a **chain of command,** or the channel of communication, coordination, and control. The first-line manager reports to a middle-level manager, who reports to an executive-level manager.

Exhibit 7-3 is a pyramid diagram of a managerial hierarchy. The pyramid is used for many medium- and large-sized businesses because it geographically depicts the number of managers at each level and the authority relationships among them.

Three levels of management are shown in the pyramid: executive, middle, and first-line. Executive-level managers have more authority in decision making than middle-line managers; middle managers have more authority in decision making than first-line managers. Some titles typically associated with the various levels are also shown in Exhibit 7-3.

7-6a Executive

At the top of the management pyramid sits the president or chief executive officer and other managers engaged primarily in charting the overall mission, strategy, and objectives of the business. The executive management team must be skilled in general planning, recruiting key personnel, and developing strategic plans. In addition, executive-level managers often are asked to represent the organization in community activities, dealings with the government, and seminars and the like at educational institutions. They function externally for the business and are important spokespersons for everything the company is attempting to accomplish.

The obligations and responsibilities of executive managers in large organizations are many. Consequently, the monetary rewards are often relatively large. The pay of executive-level managers—including base salary, bonus, and other monetary considerations—is often in six figures. An effective executive is usually very mobile; each year at least one out of five moves to a new geographic location. Many executive-level managers move from one

Managerial Hierarchy
The levels of management in an organization, typically three distinct levels: executive, middle, and first-line.

Chain of Command
A channel in which communication, coordination, and control flow through the various levels of management to subordinates.

company to another. Thus the question is not *whether* the successful executive-level manager will move but where and when.

7-6b Middle

The middle level of the management hierarchy includes plant supervisors, college deans, project directors, and regional sales coordinators. These managers receive the broad overall strategies, missions, and objectives from executive-level managers and translate them into specific action programs. The emphasis is on implementing the broad organizational plans. Basically the middle manager is a conduit between the top policymakers (executive management) and the supervisory personnel responsible for producing products and/or services so that the company achieves its objectives.

7-6c First-Line

The third level of management, the first-line or supervisory level, is directly responsible for the minute details needed to coordinate the work of nonmanagers. Supervisors must work directly with employees and motivate them to perform satisfactorily. The supervisor in a factory, the departmental chairperson in a college, and the product manager in a marketing department must translate overall corporate goals into action plans. This management level is the link between managers and nonmanagers. This is typically the entry level into management for college and associate degree graduates.

The cornerstone that separates the three levels of managers from nonmanagers is decision making. Managers at any level, performing any managerial function and applying any management principle, must make decisions. Executive-level managers must determine the overall direction of the company. The middle manager must decide how to implement the overall plan at the supervisory level: How should the plan be communicated? How should supervisors be motivated? When should the supervisor be informed about the overall plans? The first-line supervisor must decide how to motivate employees and reward the best performers.

The world of business is constantly changing.[12] Some trends that managers face because of the changing workplace include the following:

- The average size of companies, measured by the number of individuals they employ, is decreasing. More people each year are starting their own businesses.
- The traditional hierarchical organization characteristic of industry giants is giving way to a variety of organizational forms with greater focus on teamwork.
- The concept of doing business means providing a service for over 75 percent of businesses.
- Workers' pay is tied less to a person's position or tenure and more to the changing market value of his/her skills or competencies.
- Work involves continuous learning and education.
- An increasing number of people (over 12 million) now work away from a main office. Many of them are referred to as telecommuters.

In addition to meeting the challenges of the preceding trends, tomorrow's managers at all managerial levels—executive, middle, first-line—must rely on their expertise and diplomatic coordination skills to motivate newly specialized employees and to handle special circumstances to attain organizational goals while still making their jobs meaningful.

---

12. Ira Mattathia, *Next: Trends for the Near Future* (New York: Overlook, 2000).

EXHIBIT 7-4

How Managers Spend Their Time

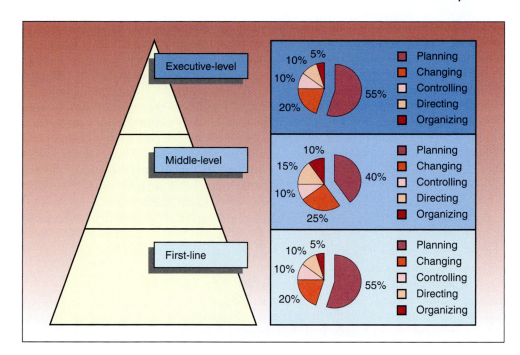

7-7 WHAT DO MANAGERS DO WITH THEIR TIME?

Managers at different levels in the hierarchy allocate their time in various ways. As shown in Exhibit 7-4, managers at different levels generally focus on different tasks. One study found that executive managers concentrate a significant portion of their workday on planning, managing, and coping with change, and organizing. First-line managers focus primarily on directing operating employees. They spend far less time in such conceptually oriented areas as planning and in developing change programs.[13]

Another study of managerial time examined how time was used by middle-level managers in various departments.[14] Four departments were examined: production, marketing, finance, and human resource management. Four management functions were used, including planning, organizing, controlling, and a miscellaneous "other" category. The study found distinct uses of time across functions, as illustrated in Exhibit 7-4. Production, marketing, and finance managers all spend the greatest percentage of their time on controlling activities. Personnel/human resource managers, however, spend the largest proportion of their time on planning activities. Over the years, different researchers have confirmed the diversity in time use between levels of management and functions of management.

Professors and consultants who have studied real-life bosses have found that a fluid time style that includes plenty of unstructured time allows good managers to stay plugged in to their organizations. One study conducted by Stephanie Winston (a New York-based expert on organizing) found that only two hours of a CEO's nine- to ten-hour working day consisted of prebooked appointments. Joseph Vittoria, CEO of Avis, blocks out two to three hours of his workday just for unscheduled encounters.

However, to accomplish necessary tasks, managers must still set aside private time each day, even if it means having to leave the desk or office or working at unconventional

13. "New Work Order," *The Economist*, April 9, 1994, p.76; and Henry J. Mintzberg, *The Nature of Managerial Work*, New York: Harper & Row, 1973.

14. J. Horne and Tom Lupton, "The Work Activities of Middle Managers: An Explanatory Study," *Journal of Management Studies*, January 1965, pp. 14–33.

hours to do so. Cosmetics tycoon Mary Kay Ash had her own method for finding such private time. She made a habit of rising by 5 A.M. at least six days a week to give herself an early start on the workday. Regardless of which technique a manager chooses to employ, the efficient use of time is clearly a must in a workday that includes the number and variety of duties of today's manager.

As you read this chapter and attend to other parts of your life, you may think you're really busy. E-mail, pagers, a lack of clear objectives, drop-in visitors, and meetings seem to plague managers and nonmanagers alike. However, take a peek at the fully packed schedules kept by chief executive officers of various organizations. What sets the CEO's job apart from others on the management team is not the amount of time worked but the number of people and the variety of tasks that must be dealt with every day. Time demands on CEOs come from every direction—subordinates, the board of directors, customers, lawyers, consultants, civic organizations, and suppliers. Donald Schuenke, CEO at Northwestern Mutual Life Insurance, estimates that he would need to work at least twenty-four hours a day if he were to accept all the requests he receives from people wishing just a little of his time. In fact, he devotes about sixty hours a week to the job.

The ability to delegate work to others is one of the CEO's most important skills for managing time efficiently. Allen Rosenshine, CEO at the Omnicom Group (a holding company that controls two of the three largest U.S. advertising agencies), states, "For me, the first decision is, do I handle it or do I delegate it to somebody else and forget about it?" Delegation means giving jobs to others without always checking on them. It is tough for CEOs to give up important, crucial jobs.

Staff assistants are an important tool in the CEO's time management program. CEOs vary widely in the degree to which they allow secretaries to screen people, requests, and information. Most often the assistant is not an arbiter of access but rather helps screen and schedule the bidders for the CEO's time—subject to later approval or rearrangement. Rosenshine, like a growing number of CEOs, has two support personnel. One handles typing, filing, and other clerical chores. The other helps him manage his time, both by keeping the appointment book straight and by serving as a go-between when Rosenshine can't immediately get in touch with someone.

Because CEOs must so often play important roles outside their firms, many designate special assistants to take up some of these responsibilities. Barry Sullivan, CEO at First Chicago Bank, is a trustee of the University of Chicago, a trustee of the Art Institute of Chicago, a cochairperson of the financial advisory committee for the city, and a participant in many other civic endeavors. He assigned Michael Leyden of First Chicago to help him with these demands. Now Sullivan and Leyden share the civic responsibilities.[15]

In the busy world of CEOs, there is concern about establishing objectives, applying the functions of management, performing multiple roles, and learning relevant management skills. However, there is also a lot of concern about stretching time, using it wisely, and establishing tactics to make the most of each minute.

7-8 CORE MANAGEMENT SKILLS

Regardless of what level a manager occupies within the managerial hierarchy or how much uninterrupted time he or she has, it is essential to master and apply certain fundamental skills to become an effective leader of the organization or department.

Management skill is the ability to use knowledge, behaviors, and aptitudes to perform a task. Skills are learned and developed with experience, training, and practice. Management writers have attempted to define the skills that successful managers use. Robert Katz classified management skills as technical, human relations, and conceptual.[16] **Technical skills** are those involved in making a product or providing a service.

> **Management Skill**   The ability to use knowledge, behaviors, and aptitudes to perform a task.
>
> **Technical Skill**   Skill involved in making a product or providing a service.

15. "The CEO's Secret of Managing Time," *Fortune*, June 1, 1992, p. 135.

16. Robert L. Katz, Skills of an Effective Administrator," *Harvard Business Review*, September–October, 1974, pp. 90–102.

Katz	Mintzberg
Technical (having the required knowledge to perform job)	Technical (especially required at first-line management due to closeness to the operation)

Human relations (listening to, observing, and working effectively with people)	Human relations: Peer
	                     Leadership
	                     Conflict resolution

Conceptual (understanding the organization as a whole, and its future)	Conceptual: Information processing
	                  Decision making
	                  Resource allocation
	                  Entrepreneurial
	                  Introspection

EXHIBIT 7-5

The Katz and Mintzberg Skill Categories

Katz points out that technical skills are especially important at the first-line management level. **Human relations skills** involve relating and interacting with subordinates, peers, superiors, and customers or clients. **Conceptual skills** are the manager's ability to organize and integrate information to better understand the organization as a whole. Conceptual skills are especially important at the executive level of management.

Henry Mintzberg provided a broader classification. He expanded the human relations skill to include three categories and the conceptual skills to include five categories. Exhibit 7-5 provides a comparison of the Katz and Mintzberg classification systems.

Human Relations Skills   The ability to relate and interact with subordinates, peers, superiors, and customers or clients.

Conceptual Skills   The ability to organize and integrate information to better understand the organization as a whole.

7-8a Studies of Management Skills

Virginia Boehm conducted an extensive study of managerial skills by assessing 1,000 managers from all levels at Sohio Corporation.[17] She wanted to determine which skills should be emphasized in selection and training at Sohio. Boehm asked each manager to describe what skills and abilities he or she used to accomplish the job objectives. In addition, each manager was rated on overall job performance.

Boehm's results showed that interpersonal skills were only of moderate importance in this sample. Six of the top ten skills related to problem solving and change. When the study was conducted, however, the company was growing rapidly. Change was therefore a fact of everyday life for managers. Under these conditions, successful managers had to possess skills to cope with managing uncertainty.

The Katz and Mintzberg classifications and the Boehm research results point to four core management skills that you will have to learn, practice, and become proficient in to be a successful manager. These skills, highlighted in Exhibit 7-6, are decision-making/problem-solving skills, communication skills, interpersonal skills, and objective/goal-setting skills. Whether we discuss a small convenience shopping store (e.g., 7-Eleven, Circle K) or an organization with thousands of employees (e.g., J C Penney), these skills are still important.

7-8b Decision-Making/Problem-Solving Skills

Decision making and problem solving involve the type of activities listed in Exhibit 7-6: identifying problems, creatively generating alternative solutions, selecting a specific alternative, delegating authority to implement a solution, making decisions under uncertain and risky circumstances, and evaluating the success or failure of the alternative selected. These specific skill activities must be applied by managers at all levels in the management hierarchy.

17. Virginia R. Boehm, "What Do Managers Really Do?" (Paper researched at the annual meeting of the AACSB Graduate Managerial Admissions Council, Toronto, June 1981.)

EXHIBIT 7-6

Core Management Skills and Their Characteristics

Decision Making/ Problem Solving	Communication	Interpersonal	Objective/ Goal Setting
Identifies problems	Writes clearly and concisely	Shows empathy	Establishes meaningful, challenging, and clear objectives
Creates feasible alternatives	Speaks effectively	Uses power and influence fairly	Sets priorities
Selects an optimal alternative	Listens carefully	Projects a positive image to others	Evaluates success of objectives/goals approach
Delegates	Has computer skills	Leads effectively	Uses objectives/goals as standards to establish reward program
Makes decisions under risk and/or uncertainty	Makes effective presentations	Behaves ethically	Provides effective feedback on progress, expectations, and modifications
Evaluates alternatives used to solve problems	Uses appropriate etiquette	Resolves conflict	

7-8c Communication Skills

The majority of time a manager spends applying the functions of management is spent communicating with others via e-mail, faxing, speaking, listening, or videoconferencing.[18] Today, among many communication requirements, managers are expected to give speeches, make inspirational talks to employees, and write clear memos, letters, and reports. Computers are here to stay, so managers will also have to use the computer efficiently. They don't have to be computer programmers, but they will have to know how to use computer software to make their job easier.

According to Madelyn Burley-Allen, author of *Listening: The Forgotten Skill*, a survey of Fortune 1,000 company presidents indicated that listening is a major problem for most people.[19] For example, managers report that subordinates' failure to receive critical information and to accept and/or carry out responsibilities is a major problem in business. Both of these failures imply deficient listening skills. With regard to all communications, listening takes about 40 percent of a manager's time (speaking is 35 percent, reading is 16 percent, and writing is 9 percent).

We tend to equate listening with hearing, but this is not correct. Good listening means being aware of what you hear, accurately receiving the information you hear, and combining the information you hear in a way that is useful to you. The values and attitudes quiz in Exhibit 7-7 will help you determine your current level of listening skills.

In August 2001, the state of New York passed a law that might impact listening with handheld cell phones that occurs in cars. The New York law prohibits the use of handheld cell phones by drivers. It is estimated that about 65 percent of all cell phone use takes place when people are driving. Research has established there is a fourfold increase in the probability of a car wreck when drivers use handheld cell phones.[20]

18. Clarke L. Cayewood, ed., *The Handbook of Strategic Public Relations and Integrated Communications* (New York: McGraw-Hill, 1997).

19. Madelyn Burley-Allen, *Listening: The Forgotten Skill* (New York: John Wiley, 1982).

20. Dennis W. Organ, "Listening Can Be Dangerous," *Business Horizons*, September 2001, pp. 10–11.

Listening Skills

Directions: Place an X on the number that indicates how important you think the specific skill is for good listening. Then place a circle around the number to indicate your estimation of your present skill level in listening to people.

Skill areas	High/ excellent				Low/ poor
1. Regarding what the other person says as important—at least to the speaker.	5	4	3	2	1
2. Listening without interrupting.	5	4	3	2	1
3. Not rushing the other person.	5	4	3	2	1
4. Giving full attention to the other person.	5	4	3	2	1
5. Not responding judgmentally.	5	4	3	2	1
6. Adjusting to the other person's pace of speaking.	5	4	3	2	1
7. Listening objectively.	5	4	3	2	1
8. Responding both to what is said and to what is left unsaid.	5	4	3	2	1
9. Checking to be sure that the other person heard correctly.	5	4	3	2	1
10. Maintaining confidentiality.	5	4	3	2	1

Give your overall rating of the quality of your listening skills (circle one):

Very high   10   9   8   7   6   5   4   3   2   1   Very low

Feedback: Both students and managers have completed the Listening Skills quiz. Based on many responses, the two skill areas in which respondents seem to be the weakest are (2) listening without interrupting and (4) giving full attention to the other person. People seem to have a knack for interrupting others and of not listening to what is being said. Any item that has an X on the 1 or 2 rating may require attention on your part. Also, an X-O gap of two or more numbers indicates a discrepancy between importance and skill level. Each of these ten areas is extremely important.

Listening skills can be improved by:

- Talking less.
- Avoiding hasty judgments.
- Taking notes.
- Letting the person finish talking.
- Asking questions.
- Paying attention.

Students need to practice good listening skills in all of their classes. Without listening ability, learning is difficult. Are you a good listener? How can you determine your listening skill weaknesses?

7-8d   Interpersonal Skills

Interpersonal relations in the work environment are the primary glue in a successful organization.[21] Talking, listening, cajoling, facilitating, and showing concern are all important in developing relationships with people. Using power and influence skillfully and serving as a referee are also crucial parts of the manager's network of interpersonal relationships with people. A manager's ability to empathize affects subordinates' behavior and attitudes significantly. Empathy is a skill with two main characteristics: accurately perceiving the

---

21. Gerry Lane and Todd Domke, *Cain and Abel at Work: How to Overcome Office Politics and the People Who Stand Between You and Success* (New York: Broadway Books, 2001).

content of another person's message and giving attention to the message's emotional components. Positive changes in behavior and attitude and interpersonal growth are associated with the superior's show of empathy in an interaction.

Rick Hess, chief operating officer of M/A-Com, a Massachusetts defense company, knows the importance of interpersonal skills. He knows his employees are under a lot of stress, so, to make sure they avoid job burnout, he tries to stay close to them by taking them to lunch, expressing an interest in what is going on in their personal lives, and even playing softball or basketball with them one night a week.[22]

7-8e Objective/Goal-Setting Skills

The fourth skill area—setting objectives and goals—is concerned with establishing organizational, departmental, subunit, and individual objectives. Carefully set and attended to objectives (specific targets) and goals (general targets) can affect individuals' motivation and performance. Priorities must be set and an evaluation program developed. The evaluation program must then be used as the basis for creating an equitable, timely, and clearly communicated reward system.

The four core management skills apply to managers at each level of the management hierarchy. These skills are used to perform the planning, organizing, staffing, directing, and controlling functions of management. How well managers do their jobs depends on how proficient they are in these skills; deficiency in any area diminishes the manager's chance of success. Learning, practicing, receiving feedback on, and observing (through videotaping in training programs) these skills will help shape and refine them so that optimal results are achieved.

7-9 CONCLUSION

Managers can make a difference in organizational performance. The way they work, use their skills, and apply the functions of management affects the actions of others and the accomplishments of businesses. Since managers are human, they may make mistakes, err in judgment, act unethically, and behave selfishly or insensitively. When this happens, people on the receiving end of such behavior get hurt, and objectives may be jeopardized. At other times, managerial behavior is very positive. Managers anticipate errors, help a floundering employee, create career opportunities for others, behave ethically, and act decisively. When this happens, people working with a manager blossom and gain self-confidence, and organizational objectives are accomplished.

The study of management and leadership will prepare you for a career in any size organization, in any industry, and in any country in the world. The future is especially bright for managers with a range of skills and global understanding. In a world that is becoming borderless in terms of economic and business transactions, understanding what work managers and leaders must perform and what skills are mandatory is a good first step for students.

SUGGESTED WEBSITES

Note: These websites were functional when we went to press. Please access the online text for the most up-to-date URLs.

1. www.cvs.com
2. www.sears.com
3. www.wlgore.com
4. www.btm.co.jp

5. www.aurorafoods.com
6. www.bluebell.com
7. www.tomsofmaine.com

22. Jerry Jasinowski and Robert Hamrin, *Making It in America* (New York: Simon & Schuster, 1995).

SUMMARY OF LEARNING OBJECTIVES

1. *Define the terms* management *and* leadership. Management is the application of planning, organizing, staffing, directing, and controlling functions in the most efficient manner possible to accomplish meaningful organizational objectives. Management is carried out by one or more managers to get things done through other people. Leadership is different from managing. Leadership is not always associated with a position in a hierarchy. It is a process of influence exercised over followers.

2. *Explain what is meant by the term* organizational objectives *and describe the four levels of such objectives.* Objectives are desired results of targets to be reached by a certain time. They are specific, state what is to be accomplished, and indicate when it will be achieved. Objectives are tailored to four important levels: organizational, departmental, subunit, and individual.

3. *Discuss the five functions that successful managers must perform.* Planning involves developing a set of actions to achieve objectives. Organizing consists of grouping people and assigning activities so that job tasks and the mission can be carried out. Staffing involves the selection, placement, training, development, and compensation of subordinates. Directing involves taking charge, initiating action, and directly motivating employees. Controlling is monitoring or checking employees and objectives and taking action to correct discrepancies between objectives and performance.

4. *Compare the three levels of management in terms of authority, responsibility, and accountability.* Executive-level managers are engaged primarily in charting the overall mission, strategy, and objectives of the business. These managers must be skilled in planning product distribution, recruiting key personnel, and developing plans. They often represent the company in the community and in dealing with the government. Middle-level managers receive the overall strategies, missions, and objectives from the executive managers and translate them into specific action programs. They function as a conduit between executive managers and supervisory personnel. First-line managers are directly responsible for coordinating the work of nonmanagers. They work directly with employees and motivate them to perform satisfactorily.

5. *Identify the four core skills that managers should acquire and practice.* The core skills are decision making/problem-solving, communication, interpersonal, and objective/goal-setting skills.

KEY TERMS

autocratic leadership (p. 161)
chain of command (p. 165)
conceptual skills (p. 169)
controlling (p. 162)
democratic leadership (p. 162)
directing (p. 161)
empowerment (p. 162)

goals (p. 158)
human relations skills (p. 169)
laissez-faire leadership (p. 162)
leadership (p. 156)
management (p. 156)
management skill (p. 168)
managerial hierarchy (p. 165)

mission statement (p. 159)
objectives (p. 158)
organizing (p. 161)
planning (p. 160)
staffing (p. 161)
technical skill (p. 168)

QUESTIONS FOR DISCUSSION AND REVIEW

1. What is challenging about being a middle-level manager? Try to locate such a manager and ask him or her what makes the job challenging.

2. What is meant by the phrase "all business is show business"?

3. Can female and male managers apply each of the four core management skills discussed in this chapter with equal effectiveness? Explain.

4. Are leaders always formally recognized by an organization? Why?

5. Why are communication skills so necessary for success in the field of management?

6. How could a manager develop and improve his or her decision-making/problem-solving skills?

7. The need to practice good or efficient time management seems to apply to everyone. Why is it so important to managers? How can you personally improve your own time management skills?

8. Do you set individual objectives? Describe how you can improve upon the establishment of objectives and the monitoring of your progress.

9. Why would some traditional managers resist empowering their subordinates?

10. What management and leadership skills are you responsible for in terms of your own self-development?

END-OF-CHAPTER QUESTIONS

1. There are more than 21 million business establishments in the United States.   **T** or **F**

2. The amount of formal power and authority that accompanies a leadership position directly impacts how effective the leader is. **T** or **F**

3. Autocratic leadership means granting employees the authority and power to make work-related decisions.   **T** or **F**

4. With democratic leadership, the supervisor avoids power and responsibility.   **T** or **F**

5. The average size of companies, measured by the number of individuals it employs, is decreasing.   **T** or **F**

6. To accomplish necessary tasks, managers must set aside private time each day, even if it means leaving the desk or office or working at unconventional hours.   **T** or **F**

7. Conceptual skills involve relating and interacting with subordinates, peers, superiors, and customers or clients.   **T** or **F**

8. A survey of Fortune 1,000 company presidents indicated that listening is a major problem for most people.   **T** or **F**

9. _____ managers focus primarily on directing operating employees. They spend far less time in such conceptually oriented areas as planning and in developing change programs.
   a. Executive
   b. First-line
   c. Middle
   d. All of the above

10. The cornerstone that separates the three levels of managers from nonmanagers is _____.
    a. pay scale
    b. title
    c. longevity
    d. decision making

11. Which of the following is *not* one of the three distinct levels of management?
    a. Executive
    b. Middle
    c. First-line
    d. Entry level

12. The _____ function of management consists of grouping people and assigning activities so that job tasks and the mission can be properly carried out.
    a. staffing
    b. directing
    c. leading
    d. organizing

13. The Northeast Insurance Company relies on _____ to sell policies.
    a. advertising
    b. word of mouth
    c. its sales force
    d. a lack of competition

14. To which company does the mission statement "To give unlimited opportunity to women" belong?
    a. Wal-Mart
    b. 3M
    c. Mary Kay Cosmetics
    d. Merck

15. Experts thought that Darwin Smith, CEO of Kimberly Clark, had lost his mind when he _____.
    a. reduced his workforce
    b. bought out the competition
    c. sold his paper mills
    d. reduced his salary by half

INTERNET EXERCISE

Women As Leaders

Leadership is not a male-only concept. Although in the Fortune 500 only a small percentage of the CEOs are females, more and more women are moving into the top positions in small and medium-size companies. Meg Whitman of e-Bay; Andrea Jung at Avon; Ann Moore, executive vice president at Time; and Dawn Lepore, Charles Schwab's chief information officer are examples of women in powerful, meaningful leadership positions.

Using the Internet, collect and report on:

1. The backgrounds of these four leaders—Whitman, Jung, Moore, and Lepore.

2. Three women presidents of major universities. What is their background and experience?

3. Three women politicians: Barbara Boxer, Hillary Clinton, and Kay Bailey Hutcheson. What is their background and experience?

4. Are there common characteristics and experiences reflected in the backgrounds of the leaders examined in questions 1–3?

EXPERIENTIAL EXERCISE

Setting Objectives for Your College

Activity

Each student will develop a written list of objectives, which his/her college might consider accomplishing. Since the one organization all class members and the instructor have in common is their college, this exercise will allow students to work through objective setting in an organization of familiarity. One hour of time outside of class and approximately twenty minutes of class time to review objectives will be needed for this exercise.

Directions

1. The instructor should review the textbook chapter's material on setting objectives and relate the importance of this process to the overall success of an organization, including the students' college.
2. Assign each student the task of developing at least three organizational objectives for the college as a whole and at least three departmental objectives for the business department. Both sets of objectives should have short-range and long-range examples. The assignment is to be written and turned in at the next class meeting.
3. On the due date of the assignment, ask for volunteers to share their objectives with the class. Since some students may feel insecure sharing their work on an assignment like this, the instructor may need to call on class members in the absence of volunteers. When calling on students to participate, limit each student to only one or two objectives each. This will allow the instructor sufficient time to include a large number of participants.
4. While the students are orally sharing their objectives with the class, the instructor might wish to list the objectives on a chalkboard or overhead transparency under the categories "Organization Objectives" and "Departmental Objectives."
5. The instructor may analyze and clarify how the various organizational departmental objectives are or are not related.
6. Collect assignments and grade according to the instructor's style and standards.

BUSINESS APPLICATION

Establishing Control Guidelines for a Restaurant

Activity

This activity is to be conducted during class and will involve reviewing the basic steps of the managerial controlling function and applying such to a restaurant setting. Approximately twenty-five minutes of class time will be needed.

Directions

1. The instructor should review the following four basic steps to the controlling function identified in the chapter:
   - Set standards for time, quality, and so on.
   - Measure performance (results).
   - Compare performance to standards.
   - Make necessary modifications.
2. The instructor should then explain how these four steps could be successfully applied to many organizations, including fast-food restaurants.
3. Beginning with the first step of the controlling process, ask students to write down examples of standards the manager of a fast-food restaurant might use. Indicate the standard should be numerically based if at all possible.

   After the class has been given an opportunity to come up with a list of standards, begin calling on various students to share their list with the class. As the students are sharing their standards with their peers, the instructor might begin writing some of the standards down on the chalkboard/overhead transparency.

   The instructor should review the list of standards obtained and lead the class in a discussion on how the manager might measure the performance (step 2 of the process).

   After comparing performance to standards (step 3 of the process), the instructor should lead the class in a discussion on what actions might be taken if performance either is short or exceeds the standards set.

Case

Balmer's Microsoft Style

Who is the Microsoft CEO? Bill Gates. No, it is Steve Balmer. At Microsoft, Bill Gates is still involved as the chairman and chief visionary, but the main manager and leader is Balmer. Both Gates and Balmer actually share power. However, Balmer leads the day-to-day operations.

Balmer's style is described in a lot of different ways. He is a team player, who has increased his power and authority over the years. Early in his Microsoft career, Balmer was the super-salesman and motivator. He was not an expert in how the company built products. He also was short of experience in how service had to be delivered. Now, as the leader, he must be involved with sales, production, marketing, and service. This involves a much broader set of roles than focusing on only one of these crucial areas.

It is Balmer's belief that his best style of managing and leading is to serve as a coach. He interprets coaching to mean you have to observe, support, facilitate, and encourage people. A coach also has to pick the right people. Once good people are in place, the coaching can take hold.

In addition to serving as "head coach," Balmer wants to empower Microsoft employees. He encourages Microsoft employees to build and nurture closer relationships with Microsoft customers and partners by using personal relationships and software to build a stronger bond with them.

The leadership attributes that are used to describe Balmer are the following: focused, hard charging, dynamic, sincere, funny, and passionate. Whether a person can be trained to improve any of these attributes to lead a company is debatable.

With his college friend Bill Gates, Balmer has helped to create a very powerful company. Through his style and leadership attributes, Steve Balmer is steering the company and using his style to create a high charged, motivationally rich atmosphere. Most Microsoft employees thrive in this kind of atmosphere. Balmer's ability to lead over an extended period of time will be tested more and more as Microsoft is challenged by competitors and also attempts to respond to government reviews of the firm's business practices.

Questions for Discussion

1. Would Steve Balmer's college friendship with Bill Gates be the primary reason for promoting and retaining him as Microsoft's CEO?
2. Is Balmer a manager or a leader? Why?
3. How can two individuals such as Gates and Balmer share power at Microsoft?

Sources: Dan Gilmor, "Balmer at the Helm," *Silicon Valley News*, March 1, 2001, pp. 1–4; and "Steve Balmer, Chief Executive Office, Microsoft Corp.," *Microsoft News*, January 2, 2002, p. 8.

8

Organizational Design and Teamwork

Photo: comstock.com

Chapter Objectives

After completing this chapter, you should be able to:

1 **Define** the term *organizing*.

2 **Describe** formal and informal organizations.

3 **Distinguish** between line and staff authority.

4 **Discuss** centralized versus decentralized decision-making authority.

5 **Identify** what a manager can learn about an organization by reviewing an organizational chart.

6 **Identify** the principles of organizing.

7 **Compare** the advantages and disadvantages of functional, product, and territorial structures.

8 **Explain** what types of structures combine to form a matrix organization.

9 **Discuss** modern organizational designs such as virtual and adaptive organizations.

Ameritrade Attempts Structural Changes

1 ☞ **A**meritrade Holding Corp., the Omaha discount broker that made its name offering cheap online trades at the height of the bull-market-driven web trading frenzy, is looking to reinvent itself—though not dramatically—for a starker market environment. In mid-2001 the company reorganized its businesses into two units—one focusing on private clients and retail customers, the other on institutional clients. Ameritrade said it would pursue a segmentation strategy dictated by customers' service requirements and charge fees accordingly.

The company also reshuffled its executives and formed a new management committee, whose head is chief executive Joseph Moglia. Mr. Moglia joined Ameritrade in spring 2001 and was given the task of making it better able to weather rougher times. Ameritrade, along with its competitors, has had to lay off staff in an effort to plug up revenue leaks.

Ameritrade's restructuring is somewhat similar to initiatives at other discount brokers that have sought to target different customer brackets—in some cases higher-net-worth individuals—to counter declining revenues.

2 ☞ Several of its competitors, including Charles Schwab 3, 4 ☞ Corp., CSFBdirect, and E-Trade Group, have also embraced a bricks-and-mortar approach, opening service centers to aid and advise the newly gun-shy. But setting up a branch network is not currently on Ameritrade's agenda, Mr. Moglia, said. "Is bricks-and-mortar in the best interest of our clients? We would have to look at it from a cost-benefit analysis," Mr. Moglia said. "It may be a good thing, but it would be very expensive to build. One solution would be to seek alliances with a company that already has branches," he said.

"The current changes at Ameritrade will make it more nimble," Mr. Moglia said. On the private client side, it will offer services for four market segments. For its customers who require no tools and no customer service it will extend its existing Freetrade offering. Customers trade for free because Ameritrade makes money on "payment for order flow" deals with brokers in exchange for steering business their way. Those who want more tools and services can still use Ameritrade Brokerage, for $8 a trade. But analysts wondered whether Ameritrade's efforts were too little too late. "This is not new—they're the laggards," said Eric Wasserstrom, an analyst with UBS Warburg. "Their model was ☜ 5 appropriate for a certain market environment that will likely not exist again."

Time will tell if Ameritrade's attempts to reinvent itself through organizational structure changes pay off. In reality, the firm had little choice in the matter. Severe market conditions required some type of internal changes. Worth considering is whether more astute leadership could have instituted changes before the crisis and whether that would have made a difference in the firm's competitive position.

Source: Adapted from Niamh Ring and Deborah Bach, "Ameritrade Revamps Structure and Lineup," *American Banker*, June 28, 2001, pp. 1–2.

8-1 INTRODUCTION

Organizational structure is an incredibly important, yet often overlooked, component of the success or failure of a business. The way businesses arrange and manage lines of authority, decision making, and communication can impact profitability, customer service, and employee morale. Structures that require too much formality and long decision-making processes are often derided as "bureaucracies." Employees often report being stifled in such environments, feeling as though they cannot act on even the most routine issues without permission from one or more superiors. Other structures are far too loose, resulting in sloppy service, lost business, and employee grievances. Badly structured organizations are difficult for customers to work with and tend to have a "no one's in charge" culture.

Businesses such as Ameritrade, discussed in the opening vignette, must find the correct balance between structure and freedom, authority and empowerment, and between speedy decision making and sound decision making. As an organization's competitive environment changes, as it did in the case of Ameritrade, managers must confront the possibility that the organizational structure may also have to change. A new focus on "adaptive organizations" suggests that firms that are able to change their structure rapidly in response to environmental and competitive challenges are more likely to sustain long-term profitability.

The issues and choices involved in organizational structure decisions is the subject of this chapter. First, we discuss why businesses organize, and then we examine some basic decisions made in organizing a business. Next, we review the principles of organizing, followed by a discussion of the various structures for organizing a business. Finally, we discuss several factors affecting organizational structure in recent years, including downsizing, virtual organizations, and adaptive organizations.

8-2 WHY ORGANIZE?

Organizing   The management function of grouping people and assignments to carry out job tasks and the mission.

Organizing is the management function of assigning activities and grouping people (designing and developing a blueprint or structure) so that the firm's objectives can be accomplished.

When a business grows from a one-person operation to one with several or more employees, structure becomes necessary. For example, as a firm grows, some employees may need to specialize, more interpersonal interactions may be required to accomplish complex goals, and integrating diverse viewpoints to improve competitiveness may be necessary. Some type of organizational structure is needed for things to run smoothly. Managers must design and implement the way a business will be organized. Unfortunately, for many businesses, organizational structure is not planned. Most organizations have structures in place that evolved over time in fits and starts, shaped more by internal politics than by competitive pressures.[1]

Organizational Structure   The arrangement of work to be done by a business.

In organizing a business, management (an individual or a group) usually decides what each person will do and how much authority each will have. The **organizational structure** is intended to help the business accomplish its objectives by arranging the work to be done. There is really no one best way to organize.[2] The "how to organize" decision for a particular business depends on many different factors, including organizational size, market, number of employees, competition, history, and available financial resources. Each firm must find the particular organizational structure that works best for its people and organizational goals. What works for Oracle, for example, may not be what is best for Sun, Microsoft, Cisco, or other competitors. If there is a sound lesson about organizing, it would be: "Observe what your competitors are doing, but arrange your structure in a way that is best for your firm, its employees, and the objectives the enterprise seeks to accomplish."

6 ☞
7, 8, 9 ☞

8-3 ORGANIZING FUNDAMENTALS

Although differences in objectives, resources, and markets mean that different organizing strategies should be used, a knowledgeable manager will proceed with caution. Understanding the fundamentals can be helpful in earning a reasonable profit or operating a business efficiently. Reengineering is a concept that emphasizes rethinking how organizing occurs.

A number of issues that managers need to consider in any type of organizing decision are discussed next to illustrate that managerial action is needed to help make organizations efficient.

8-3a Clear Objectives

As discussed in Chapter 7, *objectives* are desired operating results or targets. Having clearly stated, meaningful, specific, and challenging objectives is important for organizations to be effective. They give meaning to the business—and to the work done by employees—by determining what it is attempting to accomplish. The multiple objectives (e.g., profit, market share, human resource development) of a business provide the direction for those organizing the firm. Objectives also provide the framework for recruiting and hiring the

1. Michael Goold and Andrew Campbell, "Do You Have a Well Designed Organization?," *Harvard Business Review,* March 2002, pp. 117–124.

2. Lee Tom Perry, *Offensive Strategy* (New York: Harper & Row, 1990), p. 13.

type of human resources needed. Organizational structure is a major part of setting and realizing business objectives. Genzyme Corporation, one of a handful of biotech companies that actually make money, uses an innovative structure to ensure it meets business objectives. For example, the company has a nine-lawyer patent office. Each lawyer works for a separate research and development (R&D) division of the company to ensure that its intellectual property, licensing, and patent contracts and paperwork are in order. This enables the R&D people to focus on what they do best—creating new products for Genzyme markets.[3]

10

8-3b Coordination

Organizational, departmental, subunit, and individual objectives must fit together. This means the efforts of individual employees must be coordinated, or interwoven. **Coordination** requires everyday, informal communication with and among employees.

Any organizational structure, no matter how complicated, requires someone or some group to work continually on coordinating the activities of others. Managers and leaders can be the coordinators if they are respected and skilled in integrating the efforts of their subordinates or followers. Managers should not underestimate the effort that must go into coordination. Researcher Roger D'Aprix has identified the leader's communication skills as critical in coordinating the strategic efforts of the organization. As individuals work within discrete units, they can occasionally lose track of the larger organizational goals and objectives. D'Aprix says business leaders must ensure that employees have answers to six fundamental questions:

1. What is my job?
2. How am I doing?
3. Does anyone care?
4. How are we doing?
5. What are our vision, mission, and values?
6. How can I help?

Business leaders must ensure that they are communicating with employees across the organizational structure on these six questions.[4]

> **Coordination** Procedures that link the different plans, units, and parts of an organization to help achieve a firm's mission.

8-3c Formal and Informal Organizations

Two distinct organizations influence a company's employees. The **formal organization** is the one put together by management, created by those who have authority, responsibility, and accountability. The formal organization is displayed in the *organizational chart*, the graphical representation of the formal structure of the business. A formal organization dictates the relationships among people and resources. Ideally, these are organized in an optimal way to facilitate the accomplishment of the work of the organization. A company puts in place a formal organization to maximize its human and other resources; this formal organization depends greatly on what the company wants to accomplish.[5]

Informal organizations exist in every business. Not planned or displayed on an organizational chart, the **informal organization** is the network of personal and social relationships that emerges when people work together. The informal organization is a complex network in that the relationships between its members cannot be diagrammed like the formal organization, yet they are just as important to the smooth operation of a company. By their nature, they are different for every company and are continually experiencing change. This organization is made up of ad hoc work groups and friendships among employees that

> **Formal Organization**
> The management-designed, official structure of the business.

> **Informal Organization**
> The network of personal and social relationships that emerges when people work together.

3. Bruce Rubenstein, "Working with Business Units, Genzyme Finds Patented Success," *Corporate Legal Times*, February 1, 2002, p. 14.

4. "Reinventing the Strategic Communicator," *Strategic Communication Management*, August/September, 2001, pp. 32–35.

5. W. H. Weiss, "The Science and Art of Managing," *Supervision*, March 1999, pp. 11–15.

cross functional lines. Noted for its spirit of cooperation and service, the informal organization is seen as the human side of the formal organization. The intangible nature or culture of the organization distinguishes one company from another.[6]

8-3d Organizational Chart

Organizational Chart
A graphic blueprint, or map, of positions, people, and formal authority relationships in the organization.

A graphical presentation of the formal structure of a business is the **organizational chart.** It maps positions, people, and their authority and reporting relationships. The organizational chart shows authority, the location of responsibility, and to whom subordinates report. Exhibit 8-1 illustrates a simple line authority organizational chart. Each position is represented by a box (with a title), and straight lines represent the flow of authority. Exhibit 8-2 shows a chart expanded to include staff authority. The legal counsel is a staff position advising the president on legal matters. By way of contrast, the director of engineering exercises line authority over three project engineer supervisors.

Because it cannot picture informal relationships, the chart does not show exact communication patterns. For example, a worker communicating directly with another worker in a different department would represent an informal organizational activity. Organizational charts also don't picture workplace teams that leaders have organized to solve particular problems. Working on cross-functional teams can be difficult for some employees if they become confused about to whom they are to report and how their performance will be evaluated. Businesses that use such teams must be sure to provide team members with clear instructions, including their reporting responsibilities.[7]

Organizational charts offer only a general view of the formal structure at a specific time. Every chart needs continual updating as changes in environment, personnel, resources, size, and technology occur.

8-3e Formal Authority

Formal Authority The right to give orders.

Hierarchy Refers to the authority and reporting lines within an organization.

Delegation Giving an employee at a lower level in the organization the responsibility for a given task as well as the authority to carry it out.

The right to give orders and set policy constitutes **formal authority.** In organizations, formal authority is organized according to a **hierarchy,** where one manager may have authority over some employees, while simultaneously being subject to the formal authority of a superior.

It is widely recognized today that effective organizations require that managers delegate much of their authority to employees. **Delegation** is the process by which authority is distributed or pushed downward in an organization. Failure to delegate creates two problems: (1) It forces managers to do work that others could do more effectively and more economically, and (2) managers will have less time to focus on the projects and tasks for which they are better qualified.[8]

Organizational structure determines the pattern for delegation of authority. It establishes common understanding between the manager and the employee about the degree and type of authority delegated. Two major types of authority used in organizational structural arrangements are line and staff. Managers should understand these distinctions to know how much decision-making freedom they have.

Line Authority

Line Authority Unquestioned, direct authority to make decisions and take action.

11 ☞

Each position in the managerial hierarchy has **line authority,** or direct authority over lower positions in the hierarchy. A manager with line authority is the unquestioned superior for all activities of his or her subordinates. At a McDonald's restaurant, for example, the manager has authority over the salesclerks and the cooks. In a manufacturing firm, the foreman has authority over line workers, and the division manager has authority over the foreman.

---

6. Ibid.

7. Thomas J. Hackett, "Giving Teams a Tune-Up," *HR Focus,* November 1997, pp. 11–12.

8. Susan Wilson and Malia Boyd, "Delegate!," *Incentive,* April 1995, pp. 67–69.

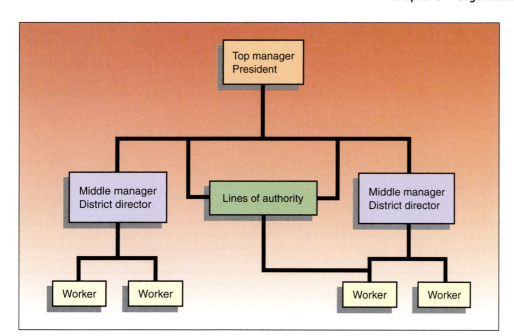

**Organizational Chart:
Line Authority**

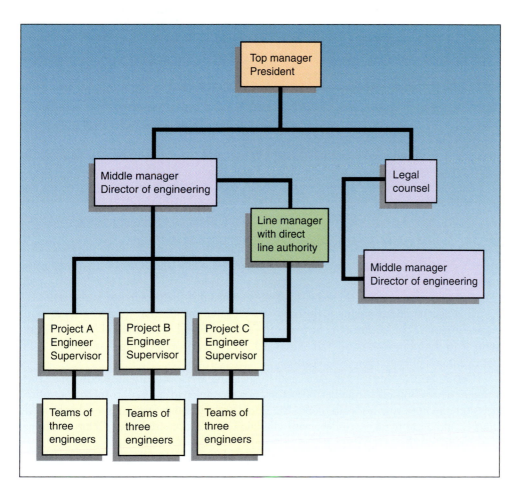

E X H I B I T 8 - 2

**Organizational Chart:
Line and Staff Authority**

Advantages and Disadvantages of Line and Staff Authority

Advantages	Disadvantages
Line Authority	
Everything kept simple.	Neglects advisers.
Authority relationship graphically illustrated by hierarchy.	Too many decisions to make in short time period.
Close to employees so decisions can be made quickly.	Requires very skilled line managers.
Staff Authority	
Uses the best experts.	Confusing to some employees.
Frees line managers for day-to-day activities.	Creates line-staff conflicts.
Can be used as screening and training arena for future line managers.	Places staff in subservient role.

Staff Authority

Staff Authority An advisory authority in which a person studies a situation and makes recommendations but has no authority to take action.

A person with **staff authority,** which is advisory authority, studies a situation and makes recommendations but has no authority to take action. For example, many firms have a legal department that provides counsel on legal issues important to the firm. The legal department can make recommendations about actions and their implications, but as a staff function, it has no authority to carry out those recommendations.

The backbone of most organizational structures is line authority. Staff authority is narrower because staff expertise comes as advice, which may not be used by the line manager. In structuring a business, managers may use both line and staff authority. Managers should be aware of potential conflict between line and staff divisions of an organization. Since line functions are typically considered to be "operational" (i.e., contributing to the "bottom line") and staff functions are considered to be "support," tensions can arise between line and staff units. Being aware of this possible tension can help to minimize its impact if it should occur.[9]

Exhibit 8-3 summarizes some of the advantages and disadvantages of each of these forms of authority.

8-3f Centralization and Decentralization

Centralized Business
An organization in which all, or nearly all, authority to make decisions is retained by a small group of managers.

Decentralized Business
An organization in which a significant amount of the authority to make decisions is delegated to lower-level managers.

Another important organizational consideration is the amount of authority to delegate. In a **centralized business,** only a small amount of authority is delegated. A relatively small number of managers make the decisions and hold most of the power and authority.

In a **decentralized business,** authority is delegated rather than held by a small management group. The authority continuum in centralized and decentralized business is presented in Exhibit 8-4. The table includes a comparison of some advantages and disadvantages of each type of delegation.

Organizations often move back and forth along the centralized-decentralized continuum, depending on a number of factors. For example, in a crisis, a more centralized decision-making structure is often both warranted and desirable. Decisions need to be made quickly and actions taken to deal with changing or volatile situations.[10] During normal

9. Peter G. Spanberger, "Line vs. Staff: Minimizing the Friction," *Executive Female*, January/February 1997, pp. 21–23.

10. Zhiang Lin and Kathleen M. Carley, "Organizational Design and Adaptation in Response to Crises: Theory and Practice," *Academy of Management Proceedings*, 2001, pp. B1–B6.

Advantages	Disadvantages

Most organizations lie somewhere on a continuum from centralized to decentralized authority.

Centralized

Increases uniformity of policies, rules, and procedures.	Places demands and pressure on a few managers.
Helps avoid duplication of effort and use of resources.	Reduces sense of involvement.
Increases uniformity of decision.	Gives large amount of power to a few managers.

Decentralized

Places decision making closer to action.	Makes coordination more difficult.
Gives individual decision makers more responsibility for their actions.	Limits availability of capable managers.
Helps develop managers for the future.	Lacks uniform policies.

Decentralized operation	**Centralized operation**
Maximum delegation of authority.	Little or no delegation of authority.

EXHIBIT 8-4

The Centralized-Decentralized Continuum of Authority

(i.e., noncrisis) periods, most firms today prefer a more decentralized structure that encourages employee empowerment and delegation of authority.[11]

An important management skill in a decentralized operation is delegation. This skill is the ability to pass on to an employee the responsibility for a given task, as well as the authority to carry it out. Can you delegate? Complete the values and attitudes quiz in Exhibit 8-5 and learn about your delegation skills.

8-4 PRINCIPLES OF ORGANIZING

Are delegation of authority, organizational charts, and formal and informal organizations all there is to organizing? No, other principles of organizing have been found to be effective through practice and experimentation. These principles have been considered in organizing large businesses (e.g., Procter & Gamble and Boeing), medium-sized businesses (e.g., Starbucks, SmartForce), and small businesses (e.g., Pragmatech).

Principles are guidelines for decision making; they are not laws etched in stone. Sometimes principles should be used exactly as they are stated; other times they should be modified or completely ignored. Managers must learn through experience when and where to use principles or to modify them. In general, those responsible for developing organizational structure keep a number of principles in mind. Many principles are available to consider, but we have selected just a few of the more important ones that need to be kept in mind in nearly any type of organization:

- Division of labor
- Unity of command
- Scalar principle
- Span of control
- Workplace teams

📧 12, 13
📧 14, 15, 16

Principles Guidelines that managers can use in making decisions.

11. Riccardo Peccei and Patrice Rosenthal, "Delivering Customer-Oriented Behavior Through Empowerment: An Empirical Test of HRM Assumptions," *Journal of Management Studies*, September 2001, pp. 831–857.

Directions: Place an **X** on the number that indicates how important you think the skill is for delegating job assignments or decision-making power. Circle the number that indicates how much of the skill you now possess.

	Very important/ significant				Not important/ little
1. Trusting the ability of other people.	5	4	3	2	1
2. Delegating meaningful, not just routine, jobs to others.	5	4	3	2	1
3. Coaching and helping others with a new job.	5	4	3	2	1
4. Sharing power and authority.	5	4	3	2	1
5. Following up to let individuals know how they are doing.	5	4	3	2	1
6. Setting reasonable goals on what is to be accomplished.	5	4	3	2	1
7. Determining others' ability to make decisions.	5	4	3	2	1
8. The challenges of the delegated job are motivational.	5	4	3	2	1

Feedback: A person with a strong orientation toward delegation would score between 33 and 40. A score of 40 would result from placing an **X** on the number 5 for all eight items. Being a good delegator has several payoffs for a manager. First, delegating regular, routine tasks frees the manager's time for more important tasks. Second, employees develop and become more involved with the job because they have added responsibility. Third, having more varied tasks can break the monotony for the employee of doing the same job over and over again.

   Although delegation seems simple, it requires the manager to look closely at these factors:

1. Can the employee handle delegation?
2. What will be delegated? Is it clearly stated?
3. How will the person know he or she is doing a good job, especially in terms of the delegated tasks? Are there standards of performance?
4. Is the delegator available to answer questions, coach, and provide feedback?
5. Does the employee feel good after completing the delegated task?

Instead of rushing into delegation, the manager must carefully think these factors through. The quiz points to such managerial concerns as trust, coaching, sharing of power, and building in job challenge. The quiz also highlights points that managers need to address before deciding whether delegation is a useful organizing strategy for them. Think of a time when you delegated a job or task to someone. Did you feel comfortable about delegating?

8-4a   Division of Labor

Organizations of all sizes perform a wide variety of tasks. A basic principle of organizing is that a job can be performed more efficiently if the jobholder is allowed to specialize. This principle, called the **division of labor,** involves dividing a major task into separate smaller tasks or jobs. The major task of manufacturing textiles is divided into smaller tasks (jobs) of weaving, finishing, and needling. Adam Smith famously highlighted the power of the division of labor principle in his seminal book *The Wealth of Nations.* In that eighteenth-century economic treatise, Smith pointed out that an individual working alone could produce only a fraction of what a group of people, dividing labor logically among them, could produce. Using the simple example of a pin factory, Smith pointed out that a single person could only produce a small number of pins each day if that person had to perform all of the procedures in pin making. However, Smith pointed out, if labor were divided into

Division of Labor   A principle of organization that a job can be performed more efficiently if the jobholder is allowed to specialize.

separate production tasks handled by separate individuals, the number of pins that could be produced was exponentially greater than the number that could be produced by those individuals working alone.[12]

The efficiency achieved by becoming an expert in a small task can be significant. However, breaking a job into smaller and smaller tasks can be overdone. Dividing labor into small, boring jobs that offer no mental challenge can result in employees feeling frustrated, having low levels of job satisfaction, and seeking employment elsewhere.

8-4b Unity of Command

The principle of **unity of command** states that no member of an organization should report to more than one superior. Subordinates need to know from whom they receive the authority to make decisions and do the job. Conflicting orders from different superiors should be avoided; they can cause confusion, result in contradictory instructions, and create frustration about which order to follow. This principle can be followed easily in an organization having only line authority. However, when a staff and line authority structure is used, the unity of command principle is often violated.

> **Unity of Command**
> The principle of organization that no employee should report to more than one superior.

8-4c Scalar Principle

That authority and responsibility should flow in a clear, unbroken line from the highest to the lowest manager is called the **scalar principle.** When managerial levels are arranged in a hierarchy, the importance of the scalar chain from top to bottom is obvious. Breaking the chain would result in uncertainty about authority relationships, which would in turn lead to confusion and frustration for employees.

An extension of the scalar principle is the notion that authority should equal responsibility. For example, suppose a production supervisor at Lockheed-Martin has been assigned the responsibility to purchase new plant equipment. It would be important for this supervisor to have the authority to determine what price should be paid for the new equipment. Without this authority, how could the supervisor be held responsible for the decision?

> **Scalar Principle**   The principle of organization that authority and responsibility should flow in a clear, unbroken line from the highest to the lowest manager.
>
> ✍ 17

8-4d Span of Control

The concept of **span of control** refers to the number of subordinates reporting to a supervisor, or boss. The span of control principle says there is a limit to the number of subordinates one superior can supervise effectively. Managers using this principle often specify an exact number of subordinates. This is unrealistic, however, because some supervisors can handle more subordinates than others. The optimum span of control depends on many factors, such as the type of skill and the experience levels of subordinates, the nature of the job, the supervisor's skill in handling subordinates, the situation, and the time available to do the job.

In general, highly skilled employees require less supervision than the less skilled. This permits the manager to have a wide span of control—that is, a larger group of employees reporting to him or her. For example, a single manager can supervise a large group of highly skilled technicians in a 3M research and development unit. On the other hand, an open-heart surgery team at St. Joseph Hospital in Chicago involves highly skilled employees but a narrow span of control. Exhibit 8-6 illustrates wide and narrow spans of control.

The optimum span of control depends on many factors. Rather than a universal set of numbers, managers have only general suggestions to examine the total picture—the managers, subordinates, job, resources, and time available. Additionally, some companies have been able to widen the span of control, and eliminate layers of middle managers, through use of information technology. In fact, some of the employees managed through

> **Span of Control**   The principle of organization that limits the number of subordinates reporting to a supervisor.
>
> ✍ 18

---

12. Adam Smith, *The Wealth of Nations* (London: Dent Publishing, 1957).

8-5 HOW TO ORGANIZE A BUSINESS

A person involved in organizing a business should identify the business objectives, the types of people working for the business, the technology, and the environment in which the business operates. If you've ever been in a house in which the rooms are too small or poorly arranged, you know the importance of the notion that "form follows function." That principle is also important in making organizational structure decisions. People making decisions about structure need to examine the functions before selecting a form (i.e., the structure).

Numerous forms, or designs, of structure are available to managers. Each way of organizing a business has advantages and disadvantages. A manager has to weigh all of these in making a selection. When the decision is made without considering disadvantages, the resulting choice may be the least effective or least suitable structure. The designs we present here are the most popular and widely used structures in business organizations.

8-5a Functional Structure

> **Functional Structure**
> A structure in which each unit or department has a different set of activities and responsibilities.

Each unit or department in the **functional structure** has a different set of activities and responsibilities. In a manufacturing firm, this means that engineering, manufacturing, and marketing would be separate departments. In a hospital, functional structure would include departments of nursing, housekeeping, medical records, radiology, and so forth. A functional structure for a county hospital is shown in Exhibit 8-7.

Advantages

The functional structure orients workers toward a specific set of activities. For example, the engineer focuses on product design and improvement, and the salesperson works on selling. These functional experts become even more skilled in their areas. Research shows that the functional structure works well for a firm operating in a relatively stable (unchanging or slowly changing) environment.[15] Glass and building material companies such as Corning, PPG Industries, and Johns Manville operate in a normally stable environment. Product lines change little from year to year, so the arrangement used is a functional structure.

20, 21, 22 ☞

Disadvantages

The functional structure de-emphasizes the exchange of ideas and cooperation with other departments. The boundary between, say, marketing and engineering is imaginary, but it can in some organizations be as impregnable as the Great Wall of China. Some companies, and even entire industries, have become inefficient because of the functional "silos" into which they have been divided. For example, financial services companies are beset with traditional functional distinctions that often prevent them from offering high levels of customer service.[16] This happens in large measure because each department is evaluated on the basis of its own performance. Knowing they will be evaluated this way, managers concentrate on departmental matters instead of overall organizational objectives.

If the business's objectives and environment require coordination across departments, the functional structure becomes an obstruction. Problems arise that have no single departmental solution. As a result, the problems go unresolved, the buck is passed, or problems are pushed up to top management.

In summary, functional structures are best suited for businesses with a relatively stable environment, such as Corning. At Corning the organizational structure takes advantage of technical expertise. On the other hand, in an environment with numerous style changes, such as that of Liz Claiborne, a functional structure would lack flexibility and be slow in reacting. Liz Claiborne has to react quickly to fashion changes.

23 ☞

---

15. Chris Argyris, *Overcoming Organizational Defenses* (Englewood Cliffs, NJ: Prentice Hall, 1990).

16. Lawrence W. Borgen, "Focus on Customers," *Best's Review,* November 2001, pp. 49–51.

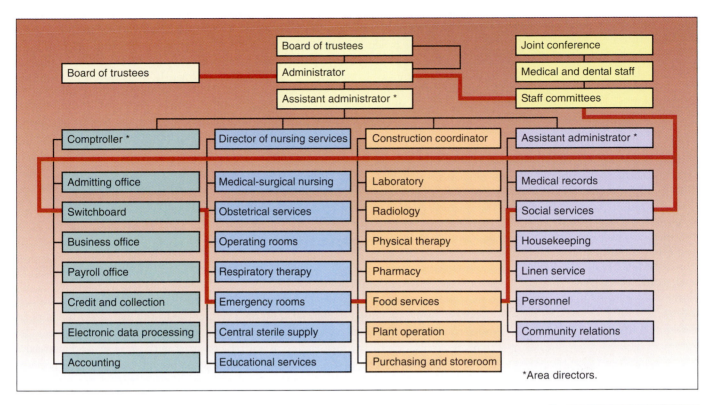

Board of trustees		
Board of trustees	Administrator	Joint conference
	Assistant administrator *	Medical and dental staff
		Staff committees

Comptroller * — Director of nursing services — Construction coordinator — Assistant administrator *

Admitting office	Medical-surgical nursing	Laboratory	Medical records
Switchboard	Obstetrical services	Radiology	Social services
Business office	Operating rooms	Physical therapy	Housekeeping
Payroll office	Respiratory therapy	Pharmacy	Linen service
Credit and collection	Emergency rooms	Food services	Personnel
Electronic data processing	Central sterile supply	Plant operation	Community relations
Accounting	Educational services	Purchasing and storeroom	

*Area directors.

8-5b   Product Structure

Businesses producing a wide variety of products often establish a **product structure.** Consumer products giant Procter & Gamble (P&G) used the product structure as early as 1927. At that time, a new women's soap product, Camay, was not selling well. A young executive, Neil McElroy (who later became the company's president), was told to give his exclusive attention to increasing the sales of the product. McElroy took the (at the time) revolutionary step of introducing product managers into the structure of the sales division. This simple change led to rapid increases in sales of Camay, due to the increased focus of product managers. Soon afterward P&G added other product managers in other lines of its business.

Today many firms, especially those in the food (Pillsbury), toiletries (Gillette), and chemical (W. R. Grace) industries, use product structures. Kraft Foods, for example, uses a product structure in its Post Division, in which separate product managers are in charge of cereals, pet foods, and beverages.

Advantages

The product structure places responsibility for a product or product line with the managers. For example, in the wake of the dramatic drop in spending on consumer electronics, Ericsson undertook a product structure to place increased focus on individual product markets. This reorganization helped the Swedish consumer electronics maker generate new business in a range of international markets.[17] Instead of a department orientation, as with the functional structure, the focus is on product.

In addition, the product structure encourages creativity. One study found that businesses with product structures were more successful in creating and selling new products than were businesses without product structures.[18] The product structure also is flexible enough to cope with changing environments. People have to cooperate so that the product will perform well.

17. Phil Jones, "Ericsson Unveils New Structure and Appoints COO to Govern It," *Network Briefing Daily*, August 20, 2001, p. 1.

18. Authur H. Walker and Jay Lorsch, "Organizational Choice: Product versus Function," *Harvard Business Review*, November/December 1968, pp. 129–138.

EXHIBIT 8-7

Functional Structure in a Hospital

This chart reflects the line responsibility and authority in the hospital organization. However, a great part of the work of the hospital is accomplished through informal interaction between the identified services and functions. These functional working relationships are encouraged. Where there is difference in understanding or changes in procedure are required, the line organization should be carefully observed.

✆ 24, 25, 26, 27

✆ 28

Product Structure
An organizational structure in which a manager is placed in charge of and has responsibility for a product or product line.

Disadvantages

The price of the product structure can be high. Product managers often are not given enough authority to carry out responsibilities; therefore, they have to spend a lot of time coordinating activities so that people work together efficiently. This means less time for planning. Often they are told that they are like presidents in their product area, but in fact they are usually only referees and low-level coordinators.

Managers have also found that, compared with employees in functional structures, employees in product structures are more insecure and anxious about unemployment and personal development.[19] Perhaps this results from using product structures in relatively unstable, unpredictable environments. (Such environments reject products, even certain kinds of packages and names of products.) This unpredictability sometimes is stressful and produces anxiety because people's success depends on their product's success.

> **Territorial (Geographical) Structure** An organizational structure in which units are divided on the basis of territory or geographical region.

8-5c Territorial Structure

29 ☞

Businesses that divide units on the basis of location are using **territorial,** or **geographical, structure.** When adjustments to local conditions, markets, or resources are important, responsibility assigned on the basis of territory has advantages. For example, British Columbia furniture importer Hamilton & Spill reorganized itself based on territory in order to improve customer service in the face of increasing and stiff competition. The company undertook this reorganization as a means to assist with pre-sales and after-sales activities, service, and support.[20] This simple shift in structure has helped the firm maintain its competitive edge, without having to resort to costly price-based competition.

30, 31 ☞
32, 33, 34 ☞

Other merchandising organizations, such as Wal-Mart and Federated Department Stores, have found territorial structure attractive. Kroger, Safeway, and HEB also use territorial division structures, coupled with centralization of certain functions (e.g., purchasing and distribution). Division managers have authority to take advantage of regional cost, resource, and competitive conditions.

35 ☞

Transportation companies may also be structured by territory. Low-cost airline prices have eaten into long-distance bus travel. Today the average bus trip has decreased from about 500 miles to slightly over 200 miles. This type of competition encouraged Greyhound Lines' management to change the company from a functional to a territorial structure. Greyhound now has four territorial divisions: eastern, central, southern, and western. Customer needs in Phoenix are monitored and then met by the western division, while customer needs in Chicago are observed and handled by the central division. The territorial structure helps Greyhound be more responsive to consumer needs and better able to coordinate schedules, maintenance, replacement, and employee preferences in each region.[21]

Multinational corporations (MNCs) will typically use a territorial structure, dividing up the business by countries of operation. MNCs will usually appoint a "country manager," someone who is familiar with the country in which they are operating. IBM has recently abandoned that structure in favor of a product structure. Only time will tell whether that move will help its international business.[22]

Advantages

The main advantage of the territorial structure is that it allows coordination at the point of sale. This coordination can lead to more personalized and speedier service. In a territorial arrangement, customer needs can be better addressed.

---

19. E. Raymond Corey and Steven H. Star, *Organization Strategy: A Marketing Approach* (Cambridge, MA: Division of Research, Graduate School of Business Administration, Harvard University, 1970).

20. "Hamilton & Spill Changes Reps' Titles," *Furniture/Today,* December 24, 2001, p. 14.

21. "Greyhound Splitting into Four to Go After Short Haul Trade," *Chicago Tribune,* April 30, 1986 pp. 3, 8.

22. Ira Sager and Gail Edmondson, "Big Blue Wants the World to Know Who's Boss," *Business Week,* September 26, 1994, p. 78.

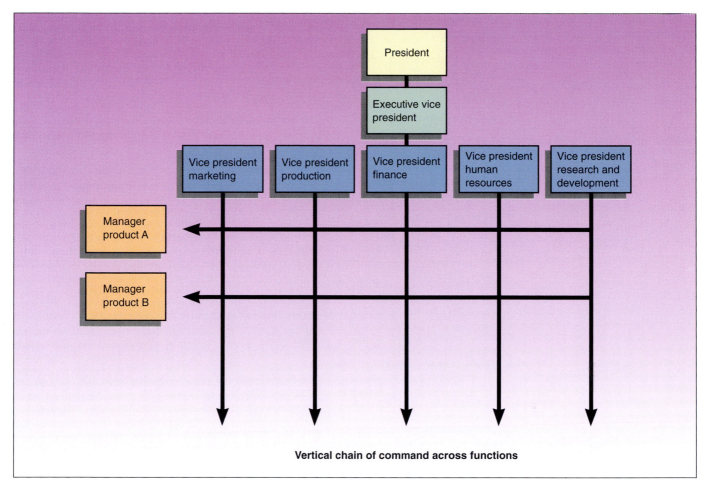

Vertical chain of command across functions

EXHIBIT 8-8

A Matrix Structure

Disadvantages

Some duplication of effort occurs in the territorial structure. Also, the corporation needs to hire, train, and develop managers with the broad-based ability and technical knowledge required to manage multiple functions such as sales, production, and marketing.

8-5d Matrix Structure

Occasionally a company utilizes a functional structure and either a product or a project structure simultaneously; that is, it combines functional structure and a second management arrangement into a **matrix structure.** This structure runs counter to the unity-of-command principle of organizing because employees report to more than one boss. In a matrix structure, employees are assigned to both a functional department (permanent home) and a particular product or project (temporary home).[23] Exhibit 8-8 shows a matrix structure with five functional departments and three projects staffed by employees from the departments.

Why have the matrix, when it obviously runs counter to the principle of unity of command? Recall the weaknesses of functional and product structures. The functional structure de-emphasizes the exchange of ideas and cooperation, although it does permit specialists to interact and strive for technical excellence. The product structure is weaker at encouraging job security, although it is strong at inducing cooperation, adhering to schedules, and controlling costs. The matrix design gains the strengths of both while

Matrix Structure A functional structure combined with either a product or a project structural arrangement.

23. Steven C. Dunn, "Motivation by Project and Functional Managers in a Matrix Organization," *Engineering Management Journal*, June 2001, pp. 3–9.

avoiding the disadvantages of either. Matrix structures have been used in diverse organizational types:

- Manufacturing: aerospace, chemicals, electronics
- Service: banking, insurance, retailing
- Professional: accounting, consulting, law
- Nonprofit: hospitals, United Nations, universities

Advantages

The matrix structure responds effectively to three conditions. First, a matrix can handle a dual focus. For example, the company may need to respond to two equally important environmental pressures. Aerospace firms such as Lockheed Martin and Boeing must meet both technical requirements and customer cost constraints. While the manager argues for more money to improve the product technically, the product manager argues for meeting budget constraints. The dual focus of technical and cost interests is possible in the matrix structure.

Second, requirements for communication among employees may exceed the capacity of a traditional functional structure. Environmental uncertainty, work complexity, and interdependence of departments increase as a business grows and diversifies its products and markets. The functional structure does not encourage cooperation and a total team spirit.[24] A structure is needed that encourages the sharing of information. The matrix gives the cross-functional benefits of a product structure while keeping the administrative controls of the functional structure.

Third, performance, cost, and time pressures require greater sharing and use of resources. Placing limited resources in only one department results in a monopolization of the resources. When talented engineers, physicists, computer specialists, and other skilled professionals are in scarce supply, several groups, projects, or units must share the talent and resources. In the matrix structure, talent and resources can be moved from project to project. Priorities for the use of the limited resources are measured against the overall business objectives and interests. The matrix makes this shifting of resources easier.

Disadvantages

If the matrix always worked for every business, it would always be used. There are, however, problems with the matrix. Some of the most frequently cited include:[25]

- Confusion about who reports to whom, and when.
- Power struggles between functional and product managers.
- Groupthink, or too much group decision making.
- "Meetingitis," or just too much time wasted in one meeting after another.
- The tendency to become "papermills." To ensure cooperation and coordination, everyone puts everything in writing. The result is a seemingly endless paper output.
- Excessive costs of having more managers to compensate.

The advantages of the matrix structure seem to outweigh its problems. Nevertheless, this type of organizational structure is not for everyone. The manager with two bosses must work very well with people. Would you be able to work with two bosses—one functional and one product? Think about some of the conflicts you might face. Suppose each wanted you to attend a different important meeting at 10 A.M. or to attend training seminars, one in Los Angeles and one in Boston, on the same date. Having more than one boss contradicts the principle of unity of command.

24. David R. Belasco, "Team Up for Success," *Strategic Finance,* May 2000, pp. 54–59.

25. John M. Ivancevich, Peter Lorenzi, Steven J. Skinner, and Philip B. Crosby, *Management: Quality and Competitiveness* (Burr Ridge, IL: Irwin, 1994), pp. 271–273.

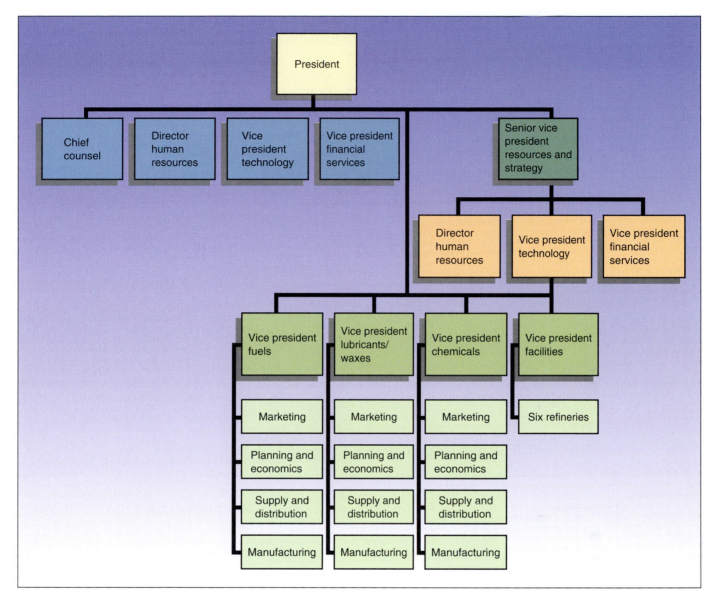

8-5e Multiple Structures

We have been discussing forms of structure as if they were an either/or choice. In reality a business is free to use any form or combination of structures. An example of a *multiple structure* appears in Exhibit 8-9. Each division has its own functional departments of marketing, planning and economics, supply and distribution, and manufacturing. Sun also has a number of centralized functions, such as human resources, technology, public affairs, and facilities. The multiple organizational structures enable the refineries to produce products for the three product divisions.

A Multiple Structure

Advantages

Companies use multiple structures to gain the benefits of each arrangement. Perhaps the biggest advantage of the multiple structure is that it encourages management to look at the total picture of organizing. This overall view stimulates a total-company enthusiasm and a realization that each part or unit is important in accomplishing corporate objectives.

Disadvantages

Potential drawbacks to multiple structures are increased management overhead expenses, duplication of resources, and conflict between headquarters and product divisions. Problems in coordination of policies, programs, and resources arise often. Finally, a successful move from a single-structure arrangement to a multiple-structure system may take significant time and resources.

8-6   RECENT DEVELOPMENTS IN ORGANIZATIONAL STRUCTURE

We have been stating in this chapter that there is no single best way to structure an organization, while at the same time emphasizing that there are principles and guidelines that managers should follow. Many of the principles that have been described in this chapter apply to nearly any type of organization in nearly any competitive environment. As organizational research forges ahead, and as managers find new and better ways to organize, the old principles still apply and new ones are created.

Over the past several decades, a number of dynamic forces have been at work to change the way organizations must function to survive. For example, during the late 1980s and early 1990s, most organizations were thought to have accumulated too many layers of management and were becoming inefficient. A popular movement, known as **reengineering,** swept through organizations of all types, leading to the slashing of middle management layers. This *downsizing* process resulted in dramatically leaner organizations. We examine downsizing with the wisdom of hindsight in the next section, 8-6a. We also look at two other popular schools of thought regarding organizational structure: virtual organizations (section 8-6b) and adaptive organizations (section 8-6c).

Reengineering
An organizational change strategy that involves removing layers of middle managers and generally flattening the organizational hierarchy.

8-6a   Downsizing

The procedure of keeping levels in a managerial hierarchy to a minimum often means that **downsizing,** or cutting out entire layers of managers, is necessary. Communication, message distortion, personal contact, and feeling like a part of a team are factors addressed by this principle. As the levels, or layers, of management increase in an organization, so do the problems. The more levels of management, the longer the communication chain. This means more potential for message distortion. Moreover, top management and the lower levels have less contact as the distance from top to bottom increases. Finally, people feel more isolated as this distance increases, and there is a loss of team spirit, of pulling and working together.

Downsizing   Cutting out entire layers of management in the organization.

Organizations of all types and all over the world have from time to time needed to downsize in order to adjust to changing market or competitive conditions. For example, Nippon Petrochemicals decided to cut 200 jobs as part of a restructuring effort designed to cut costs amid low product prices and weak demand. The restructuring is designed to cut costs by $74 million.[26] This type of cost cutting, involving downsizing and/or layoffs, is common in many industries that are subject to regular business cycles. Many firms organize their downsizing efforts to minimize the impact on the employees that are let go. For example, it is possible for firms to reduce the labor force through natural attrition, early retirement plans, or even voluntary contract buyouts. It is becoming increasingly common for firms to be concerned about their laid-off employees since many of them could be rehired when business gets better. Another common tactic that firms use is to lay off employees and then retain them as contract laborers. This enables the firm to use the employees only as much as needed and avoids the need to pay for costly benefits and retirement programs.

36 ☞

26. Ian Young, "Nippon Petrochemicals to Cut Jobs as Part of Restructuring Effort," *Chemical Week*, February 20, 2002, p. 19.

FOCUS ON TECHNOLOGY

Extreme Telecommuting

It's 9:00 A.M., the start of another busy day, as Paolo Conconi logs on to read his e-mails. But instead of a business suit, he sports a bathing suit. And although his work is in Europe and China, his office is a table by the pool of his villa in Bali, Indonesia. As he goes through his mail, he sips his favorite Italian coffee. An attendant lights his cigarette.

Mr. Conconi has a lifestyle known as "extreme telecommuting"—work wholly unfettered by physical location. Pushing the promises of technology to the limit, this rare breed of telecommuters live countries—even continents—apart from their companies' home offices, indulging in a way of life others only dream about.

For American Greg LaMoshi, extreme telecommuting is the fulfillment of years of idle cubicle fantasies. Mr. LaMoshi works as the night editor for eRaider.com, a Manhattan-based financial website dedicated to corporate takeovers. He is not in Manhattan. Mr. LaMoshi makes his home along the shores of Bali, where there is roughly a twelve-hour time difference with New York. So, as night falls on New York, Mr. LaMoshi begins his overnight shift as the sun is rising in Bali, editing columns and message boards, and combing the Internet for new items. He often works from a garden terrace overlooking a water lily pond. Having long daydreamed of retirement on sunny beaches in an exotic locale, he says, "This was the opportunity to do all that, without the retire part."

Source: Kevin Voigt, "For 'Extreme Telecommuters,' Remote Work Means Really Remote," *The Wall Street Journal,* January 31, 2001, pp. B1, B7.

8-6b Virtual Organizations

Communications and information technologies have enabled a new way of organizing that has been growing increasingly popular—the virtual organization. The **virtual organization** is characterized by individual professionals who may or may not share office space, and who regularly communicate and collaborate via technology. In this regard, the notion of a virtual organization means a distributed workforce that is able to interact meaningfully and work together using computer and telecommunications technologies. Today, many firms boast workers who contribute significantly to the firm's bottom line but who have never set foot in the office. The Focus on Technology box, "Extreme Telecommuting," highlights several workers who have found they are able to make significant contributions to their organizations while working several thousands of miles from headquarters.

The virtual organization is based on the Internet. The file sharing and interactivity of the Web has made it possible for people to work together on projects no matter where they are, as long as they can connect to the Web. A fairly recent development is the use of corporate intranets or corporate portals for employees to collaborate on complex projects. As more employees familiarize and become comfortable working online, the virtual workplace continues to evolve. It's likely that this evolutionary process will continue to unfold and take on new configurations into the foreseeable future.

Virtual Organization
An organization that operates across space, time, and boundaries with members who communicate primarily through electronic technologies.

Advantages of Virtual Organizations

The following are some of the advantages of virtual organizations:

Reduced real estate expenses.   IBM saves 40 to 60 percent per site annually by eliminating offices for all employees except those who truly need them. Others estimate the savings at $2 for every $1 invested.

Increased productivity.   USWest reported that the productivity of its teleworking employees increased, some by as much as 40 percent.

Higher profits.   Hewlett-Packard doubled revenue per salesperson after moving its salespeople to virtual workplace arrangements.

Improved customer service.   Andersen Consulting found that its consultants spent 25 percent more time face-to-face with customers when they did not have permanent offices.

Access to global markets.   John Brown Engineers & Constructors Ltd., a member of the engineering division of Trafalgar House, the world's third-largest engineering and construction organization, with 21,000 employees around the globe, was able to access local pharmaceutical engineering talent at a project site in India. Using virtual work arrangements, the firm traversed national boundaries, enabling it to work with and present a local face to its global clients. This enhanced its global competitiveness.

Environmental benefits.   At Georgia Power, 150 people, or 13 percent of the workers at headquarters, are teleworkers. This has reduced annual commuting mileage by 993,000 miles, and automobile emissions by almost 35,000 pounds.

Disadvantages of Virtual Organizations

Offsetting these advantages, however, are some potentially serious disadvantages that managers should consider carefully before institutionalizing virtual organization arrangements:

Setup and maintenance costs.   For individual employees, the additional cost required to equip a mobile or home office varies from roughly $3,000 to $5,000, plus about $1,000 in upgrades and supplies every year thereafter. In addition, to be viable, virtual offices require online materials that can be downloaded and printed: databases on products and customers that are accessible from remote locations; well-indexed, automated central files that are accessible from remote locations; and a way to track the location of mobile workers. Technology is the remote worker's lifeline. In the absence of the administrative and technical support that one might find at the home office, the technology must work flawlessly, and technical support should be available twenty-four hours a day, seven days a week. Decision makers need to consider the incremental costs associated with setting up and maintaining virtual workplaces.

Loss of cost efficiencies.   When expensive equipment or services are concentrated in one location, multiple users can access them. When the same equipment or services are distributed across locations, cost efficiencies may be lost. For example, in the securities industry, certain real-time information sources are necessary. Most stock quotes are available on the Internet on a fifteen-minute delay, which is adequate for most people's needs. However, for brokers and traders quoting prices to customers, it is imperative that quotes be up-to-the-second. When a securities firm needs this information for fifty brokers, along with related services, it is more cost-effective to have all employees at one location, rather than working at many different locations.

Cultural issues.   Virtual organizations operating in the global arena often have to transfer their business policies and cultures to work with dispersed business teams across collaborating organizations, geography, and cultures. This can lead to potential clashes of business and national cultures, which, in turn, can undermine the entire alliance. If the members of a virtual organization or a virtual team are not empowered to make decisions, the technology that enables their collaboration will add little value, and the competitive advantage associated with rapid responses to demands in the marketplace will be lost.

Feelings of isolation.   Some level of social interaction with supervisors and coworkers is essential in almost all jobs. Without it, workers feel isolated and out of the loop with respect to crucial communications and contact with decision makers who can make or break their careers.

Lack of trust.   A key ingredient to the success of virtual work arrangements is trust that one's coworkers will fulfill their obligations and behave predictably. Lack of trust can undermine every other precaution taken to ensure successful virtual work arrangements, such as careful selection of employees to work in the virtual environment, thorough training of managers and employees, and ongoing performance management.[27]

To accomplish organizational goals in a virtual workplace, managers must learn to communicate effectively over new channels. Projects must be clearly delineated, with reasonable goals and performance benchmarks at regular intervals. Remote workers should be allowed to participate in decision making regarding who will be assigned to which projects.[28] In other words, remote employees should be treated the same as workers who are physically proximate. The virtual workplace, just like any other workplace, must treat individuals fairly and provide equal rewards for equal contributions to the firm. While remote workers often are individual "stars" who are self-motivated and highly creative, they should not be accorded special status.

8-6c Adaptive Organizations

Recent thinking in organizational design argues that fast, flexible workforces and information technologies are enabling organizations to become exceedingly adaptable. Many firms, in fact, have taken advantage of temporary help agencies and contract or "outsourced" labor to grow and shrink according to consumer and competitive demands. Some firms use novel techniques for launching new products or spinning off new ventures without risking their flagship brand.

Many modern business theorists use the analogy of biological systems when describing the **adaptive organization.** For example, in his book *Shaping the Adaptive Organization*, William Flumer says that managers, executives, and other business leaders must survey their organizational landscape. They must ask themselves: What is my business environment? Is it hierarchical or flat? How does it relate to other similar organizations? Leaders must first understand their organization before they can begin to change its structure to fit present circumstances.[29]

> **Adaptive Organization**
> An organization that is flexible enough to adjust or adapt to environmental changes, trends, and shifts.

In the adaptive organization, the role of the manager/leader is different from other types of organizations. For example, in creating a territorial structure, a manager lays down clear lines of responsibility and accountability. By way of contrast, the manager's role in creating an adaptive organization is to facilitate learning and adaptability on the margins of the organization. The learning and adapting is typically complex and subtle, best carried out by those who are on the front lines, so to speak. The manager's role in this situation is better described as facilitating or nurturing. People on the front lines are empowered to create structures best suited for them to achieve their objectives.

In general, the adaptive organization focuses on designing structure around business *processes* rather than *functions*. For example, one organization that's done a very good job of this is 3M Telecommunications Products. Roger Lacey, the head of the unit, has turned it into a process enterprise. When asked how he did it, Lacey said it was "muddling with a purpose." In other words, he knows where he want to get, but he's not going to try to get there all at once. He's going to adapt and learn along the way.[30]

27. Wayne F. Cascio, "Managing a Virtual Workplace," *Academy of Management Executive*, August 2000, pp. 81–90.

28. John M. Ivancevich and Thomas N. Duening, *Managing Einsteins: Leading High Tech Workers in the Digital Age* (Chicago: McGraw-Hill, 2002).

29. William E. Fulmer, *Shaping the Adaptive Organization* (New York: AMACOM, 2000).

30. Michael Hammer, "Processed Change," *The Journal of Business Strategy*, November/December 2001, pp. 11–15.

Of course, this adaptive approach to structure is not appropriate to all types of organizations. It is highly suited to start-up ventures seeking to find a fit for their products and/or services. It is also suited to organizations that have been through a crisis and are attempting to reestablish themselves. Established businesses with well-functioning territorial or product structures can use adaptive structures to explore new markets or new product lines.

Ultimately, the choice of the best organizational structure resides with managers. As we have been stating, the choice will be driven by a host of factors, such that it is impossible to prescribe the "one best approach" in a textbook. However, there are circumstances and situations in which particular structural types have proven to be effective. Using the principles and examples in this chapter should help you shorten your learning/experience curve when creating effective organizational structures to meet the inevitable challenges of organizational design.

SUGGESTED WEBSITES

Note: These websites were functional when we went to press. Please access the online text for the most up-to-date URLs.

1. www.ameritrade.com
2. www.charlesschwab.com
3. www.cfsbdirect.com
4. www.etrade.com
5. www.ubswarburg.com
6. www.oracle.com
7. www.sun.com
8. www.microsoft.com
9. www.cisco.com
10. www.genzyme.com
11. www.mcdonalds.com
12. www.pg.com
13. www.boeing.com
14. www.starbucks.com
15. www.smartforce.com
16. www.pragmatech.com
17. www.lockheedmartin.com
18. www.mmm.com
19. www.xerox.com
20. www.corning.com
21. www.ppg.com
22. www.jm.com
23. www.lizclaiborne.com
24. www.pillsbury.com
25. www.gillette.com
26. www.grace.com
27. www.kraftfoods.com
28. www.ericcson.com
29. www.hamiltonspill.com
30. www.walmart.com
31. www.federated-fds.com
32. www.kroger.com
33. www.safeway.com
34. www.heb.com
35. www.greyhound.com
36. www.npcc.co.jp/english/

SUMMARY OF LEARNING OBJECTIVES

1. *Define the term* organizing.   Organizing is the management function of grouping people and assigning activities so that the company's objectives can be accomplished.
2. *Describe formal and informal organizations.*   The formal organization is put together by management, created by individuals who have authority, responsibility, and accountability. The formal organization is depicted in the organizational chart. The informal organization is the network of personal and social relationships that emerge when people work together.
3. *Distinguish between line and staff authority.*   Managers with line authority have direct control over lower positions in the management hierarchy. Managers with staff authority can study a situation and make recommendations, but they have no authority to take action.
4. *Discuss centralized versus decentralized decision-making authority.*   In a centralized business, a relatively small number of managers make the decisions and hold most of the power and authority. Advantages of centralization include uniformity of policies, rules, and procedures; avoiding duplication of effort and use of resources; and uniform decisions. The disadvantages include greater pressure and demands on a few people, a reduced sense of involvement, and large amounts of power concentrated in a few people. In a decentralized business, authority is delegated to more levels of management. Decentralization places decision making closer to the action, gives decision makers more responsibility for their actions, and develops managers of the future—all advantages. The disadvantages include more difficult coordination, possible lack of capable managers, and lack of uniformity in policies.
5. *Identify what a manager can learn about an organization by reviewing an organizational chart.*   An organizational chart is a graphical presentation, or blueprint, of the formal structure of an enterprise. The chart shows people, their positions, and their authority relationships.
6. *Identify the principles of organizing.*   Division of labor involves dividing a major task into separate, smaller tasks to achieve greater efficiency. Unity of command means subordinates report to no more than one supervisor. The scalar principle states that authority should equal responsibility. Under span of control, the number of subordinates who should report to a supervisor is limited.
7. *Compare the advantages and disadvantages of functional, product, and territorial structures.*   The functional structure orients people toward a specific set of activities. As a result, they become more skilled in their areas. It works well in a relatively stable environment. However, the exchange of ideas and cooperation with other departments is lessened, and problems may arise that cannot be solved by one department. In the product structure, managers are responsible for one product or product line. They devote all their energy and skill to containing product costs, meeting schedules, and earning a profit. This structure encourages creativity. Its disadvantages include managers not having enough authority to carry out their responsibilities, the extra time required for planning, more insecure and anxious employees, and more stressful environments. The territorial structure's main advantage is coordination at the point of sale, leading to more personalized and speedier service. Disadvantages include some duplication of effort and the need to have managers who can perform multiple functions within their territories.
8. *Explain what types of structures combine to form a matrix organization.*   This matrix organization is a combination of the functional structure and either a product or project structure. As a result, subordinates have a functional boss (their permanent home is in the functional unit) and a product/project boss (a temporary home).
9. *Discuss modern organizational designs such as virtual and adaptive organizations.*   Virtual organizations are a function of electronic and communications technologies and dispersed workers. With the aid of modern technologies, many people are able to make significant contributions to their organizations without ever setting foot in the office. This technology-mediated work environment poses unique challenges for managers but can be very effective for retaining and motivating highly intelligent and mobile workers. Adaptive organizations are those that don't put a single organizational structure in place and use it to confront the competitive environment. Instead, adaptive organizations stay flexible on the margins and empower employees to craft structures that best help them achieve organizational goals and objectives.

KEY TERMS

adaptive organization (p. 199)
centralized business (p. 184)
coordination (p. 181)
decentralized business (p. 184)
delegation (p. 182)
division of labor (p. 186)
downsizing (p. 196)
formal authority (p. 182)
formal organization (p. 181)

functional structure (p. 190)
hierarchy (p. 182)
informal organization (p. 181)
line authority (p. 182)
matrix structure (p. 193)
organizational chart (p. 182)
organizational structure (p. 180)
organizing (p. 180)
principles (p. 185)

product structure (p. 191)
reengineering (p. 196)
scalar principle (p. 187)
span of control (p. 187)
staff authority (p. 184)
territorial (geographical) structure (p. 192)
unity of command (p. 187)
virtual organization (p. 197)

QUESTIONS FOR DISCUSSION AND REVIEW

1. Would a large organization such as ExxonMobil, IBM, or Kraft Foods use multiple structures? Why?
2. What skills does a manager need in an organization that uses a matrix structure to overcome the violation of the unity-of-command principle? Explain.
3. Some small-business owners claim that they don't need to worry about organizing principles of management because they are small. Do you agree with this claim? Explain.
4. Most organizations are a combination of centralized and decentralized structures. What are relevant factors for managers to think about when considering decentralizing the organizational structure?
5. In what unit of the U.S. government is the scalar principle most obviously used and applied? Explain why this is the case.
6. What purposes does the informal organization serve?
7. What are some unique challenges managers will face in a virtual organization? In an adaptive organization? List the challenges for each type. How can managers best deal with these challenges?
8. Why is it important for a manager to be flexible in terms of how he or she structures the unit being supervised? Inflexibility can result in what types of problems?
9. Explain the difference between line and staff positions. Use an organizational chart to illustrate your explanation.
10. What factors should be considered to determine the optimum span of control for a particular manager?

END-OF-CHAPTER QUESTIONS

1. Organizational structure is an incredibly important, yet often overlooked, component of the success of a business.   **T** or **F**
2. Coordination requires everyday, informal communication with and among employees.   **T** or **F**
3. The organizational chart shows exact communication patterns.   **T** or **F**
4. In a crisis, a more centralized decision-making structure is often both warranted and desirable.   **T** or **F**
5. The principle of *span of control* states that no member of an organization should report to more than one superior.   **T** or **F**
6. Each unit or department in the *functional structure* has a different set of activities and responsibilities.   **T** or **F**
7. Consumer products giant Procter & Gamble used the *product structure* as early as 1927.   **T** or **F**
8. Businesses that divide units on the basis of location are using territorial or geographical structure.   **T** or **F**
9. It is a common tactic for firms to lay off employees and then retain them as contract laborers.   **T** or **F**
10. Social interaction between supervisors and coworkers is prohibited in almost all jobs.   **T** or **F**
11. Many firms take advantage of temporary help agencies and contract or "outsourced" labor to grow and shrink according to consumer and competitive demands.   **T** or **F**
12. In general, the adaptive organization focuses on designing structure around business *processes*, rather than functions.   **T** or **F**
13. IBM saves _____ per site annually by eliminating offices for all employees except those who truly need them.
    a. 5 to 10 percent
    b. 15 to 20 percent
    c. 30 to 40 percent
    d. 40 to 60 percent
14. Each person in the managerial hierarchy has _____ authority over lower positions in the hierarchy.
    a. staffing
    b. delegation
    c. line
    d. formal
15. A graphical presentation of the formal structure of a business is the _____.
    a. matrix structure
    b. functional structure
    c. road map
    d. organizational chart

INTERNET EXERCISE

Adam Smith on Division of Labor

As part of this exercise, students should be instructed to visit the following website:

http://www.wsu.edu:8080/~dee/ENLIGHT/WEALTH1.HTM

This website extracts verbatim the relevant passages in Adam Smith's *The Wealth of Nations* pertaining to division of labor. Students should be encouraged to read the original words of Smith and relate them to labor as it exists today. They should think about the following questions while reading the passage.

1. What unique conditions existed in work and organizations when the division of labor concept emerged in the eighteenth century? Why wasn't it discovered sooner?
2. Why did Smith choose such a simple example (pin making) to make his point?
3. What role does division of labor play in modern organizations focused on:
    - Manufacturing?
    - Service?
    - Retail?
4. What problems does the division of labor principle create, and what are some ways of solving those problems?

EXPERIENTIAL EXERCISE

Investigating Organizational Design

Activity

Each student will examine an organization or organizational unit of his or her choice. He or she should contact a manager in the chosen organization and conduct a fifteen-minute interview. Students should briefly write up their findings and be prepared to discuss them in class.

Directions

The interview can range over any organizational design issues discussed in Chapter 8 but should include the following questions:

1. What is the primary purpose or mission of the unit? What functions must be performed to accomplish the mission? What customers does the unit serve with what products or services? What are the primary environmental factors that influence the unit's performance?
2. Describe the existing organizational structure. Draw an organizational chart showing both line and staff positions.
3. Which organizational design studied in this chapter most accurately describes the existing organizational structure?
4. Is the existing organizational design appropriate for the unit given its mission, functions, customers, products/services, and environment? Justify your answer.

BUSINESS APPLICATION

Assessing Organizational Structures

Activity

Following the discussion of various types of organizational structures, each student will develop a list of advantages and disadvantages for each type of structure. The activity will take approximately thirty minutes of class time.

Directions

1. The instructor draws a simple organizational chart focusing on the top two levels of a national retail clothing store corporation. The top level would have the CEO title written in the box, with the second level showing vice president with functional-oriented titles (e.g., VP of Human Resources, VP of marketing, etc.).
2. Ask students to write down the advantages and disadvantages of the functional type of structure for this organization. After giving students about five minutes to work on their lists, the instructor will conduct a class discussion on the functional structure by having students share their lists with the class.
3. Repeat Step 1 for the national clothing retailer, except this time a product type of structure should be used. Job titles for the second level of the chart might be VP of Footwear, VP of Coats & Sweaters, VP of Sporting Wear, and so on.
4. Repeat Step 2, except have the focus be on the product structure.
5. Repeat Step 1 for the national clothing retailer, except this time a territorial type of structure will be used. Job titles could possibly include VP of Southeast Division, VP of Northeast Division, VP of Midwest Division, and so on.
6. Repeat Step 2, except have the focus be on a territorial structure.

The instructor closes out the activity by summarizing the advantages and disadvantages of the functional, product, and territorial types of organizational structures.

Case

General Motors Restructures to Regain Competitive Edge

At General Motors, designers and engineers have been arm wrestling for years over something they call "tumble home." It's boatbuilding jargon for the curvature in a hull, and Detroit has appropriated the expression to describe the deviation from the vertical in a side window. Designers want a sleek inward curvature of the glass toward the roof. Engineers fought it: Without somewhat costly adjustments, more tumble home results in less headroom and a weaker roof. At General Motors the engineers always won. That's one reason GM cars looked boxy.

Then Richard Wagoner, GM's CEO, hired Robert Lutz, a former Chrysler executive, as vice chairman. Lutz let it be known that he wanted more tumble home. He tossed in a suggestion explaining how other companies were able to thin down a roof beam to allow for angled windows. The cost? Just do it. Suddenly any GM car that needs more tumble home can get it. "It is like the laws of physics changed," says Edward Welburn, a senior GM designer.

Since joining General Motors Corp. (GM) development chief Robert A. "Bob" Lutz has been working to make product development more efficient. The ex-president of Chrysler Corp. is taking a leaf from his former employer's book and pushing designers and engineers to use more off-the-shelf hardware in crafting new models. In addition to giving stylists greater freedom, Lutz also has asked GM's designers to find inspiration in classic models, the goal being nostalgia-inducing cars—rather like Chrysler's PT Cruiser. Lutz has a distinguished record of introducing products that consumers crave. For example, he was responsible for the popular Dodge Ram truck line that he developed as president of Chrysler.

Now, he's doing something else that is very un-GM. In a broad restructuring of the automaker's product-development organization, Lutz is ditching the brand-management philosophy of design implemented by retired board member John Smale and recently departed GM North America President Ronald L. Zarrella. He's also stripping layers of bureaucracy from the product-development process and making GM's different business groups—such as engineering, manufacturing, and design—work more closely together.

A lot is changing. No longer bound by rigid rules, designers will be empowered to style cars in the spirit of their divisions. Under Zarrella, who departed to become CEO of Bausch & Lomb, GM would identify a demographic and try to win it over with a vehicle and brand image tailored to the market segment's tastes and desires. The resulting models, however, rarely hit the mark. Now, Lutz wants GM to focus on making better vehicles. "Products drive brands," Lutz said in December. "You cannot transform great brands without great products."

His proposal sounds good in theory, but Lutz needs to prove that his new organizational structure can work. While his approach puts a focus on product development, he'll have to make sure that the different departments within the huge corporation work together. Nor will the restructuring matter, says James N. Hall, vice president of auto research firm AutoPacific, "if they're not coming up with anything that people like."

At the very least, Lutz is sharpening GM's focus. Each new-vehicle program will boast a team of engineers, designers, bean counters, researchers, and product planners working in concert. In the past, a new vehicle would start with designers who created the concept. Next, it would go to brand managers for their input. Then manufacturing bosses would take their turn and decide what chassis, platform, and parts to use. Finally, engineers would make a few more alterations. It was a process of change and compromises every step of the way. In some cases, new cars were approved and money spent before the styling had been thoroughly reviewed.

Under the new system, design moves to the forefront. For every vehicle idea, three teams will compete to create what will eventually make it to market. Lutz held just such a contest to develop the Pontiac Solstice concept car—a two-seat roadster that was lauded for its looks at last month's auto show in Detroit. If cars destined for dealers' showrooms can inspire similar reactions, Lutz's bold reorganization will have been a success.

Questions for Discussion

1. How long do you think it will take Robert Lutz to change the organizational structure of General Motors (a company with a complex product line, 360,000 employees, and international alliances)? How much time does he have?
2. Where would you begin changing the organizational structure of a company as large and historic as General Motors?
3. What are the dangers of undertaking massive structural change with a company like GM? What are the dangers of *not* undertaking structural change?

Sources: Adapted from David Welch, "At GM, Bob Lutz Maps a Different Route," *Business Week*, February 1, 2002; Robyn Meredith, "Car Guy," *Forbes*, January 21, 2002; Jerry Flint, "Time to Praise GM," *Forbes*, December 12, 2001; and David S. Pottruck and Terry Pearce, "Listening to Customers in the Electronic Age," *Fortune*, May 1, 2000.

Managing Production and Operations

Photo: comstock.com

After completing this chapter, you should be able to:

1 **Define** the production and operations management function.

2 **Discuss** two or three critical issues facing production and operations management.

3 **Compare** traditional company organization with cellular organization.

4 **Describe** what is meant by the concept of managing the supply chain effectively.

5 **Evaluate** the effects of computerization on production and operations management functions.

6 **Explain** the importance of productivity and quality to business.

7 **Review** the role of the production and operations unit in safety and environmental concerns.

Lean Manufacturing Works at GSI Lumonics

SI Lumonics (GSI) had the kind of problem that most organizations dream about and hope for: an overwhelming demand for its products. Conversely, it also had the kind of problem that companies work hard to avoid: difficulty meeting the demand. From its plant in Wilmington, Massachusetts, GSI produces laser-based advanced manufacturing systems and components and supplies products and services for companies in the semiconductor, electronics, automotive, and other industries.

To avoid the problems resulting from meeting overwhelming demand, GSI instituted a lean manufacturing program to decrease manufacturing cycle time and increase production. The company also wanted to gain better control over its information flows. A lean manufacturing process helped make GSI more agile.

As part of its shift to lean manufacturing, GSI adopted a real-time locating system to provide live asset visibility throughout the production process. Asset tracking now drives lean manufacturing. The solution is an integrated platform that supplies live location, event, and status information to application software packages and delivery devices, which enables lean practices and asset visibility.

GSI's system allows it to track the flow of information. For example, defective material is moved to a special area where it's examined and awaits disposition. The material is tagged, which means that GSI can track it and see where it is going. This is most important for reducing the size of inventory. If GSI has an expensive piece of equipment that sits idly in a deficit state for any length of time, the firm is carrying too much inventory.

Being lean, tracking work flow, and providing information to managers are extremely important for GSI to keep its competitive edge. Agility, quick cycle times, and high quality are all made possible through GSI's commitment to lean manufacturing.

Sources: Ken Krizner, "Lean Manufacturing Gets Boost at GSI Lumonics," *Frontline Solutions*, February 2001, pp. 1–3; and William M. Field, *Leaning Manufacturing: Tools, Techniques, and How to Use Them* (New York: CRC Press, 2000).

9-1 INTRODUCTION

Firms in many industries are faced today with customer demands for greater product variety, high quality, and reduced delivery times. The opening vignette illustrates how GSI Lumonics meets customer demands. This combination is difficult for many companies to achieve because quick delivery is usually based on standardization, whereas product variety requires the organization to be flexible and innovative. One common response to these pressures is to begin production of expensive, specialized products prior to receiving orders. Firms using this strategy build up an inventory of unsold products that is expensive to store in a warehouse.

Every consumer's dream, when making a major purchase, is to get exactly the features that they want. Although Detroit isn't about to offer this to customers any time soon, Dell Computer, the number one marketer of PCs with annual sales of over $32 billion, is doing it today.[1] Dell's build-to-order system has enabled the company to compete with the major computer makers since 1984 when Michael Dell got his start assembling machines in his college dorm room (see the Focus on Innovation box, "A Day at Dell").

Dell delivers customized computers practically overnight. That is the firm's distinctive competence. Why do you think other computer makers have had difficult competing with Dell on this basis? Dell has had problems competing in the laptop computer market. What special problems do you think this market holds for Dell?

To meet the needs of their customers, businesses strive for the perfect blend of management and machine. Creating and maintaining that blend is the task of the production and operations manager. The task has not been easy. In the 1970s, double-digit inflation plus a recession dealt heavy blows to industry in the United States, along with the rest of the industrial world. Consumers could no longer afford to buy as much, so they wanted goods that would last. The cost of money soared, and financing the growth of companies became

1. Tish Williams, "Dell Tops Raise Expectations," *The Street.com,* February 14, 2002.

FOCUS ON INNOVATION

A Day at Dell

Wednesday, 10:49 P.M. (CENTRAL TIME) Dave Cozzette, an accountant at Rothfos Corporation, a twenty-employee coffee broker in White Plains, New York, calls in his order for a Dell PC. At Dell's order center, sales representative Cassye Ewald promises the PC will be delivered within five business days. (She estimates it will arrive sooner, but sales representatives are trained to keep customer expectations low.)

12:50 P.M. Dell's financial services unit verifies the charge with Cozzette's credit card company, and the details of his $2,700.22 order print out on the production floor across the street at Dell's factory. Laquitta Lister checks the information sheet—called a traveler—which lists the sixty items that Cozzette's computer must include, from cables to software. The order is branded with a serial number that will identify the PC for its lifetime, regardless of who owns it.

1:00 P.M. The assembly process starts with the installation of an Intel 486 DX2 chip—the brains of Cozzette's computer—onto the machine's main circuit board, known as the motherboard.

1:55 P.M. Ronda Pena applies a sticker bearing the nascent PC's serial number to the chassis, then lays in the motherboard, fastening it with screws.

2:01 P.M. Anthony Garcia inserts Cozzette's fax modem, a device that can send documents created on the PC to fax machines or other computers via telephone lines.

2:10 P.M. Manuel Brito installs the floppy drive that was prepared earlier, along with a tape backup unit. It will let Cozzette make up-to-date duplicates of his hard disk files in the event his machine has a breakdown.

2:20 P.M. The power supply, a transformer that converts electrical current for use in the PC, goes into the unit, and Ronnie Hines affixes the PC's faceplate with the Dell logo subtly displayed.

2:26 P.M. Shena Galvan scans the computer's bar code to update Dell's inventory. The components that have been installed in Cozzette's PC are now listed as removed from the company's storage facility in another area of the plant.

2:27 P.M. The PC gets its first quality inspection. Steve Geil checks the traveler to make sure his coworkers have installed every component the computer should have. Then he creates a test diskette that will keep track of which software Cozzette has ordered and which components will need to be tested.

---

very expensive. Millions of employees lost their jobs. Vulnerable in key areas such as automotive, textiles, machine tools, and steel, the United States gradually lost its number one position in those markets to the competition—Japan, Germany, Korea, and other nations.

To recapture markets, top management asked production and operations managers to increase productivity, improve quality, and cut costs. Although progress has been made in all three areas, much work needs to be done to complete a turnaround. Because technology, competition, products, and worker skills have changed so much in the last twenty years, the job of the production and operations manager requires a wide range of analytical and communication skills. These managers must understand sophisticated technology, delegate tasks, and forfeit some decision-making power. Office technology used to be mechanical; now it is electronic, emphasizing computers, networks, and shared information.

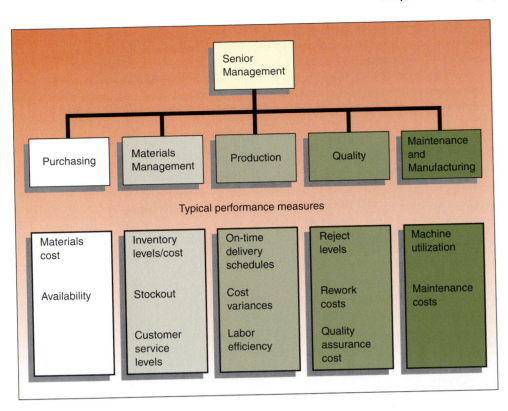

Senior Management

| Purchasing | Materials Management | Production | Quality | Maintenance and Manufacturing |

Typical performance measures

| Materials cost | Inventory levels/cost | On-time delivery schedules | Reject levels | Machine utilization |

| Availability | Stockout | Cost variances | Rework costs | Maintenance costs |

| | Customer service levels | Labor efficiency | Quality assurance cost | |

Manufacturing refers only to the physical process of producing goods; services are not manufactured. The word *manufacturing* comes from the ancient Latin words *manu* (hand) and *facto* (create, or make)—in other words, handmade. In ancient Rome, distinguishing between machine made and handmade was not an issue; all goods were handmade. If someone sang for the Romans, it was a service; if someone crafted a brand-new jar for storing olive oil, it was a manufactured good, something created by the work of hands.

9-3 A SHORT HISTORY OF PRODUCTION AND OPERATIONS MANAGEMENT

Until the nineteenth century, manufacturing was done largely by hand, using only hand-operated tools. Modern industry began with (1) the use of fuel energy in manufacturing and (2) the development of mass production.

9-3a Early and Crucial Innovations

A number of factors have contributed to the growth and development of industries and economic markets.

The Use of Fuel Energy

Fuel energy made it possible to use large machinery in factories; the use of large machinery made mass production possible. In the United States, the steam-powered mills of the nineteenth century were the first indication of the growth of industry that would follow.

Scientific Management

As the twentieth century began, managers became very interested in improving production of individuals and of the total organization. Frederick Taylor, the "father of scientific management," pioneered the use of scientific methods to improve productivity.[3] The

3. Jill R. Hough, Using Stories to Create Change: The Object Lesson of Frederick Taylor's Pig Tale," *Journal of Management*, September–October 2001, pp. 585–601.

EXHIBIT 9-2

The Traditional Plant

INTERACTIVE EXHIBIT

Manufacturing The actual processes of making products or of materials and parts. Literally creating something by the work of one's hands.

2:28 P.M. The PC powers up for the first time during a "quick test" that checks memory, video circuits, and floppy and hard disk functions. If the test diskette finds a bad sector on the hard disk—a portion that cannot properly store data—Sophia Finney will install a new hard disk. The test diskette sets the computer's clock to Central Time.

2:40 P.M. Engritte Brooks slides on the PC's hood.

2:45 P.M.–7:45 P.M. Cozzette's computer sits on a rack for an extended test called "burn in." Before it starts, Aaron Whitley plugs the PC into the factory's network. For five hours the diskette runs the PC's components through grueling tests that simulate heavy use. An indicator light hooked to the back of the PC changes color to help workers monitor the testing. Only 2 percent of the PCs fail. Finally, the test diskette uses the network to download the programs Cozzette has ordered, such as Microsoft Windows, and installs them on the hard disk.

8:20 P.M. Jaye Mireles shoots a 10,000 volt charge into the PC's power supply. If the PC handles the jolt without going haywire, it earns a Federal Communications Commission Class B Certification that it is safe to use in homes and offices.

8:32 P.M. During the PC's final test, the system is hooked up to a monitor and keyboard and operated without its test diskette, just as Cozzette will use it. Lonnie Gilliland looks for glitches in the newly installed software.

8:35 P.M. Julie Goodman puts the PC through "wipe-down," which is not code language for some top-secret Dell process but a cosmetic inspection that includes scrubbing off grubby fingerprints.

8:37 P.M. Ramon Lopez puts Cozzette's computer in a box with its keyboard, manuals, and warranty papers; Darrell Arvie slaps on the Rothfos Corporation address.

9:25 P.M. Airborne Express loads the PC onto a truck. If Cozzette had called Dell a few hours earlier, his PC would have made it onto a truck before the 7 P.M. deadline for next-day delivery. Instead, he'll get it on Friday.

Friday, 10:31 A.M. (EASTERN TIME) Airborne drops off the package at Cozzette's office. He plugs in his PC, and Dell's greeting software offers its congratulations.[2]

This chapter portrays how production and operations managers do their jobs. We start with a description of production and operations, followed by a brief history of manufacturing. We then discuss the various responsibilities of the production and operations manager, including organizing the production process, planning site location and layout, controlling materials, purchasing, inventory, and production scheduling. Other topics covered include using technology such as computers and robots, increasing productivity while maintaining quality control, and maintaining safety for employees, consumers, and the environment. Finally, we examine some critical issues and their implications for the future.

2. William J. Stevenson, *Operations Management* (New York: McGraw-Hill, 2002).

EXHIBIT 9-1

Several Types of Production

Organization	Inputs	Production Processes	Outputs or Products (Type)
Magazine publisher	Information in various forms: written, verbal, and photo or art pictorials Labor, energy, capital, ink, paper, tools, equipment, technology	Planning, budgeting, scheduling, design and layout, writing, editing, typesetting, art, and photo preparation, management control, printing, folding, cutting, binding, shipping on time	Magazines (nondurable goods)
Hair styling salon	Clients, hair knowledge, skills, information. Hair care supplies, tools, technology, equipment, labor, energy, capital, water.	Planning, budgeting, scheduling, materials ordering and handling, design, hair preparation, washing, conditioning, coloring, styling, meeting schedules, maintaining customer satisfaction (quality control)	Personal hair care (service)
Steel conduit manufacturer	Steel, chemicals, labor, energy, capital, tools, technology, equipment, water, location	Planning, budgeting, scheduling, materials ordering and handling, metal processing, labor organization, employee relations and safety, quality control, forming, cooling, storage and distribution, meeting schedules	Steel wire and pipe products (durable goods)

9-2 WHAT ARE PRODUCTION AND OPERATIONS?

Production The total process by which a company produces finished goods or services.

Operations Any functions needed to carry out a strategic plan, to keep the company producing.

Many people confuse the terms *production*, *operations*, and *manufacturing*. **Production** the total process by which a company produces finished goods or services. This proce might involve the work, ideas, and plans of the design engineers; the production manage the plant manager, the plant superintendent, and their crews; and any other departmen actually involved with bringing forth the product. Exhibit 9-1 illustrates different types businesses, products, and the processes involved. Production is not limited to the man facture of goods; it applies to the service sector as well. For example, a company mig produce shampoo and cream rinse for hair, which are manufactured goods; another con pany might operate a chain of hair salons, which provide a service. The word *producti* can also be used to name the total amount of product brought forth, as in the stateme "Total production increased by 20 percent in 2002."

    Operations are the functions needed to keep the company producing, literally a function or series of functions enacted to carry out a strategic plan. In a firm such as Fo Motor Company, operations will usually include purchasing, materials management, pr duction, inventory and quality control, maintenance and manufacturing engineering, a plant management. See Exhibit 9-2 for the activities managed by operations in the tra tional plant.

essence of his philosophy was that scientific laws govern how much a person can produce per day and that it is the function of management to discover and use these laws in the operation of productive systems.

    Taylor's approach was not greeted with universal approval. Some unions feared scientific management because it was rigid; unions played almost no role in Taylor's setup of jobs, and they had little idea of Taylor's ultimate goal. In some cases, managers embraced Taylor's time study and incentive plans but ignored the need to organize and standardize the work to be done. The result was poorly designed production operations and overworked employees.[4] For example, in the steel industry, many workers unionized to fight some of the demands made by management. In the automobile industry, scientific management led to strict division of labor and the eventual collapse of competitiveness. Japanese automakers that encouraged employees to develop expertise in more than one area were more productive and had better quality.

    Despite critics and inept application, Taylor's philosophy and work helped shape work flow systems, incentive packages, and the design and arrangement of jobs. His principles of scientific management are still a part of the procedures used in production and operations. For example, the New United Motor Manufacturing Company (NUMMI), a joint venture between Toyota and General Motors, employed a new form of Taylor's scientific management.[5]

Mass Production

Mass Production Rapid manufacture of large quantities of goods accomplished through division of labor, specialization, and standardization.

Mass production refers to the production of a large number of standard products for sale to consumers. In the age of individual craftsmen, mass production was not used because individuals were limited in the number of goods they could produce. When fossil fuels were used to power industrial plants, it became possible to produce large quantities of products for wide distribution. Early textile mills and steel plants are good examples of mass production in action. Of course, consumers sacrificed the customized goods of the individual artisan, but mass-produced goods could be purchased more cheaply, and they were more widely available.

    In the early twentieth century several other developments made mass production more efficient: the assembly line, division of labor, and standardization of parts.

The Assembly Line

Assembly Line A production line made up of workers who each perform one specific task as the product moves past, toward completion.

Around 1913 a significant breakthrough occurred with the establishment of the moving assembly line for the manufacture of Ford automobiles. In the mass production of the early Ford cars, one worker attached the headlamps, another attached the hood, and so on. Each worker performed one function on each and every car as its chassis came down a moving conveyor belt, or **assembly line.** The belt carried work from one workstation to the next. Ford's assembly line began at the entrance to a long shedlike factory building and emerged bearing finished cars at the other end. When a finished automobile emerged at the end of the assembly line, workers had given utility to the materials used.

Division of Labor

Industrial plants that mass-produce goods generally use a rigorous division of labor. This allows workers to focus their knowledge, skills, and concentration on a single aspect of the production process. The practice of dividing labor into discrete functions is common in manufacturing today, but it has been modified to eliminate the problem of worker boredom from repeating the same task day in and day out. Many plants today train workers to perform more than one specialized task and then rotate them to different processes. In this way, division of labor is maintained, but workers do not become bored from repeating routine behaviors. W. L. Gore Associates, the maker of Gore-Tex, for example, does not have division of labor. When new workers are hired in the plant, they are told

4. Ibid.

5. Ibid.

to find a place for themselves among the myriad of teams that are performing the tasks necessary to produce the final product. There are no job descriptions, no departments, and no boundaries.[6]

Standardized Parts

Standardization of parts was another essential factor in the development of mass production. At Ford each headlamp was exactly the same size and was connected to the same spot on identical car frames as they came down the assembly line. Thus one worker could attach headlamps over and over rather quickly and easily with a standard level of quality because the parts were standardized.

Some workers and social critics complained about the "human machines" who moved their arms and hands over and over again, in the same motions, to the rhythms of the inescapable assembly line. Comedian Charlie Chaplin even imitated and mocked them. But mass production and the assembly line were here to stay. No significant business operation could afford to ignore the technological advances they represented. Their tremendous production capacity would eventually make the United States the most productive and richest nation in the world.

9-3b Industrialization and America's Postwar Supremacy

During the 1920s, the nations of the world became increasingly industrialized and some of them increasingly competitive. Most, however, were seriously damaged by World War II. With its superior production and manufacturing achievements and the fact that its production capacity was not destroyed or badly damaged, the United States emerged from World War II the leader in production and manufacturing.

During the 1950s, 1960s, and most of the 1970s, American goods and services were the most sought after in the world. The holds of cargo planes and ships carried American cars and trucks, mechanical and electrical parts, chemicals, commodities, wearing apparel, medicines, food products, toys, soft drinks, and recordings to every major port in the world. In the passenger compartments of planes and ships, American services and technical know-how were being exported as well. Doctors, nurses, dentists, X-ray technicians, teachers, broadcaster, engineers, agricultural advisers, and hundreds of other specialists carried their know-how to foreign markets. Soon the workers, entrepreneurs, and governments of those markets began to respond in kind. As Europe and Japan recovered from the devastation of war, they began to rebuild their industries. They began to export goods and services, competed with each other, and created an industrial and marketing basis for competing in world markets.

9-3c Consumerism and Planned Obsolescence

In the U.S. expansion of the late 1950s and the 1960s, the pace of life—and the pace of production and consumption—escalated to unimagined speed. Salaries rose, prices increased, production rates climbed. By the 1970s, new and unexpected pressures appeared. An uneasiness and dissatisfaction began to spread. Americans became disillusioned with leadership at national, local, and even trade and labor union levels. With disillusionment came cynicism. Manufacturers talked of planned obsolescence—goods made to last only a short period of time so consumers would have to buy again. Consumers began to question the quality of products and services and the prices charged for them. Critics also questioned the facilities being used for manufacturing; many factories were old, outdated, inefficient, and dirty.

In addition to leadership, quality, and facility problems, the pressures to produce more and faster made pride of accomplishment all but impossible. Goods and services were

---

6. Frank Shipper and Charles C. Manz, "Alternative Road to Empowerment," *Organization Dynamics*, Winter 1992.

needed so fast that the prevailing cry was, "Never mind about the details—it's got to get out!" And, "If there's anything wrong with it, they can send it back!" And they did. In the 1940s, products might be returned once in a while; by the mid-1970s, corporations maintained whole departments solely to handle returns of defective items.[7]

9-3d American Manufacturing Joins the Global Marketplace

The decline in confidence in once invincible "Made in the USA" products became a crucial issue. The manufacturing community developed a new interest in what production and operations managers do and how to improve it. Today U.S. firms are searching for new ways of manufacturing goods and delivering services.

In the United States, fears of economic decline have been linked to the nation's inability to manage production and operations efficiently over the past two decades. Can the United States produce as well as it should or as well as some other nations (e.g., Germany, Japan, and Korea)? Check your understanding by completing the values and attitudes quiz in Exhibit 9-3.

Why does the United States need to find new manufacturing methods? Traditional mass-production methods have been changing as other countries, such as Germany and Japan, have used alternatives successfully. For example, the success of the Japanese auto industry is based on a system different from Detroit's. The Japanese make products that are different (in color, shape, weight) for each market segment. They have had to develop manufacturing technologies, job designs, and work flows that enable them to change production runs on assembly lines with little downtime, adapt to low-volume production of some models, and at the same time decrease the new-product development cycle. Such production innovations as just-in-time inventory, statistical process control, and quality circles originated in Japan. The Japanese emphasize quality, service, and cost.

U.S. industry today is competing globally, as companies worldwide are eyeing global markets rather than relying on domestic markets. The United States must sell abroad to pay for the goods and services it purchases abroad and for the money it has borrowed from abroad. To compete successfully for foreign markets, it must explore foreign innovations and manufacturing technologies.

For decades, American businesses largely ignored technological innovations coming from foreign laboratories and companies.[8] Most production and operations experts scoffed at Korean steel-processing procedures, Japanese inventory systems, Swedish assembly-line team concepts, and Taiwanese electronics procedures. But today more and more U.S. managers are scanning foreign projects, activities, and innovations. Importing ideas and methods of potential benefit is now an accepted practice.

Using a technique known as *benchmarking,* production and operations managers seek to identify a company that is the best in the world at some process, and then copy it. Benchmarking should not be confused with industrial espionage. Rather, it is the art of finding out, in a perfectly legal and aboveboard way, how other companies do things better than your company so you can imitate—and perhaps improve—their techniques. The American Quality Foundation and Ernst & Young report that 31 percent of American enterprises regularly benchmark their products and services. AT&T, Du Pont, Ford Motor, IBM, Eastman Kodak, Milliken, Motorola, and Xerox are just some of the major American companies that use benchmarking in their drive for quality and productivity.[9]

7. Earl Nauman, "How to Implement a Customer Satisfaction Program," *Business Horizons,* January 2001, pp. 37–46.

8. Thomas C. Fisher, *The United States, The European Union, and the Globalization of World Trade* (New York: Greenwood Publishing, 2000).

9. Mark T. Czarnecki, *Managing by Measuring: How to Improve Your Organization's Performance Through Effective Benchmarking* (New York: ANACOM, 1999).

Directions: The MIT Commission on Industrial Productivity published a book entitled *Made in America*. The book emphasized that some U.S. industries and products have lost 50 percent or more of their share of world markets since 1960. Which of these industries do you think have lost 50 percent or more of their world markets?

	Yes	No
Automobiles	___	___
Color TV sets	___	___
Cameras	___	___
Stereo equipment	___	___
Microwave ovens	___	___
Steel	___	___
Machine tools	___	___
Copiers	___	___
Optical equipment	___	___
Commercial aircraft manufacturing	___	___

EXHIBIT 9-3

The U.S. World Market Share

Feedback: Every checkmark should be yes, except for the manufacturers of commercial aircraft. Each of the other U.S. industries or products listed has lost 50 percent or more of the world market since 1960. The decline of the manufacturing or production part of business has been one reason why market share has dwindled.

How to speed product development is a top priority of all managers, especially those in production and operations. Compaq, Boeing, Merck, Microsoft, Honda, 3M, and Toyota are known for their ability to develop, manufacture, and market what consumers want, when they want it, and at an affordable price. Typically these cutting-edge product developers are global, and 35 to 70 percent of their sales come from outside their home market.[10]

In the search for new and better manufacturing methods, production and operations managers are playing more significant roles in their organizations. As markets and technologies globalize, these managers will increasingly need to understand foreign customers' needs, preferences, and price limitations. The basis for successful global competition lies in the successful adaptation of the production and operations functions of U.S. business. Unless production and operations can restore the stature of "Made in the USA" goods and services, the economic quality of life of Americans is likely to suffer. Products that cannot compete in the global market in terms of quality and price are unacceptable for the future of business in the United States.

1, 2, 3, 4, 5, 6
7

9-3e Production and Operations Management in the Service Sector

Most of the discussion to this point has concerned the role of production and operations management in manufacturing companies. Increasingly today, however, people are employed in the service sector of the economy. Services have been broadly defined as "anything that you can't drop on your foot." Businesses from retail sales to legal advice to health care have sophisticated operations that must be monitored, assessed, and continuously improved. Wal-Mart, for example, derives much of its competitive advantage over rivals from its sophisticated product tracking system. The retail giant's managers know almost instantly which products are selling well, thus deserving more prominent shelf space, and which items are not selling well.

10. Rekha Baler, "Act Local, Think Global," 1999, *Fast Company*, March 2001, p. 67.

FOCUS ON TECHNOLOGY

Technicians Will Be in High Demand

Technological advances in modern organizations, coupled with the trend toward downsizing, has left the technician in a commanding position. As the farmhand was to the agrarian economy of a century ago and the machine worker was to the electromechanical industrial era of recent decades, the technician is becoming the core worker of the information age. Since 1950 the number of technical workers has increased nearly 300 percent—triple the growth of the workforce as a whole—to over 20 million. With one out of every four new jobs going to a technical worker, the U.S. Bureau of Labor Statistics forecasts that such workers will represent one-fifth of total U.S. employment by 2004.

As corporate hierarchies collapse and the boundaries between organizations dissolve, employers are beginning to develop a new appreciation for the work technicians do. In the new economy, says Michael Arthur, a management professor at Suffolk University in Boston, it is competence rather than a place in a hierarchical pecking order that defines an employee's value. He says, "Technical occupations are becoming the new anchor for people's careers."

What are these technical careers? They cover a wide range of occupations, including computer programmers, drafters, clinical laboratory technologists and technicians, emergency medical technicians, paralegals, and many more. For example, automation has taken jobs away from many semiskilled industrial workers. But for factory technicians who know how to operate the new computer-controlled production equipment, opportunities abound. As manufacturing consultant Tom Blunt puts it, "Employers who automate but take people out of the process are lobotomizing their factories."

Technical work is the wave of the future. Employers must offer technicians career opportunities that will keep them motivated, productive, and creative. The technical worker freed from the monotony of the old organizational structures can provide companies with new ideas and innovations that help them compete. Intellectual capital is a high-value asset to companies. Research done by Dartmouth School of Business Professor James Brian Quinn has shown that, even in manufacturing, perhaps three-fourths of value added derives from technical knowledge. In the information age, technical skills are the foundation of long-term organizational competitiveness.

The technical worker has suddenly become very important to many businesses. Can you think of some industries that can't benefit from technical support? What advances in technology do you think have been the most critical in lifting the technical worker's status?

Sources: From Bureau of Labor Statistics, which provides continual updates.

United Parcel Service produces nothing, yet it has a highly developed operations function that rigorously determines the flow of packages through the system. UPS drivers are instructed how to enter and leave their trucks to maximize efficiency. Operations managers even went so far as to shave off the outside corner of drivers' seats to enable smoother exit from the vehicle.[11] The Focus on Technology box, "Technicians Will Be in High Demand," examines the supply and demand for technical workers.

11. Sunil Chopra and Peter Meindl, *Supply Chain Management: Strategy, Planning, and Operation* (Upper Saddle River, N J: Prentice-Hall, 2001).

9-4 WHAT DOES THE PRODUCTION AND OPERATIONS MANAGER DO?

Production and operations managers are responsible for producing the goods that business needs to sell. There are many kinds of production and operations systems, just as there are many kinds of products—goods and services—wanted by people in the marketplace. Production and operations can vary in size from a single person in a very small company (e.g., a family-owned bakery such as La Madeliene) to thousands of employees in a huge, multinational corporation such as Procter & Gamble.

Every business's production goals focus on producing products or delivering services. Companies want to make the best products at the lowest cost, or deliver the best services that money can buy. Thus the production and operations manager must produce with effectiveness and efficiency while maintaining quality control. Richard Bodine, president of Bodine Corporation, knows about speed, efficiency, and effectiveness. He manufactures assembly lines for organizations.[12] His firm is now working on an electromechanical system that will assemble 2,400 alkaline batteries an hour. Bodine manufactures about thirty machines a year at a rate that is fast, is efficient, and maintains high quality.

A production and operations manager's job is to see that the operations necessary to achieve the company's production and service goals are carried out. To do this, these managers oversee a number of company operations. The following functions are typical:

- Product planning
- Site location and layout
- Inventory control
- Purchasing and materials management
- Manufacturing and production
- Production control
- Quality control
- Plant management

In moderate-sized firms, the production and operations manager is often a vice president who reports directly to top management; managers or supervisors representing the preceding functions report to the production and operations manager.

Production and operations managers have *product planning* responsibilities, such as preparing forecasts, schedules, and budgets in collaboration with top management, finance, and marketing. In start-up operations, they oversee site location and layout. They also oversee the hiring, training, and development of personnel for departments involved with production and operations. Working with all other departments in the company—especially marketing, physical distribution, warehousing, and shipping—is important as well.

9-4a Organizing the Production Process

Chapter 8 presented different ways to organize businesses, depending on needs, types of production, strengths and weaknesses of company managers, and the like. Titles vary also. The inventory control manager in one company may be called the purchasing and inventory control manager in another company. Knowing the exact titles and type of organization in place enables managers to have appropriate expectations and communicate effectively. Production and operations managers must fit into different types of organizations.

---

12. Gary Slutsker, "Struggling Against the Tide," *Forbes*, November 12, 1990, pp. 312–314.

**Traditional Organization:
Manufacturing Firm**

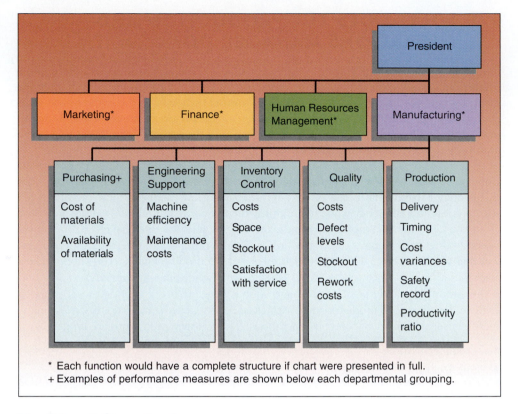

EXHIBIT 9-4

* Each function would have a complete structure if chart were presented in full.
+ Examples of performance measures are shown below each departmental grouping.

Traditional Organization

The organizational chart shown in Exhibit 9-4 follows the most traditional form. It gives each manager a specific area of authority and responsibility; however, it also sometimes pits managers against each other. For example, if a purchasing manager has budgeted $100,000 for a quantity of a specific part and the inventory control manager must order them on a rush basis for $60,000, the purchasing manager's responsibility and authority are subordinated to the inventory manager's needs.

Exhibit 9-4 shows typical departments in this type of organization and some common measures used in judging departmental performance. For example, the quality manager's performance would be appraised on the basis of costs, defect levels, and rework costs.

Companies that use an assembly-line approach to producing goods have typically been structured according to a job-shop design. Under this design, separate departments or divisions are responsible only for making a specific part and then sending it out the door to the next department. Machines that are similar to one another are all grouped together in a job shop. Anything that needs mill work is sent to the mill shop. Anything that needs grinding is sent to the grind shop. This often leads to lengthy travel distances for some parts that are sent to many different shops. In addition, because the product or subassembly is handled by so many different shops, the potential for error and the introduction of defects are increased. The more defects produced, the greater the cost to the company in terms of rework, lost customers, or worse. To eliminate some of the problems with the job-shop design, some firms have been using a cellular design.

Cellular Organization

In the past decade, more and more companies have begun to use a cellular organization. In this type, workers cooperate in teams, or cells, to manufacture total products or subassemblies. Each cell is responsible for the quality and quantity of its products. Each has the authority to make adjustments to improve performance and product quality. Exhibit 9-5 illustrates how, in the cellular arrangement, machines are arranged to handle all of the operations needed to assemble the products. The parts follow a path through each cell to final assembly.

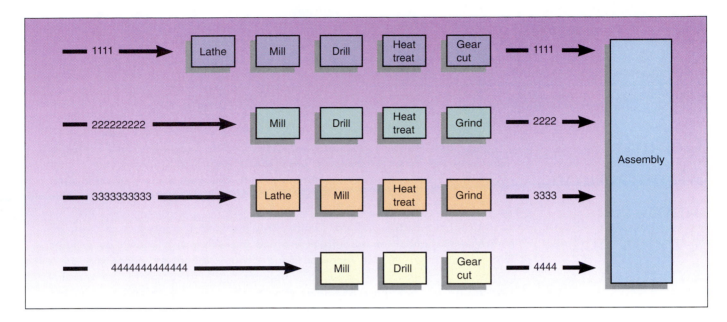

EXHIBIT 9-5

Cellular Manufacturing Layout

The basic difference between the cellular and the traditional organization is that workers in the cells are all responsible for their output. The linear competitiveness of the traditional structure is avoided. Instead each individual is pressured to perform so that the group will succeed. Cells tend to be tightly self-monitoring and self-correcting. In a cellular organization, companies tend to have much smaller staffs overall, with middle management positions reduced and lean management numbers at the top. Sony has been pioneering a new form of cellular manufacturing that takes a page from the craft workshops of the past. In a snail-shaped shop known as the "spiral line," Sony workers assemble entire cameras by themselves, doing everything from soldering to testing. Output per worker on the experimental line is 10 percent greater than the conventional assembly line. According to one consultant who helped Sony develop the spiral line, "there is no future in conventional conveyor lines. They are a tool that conforms to the person with the least ability."[13] Cummins Engine Company's use of a cellular design is described in the Focus on Innovation box, "Cellular Manufacturing Improves Quality and Productivity."

9-4b Planning Site Location and Layout

When a company starts up or opens a new branch, the production and operations manager is heavily involved in planning the site location and layout. Company officers, engineers, and heads of departments add their ideas and lists of requirements.

Site Selection

A site may be bought or leased, with or without a building already in place. If the site is to be leased, all managers involved will make their plans and submit their needs to a commercial or industrial real estate broker. The broker will then submit a list of properties available in the area within the price range required. Sites may come with a "build to suit" lease or may be a turnkey location, in which the building and interior facilities are already completed.

The type of business dictates the kind of facility. Service sector businesses often require small office facilities in heavy traffic areas convenient to customers or to the electronic communications and other services the business itself requires. Heavy industry, on the other hand, requires vast space near ship or rail transportation, often beside bodies of water that can be used for cooling operations as well as transportation to market. Most if

13. Yiannis Gabriel, "Organizations in Depth," *Organization Studies*, May 2001, p. 526.

FOCUS ON INNOVATION

Cellular Manufacturing Improves Quality and Productivity

For most of the twentieth century, factories were laid out according to process, with like machines located near like machines. This layout is known as the *job-shop design*. In other words, jobs of a similar nature are all done in the same shop. Under such a layout, batches of parts or unfinished product shuffle from one department to another. A major drawback to this design is convoluted flow paths.

To eliminate the time-consuming flow paths of the job-shop design, an increasing number of manufacturers use an alternative known as *cellular manufacturing*. Cellular manufacturing groups machines according to a process. Some processes require multiple machines to complete, and a cellular design will put these machines together to complete the process in one plant location. In that way, the lengthy flow paths of the job-shop design are eliminated.

Another benefit of the cellular approach is that workers receive training on more than one machine. In each cell, a worker can be trained to operate all of the machines that are required to complete the process. This gives workers stronger insight into the product and its manufacture. It also enables them to make stronger contributions to the company's quality improvement efforts. A worker who is familiar with the entire system is better able to recommend improvements than one who is only familiar with a small fraction of the system.

Cummins Engine Company is a notable example of a manufacturer that switched from the job shop to the cellular design. This change helped the maker of heavy-duty diesel engines for trucks and tractors become more flexible and responsive to customer needs. Facing declining market share in the early 1990s, the company knew its primary competition was from foreign companies that were better able to tailor their production to meet individual needs of customers. Following a switch to cellular manufacturing Cummins has rebounded in its global competitiveness. Cummins serves it customers through 500 company-owned and independent distributors in 131 countries. With over 24,900 employees worldwide, Cummins reported sales of $5.7 billion in 2001. Besides cellular manufacturing, the company lists worker training, worker quality groups, worker management, teamwork, and worker suggestions as the keys to its turnaround.

Cellular manufacturing replaces the standard assembly line approach to manufacturing. By placing people in cells where the product is produced from start to finish, travel distances are cut, quality is improved, and productivity is increased. What do you think are some barriers to converting a plant to a cellular design? Large manufacturing firms are more likely to use a cellular design than smaller firms. Why do you think smaller manufacturers have been reluctant to adopt this design?

Sources: Adapted from Cummins Engine, Annual Report 2001, Stephanie M. Rehta, "Cell Manufacturing Gains Acceptance at Smaller Plants," The Wall Street Journal, September 15, 1994, p. B2; "Rust Belt Resurgence," Challenges, February 1994, p. 7; and Kevin Kelly, "A CEO Who Kept His Eyes on the Horizon," Business Week, August 1, 1994, p. 32.

- Economics of cost or other economic advantages for land, buildings or units, taxes, insurance, and so on
- Nearness to related industries and suppliers, warehouse, or service operations
- Availability of appropriate labor force, considering such factors as average educational level, quality, and cost
- Availability of economical transportation for materials and supplies as well as for finished goods
- Nearness to market for goods
- Air and water conditions
- Nearness to plentiful and economical energy sources
- Climate and environment in line with needs for the kind of industry and amenable for employees' lifestyle
- Ample space for planned needs of business and for later expansion
- Nearness to such employee needs as housing, schools, mass transportation, religious facilities, day care, shopping, and recreational facilities
- Community receptiveness

EXHIBIT 9-6

Site Selection Factors

not all of the factors in Exhibit 9-6 will be considered in the production and operations manager's plan for site location.

Some site choices may be based on the overriding advantages of one factor, such as availability of labor or market, or the low cost of land. In recent years, for example, many American companies have chosen to locate in Mexico because of the low costs of facilities, land, and labor. Clothing manufacturers have settled in Korea and Taiwan because of the abundant supply of cheap labor. Another production site growing in popularity is Eastern Europe. Major changes in the business climate and a large untapped market have made the former Soviet Union, Poland, Hungary, and other central and eastern European countries intriguing options for joint ventures and new plants.

Site Layout

Just as it dictates the kind and location of facility, the type of business also determines the layout of the site selected. Different kinds of production require varying space for assembly lines, workstations, or other specific arrangements for the work layouts.

The manager must plan the layout in detail before the site is chosen. The plan must account for the needed square footage, work areas, office and conference areas, storage, and shipping needs. To draw up specific plans, managers use templates, models, drawings, and the latest computer techniques.

9-4c Managing Materials, Purchasing, and Inventory

Materials management, purchasing, and inventory control cover the planning, ordering, and internal storage and distribution of the supplies and materials needed for production. Other names used for these areas include material handling, procurement, supply room management, and inventory management. You will encounter many variations.

Some variations also occur in the way authority and responsibility are organized. In some companies, the purchasing department purchases all goods or services bought from outside sources. In others the purchasing function covers only those materials and supplies used in the actual production process.

In large companies, the materials manager may oversee the functions of purchasing and inventory control, or inventory control may be part of production control, depending on its scope. Inventory control may handle only inventory of components and subassemblies, or it may cover all inventories—of supplies, raw materials, components and subassemblies, and even finished products.

In recent years, two important systems have been created to handle materials management and inventory control. Just-in-time (JIT) inventory control and materials requirements planning (MRP) have greatly refined the degree to which materials and inventory control can be managed and scheduled.

Just-in-Time (JIT)   A system for decreasing inventory by using suppliers who agree to deliver the fewest possible items at the latest possible moment to keep production moving smoothly.

The **just-in-time (JIT)** inventory control approach was developed by Taiichi Ohno at Toyota Motor Company of Japan.[14] "Just-in-time" aptly names a production system in which operations (purchase orders, movement of materials, etc.) occur just at the time they are needed. As a result, very little inventory is carried. Under Ohno's JIT system, Toyota factories carry very little inventory. When parts are needed, they are delivered from other Toyota plants or from outside suppliers.

The Toyota system is called *kanban*. Kanban is the Japanese word for the piece of paper enclosed in clear plastic that accompanies each bin of parts. When a worker on the line takes a part from a new bin, the kanban is removed and routed back to the supplier. This signals the need to place a new order for a bin of parts.

An efficient JIT system can result in low inventories of purchased parts and raw materials, work in process, and finished goods. It saves warehouse and work area space as well as lowering the costs of carrying large inventories. Reducing inventory can also expose other production problems. A sometimes tardy supplier can be covered if the firm carries a large inventory. Smaller inventories spotlight the efficiency of all sources. A delinquent supplier will be replaced.

Just-in-time systems have been more common in Japan where groups of companies have traditionally associated in tight supplier-manufacturer relationships known as *keiretsu*. In these relationships, companies will mutually invest in one another to increase their commitment. American companies have been establishing closer ties to suppliers through electronic technology known as *electronic data interchange,* or EDI. EDI is a direct electronic link where manufacturers can begin the order cycle directly on the supplier's computer. This eliminates costly and time-consuming paperwork and also facilitates the tracking of orders.

Since JIT systems have little finished-goods inventory, machine breakdowns are very costly. Thus, careful attention to maintaining efficient equipment becomes a top priority. Machines must be in tip-top working order to fulfill the JIT demands. A top-quality repair team that can move into immediate action must be available if JIT is to work effectively.

Materials Requirements Planning (MRP)
A computerized forecasting system used to plan ordering of parts and materials for manufacturing.

Materials requirements planning (MRP) is a computer-driven system for analyzing and projecting materials needs and then scheduling their arrival at the work site at the right time. MRP works closely with the master production schedule and takes into account such variables as lead time in ordering.

MRP focuses on "getting the right materials to the right place at the right time." In most cases, making "right" decisions requires a computer to handle all of the materials and components involved. The MRP program analyzes data from inventory, the master production schedule, and the bin of materials. The output includes inventory status, planned order timing, and changes in due dates because of rescheduling.

MRP is used in companies involved in assembly operations. Firms that produce large volumes of tools, generators, turbines, appliances, and motors are particularly attracted to MRP. It is also very useful in companies that order a high number of units.

Together JIT and MRP provide a system that saves time and dollars. They have helped managers control the amount of inventory required to keep production moving smoothly. With JIT and MRP, suppliers of parts and subassemblies can plan in much closer time tolerances. In very large operations, such as the Detroit automobile assemblies, nearby suppliers are actually hooked up by computer to follow the progress of assembly-line work. From this vantage point, their trucks can arrive very nearly at the moment the materials are needed. Lead times on orders are greatly reduced, and costs of storing inventory drop sharply.

Materials Resources Planning (MRPII)   Developed around 1988 to enhance MRP.

Materials resources planning (MRPII) was developed around 1988 to enhance MRP. It incorporates a computerized system to integrate data from functional areas such as marketing, accounting, engineering, and production. MRPII systems then produce a production plan that provides forecasts, reports, charts, and financial statements. Managers can

14. Terry Hill, *Manufacturing Strategy: Text and Cases* (New York: McGraw-Hill, 2000).

use MRPII-generated information to make production, scheduling, and break-even analysis decisions.[15]

Enterprise resource planning (ERP) systems pull together data, information, and facts from suppliers and customers. ERP aggregates all of the data, information, and facts into a single software program. National Semiconductor started to use an ERP system to make better and faster decisions. The firm put together a financial system, a production system, and a SAP R 13 financial and resource system. The integrated approach enables the firm to answer supplier questions quickly and to provide advice to customers. By sharing real-time information with customers, suppliers, and workers, better inventory, production scheduling purchasing, job assignment, and work design decisions can be made. Guessing about what to place in inventory, who will work on a project, and when products can be delivered is reduced by using an ERP system.

Enterprise Resource Planning (ERP)   A program or system that attempts to integrate departments, tasks, and functions across a company into a single computer system that can satisfy the needs of those using the ERP.

9-4d Supply Chain Management

There has been a concentrated effort to improve relationships among manufacturers and their channel partners. This effort is referred to as **supply chain management (SCM)**.[16] The concept is to manage the relationships between supply chain members so that, in concert, costs, wastes, and inefficiencies can be reduced. One end result of effective SCM is more satisfied customers. Over the past decade SCM has become acknowledged as an effective approach to bring about efficiencies.

Xerox reported that its supply chain reengineering approach simultaneously cut inventories by $650 million, reduced annual operating expenses by $150 million, and significantly improved the success rate in meeting customer-requested dates for product delivery.

At Hewlett-Packard, the "DaVinci" supply chain integration project has achieved dramatic results. Business partners and end customers report that doing business with Hewlett-Packard is now easier and much more responsive.

Today's consumers expect far more than previous generations did in terms of instant and universal product availability. If we can have a vast variety of ready-to-eat foods delivered to our homes in a few minutes, why do we need to travel long distances and wait longer for other products? The world of "real-time everything" requires efficient SCM. Those companies that are faced with supply friction and inefficiencies will eventually suffer by losing customers and market share.

Supply Chain Management (SCM)   The process of managing the flow of materials, parts, work in progress, finished goods, the return of goods, and information by coordinating activities of all the organizations in the chain.

9-4e Basic Supply Chain Management Components

SCM involves a number of basic components:

1. *Plan*—the strategic planning portion of SCM. You need a plan and strategy for managing all the resources that go into meeting customer demand for your product or service.
2. *Source*—the selection of the suppliers that will and can deliver the needed goods and services.
3. *Make*—the manufacturing step involving scheduling, testing, packaging, and preparing for delivery.
4. *Deliver*—involves the logistics and timing.
5. *Return*—often the "soft" link in the chain; supporting customers who are returning or who have problems with the products or service must be a part of this process.

These five core steps are essential (see www.supply-chain.org for a more detailed explanation). SCM software can help in providing what is needed for each of the five basic steps. Many vendors have prepared software that attempts to deal with one or more of the five

---

15. Dough Bartholomew, "A Shower of Software," *Industry Week*, January 15, 2001, p. 39.
16. Samuel Greengard, "New Connections," *Industry Week*, August 13, 2001, p. 45.

FOCUS ON BUSINESS

Hogs and Supply Chains

The name the "Hog" has worked its way into the vocabulary of a growing number of motorcycle enthusiasts. Harley-Davidson has evolved into a worldwide economic success story through supply chain management, total quality management, and lean manufacturing.

In the early 1980s, Harley-Davidson was on the brink of bankruptcy. Declining sales brought on by deteriorating product quality were major problems, so the company's owners, American Machine and Foundry, put it up for sale. When no buyer or offer came forward, a group of Harley executives purchased the company.

Harley incorporated a strong emphasis on supply chain management to improve relationships with suppliers and the quality of motorcycles, the "Hogs." Harley worked hard to develop mutually advantageous relationships with its suppliers. Over 125 suppliers were given special attention so that they and Harley improved their mutual level of trust.

In turn, Harley's suppliers were expected to meet high expectations for timely service, the highest-quality products, and open communications. The performance of each supplier is continually reviewed in a manner similar to employee performance reviews.

The principles used by Harley with supply chain partners have yielded astounding results. The firm now annually produces more than 200,000 motorcycles and is generating over $3 billion in sales revenue.

The one major threat facing Harley-Davidson is to become complacent. Becoming lazy and less concerned about supply chain effectiveness could stop Harley's growth and profitability. The near bankruptcy experiences and history are enough to remind Harley's managers and employees that they are responsible for preserving the economic success story.

Source: Martha Richards, "High on the Hog," *Manufacturing.Net*, September 30, 2001, pp. 1–2.

basic steps. The Internet has allowed a company's supply chain to be connected to the supply chains of their suppliers and customers. Harley-Davidson has had significant success by using SCM as described in the Focus on Business box, "Hogs and Supply Chains."

Cisco Systems, which makes equipment to hook up to the Internet, is another example of how to bring about supply chain effectiveness and collaboration.[17] Cisco has a network of component suppliers, distributors, and contract manufacturers that are linked through Cisco's extranet to form a virtual, JIT supply chain. When a customer orders a Cisco product—for example, a router that directs Internet traffic over a company network through Cisco's website—the order triggers a series of messages to contract manufacturers of printed board assemblies. Distributors meanwhile, are alerted to supply the generic components of the router. Cisco's contract manufacturers know what is coming in terms of orders because they've logged on to Cisco's extranet and linked in to Cisco's own manufacturing execution systems.

This type of collaboration is made possible because of Cisco's use of the Internet and SCM software. It is important, however, to be patient with the SCM software used since

17. "McKesson: Empowering Healthcare," *Healthcare Financial Management*, January 2002, p. 26.

it will undoubtedly need some initial tweaking. In most cases the software program has to absorb a company's history and processes. That is, learning, adjustments, and patience are needed before a SCM system can optimize the use of software.

9-4f Controlling Production: Scheduling

The production manager is responsible for the main goal of the company: producing goods or delivering services. In the case of the production of goods, the production or manufacturing manager must be concerned with volume, production sequence, and the type of product to be produced. In a service organization, the production manager is also concerned with volume and the style in which services are delivered to customers.

Three elements of management—planning, organizing, and controlling—can clearly be seen in the tasks of the production manager. In the case of manufacturing, for example, planning the use of labor, facilities, and materials for fulfilling the production schedule is a complex, ongoing task. The manager will usually have more than one product to plan for, with the resultant needs for changes in materials, production processes, energy, and labor.

Master Production Schedule

A *master production schedule* must be created. It will show when the manager plans to produce each product and in what quantities. The production manager is responsible for meeting the dates, quantities, and cost commitments on the schedule. The master schedule affects the efforts and success of every department in the company. Therefore, it should also reflect the needs of the finance, marketing, shipping, and all other departments.

Production managers must plan for flexibility to be able to change from one process to another on short notice. They may use a number of tactics to meet emergencies or make changes in the plan. Requesting overtime, hiring temporary workers, cross-training workers so they can do more than one job, and many other methods are available.

PERT Charts

Flexibility as well as adherence to schedule can be achieved with the use of the program evaluation and review technique **(PERT) chart.** PERT developed in the 1950s from the joint efforts of Lockheed Aircraft, the U.S. Navy Special Projects Office, and the consulting firm of Booz-Allen & Hamilton. They were working on the Polaris missile project and wanted to provide the United States with an advantage over the Soviet Union in time of completion.

An important part of PERT is the construction of a chart, a graphical system for tracking the events that must take place to accomplish a task. A PERT chart is one of the most effective tools of modem management. To create one, five steps are followed:

PERT Chart   Program evaluation and review technique that tracks a project's progress and enables management to make optimal allocation of resources.

1. Break the project to be accomplished into events, or completed actions; label each with the amount of time needed to do it.
2. List the first event of the task.
3. List the event that follows the first one; draw a line with an arrow from the first event to the next one, showing the sequence. (If two events follow, draw arrows to both events to show that one event leads to two or more events.)
4. Chart all the events needed to complete the project in the same way, to completion.
5. Label the arrows with the amount of time it takes to complete each activity.

Exhibit 9-7 presents a PERT chart for the assembly of an engine. The interdependency of the events is spelled out in the column of prerequisites. That is, the development of the production plan, circle 5, requires that activities 1, 2, and 3 be completed. To reach the final assembly event, all seven other events must be completed.

EXHIBIT 9-7

PERT Chart

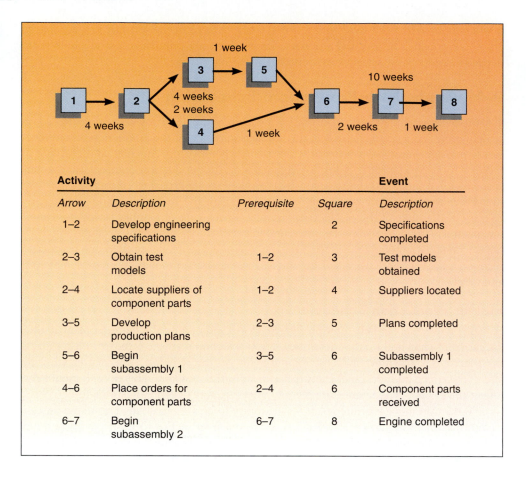

Activity				Event	
Arrow	Description	Prerequisite	Square		Description
1–2	Develop engineering specifications		2		Specifications completed
2–3	Obtain test models	1–2	3		Test models obtained
2–4	Locate suppliers of component parts	1–2	4		Suppliers located
3–5	Develop production plans	2–3	5		Plans completed
5–6	Begin subassembly 1	3–5	6		Subassembly 1 completed
4–6	Place orders for component parts	2–4	6		Component parts received
6–7	Begin subassembly 2	6–7	8		Engine completed

When the chart is completed, the longest path from start to completion of the project (in time needed to complete the activities) is called the *critical path*. Path 1-2-3-5-6-7-8 will require twelve weeks, while path 1-2-4-6-7-8 will require ten weeks. Thus path 1-2-3-5-6-7-8, as the longest, is called the critical path.

The PERT chart can be used to track exactly where a product is in its development and what needs to be done next to keep it on its path. Bottlenecks can be identified, and managers can organize employees in that part of the operation to devise ways to improve the process and reduce or eliminate the problem. For example, if the third event in a sequence always involves a delay, the production manager can form a team of employees from that process who can identify ways to improve productivity. By involving the employees in the improvement process, the manager is using the people closest to the process who probably have the best knowledge of how it works and how it can be improved.

The PERT chart is only as good in planning as the ability of its users to identify all of the steps in a chain of events. Because it helps break down the production tasks into clearly separate segments, PERT also helps to identify needs and uses for computerized manufacturing programs, temporary workers, and overtime techniques. This breakdown is very helpful in the current climate of rapid change in production techniques, numbers of products, and kinds of new products. The public presents an ever ready market for newer, more appealing products; getting the products to the consumer is up to the production staff. In the recent past, companies could expect to bring out a new product line or new models in the line no more frequently than every year. Now, in many industries, new products are inserted into the master schedule—and from there into the marketplace—as fast as they can be designed. With the increased capability offered by computerized design and engineering, that is very fast indeed.

9-5 USING TECHNOLOGY

Increased production is not achieved only through efficient planning. Computers have added flexibility and speed to the production process.

9-5a Computer-Aided Design, Engineering, and Manufacturing

Computer-aided design (CAD) and **computer-aided engineering (CAE)** have made possible the development of millions of new designs. Designs can be drawn, extended, contracted, added to, or taken from within the computer. Engineers can test designs for function and stress and try out variations without the cost or risk of building models or samples. Drafters using CAD can perform many of these tasks once the initial design has been developed. The computer does much of the calculation and the drawing, in two or three dimensions as needed.

CAD has been used to design buildings, ships, and even chips. Frito-Lay used CAD to design its O'Grady's double-density ruffled potato chip. An improperly designed chip is not attractive, may be too brittle and break into small pieces, or may not be suitable for using with dips.[18]

Computer-aided manufacturing (CAM) includes the use of computers for controlling the operation of traditional, modified, and electronic machines, including robots. In Japan the Fujitsu plant in Akashi was using robots effectively in the 1980s. The plant specializes in sheet-metal manufacture, producing more than 100,000 parts each month for 1,500 different products. The production order, specifying the parts, the number, and the materials to be used, is given to the main computer. The computer then selects the most efficient way to make the parts and creates a layout for the automated shear machines and punch presses to follow. The Fujitsu plant is estimated to be 40 percent more productive with the CAM system, saving approximately $10,000 worth of material a month.

9-5b Robotics

In the United States, the automotive industry is the best-known user of **robots** for manufacture. Robots paint, sand, test, and weld car parts; robots track individual cars on the assembly line and perform dozens of repetitive, exacting, unwieldy, or dangerous tasks.[19]

In 1988 approximately 51 percent of robots in operation in the United States were used in the automotive industry. As of 2001, however, less than 25 percent of the robots

> **Computer-Aided Design (CAD)**   The use of computers to draw plans for a product.
>
> **Computer-Aided Engineering (CAE)**   The use of computers to plan engineering processes and test designs.

> **Computer-Aided Manufacturing (CAM)**   The use of computers to guide or control the actual production of goods.

> **Robots**   Computerized, reprogrammable, and multifunctional machines that can manipulate materials and objects in the performance of particular tasks.

18. Frito-Lay Annual Report, 2001.

19. Richard B. Chase, F. Robert Jacobs, and Nicholas J. Aquiliano, *Operations Management for Competitive Advantage* (Burr Ridge, IL: McGraw-Hill/Irwin, 2004), p. 83.

in operation were in the automotive industry as increased robot use has swept into the service sector and other areas. However, robots still play a significant role in automotive production and will probably continue to do so.

The ability to manipulate other objects makes a robot unique compared with other kinds of computerized machinery. Robots also can perform the same tasks, such as welding a piece in place over and over again, hundreds and hundreds of times, without becoming tired or being endangered, as the human worker would be in the same function. Robots are therefore used especially in situations that are too repetitive or dangerous for human beings. For example, a robot can be more efficient, consistent, and cost-effective than its human counterpart in the task of opening and closing a car door thousands of times. In applying acid to the surface of metal parts, a robot can perform at a constant pace for thousands of hours without danger or exhaustion.

From the early, simple machines (e.g., automated mail delivery carts) to the sensor-monitored "intelligent" machines of today, robotics has made a rapid ascent indeed. An estimated 95,000 robots are currently at work in American industry, most of them in the automotive, appliance, aerospace, chemical, electronics, food processing, home furnishings, pharmaceuticals, and textiles manufacturing areas. Technologies such as machine vision and tactile sensing promise to expand robot use in service industries such as education, health care, security, and training and development.

9-5c Flexible Manufacturing Systems

> **Flexible Manufacturing Systems (FMS)**   The use of computers to change from one production process to another in order to produce different goods.

Robots and other computerized machines programmed to switch fairly easily from producing one kind of product to another can be grouped in **flexible manufacturing systems (FMS).** Parts and materials flow to the operation by automated equipment, and finished products are removed automatically. Their flexibility allows FMS to be used in JIT inventory control projects as well as for small batches of customized parts or products without raising costs drastically.[20]

The National Bicycle Industrial Company, a subsidiary of Japanese electronics giant Matsushita, has used FMS with great success. Robots, computers, and people work together to turn production on a dime.[21] With twenty employees and a design-smart computer, the firm can produce any of 11,231,862 variations of eighteen models of racing, road, and mountain bikes in 199 different color patterns and about as many sizes as there are people. Production doesn't start until an order is placed. But within two weeks, the customer is riding his or her personalized bike.

National Bicycle designs and manufactures the bicycle to fit the size, shape, and strength of the customer. The bicycle store sends the specifications, by mail or fax, to the firm. A computer operator punches the data into a microcomputer. The bicycle is bar coded for one customer. The bar code is fed into the computer that instructs a robot where on the frame to build or what color the bicycle should be painted. The customer's name is imprinted on the frame. The personalized, flexibly manufactured bicycles sell for $545 to $3,200, compared with $250 to $510 for standard bicycles.

9-6 IMPROVING QUALITY

Computers, JIT systems, production schedules, and robots are all used in production and operations to improve quality, cost, service, and productivity. Improvements in productivity and quality have long-term effects on the success of business.

The term *quality* and its implications are now very important throughout the industrialized world. Germans brag about the quality of their automobiles. The Swiss praise the quality of their watches. The quality of Italian marble and tile work sets the standard for

---

20. Mikell Groover, *Automation, Production Systems and Computer-Aided Manufacturing* (Englewood Cliffs, NJ: Prentice-Hall, 2001).

21. Susan Moffat, "Personalized Production," *Fortune*, October 22, 1990, pp. 132–135.

Dimension	Example
Performance: Good/service's primary operating characteristics.	Sony TV's richness of color, clarity of sound.
Feature: Secondary, "extra" characteristics.	Hyatt Regency's complimentary breakfasts.
Reliability: Consistent performance within a specific period.	Honda Acura's rate of repair in the first year of purchase.
Conformance: Degree to which design and characteristics meet	Apple computer's compatibility with IBM software.
Durability: Length of a good/service's useful life.	Average 17-year life of Kirby vacuum cleaners.
Serviceability: Speed, courtesy, competence, and ease of repair.	Caterpillar Tractor's worldwide guarantee of 48-hour delivery of replacement parts.
Aesthetics: Look, taste, sound, smell of a good/service.	Flavor, texture of Baskin-Robbins ice cream.
Perceived quality: Quality conveyed via marketing, brand name, reputation.	Bose's reputation in stereo speakers.

EXHIBIT 9-8

Dimensions of Quality

Source: James H. Donnelly, Jr., James L. Gibson, and John M. Ivancevich, *Fundamentals of Management*, 10e (Burr Ridge, IL: Irwin, 1998), 536.

everyone in that industry. At times quality refers to workmanship or an evaluation (e.g., the "Good Housekeeping Seal of Approval"). From the consumer's perspective, quality is best defined as "perceived excellence." It is how a person views the product or service.

The perception of quality generally depends on how well the product or service meets or exceeds the customer's specifications and requirements. A consumer makes decisions about quality by evaluating one or more of its dimensions. Exhibit 9-8 illustrates eight such dimensions, including performance, features, durability, and aesthetics. In judging the quality of a Ford Taurus or an Oldsmobile Aurora, a car buyer may compare the vehicles on performance, features, serviceability, aesthetics, and perceived quality before making the purchase decision. Whether the buyer purchases a second Taurus or Aurora three years later will depend on how well the first car meets his or her expectations of quality. Ronald E. Goldsberry, Ford's vice president for customer service, expressed his company's emphasis on building long-term relationships: "In the past, the division's mission was to generate revenue through selling parts and taking care of service through warranties. Now we don't look at ourselves as parts, warranty and service providers. We want to provide an ownership experience so good that the customer will reward us by buying another Ford." Ford estimates that each one-point gain in owner loyalty is worth $100 million in profit.[22]

As we discussed earlier in this chapter, the quality of American goods—unquestioned before and just after World War II—slipped in the 1960s, 1970s, and 1980s. Many reasons have been advanced for this. The postwar economic boom created a seemingly ever-expanding market as demand for goods and services rose. Consumers, looking for the latest models in cars, cameras, tape recorders, and televisions, bought more and faster products. Technological change accelerated and business hurried to keep pace, while workers complained they had no time or authority to maintain quality. In the midst of plenty, imperfections in the production process began to erode the confidence of consumers and the optimism of industry.

As American-made goods no longer were seen as top quality, foreign competitors' products began to gain acceptance as meeting top-quality standards. In major markets (automobiles, steel, electronics), this loss of sales cut deeply into the U.S. economy.

Greater pressure from competitors increases the importance of high quality in products. For example, foreign competitors—Japanese automakers, BMW, Daimler-Benz, and Volvo—have stimulated the improvements in quality now taking place in the American

22. Stevenson, *Operations Management*, pp. 223–225.

Deming's 14 Points of Quality

1. Drive out fear.
2. Eliminate quotas and numerical goals.
3. Break down all barriers between departments.
4. Eliminate inspection. Learn to build products right the first time.
5. Institute a vigorous program of education and self-improvement.
6. Remove barriers that rob workers of their right to pride of workmanship.
7. Institute leadership. The aim of leadership should be to help people do a better job.
8. Eliminate slogans, exhortations, and production targets.
9. Adopt a new philosophy. This is a new economic age. Western managers must awaken to the challenge, learn their responsibilities, and take on leadership for change.
10. End the practice of awarding business based on the price tag. Move toward a single supplier for any one item. Base this long-term relationship on loyalty and trust.
11. Improve constantly and forever the system of production and service.
12. Put everybody to work to accomplish the transformation.
13. Institute job training.
14. Create constancy of purpose toward improvement of product and service to become competitive and to stay in business and to provide jobs.

Source: John Hillkirk, "On Mission to Revamp Workplace," *USA Today,* October 15, 1990, p. 4B. Copyright, USA TODAY. Reprinted with permission.

automobile industry. Meanwhile the Japanese have redefined and expanded their notion of quality with a concept called *miryokuteki hindshitsu:* making cars that are more than reliable, that fascinate, bewitch, and delight.[23] Japanese engineers are working to give each car a special look, sound, and feel without sacrificing reliability. They call this the "second phase of quality." (The first phase of Japanese quality was inspired by American engineer W. Edwards Deming. Exhibit 9-9 highlights Deming's fourteen principles of quality.)

American automakers have been steadily regaining domestic market share from foreign competitors and are also making inroads abroad. This turnaround in fortunes is in large measure due to improved quality and innovation. All told, U.S. automakers moved out nineteen new models in 1995. As competition heats up, the biggest challenge will come in the 2.3 million-car family sedan market. Ford's new entries, the Contour and its Mercury Mystique sibling, along with Chrysler's Cirrus and Stratus, represent Detroit's first credible challenge to Japan's biggest U.S. stronghold. The new models come close to matching the performance and quality of such Japanese standards as the Toyota Camry, Honda Accord, and Nissan Altima, but they sell for up to $7,000 less.[24]

Consumer pressure, lost market share, good business thinking, and competition, then, all motivate companies (whatever their nationality) to focus on quality. The unit in the company that controls quality is sometimes called *quality assurance (QA).*

9-6a Managing Quality Control

The quality control manager may be responsible for defining standards with exact specifications or for issuing guidelines regarding exact specifications set by an outside agency. Standards are set by agencies such as the Food and Drug Administration (FDA), the Bureau of Standards, and hundreds of other regulating groups. These standards affect the color, size, shape, taste, texture, durability, and many other properties of goods produced in the United States. From toothpaste to rocket fuel, American products are tested and standardized to a greater degree than any others in the world. Government contracts can be lost and consumer purchasing can fall rapidly if standards are not met.

The quality control manager must select or devise procedures to test the quality of products, establish troubleshooting procedures, pinpoint causes of any defects in products, and rapidly correct any problems to minimize losses. Customer complaints or returns of defective products must also be analyzed so that necessary corrections can be made.

23. Jerry Bowles, "Quality 2000," *Fortune,* September 19, 1994, pp. SA1–SA4.
24. David W. Woodruff, "A New Era for Auto Quality," *Business Week,* October 23, 1990, pp. 84–96.

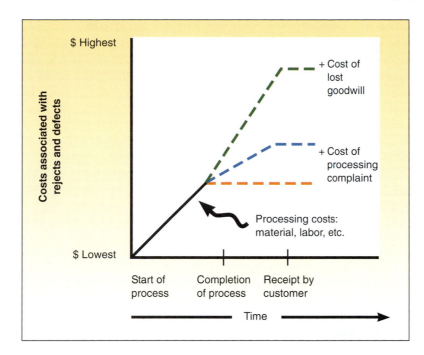

EXHIBIT 9-10

The Quality Funnel Principle

Source: Adapted from David Bain, *The Productivity Prescription: The Manager's Guide to Improving Productivity and Profits,* © 1982 McGraw-Hill, Inc. Reproduced by permission of the publisher.

Complaints and returns from customers can build up and result in lost customers and sales. Therefore, a quality control expert must develop a system that reduces the chances that low-quality products or services get to the customers. A four-step program can help keep the perception of poor quality from being associated with the company.

Step 1: Define Quality Characteristics

The first step involves defining the quality characteristics the customer or client desires. Examining customer preferences, technical specifications, marketing suggestions, and competitive products provides necessary information. Customer preferences are extremely significant, since repeat sales will likely depend on a reasonable degree of customer satisfaction. A Rolex customer wants accuracy, a long service life, and a stylish watch. But a Timex watch customer has other quality standards and preferences. The Timex keeps reasonably accurate time and sells at a much lower price than the Rolex. The exact quality characteristics for the Rolex and Timex watches meet, and depend on, different customer preferences.

Step 2: Establish Quality Standards

Once the quality characteristics have been defined (e.g., a Rolex or Timex), the next step is to establish the desired quality levels. Quality standards serve as the reference point for comparing the ideal to what actually is. Management sets standards for factors such as size, color, weight, texture, accuracy, reliability, time of delivery, and support.

The cost of achieving and sustaining a specific level of quality must be estimated and compared with the cost of potential rejections. Exhibit 9-10 represents what is often called the *quality funnel principle:* The closer to the start of the production process, the lower the cost of rejection. As the product or service progresses through the process, more resources are invested; the greater the amount of resources invested, the higher the cost of rejection. The greatest cost is incurred when the customer or client is the source of rejection. In that case, the cost of processing the complaint and the cost of lost goodwill are added to the cost of resources. For example, complaints about Dell's first notebook computers were costly in the form of lost repeat sales and recalls to repair defective parts. Dell learned the hard way that superior quality is very important to modern consumers. Its first notebook computers had many defects, and their failure hurt the company's reputation.

Step 3: Develop the Quality Review Program

The methods for quality review, where and by whom reviews will be reported and analyzed, and other review procedures must be formalized. One important decision involves how many products will be checked for quality. Will all products be inspected or only a representative sampling? The greater the number of products inspected, the greater the costs associated with quality review. Representative sampling is less costly but creates (1) the risk that more low-quality products will get into the hands of customers, (2) a greater likelihood that customer goodwill can be tarnished, and (3) the need to decide on what number of defects or poor-quality products will be acceptable.

Sampling procedures can take many forms. Some organizations use a random spot check, in which a random selection of products (e.g., cars, generators, computers) is inspected for quality. When a formal random spot check is used, the results can be meaningful and can provide adequate control. Other forms of sampling plans using statistical analysis are also available.[25] In each case, the decision about which plan to use involves making inferences about the entire production, based on samples. Representative sampling presupposes that defective products will occasionally slip through the quality check network.

Step 4: Build Quality Commitment

A commitment to quality among the workforce within an organization has three ingredients:

- *Quality focus.* There must be a sincere belief by employees, from top management to operating employees, that quality of all outputs is the accepted practice. Satisfying customer or client quality needs must be a goal of all employees.

- *Quality intelligence.* Employees must be aware of the acceptable quality standards and how the standards can be met.

- *Quality skills.* Employees must have the skills and abilities to achieve the quality standards set by management.

The employees' commitment to producing high-quality output is imperative.[26] It can be created with motivational programs or with programs involving job enrichment, goal setting, positive reinforcement, and team development. An approach with many adherents, participative management, involves employees in important management decisions.

9-6b Quality Circles

Quality Circles Small groups of employees who meet regularly to identify, and sometimes solve, work-related problems.

Quality circles are based on the belief that the people who work with the process are the best able to identify, analyze, and correct the problems in any given production situation. They are said to have begun in the United States but were expanded into a highly developed system by Japanese firms. Quality circles usually consist of seven to eleven people working in a related area. They meet about once a week and discuss the flow of work, its problems, and potential solutions. Participation in the circle is voluntary, and the workers establish a moderator or team leader to lead discussions. Findings and proposals of the group are forwarded to management.

Experience with quality circles suggests that several preconditions are required for success. First, those involved must be intelligent. They must know how to use statistics and work design analyses. They must know the technical aspects of the job. Second, management must trust the participants enough to provide them with confidential cost information (from competition). Third, the participants must be dedicated to working together as a team. They must have a team spirit, since groups, not individuals, are rewarded for success. Fourth, quality circles work best as part of what is called *total quality control*. This philosophy follows three principles:

---

25. Wallace J. Hoop and Mark L. Spearman, *Factory Physics* (New York: McGraw-Hill, 2001).

26. Gary K. Griffith, *The Quality Technician's Handbook* (Upper Saddle River, NJ: Prentice-Hall, 2000).

1. The goal is to achieve a constant and continual improvement in quality year after year.
2. The focus extends beyond the actual product or service that a firm provides, to every process in the organization (e.g., finance, accounting, research and development).
3. Every employee bears the responsibility for quality improvement.

The implementation of total quality control involves the same steps used to develop the quality control system. However, the breadth of the quality focus—that every employee is responsible—and the challenge of continual improvement require extra effort.

The extra effort has paid off in the Metal Stamping Division of Irvin Industries, of Richmond, Kentucky. After receiving quality improvement training, the firm declared that quality was a must and that each quality circle would set zero defects as a goal. Each Irvin employee has accepted the goal.[27] The quality circle improvements have resulted in many cost savings, a reduced injury rate, and increased morale.

Quality is also important in services. For example, a plastic surgeon who performs a poor-quality surgical procedure on a patient's face can have it result in permanent disfiguration. Businesses trying to provide quality services need to use every single step of the process applied to product quality control.

9-7 IMPROVING PRODUCTIVITY

The rate at which goods and services are created is called **productivity.** In a healthy economy, productivity must be high and also steadily increasing. One common measure of productivity is expressed in dollars of output (adjusted for inflation) per hour worked. Another important factor in productivity is technology and how it is being used by employees. Labor and technology combined generate the outputs that are priced and sold to consumers.

In the presence of increasing labor, material, and opportunity costs, uncertain world events, fast technological change, and shifting investment policies, the productivity of a company must continually increase in order for the company to stay in business. The challenge facing managers and nonmanagers in firms of all sizes is immense. Ignoring either quality or productivity improvements is likely to result in lost markets, layoffs, foreclosures, and general business decay. Consumers are demanding more quality, and companies need to improve the output per labor and technological input.

9-8 MAINTAINING SAFETY: FOR EMPLOYEES, PRODUCTS, AND THE ENVIRONMENT

A productivity and quality improvement strategy and motivated workers are key ingredients for business success. However, these can be diminished if the company shows little regard for the environment or sacrifices safety. It is important to improve productivity and quality without jeopardizing the well-being and future of the employees or the environment.

9-8a Employee and Product Safety

Chapter 6 has a detailed discussion of safety and social responsibility. Here we view these issues in relation to the operations and production areas, where many of the most potentially hazardous materials, processes, and products are found. Although safety is a part of the responsibility of every employee in the workforce, corporate responsibility for safety is most often delegated to the production and operations manager. Employee safety is mandated by a number of government regulations and laws; the production and operations manager is responsible for the implementation of these regulations in the plant.

Productivity   A measure of output per unit of a particular input.

---

27. Kevin Hendricks and Vinod R. Singhal, "Don't Count TQM Out," *Quality Progress*, April 1999, pp. 35–41.

The Monsanto Pledge

- Reduce all toxic releases, working toward a goal of zero.
- Ensure that no Monsanto operation poses undue risk to employees and communities.
- Work to achieve sustainable agriculture through new technology and practices.
- Ensure groundwater safety—making our technical resources available to farmers dealing with contamination, even if our products are not involved.
- Keep our plants open to our communities, bringing the community into plant operations. Inform people of any significant hazard.
- Manage all corporate real estate to benefit nature.
- Search worldwide for technology to reduce and eliminate waste from our operations, with the top priority being not making it in the first place.

Source: Business and Society Review, Spring 1990, p. 66.

Compliance costs time, work, and money that must be provided for in schedules and budgets. Production and operations managers should realize that unsafe practices and contamination of the environment can implicate them and their failure to practice sound management.

Johnson & Johnson, maker of bandages and other health care products, is intent on being known as the number one firm in safety.[28] When any workplace accident causes death or a fracture, injury, or burn resulting in at least one lost day of work, the head of the company unit involved must file a written report to top management within twenty-four hours. The head must then travel to company headquarters in New Brunswick, New Jersey, and personally explain to a top-level committee what went wrong. Johnson & Johnson slashed its annual lost workday incidence per 100 workers from 1.81 to 0.14 in eight years (1981–89). Corporate workers' compensation expenses now average about $50 billion annually. It pays to be as safe as possible.

Not only must employees have safe working conditions, the goods produced must be safe for the consumers who ultimately buy them. Product safety is the specific responsibility of the quality control department. Growing consumer consciousness of the issue has increased efforts to make products that are accident-proof. Automatic testing devices tug and pull plastic eyes and noses on toy rabbits to make sure they will not come off in the mouths of eager 2-year-olds. Medicine bottles are made tamperproof, and sharp products such as paring knives bear brightly colored labels to prevent consumers from cutting themselves accidentally.

Production in the United States is the most highly regulated in the world. Compliance, a production cost, has become increasingly expensive; research and development, testing, and fulfillment functions also add to the cost of production. The increased expenditures show that most companies and employees at all levels have begun to take safety issues seriously: Consumer accidents receive greater attention and investigation today than they did a decade ago.

Monsanto, the United States' fourth-largest chemical producer, has developed a program to help clean up the environment. Their pledge is reproduced in Exhibit 9-11.

9-8b Globalization of Environmental Pollution

In recent years international concern has focused on some alarming issues. The atmosphere's ozone layer is thinning. World climate is changing as a result of deforestation of large areas such as the Amazon rainforest. The Chernobyl nuclear accident released radiation on people hundreds of miles from its source, which is now enclosed in a giant sarcophagus-like enclosure.[29] In addition to workers and consumers, our very environment

28. "Quality Circles: A Worthy Tool to Use Under the QIP Umbrella," *Quality Update*, Fall 1990, pp. 26–29.

29. Albert R. Karr, "The Corporate Race Belongs to the Safest," *The Wall Street Journal*, July 5, 1990, pp. B1–B5.

is at risk from the dangers of industry. Major corporate safety issues are chemical casualties, air/water/land pollution, waste disposal, site location and maintenance, and general environmental protection from products or by-products of industry.[30]

Industry will continue to come under pressure to produce more, yet do it safely, cleanly, and efficiently. As globalization in all areas emphasizes the limitations and the vulnerability of our ecosystem, production managers all over the world will continue to be challenged to find new and better ways to produce.

9-9 THE CHALLENGE FOR PRODUCTION MANAGERS

If the problems of and pressures on production and operations management are unprecedented, perhaps so too are the opportunities for positive solutions. Most of these solutions have become possible as a result of the electronics revolution. It has been said that if the first Industrial Revolution multiplied the power of production 100 times, the second Industrial Revolution—empowered by the microcomputer—has increased it thousands of times.

Today, with the aid of CAD, CAE, CAM, and a wealth of other computer-based management tools, managers can plan, forecast, design, do research, and modify an infinite number of systems and products without the expense of trial and error. The expansion or contraction of schedules, the addition of a different wing to an experimental airplane plan, and the modification of a chemical coating for a 300-foot antenna that must last twenty years can all be planned and tested on the computer, with great accuracy. The computer was the single most important technological change to occur in industry in the twentieth century, and the change has only begun.

Microelectronics represents not only the most powerful avenue of positive change for industry but also the greatest potential arena for error. As with all forms of power, the test is in how the power is used. Already in the last two decades, we have witnessed major problems caused by error or misuse of microelectronics—from the space shuttle disaster to the failure of AT&T's electronic programs, which tied up half the country's telephone lines for nearly an entire day. A high degree of skill is needed to use the new technology well. Keeping up with technological change is, therefore, the primary challenge to the production managers of today and tomorrow.

SUGGESTED WEBSITES

Note: These websites were functional when we went to press. Please access the online text for the most up-to-date URLs.

1. www.compaq.com
2. www.boeing.com
3. www.merck.com
4. www.microsoft.com
5. www.honda.com
6. www.3m.com
7. www.toyota.com

30. Terry Golway, "Chernobyl's Children Call Out for Help," *New York Observer*, April 30, 2001, p. 1.

SUMMARY OF LEARNING OBJECTIVES

1. *Define the production and operations management function.* Production refers to the total process by which a business brings forth finished goods or services. Operations refers to the functions needed to keep the company producing. Functions such as purchasing, materials management, production, inventory and quality control, and maintenance are included. The process and functions needed to produce and/or deliver goods or services make up the production and operations management function.

2. *Discuss two or three critical issues facing production and operations management.* The concept that to live well a nation must produce well is a critical issue. The United States and other developed nations must find a way to improve the stature, performance, and quality of manufacturing firms. Another crucial issue involves finding the skilled workers needed to work with more sophisticated production techniques and processes.

3. *Evaluate the effects of computerization on production and operations management functions.* The effects have been significant in terms of speed, efficiency, and productivity. CAD, CAE, MRPII, and ERP have made possible tremendous flexibility and experimentation. The computer has become a major tool that must be understood by all production and operations employees.

4. *Explain the importance of productivity and quality to business.* Improvements in productivity and quality have long-term effects on the success of business. Ignoring either quality or productivity decreases the output per labor and technological input.

5. *Compare traditional company organization with cellular organization.* The traditional organization emphasizes specialists in areas linked to manufacturing. Cellular organizations have a layout in which machines are grouped into what is called a cell. Groupings are determined by the operations needed to perform work for a set of similar items. In the cellular arrangement, units are completed by a team. The layout speeds up the assembly from start to finish.

6. *Describe what is meant by the concept of managing the supply chain effectively.* Managing a supply chain effectively means that proper planning, organizing, and control mechanisms are in place to intiate, monitor, and evaluate the performance of members and processes in the chain. Through the management of monitoring and evaluation, adjustments, changes, and corrections in schedules, procurement, and the transformation of materials into products can be made.

7. *Review the role of the production and operations unit in safety and environmental concerns.* Corporate responsibility for employee safety is often delegated to the production and operations manager. Product safety is the specific responsibility of the quality control department. Concerns about pollution, global warming, toxic wastes, and preserving the earth's forests have made these topics of debate. The production and operations unit is expected by the corporation to oversee environmental matters. Environment-friendly technologies are needed in all areas, especially manufacturing. Production and operations units will be asked to work more on minimizing pollution at the same time they are expected to contribute to a firm's profit margins.

KEY TERMS

assembly line (p. 212)
computer-aided design (CAD) (p. 227)
computer-aided engineering (CAE) (p. 227)
computer-aided manufacturing (CAM) (p. 227)
enterprise resource planning (ERP) (p. 223)
flexible manufacturing systems (FMS) (p. 228)

just-in-time (JIT) (p. 222)
manufacturing (p. 211)
mass production (p. 212)
materials requirements planning (MRP) (p. 222)
materials resources planning (MRPII) (p. 222)
operations (p. 210)

PERT chart (p. 225)
production (p. 210)
productivity (p. 233)
quality circles (p. 232)
robots (p. 227)
supply chain management (SCM) (p. 223)

QUESTIONS FOR DISCUSSION AND REVIEW

1. What is the difference between operations and production? Why is it important to make this distinction?

2. What features of quality are important to you when you purchase a product or service?

3. If you were going to open a retail clothing store, what factors would be important in selecting a site layout?

4. Develop a PERT chart that depicts your plans for a college education. What important events should be noted?

5. How could an organization use ERP systems to improve their inventory control approach?

6. What is the meaning of the statement that quality is "perceived excellence"?

7. Do you think that inventory control systems such as the JIT technique can be applied to the operation of a service business? Give an example of why or why not.

8. CAD, CAM, ERP, MRPII, and FMS are abbreviations of innovations in production. Provide the meaning of each abbreviation and tell, in your own words, how each has affected the production function.

9. Explain why SCM has become such an important concept for organizational success.

10. Explain how a firm using cellular manufacturing differs from a traditional manufacturing organization.

END-OF-CHAPTER QUESTIONS

1. Dell computer delivers customized computers practically overnight.   **T** or **F**
2. Early textile mills and steel plants are good examples of *mass production*.   **T** or **F**
3. Industrial plants that mass-produce goods generally use a rigorous division of labor.   **T** or **F**
4. Production and operations managers can legally use *industrial espionage* to identify a company that is the best in the world at some process.   **T** or **F**
5. UPS drivers are instructed how to enter and leave the trucks in order to maximize efficiency.   **T** or **F**
6. Companies that use an assembly-line approach to produce goods have typically been structured according to a job-shop design.   **T** or **F**
7. The size of the business determines the layout of the site selected.   **T** or **F**
8. Because JIT systems have little finished-goods inventory, machine breakdowns are very costly.   **T** or **F**
9. Computer-aided design (CAD) has been used to design potato chips.   **T** or **F**
10. American automakers have been steadily losing domestic market share to foreign competitors.   **T** or **F**
11. Quality circles usually consist of seven to eleven people working in a related area.   **T** or **F**
12. In the past decade, more and more companies have begun to use _____ that allows workers to work in teams to manufacture products or subassemblies.
    a. an operations function
    b. a spiral line
    c. as assembly-line approach
    d. a cellular organization structure
13. Standardization of _____ was an essential factor in the development of mass production.
    a. wages
    b. parts
    c. workers
    d. transportation
14. The use of large _____ made mass production possible.
    a. groups of workers
    b. machinery
    c. warehouses
    d. volumes of natural resources
15. The physical process of producing goods is called _____.
    a. production
    b. manufacturing
    c. operations

INTERNET EXERCISE

Links to Terms

Visit the website www.alltheweb.com and use the following key phrases:

- Lean manufacturing
- CAD/CAM
- MRPII
- Quality management
- ERP software

1. What does your search show?
2. Find "links" on various sites that appear for each of the phrases.
3. Visit www.nam.org (National Association of Manufacturers) and use the five phrases in this site's search engine. What do you find?

EXPERIENTIAL EXERCISE

Learning about Production and Operations Managers

Activity

To gain firsthand knowledge of the duties and job environment of production and operations managers, students will identify and interview someone in that profession at their place of work. Interviews should be limited to twenty minutes.

Directions

1. Instructors should describe the roles of production and operations managers, emphasizing that management of production and operations often involves a large number of people.
2. Develop a short list of questions in class that each student should use for an interview with a manager.

   Encourage students to identify someone in an industry they are interested in and then arrange an interview with that person at the workplace. The interview should be arranged at a time convenient for the manager.
3. Students should complete the interviews within two weeks.
4. Each student should write a two-page report on his or her impressions of the duties of the manager, as well as his or her impression of the workplace.
5. If class time allows, students should share and debate their impressions in class.

BUSINESS APPLICATION

Selecting Site Location for Branch Campus

Activity

In groups of three to five, students will review the factors in site selection contained in Exhibit 9-6 and apply the criteria to the process of establishing a branch campus for the college. Approximately three hours outside of class will be needed to complete the application.

Directions

1. The instructor reviews the textbook material on factors involved in site selection.
2. Explain to the students that if the college were to expand its operations by opening a branch campus, then considerable time would be spent studying site location.
3. Assign students the task of making a recommendation for a site selection of the college's branch campus by applying the criteria reviewed from the textbook. The work is to be done in groups of three to five. Each group will be asked to present its findings to the class.
4. Encourage students to include additional factors not necessarily included in Exhibit 9-6.
5. On the due date of the assignment, ask the groups to make a five- to ten-minute presentation to the class on their site selection and the rationale behind it.

Case

The Application of Supply Chain Management

Longs Drug Stores and Seven-Eleven Japan are proving that successful demand chain management (DCM) can be a core competitive differentiator. Both companies have mastered the art of capturing and using information to respond to actual customer demands quickly and accurately.

Supply chain management (SCM) is widely recognized as a core component of global competitiveness, but DCM is often overlooked. Understanding demand requires a comprehensive knowledge of who your customers are, what products/services they like, how they make their purchases, how often they order, and what constraints they place on the purchasing process. Demand knowledge can then be used to drive a replenishment system that generates the right inputs from suppliers and reliably delivers the products and services to customers. The key to successfully using DCM is the smart use of information.

Longs Drug stores is a major U.S. drug chain with more than 400 retail outlets and $3.7 billion in annual sales. Today, drug chains like Longs cannot ignore the high cost of inventory. Price pressures from HMOs, insurance companies, Medicaid, and medicine, combined with higher costs of opening, stocking, and operating stores have been squeezing margins and increasing capital requirements.

Longs' senior managers recognized that the collective wisdom of pharmacists and buyers was no longer sufficient to manage inventory in a fast-changing environment. The firm decided a comprehensive information system was needed. Longs adopted a new technology supplied by NONSTOP Solutions. The NONSTOP solutions technology uses state-of-the-art methodologies to optimize demand chain activities: forecasting, inventory control, transportation, materials handling, and warehousing. The NONSTOP system uses daily demand as the unit of analysis. As new sales data are collected at the stores, Longs sends the data to NONSTOP via a secure intranet.

Seven-Eleven Japan (SEJ) is the country's largest convenience store chain. SEJ has more than 8,200 stores in Japan, a number that is growing by 400 to 500 per year. SEJ uses an integrated service digital network (ISDN) to link its retail stores with the central headquarters. The two-way communication gives franchises direct access to the host computer and the central database containing point-of-sale (POS) data and analysis.

When an SEJ customer comes to the checkout counter with a basket of items, the clerk first keys in the person's gender and age (estimate) on a separate key pad. The clerk then scans the bar codes of purchased items. These sales data are passed on to headquarters via the ISDN. At the same time, the data are processed by an in-store computer system that controls all equipment and peripherals in the store. The in-store computer enables both the store manager and SEJ headquarters to update and analyze POS data simultaneously. Headquarters aggregates the data by region, product, and time and makes the information available to all stores and suppliers by the following morning.

Longs and SEJ both enjoy financial success. One contributor to this success is very efficient DCM. Both companies recognize that data are the key to continuing success.

Questions for Discussion

1. Explain in your own terms the similarities and differences between demand and supply chain management.
2. What are Longs and Seven-Eleven Japan doing in terms of demand chain management that allows them to stand out among competitors?
3. Would you consider Longs and Seven-Eleven Japan to be agile, quick-reacting businesses? Why?

Sources: Hau L. Lee and Seungjin Whang, "Demand Chain Excellence: The Tale of Two Retailers," *Supply Chain Management Review*, March 2001, pp. 21–26; and *Supply Chain Management: Strategy, Planning, and Operations* (Englewood Cliffs, NJ: Prentice-Hall, 2001).

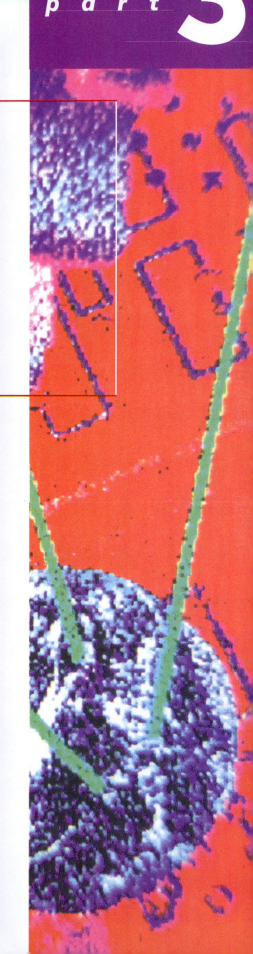

part 3

Human Resources Practices

10

Human Relations and Motivation

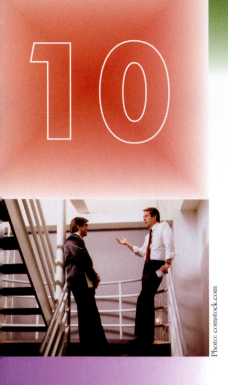

Photo: comstock.com

After completing this chapter, you should be able to:

1   **Define** the term *scientific management*.

2   **Explain** what the Hawthorne studies revealed about the role that groups play in motivating employees.

3   **Define** the term *motivation*.

4   **Discuss** Maslow's view of needs and motivation.

5   **Compare** and contrast the Theory X, Theory Y, and Theory Z approaches to motivating employees.

6   **Explain** why Herzberg's view of motivation is so popular with practicing managers.

7   **Describe** the principles of goal setting.

McKinsey's Motivational Approach

The global management-consulting firm McKinsey & Co. is a company that is concerned with the well-being, motivation, and personal development of its employees. Training programs, reward systems concerned about fairness, coaching, and leadership are all part of the McKinsey approach to create a positive and motivational work environment.

McKinsey uses intensive feedback and coaching as part of the motivational approach. Such activities absorb 15 to 20 percent of the average partner's time. Every McKinsey consultant receives a formal performance review from his or her office's partner group twice a year, with the individual's designated development director offering detailed feedback, counseling, and career advice. The input of the biannual review comes from reports prepared by each of the clients, engagement managers, and senior-level consultants who are responsible for the day-to-day management of the team to which the individual belongs and who have supervised the individual's work.

McKinsey has decided that an individual's internal motivation can be triggered and sustained by receiving feedback that is work related. The individual's knowledge of how he or she is doing helps direct behavior. People value feedback, and it is considered to be one of the key reasons why individuals enjoy working at McKinsey.

The McKinsey approach is to not only address monetary needs of individual employees, but to also pay attention to job performance. McKinsey's consultants are considered knowledge workers who place a high value on receiving feedback about their performance. Apparently, McKinsey has found through the intense feedback and coaching used that their knowledge workers value this approach and consider it motivational.

Sources: Adapted from Christopher A. Bartlett and Sumantra Ghoshal, "Building Competitive Advantage Through People," *MIT Sloan Management Review*, Winter 2002, pp. 34–41; and Jonathon D. Day, Paul Y. Mang, Ansgar Richter, & John Roberts, 2002, "Has Pay for Performance Had Its Day?" *McKinsey Quarterly*, 2002, accessed online at www.mckinseyquarterly.com.

10-1 MOTIVATION AND PERFORMANCE

In any attempt to motivate, the psychology of individuals—why they behave the way they do—is important. Motivation attempts to influence or cause certain behaviors.[1] In fact, many people equate the causes of behavior with motivation. The importance of the behavior concept is spelled out in advice Ross Perot once gave to General Motors: A positively motivated person behaves enthusiastically, forcefully, and with a clear purpose. This is also what McKinsey's top management believes as indicated in the opening vignette.

One of the most difficult tasks facing managers is motivating employees. Managers are responsible and accountable for meeting important organizational objectives. Therefore, they must be concerned about the performance of employees in such important tasks as answering a customer complaint, interpreting a computer printout, or selling a graphic computer disk player to a customer. Successful business managers must create an atmosphere that motivates employees to use their skills and abilities. When a skilled employee does not perform up to his capabilities, is this a motivation problem? Yes, it probably is.

10-2 HUMAN RESOURCE MANAGEMENT AND RELATIONS

Frederick Winslow Taylor's principles of scientific management introduced the importance of managing human resources and relations. Taylor studied workers in the Midvale and Bethlehem steel plants in 1885. His most famous experiment involved a pig iron shoveler he called Schmidt (his real name was Henry Noll). Using a time-and-motion approach and a stopwatch, Taylor studied Schmidt's every move and work activity. He presented improvements in how to handle pig iron. Schmidt increased his productivity from 12.5 long tons (a long ton equals 2,240 pounds) to 47.5 long tons per day!

1. Kenneth W. Thomas, *Intrinsic Motivation at Work: Building Energy and Commitment* (San Francisco: Barrett-Koehler, 2000).

Scientific Management
The scientific study and breakdown of work into its smallest mechanical elements, and their rearrangement into the most efficient combination.

Hawthorne Studies A series of experiments that found that work groups significantly affected the way workers behave and perform.

This is **scientific management**—the systematic study and breakdown of work into its smallest mechanical elements, and then the rearrangement of these elements into their most efficient combination. The application of scientific management principles has resulted in many cases of increased or improved productivity. However, some of the principles, such as introducing a high degree of specialization or routine work, result in boredom and poor morale among some individuals.

10-2a The Hawthorne Studies

The **Hawthorne studies** were conducted from 1927 to 1932 at a Western Electric plant in Cicero, a suburb of Chicago.[2] The team of Harvard University researchers included Elton Mayo, Fritz Roethlisberger, and William Dickson. This series of experiments is the single most important event in the historical foundation of the behavioral study of employees.

In an illumination experiment, employees were divided into two groups. One group worked in a test room where the intensity of lighting was varied, and the other group worked in a room with constant lighting over the time of the experiment. When light levels were raised in the test room, production increased; when light levels were lowered, production still increased. Puzzled, the researchers decided to change working conditions. They introduced shorter rest periods, longer but fewer rest periods, and other changes. Once again, no matter what change was introduced, production still improved.

The researchers next interviewed many of the employees involved in the study, asking questions about their reactions to working conditions. The researchers found that a change in morale occurred because the employees felt more responsible. They also did not want to let down coworkers. This was a form of self-imposed pressure. They also felt good about being a part of the experiment. Labor turnover stopped, and absences were drastically reduced. An employee who had been absent eighty-five times in the thirty-two months before the experiment went for sixteen months without an absence.

A second experiment, which lasted for only sixteen weeks, was designed to measure the effect of group incentive plans on productivity. Although economical incentives were offered for increased productivity, the members of the group set informal production quotas that would allow most group members to work at a comfortable pace. Productivity levels were not significantly increased. The power of the informal group, not the economic incentive, controlled production.

The Hawthorne findings offered no perfect answers or specific motivation programs for managers. But the studies did show that informal groups can influence productivity. Productivity increased through self-imposed pressure in the first experiment, but it was restricted by group pressure in the second. Both experiments used highly cohesive, or tightly knit, groups.

The major difference in the two experiments was the supervisory style used. The first used general supervision. The employees stated that they had freedom and were treated well. They felt special and good about themselves. The self was recognized, and employees liked this kind of recognition. In the second experiment, a closer supervisory style was used.

There were other dissimilarities. The employees were women in the first experiment, men in the second. In the second experiment, the room in which the employees worked was set up just for the experiment and involved no researcher-introduced changes. In the first experiment, the researchers changed lighting and rest periods.

Regardless of the differences, the Hawthorne studies showed how group characteristics and type of supervision, among other things, influence motivation and productivity. The studies have been interpreted in different ways, but one message is clear. Managers attempting to create a favorable climate for motivation need to consider (1) the group, (2) helping employees improve their self-esteem, and (3) style of supervision.

2. Robert D. Smithers, *The Psychology of Work and Human Performance* (New York: Longman, 1998).

The importance of helping people to feel good about themselves, to feel special, is captured in Roethlisberger's own words: "If one experiments on a stone, the stone does not know it is being experimented upon"—which makes things simple for people experimenting on stones. But a human being who is being experimented upon is likely to know it. Therefore, attitudes toward the experiment and toward the experimenter become very important factors in determining the subjects' responses. This phenomenon is known as the "Hawthorne effect."[3]

Scientific management and the Hawthorne studies have contributed many insights, methodologies, and ideas to the area of human relations; that is, the study of how organizations manage their employees individually and within groups to improve productivity. The Hawthorne studies are so important in understanding motivation, groups, and productivity that the original readings are now considered classics and are required reading for scholars and researchers around the world.

10-2b Motivation Concepts

Motivation is the way in which drives or needs direct a person's behavior toward a goal. It concerns the level of effort put forth to pursue specific goals. Managers cannot observe the motivational process directly since it occurs internally. So they observe behaviors and then reach conclusions about a person's motivation. For example, Anne, a fifth-grade teacher, knows that José and Mike have similar intelligence and ability. José does well in school, but Mike continually struggles with school work. She concludes that José is motivated but Mike is not. Why? That's the motivational puzzle Anne must solve.

> **Motivation** The way drives or needs direct a person's behavior toward a specific goal; involves the level of effort put forth to pursue the goal.

Managers become concerned about motivation when employees exhibit productivity problems, reduced commitment to quality, and resistance to management programs. Managers know it is not simple to motivate employees. In fact, managers realize they must understand how to use an array of tools (e.g., techniques, programs, rewards) to create the best motivational atmosphere possible.

Generally speaking, rewards and punishments are the tools managers use to motivate employees. Rewards can be extrinsic or intrinsic. **Extrinsic rewards** are external to the work itself, they are administered by someone else, such as a manager. Examples include pay, fringe benefits, recognition, and praise. **Intrinsic rewards** are related directly to performing the job. In this sense, they are often described as self-administered. Intrinsic rewards include feeling good about accomplishing an objective and about being able to make job-related decisions without consulting a supervisor. On the other hand, **punishment** involves taking something away from a person or administering an undesirable consequence for a particular behavior. For example, a frequently tardy worker would be punished by having his or her pay docked for the time missed.

> **Extrinsic Rewards** Rewards external to the work itself and administered by someone else, such as a manager.
>
> **Intrinsic Rewards** Rewards derived from a sense of gratification directly related to performing the job.
>
> **Punishment** An undesirable consequence of a particular behavior.

Communicating and administering rewards and punishments are part of the manager's job in creating the best motivational atmosphere. Both types of rewards appear to produce higher levels of performance than punishment does.

Motivation is goal oriented. It can work this way: First, the person experiences tension created by unfulfilled needs. A need indicates a deficiency; for example, when you are hungry, you have a need for food. Second, the person starts a search to find a reasonable way to satisfy these unfulfilled needs. Third, when some of the needs are fulfilled and some of the goals are accomplished, the process begins again. Exhibit 10-1 illustrates the goal-oriented process of motivation.

To create the atmosphere their subordinates need to perform efficiently, managers must have some grasp of the motivation process. As recognized management guru, educator, and consultant Peter Drucker stated: "No matter how authoritarian the institution, it has to satisfy the ambitions and needs of its members and do so in their capacity as individuals."[4] The rest of this chapter discusses various types of needs and how they can be used to motivate and manage employees.

---

3. Bent Blyvbjerg, *Making Social Science Matter* (Cambridge, England: Cambridge University Press, 2001).

4. Peter Drucker, *Management Tasks, Responsibilities, Practices* (New York: Harper & Row, 1974), p. 504.

EXHIBIT 10-1

The Process of Motivation in the Individual

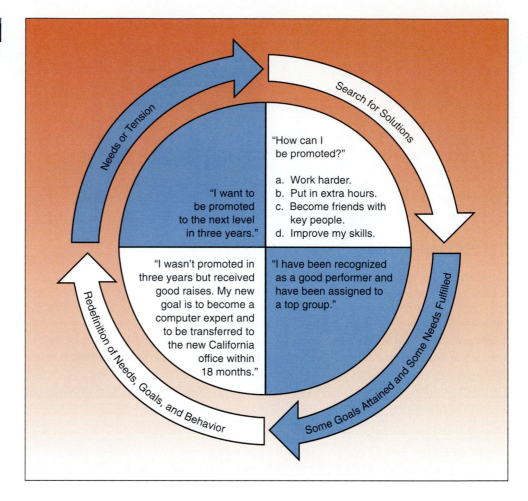

10-3 THEORIES OF MANAGEMENT AND NEEDS

A number of traditional and classical motivation theories and explanations have found their way into the literature and practitioner debates. A few of these classic theories are presented as examples.

10-3a Maslow's Needs Hierarchy

A popular theory of human needs that helps us understand motivation is psychologist Abraham Maslow's **needs hierarchy.** He identified five basic needs that explain the internal motivational process: physiological, safety, social, esteem, and self-actualization needs.[5]

The needs Maslow identified fall into a hierarchy, or arrangement, of power to motivate behavior, as illustrated in Exhibit 10-2. Each higher-order need becomes active and motivates a person only when lower-level needs have been fulfilled. Each person is assumed to have needs in each category. Examples of job satisfiers that can fulfill the needs are also included in Exhibit 10-2.

The starting point for understanding motivation is **physiological needs.** The person who is hungry or tired is thinking about food or sleep, not work. But once physiological needs are fulfilled, they lose their power to motivate. Then **safety needs** become important. For instance, workers are concerned about keeping their jobs and about being financially secure when they retire. "How safe is my job?" is a question being asked around the United States.

Needs Hierarchy
A motivational theory, offered by Maslow, that people have five needs arranged in a hierarchy from physiological to self-actualization.

Physiological Needs   Biological needs, such as for food, air, water.

Safety Needs   Security needs, such as the need to be financially secure and protected against job loss.

5. Abraham Maslow and Deborah C. Stephens, *The Maslow Business Reader* (San Francisco: Jossey-Bass, 2000); and Leslie W. Braksick, *Unlock Behavior, Unleash Profits* (New York: McGraw-Hill, 1999).

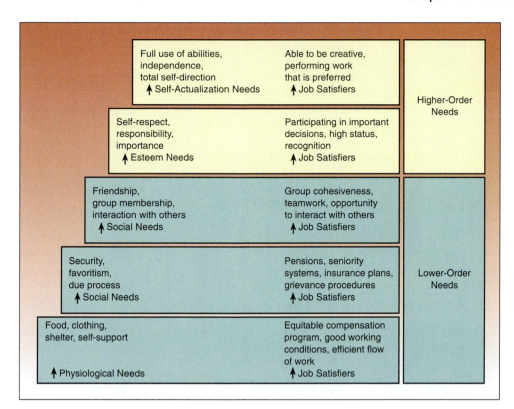

Around the world each year, jobs are eliminated and cut from the payroll because of mergers, economic setbacks, and organizational changes. For example, every year thousands of employees learn they are losing their jobs.[6] Such cutbacks threaten an employee's sense of job security. Safety needs can be satisfied by the creation of seniority systems, pensions, and insurance plans. As with physiological needs, once most of the safety needs have been satisfied, the next level of needs becomes more important.

Employees want to belong, to interact with other employees. Thus the friendly behavior of individuals in small groups within organizations is a major source of satisfaction for **social needs.** In a small group, individuals support and encourage one another; as a by-product, they get a sense of being an accepted member of the group. Once social needs have been largely satisfied, they also begin to lose their power to motivate.

The **esteem needs** are needs for self-respect and respect from others. An important part of this area is that an employee's work efforts and output be recognized and appreciated by others. When the need for esteem is strong, the individual will often set difficult goals, work hard to achieve the goals, and expect to receive recognition for these efforts. Goal accomplishment and the resulting recognition lead to feelings of self-esteem and self-confidence.

The top of the needs hierarchy is self-actualization, the ability to display and use one's full potential. **Self-actualization needs** take over when an adequate level of satisfaction has been reached in the other four need levels. A person who reaches self-actualization has come close to using his or her full set of skills. Maslow noted that self-actualizing people display certain characteristics:

- They tend to be serious and thoughtful.
- They focus on problems outside themselves.
- Their behavior is unaffected and natural.
- They are strongly ethical.

Social Needs   The need to belong and to interact with other people.

Esteem Needs   The need for self-respect and respect from others.

Self-Actualization Needs   The need to use and display one's full range of skills and competence.

6. Ann Fisher, "Staying Put in a Mediocre Job, *Fortune*, March 4, 2002, p. 146.

Most people think of artists, composers, and scientists as seeking self-actualization. Because people work to satisfy the more basic needs, managers often overlook employees' self-actualization needs.

Reaching a level of complete self-actualization rarely occurs. Certainly it is hard to achieve if other needs are not being adequately satisfied. But everyone is capable of partially satisfying the self-actualization need. Steve Jobs, one of the original founders of Apple Computer in Cupertino, California, achieved a sense of accomplishment by nurturing the personal computer concept. He had an insatiable desire to commercialize the Apple computer. Through his work and creativity he reached a state of satisfying his self-actualization needs.[7]

Of course, employees differ in the intensity of their needs. Some have an intense security need that will dominate their behavior no matter what managers do. Others are more strongly influenced by esteem needs. Managers have no standard program to follow when attempting to encourage a high level of motivation. Differences in personal background, experience, and education are powerful; conditions that work for one individual may not work for another.

10-3b McGregor's Theory X and Theory Y

Although managers should try to understand needs, they often don't. Douglas McGregor, a professor of management, introduced a theory of managerial style, referred to as Theory X and Theory Y, to explain this phenomenon.[8]

Theory X managers believe the average employee

Theory X Managerial assumptions that employees dislike work, responsibility, and accountability and must be closely directed and controlled to be motivated to perform.

- Dislikes work and finds ways to avoid it as much as possible.
- Responds to threats of punishment or control because of the dislike of work.
- Avoids responsibility because of a lack of ambition.
- Wants to be directed and have security.

A problem with making such assumptions about people is that they can become self-fulfilling. A manager with a Theory X view of workers will probably focus on creating conditions to satisfy physiological and safety needs, closely controlling and supervising subordinates. Some employees respond favorably to this style, but others feel frustrated, anxious, and very much in conflict. Their goals for self-esteem and self-actualization cannot be achieved.

Theory Y is a set of managerial assumptions that results in looser control and more delegation of authority. The Theory Y manager assumes that the average employee

Theory Y Managerial assumptions that employees want to be challenged, like to display creativity, and can be highly motivated to perform well if given some freedom to direct or manage their own behavior.

- Enjoys work and does not want to avoid it.
- Wants to achieve organizational goals through self-directed behavior.
- Responds to rewards associated with accomplishing goals.
- Will accept responsibility.
- Has initiative and can be creative in solving organizational problems.
- Is intellectually underutilized.

According to McGregor, Theory Y assumptions reflect a managerial emphasis on human growth and development instead of coercive authority.

Theory X and Theory Y represent two extremely different positions—an autocratic management style and a democratic management style. Many workers prefer Theory Y behavior from managers. They want to satisfy some of their social, esteem, and self-actualization needs on the job, and Theory-X-oriented management behavior only produces frustration and anxiety. Because of our democratic political heritage, the idea of

7. Julie Rose, "The New Risk Takers," *Fortune Small Business,* February 15, 2002, pp. 30–33.

8. Manuel London (ed.), *How People Evaluate Others in Organizations* (Mahwah, NJ: Erlbaum, 2001).

Theory Y is appealing to most people. On the other hand, there are some workers who don't respond well in a Theory-Y-oriented organization; some job situations call for autocratic controls. These individuals want their job duties spelled out specifically and prefer to work within a tightly controlled set of expectations. Managers must apply their own unique diagnostic skills to determine what each employee prefers—Theory X, Theory Y, or some combination of these two positions. He or she must observe, review, and contemplate the people involved and the situation and then determine which particular style best optimizes motivation.

10-3c Ouchi's Theory Z

The Japanese performance miracle in the 1970s and 1980s, which is still impacting many of today's managerial practices, is attributed to many factors, such as business-government cooperation, operating with relatively new (post–World War II) plants and equipment, a homogeneous ethnic population, a group-oriented culture, and even a rigorous educational system.

Another factor in the successes achieved by a highly motivated workforce is called the **Theory Z** style of management. William Ouchi's Theory Z approach draws on characteristics of successful U.S. and Japanese management styles and organizational practices. Ouchi, a management researcher, emphasizes these characteristics of Theory Z practices:[9]

- Lifetime employment (to help satisfy physiological and safety needs)
- Consensus decision making (to help satisfy social needs)
- Individual responsibility (to help satisfy self-esteem needs)
- Careful evaluation and promotion (to build confidence and self-esteem)
- Opportunity to use skills (to help satisfy self-actualization needs)

Theory Z   Management theory that draws on the characteristics of successful Japanese and American managers; emphasizes consensus management practices.

A comparison of U.S., Japanese, and Theory Z styles (see Exhibit 10-3) illustrates the blending of the first two approaches into the third.

Theory Z places a special emphasis on participative management; that is, employees participate in goal setting, decision making, problem solving, and designing and implementing changes. Participation, or being involved, is thought to improve employee motivation. Of course, some workers may prefer not to participate in these areas. This point should be kept in mind when an enthusiastic advocate of Theory Z and participation attempts to get everyone involved. Some people simply want to do their job well and go home. Likewise some firms or jobs have a culture or atmosphere in which participation will not work. For example, in a business with only one trained scientist working in research and development, the scientist would listen to others but the experimentation and testing of new ideas can and should be carried out by only the one trained person.

As with Theory X and Theory Y, the Theory Z assumptions and suggestions have not been subjected to extensive scientific testing or evaluation. There is no solid evidence to support any of these explanations. However, each offers a perspective on the behavior of employees in organizations. And proactive, inquisitive managers are interested in each perspective to help explain the differences they observe daily among their employees.

10-3d Herzberg's Two-Factor Model of Motivation

In the 1950s, Frederick Herzberg, a social psychologist and consultant, proposed a **work motivation model** that is still popular among business managers.[10] Herzberg surveyed accountants and engineers, asking them to describe when they felt good or bad about their

Work Motivation Model   An explanation of motivation that defines hygiene factors and motivator factors, and how they affect job satisfaction and dissatisfaction.

9. Masao Nakamura, *The Japanese Business and Economic System: History and Prospects for the 21st Century* (New York: Palgrave, 2001).

10. J. Michael Syptak, David W. Marsland, and Deborah Ulmer, "Job Satisfaction: Putting Theory into Practice," *Family Practice Management*, October 1999, pp. 22–28.

EXHIBIT 10-3

Blending American and Japanese Styles into Theory Z

	Management Style		
Characteristic	**American**	**Japanese**	**Theory Z**
Length of employment	Relatively short-term; layoffs when business slow	Long-term; lifetime when possible	Retain employees in good and bad times
Evaluation and promotion	Short-term and rapid promotions	Longer-term and moderate promotion schedule	Evaluate skills and promotions based on contributions, not tenure
Decision making	Individual	Collective, with input from all parties	Use of a democratic process that strives for consensus
Responsibility	Individual	Shared by group	Responsibility remains with key individuals
Control	Control by use of policies and rules	Self-control	Informal but with an emphasis on objective facts and data
Concern for workers	Emphasis on work itself	Focus on entire life of workers	Concerned with worker's life and family

Source: A. Parasuraman, *Marketing Research,* © 1995 by Addison-Wesley Publishing Co., p. 20. Reprinted by permission of the Addison-Wesley Publishing Co., Reading, MA.

jobs. He found that one set of job and personal factors produced good feelings and that another created bad feelings.

One set of factors Herzberg called **hygiene factors** (also called *maintenance factors*). These factors, if present and available, are essential to job satisfaction, although they cannot motivate an employee. They include the following:

Hygiene Factors External characteristics essential to avoiding job dissatisfaction.

Salary	Working conditions	Technical supervision
Job security	Status	Company policies
Personal life	Interpersonal relations	

Hygiene factors, if absent or inadequate, cause job dissatisfaction. Herzberg believes that by providing these factors, managers can prevent job dissatisfaction but cannot motivate employees to perform any better.

Herzberg described the second set of factors as **motivators** of on-the-job behavior. They include the following:

Motivators Content-oriented characteristics that contribute to job satisfaction.

Achievement	Advancement	Growth opportunities
Recognition	The job itself	Responsibility

Whereas hygiene factors deal with external features of the job, motivators are job-content oriented, or tied to the job itself.

The employee appreciates the hygiene and motivator factors at different times. For example, the employee takes a paycheck (hygiene factor) to a bank, cashes it, and receives some satisfaction when the money is received. While actually performing the work, the employee can receive and enjoy such motivators as responsibility, recognition, and growth opportunities. These and other motivator factors make up the fabric of the job.

Omni Hotels has established a motivator-based program for its hardworking employees.[11] The Omni Service Champion (OSC) program recognizes employees who go beyond

11. Ronald Whipple, "Rewards Have Value," *Personnel Journal,* September 1990, pp. 92–93.

Job factors	Worker dissatisfaction with the job	Neutral about the job	Satisfaction with the job
Motivators		Little or no satisfaction with motivators "I'm not being challenged by my job."	Satisfaction "My job is now really challenging me."
Hygiene factors	Dissatisfaction with the hygiene factors "I am dissatisfied with my working conditions."	Little or no dissatisfaction "My job is OK, I guess."	

EXHIBIT 10-4

The Dissatisfaction-Satisfaction Relationship: An Application

the call of duty to ensure guest satisfaction. Employees observed doing something extra to help a guest are given OSC commendations on the spot. Commendations have been given for packing luggage for a guest with a broken hand, saving someone's life at the hotel pool, or taking a taxi to another location to get something fixed for a customer. On the first, fifth, tenth, fifteenth, and twentieth days of each month, the recognized employees receive the OSC medal that is worn on the uniform. At the end of the year, the three employees from each Omni hotel who received the most medals are awarded medals and cash prizes, and they attend a gala celebration to culminate the program for the year.

Hygiene factors can result in not being dissatisfied, but they are not motivational. Managers need to know this because the elimination of job dissatisfaction will not necessarily motivate employees. Exhibit 10-4 presents Herzberg's thinking on this issue. If motivation is what the manager wants to achieve, then he or she must emphasize recognition, achievement, and growth, the motivators.

10-3e Maslow and Herzberg: A Comparison

Maslow's needs hierarchy and Herzberg's work motivation model have many similarities, as Exhibit 10-5 shows. The lower-level needs are similar to the hygiene factors. These needs are satisfied for many employees, but some have not adequately fulfilled their lower-level needs. Then hygiene factors may be motivators. Today managers pay more attention to the higher-level needs, or motivator factors, than they did in the 1950s when Herzberg presented his theory.

Although Herzberg's model is popular and makes sense, it has been criticized. Some critics remind us that the original study group from which the model was developed included only engineers and accountants. These two occupational groups do not represent most employees (salesclerks, computer operators, teachers, police officers, scientists, nurses) in organizations. In response, Herzberg cited studies that used nurses, supervisors, scientists, food handlers, and assemblers and found results similar to his original study. Other critics question the manner in which Herzberg collected his information. They believe that his method of asking questions influenced the way the accountants and engineers responded.

Despite these criticisms, many managers use the work motivation model, because it is logical and uses language that managers understand. However, it was not Maslow, McGregor, or Herzberg who really stimulated management thinking about motivation at work. It was the previously mentioned Hawthorne studies.

We have discussed types of needs that employees have. The values and attitudes quiz in Exhibit 10-6 on page 253, examines the Maslow needs hierarchy. Take a few minutes and complete the scale. Maslow's needs hierarchy provides a useful framework for managers.[12]

12. Longer, more detailed survey scales are available in the organizational behavior and management literature.

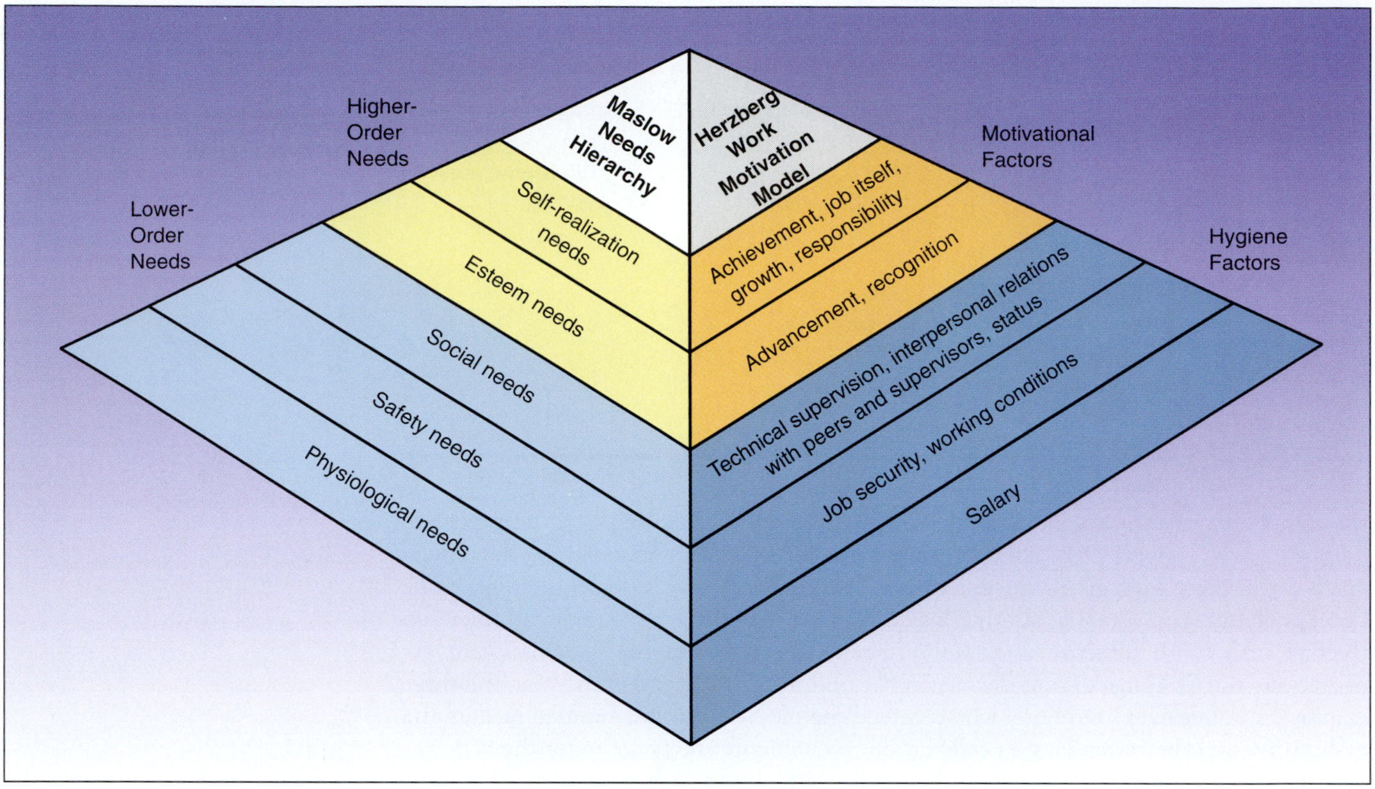
Maslow Needs Hierarchy
Herzberg Work Motivation Model
Higher-Order Needs
Lower-Order Needs
Motivational Factors
Hygiene Factors
Self-realization needs
Esteem needs
Social needs
Safety needs
Physiological needs
Achievement, job itself, growth, responsibility
Advancement, recognition
Technical supervision, interpersonal relations with peers and supervisors, status
Job security, working conditions
Salary

EXHIBIT 10-5

Similarities in the Needs Hierarchy and Work Motivation Model

INTERACTIVE EXHIBIT

10-4 MOTIVATING EMPLOYEES

The group incentive plan in the Hawthorne studies did not motivate the employees as expected. Those and other studies show that there is no magic formula for providing employees with the interest and desire to perform well—although some programs work better than others. The manager's job is to find the best motivational trigger for his or her group and situation. For some, money is a key, whereas others prefer more job authority, and still others like to have clear objectives to use as targets. The example of Warren Buffet in the Focus on Business box on page 254, "Motivation Is Personal," illustrates how personal motivation is for each employee.

10-4a Goal Setting

Goal Setting The process of identifying specific levels of performance to be achieved in a certain time frame.

The notion that employees' motivation and performance may be enhanced by setting specific job performance goals has gained popularity in the past thirty years. As a result of research, some specific principles of goal setting have been established.[13] **Goal setting** is the process of identifying specific levels of performance that a person seeks to accomplish in a certain time frame.

Probably the best-established goal-setting principle is that workers perform at higher levels when asked to meet a specific challenging goal than they do when simply asked to "do your best" or when no goal at all is assigned. This principle relates the effectiveness of goal setting not only to specific goals but also to challenging goals. However, when goals become too difficult, performance drops because the goals are seen as unrealistic. For example, a usually average student setting a goal to be the number one person in the class might be unrealistic.

Another interesting goal-setting concept is to involve workers in the process. Meaningful goals that employees have helped to set may enhance performance more than goals

13. Gary R. Blair, *Goal Setting Forms: Tools to Help You Get Ready, Get Set, and Go for Goals* (New York: The Goals Guy, 2000).

Directions: Circle the number under the response that best describes your own feelings about the statement. There are no right or wrong answers; the purpose of this questionnaire is simply to organize your own thoughts about your personal preferences.

	Strongly Disagree	Agree	Neither	Disagree	Strongly Agree
1. I value friendship more than almost anything else.	5	4	3	2	1
2. Just knowing I've done something well gives me satisfaction; I don't need praise from others.	1	2	3	4	5
3. Being happy is more important to me than making money.	5	4	3	2	1
4. I need a lot of time by myself.	1	2	3	4	5
5. My first priority is high income and job security.	5	4	3	2	1
6. I don't believe people should waste their time pursuing dreams.	1	2	3	4	5
7. I feel disgusted if someone else gets credit for my accomplishments.	5	4	3	2	1
8. I'm more concerned with whether or not I enjoy my work than what I get paid for doing it.	1	2	3	4	5

Feedback: This quiz measures one's current motivational interest. This insight will help you understand why you view the interests of others to be similar or different.

Score your answers by filling in the numbers you have circled in the form below. Your scores will range from 2 to 10 on each of the four need scales. The four need scores correspond to the four higher-order categories of needs (or motives) identified by Abraham Maslow. The lowest-level need category, physiological needs (food, shelter, water, etc.), is not included. High-scale scores are 8, 9, or 10. Did you score high on more than one scale? Which ones? Do you think your scores accurately describe your own predominant motives?

Items	Scores	Need Scale
5 + 8	___ + ___ = ___	Safety, security
1 + 4	___ + ___ = ___	Belongingness, social
2 + 7	___ + ___ = ___	Self-esteem
3 + 6	___ + ___ = ___	Self-actualization

that are simply assigned by a manager. The logic is that, by participating, a person becomes more committed and develops a stronger drive to accomplish the goal.

Feedback on goal accomplishments is also important.[14] People want to know how they are doing. Whether the accomplishment concerns schoolwork, hitting a baseball, or drawing a picture, people value feedback. A study of different units in the U.S. Air Force showed that feedback and goal setting together helped improve performance for work groups as opposed to individuals.[15]

Managers can use goal setting to motivate employees. Setting specific, challenging goals and providing feedback about goal accomplishment enhance motivation and

14. Stephen C. Lunden, Harry Paul, and John Christensen, *Fish!* (New York: Hyperion, 2000).

15. R. D. Pritchard, S. D. Jones, P. L. Roth, K. K. Steubing, and S. E. Ekeberg, "Effects of Group Feedback, Goal Setting, and Incentives on Productivity, *Journal of Applied Psychology*, April 1988, pp. 337–358.

FOCUS ON BUSINESS

Motivation Is Personal

Warren Buffett is the founder, chairman, and CEO of Berkshire Hathaway, a very successful and world-famous investment firm located in Omaha, Nebraska. He is an unassuming, wealthy, and interesting individual who has his own opinions about work, happiness, and motivation. Buffett, in talking to a group of college students at the University of Washington, stated:

I can certainly define happiness, because happy is what I am. . . . I get to do what I like to do every single day of the year. I get to do it with people I like, and I don't have to associate with anybody who causes my stomach to churn. I tap dance to work. . . . I'd advise you that when you go to work, work for an organization of people you admire, because it will turn you on. I always worry about people who say, "I'm going to do this for 10 years; I really don't like it very well. And then I'll do this. . . . That's a little like saving up sex for old age. Not a very good idea. I have turned down business deals that were otherwise decent deals because I didn't like the people I would have to work with. I didn't see any sense in pretending.

Buffett's statement shows that he is motivated by his job, the work environment, and colleagues. He is like most people, motivated by a number of factors.

Sources: Keith H. Hammonds, "Norman Lear's Not Laughing," *Fast Company*, January 2001, pp. 48–50; and S. Nearman, "The Simple Billionaire," *Selling Power*, June 1999, p. 48 (quote).

performance. Management by objectives (MBO) involves the use of goal setting either throughout an organization or within units.

One excellent goal setter and goal accomplisher is Harvey Cook, the author of *Scientific Success*. He sells insurance only two days a week for seven months out of the year. He sells $4 million of insurance in the first eight days.[16] His advice: "Don't compete for number 1; compete with yourself." Cook uses a fifteen-minute time guide for his goals by breaking his day into fifteen-minute increments.

According to Cook, a person must decide what to accomplish in each fifteen-minute period of the day. A salesperson's game plan might be:

- Every fifteen minutes, make the three telephone calls you'll need to get one qualified appointment.
- Spend thirty-five minutes of selective canvassing with potential clients to get one appointment.
- Line up sixteen appointments to make the eleven client presentations you need to close at least ten sales every two days.

Don't just set goals to increase numbers. Use tools of motivation to improve effectiveness. Novelists such as Irving Wallace and Ernest Hemingway used reinforcement systems and goals to increase their writing productivity. Day by day they would chart the number of words they had written. That number compared to a goal scolded or encouraged the author. Hemingway accumulated words he'd written over his goal so he could reward himself with a day off. Goal setting is a powerful technique that, when combined with rewards, sanctions, and self-discipline, can be a powerful motivating force.

16. "The Science of Success: How to Develop New Performance Habits, " *Success*, September 1990, pp. 48–49.

10-4b Job Enrichment

In his work motivation model, Herzberg introduced **job enrichment,** a method intended to increase the motivation and satisfaction of employees and to improve production through job design. By adding more motivators to the job, job enrichment can make work meaningful, stimulating, and challenging. The employee comes to view the job a lot like play. Don Ritcher owns an Arby's Restaurant in Chicago. Rather than using authority, commands, and directives to motivate his employees to be courteous to customers, show up for work on time, help keep the restaurant immaculate, and work hard, Ritcher created an achievement-oriented franchise. He permitted his workers to establish flexible work schedules to fit their needs, instituted an "employee of the week" reward program, held discussion meetings and allowed each employee to present opinions on how to improve business and service, and let employees attend development seminars to improve their skills. He made working at Arby's more meaningful and interesting.

> **Job Enrichment**
> A motivational technique that involves incorporating variety, feedback, and autonomy in the job.

The first step in job enrichment is to determine which characteristics of a job increase motivation. Picture the golfer hitting a bag of practice balls. Such practice is meaningful because the hitting skill can be improved. The golfer is in charge of every shot attempted. Once a shot is made, the golfer receives immediate feedback on how well the ball was hit. The sense of hitting the ball well is important in determining the golfer's "psychological feelings" about practicing; it serves to motivate him or her to continue or to come back for another practice session.

The same is true for an employee doing a job. Motivational jobs contain the following characteristics:

- *Meaningfulness*—the work must be perceived as worthwhile.
- *Responsibility*—the employee must be personally responsible for any effort expended.
- *Knowledge of results*—the employee must receive, on a regular basis, feedback about how well he or she is performing.

When these conditions are present, jobholders usually feel good about the job and their contribution. These good feelings motivate employees to continue to do well. But if one of these three conditions is missing, the internal feeling (motivation) drops off dramatically.

Studies indicate that five job characteristics create good psychological feelings about a job.[17] These characteristics can be enriched by a manager. Three of the five characteristics contribute to the meaningfulness of a job:

- *Skill variety*—the degree to which a job requires activities that are challenging.
- *Task identity*—the degree to which the job requires the completion of a "whole" piece of work. For example, building an entire generator has more tasks than just placing a flywheel on the generator as it passes by on a conveyor belt.
- *Task significance*—the degree to which the job is significant to the organization or other individuals.

A fourth job characteristic leads an employee to experience more responsibility: *Autonomy* is the degree to which the job gives the worker freedom, independence, and leeway to carry out what is required. The fifth job characteristic, *feedback*, is the degree to which a worker gets information on his or her effectiveness in carrying out the job.

Organizations such as AT&T, Saab-Scania, Volvo, and General Foods have used job enrichment to motivate employees; they have redesigned or changed job characteristics for various employees or groups. But like all sound motivation programs, job enrichment must be used selectively. Management must also provide enough time for the approach to be understood. The user must consider the situation, the job, and the people involved (see Exhibit 10-7). Job characteristics that can be enriched are especially important for

✍ 1, 2, 3, 4

17. Sharon K. Parker and Toby D. Wall, *Job and Work Design* (Thousand Oaks, CA: Sage, 1998).

EXHIBIT 10-7

Job Characteristics, Individual Differences, and Reactions

INTERACTIVE EXHIBIT

Job Characteristics That Can Be Found	Individual Differences and Need Strengths	Potential Reaction to Jobs

Skill variety
Task identity
Task significance
Autonomy
Feedback

Employees who desire job enrichment

High internal motivation
High job satisfaction
High pride in work that is done
Lower absenteeism

Employees with low desire for job enrichment

Possible lowered job satisfaction
Frustration with changes
Internal motivation not encouraged by the job

employees who desire enrichment. The potential consequences for these workers are spelled out in the figure. Usually, if the organization supports enrichment, more employees desire the job changes.

10-4c Behavior Modification

The application of a set of learning principles called operant conditioning, developed by psychologist B. F. Skinner (1904–1990), is called **behavior modification.**[18] Behavior modification grew out of the idea that changing the attitude of a person does not necessarily improve performance. Instead the person's behavior must be changed. This is done by changing the environment in which the person behaves.

Skinner believed that the way people behave is a function of heredity, past experiences, and the present situation. Managers can control only the present situation. Therefore, Skinner recommends that managers consider these two points: (1) If an act (behavior) is followed by a pleasant consequence (say, a pat on the back), it probably will be repeated; (2) if an act is followed by an unpleasant consequence (a reprimand, a harsh glare), it probably will not be repeated. The manager's job is to design the present situation so that good performance will result.

The manager can shape the behavior of subordinates by controlling the reinforcers. A **reinforcer** is a consequence of behavior, one that can improve the likelihood that the behavior will or will not occur again. For example, praise—a **positive reinforcer**—given immediately after an employee completes a job on time may increase the occurrence of finishing work on time. Or a reprimand—a **negative reinforcer**—given immediately for not finishing on time may also increase the likelihood of work being done on time. By finishing on time, the employee creates a situation in which the supervisor will not issue a reprimand.

An interesting reinforcer-based program is used by a Chicago firm, Mediatech. Each week the firm contributes $250 to the Mediatech Employee Lottery.[19] All of the 350 full-time and 25 part-time employees in the firm's offices in New York, Los Angeles, and Chicago are eligible for the lottery. Their hopes of winning rest on the employees' last four digits of their payroll identification number. Every Monday, a different employee spins a

Behavior Modification
Application of learning principles called operant conditioning that is designed to modify behavior.

Reinforcer A consequence of behavior that improves the chances it will or will not reoccur.

Positive Reinforcer
A consequence of behavior such as praise or other rewards that, when administered, increases the chances that the behavior will be repeated.

Negative Reinforcer
A consequence of behavior such as a reprimand that, when administered, encourages an employee to adapt more desirable behavior to avoid the unpleasant consequence.

18. Alan E. Kazdin, *Behavior Modification in Applied Settings* (Cincinnati, OH: Wadsworth, 2000).

19. Charles Storch, "A New Spin on Job Motivation," *Chicago Tribune,* September 23, 1990, p. 9E.

wheel at Mediatech's headquarters. Depending on where the wheel lands, there is either a Friday afternoon drawing or the prize money rolls over until the next week. The money accumulates. The biggest winnings on a Friday so far have been $1,000. Other prizes are also given for $600, $300, and $100. Attendance on Friday has improved significantly in all of Mediatech's offices. The reinforcer (winning the lottery) increases the likelihood of coming to work.

Punishment influences behavior by presenting something distasteful or withdrawing something that is liked. For example, a manager says something rude to an employee and receives disapproval (punishment) from other managers. If the disapproval is unpleasant enough, the manager's rudeness is less likely to occur in the future. Another kind of punishment takes something pleasant away. Suppose Nick Rodman, a project engineer, is assigned temporarily to a group that is important to him. Because Rodman frequently arrives late to work for the new assignment, he is placed back in a regular work group. Rodman is not able to work with the group he likes because of his tardiness. He has been punished.

Punishment and negative reinforcement are not the same. In negative reinforcement, an act (completing work on time) that allows the person to avoid some unpleasant event (supervisor's reprimand) is reinforced when the unpleasant event is removed. In punishment, one of two things happens: (1) An unpleasant event (group disapproval) follows a behavior (rude remark), or (2) a pleasant event (being a member of a group) is taken away after a behavior (tardiness).

Managers applying behavior modification on the job must do the following:

1. Identify the elements of a job that are observable and measurable.
2. Measure how frequently behaviors occur.
3. Positively reinforce the person when a correct behavior occurs.

These procedures have met with some success at Emery Worldwide, the air freight carrier. Emery personnel load containers with packages and ship them by air. Management had assumed that containers were always being loaded to capacity, but a check found that containers were being fully loaded only 45 percent of the time. A list of employee activities and goals for filling containers was developed. Results were recorded in terms of container use so that team results could be compared. By correcting deficiencies and providing feedback and recognition for good performance, management increased container capacity.

Like other motivation programs, behavior modification has its critics. Some view it as a technique that Skinner transferred to humans after conducting trial experiments with animals such as pigeons. They claim that employees are not pigeons and do not respond like pigeons. Another criticism is that behavior modification is too artificial. The employee who receives reinforcement should know why he or she receives a reward. In most behavior modification programs, positive reinforcers are provided without an explanation. The complexity of the work environment often leaves no time to explain their use. Finally, behavior modification has a manipulative aspect. Behavioral consequences are controlled, and people are forced to change behavior instead of changing behavior on their own initiative. This approach is not consistent with the theme that people should act freely. The need for self-actualization is not recognized, which is considered dehumanizing.

10-4d Rewards and Motivation

As indicated earlier in the chapter, formal financial rewards are not the only way to motivate employees. Job design alteration and exceptional goals can be very motivational and rewarding. However, it must be stated that financial rewards should also be considered to be part of a firm's reward and motivation program. Some so-called experts emphasize that financial rewards are not motivational.[20] We are not so sure of such an all-encompassing claim and statement.

20. Carol Beatty and Harvey Schachter, *Employee Ownership: The New Source of Competitive Advantage* (San Francisco: Jossey-Bass, 2001).

A portion of any employee's paycheck is based on membership and seniority. Employees earn a wage or salary and also benefits. One reason for increasing the size of the paycheck and benefits is the person's seniority in the firm. Seniority-based rewards can reduce turnover because the cost of quitting increases with each year of service. This type of reward is not directly motivational or linked to performance. However, abruptly eliminating seniority-based rewards could cause problems since employees are used to this method of reward allocation.

Another type of reward system is one that focuses on competencies or the abilities, values, traits, and characteristics that lead to excellent performance. Competency-based rewards pay employees for their specific skills, knowledge, and traits that lead to desired behaviors. In some firms those employees with a set of desired competencies can earn more than their superiors. This opportunity motivates employees to acquire the skills, knowledge, and traits.

Skill-based pay represents a form of competency-based rewards.[21] In a skilled-based plan employees earn higher rates of pay based on the number of skill modules they have mastered. For example, Marley Cooling Tower Co. has over thirty skill modules to master for the production operation. Unskilled workers start at a wage of $6.30 per hour and this increases to more than $15 per hour for those showing mastery of all thirty skill modules. On-the-job training, experience and practice, and special training courses are used to master the skills. Finally, the employee must pass a written and a hands-on test before earning the higher pay rate for each module mastered.

Piece-rate (pay for number of units produced), merit pay (pay based on performance appraisal), gainsharing (rewards based on team members reducing costs of production and increasing labor efficiency), and **employee stock ownership plans (ESOPs)**—plans that encourage employees to buy shares of the company stock—are all approaches that attempt to provide positive motivational for employees. For some employees, any one of these plans can be motivational. It is not, however, correct to assume that any reward approach will be motivational for all employees. An individual's needs, preferences, and expectations will play some role in what reward system or combination of rewards will be motivational.

Motivation is more than just work-related rewards. Outside-of-work issues also play a role in motivation.

A few strategies that managers should consider when attempting to use rewards to motivate are these:[22]

1. Make sure performance is accurately measured. Rewards won't work unless performance is accurately measured and is tied to the reward. Linking performance and pay increases in the minds of employees is easier said than done.
2. Make sure the rewards are meaningful. Rewards that are inconsequential or unimportant will not be motivational. Finding out what is meaningful is an important step for managers.
3. Use team rewards when they fit. In jobs that are interdependent, team rewards can be powerful motivators. For example, if one employee's work is connected in some way to the work of three other employees, tie their rewards together. Team bonuses, incentives, and sharing can help everyone pull in the same direction so that others on the team are not disappointed.

Performance-based rewards have the potential to be motivation if they are carefully used and monitored. These types of rewards are not new, and they come in many variants. They can be applied to individuals (merit), teams (gainsharing), or organizations (ESOPs), and each can be motivational for some employees.

Skill-Based Pay   A form of competency-based rewards/skilled-based plan where employees earn higher rates of pay based on the number of skill modules they have mastered.

Employee Stock Option Plans (ESOPs)   Plans in which employees are given an opportunity to purchase stocks and own a portion of the company at a fixed price.

21. Richard Henderson, *Compensation Management in a Knowledge-Based World* (Upper Saddle River, NJ: Prentice-Hall, 2000).

22. Joseph J. Martocchio, *Strategic Compensation: A Human Resource Approach* (Upper Saddle River, NJ: Prentice-Hall, 2001).

SUGGESTED WEBSITES

Note: These websites were functional when we went to press. Please access the online text for the most up-to-date URLs.

1. www.att.com
2. www.saab.com
3. www.volvo.com
4. www.generalmills.com

SUMMARY OF LEARNING OBJECTIVES

1. *Define the term* scientific management.   Scientific management is the scientific study and breakdown of work into its smallest mechanical elements, and then rearrangement into their most efficient combination.

2. *Explain what the Hawthorne studies revealed about the role that groups play in motivating employees.*   The Hawthorne studies at the Western Electric plant showed the importance of informal work groups as motivators of employees. Work groups can affect individual behavior. The studies also showed that the employees felt they were special because they were involved in the experiment. This feeling of specialness caused their work performance to improve.

3. *Define the term* motivation.   Motivation is the way in which drives or needs direct a person's behavior toward a specific goal. A nonobservable phenomenon that takes place inside everyone, motivation determines the level of effort a person puts forth to achieve the goal. Managers can readily observe a person's behavior, but they can only make assumptions about what causes the person to behave in that way.

4. *Discuss Maslow's view of needs and motivation.*   Maslow believed that people's behavior was motivated by their desire to fulfill needs. These needs were arranged in a hierarchy from the most basic survival needs at the bottom to self-fulfilling needs at the top. The need levels are physiological, safety, social, esteem, and self-actualization. After needs on the lowest level have been satisfied, people are motivated to fulfill needs at the next highest level.

5. *Compare and contrast the* Theory X, Theory Y, *and* Theory Z *approaches to motivating employees.*   Managers have the challenging task of identifying their employees' needs in order to motivate them to perform better. They can also determine how their style of managing influences employee behavior. McGregor's *Theory X* manager is concerned with helping employees satisfy lower-level physiological and safety needs; such managers are more autocratic and controlling. *Theory Y* managers are concerned with fulfilling their employees' higher-level needs; their managerial style results in looser control and more delegation of authority. *Theory Z* managers emphasize lifetime employment, consensus decision making, and giving employees the opportunity to use their skills.

6. *Explain why Herzberg's view of motivation is so popular with practicing managers.*   Herzberg's theory of motivation uses understandable managerial language and instructs managers that motivators should be used to create a more positive work environment. Motivators are conditions such as employees having increased responsibility, more advancement opportunities, and more recognition for good work.

7. *Describe the principles of goal setting.*   Goal setting is a way to motivate employees. One principle holds that employees perform better when given specific, challenging goals than when they are given no goals at all or simply told to do their best. Workers also should be involved in the goal-setting process and should be given timely, meaningful feedback on their performance.

8. *Reward systems have the potential to be motivational.*   Rewards can be administered at the individual, team, or organizational level. Do not assume that a particular reward system is preferred or fits every individual the same way. For some a reward may be motivational, while others may interpret a reward to be demanding or trivial. Individual differences play a role in how rewards are interpreted and how they serve in terms of motivational power.

KEY TERMS

behavior modification (p. 256)
employee stock option plans (ESOPs) (p. 258)
esteem needs (p. 247)
extrinsic rewards (p. 245)
goal setting (p. 252)
Hawthorne studies (p. 244)
hygiene factors (p. 250)
intrinsic rewards (p. 245)
job enrichment (p. 255)

motivation (p. 245)
motivators (p. 250)
needs hierarchy (p. 246)
negative reinforcer (p. 256)
physiological needs (p. 246)
positive reinforcer (p. 256)
punishment (p. 245)
reinforcer (p. 256)
safety needs (p. 246)

scientific management (p. 244)
self-actualization needs (p. 247)
skill-based pay (p. 258)
social needs (p. 247)
Theory X (p. 248)
Theory Y (p. 248)
Theory Z (p. 249)
work motivation model (p. 249)

QUESTIONS FOR DISCUSSION AND REVIEW

1. What are some of the motivational advantages of a skill-based reward system?
2. Theory Z, like Theories X and Y, has not been proven scientifically. Why has Theory Z had an impact on management practices when it has not been scientifically proven?
3. Can the principles of goal setting be applied to nonwork settings such as school, family, or leisure activities? Explain.
4. What are the challenges that will face managers attempting to help motivate an increasingly diverse (e.g., ethnic, gender, age) workforce?
5. Can the Hawthorne effect influence motivation negatively? Explain.
6. Why would behavior modification appeal to some managers?
7. How does goal setting work in terms of motivating an employee? A student?
8. Is the concept of individual, team, and organizational rewards systems relevant for large organizations?
9. Explain the concept of intrinsic motivation. What should a manager know about intrinsic motivators?
10. How can managers improve their ability to motivate employees?

END-OF-CHAPTER QUESTIONS

1. *Scientific management* is the systematic study and breakdown of work into its smallest mechanical elements, and then the rearrangement of these elements into their most efficient combination.   **T** or **F**
2. The Hawthorne studies showed how group characteristics and the type of supervision, among other things, influence motivation and productivity.   **T** or **F**
3. *Intrinsic rewards* are external to work itself, they are administered by someone else, such as a manager, and include such things as pay, fringe benefits, recognition, and praise.   **T** or **F**
4. Theory X managers believe that the average employee dislikes work and finds ways to avoid it as much as possible.   **T** or **F**
5. Theory Z places a special emphasis on participative management.   **T** or **F**
6. In the 1950s, Frederick Herzberg proposed a work motivation model that contained three factors, *hygiene*, *maintenance*, and *motivators*.   **T** or **F**
7. Goal setting is the process of identifying specific levels of performance that a person seeks to accomplish in a certain time frame.   **T** or **F**
8. Skill-based pay represents a form of competency-based reward.   **T** or **F**

9. *Gainsharing* is pay based on performance appraisal.   **T** or **F**
10. To motivate employees, managers must choose rewards that are meaningful to the employees.   **T** or **F**
11. Maslow believed that people's behavior was motivated by their desire to fulfill needs.   **T** or **F**
12. The Hawthorne Studies were conducted in _____.
    a. America   c. Brazil
    b. England   d. Germany
13. Salary, working conditions, and job security are considered _____ factors by Herzberg.
    a. motivational   c. perks
    b. hygiene   d. technical
14. The top level of the needs hierarchy is _____.
    a. social needs   c. esteem needs
    b. self-actualization d. safety needs
15. _____ employees is one of the most difficult tasks that managers face.
    a. Hiring   c. Motivating
    b. Transferring   d. Training

INTERNET EXERCISE

Analyzing Motivation Programs

Are you now aware after studying the chapter that there is no one best theory of motivation that is effective with every employee? Different approaches work for different people. You can examine what private and public companies are using to motivate their employees by visiting the website for The Foundation for Enterprise Development at www.fed.org. This is a not-for-profit organization that provides valuable motivation information. Select the "resource library" and follow up by choosing to examine the library for subject review categories such as: "case studies for public companies," "case studies for private companies," "ESOP," and other related issues. Pick a few samples from those available and analyze the motivational programs.

EXPERIENTIAL EXERCISE

Profiling Leaders as Motivators

Activity

Students will review the motivational skills of leaders they have known or observed and develop profiles of such leaders. Approximately thirty minutes of class time will be needed.

Directions

1. The instructor will review some of the motivation theories identified in the chapter.
2. Following the review of motivation theories, each student is to think about a leader he or she has known or observed who was an effective motivator.
3. Each student is to write down the characteristics of the leader that contributed to being an effective motivator.
4. The instructor calls on a large number of students to individually share part of the list of personal characteristics of motivators.
5. The instructor is to write down the information shared by the students. The developing profile should be written on a chalkboard or overhead transparency.

   At the conclusion of the exercise the instructor is to summarize the characteristics included in the profile of an effective motivator.

BUSINESS APPLICATION

Motivating Workers in Different Job Settings

Activity

Students will participate in small-group sessions analyzing motivation strategies in various types of job settings. About forty minutes of class time will be needed.

Directions

Divide the class into three groups of students, with each group electing a spokesperson/recorder.

1. Each of the three groups will develop strategies for motivating workers applicable to the job setting assigned.
   - Group 1 is to focus on motivating factory workers who are used to dull repetitious work.
   - Group 2 is to focus on sales workers in a department store.
   - Group 3 is to focus on motivating nurses in a hospital setting where turnover is high and morale is low.
2. Clarify that each group is to view the assignment from the management perspective of developing strategies to motivate workers within the particular work setting. (Allow twenty minutes for this part of the exercise.)
3. Each group's spokesperson is to report the group's motivational strategies applicable to the particular setting.
4. The instructor should write the strategies on the chalkboard adjacent to the applicable setting. Following the reporting of strategies, each group is to explain the rationale for selecting the particular strategies.
5. The instructor will summarize the strategies and supporting rationale provided by the groups.

Case

Roadway Express

Roadway Express is attempting to come to grips with what can be done to improve the morale and motivation of employees. Management has some ideas and the unionized workforce also has some suggestions. Management and employees are well aware of the fact that to compete in the trucking industry in which net profit margins are less than 5 percent per year, employees must be motivated. Motivating all 28,000 Roadway employees at multiple facilities is a challenging task.

Since about two-thirds of every revenue dollar is consumed by wage and benefits, the motivation state of employees is crucial. Being motivated, staying motivated, and helping others become motivated is what Roadway management is continually coping with by examining various approaches.

The company adopted a collaborative process called "appreciative inquiry" and used it at its Akron, Ohio, facility. A steering committee of workers was put together offsite to chart the course. Their first task was to decide who would be invited to attend the appreciative inquiry first session. A total of eighty-eight employees were picked to attend a three-day offsite work session.

One of the tasks for the attendees was to "talk about a time when you felt the most alive, the most engaged, in your job at Roadway." The wording was intentional so that the session didn't turn into the usual labor-management gripe and complain session. The session produced an interesting result. It didn't matter what the person's job was. Everyone wanted similar core things. The final lists included:

- Personal growth
- Satisfied and pleasant customers
- Job security

Once the list was finalized, the participants moved to produce a plan, which was called an "opportunity map" of needs and priorities. Votes were taken on the most important needs, and seven action teams were established. Teams were asked to address such items as trust between management and workers, communication, performance review and monitoring, and employee development.

The participants served as the firm's leaders to trigger a more positive motivational atmosphere at Roadway. The same approach will be used at a number of Roadway facilities so that action can be guided and crafted to fit the management and employees at each location.

Questions for Discussion

1. What is different about Roadway's "appreciative inquiry" approach than what one would expect in the trucking industry?
2. How should Roadway evaluate the effectiveness of its action teams? Prepare a "to do" list of items that should be included.
3. How can management sustain the goodwill that comes from paying attention to Roadway employee needs and priorities?

Sources: Keith H. Hammonds, "Leaders for the Long Haul," *Fast Company*, July 2001, pp. 56–58; and *Leading Edge Technology*, Reimer Express Lines Monograph, January 2002.

11

Managing Human Resources

Photo: comstock.com

After completing this chapter, you should be able to:

1 **Define** the term *human resource management (HRM)*.

2 **Explain** why human resource planning, recruiting, and selecting are important.

3 **Describe** job analysis, job descriptions, and job specifications.

4 **Explain** the role of the federal government in providing equal opportunities for employment to all Americans.

5 **Discuss** training and development programs for hourly and salaried employees.

6 **Identify** examples of direct and indirect compensation.

7 **Discuss** comparable worth.

8 **Discuss** modern workplace issues such as sexual harassment and workplace safety.

Sexual Harassment Is a Time Bomb for Employers

If coworkers are guilty of sexual harassment, an employer is liable if the employer knew or should have known of the misconduct, and unless immediate and appropriate corrective action was taken. The extent of company liability for harassment by supervisors will vary with the employer's precautions and response to the actions that prompted the harassment charges. Employers need to take appropriate action to protect their firms from potentially devastating consequences from legal action and large jury awards. They must be vigilant to ensure that everyone in their organization is informed, educated, and committed to preventing sexual harassment.

Without a coordinated plan of education and enforcement based on zero tolerance of sexual harassment, unacceptable incidents of employee behavior can multiply to create a hostile and litigious environment. The Supreme Court ruled on such a situation in the landmark case of *Faragher v. City of Boca Raton*. Beth Ann Faragher worked part-time as an ocean lifeguard for the Marine Safety Section of the Parks and Recreation Department for the City of Boca Raton, Florida. During her five years of employment, Faragher suffered repeated, uninvited, and offensive touching by two supervisors.

During her employment, Faragher did not complain to higher management. She resigned, but two years later, in 1992, she brought an action against the supervisors and the city. A federal district court found that the behavior of the male supervisors was sufficient to create a hostile working environment and ruled in Faragher's favor. The question raised in the Supreme Court appeal case was whether the employer could be held responsible for the actions of the supervisors. The Supreme Court concluded that the employer was liable. The City of Boca Raton was required to pay the damages assessed by the lower court.

The long-term consequence of the Faragher decision for managers is that the courts described the means by which employers could protect themselves in the event of a future lawsuit. The defense has two elements. First, the employer must have exercised reasonable care to prevent and correct promptly any sexually harassing behavior. Second, the employee must have unreasonably failed to avoid harm or failed to have taken advantage of preventive or corrective opportunities provided by the employer.

To avoid liability, an employer must strive to prevent harassment from occurring and be in a position to successfully defend against a claim should a harassment case be filed. For many companies, these changes mean that the firm's policies and procedures must be revised to reflect the court's new pronouncements on sexual harassment.

Sources: Adapted from John A. Pearce, II and Samuel A. DiLullo, "A Business Policy Statement Model for Eliminating Sexual Harassment and Related Employer Liability," *Advanced Management Journal*, Spring 2001, pp. 12–21.

11-1 INTRODUCTION

Many business leaders will readily agree that the key to business success today is talented people who are motivated and rewarded to perform at a high level. The relative importance of "human capital" in the modern organization compared with other forms of capital (e.g., land, machinery, money) places it at a premium value. Despite this relatively high value, however, most human resource issues and problems have played a secondary role to other business decisions. In many organizations, financial, production, and marketing judgments are made first, before people-related decisions. This second-class status is changing fast, though, as people—workers and managers—are recognized as a delicate, scarce commodity.

Business leaders from Jack Welch, former CEO of GE, to the single-site retail store owner, such as Houston's Jim "Mattress Mack" McIngvale, will tell you that their employees are their most important assets. Welch is famous for his use of teams and "work-out groups" for setting corporate strategy and action plans. Welch is equally famous for his no-nonsense approach to performance evaluation. He instructed GE's managers to make sure they fired a certain number of low-performing individuals each year. They managed this through a forced rating system that ensured a certain number of people would be evaluated at the lower end of the scale—and fired for poor performance.[1] McIngvale is famous

---

1. Jack Welch and David A. Byrne, *Jack: Straight from the Gut* (New York: Warner Books, September 11, 2001).

for his enthusiastic approach to motivating and rewarding his workers. McIngvale's single-site store sells more than $150 million worth of furniture per year—more furniture than many chain stores. He does this through an unrelenting focus on developing his human resources and rewarding people for their efforts.[2]

At the same time, managers are faced with an increasingly complex and litigious work environment. New federal regulations, constantly shifting sociocultural sensitivities and "political correctness," as well as new demands from employees themselves for more meaningful work has made the "personnel" function of management an increasingly vital part of a healthy organization. As the opening vignette shows, simple procedures and policies, such as a "zero tolerance" policy toward sexual harassment, can help firms avoid costly legal fees. "Personnel" has become "human resources," and the scope of issues this function deals with has grown exponentially. From monitoring compliance with federal employee regulations to actively pursuing employee well-being with specific employee assistance programs, human resources management is critical to an effective organization.

11-1a The Changing Demographics of the Workplace

With the changes occurring in technological development, people performance, operating costs, and demographics, human resources has become a key issue for business and industry. The civilian labor force in the United States is projected to increase by 17 million over the 2000–2010 period, reaching 158 million in 2010. This 12 percent increase is slightly greater than the 11.9 percent increase over the previous ten-year period, 1990–2000, when the labor force grew by 15 million. The projected labor force growth will be affected by the aging of the baby-boom generation, persons born between 1946 and 1964. In 2010, the baby-boom cohort will be ages 46 to 64, and this age group will show significant growth over the 2000–2010 period. The median age of the labor force will continue to rise, even though the youth labor force (ages 16 to 24) is expected to grow more rapidly than the overall labor force for the first time in twenty-five years.

A closer view of the 2000–2010 labor force reveals that certain demographic groups are projected to grow more rapidly than others. For women, the rate of growth in the labor force is expected to slow, but it will still increase at a faster rate than that of men. As a result, the share of women in the labor force is projected to increase from 47 percent in 2000 to 48 percent in 2010. The number of men in the labor force is projected to grow more rapidly even though the aggregate labor force participation rate for men is projected to continue declining (from 74.7 percent in 2000 to a projected 73.2 percent in 2010). Hispanic origin groups have shown and are projected to continue to show widely varied growth rates because of divergent rates of population growth in the past. Among race and ethnic groups, the "Asian and other" labor force is projected to increase most rapidly. By 2010, the Hispanic labor force is projected to be larger than the black labor force,

2. Jim McIngvale, Thomas N. Duening, John M. Ivancevich, *Always Think Big* (Chicago: Dearborn Trade, May 2002).

primarily because of faster population growth. Despite slower-than-average growth and a declining share of the total labor force, white non-Hispanics will continue to make up more than two-thirds of the workforce.[3]

11-1b Implications of Changing Demographics

These rapidly changing demographics mean that human resource experts will work harder and longer to solve problems. In businesses of any size—large, medium, or small—human resources must be recruited, compensated, developed, and motivated. Small organizations typically cannot afford to have a separate human resource management (HRM) department that continually follows the progress of individuals and reviews the accomplishment of goals. Larger firms usually have an HRM department that can be a source of help to line managers. In large or small firms, with or without HRM departments, however, each manager is responsible for using the skills and talents of employees. And in either case, much of the work in recruitment, compensation, and performance appraisal must be finalized and implemented by managers.

In this chapter, we discuss the HRM function's importance to business. We begin with human resource planning, recruitment, and selection. Laws governing recruitment and recruitment sources are discussed, as are drug and AIDS testing as a condition of employment. We explain how a company arrives at a decision to hire a candidate for a job. In the section on training and development, we cover orientation, training, and management development, including performance appraisals. The next topic, compensation and benefits, includes direct and indirect compensation, individual and group incentives, comparable worth, benefits and services, and protection programs. The chapter concludes with a discussion of safe work environments.

11-2 THE WORK OF HUMAN RESOURCE MANAGEMENT

Human resource management (HRM) can be defined as the process of accomplishing organizational objectives by acquiring, retaining, developing, evaluating, rewarding, and properly using the human resources in an organization.

> **Human Resource Management (HRM)**   The process of acquiring, retaining, terminating, developing, and properly using the human resources in an organization.

The success of any HRM program requires the cooperation of managers at different levels who must interpret and implement HRM policies and procedures. Line managers must translate into action what an HRM department decides are in the best interests of the organization. For example, the HRM department may enact a particular employee evaluation approach. The managers of each unit must implement that approach or it will not have an impact on the organization. Without managerial support, HRM programs cannot succeed. This need for HRM to enact its policies and procedures through other managers is complicated by the fact that most HRM departments are staff rather than line functions. Therefore, human resource managers need to understand clearly how to communicate their policies and procedures to the other units of the organization.

There are as many different approaches to effective HRM as there are companies. For example, the human resource program at IBM serves the needs of the organization and facilitates the accomplishment of IBM's objectives. But this program would probably not be well suited for Apple or Dell without modifications. Each company develops its own HRM program after considering such factors as size, types of skills needed, number of employees required, unionization, clients and customers, financial posture, and geographic location.

Acquiring skilled, talented, and motivated employees is an important part of HRM. The acquisition phase involves recruiting, screening, selecting, and properly placing personnel. Prudential Financial and other firms are finding that acquiring the talent

☞ 1

☞ 2, 3

☞ 4

---

3. Howard N. Fullerton, Jr., and Mitra Toosi, "Labor Force Projections to 2010: Steady Growth and Changing Composition," *Monthly Labor Review Online*, November 2001.

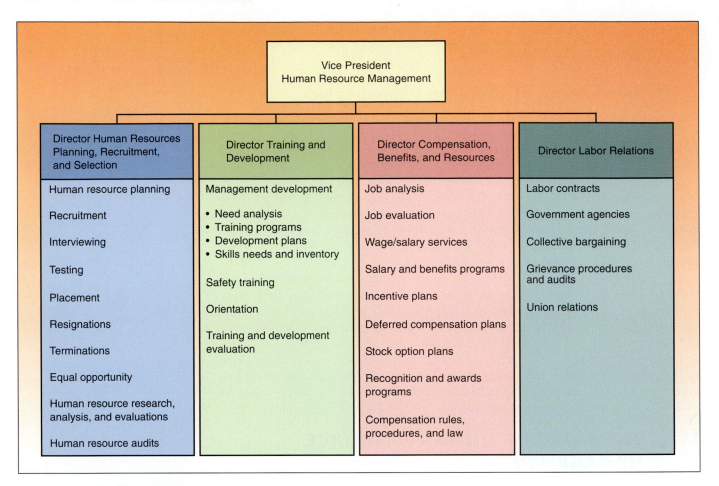

Vice President Human Resource Management			
Director Human Resources Planning, Recruitment, and Selection	**Director Training and Development**	**Director Compensation, Benefits, and Resources**	**Director Labor Relations**
Human resource planning	Management development	Job analysis	Labor contracts
Recruitment	• Need analysis	Job evaluation	Government agencies
Interviewing	• Training programs	Wage/salary services	Collective bargaining
Testing	• Development plans	Salary and benefits programs	Grievance procedures and audits
Placement	• Skills needs and inventory	Incentive plans	Union relations
Resignations	Safety training	Deferred compensation plans	
Terminations	Orientation	Stock option plans	
Equal opportunity	Training and development evaluation	Recognition and awards programs	
Human resource research, analysis, and evaluations		Compensation rules, procedures, and law	
Human resource audits			

EXHIBIT 11-1

Sample Human Resources Department

Retention   Refers to efforts companies take to retain productive employees.

needed to survive is becoming more difficult; talented candidates are in short supply compared with the demand from multiple competitors both domestic and abroad. If qualified individuals regularly leave a company, then that company must continually seek new personnel. Seeking, screening, hiring, and training new employees are costly and time-consuming activities. Thus, many firms today have placed an increased emphasis on **retention** of productive people.

Developing human resources involves training, educating, appraising, and generally preparing personnel for present and future roles within an organization. These activities are important for the employees' economic and psychological growth. Self-actualization needs cannot be satisfied in an organization that does not have a set of development activities. Many firms develop people through specialized training programs. Manufacturing and direct service companies offer extensive on-the-job training, giving new employees exposure to their roles in actual workplace settings. Other companies use on-site or off-site trainers, individual experts on a topic or subject who present short course in their area of expertise. Milliken & Company, for example, annually spends in excess of $30 million training its 16,000 employees through Milliken University. The company has a policy that each employee is to obtain at least forty hours of continuing education training each year. The Internet Exercise at the end of this chapter guides you through the company's training programs.

The proper use of human resources involves understanding both individual and organizational needs. This aspect of HRM suggests the importance of matching individuals over time to shifts in organizational and human needs. Exhibit 11-1 is an example of an HRM department in an organization large enough (usually over 1,000 employees) to have such a unit. In smaller firms, there may not be a formal "HRM Department," but someone or some group must perform the jobs shown in the figure. The objectives of HRM are to clarify the firm's human resource problems and develop solutions to them. HRM focuses on action, satisfying individual needs, and the future.

11-3 HUMAN RESOURCE PLANNING, RECRUITMENT, AND SELECTION

An organization can only be as effective as the people who operate it. Thus, acquiring the people necessary to operate the business is an important function of any HRM program. To begin the recruitment process, managers throughout the organization need to establish human resource plans. Recruitment, selection, placement, and other HRM actions stem from this basic plan.

11-3a Planning

Human resource planning has been defined as the process of "analyzing an organization's human resource needs under changing conditions and developing the activities necessary to satisfy these needs."[4] The first part of this definition refers to human resource needs forecasting, which can be further divided into two parts: current and future needs. Research indicates that the more dynamic and changeable is the organization's environment, the less accurate is the human resource forecast.[5] Complicating factors include changes in economic conditions, changes in the labor supply, and/or changes in the political environment.

> **Human Resource Planning** The steps taken in estimating the size and makeup of the future workforce.

Formal and informal approaches to human resource planning are used. Many organizations use an informal "pull" model of human resource planning. Under this approach, human resource planning assumes that promotions will occur as a result of higher-level organizational vacancies that, in effect, *pull* lower-level people up through the organization. This process includes a "ripple" effect in that, as each higher position is filled, a lower-level position opening is created. These pull models usually assume a relatively stable organizational structure and competitive environment.[6]

More formally, many organizations use stochastic (probabilistic) or **Markov models** to forecast human resource needs. These models enable managers to forecast flows to and from various positions based on the past probabilities of such changes. These probabilities are arranged in a table known as a "transition matrix" (see Exhibit 11-2). In such a table, the rows generally represent the positions of personnel at time 1, and the columns the positions at time 2. The period of analysis usually is one year, and the transitions used vary from job, grade, department, or some combination.

> **Markov Models** Models used to forecast human resource needs.

The data in a transition matrix are generally gathered over a period of several years to determine the stability of the probabilities. The staffing levels at the end of the next year may be multiplied by the probabilities of various transitions to obtain a forecast for the following year.

Consider the importance of human resource planning to a large firm such as DaimlerChrysler, which employs over 100,000 people in multiple countries. Every day some new people begin jobs with the multinational corporation, while others retire or leave for other jobs. This inflow and outflow is constant. Paying attention to inflow, outflow, future plans, and competitors is vital to the effective operation of DaimlerChrysler.

To have the right number and type of people in the night place at the right time, a firm must engage in human resource planning. By having a sound human resource planning system, a firm can translate its objectives and plans into the number of employees needed to do the job.

---

4. J. W. Walker, *Human Resource Planning* (New York: McGraw-Hill, 1980).

5. Thomas H. Stone and Jack Fiorito, "A Perceived Uncertainty Model of Human Resource Forecasting Technique Use," *Academy of Management Review*, Fall 1986, pp. 635–642.

6. J. Benjamin Forbes, "Human Resource Planning: Applications and Evaluation of Markov Analysis," *Academy of Management Proceedings*, 1983, pp. 287–291.

Transition Matrix

		\multicolumn{10}{c}{**Job Class Transitions (2002 and 2003)**}									

Job Class Transitions (2002 and 2003)

		To									
		1	**2**	**3**	**4**	**5**	**6**	**7**	**8**	**Exit**
From	**1**	88								9
	2		77			5				16
	3		2	75	4	3				15
	4				73	4	10	2		10
	5				1	84	4	2		9
	6					1	82	13		4
	7						1	83	11	4
	8							8	86	5
Hires		28	32	4	10	17	3	3	2	—

Figures are average percentage moving from one state to another.

Category Definitions:

1. Hourly (Maintenance, Laborers, Operatives)
2. Clerical and Service
3. Nonexempt Technical
4. Exempt Technical/Professional
5. Supervisory/Staff/Sales
6. Management/Specialists-Lower Level
7. Management/Specialists-Middle Level
8. Management/Specialists-Upper Level

Recruitment Steps taken to staff an organization with the best-qualified people.

Job Analysis The process of determining the tasks that make up a job and the skills, abilities, and responsibilities needed to perform the job.

Knowledge Refers to the body of information in a subject area that is needed to adequately perform a job.

Skills A term that describes observable capabilities to perform a learned behavior.

Abilities Innate or natural attributes a person has that can be developed into skills or knowledge.

Job Description A written statement that furnishes information about a job's duties, technology, conditions, and hazards; based on data from the job analysis.

Job Specification A written statement of the human qualifications, education, and experience needed to perform a job.

11-3b Recruitment

Recruitment is an essential step in staffing. Virtually every company has to perform this function.[7] The primary objective of **recruitment** is to find and attract the best-qualified applicants to fill vacancies. However, before that can be done, those involved in the recruiting process must clearly understand the position to be filled. The procedure used to acquire an understanding about a job is called job analysis.

Job analysis is the process of determining the tasks that make up the job and the knowledge, skills, and abilities (KSAs) an employee needs to successfully accomplish the job. **Knowledge** refers to the body of information in a subject area that is needed to adequately perform a job (e.g., knowledge of MSExcel spreadsheet; knowledge of contract law). The term **skills** describes observable capabilities to perform a learned behavior (e.g., operating a wood lathe). **Abilities** refer to those innate or natural attributes a person has and that can be developed into skills or knowledge. For example, a person with the ability to operate a lathe has to be trained appropriately to develop the skill.

From the data gathered through job analysis, job descriptions are generated. A **job description** provides details about the activities involved in performing a job and the conditions under which the employee will work. A statement of the qualifications (KSAs), education, and experience needed for a job is called **job specification.** Both job descriptions and job specifications are often produced in written form.

---

7. Daniel B. Turban and Thomas L. Keon, "Organizational Attractiveness: An Interactionist Perspective," *Journal of Applied Psychology*, April 1993, pp. 184–193.

EXHIBIT 11-3

Job Description for a Human Resources Manager

Job Title: Human Resource Manager	Department: HRM
	Date: January 2, 2003

General Description of the Job

Performs responsible administrative work managing personnel activities of a large state agency or institution. Work involves responsibility for the planning and administration of an HRM program that includes recruitment, examination, selection, evaluation, appointment, promotion, transfer, and recommended change of status of agency employees, and a system of communication for disseminating necessary information to workers. Works under general supervision, exercising initiative and independent judgment in the performance of assigned tasks.

Job Activities

Participates in overall planning and policymaking to provide effective and uniform personnel services.

Communicates policy through organization levels by bulletins, meetings, and personal contact.

Interviews applicants, evaluates qualifications, and classifies applications.

Recruits and screens applicants to fill vacancies and reviews applications of qualified persons.

Confers with supervisors on personnel matters, including placement problems, retention or release of probationary employees, transfers, demotions, and dismissals of permanent employees.

Supervises administration of tests.

Initiates personnel training activities and coordinates these activities with work of officials and supervisors.

Establishes effective service rating system, trains unit supervisors in making employee evaluations.

Maintains employee personnel files.

Supervises a group of employees directly and through subordinates.

Performs related work as assigned.

An efficient job analysis program provides information used to make important decisions. For example, to recruit and select effectively, the HRM department must match qualified personnel with job requirements. The job description and job specification are also used to establish proper rates of pay. A job description for an HRM manager appears in Exhibit 11-3.

11-3c Laws Governing Recruitment

Individuals responsible for recruiting must comply with legal requirements to ensure non-discrimination in employment practices. Laws administered by the Equal Employment Opportunity Commission (EEOC) enforce these requirements. Through Title VII of the **Civil Rights Act of 1964,** the **Civil Rights Act of 1991,** and the **Equal Employment Opportunity Act of 1972,** the federal government attempts to provide equal opportunities for employment without regard to race, religion, age, creed, sex, national origin, or disability. These laws have broad coverage and apply to any activity, business, or industry in which labor disputes would hinder commerce.[8] The laws also cover state and local governments, government agencies, and agencies of the District of Columbia. Specific provisions of the Equal Employment Opportunity Act of 1972 include the following:

Equal Employment Opportunity Commission (EEOC)
A federal agency whose purpose is to increase job opportunities for women and minorities.

Civil Rights Act of 1964
An act that makes various forms of discrimination illegal. Title VII of the act spells out the forms of illegal discrimination.

Civil Rights Act of 1991
Increases the scope of Title VII of the Civil Rights Act of 1964. Victims are now entitled to jury trial and punitive damages.

Equal Employment Opportunity Act of 1972 A law that has specific provisions about equal opportunities for employment; provided for the establishment of Equal Employment Opportunity Commission.

7

---

8. David P. Twomey, *Equal Employment Opportunity Law* (Cincinnati: South-Western, 1994).

It is unlawful for an employer to fail or to refuse to hire, or to discharge, any individual or otherwise to discriminate against any individual with respect to compensation, conditions, or privileges of employment because of race, color, religion, sex, age, or national origin. This applies to applicants for employment as well as current employees.

Employers may not limit, segregate, or classify employees in such a way that would deprive them of employment opportunities because of race, color, age, religion, sex, or national of origin.

The EEOC has the power to file action in a federal district court if it is unable to eliminate alleged unlawful employment practices by the informal methods of conference, conciliation, and persuasion.

Employment tests may be used if they can be proved to be related to the job or promotion sought by the individual. Tests should be validated for each company. No discriminatory statements may be included in any advertisements for job opportunities.

Immigration Reform and Control Act (IRCA)   A law, passed in 1986, that places a major responsibility on employers to stop the flow of illegal immigrants into the United States by not employing unauthorized aliens.

The **Immigration Reform and Control Act (IRCA)** of 1986 places a major responsibility on employers for stopping the flow of illegal immigrants into the United States.[9] The employer must:

1. Not recruit, hire, or continue to employ unauthorized aliens.
2. Verify the identity or work authorization of every new employee.
3. Not discriminate on the basis of citizenship or national origin.

The IRCA requires every individual who is recruited and hired to provide acceptable documentation of his or her status. The Immigration Act of 1990 provides for 140,000 visas annually for employer-sponsored immigrants. The Act includes aliens with extraordinary ability, such as outstanding scientists and researchers.

Americans with Disabilities Act (ADA)   Comprehensive antidiscrimination law, passed in 1990, aimed at integrating the disabled into the American workforce; prohibits all employers from discriminating against disabled employees or applicants.

An estimated 43 million Americans have some type of disability. Although many would like to work, some cannot because of discrimination. In May 1990, the **Americans with Disabilities Act (ADA)** was passed.[10] This comprehensive antidiscrimination law aims at integrating the disabled into the American workforce. The ADA prohibits all employers, including privately owned businesses and local governments, from discriminating against disabled employees or job applicants when making selection decisions.

Typically, discrimination against disabled applicants takes the form of application forms and pre-employment interviews that inquire into the existence of a disability rather than the ability to perform the required job activities. Title I of the ADA prohibits these and other practices that may prevent a disabled person from obtaining and maintaining employment.

Reasonable Accommodations   Owners must make an attempt to provide accommodations for people with disabilities.

To be in compliance with the ADA, business owners must make their premises accessible to the disabled by providing **reasonable accommodations.** This edict to accommodate persons with disabilities applies to both employees and customers of the business. While the term *reasonable accommodation* is open to interpretation, there are limits on what the law expects. Employers are protected from incurring inordinate costs to accommodate handicaps in that the law also has a provision that such accommodation should not require the business to experience **undue hardship.** The ADA publishes a booklet to help business owners determine how to make their workspace accessible to handicapped individuals without excessive costs. For example, installing wider doors on restrooms to accommodate wheelchairs, using doorknobs in public access points that can be opened without grasping, or having ramps in lieu of or in addition to stairs are simple and inexpensive fixes. All new businesses started after the ADA was enacted and any business older than May 1990 but undergoing renovation must make reasonable accommodations.

Undue Hardship   Refers to provisions in the Americans with Disabilities Act that state that accommodations for people with disabilities should not require the business to experience excessive hardship.

---

9. David P. Twomey, *Labor and Employment Law* (Cincinnati: South-Western, 1994), pp. 613–616.

10. Francine S. Hall and Elizabeth L. Hall, "The ADA: Going Beyond the Law," *Academy of Management Executive*, February 1994, pp. 17–26.

Businesses that fail to comply face civil penalties of as much as $50,000 for the first violation and $100,000 for subsequent violations. Also, a disabled person can obtain an injunction against the business. Additionally, courts can award monetary damages to disabled persons victimized by discrimination.

11-3d Recruitment Sources

Internal sources of recruitment include present employees, friends of employees, former employees, and previous applicants. By carefully screening these files, some good applicants can be added to the pool of candidates.

If needed human resources are not available within the company, outside sources must be tapped. New applicants can be found through advertisements in newspapers, trade journals, and magazines. Responses to ads come from both qualified and unqualified individuals. Occasionally a company will list a post office box number and not provide the company name. This is called a **blind advertisement.** (Such an ad appears in Exhibit 11-4.) Blind ads eliminate the need to contact every applicant, even the unqualified ones. However, a blind ad does not permit the company to use its name or logo, which is a form of promotion.

To locate experienced employees, organizations can use private employment agencies, executive search firms, state employment agencies, or one of the many online job recruitment services such as Monster. Most are no-fee agencies, which means the employer rather than the applicant pays the fee (if there is one). An organization is not obligated to hire any person referred by an agency, but the agency is usually notified when an applicant is hired.

Another important source for lower-level or entry-level management recruits is the college campus. Many colleges and universities have placement centers that work with organizational recruiters. The applicants read advertisements and information provided by the companies and then are interviewed. The most promising students are invited to visit the company, where other interviews are conducted.

Blind Advertisement   A post office box number provided by a company which does not provide the company name to job applicants.

 8

Training and Development Manager

A large profit-oriented company with headquarters in Houston is currently expanding its management development and training program. We seek a manager whose responsibilities will include the overall planning, development, and direction of the corporate training and development program. The qualified candidate for this position will report directly to the Vice President of Personnel Services.

The qualified candidate must have a Bachelor's degree with a minimum of 8 years directly related experience in training and development, with a demonstrated record of results in private industry. The individual must communicate effectively with different organizational levels to include working directly with high-level management and company officers.

Initial selection of qualified candidates will be based on detailed resume and any other material the candidate wishes to submit, along with salary history and salary requirements. For prompt confidential reply, send resume to:

Confidential Reply Service
Nationwide Advertising Service Inc.
Dept. 6-GC-28
58-5 Richmond Ave.
Houston, Texas 77057

Our client is an equal opportunity employer. M/F.

EXHIBIT 11-4

Blind Advertisement

11-3e Selection

The selection and placement of employees must comply with legal requirements. Discriminatory practices in recruiting, testing, and hiring are illegal, as stated in the Civil Rights Act of 1964 and the Equal Employment Opportunity Act of 1972.

The **selection** process is a series of steps that starts with the initial screening and ends with a decision to hire the person. Exhibit 11-5 is a flow diagram showing each step in the process. Preliminary interviews screen out unqualified applicants. This screening is often the first personal contact an applicant has with a company.

Applicants who pass the preliminary screening often complete an application form. The form asks for information that can be used in reaching an employment decision. Answers to the questions can also, in a general sense, predict job success. The appropriate questions are usually developed after a careful job analysis is completed. The application should provide all necessary information and yet be concise enough not to request information that is not germane to the job. The latter serves to ensure the job application will be useful in the selection process, and to help avoid possible litigation. It is imperative for employers to be aware that questions asked in job interviews, testing, screening, and selecting *must* be directly related to the performance of the job. Any questioning that goes beyond that could be construed as potentially discriminatory and result in litigation.

Interviews occur throughout the selection process, but each includes three basic steps: (1) interviewers must acquaint themselves with the job analysis; (2) they must analyze the information on the application; (3) they need to ask questions that will add to information on the application. Because of the extensive regulation of employment in the United States, there are many interview questions that cannot legally be asked. Many businesses are unaware of these constraints and find themselves in lengthy and costly law-

Selection In employment, a series of steps that starts with the initial screening and ends with a hiring decision.

EXHIBIT 11-5

Typical Selection Decision Steps

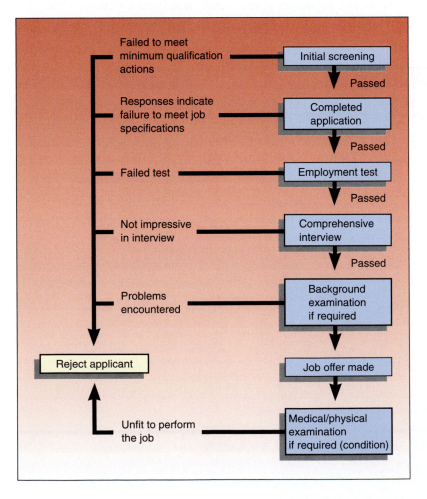

suits as a result. Many of the illegal questions are straightforward: For example, it's illegal to ask someone their racial background. However, other illegal questions are subtler. Exhibit 11-6 presents a list of possible interview questions. See if you can determine why each of these questions is illegal.

11-3f Testing

For years selection tests have been widely used to screen applicants. Frequent use started with World War I, when the Army Alpha test was used to measure intelligence. Installing an effective testing program is costly and time-consuming, and it must be done by experts. Just because a test was useful for selecting sales personnel in one company does not mean it will be useful in another. Exhibit 11-7 presents the results of a Bureau of National Affairs study of firms involved in making selection decisions. The study results indicate which selection procedures are often used and which procedures are not widely used.

9

The advantages of an effective testing program include:

- *Improved accuracy in selecting employees*. Individuals differ in skills, intelligence, motivation, interests, and goals. If these differences can be measured and if they are related to job success, then performance can be predicted to some extent by test scores.

- *An objective means for judging*. Applicants answer the same questions under the same test conditions, so one applicant's score can be compared with the scores of other applicants.

- *Information for current employee needs*. Tests given to current employees can provide information about training, development, or counseling needs. Thus they can objectively uncover needs.

Important legal rulings and fair-employment codes have resulted in strict procedures for developing tests. The following criticisms have been directed at testing programs:

- *Tests are not infallible*. Tests may reveal what people *can* do but not what they will do.

- *Tests are given too much weight*. Tests cannot measure everything about a person. They can never be a complete substitute for good judgment.

- *Tests discriminate against minorities*. Ethnic minorities may score lower on certain paper-and-pencil tests. Title VII of the Civil Rights Act of 1964 prohibits employment practices that artificially discriminate against individuals on the basis of test scores.

Disabilities and Physical Skills

1. How tall are you?
2. What color are your eyes?
3. Do you work out regularly?
4. Is it true that you have the HIV virus?
5. Did you get any workers' comp from your last job?

Personal History

1. How old are you?
2. When was the last time you were thrown in jail?
3. Are you really a woman?
4. Do you rent or own your home?
5. Have you ever declared bankruptcy?

Race Creed or Color

1. Where are your parents from?
2. Do you consider yourself a minority?
3. Is English your first language?
4. I can't tell if you're Korean or Chinese. Which is it?
5. Do you follow all of the pope's instructions?

Family and Relationships

1. Do you have dependable child care in place?
2. How many times have you been married?
3. We were just wondering: Are you gay?
4. Are you in a committed relationship right now?
5. How does your husband feel about you working here?

EXHIBIT 11-6

Illegal Interview Questions
Source: Evan Harvey, "Illegal Interview Questions: Prospective Employers Can Only Go So Far," *CareerBuilder.com*, http://www.careerbuilder.com/subcat/int/gint040101.html.

EXHIBIT 11-7   **Results of Bureau of National Affairs Study**

	Percentage of Companies					
	Any Job Category*	Office/ Clerical	Production/ Service	Professional/ Technical	Commissioned Sales	Managers/ Supervisors
(Number of companies)	(245)	(245)	(221)	(237)	(96)	(243)
Skill performance test/ or work sample	63%	55%	19%	10%	4%	3%
Medical examination	57	43	57	47	46	45
Mental ability test	31	23	10	8	9	9
Job knowledge test	27	14	14	14	3	5
Drug test	26	21	26	22	23	21
Personality test	17	1	2	6	23	13
Assessment center test	12	**	1	3	4	10
Physical abilities test	11	1	12	2	1	1
Written honesty test	7	4	6	2	4	3
Polygraph test	5	2	4	2	5	2
Genetic screening	3	2	2	2	—	1
AIDS test	1	**	**	1	—	**
Other	2	**	1	1	1	1

*Percentages in this column show the proportion of all responding organizations that administer a preemployment test to applicants in any job category.
**Less than 0.5%
Source: Reprinted with permission from *Recruiting and Selection Procedures*, Personnel Policies Forum Survey No. 146, p. 17 (May 1988). Copyright 1988 by The Bureau of National Affairs, Inc. (800-372-1033).

As mentioned earlier, employers who use testing to select employees must ensure that the test questions measure abilities that are required for the performance of the job. This is true whether the testing is related to intelligence or skills. For example, it would be discriminatory if a firm tested whether job candidates could lift 100-pound sacks of wheat if the job in question had no such tasks associated with it. The Focus on Technology box, "Armchair Testing," highlights a firm that uses the Internet to test salespeople on specific skills.

11-3g Drug Testing

Drug-Free Workplace Act of 1988   An act passed to help keep the problem of societal drug abuse from entering organizations.

The **Drug-Free Workplace Act of 1988** was passed to help keep the problem of societal drug abuse from entering organizations. The act specifies that government agencies, federal contractors, and those receiving federal funds ($25,000 or more) must actively attempt to maintain a drug-free workplace. In addition, the act requires that employees of companies regulated by the Department of Transportation and the Nuclear Regulatory Commission who hold certain jobs such as long-haul truck driving must take drug tests.

More and more employers have adopted drug and alcohol screening programs for both applicants and current employees. There are good reasons to avoid hiring substance abusers. Drug and alcohol abusers have higher rates of absenteeism and accidents. In addition, employers may be liable for negligent hiring if a drug-user employee causes an accident that injures or harms others. Forty percent of all on-the-job injuries and about half of all work-related deaths are attributed to substance abuse. Also, it has been estimated that the United States loses over $600 billion annually in productivity because of substance abuse.[11]

A major concern for opponents of drug testing is how the process works and how the information is used. Drug testing when conducted to eliminate drugs in the workplace is more acceptable than using a testing program to catch those doing drugs. Motorola uses a

10, 11 ☞

12 ☞

11. Bill Oliver, "How to Prevent Drug Abuse in Your Workplace," *HR Magazine,* December 1993, pp. 78–82.

FOCUS ON TECHNOLOGY

Armchair Testing

Phoenix-based Inter-Tel, a telecom software company, used to have its sales applicants take a written personality test to see who was self-motivated, outgoing, and energetic. Each three-hour test cost the company about $60, and it took days to get results from the testing firm. All told, testing ran $600 per hire because only one out of ten candidates got a job. In 2001 the company swapped its paper-and-pencil version for an online test. Applicants now take a test from their own computers before being considered for an interview. A computer-generated report is available in minutes to hiring managers. Because it weeds out people up front, recruiters waste less time interviewing unqualified candidates. Cost: $25 each hire.

The Internet has already revolutionized the job hunt. Now, in the next step, online testing is being hawked as a tool to screen job applicants. A slew of

13 ☞ small outfits, such as Fitability Systems, Q-Hire, and Epredix.com, are crowding into the market, while big test providers, like Chicago-based Reid London House, are exploring the Internet, too.

Sources: Adapted from Joanne Gordon, "Armchair Testing," *Forbes*, April 16, 2001, p. 1; and Barbara Ehrenreich, "What Are They Probing For?," *Time*, June 4, 2001, p. 86.

well-publicized and rigid drug-testing program. Individuals who refuse the Motorola drug test are terminated immediately.[12] The company believes that a firm stand against substance abusers is necessary. Other companies are not as harsh when they identify employees who fail a drug test. These firms place the individuals failing a drug test into rehabilitation programs.

Job applicants who test positive for substance abuse are usually dropped from the pool of candidates. Companies do not want to hire substance abusers because of the cost, liability, and research findings that abusers have more accidents and higher absenteeism.

A reliable and valued drug-testing program that protects the dignity of individuals being tested can be beneficial. However, there are still cases where drug testing gives false readings or the specimen is inappropriately handled. Companies need to use precise and dignified drug-testing programs so that substance abusers are correctly identified.

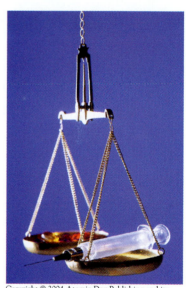

11-3h AIDS Testing

The human costs of acquired immune deficiency syndrome (AIDS) are incalculable. For those who suffer from AIDS and for their families, the emotional toll is terribly high. For employers AIDS presents the specter of a major economic drain. Benefits paid out for an employee with AIDS typically exceed $100,000.

The spiraling costs of caring for AIDS patients require the immediate attention of employers and insurers. Since the law states that an employer cannot discharge or refuse to hire someone with AIDS, employers need to check their health, life, and disability insurance coverage. In many federal and state courts, persons with AIDS have been extended the protection of laws for the disabled. A disability can be a reason for dismissal or refusal to hire only if it prevents the person from doing the job.[13]

12. Twomey, *Labor and Employment Law*, pp. 605–607.

13. Clifford Pugh, "Quilting Bee Creates Camaraderie That Helps to Heal the Heartbreak," *Houston Post*, March 30, 1995, pp. D1–D2.

Rehabilitation Act of 1973
A law that protects employees with AIDS.

The **Rehabilitation Act of 1973** protects employees with AIDS. Section 504 of the act states:

> No otherwise qualified individual with handicaps . . . shall, solely by reason of his handicap, be excluded from the participation in . . . or be subjected to discrimination under the program or activity receiving federal financial assistance.

The Americans with Disabilities Act now requires employers to provide reasonable workplace accommodations for an employee with HIV/AIDS.

Because AIDS is a major challenge and a serious problem, organizations are now establishing guidelines for dealing with it. Some of the guidelines found in policies at IBM, Johnson & Johnson, and BankAmerica include:

- People with AIDS or who are infected with HIV, the AIDS-causing virus, are entitled to the same rights and opportunities as people with other serious illnesses.
- Employment policies should be based on the scientific evidence that people with AIDS or HIV infection do not pose a risk of transmitting the virus through ordinary workplace contact.
- Employers should provide workers with sensitive and up-to-date education about AIDS and risk reduction in their personal lives.
- Employers have the duty to protect the confidentiality of employees' medical information.

Knowledge and information in the form of a policy document can be helpful in alleviating fear and correcting misinformation about AIDS. The devastation of AIDS is well documented. It is a disease caused by a virus that breaks down part of the body's immune system. A firm's policy can't help the body fight the disease, but it provides useful information to help employees understand that AIDS victims will be treated with human dignity and concern. This important message to those with AIDS, as well as to their colleagues, says that the firm cares and wants to help.

11-3i Decision to Hire

After preliminary screening, evaluating the application, interviewing, and testing, the company may decide to make a job offer to an applicant. If so, a background check is often made. The background check verifies information by consulting the references the applicant provided. This information may be obtained by letter, by telephone, or in person. One important group of references is previous employers; the company tries to gather information about the applicant's previous job performance. Under the **Fair Credit and Reporting Act,** the prospective employer must secure the applicant's permission before checking references.

Fair Credit and Reporting Act
Prospective employers must secure an applicant's permission before checking references.

When the reference check yields favorable information, the line manager and an HRM representative meet to decide what the offer will be. The offer is sometimes made subject to successful completion of a physical examination, which can be conducted by a company physician or by a doctor outside the organization. The objective is to screen out people whose physical deficiencies might be expensive liabilities and to place people in jobs they are physically able to handle.

11-4 TRAINING AND EMPLOYEE DEVELOPMENT

Training   A continual process of helping employees perform at a high level.

Employee Development
Anything a company does to increase the effectiveness of employees to perform their jobs.

Training and **employee development** programs include orientation activities that inform employees of basic company policies and procedures, training programs to educate people in job skills and develop them for future advancement, performance appraisal to assess whether an employee is contributing at peak efficiency, and employee assistance programs to help employees with work/life issues. The importance of a firm's training and development program to the overall effectiveness of the organization cannot be overemphasized.

Through recruitment and placement, good employees can be brought into the company. They then need continual training and development so that both their needs and the objectives of the firm can be achieved.

11-4a Orientation

Most large companies have formal **orientation programs** for new employees. Although new hires usually know something about the firm, they often lack specific information about working hours, pay, parking, rules, facilities, and so on. The HRM department usually coordinates the orientation, but the immediate supervisor is the key to the process. He or she and the new employee must eventually establish a cordial relationship that will encourage communication.

All organizations large and small should have some type of orientation to help new employees learn about and adjust to their new workplace. Entering a work environment for the first time can be unsettling for a lot of people, especially those who are beginning entry-level positions. Most orientation programs introduce employees to the firm's policies and procedures. Legally, it is not required to have an orientation program, but it is a good idea to make sure that employees know a firm's policies and its grievance procedures. In addition, employees should be made aware of any safety issues, including exit routes in case of emergency and locations of first aid equipment. Precautions such as these can help in the event of an emergency, and they can minimize a firm's exposure to litigation in the case of an actual situation arising.

Beyond the perfunctory training in policies and procedures, many firms also use the orientation session to introduce employees to the organization's culture and history. This type of information provided early on can help the employee in the assimilation process. Knowing a firm's history and its internal "lore" can be a big help when new employees attempt to fit in with the rest of the workforce.

In lieu of lengthy formal orientation training sessions, many firms have short sessions that are supplemented with employee handbooks. Although that is not the ideal way to introduce new employees to large organizations, the approach can be effective for small firms with less complex policies, procedures, and cultures. Employee handbooks should include organizational policies and procedures. Many firms elect to include tear-out forms that employees sign and turn in, indicating they have read and understand the policies. This can be especially useful for sensitive issues such as sexual harassment, where firms can protect themselves from liability merely by having a policy of zero tolerance that they communicate to all employees.

> **Orientation Programs**   A series of activities (e.g., meetings, Q&A sessions, discussions) to bring new employees up to speed on the company, its cultures, policies, expectations, and programs.

11-4b Training

Training is a continual process of providing employees with skills and knowledge they need to perform at a high level. It begins on the person's first day at work. Training may occur in the workplace or at a special training facility, but training experts should always supervise the curriculum and delivery of training.

To be effective, a training program must accomplish a number of objectives. First, it must be based on both organizational and individual needs; training for training's sake is not the objective. Second, the objectives of training should spell out what problems will be solved. Third, all training should be based on sound theories of learning. This is the major reason why training and management development are not for amateurs. Finally, a training program must be evaluated to determine whether it is working.

Before a training program can be developed, problem areas must be pinpointed. Companies use a number of techniques to identify problems, including reviewing safety records, absenteeism data, job descriptions, and attitude surveys to see what employees think about their jobs, bosses, and the company.

Skill Objectives Objectives that focus on developing physical abilities.

Knowledge Objectives Objectives that are concerned with understanding, attitudes, and concepts.

On-the-Job Training A supervisor or other worker may show a new employee how to perform the job.

Vestibule Training Training in a mock-up or simulation of the actual work area.

Classroom Training Training method used to help employees reach skill and knowledge objectives.

Once training needs have been identified, objectives need to be stated in writing. They provide a framework for the program. Objectives need to be concise, accurate, meaningful, and challenging. There are usually two major categories of objectives—skills and knowledge. **Skill objectives** focus on developing physical abilities; **knowledge objectives** are concerned with understanding, attitudes, and concepts.

Various methods are available for reaching the skill and knowledge objectives. Such factors as cost, available time, number of persons to be trained, background of trainees, and skill of the trainees determine the method used. Some of the more widely used training methods are as follows:

- **On-the-job training:** A supervisor or other worker may show a new employee how to perform the job.

- **Vestibule training:** This is training in a mock-up or simulation of the actual work area.

- **Classroom training:** Numerous classroom methods are used by business organizations. The lecture—a formal, organized presentation—is one method. A conference or small discussion group gets the student more involved than the lecture method. Interactive video (IAV) lecturing is becoming a popular technique. In IAV training, employees communicate with a computer to acquire knowledge and skills.

14 ☞

Corporate training programs can be an important aspect of employees' sense of well-being and productivity. If they know the company will help them build their skills and advance their career, they can make a full commitment to the firm. Abbott Foods, for example, prides itself on a developing a corporate culture that brings out the best in its more than 450 employees, or, "associates," as they all are called. "People are the key to our success now and in the future," notes Larry Abbott, president. "We want to recruit the best and retain our associates, particularly in the tight labor market here in central Ohio, where unemployment is less than 3 percent."

Abbott boasts a strong record of continuity. Average length of service for senior managers is 15.2 years. All employees are encouraged to feel part of and take ownership in the organization. A combination of training and an atmosphere of inclusiveness and fun help to foster an upbeat attitude and teamwork. "We have a general initiative to recognize people and a job well done," points out Cynthia Alls, Abbott Foods' human resources manager, herself a fourteen-year veteran. A "Pay Attention" program, for example, helps employees to focus their personal goals within the company. An emphasis is placed on promoting from within, and supervisors—to whom HR acts as advisers on personnel issues—are expected to help ensure the success of their charges.

Toward this end, Alls provides semiannual training for all supervisors on human dynamics—how, for instance, to keep people accountable and how to interview—as well as changes in laws and policies. "We view this training as a means of appreciating our associates," she points out. "It has been really helpful. One night supervisor, for example, has said that this training has refocused him, and he is now writing job descriptions and is eager to help HR and the company's associates."[14]

11-4c Management Development

Management Development Programs and processes used to educate managerial personnel to prepare them for additional responsibilities.

Training is generally associated with operating, or nonmanagerial, employees; management development is associated with managerial personnel. **Management development** refers to the process of educating and developing selected personnel so that they have the knowledge, skills, attitudes, and understanding needed to manage in future positions. The process starts with the selection of a qualified individual and continues throughout that individual's career.

14. "People: Abbott's Key to Future Success," *ID: The Information Source for Managers and DSRS,* September 2001, pp. 59–60.

Companies use management development to ensure the long-term success of the organization, to furnish competent replacements, to create an efficient team that works well together, and to enable managers to reach their potential. Management development may also be needed because of high executive turnover, a shortage of management talent, and our society's emphasis on lifelong education and development.

Employees can acquire the knowledge, skills, attitudes, and understanding necessary to become successful managers through two types of programs: on-the-job training and formal development. On-the-job programs include:

- **Understudy programs.** A person works as a subordinate partner with a boss, with the goal of eventually assuming the full responsibilities and duties of the job.

- **Job rotation.** Managers are transferred from job to job on a systematic basis. Job assignments can last from two weeks to six months.

- **Coaching/mentoring.** A supervisor teaches job knowledge and skills to a subordinate. The supervisor instructs, directs, corrects, and evaluates the subordinate.

On-the-job development programs emphasize actual job experience. They are designed to increase the employee's skill, knowledge, and confidence.

Formal management development programs are often conducted by training units within organizations or by consultants in universities and specialized training facilities around the country. In very large corporations, full-time training units conduct regular management development courses. For example, General Electric's Advanced Management Course, designed for the four highest levels of management, lasts thirteen weeks. It covers business policy, economics, social issues, and management principles. Many smaller firms send managers to development programs at universities. Publicized and well-attended programs are found at the University of Michigan, Columbia University, Duke University, the University of Houston, and Pennsylvania State University.

11-4d Performance Appraisals

Training and development also involve **performance appraisals.** Managers use appraisal programs to communicate expectations and to help subordinates improve personal deficiencies. Most employees want to know how well they are performing, and appraisals provide a basis for reviewing their performance. Appraisals also give employees a chance to discuss their career plans with their supervisor.

Properly handled, formal performance appraisals can help supervisors and subordinates develop mutual trust, respect, and understanding. But to do that, managers must divorce performance appraisals from the review of salary.

Perhaps the oldest performance appraisal technique is the **graphic rating scale.** Usually the supervisor is supplied with a printed form for each person to be rated and is asked to circle or check the phrase that best describes the individual on the particular trait. Exhibit 11-8 shows a sample rating scale.

This type of scale is easy to use but has serious disadvantages. First, scoring is difficult. Second, it doesn't tell which traits are most important. For example, is quality more important than cooperation? Third, ratings usually cluster around the more positive statements. Finally, this system doesn't tell a manager how to help subordinates correct identified deficiencies.

The perfect system would be accurate, reliable, fair, informative, and designed for each key feature of a job. Furthermore, the supervisor and subordinate would know exactly what is expected in the job and that performance results are linked to preestablished criteria. Such a perfect system simply is not available. But the search has gone on for years.

In addition to this performance appraisal technique, there are numerous others that managers can use. One of the more popular contemporary appraisal approaches goes by

Understudy Programs
Programs in which a person works as a subordinate partner with a boss, with the goal of eventually assuming the full responsibilities and duties of the job.

Job Rotation Method of transferring managers from job to job on a systematic basis with assignments lasting from two weeks to six months.

Coaching/Mentoring
A method in which a supervisor teaches job knowledge and skills to a subordinate. The supervisor instructs, directs, corrects, and evaluates the subordinate.

15

Perfomance Appraisals
Programs used to communicate expectations and to help subordinates improve personal deficiencies.

Graphic Rating Scale
Performance appraisal technique where supervisor is supplied with a printed form for each person to be rated and is asked to circle or check the phrase that best describes the individual on the particular trait.

EXHIBIT 11-8

Example of a Graphic Rating Scale

Name _____	Dept. _____			Date _____	
	Out-standing	Good	Satis-factory	Fair	Unsatis-factory
Quality of work: volume of acceptable work under normal conditions Comments:					
Quality of work: thoroughness, neatness and accuracy of work Comments:					
Knowledge of job: clear understanding of the facts or factors pertinent to the job Comments:					
Personal qualities: personality, appearance, sociability, leadership, integrity Comments:					
Cooperation: ability and willingness to work with associates, supervisors, and subordinates toward common goals Comments:					
Dependability: conscientious, thorough, accurate, reliable with respect to attendance, lunch periods, reliefs, etc. Comments:					
Initiative: Earnestness in seeking increased responsibilities. Self-starting, unafraid to proceed alone Comments:					

360-degree feedback
A performance appraisal approach that requests feedback on each employee from others who work for, with, and manage the individual.

the name of **360-degree feedback.** This approach requests performance feedback on each employee from others who work for or with the individual and manage the individual. This approach provides the ratee's manager with a complete, "360-degree" view of his or her performance. Many firms have adopted this technique to great effect, while others have stumbled with it. Whatever performance appraisal technique is chosen, it must be objective, be clear to all involved, and provide useful feedback to the employee for performance improvement and career development. Too many performance appraisal systems become perfunctory, undesirable "tasks" that have no benefits for the organization or employees. Managers can avoid that by selecting and using an appraisal system that meets the needs of their particular workplace and business goals.

11-4e Employee Assistance Programs

In today's complex social and business world, from time to time many employees find they are unable to cope with the stresses in their personal lives. Although in general a business does not get involved with employee lives beyond the business, many firms are finding that personal issues impact individual productivity and effectiveness. To help employees who are going through stressful personal issues, businesses have adopted **employee assistance programs (EAPs).** These programs cover a wide range of topics, including stress management, personal financial management, coping with alcohol or other addictions, caregiving to elderly family members, and other topics. Although they are not intended to replace the formal medical or mental health system, EAPs are discreet and effective ways for employees to deal with personal issues and remain productive at work.

Do all of these HRM functions work? That question has been put to more than a few human resources vice presidents over the years. Especially in difficult economic environments, CEOs seek ways to cut costs. If they believe some units are not contributing to the "bottom line" they will be the first ones scrutinized for cost cuts. To help bolster the argument for the significance of an effective HRM function in organizations, research has shown a direct link between HRM and profits. The Focus on Business box on page 284, "HR Makes a Financial Difference," highlights recent research into this issue.

11-5 COMPENSATION AND BENEFITS

In modern society, money is important both economically and psychologically. Without it a person can't buy the necessities or luxuries of life, but it is equated with status and recognition. Because money is so important, employees are quite sensitive about the amount of pay they receive and how it compares with what others in the company and in society are earning. Employees need to believe they are being compensated fairly for the work they do.

A compensation system has one objective: to create a system of rewards that is equitable to both employer and employee. The system must motivate the employee to work hard and accomplish goals. An employer views compensation in terms of cost-effectiveness, fairness, and adequacy. An employee views compensation in terms of equity, security, motivation, and meaningfulness.

Compensation is direct or indirect. **Direct compensation** includes an employee's base pay (wages or salary) and performance-based pay (incentives). **Indirect compensation** consists of federally required and state-mandated protection programs, private protection programs, paid leave, and miscellaneous benefits. (We discuss protection programs and benefits later in the chapter.) The total (direct and indirect) compensation package is used to:

- Attract potential job applicants.
- Retain good employees.
- Motivate employees.
- Administer pay within legal regulations.
- Gain a competitive edge.

Many people take part in compensation decisions. Top management determines the total amount of the budget that goes to pay, the pay form to be used (wages versus incentive plans), and pay policies. The manager working with employees makes inputs into the pay decision. An HRM unit advises management (top and operating) on pay strategy, legal issues (regular pay, overtime pay), competition, and market conditions.

Employee Assistance Programs (EAPs)   A program created to provide counsel, support, and resources to employees who are going through stressful personal issues such as stress management, personal financial management, coping with alcohol or other addictions, and caregiving to elderly family members.

Direct Compensation An employee's base pay (wages and salary) and performance-based pay (incentives).

Indirect Compensation Federally required and state-mandated protection programs, private protection programs, paid leave, and miscellaneous benefits.

FOCUS ON BUSINESS

HR Makes a Financial Difference

16 ☞ **R**esults of a study by HR consulting firm Watson Wyatt prove for the first time that there is a cause and effect relationship between human capital management and financial performance. Watson Wyatt's 2001 "Human Capital Index (HCI)" study shows that superior human resources practices are not only correlated with improved financial returns, they are, in fact, a leading indicator of increased shareholder value.

The year-long study, a follow-up to the firm's HCI study in 1999, reports that companies with the best HR practices provided a 64 percent total return to shareholders (TRS) over a five-year period—more than three times the 21 percent of the TRS for companies with the weakest HR practices. Bruce Pfau, head of organization effectiveness consulting at Watson Wyatt and author of the study, says, "Evidence from this new research clearly favors superior human capital management as a leading, rather than lagging, indicator of improved financial outcomes."

The HCI study is based on a comprehensive survey of human resource practices at 750 North American and European companies with a track record of at least three years of total returns to shareholders, 1,000 or more employees, and a minimum of $100 million in revenues or market value. Other highlights of the research include:

- Making a stronger effort to link pay to performance—that is, through stock programs, incentive/profit-sharing plans, or higher pay for top performers—is associated with a 6.3 percent increase in market value overall.
- Capitalizing on basic communication technology holds tremendous potential for financial payoff—companies that give employees easy access to these technologies see a 4.2 percent gain in market value.
- Companies that support flexible work arrangements, such as flextime, telecommuting and job sharing, have 3.5 percent higher market value.

Sources: Adapted from "HR Practices Are Leading Indicators of Financial Success," *Management,* February 2002, pp. 8–9; "HR Technology and Impact on Firm's Value," *Business Times,* January 10, 2002; and Steve Bates, "Study Links HR Practices with the Bottom Line," *HR Magazine,* December 2001, p. 14.

11-5a Wages

Wages A traditional payment method based on an hourly or daily rate.

The most common system for compensating operating or nonmanagerial employees is **wages,** based on time increments or number of units produced. Blue-collar workers have traditionally been paid at an hourly or daily rate, although some are now being paid biweekly or monthly.

11-5b Individual Incentives

Individual Incentive Plan The oldest type of compensation, which can take several forms: piecework, production bonuses, and commissions.

The oldest form of compensation is the **individual incentive plan,** which by definition pays for performance. Individual incentive plans take several forms: piecework, production bonuses, and commissions.

Piecework A plan in which the employee is paid a certain rate for each piece produced, with no other form of compensation.

Straight **piecework** means the employee is paid a certain rate for each piece produced, with no other form of compensation. A modified piecework plan works like this. The employer guarantees the employee an hourly rate for performing the expected minimum output. For production over the standard (set through work measurement studies), the employer pays so much per extra piece produced. For example, suppose the hourly rate

is $5.00 and the standard of production is ten units per hour. Management determines that paying $.50 per unit produced above the standard level is fair. Thus an employee who produces fifteen units per hour (rather than the standard ten units) would earn $2.50 more per hour, or a total of $7.50 per hour ($5.00 hourly rate + $2.50 incentive for being above standard).

Production bonus systems pay an hourly rate. A bonus—something extra—is paid when the employee, or the total output, exceeds the standard.

Sales employees often receive commissions. A **commission** is payment tied directly to performance standards. Straight commission, the equivalent of straight piecework, is typically a percentage of net sales.

> **Production Bonus**   A bonus or payment to employees based on a formula that encourages quantity and quality of output.
>
> **Commission**   Payment to an employee that is tied directly to performance standards.

11-5c Group Incentives

To provide broader motivation than that furnished by individual incentive plans, several group-based approaches are used. Their aim is to increase productivity and improve morale. Group incentive plans give each group member a chance to receive a bonus based on the output or performance of the group.

Scanlon Plans

A combination group incentive, suggestion, and employee participation arrangement, the **Scanlon plan,** has been popular in small and medium-sized manufacturing firms.[15] Such plans require management and employee involvement, interaction, and cooperation. In a Scanlon plan, named after its designer, Joseph Scanlon, each department of the firm has a production committee. Members include the supervisor and employee representatives elected by coworkers or appointed by the union. The committee receives and reviews employees' and managers' suggestions for improving work practices and procedures. The number of suggestions in a Scanlon plan company is usually double the typical suggestion-plan rate.

A Scanlon plan formula is used to calculate productivity gains resulting from the suggestions. Workers typically receive about 75 percent of the cost savings from improvements resulting from the suggestions, while the remainder goes to the firm. The savings are distributed to employees based on their wage levels.

> **Scanlon Plan**   A plan in which each department of the firm has a production committee that receives and reviews employees' and managers' suggestions for improving work practices and procedures.

Profit-Sharing Plans

The Gallatin glassworks factory in New Geneva, Pennsylvania, used the first recorded **profit-sharing plan** in 1794. Today over 430,000 such plans are used by American businesses.[16] In profit sharing, an employer pays or makes available to regular employees

> **Profit-Sharing Plan**   A plan in which an employer pays employees an amount based on profits earned plus regular salary.

---

15. Jay R. Schuster and Patricia K. Zingheim, "New Pay Strategies That Work," *Journal of Compensation & Benefits,* May–June 1993, pp. 5–9.

16. U.S. Department of Labor, Bureau of Labor Statistics, "Employee Benefits in Medium and Large Firms, 1988," August 1989, p. 406.

special current or deferred sums based on profits earned in addition to their regular pay. There are three types of profit-sharing plans:

- *Cash, or current, payment.* Profits are immediately distributed quarterly or annually.
- *Deferred.* A portion of profits is credited to employee accounts, with payment made at the time of retirement, disability, or severance (when an employee leaves the company). This is the most popular plan because of the tax advantages of deferring income.
- *Combined.* This plan incorporates features of the current payment and deferred plans.

In the United States, profit sharing is the most common method firms use to provide retirement income for their employees. Advocates contend that the plans encourage better performance by employees. However, profit sharing has some potential problems. What does management do in down years, when there are no profits? Even though employees have worked hard, an ineffective advertising program or a new product from a competitor may wipe out any profits. After several difficult and lean years, employees may begin to wonder whether hard work is worth the effort. Even in good years, it is often difficult to see how hard work is significant to profits received a year away or, worse, at retirement many years later.

Lincoln Electric Plan

Lincoln Electric Plan A plan which rewards good performance by issuing a bonus that an employee receives based on his (her) contributions.

The majority of group incentive plans are customized to fit a particular organization. The most publicized and successful has been the **Lincoln Electric plan.** Lincoln Electric employees are rewarded for good performance. At Lincoln Electric, all jobs are compensated on the bonus system. The year-end bonus is intended as a sharing of the results of efficient operation based on each individual's initiative, quality, and teamwork. Lincoln has used this effective merit-rating system since 1934.[17] Needless to say, Lincoln Electric jobs are in great demand.

11-5d Wage Determination

Job Evaluation Systems Processes by which the relative values of jobs within the organization are determined.

In many organizations, the relative worth of a job and the wage adjustments for it are determined by using **job evaluation systems** in which a job is compared with others within the organization. Under the ranking method, all jobs are ranked from highest to lowest on the basis of skill, difficulty, working conditions, and importance to the success of the organization. The work attitudes or personalities of the current jobholders often distort rankings. In most cases, unions are not enthusiastic about job evaluation. With such a system, the union negotiator has almost no role to play.

Unions generally prefer the daily rate of pay over systems that involve piecework or incentive payments. Because time standards and records of the employee's output are not needed, a daily rate of pay is easier to understand and use than are piece rates, bonuses, or commissions. Unions also believe that a piecework system reduces the group orientation, the need for union solidarity; a worker paid on the basis of individual effort can produce at any level he or she wants to. Unions prefer to encourage group solidarity and a united front.

Many factors help determine the wage rate for a nonmanagerial job. Wages for certain jobs are affected by the supply of, and demand for, qualified personnel, although unions and the government may hinder these effects. Unions, for example, using strike threats and contract agreements, can prevent employers from lowering wage rates even when qualified personnel abound.

Existing wage rates in competing companies or in the community also influence wage determination. Organizations typically conduct wage surveys to assess hourly rates, piecework or other incentive rates, and fringe benefits offered by other organizations. If the wage rates of a firm are too low, it may be difficult to attract qualified personnel.

17. Carolyn Wiley, "Incentive Plan Pushes Production," *Personnel Journal*, August 1993, pp. 86–91.

Wage and salary administration, like other areas of HRM management, has been the target of various laws. For instance, full-time employees must be paid at least the minimum wage per hour of work. Since the first minimum wage law was enacted in 1938, the rate has risen from $.25 to $5.15 per hour. In addition, the Fair Labor Standards Act of 1938 forbids the employment of minors between 16 and 18 years of age in such hazardous occupations as coal mining, logging, and woodworking.

11-5e Comparable Worth

In an effort to close the earnings gap between men and women, a growing movement has worked to have the widely accepted concept of equal pay for equal jobs expanded to include equal pay for comparable jobs. The issue is known as **comparable worth.** In *Gunther v. Washington*, the Supreme Court ruled five to four that a sex discrimination suit can be brought under the 1964 Civil Rights Act on the basis of "equal or substantially equal work."[18] In that case, male prison guards received significantly higher pay than female prison guards doing similar work. The county had evaluated the male prison guards' jobs and found them to have 5 percent more job content than the female jobs. However, the males were paid 35 percent more.

The **Equal Pay Act of 1963** was designed to lessen the existing gap between male and female pay rates. Although some progress has occurred, women in general still earn about 75 percent of what their male counterparts earn. Some of this difference exists because of male- versus female-dominated occupations. There is also the fact that women have often spent less time in various jobs and because of less seniority do not receive the same salary or wage as those with more seniority. Exhibit 11-9 presents the Bureau of the Census analysis on the difference between men and women's median incomes across different occupations.

Comparable Worth
The concept of equal pay for jobs that require similar levels of skills, training, and experience.

Equal Pay Act of 1963
Designed to lessen the existing gap between male and female pay rates.

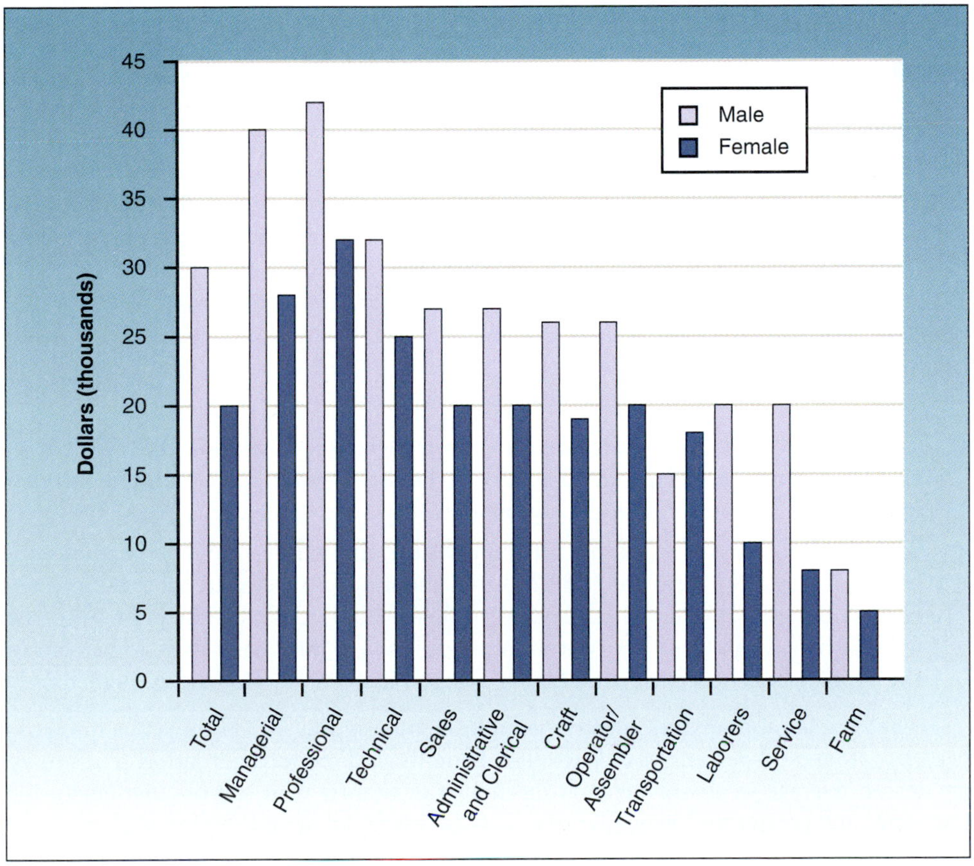

EXHIBIT 11-9

A Comparison of Median Income of Male and Female, Year-Round, Full-Time Workers

18. "Comparable Worth in Industrialized Countries," *Monthly Labor Review*, November 1992, pp. 40–42.

The Equal Pay Act requires employers to eliminate pay differences for the same job. For example, if a firm is hiring a laboratory lecturer, the position must be paid the same irrespective of the sex of the jobholder. If two workers, however, one male and one female, perform at different levels during a period of time, they could be compensated differently based on the notion that performance is rewarded.

Using comparable worth principles requires a sound job evaluation system, regular comparison of pay across jobs, and a documented pay system. A job evaluation point system is widely used. It requires the evaluator to quantify the value of the elements of a job. For example, job knowledge may receive twenty points; quality of work, thirty points; and so forth. The points are then added up and are used to rank jobs.

11-5f Salaries

Salaries Compensation paid to employees on a weekly or longer schedule.

Employees compensated on a weekly or longer schedule are paid **salaries.** Salaried employees are assumed to be able to influence the way they perform their jobs more than can employees who are paid wages. But the approach to developing an equitable compensation system for executives is similar to that for hourly workers. Companies make comparisons, conduct surveys, and analyze supply and demand, job duties, and job responsibilities.

Hay Associates developed one method specifically for evaluating middle- and top-management positions. First, analysts evaluate each position from information provided in the job description. They consider three factors: job know-how, problem solving, and accountability. Then, through a statistical procedure, they convert evaluations for the jobs in a particular company to the Hay control standards, a special ranking system. Hay Associates publishes annual surveys showing the compensation practices of a number of companies for jobs of similar control standards. All Hay clients use the same evaluation method, so they can compare management salaries.

11-5g Benefits and Services

Benefits Forms of indirect compensation that are financial in nature; examples include health insurance and pension fund contributions.

Services In business, intangible products that cannot be physically possessed and that involve performance or effort; examples include teaching, nursing, air travel, tailoring, accounting, and the opera. In employee compensation, indirect compensation in the form of programs, facilities, or activities supplied by employers for employees' use.

Consolidated Omnibus Budget Reconciliation Act (COBRA) Law passed in 1985 ensures that terminated or laid-off employees have the option to maintain health care insurance by personally paying the premiums.

Tax Reform Act of 1986 A law with provisions that affect indirect compensation.

Benefits and services are forms of indirect compensation. They are monetary and nonmonetary payments over and above wage and salary rates. **Benefits** are financial in nature (e.g., health insurance payments, contributions to a pension fund), whereas **services** are employer-supplied programs, facilities, or activities (e.g., parks, gymnasiums, housing, transportation, child care, company cafeterias) useful to employees.

To yield a return to the employer and provide something positive to employees, benefits and services must be developed and used systematically. Too often, the so-called benefits are improperly installed. The company must first determine what benefits and services employees prefer and what resources are available and then select the best package the company can afford. In developing a benefit and service package, the employer must consider two important Internal Revenue Service issues:

- Passed in 1985, the **Consolidated Omnibus Budget Reconciliation Act (COBRA)** ensures that terminated or laid-off employees have the option to maintain health care insurance by personally paying the premiums.

- The **Tax Reform Act of 1986** has two provisions that affect indirect compensation. Essentially in 1995 it capped at $9,240 the amount of tax-deferred contributions (to be paid out at a later date) employees can make into a deferred-pay plan. Also the average benefits to employees not highly compensated must be at least 75 percent of the average benefits provided to highly compensated employees (top 20 percent).

The benefits and services offered to employees are significant. The average firm pays between 30 and 50 percent of its payroll to benefits. Indirect compensation tends to be greater on average in the manufacturing industries than it is in the nonmanufacturing industries and greater for blue-collar than it is for white-collar and service workers.

11-5h Protection Programs

Protection programs are designed to assist employees and their families if direct compensation is terminated and to alleviate the burden of health care expenses. Public protection programs grew out of the Social Security Act of 1935. They include social security benefits, unemployment compensation, and workers' compensation.

Funding of the **social security** system is provided by equal contributions from the employer and employee under terms of the Federal Insurance Contribution Act (FICA). The average social security benefit per year for a single person is $8,376 (for a married couple, $14,136), with adjustments periodically for increases in the consumer price index.

The Social Security Act dictates that **unemployment compensation** (given when a person loses a job) be jointly administered by the federal and state governments. Because income levels vary from state to state, unemployment compensation also varies by state. With the exception of Alabama, Alaska, and New Jersey, only employers contribute to the unemployment fund. All profit-making firms pay tax on the first $7,000 to $10,000 of wages earned by each employee. Their contribution rate, however, varies based on the number of unemployed people drawing from the fund.

To be eligible for unemployment compensation benefits, a person must:

- Have worked a set number of weeks (established by the state).
- Be available and ready to work.
- Be actively searching for a job.
- Not be unemployed due to a labor dispute (except in New York and Rhode Island).
- Not have been terminated for gross misconduct.
- Not have terminated voluntarily.

The time period that the employee receives benefits is a function of how long the person worked prior to termination; in general the standard maximum period is twenty-six weeks. Benefits can be extended up to thirteen weeks during periods of high unemployment or when jobs are lost due to foreign competition. The benefits vary across states but are about $225 per week.

Workers' compensation benefits are provided for temporary and permanent disability, disfigurement, medical expenses, and medical rehabilitation. Several benefits, the terms of which vary by state, are provided following fatal injuries.

Private protection programs are provided by firms but are not required by law. They include such benefits as health care, income after retirement, insurance against loss of life or limb, and, in some firms, guaranteed work and pay programs.

Another category of indirect compensation includes programs for elder care, child care, and employee services. The U.S. population 80 years old and older is expected to grow from 5 million in 1980 to over 23 million in 2040. The Travelers Companies in Hartford, Connecticut, has established an elder care program to help employees with the cost of care for aging parents or dependents.

Until the early 1980s, the U.S. workforce was largely composed of traditional family heads—husbands who worked as the employed breadwinner. Increasingly, both spouses are working for pay; dual-career couples now account for over 40 percent of the workforce. One problem faced by dual-career couples and single parents is child care. Organizations, now aware of the child care problem, address it in a number of ways. More than 8,000 firms provide day-care services, financial assistance, or referral services for child care. A growing number of firms have on-site or near-site centers.[19] Other firms allow flexible work schedules, and employees can use the time to care for sick children or for special activities such as dental appointments or meetings with school counselors.

Protection Programs   Programs designed to assist employees and their families if direct compensation is terminated and to alleviate the burden of health care expenses.

Social Security   A system in which funding is provided by equal contributions from the employer and employee under terms of the Federal Insurance Contribution Act (FICA).

Unemployment Compensation   Benefits given when a person loses a job, to be jointly administered by the federal and state governments.

Workers' Compensation   Benefits provided for temporary and permanent disability, disfigurement, medical expenses, and medical rehabilitation.

Private Protection Programs   Provided by firms but not required by law including such benefits as health care, income after retirement, insurance against loss of life or limb, and, in some firms, guaranteed work and pay programs.

19. Judy Nixon, Marilyn Helms, and Charles White, "What Companies Are Doing About Child Care," *Journal of Compensation & Benefits*, January–February 1993, pp. 7–24.

11-6 CONTEMPORARY WORKPLACE ISSUES

The workplace has become a microcosm of society as a whole. The forces that work to shape social interactions outside the workplace have reach and impact within the workplace itself. There are a variety of sources of this impact. Labor unions have had tremendous influence on working conditions, wages, and the authority of management. Federal agencies, such as the EEOC and the **Occupational Safety and Health Administration (OSHA),** have changed social behavior and the safety of the workplace. In this final section of this chapter, we look at two issues that all managers and business owners must consider as part of their operations: sexual harassment and workplace safety.

11-6a Sexual Harassment

To define **sexual harassment** as *illegal discriminatory conduct in violation of Title VII of the 1964 Federal Civil Rights Act* is acceptable and technically sound. However, in its 1980 guidelines, the EEOC presented a more practical definition:

> Unwelcome and unsolicited conduct of a sexual nature including, but not limited to, unwelcome sexual advances, requests for sexual favors, and other verbal or physical conduct of a sexual nature when the conduct is either directly linked to the grant or denial of an economic quid pro quo or where it has the purpose or effect of unreasonable interfering with the individual's work performance or creating a hostile, offensive, and intimidating work environment.

The EEOC guidelines state that sexual harassment is "unwelcome sexual advances, requests for sexual favors, and other verbal or physical conduct of a sexual nature" when any one of the following criteria are met:

- Submission to such conduct is made either explicit or implicitly a term or condition of the individual's employment
- Submission to or rejection of such conduct by an individual is used as the basis for employment decisions affecting the individual
- Such conduct has the purpose or effect of unreasonably interfering with an individual's work or creating an intimidating, hostile or offensive work environment

The EEOC definition describes two types of sexual harassment situations: quid pro quo and hostile or discriminatory work environment. The U.S. Supreme Court has agreed with the EEOC that both of these situations are violations of the federal law. Exhibit 11-10 shows the number of cases the EEOC has received over the years and the dollar judgments that have been levied against businesses.

For sexual harassment to be actionable it must be sufficiently severe or pervasive to alter the conditions of the employee's employment and create an abusive or hostile work environment. Federal courts and the U.S. Supreme Court accept the EEOC definition of sexual harassment. As presented in the guidelines there are two types of sexual harassment claims: quid pro quo and hostile environment.

Occupational Safety and Health Administration (OSHA)
A federal agency with the primary purpose of ensuring safe working conditions.

Sexual Harassment
Unwelcome advances and requests for sexual favors that affect a person's performance, and a hostile work environment in which employees are subjected to sexual comments, jokes, or materials.

EXHIBIT 11-10

Sexual Harassment Cases Received by the EEOC

	FY 1992	FY 1993	FY 1994	FY 1995	FY 1996	FY 1997	FY 1998	FY 1999	FY 2000	FY 2001
Receipts	10,532	11,908	14,420	15,549	15,342	15,889	15,618	15,222	15,836	
% of Charges Filed by Males		9.1%	9.1%	9.9%	9.9%	10.0%	11.6%	12.9%	12.1%	13.6%
Resolutions		7,484	9,971	11,478	13,802	15,861	17,333	17,115	16,524	16,726
Monetary Benefits (Millions)*		$12.7	$25.1	$22.5	$24.3	$27.8	$49.5	$34.3	$50.3	$54.6

Quid Pro Quo

Quid pro quo is a Latin term that means "something for something." It is used in law to describe a contractual situation in which one party gives a valuable thing in exchange for another. In sexual harassment it means the acceptance or rejection of a supervisors' sexual demands or advances in determining the terms of employment. In other words, the supervisor wants something, a sexual favor, and is willing to offer something, a pay increase or a promotion, in exchange for it. The supervisor uses his or her position to accomplish what he or she wants.

To establish a quid pro quo sexual harassment situation, the employee must clearly show that the harassment was based on sex, the employee was subjected to unwelcome and unsolicited conduct of a sexual nature, and the employee did not instigate the offensive behavior.

Hostile Environment

Hostile environment sexual harassment is not as clear-cut as quid pro quo sexual harassment. In a hostile environment situation, the victims are subjected to unwelcome advances, requests for sexual favors, and other verbal or physical behavior that interferes with performance or creates an intimidating work environment. The main difference between quid pro quo and hostile environment sexual harassment is that in hostile environment harassment, requests for sexual favors are not made in exchange for job benefits.

The EEOC suggests that courts look at the following criteria to determine if a hostile work environment exists:

- Whether the conduct was verbal, physical, or both
- How often it was repeated
- Whether the conduct was hostile or potentially offensive
- Whether the alleged harasser was a coworker or a supervisor
- Whether others joined in and continued the harassment
- Whether the harassment was directed at more than one individual
- Whether the remarks were derogatory or hostile
- Whether the alleged harasser singled out the person claiming harassment
- What the relationship was between the alleged harasser and the victim

Avoiding Accusations of Harassment

Sexual harassing behavior is easy to define but often difficult to avoid because it can be very subtle. For example, one man kept a picture on top of his desk of his wife dressed in a bikini. The picture offended women in his office. The man didn't realize that others could interpret the image of his wife as creating a hostile work environment. Some other potential forms of sexual harassment include:

- Persistent e-mails to another person with romantic or sexual overtones
- Repeatedly standing or sitting too close to another person, violating their "personal space"
- Staring at another person's body or parts of their body
- Making remarks to someone about another worker's attractiveness or sex appeal
- Casual touching of private body parts that is intended to appear accidental or inadvertent

As you can tell, harassment can occur in an infinite variety of ways in the workplace. In general, your guideline should be to avoid entirely all comments, jokes, or behaviors of a sexual nature. Remember, your behavior doesn't have to be intentional to be potentially harassing.

Quid Pro Quo   A Latin term used to describe a contractual situation in which one party gives a valuable thing in exchange for another; in sexual harassment, the acceptance or rejection of a supervisors' sexual demands or advances in determining the terms of employment.

Hostile Environment A situation in which an employee is subjected to unwelcome advances, requests for sexual favors, and other verbal or physical behavior that interferes with performance or creates an intimidating work environment.

11-6b Workplace Safety

Another important benefit for any person is a safe work environment. The December 1984 disaster in Bhopal, India, which resulted in the deaths of 3,000 people and injury to another 300,000, emphasizes the importance of safety. Americans are also familiar with the nuclear accident at Three Mile Island (1979) and the 1986 space shuttle *Challenger* disaster. Such incidents emphasize that safe equipment, practices, and procedures are crucial benefits.

Occupational Safety and Health Act Law, passed in 1970, that mandates safety and health standards for U.S. business. Provided for the establishment of the Occupational Safety and Health Administration.

Due to the efforts of unions, employees, the government, insurance companies, and society in general, the **Occupational Safety and Health Act** became law on April 28, 1970. The act directs the secretary of labor to enforce safety and health standards in over 4 million businesses and for more than 57 million employees. The core of the act is the system of standards that must be met. For example, OSHA has set an industrial noise limit of ninety decibels where workers are exposed eight hours per day. OSHA puts special emphasis on improving safety in the four industries with injury rates more than double the national average, which is 15.2 disabling injuries per minion employee-hours worked. These industries are longshoring, meat and meat products, lumber and wood products, and miscellaneous transportation equipment.

OSHA enforces standards through a system of inspectors, citations, and penalties. To inspect health and safety conditions, Labor Department representatives may enter any business at a reasonable time. (OSHA inspectors denied entry must obtain a search warrant before conducting an inspection.) They may also question the employer, employees, or employee representatives. Criminal penalties for violations can go as high as $70,000 and/or one year in prison. Four categories of violations can result from an inspector's visit:

1. *De minimis*—a minor violation not directly job related
2. Nonserious—a minor violation that is job related
3. Serious—one in which a chance of serious injury or death exists
4. Imminent danger—one that threatens serious injury or death; penalty is assessed by the federal courts

17 ☞

A workplace problem that has been receiving attention in recent years is secondhand tobacco smoke. In 1986 the U.S. Surgeon General issued a report that stated that 2,400 to 4,000 lung cancer deaths were caused annually by secondhand smoke. As a result of this report and other evidence, more and more employers are moving to restrict or abolish smoking in the workplace.[20] It is estimated that over 84 percent of employers, including the federal government, limit or have abolished workplace smoking.

11-7 CONCLUSION

18, 19, 20 ☞

This chapter emphasizes the importance of people and people-related issues. Increasingly, organizations such as Federal Express, Liz Claiborne, and 3M are indicating that managing human resources is now mandatory in business. The recruitment, selection, development, health, and safety of employees are all part of the strategic plans of more and more organizations.

Little can be done in any organization without a motivated workforce. The people doing the work, carrying out the plans, meeting the customer, finalizing the sale, working on a project theme, reviewing the purchase order, and training the recently hired engineer must be motivated. Thus, understanding people is a requirement for developing programs to encourage and sustain employee motivation, which is covered in Chapter 12.

20. Richard A. Wolfe and Donald F. Parker, "Employee Health Management: Challenges and Opportunities," *Academy of Management Executive*, May 1994, pp. 22–31.

SUGGESTED WEBSITES

1. www.ibm.com
2. www.apple.com
3. www.dell.com
4. www.prudential.com
5. www.milliken.com
6. www.daimlerchrysler.com
7. www.eeoc.gov
8. www.monster.com
9. www.bnf.gov
10. www.dot.gov
11. www.nrc.gov
12. www.motorola.com
13. www.fitability.com
14. www.abbottfoods.com
15. www.ge.com
16. www.watsonwyatt.com
17. www.surgeongeneral.gov
18. www.fedex.com
19. www.lizclaiborne.com
20. www.mmm.com

SUMMARY OF LEARNING OBJECTIVES

1. *Define the term* human resource management. Human resource management (HRM) is the process of accomplishing organizational objectives by acquiring, retaining, terminating, developing, and properly using the human resources (people) in an organization.

2. *Explain why human resource planning, recruiting, and selecting are important.* Planning is an important activity that involves estimating the size and makeup of the future workforce. Planning of human resources is the lifeblood of the firm. Without the right people in the right place at the right time, the firm could go out of business. Recruiting is important because the best-qualified applicants must be found to fill vacancies. The company wants to have the best possible pool of applicants from which to choose. Selecting is the series of steps beginning with initial screening of candidates and ending with the decision to hire one candidate. Selecting must be done in compliance with federal laws regulating employment discrimination.

3. *Describe job analysis, job descriptions, and job specifications.* Job analysis is the process of determining what knowledge, skills, and abilities (KSAs) an employee needs to successfully accomplish the job. Job descriptions use the data gathered from job analysis to outline the activities involved in the job and the work conditions. Job specifications state the qualifications necessary for a job.

4. *Explain the role of the federal government in providing equal opportunities for employment to all Americans.* Through Title VII of the Civil Rights Act of 1964 and the Equal Employment Opportunity Act of 1972, the federal government attempts to provide equal opportunities for employment without regard to race, religion, age, creed, sex, national origin, or disability. These laws are administered by the Equal Employment Opportunity Commission (EEOC). In addition, the Immigration Reform and Control Act of 1986 (IRCA) has made employers responsible for prohibiting the recruitment and employment of unautho-

rized foreign-born individuals. The Americans with Disabilities Act (ADA) prohibits employers from discriminating against disabled employees or job applicants.

5. *Discuss training and development programs for hourly and salaried employees.* Training programs inform hourly employees of company policies and procedures, educate them in job skills, and develop them for future advancement. Management development programs for salaried employees are used to educate and develop selected personnel so that they have the knowledge, skills, attitudes, and understanding needed to manage in future positions.

6. *Identify examples of direct and indirect compensation.* Direct compensation includes an employee's base pay (incentives). Wages are compensation based on time increments or number of units produced. Salaries are compensation based on a weekly or longer schedule. Individual incentives include piecework, production bonuses, and commissions. Examples of group incentives include Scanlon plans, profit-sharing plans, and the Lincoln Electric plan. Indirect compensation includes federal- and state-mandated protection programs, private protection programs, paid leave, and miscellaneous benefits. Benefits are financial in nature (e.g., child care services). Public protection programs include social security benefits, unemployment compensation, and workers' compensation. Private protection programs include health care benefits, income after retirement, insurance, and guaranteed work and pay programs (e.g., golden parachutes).

7. *Discuss comparable worth.* The concept of comparable worth is an expansion of the concept of equal pay for equal work. This has become an issue because American women working full-time earn only about 75 percent of what men earn. The idea is to rank occupation typically held by men and those typically held by women, and then assign the same pay for jobs with the same rank. Comparable worth is controversial, and its principles are difficult to practice.

8. *Discuss modern workplace issues such as sexual harassment and workplace safety.*   Sexual harassment is a pervasive issue in the workplace that can be defined as unwelcome or unsolicited conduct of a sexual nature. Two forms of workplace harassment, quid pro quo and hostile environment, are defined by the EEOC. Quid pro quo harassment refers to situations where sex is requested in exchange for workplace favors, such as a raise. Hostile environment harassment refers to situations in which sexual references, images, or gestures are used to intimidate. Workplace safety is primarily governed by OSHA. OSHA regulations ensure that employers create work environments that are safe, and that employees are instructed on safe workplace practices.

KEY TERMS

abilities (p. 270)

Americans with Disabilities Act (ADA) (p. 272)

benefits (p. 288)

blind advertisement (p. 273)

Civil Rights Act of 1964 (p. 271)

Civil Rights Act of 1991 (p. 271)

classroom training (p. 280)

coaching/mentoring (p. 281)

commission (p. 285)

comparable worth (p. 287)

Consolidated Omnibus Budget Reconciliation Act (COBRA) (p. 288)

direct compensation (p. 283)

Drug-Free Workplace Act of 1988 (p. 276)

employee assistance programs (EAPs) (p. 283)

employee development (p. 278)

Equal Employment Opportunity Act of 1972 (p. 271)

Equal Employment Opportunity Commission (EEOC) (p. 271)

Equal Pay Act of 1963 (p. 287)

Fair Credit and Reporting Act (p. 278)

graphic rating scale (p. 281)

hostile environment (p. 291)

human resource management (HRM) (p. 267)

human resource planning (p. 269)

Immigration Reform and Control Act (IRCA) (p. 272)

indirect compensation (p. 283)

individual incentive plan (p. 284)

job analysis (p. 270)

job description (p. 270)

job evaluation systems (p. 286)

job rotation (p. 281)

job specification (p. 270)

knowledge (p. 270)

knowledge objectives (p. 280)

Lincoln Electric plan (p. 286)

management development (p. 280)

Markov models (p. 269)

Occupational Safety and Health Act (p. 292)

Occupational Safety and Health Administration (OSHA) (p. 290)

on-the-job training (p. 280)

orientation programs (p. 279)

performance appraisals (p. 281)

piecework (p. 284)

private protection programs (p. 289)

production bonus (p. 285)

profit-sharing plan (p. 285)

protection programs (p. 289)

quid pro quo (p. 291)

reasonable accommodations (p. 272)

recruitment (p. 270)

Rehabilitation Act of 1973 (p. 278)

retention (p. 268)

salaries (p. 288)

Scanlon plan (p. 285)

selection (p. 274)

services (p. 288)

sexual harassment (p. 290)

skill objectives (p. 280)

skills (p. 270)

social security (p. 289)

Tax Reform Act of 1986 (p. 288)

360-degree feedback (p. 282)

training (p. 278)

understudy programs (p. 281)

undue hardship (p. 272)

unemployment compensation (p. 289)

vestibule training (p. 280)

wages (p. 284)

workers' compensation (p. 289)

QUESTIONS FOR DISCUSSION AND REVIEW

1. Some believe that drug testing as a part of job screening is a blatant invasion of privacy. Do you agree? Why or why not?

2. What do you think will be the most significant changes in the workplace from the changing demographics in the United States? Explain.

3. What do you think are the major challenges businesses face in conducting performance appraisals?

4. Do you agree that employee assistance programs can be a positive influence on employee performance? Explain.

5. Do you think sexual harassment is a problem in the modern workplace? Explain why you think the way you do.

6. Explain the difference between direct and indirect compensation plans.

7. Are there any valid, reasonable reasons why men performing a job may receive higher pay than women performing the same job? Explain.

8. Before developing a training program, what should an organization do to identify problems?

9. Has employment law become so complex that even small firms need to have access to legal advisers on most human resource management issues?

10. Most employers do not want to hire drug and alcohol abusers. Why?

END-OF-CHAPTER QUESTIONS

1. If workers are guilty of sexual harassment, an employer is liable if the employer knew, or should have known, of the misconduct. **T** or **F**

2. The success of any human resource management (HRM) program requires the cooperation of managers. **T** or **F**

3. Human resource management professionals have developed a single, standardized approach that meets the needs of most companies. **T** or **F**

4. The retention phase of HRM involves recruiting, screening, selecting, and properly placed personnel. **T** or **F**

5. The primary objective of human resource planning is to find and attract the best-qualified applicants to fill vacancies. **T** or **F**

6. The EEOC has the power to file suit in a federal district court if it is unable to eliminate alleged unlawful employment practices through conference, conciliation, and persuasion. **T** or **F**

7. Blind ads eliminate the need to contact every applicant. **T** or **F**

8. About half of all work-related deaths are attributed to faulty equipment. **T** or **F**

9. A disability that prevents a person from doing his or her job cannot be a reason for dismissal or refusal to hire. **T** or **F**

10. An employer views compensation in terms of equity, security, motivation, and meaningfulness. **T** or **F**

11. The Fair Labor Standards Act forbids the employment of minors in hazardous occupations. **T** or **F**

12. The Equal Pay Act of 1963 was designed to lessen the gap between male and female pay rates. **T** or **F**

13. The Consolidated Omnibus Budget Reconciliation Act (COBRA) ensures that terminated or laid-off employees have the option to maintain health care insurance by personally paying the premiums. **T** or **F**

14. Training in a mock-up or simulation of the actual work area is called _____.
    a. on-the-job training   b. vestibule training   c. classroom training

15. The innate or natural attributes that a person has are called _____.
    a. knowledge   b. skills   c. abilities

INTERNET EXERCISE

Training Programs at Milliken & Company

Activity

For this exercise, students should visit the Milliken & Company website at www.milliken.com. The home page has a button on the left-hand navigation column labeled "Education." Students should click on this button and view the many different employee-training programs offered through Milliken University. Students should read the Milliken University mission statement, tour the learning facilities, and examine the various course offerings. After spending twenty to thirty minutes at the site and developing an understanding of the scope of Milliken's training programs, students should address the following questions and be prepared to discuss them in class.

Questions for Discussion

1. What is the mission of Milliken University? How does that mission mesh with the overall mission of the corporation?

2. What effect do you think Milliken University has on the company's "bottom line"? What effect do you think MU has on the company's employee morale?

3. Do you think the money invested in Milliken University by the company is money well spent? Explain.

4. Do you think Milliken University would have as extensive a course offering if Milliken was a public company? Explain your answer.

EXPERIENTIAL EXERCISE

Activity

This activity is designed for classroom discussion focusing on managerial response to money missing from the store's cash register. About fifty minutes will be needed to complete the exercise.

Directions

1. Provide the class with a brief story, such as the following:
2. You (the student) are to play the role of a paint store manager who discovers that $150 is apparently missing from the cash register, as the evening receipts do not match the dollar total in the cash register. Three employees had access to the cash register that afternoon.

3. Ask each student to discuss and identify the steps to be taken by the manager. Provide about fifteen minutes. Select a few students to report individual analyses.
4. Interject a new variable into the discussions at this point by saying that one of the three employees has stepped forward and admitted taking the $150. She happens to be a single mother who has previously been on welfare. Ask the students to decide what steps the manager should now take on this case. Provide about ten minutes for further discussion.
5. Select a few students to describe their decision and underlying rationale. Allow about ten minutes.

BUSINESS APPLICATION

Managers Controlling Health Costs

Activity

This activity is designed for small-group and classroom discussions focusing on managerial strategies for controlling the soaring costs of group health insurance. About forty-five minutes should be allotted for completion.

Directions

1. Divide the class into small groups of four to seven members, asking each group to appoint a recorder/spokesperson for the group.
2. Provide the class with a brief background on the health insurance cost problem, citing aspects such as the following:
   - An employer's provision of group health insurance coverage is very important for the employee's benefit package.
   - The cost of providing group health insurance coverage is very important for the employee's benefit package.
   - Group 3 is to focus on motivating nurses in a hospital setting where turnover is high and morale is low.

   - One approach to controlling insurance costs has been to attempt to reduce the employees' utilization of the insurance by trying to curb factors that contribute to poor health, such as cigarette smoking.
   - Cigarette smoking contributes to increased sickness, which leads to increased use of health insurance.
3. Ask each group to discuss whether they would support a company's attempt to control group health insurance costs by requiring employees who smoke to pay higher premiums than those who do not smoke. Provide fifteen to twenty minutes for discussion.
4. Ask each group's spokesperson to tell the class of the group's decision and underlying rationale. Allow approximately twenty minutes for reporting and discussion.

   Note: Time permitting, the instructor may want to elicit student feedback on premium differentials for other factors contributing to sickness—for example, employees with serious health problems, family history of illness, significantly overweight people, and so forth.

Case

Deaf Waiters Serve Up Cajun Food

During the past eight years, Delcambre's Ragin' Cajun in Pike Place Market has become a fixture in Seattle's dining scene. It's always busy, has received widespread kudos (including a high ranking in the local Zagat guide), and has thrived in an increasingly competitive dining market. Chef-owner Danny Delcambre even cooked for Bill Clinton when he was president. All of that doesn't seem so surprising when you find out that Delcambre grew up in Louisiana Cajun country and apprenticed with Cajun master Paul Prudhomme at his legendary K-Paul's in New Orleans. So what's the big deal? For starters, Delcambre is deaf and legally blind (he has progressive vision loss). Furthermore, most members of his staff are deaf or hard of hearing.

But by Delcambre's account, it isn't a big deal for people who are deaf to cook, wait tables, and perform just about any other restaurant task. Sure, there are some special considerations for restaurateurs who hire the hearing impaired. Patrons, for instance, had to learn to point to what they want on the menu (though some wait staffers can read lips). Training has to be based on printed materials rather than spoken instructions. A translator has to be used in meetings between the staff and vendors, and, instead of a phone, a manual alarm alerts the authorities in an emergency.

But none of those accommodations was prohibitive, says Delcambre. Vocational rehab offices provide translators and other services for training, and the expense of adjustments like installing a teletypewriter for the phone is offset by the tax breaks that come with hiring the disadvantaged.

The bigger concern, Delcambre says, was how customers would react. "A lot of people told me I shouldn't have deaf people as wait staff," he says. "Hearing people thought customers would be afraid."

Undeterred, Delcambre learned that a reliance on visual cues can make deaf servers particularly responsive to patrons' facial expressions and needs. Guests may not have noticed their technique, but they haven't complained of any drawbacks, either. Customer Randy Silver, who counts the Ragin' Cajun among his favorite restaurants, has more to say about the "excellent food" than communication issues. "A deaf waiter was a novelty, but not an impediment," he says.

And there were definite advantages to the restaurant, above and beyond the tax breaks. For one thing, says Delcambre, his deaf employees have a more positive view of working in a restaurant. "It's harder for deaf people to get a job, so they value their jobs more," he says. "They have higher work ethics and standards and they just want to be given a chance."

He should know—he opened his own restaurant because he couldn't find anyone who would let him do more than bus tables. As a result, Delcambre says he has few problems with retention or absenteeism. Two of his deaf employees, Taika Young and Tewodros Yeshak, have been at the Ragin' Cajun almost since it opened.

Delcambre says his deaf workers are also a boon for business because they attract customers with disabilities. "I get a lot of families with children who have disabilities and deaf classes that come in to see working deaf people as role models," he says.

Though he speaks often on the matter and has received accolades such as the Presidential Award for Small Employer of the Year, Delcambre is not a cheerleader for hiring people just because they're deaf. "The thing to look at is their qualifications," he says. "I want someone with a good attitude who will be a good person on the team."

Questions for Discussion

1. What do you think are "reasonable accommodations" for deaf waiters? Do you think most small restaurants are capable of making these accommodations?
2. Do you think Delcambre would have hired deaf waiters if he was not handicapped himself? Explain.
3. What are some economic advantages Delcambre realized by hiring deaf waiters? Do you think other small-business owners can realize these advantages?

Source: Adapted from Megan Steintrager, "Impaired, Not Impeded," *Restaurant Business,* August 1, 2001, pp. 22–24.

12

Labor-Management Relations

Photo: comstock.com

United Airlines Settles Labor Dispute with Mechanics

1 ☞ **M**echanic and related employees represented by the International Association of Machinists and Aerospace Workers (IAMAW) ratified a new five-year
2 ☞ agreement with United Airlines on March 5, 2002. The accord is retroactive to July 12, 2000, and makes 13,000 IAMAW mechanic and related employees at United the highest paid in the airline industry.

"I want to thank our members at United for the strong support they gave their negotiating committee under very difficult circumstances," said Scotty Ford, District 141-M president and lead negotiator for the mechanic and related group. "Their determination and professionalism allowed the negotiating committee to obtain the best agreement possible." The pact was ratified by 59 percent of the voting membership.

The agreement followed twenty-seven months of direct and mediated bargaining that included the appointment of a Presidential Emergency Board (PEB) in December 2001. A settlement recommendation from the PEB was rejected by the membership on February 12, 2002. Subsequent negotiations produced the March 5 agreement, which was ratified in the shadow of a March 7, 2002, strike deadline.

"Both United Airlines and the White House took actions to delay these negotiations," said Robert Roach, Jr., IAMAW general vice president. "Broad support from IAMAW members and AFL-CIO transportation labor unions gave our negotiating team the ability to overcome these roadblocks and reach an agreement."

In separate negotiations, IAMAW District 141, representing 30,000 Ramp & Stores, Public Contact, Food Services, and Security Officers continued to meet in federal mediation with United Airlines.

Sources: Adapted from "Machinists at United Airlines Ratify New Pact," *Financial Press,* March 5, 2002; and "After Contract Vote Real Work Begins at UAL Corp.," *Crain's Chicago Business,* March 11, 2002, p. 10.

12-1 INTRODUCTION

Labor unions are organizations of employees who formally join together to protect, maintain, and improve their economic, social, and political power and well-being. The opening vignette highlights labor-management contract negotiations between United Airlines and the International Association of Machinists and Aerospace Workers (IAMAW). In this case, the union seems to be satisfied with the agreement it reached with the company. Negotiations such as the one between IAMAW and United are commonplace in American business. Whether you manage a company whose employees are organized in a union or work with other companies that are unionized, it's important to understand the power and politics of union activity.

For centuries people have formed labor organizations known as clubs, guilds, associations, and unions. In America, labor organizations have existed since before the Revolutionary War. They evolved as a way to combat inhumane working conditions and practices, which were commonplace during colonial times and during the early days of the Industrial Revolution.

The term *labor union* has historically referred to organizations of men and women employed in a like trade. Today, groups of professionals who formally join together to gain more power over their profession may call themselves "associations" instead of "unions." For example, the American Association of University Professors and the American Nurses Association are labor organizations that serve many of the same purposes as union membership and serve similar functions.

In this chapter, we first provide a brief history of the American labor movement. Next we consider trends in unionization and reasons for people to join unions. Then we examine the structure of unions and the federal regulations governing their operations. We also explore the processes of organizing and decertifying a union and of collective bargaining. Finally, we look at the elements of union-management contracts and nonunion organizations.

> **Labor Unions** Organizations of employees who join together to protect, maintain, and improve their economic, social, and political power and well-being.

☞ **3, 4**

12-2   A BRIEF HISTORY OF THE AMERICAN LABOR MOVEMENT

Industrial Union   A union in which all members are employed in a company or industry, regardless of occupation.

Craft Union   A union in which all members belong to one craft or to a closely related group of occupations.

Yellow-Dog Contract
A statement signed by an employee promising not to form or join a union.

Molly Maguires   An early militant union group from the Pennsylvania coal mines.

Knights of Labor   The first union federation that attracted members from local unions from all crafts and occupational areas.

American Federation of Labor
The voluntary federation of America's unions, representing more than 13 million working women and men nationwide. The AFL-CIO was formed in 1955 by the merger of the American Federation of Labor and the Congress of Industrial Organizations.

5 ☞

6 ☞

7 ☞

Congress of Industrial Organizations (CIO)   Formed in 1935 to organize industrial and mass-production employees. The CIO merged with the American Federation of Labor (AFL) in 1955.

Unions are of two general types: industrial and craft. **Industrial union** members are all employed in one company or industry (e.g., workers in the steel industry or the auto industry), regardless of occupation. **Craft union** members belong to one craft (e.g., carpenters, bricklayers, ironworkers) or to a closely related group of occupations.

As early as 1790, skilled shoemakers, printers, and tailors organized themselves into trade unions. Collectively, the unions made demands about minimum wages and pressured individuals in the craft to not accept lesser wages. Of course, employers did not sit idly by as craftsmen attempted to unionize employees. An 1806 court ruling made it a "conspiracy in restraint of trade" for workers to combine or exert pressure on management. In effect, then, unions were illegal until 1842 when the Massachusetts Supreme Court, in *Commonwealth v. Hunt,* decided that criminal conspiracy did not apply if unions did not use illegal tactics to achieve their goals.

Even then employers still resisted by discharging employees who joined unions. They also forced employees to sign a **yellow-dog contract,** a statement in which the employee promised not to form or join a union. If employees who signed such contracts later joined a union, they were discharged. Employers also obtained court injunctions against strikes.

Early unions promoted social reform and free public education. Some of the more militant groups—such as the **Molly Maguires** from the Pennsylvania coal mines—were considered socialist or anarchist. They were involved in rioting and bloodshed, initiated by both employers and union members.

The turbulent 1870s and 1880s brought growing recognition of the labor union approach to social and economic problems. These experiences helped solidify the union movement and encouraged the development of a nationwide organization.

The first union federation to achieve significant size and influence was the Noble Order of the **Knights of Labor,** formed around 1869. This group attracted employees and local unions from all crafts and occupational areas. The strength of the Knights was diluted because it failed to integrate the wide range of needs and interests of its skilled and unskilled, industrial, and craft members. Also, many workers left the Knights of Labor because they thought it was too radical.

A group of national craft unions cut their relationships with the Knights of Labor around 1886. They formed the American Federation of Labor (A.F. of L., later changed to AFL). Samuel Gompers of the Cigar-Makers' International Union was elected president. The AFL restricted its membership to skilled tradespeople. Although the AFL dominated the union scene at the turn of the century, its focus on craft unionism was not accepted by all American workers. In some places there were notable efforts to create industrial unions. For example, the United Mine Workers of America, the oldest major industrial union, was established around 1890. After 1900, three industrial unions emerged in the textile industry. The International Ladies' Garment Workers' Union (ILGWU) was the strongest of the three. However, from 1968 to the early 1990s the ILGWU lost more than 300,000 workers as a result of low-cost imports and the transfer of factories overseas. In 1995 the 125,000-member ILGWU merged with the 175,000-member Amalgamated Clothing and Textile Workers' Union to form the Union of Needletrades, Industrial and Textile Employees (UNITE).

In 1935 the **Committee** (later changed to **Congress**) **for Industrial Organizations (CIO)** was formed by John L. Lewis, president of the United Mine Workers, in cooperation with a number of presidents of unions expelled from the AFL. The CIO was formed to organize industrial and mass-production employees. At this time, the AFL began offering membership to unskilled employees also.

As shown in Exhibit 12-1, the union movement grew slowly from 1900 to 1930. The federal government's attitude toward union organizing was at different times neutral, supportive, or opposed. But with the passage of federal laws in the 1920s and 1930s that gave protection to the union organizing process, union membership began to climb.

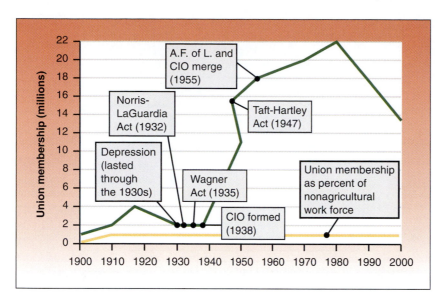

**Union Membership
in the U.S. Since 1900**

Thus, formal law helped unions grow during their formative years. From 1930 to 1947, union membership increased from 3 million to 14 million.

12-2a The AFL-CIO

Competition for new union members led to bitter conflicts between the AFL and CIO, but in 1955 they merged. The structure of the present **AFL-CIO** is shown in Exhibit 12-2. Most national and international labor unions now belong to the AFL-CIO, although a number of unions, representing over 4 million members, are unaffiliated. Such large and powerful unions as the Teamsters and the United Automobile Workers at one time broke away from the AFL-CIO, but they have now rejoined the group.

The two largest unions, with memberships of more than a million each, are the Teamsters and the American Federation of State, County, and Municipal Employees (AFSCME). Exhibit 12-3 on page 303 shows the degree of unionization by industry type.

In the United States, union membership has been on a long downward trend. After peaking at 35 percent of the nonagricultural workforce in 1954, union membership fell to 20 percent in 1981 and just 13.5 percent at the end of 2000, according to the U.S. Labor Department's Bureau of Labor Statistics (see Exhibit 12-4 on page 303).

12-2b Unions Today

In 2001, 13.5 percent of wage and salary workers in the United States were union members, unchanged from 2000. The union membership rate has fallen from a high of 20.1 percent in 1983, the first year for which comparable union data are available. Some highlights from the 2001 data are as follows:

- In both 2001 and 2000, about 16.3 million wage and salary workers were union members.

- Nearly 40 percent of government workers were union members in 2001, compared with less than 10 percent of private wage and salary workers.

- Protective service workers, a group that includes police officers and firefighters, had the highest unionization rate among all occupations, at 38 percent.[1]

Union membership and union activity have dropped over the past two decades. Why? Several factors have contributed to the decline.

AFL-CIO   The merged body of the American Federation of Labor (craft union members) and the Congress of Industrial Organizations (industrial union members).

☞ 8, 9

☞ 10

1. U.S. Bureau of Labor Statistics, "Union Members in 2001," Press release, January 17, 2002 (www.bls.gov/cps/).

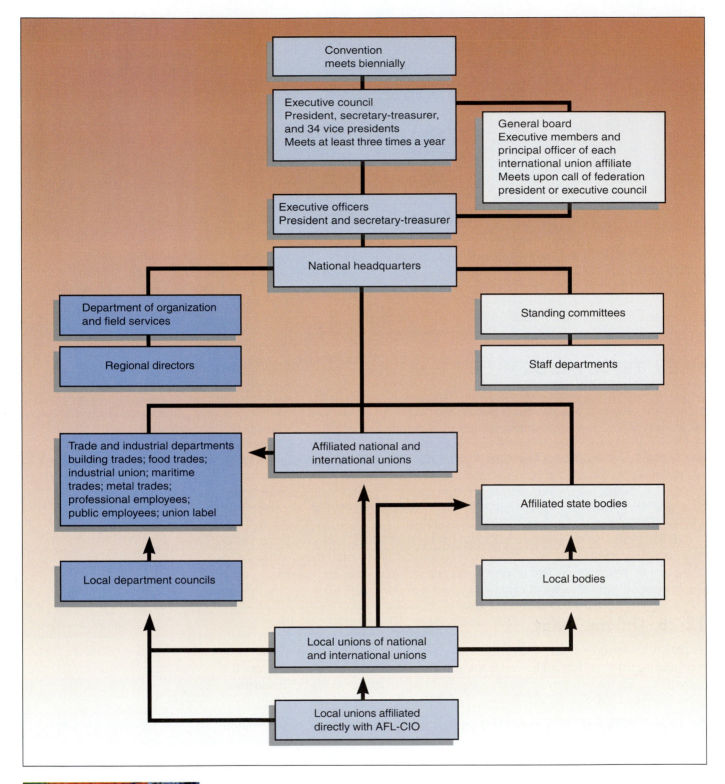

EXHIBIT 12-2

Structure of the AFL-CIO

Source: Reprinted with permission, p. 2,
Chart 1: Structure of the AFL-CIO, from
*Directory of U.S. Labor Organizations,
1994–95 Edition,* by Courtney D. Gifford.
Copyright 1994 by the Bureau of National
Affairs, Inc., Washington, DC 20037

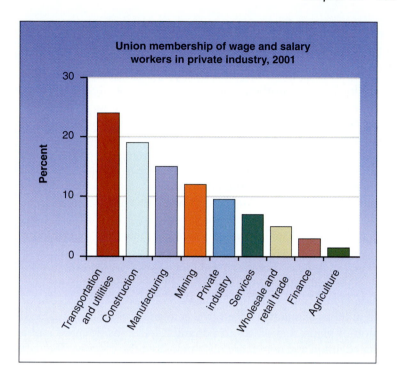

Union membership of wage and salary workers in private industry, 2001

EXHIBIT 12-3

Degree of Union Organization in Selected Industries

Source: Adapted from U.S. Department of Labor, "Current Population Survey," January 17, 2002.

EXHIBIT 12-4   **Labor Union Membership by Sector, 1983–2000**

Sector	1983	1985	1990	1995	1996	1997	1998	1999	2000
TOTAL (1,000)									
Wage and salary workers:									
Union members	17,717.4	16996.1	16,739.8	16,359.6	16269.4	16,109.9	16,211.4	16,476.7	16,258.2
Covered by unions	20,532.1	19358.1	19,057.8	18,346.3	18,158.1	17,923.0	17,918.3	18,182.3	17,944.1
Public sector workers:									
Union members	5737.2	5,743.1	5,485.0	6,927.4	6,854.4	6,746.7	6,905.3	7,058.1	7,110.5
Covered by unions	7,112.2	6,920.6	7,691.4	7,986.6	7,829.7	7,668.0	7,814.7	7,966.3	7,975.6
Private sector workers:									
Union members	11,980.2	11,253.0	10,254.8	9,432.1	9,415.0	9,363.3	9,306.1	9,418.6	9,147.7
Covered by unions	13,419.9	12,437.5	11,366.4	10,359.8	10,328.4	10,255.0	10,103.6	10,216.0	9,968.5
PERCENT									
Wage and salary workers:									
Union members	20.1	18.0	16.1	14.9	14.5	14.1	13.9	13.9	13.5
Covered by unions	23.3	20.5	18.3	16.7	16.2	15.6	15.4	15.3	14.9
Public sector workers:									
Union members	36.7	35.7	36.5	37.7	37.6	37.2	37.5	37.3	37.5
Covered by unions	45.5	43.1	43.3	43.5	43.0	42.3	42.5	42.1	42.0
Private sector workers:									
Union members	16.5	14.3	11.9	10.3	10.0	9.7	9.5	9.4	9.0
Covered by unions	18.5	15.9	13.2	11.3	11.0	10.6	10.3	10.2	9.8

Source: The Bureau of National Affairs, Inc., Washington D.C. *Union Membership and Earnings Data Book; Compilations from the Current Population Survey (2001 edition)* (copyright by BNA PLUS); authored by Barry Hirsch of Trinity University, San Antonio, TX, and David Macpherson of Florida State University. Internet site <http://www.bna.com/bnaplus/databook.html>.

First, the public has been bombarded with news of irresponsible union strikes, unreasonable wage or salary demands, some union leaders' criminal activities, and featherbedding (make-work) situations. Some of these labor stoppages have had a very high profile, such as the strike by major league baseball players in the summer of 1994. Many people have difficulty being sympathetic for striking union members whose average pay is more than $1 million annually. Such stories are poor publicity for unions. One study indicated that the monopolistic practices of unions cost the U.S. economy $5 billion to $10 billion annually. (Other estimates point out, however, that unions increase the efficiency of the economy by the same amount. How? By reducing training expenses, job search costs, and worker turnover.) The American public's confidence in unions as an institution has dropped more than in any other enterprise in the past two decades. Only 22 percent of the public holds unions in high regard. And union leaders are rated last in ethical conduct and moral practices, behind lawyers, advertising executives, government officials, and stockbrokers.[2]

Second, several economic factors, including intense international competition, poorly equipped factories, poor management, new technologies, and government regulations, have struck hardest at unionized industries—steel, autos, oil and gas, and mining. The deregulation of trucking, airlines, and communications has contributed to the erosion of union membership. Economic conditions and deregulation have caused the layoff of millions of union members, the permanent closing of unionized plants, and the relocation of plants and offices to nonunion locations. Mergers and acquisitions have eliminated union and nonunion jobs throughout the country. The reduction in union jobs has been felt the most in the states where unionization is strongest—New York, Illinois, Michigan, Ohio, California, and Pennsylvania.

Third, management in the 1970s began to resist union organizing efforts and large wage demands. They developed programs and strategies to fight back against unions. They also built new facilities in areas with less union strength—the South and the Sunbelt.[3]

Finally, since the proportion of blue-collar jobs in the workforce has decreased and the labor force is now predominantly white-collar, unions have had to redirect organizing efforts to recruit more nurses, teachers, engineers, and other professionals. Results have been spotty. White-collar employees have for years felt superior to their blue-collar counterparts. Perhaps many believe that by joining a union they would lose status, prestige, and esteem. Educational achievements, mode of dress, language, and job locations within businesses typically give the white-collar employee a more common base with management than with blue-collar employees. Also, compared to just a few decades ago, a higher proportion of women work in white-collar jobs, and women generally have been more resistant to unionization.

To sound the death knell for labor unions would be premature. Unionized workers across all industries on average earn 15 to 30 percent more than comparable nonunion workers.[4] Union advocates claim this significant difference results from union bargaining. Also, unionism has increased among government employees. The increasing numbers of better-educated, higher-status civil servants and state employees have helped improve the union's image. How much impact the image improvement will have on union membership is uncertain. But aggressive, imaginative, and fair union leadership could be effective in organizing significantly more white-collar workers. The increase in the unionization of government employees indicates that white-collar workers are listening to and watching the union message.

Another option for some unions is to purchase equity in the companies where
11 ☞ members are employed. For example, in September 1994 the United Steelworkers of America (USWA) formed a joint venture with a New York investment group to pur-
12 ☞ chase two plants that had been shut down in 1992 by Bethlehem Steel. The union

---

2. Based on Robert Hamrin, *America's New Economy: The Basic Guide* (New York: Franklin Watts, 1988), p. 442.

3. Shari Caudron, "The Changing Union Agenda," *Personnel Journal*, March 1995, pp. 42–49.

4. Thomas Karier, "Unions and the U.S. Comparative Advantage," *Industrial Relations*, Winter 1991, p. 4.

FOCUS ON GLOBALIZATION

UN Agency Focuses on Worker Rights Around the World

13 ☞
14 ☞

Labor organizations and the ongoing fight for workers' rights is an international phenomenon. The United Nations has its own labor rights agency known as the International Labour Organization (ILO). The ILO is the UN specialized agency that seeks the promotion of social justice and internationally recognized human and labor rights. It was founded in 1919 and is the only surviving major creation of the Treaty of Versailles, which brought the League of Nations into being, and it became the first specialized agency of the UN in 1946.

The ILO formulates international labor standards in the form of conventions and recommendations setting minimum standards of basic labor rights:

- Freedom of association
- The right to organize
- Collective bargaining
- Abolition of forced labor
- Equality of opportunity and treatment
- Other standards regulating conditions across the entire spectrum of work-related issues

The ILO provides technical assistance primarily in the fields of vocational training and vocational rehabilitation, employment policy, labor administration, labor law and industrial relations, working conditions, management development, cooperatives, social security, labor statistics and occupational safety and health. It promotes the development of independent employers' and workers' organizations and provides training and advisory services to those organizations. Within the UN system, the ILO has a unique tripartite structure with workers and employers participating as equal partners with governments in the work of its governing organs. Recent cases it has worked on include a pilot's dispute with Cathay Pacific Airlines, child labor in Bangladesh, and a tax on workers in Colombia to help that nation finance its war against insurgents.

Sources: Adapted from "Complaint Against Cathay Pacific Airways Launched with International Labour Organization (ILO)," *PR Newswire*, March 26, 2002; "ILO Colombia Labor Minister Against Financing War on Backs of Workers," *Business Wire News*, March 20, 2002; and "ILO Will Help Bangladesh Eradicate Child Labor," *The Independent*, March 19, 2002.

agreed to flexible work rules and pay scales that are only half what union members make at other mills. In return, workers at the new company, called BRW Steel Corporation, get a 25 percent equity stake and two seats on the board of directors—plus 800 jobs that did not exist.[5]

Organizational and recruiting efforts of unions have always varied according to changes in economic, social, and political conditions. Membership drives continue in the public sector (which includes military personnel, police, and firefighters), among professionals (teachers, medical personnel, athletes, lawyers), among employees in service industries, and among agricultural workers. In addition, labor unions have become increasingly international in scope as globalization continues. The Focus on Globalization box, "UN Agency Focuses on Worker Rights Around the World," discusses the United Nations' International Labour Organization, an agency that promotes workers' rights around the globe.

5. Keith L. Alexander and Stephen Baker, "If You Can't Beat 'Em," *Business Week*, October 24, 1994, pp. 80–81.

12-2c Famous Union Bosses

Walter Reuther and James "Jimmy" Hoffa probably are the two most recognizable names in U.S. labor history because of their charismatic and powerful leadership of their unions. They shared traits: Both came from small-town, working-class families. Neither smoked nor drank. But Reuther's and Hoffa's philosophies about what a union should be couldn't have been more different.

15 ☞

Under Reuther, the United Auto Workers was a catalyst for broad social change and essentially free of influences from organized crime. Under Hoffa, the International Brotherhood of Teamsters primarily functioned for the sake of its workers' immediate needs, such as wages and benefits. At the same time, however, the Mafia was an insidious influence on Hoffa and within the Union's **rank and file.**

The Teamsters always had problems with mob influences. Started in 1903 and fully organized in the 1930s, the union was an obvious target of mobsters who trafficked bootleg liquor across the Detroit River from Canada. After Prohibition ended in 1933, gangsters found **union racketeering** a profitable substitute for liquor smuggling.

Hoffa rose through the ranks of Detroit's Local 299, despite being beaten severely in the 1930s for organizing activities. He pushed out left-wing leaders in the local in 1941, paving the way for a more business-oriented union.

In 1957, Hoffa became national president of the Teamsters; the same year the U.S. Senate began an investigation into the union's Mafia ties. Hoffa eventually was convicted of tampering with a jury as well as fraud relating to the mishandling of a union pension fund. Although he was sentenced to thirteen years in prison, Hoffa served only about four years before he was released in 1971. Upon his release, Hoffa started to plan to regain leadership of the Teamsters. But in 1975, Jimmy Hoffa disappeared from the parking lot of the Machus Red Fox restaurant in Bloomfield Hills, Michigan. Hoffa has never been found, and the case of his disappearance has not been solved.[6]

Hoffa's son, James P. Hoffa, followed in his father's footsteps and became the head of the Teamster's Union on March 19, 1999, after serving as a labor lawyer in Detroit for twenty-five years.[7]

Rank and File   A term used to refer to union workers who vote on union matters but aren't otherwise involved in union administration.

Union Racketeering   Refers to illegal business activities such as loansharking, extortion, and bribery.

12-3 WHY DO PEOPLE JOIN UNIONS?

Many people ask, "Why do people unionize?" Of course, this question has no single answer. People join for different reasons. Research shows that people are attracted to unions because they are dissatisfied with what Fred Herzberg called hygiene factors: (1) pay and benefits, (2) supervision, and (3) job security. Recognizing the importance of job security, a growing group of companies have either contract specifications or a tradition to not lay off employees. Some of these companies believe that no-layoff policies mean higher productivity, increased loyalty, and retention of skilled workers. They cite research findings, especially reports issued by the Work in America Institute.

One study of nearly 88,000 clerical, sales, and technical employees at Sears found that the strongest predictor of unionization attempts was the employees' dissatisfaction with their supervisors.[8] What does that really mean? Is the supervisor not being fair, not being a good listener, or not being supportive? Exhibit 12-5 lists the qualities found to be important in the bond between managers and workers. They suggest that workers are satisfied with managers who possess three specific skills: technical (they know the job), administrative (they know the system), and interpersonal (they know people).

The Maslow needs hierarchy covered in Chapter 10 provides a framework for tying research findings together. Maslow portrayed humans as driven to put forth effort by the desire to satisfy needs. As research suggests, employees try to gratify important needs and

6. Jennifer Day, "Hoffa's Legacy Can't Escape Mob's Taint," *Crain's Detroit Business,* July 2, 2001, p. 42.

7. See James P. Hoffa's online biography at http://backup.teamster.org/hoffa/bio.htm.

8. W. C. Hammer and F. J. Smith, "Work Activities as Predictors of Unionization Activity," *Journal of Applied Psychology,* August 1978, pp. 414–421.

Subordinates are more satisfied with a supervisor who

- Displays technical competence.
- Sets clear work goals for subordinates.
- Gives clear instructions.
- Clearly defines subordinates' job responsibilities.
- Backs subordinates with other managers.
- Fairly appraises subordinates' performances.
- Allows subordinates adequate time to do the job right.
- Allows subordinates adequate time to learn the job's tasks.
- Informs subordinates of work changes before they are to take place.
- Displays consistent behavior toward subordinates.
- Helps subordinates to get the job done.
- Gives subordinates credit for their ideas.
- Listens to and understands subordinates' job-related problems.
- Follows through to get the job's problems solved.
- Treats subordinates fairly when they make mistakes.
- Shows concern for subordinates' career progress.
- Congratulates subordinates for doing a good job.

EXHIBIT 12-5

Factors that Determine Subordinates' Satisfaction with Supervisors

Source: Adapted from V. Scarpello and R. J. Vandenberg, "The Satisfaction with My Supervisor Scale: Its Utility in Research and Practice," *Journal of Management*, Fall 1987, pp. 447–466.

wants. When needs are unsatisfied in the workplace, the union becomes an attractive tool for change. Unionization will continue to be an alternative as long as some companies fail to satisfy their employees' economic, interpersonal, and job security needs. The quiz in Exhibit 12-6 will help you to discover your attitude about unions and management.

12-4 THE STRUCTURE AND MANAGEMENT OF UNIONS

Many unions are large organizations. They have management, leadership, and financial control problems similar to those that business firms face. Unions' national headquarters employ staff economists, engineers, attorneys, accountants, wage and salary experts, and professional managers.

12-4a Local Union Structure

The labor movement has its foundation in the local craft union. The local directly influences the membership. Through the local, members exercise their complaints and pay the dues that support the national union.

Officials elected by the members administer local union activities. Elected officers include the president, vice president, secretary-treasurer, business representative, and committee chairpersons. Elected officials of local unions often have full-time jobs in addition to their regular union duties.

In many local unions, the **business representative** is the dominant person. The major responsibilities of the business representative are to negotiate and administer labor agreements and to settle problems that may arise in connection with contracts. The business representative also collects dues, recruits new members, coordinates social activities, and arranges union meetings.

The **union steward** (sometimes called the *shop steward*) represents the interests of local union members in their relations with managers on the job. In the auto industry, the steward (called a *committee person*) devotes full time to solving disputes that arise in connection with the union-management labor contract.

Business Representative
A union official who negotiates and administers the labor agreement and settles contract problems.

Union Steward A person who represents the interests of local union members in their on-the-job relations with managers.

My Union-Management Attitude

Directions: Complete this quiz to determine your general feelings about labor (unions) and management (organizational managers). There are no correct or incorrect answers; only general impressions that you hold are of interest.

Y   N   1. Do you trust management to give a fair deal on grievances if no union (within the firm) exists?

Y   N   2. Do you believe that unions have been responsible for improved working conditions in the United States over the past 40 years?

Y   N   3. Do you believe that unions are democratically run?

Y   N   4. Do you believe that management has fairly treated nonmanagerial personnel?

Y   N   5. Do you believe that a union representative should be placed on the board of directors of a unionized company?

Y   N   6. Do you believe that police officers should have the right to strike?

Y   N   7. Do you believe that management would have raised wages and fringe benefits to generally high levels without union pressure?

Y   N   8. Do you believe that union busting or decertification should be permitted in the United States?

Y   N   9. Do you believe that management should be permitted to make promotion decisions without having to pay attention to seniority clauses (those with longer job tenure are given some preference) in a union contract?

Y   N   10. Do you believe that unions treat minority employees more fairly than management treats them?

Feedback: Now assess your attitudes toward unions and management. The following answers indicate a union or management bias or attitude.

1. Y: Management	N: Union		6. N: Management	Y: Union
2. N: Management	Y: Union		7. Y: Management	N: Union
3. N: Management	Y: Union		8. Y: Management	N: Union
4. Y: Management	N: Union		9. Y: Management	N: Union
5. N: Management	Y: Union		10. N: Management	Y: Union

If you answered 8 of the 10 questions from either the management orientation or the union orientation, you lean in favor of that particular group. For example, if you answered all 10 questions as shown (management key), the indication is that you have a strong management bias.

This is not a scientific quiz, but is used for information purposes only. Did you know that you had a bias or that you are generally neutral? Have you ever been a union member? Why did you join the union?

12-4b National-Local Relationship

The constitution of the national union establishes the rules, policies, and procedures under which the local unions may be chartered and become members. Each national union exercises some control over the local unions. These controls usually deal with the collection of dues, the admission of new members by the local, and the use of union funds. The national also provides the local unions with support for organizing campaigns and strikes and for the administration of contracts. Over 100 national union organizations support about 80,000 local unions.

12-4c Managing in the Union

The job of managing a union is challenging and time-consuming. Union officials need to be dedicated, willing to work long hours, able to counsel members on personal problems, and skilled in influencing people. Officers must periodically run for reelection.

Unions finance themselves through dues, fines, and initiation fees collected at the local level. But members resist high assessments. Union officials have to convince them that the union needs a sound financial base to have the power to secure favorable labor agreements. Most union members pay dues that come out to roughly two hours' wages per month; two major unions—the Steelworkers and Automobile Workers—have set their monthly dues at exactly this two-hour level. Initiation fees, paid once, tend to range from $50 to $150.

12-5 FEDERAL REGULATION OF LABOR-MANAGEMENT RELATIONS

State and federal laws govern union-management interaction. These laws have evolved through common law and rulings by the National Labor Relations Board and the courts. They have swung back and forth like a pendulum, at one time favoring management and at another time favoring unions. Exhibit 12-7 contains a summary of the major labor-management regulations discussed in this section.

☞ 16

Legislation	Provisions	Coverage
Railway Labor Act (1926)	Gave employees the right to organize and bargain collectively	Railroads Airlines
Norris-LaGuardia Act (1932)	Prohibited federal courts from enjoining strikes and from enforcing yellow-dog contracts	Private-sector employment
Wagner Act (1935)	Established the right to organize and engage in other concerted activities; declared certain employer actions to be unfair labor practices; established procedures for employees to elect a union; regulated collective bargaining; established the National Labor Relations Board (NLRB)	Private-sector employment • Business • Nonprofit hospitals and and nursing homes • Private colleges and universities • Performing arts
Taft-Hartley Act (1947)	Established the right to refrain from the activities protected in the Wagner Act; declared certain union actions to be unfair labor practices; provided for passage of state right-to-work laws; established the Federal mediation and Conciliation Service (FMCS); outlawed closed shops	Same as Wagner Act
Landrum-Griffin Act (1959)	Established standards for union treatment of union members; regulated internal union affairs	Same as Wagner Act and Taft-Hartley Act
Title VII, Civil Service Reform Act (1978)	Established the right to form and assist labor unions; bargaining; required arbitration of impasses and grievances; prohibited strikes and other disruptions	Federal employment (excludes some agencies, such as FBI, CIA)
The Workers' Adjustment and Retraining Notification Act (1989)	Employers with 100 or more employees or who have 100 or more employees who together work at least 4,000 hours per week excluding overtime must give employees 60 days' written notice of anticipated plant closings or other mass layoffs	Private-sector employment

EXHIBIT 12-7

Major Labor-Management Regulations

12-5a Early Labor Legislation: Pro-Labor

Railway Labor Act   A 1926 law that established collective bargaining as a means for resolving labor management disputes.

Railway Labor Act. The first labor legislation passed by Congress after the Clayton Act of 1914 excluded unions from the Sherman Antitrust Act of 1890 was the **Railway Labor Act** of 1926. It established the process of collective bargaining as a means of resolving labor-management disputes.

Injunctions   Court orders that prohibit defendants from engaging in certain activities, such as striking.

Norris-LaGuardia Act. In the 1930s, the federal government became involved in labor disputes outside the railroad industry. **Injunctions,** court decrees to stop union activities, gave employers an easy way to hinder union activities. However, in 1932 came the **Norris-LaGuardia Act** as a response to the Great Depression. This act, also called the *Anti-Injunction Act,* limited the power of federal courts to stop union picketing, boycotts, and strikes. The Norris-LaGuardia Act also made the yellow-dog contract (a contract, mentioned earlier, in which employees agree not to join any union) unenforceable.

Norris-LaGuardia Act   A 1932 law that limited the power of federal courts to stop union picketing, boycotts, and strikes; also made the yellow-dog contract unenforceable.

Wagner Act. The *National Labor Relations Act,* better known as the **Wagner Act,** was passed in 1935. This act made collective bargaining legal and required employers to bargain with the representatives of the employees. It encouraged the growth of trade unions by restraining management from interfering with them. By restricting the activities of management, this act also forced the government to take an active role in union-management relationships. Five unfair management practices specified in the Wagner Act are summarized in Exhibit 12-8.

Wagner Act   A law that made collective bargaining legal and required employers to bargain with the representatives of the employees. The law is also referred to as the National Labor Relations Act.

The power to implement the Wagner Act was given to a three-person **National Labor Relations Board (NLRB)** and a staff of lawyers and other personnel responsible to the board. The board sets up elections, on request, to determine if a given group of workers wishes to have a union as a bargaining representative. The board also investigates complaints of unfair labor practices.

National Labor Relations Board (NLRB)   A group that investigates cases of alleged unfair labor practices by employers and unions and holds elections to determine whether groups of employees want to be unionized.

12-5b Postwar Labor Laws: Restoring a Balance

Taft-Hartley Act   A 1947 labor law that prohibits the closed shop, requires unions to bargain in good faith, and makes it illegal for a union to discriminate against employees who don't join the union.

Taft-Hartley Act. The Wagner Act was considered pro-labor. To swing the pendulum back and equalize labor and management, Congress passed the **Taft-Hartley Act** (also called the *Labor-Management Relations Act*) in 1947. It amended and supplemented the Wagner Act and increased the size of the NLRB to five persons (allegedly to get rid of the NLRB's pro-union bias). Taft-Hartley guaranteed employee bargaining rights and specifically forbade the five unfair employer labor practices first established in the Wagner Act. But the act also specified unfair union labor practices; the union was restrained from the practices shown in Exhibit 12-8. Finally, the act established the Federal Mediation and Conciliation Service (FMCS).

17 ☞

Landrum-Griffin Act. In view of the corruption found in some unions, Congress assumed that the labor laws in existence still did not adequately protect the individual union member. So in 1959 Congress passed the **Landrum-Griffin Act,** which is officially designated the *Labor-Management Reporting and Disclosure Act.* It was designed to regulate the internal affairs of unions.

Landrum-Griffin Act   A 1959 labor law that requires unions and employees to file financial reports with the secretary of labor and that specifies certain activities to ensure democratic operation of the union.

This act, called the **bill of rights of union members,** gave every union member the right to (1) nominate candidates for union office, (2) vote in union elections, and (3) attend union meetings. Union members also gained the right to examine union accounts and records, while the union was required to submit an annual financial report to the U.S. Department of Labor. Employers had to report any payments or loans made to unions, their officers, or their members. This portion of the act was intended to end **sweetheart contracts,** under which the union leaders and management agree to terms that work to their mutual benefit but maintain poor working conditions for other employees.

Bill of Rights of Union Members   Another name for the Labor-Management Reporting and Disclosure Act, which gave every union member the right to (1) nominate candidates for union office, (2) vote in union elections, and (3) attend union meetings.

12-5c The Issue of Job Security

One of the most important issues for workers is **job security.** Unions also have fought and continue to fight for their own security. To establish security, unions focus on gaining the

BY MANAGEMENT

To interfere with, restrain, or coerce employees in the exercise of their rights to organize

To dominate or interfere with the affairs of a union

To discriminate in regard to hiring, tenure, or any employment condition for the purpose of encouraging or discouraging membership in any union organization

To discriminate against or discharge an employee because he or she has filed charges or given testimony under the Wagner Act

To refuse to bargain collectively with representatives of the employees—that is, to refuse to bargain in good faith

BY UNIONS

To restrain or coerce employees in the exercise of their right to join or not to join a union except when an agreement is made by the employer and union that a condition of employment will be joining the union, called a union security clause authorizing a union shop

To cause an employer to discriminate against an employee other than for nonpayment of dues or initiation fees

To refuse to bargain with an employer in good faith

To engage, induce, encourage, threaten, or coerce any individual to engage in strikes, refusal to work, or boycott where the objective is the following:

- Force or require any employer or self-employed person to recognize or join any labor organization or employer organization
- Force or require an employer or self-employed person to cease using the products of or doing business with another person, or force any other employer to recognize or bargain with the union unless it has been certified by the NLRB
- Force an employer to apply pressure to another employer to recognize a union. Examples include picketing a hospital so that it will apply pressure on a subcontractor (food service, maintenance, emergency department) to recognize a union; forcing an employer to do business only with others, such as suppliers, who have a union; picketing by another union for recognition when a different one is already certified

To charge excessive or discriminatory membership fees

To cause an employer to give payment for services not performed (featherbedding)

EXHIBIT 12-8

Unfair Labor Practices

right to represent an enterprise's workers and, where possible, to be the exclusive bargaining agent for all employees of the unit. Union job security takes several forms:

- **Union shop.** The company can hire nonunion people, but they must join the union after a prescribed period of time and pay the union dues. (Failure to join means they could be fired.)
- **Agency shop.** Employees who do not belong to the union still must pay the full union dues (assuming that the union's bargaining and agreement efforts benefit all the workers).
- **Open shop.** The workers decide whether or not to join the union. Those not joining pay no dues.
- **Maintenance of membership agreement.** Employees do not have to join a union. However, union members must maintain membership in the union over the length of the contract.

Although unions have encouraged legislation to protect their security, a number of concerns remain. First, a labor organization has no guarantee that a rival union will not replace it at a later date. Second, employees still have a number of channels through which to voice their antiunion feelings and can use these to get rid of unions. Third, no government guarantee protects unions from "free riders." A free rider is an employee who decides not to be a part of the union but still gains the benefit of unionization.

Sweetheart Contracts Agreements between union leaders and management to terms that work to their mutual benefit but maintain poor working conditions for other employees.

Job Security The relative comfort a person feels about whether his or her job will continue into the future.

Union Shop A company that requires employees to join the union after being hired.

Agency Shop A workplace where all employees pay union dues, whether or not they are union members.

Open Shop A company in which employees don't have to join a union or pay dues but can decide without pressure whether to become union members.

Maintenance of Membership Agreement Agreement that, although employees do not have to join a union, union members must maintain membership in the union over the length of the contract.

Right-to-Work Laws State laws requiring that two people doing the same job be paid the same wages, whether or not they belong to the union.

Closed Shop A company that hires only workers who are members of the union; illegal under the Taft-Hartley Act.

Title VII Part of the Civil Service Reform Act of 1978; outlawed certain unfair labor practices and created the Federal Labor Relations Authority (FLRA); granted covered employees the right to form, join, or assist any labor organization or to refrain from such activity freely and without reprisals.

18 ☞

Worker Adjustment and Retraining Notification Act (WARN) Commonly referred to as the *Plant Closing Bill,* an act that requires employers with 100 or more full-time employees to give affected employees sixty days' written notice of plant or office closing or other mass layoffs.

The Taft-Hartley Act allows states to forbid union shops by passing **right-to-work laws.** Under these laws, two persons doing the same job must be paid the same wages, whether they belong to the union or not. Unions see this as unfair because the nonunionized employees pay no dues but share in the benefits won by the union. Twenty-two states have right-to-work laws, as shown in Exhibit 12-9.

A **closed shop,** prohibited by the Taft-Hartley Act, requires that a new employee be a union member when hired. The union itself provides labor to the organization. Although this type of shop is illegal, modified closed shops are still found in the construction, printing, and maritime industries. For example, an ironworkers' union hall sends out union members to construction sites on request. A nonunion worker has little chance to be sent from a union hall to a job because the union's business agent makes the assignments. Union members elect the business agent, while the nonunion members have no vote.

12-5d Other Legislation Affecting Unions

Title VII. **Title VII** of the Civil Service Reform Act of 1978, also referred to as the *Federal Service Labor-Management Relations Act,* did for the federal government sector what the Wagner and the Taft-Hartley acts did for employment in the private sector. Title VII outlawed certain unfair labor practices and created the Federal Labor Relations Authority (FLRA), with powers similar to the NLRB.

Employees covered by Title VII are granted the right to form, join, or assist any labor organization or to refrain from such activity freely and without reprisals. Employees of some federal agencies (e.g., Federal Bureau of Investigation [FBI], Central Intelligence Agency [CIA], National Security Agency [NSA], Tennessee Valley Authority [TVA]) are exempted. Noncitizens working outside of the United States for federal agencies are also excluded.

WARN. The employee's right to notice of plant/office closing or relocation became a major issue in the 1980s. A growing number of workers in the steel, automobile, and general manufacturing industries lost their jobs because of competition, mergers, or relocation of facilities. The **Worker Adjustment and Retraining Notification Act (WARN),** commonly referred to as the *Plant Closing Bill,* was passed and went into effect in 1989. The act requires employers with 100 or more full-time employees to give affected employees sixty days' written notice of plant or office closing or other mass layoffs. WARN covers nonprofit organizations but not federal, state, or local governments. "Affected employees" are all workers, including managerial and supervisory personnel, who may suffer some employment loss as the result of a plant closing or mass layoff.

Employers violating WARN may be required to provide back pay and benefits for up to sixty days to workers laid off without proper notification. In some cases, employers may also be required to pay fines of $500 per day, up to $30,000. However, WARN allows some exceptions. A failing company actively seeking capital to prevent the plant closing or layoff is exempt, if giving notice to employees would reasonably have prevented the firm from receiving the financing. Closings due to natural disasters, such as earthquakes or floods, are also exempt from the sixty-day notice requirement.

There are humanitarian arguments to support WARN. Victims of plant closures show higher rates of stress-related symptoms such as alcoholism, ulcers, heart attacks, and suicides. Before WARN was passed, General Motors shut down its Fremont, California, plant and gave the 4,000 employees only three weeks' notice. Ford closed its San Jose, California, plant, idling 2,300 workers but giving them six months' advance notice. There were eight suicides among the laid-off General Motors employees and none among the displaced Ford workers.[9]

Critics of WARN argue that turnover, pilferage, destruction of property, and other negative behavior may occur between the time of notice and the layoff. However,

---

9. John McLaughlin, "Union Soldiers," *Restaurant Business,* November 20, 1994, pp. 66–72.

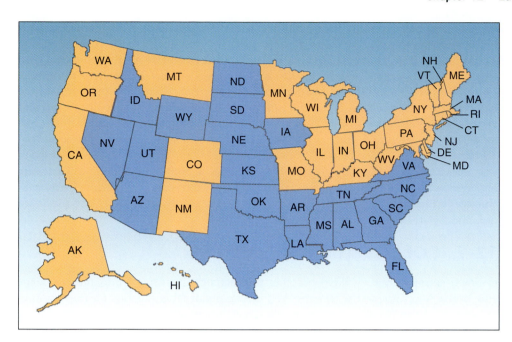

research conducted in Europe and other countries with advance notice requirements reveals no evidence to support that claim.

12-6 ORGANIZING AND DECERTIFYING A UNION

The organizing drive is the process through which a group of employees attempts to establish a legally binding relationship with the employer. The process involves three steps: (1) petition for union representation, (2) determination of appropriate bargaining unit, and (3) union representation election.

The organizing drive officially begins when employees sign authorization cards that empower the union to petition the NLRB for union representation. Thirty percent of the employees must sign, per NLRB rules. But most unions will not petition the NLRB unless a majority of the workers in the group sign the authorization cards. The union must receive 50 percent plus two of the votes cast in the election that takes place later.

After they receive the petition for union representation and check its accuracy, the NLRB notifies the employer that a particular union is seeking to be the representative of a group of employees. If 30 percent of the firm's employees are on the petition list, the NLRB notifies both the employer and the employees. The employer can then recognize the union as the representative. However, if the employer does not, the NLRB schedules a formal unit determination hearing. Employer and employees present facts and arguments about representation. The hearing enables the NLRB to determine (1) the employees' interest in being represented, (2) eligibility of employees to belong to the proposed unit, and (3) desires of employees as to who should or should not be a member of the proposed unit.

NLRB regional directors are empowered to decide the composition and appropriateness of the bargaining unit. After this is decided, the NLRB informs the employer and union that a bargaining unit has been formed. The NLRB then supervises a representation election. Again, the union must receive 50 percent plus two of the votes cast to win the election. When this happens, the NLRB certifies the union as the exclusive representative of the employees within the bargaining unit. If the union loses the election, the union must wait one year before trying again.

The NLRB is the referee, the guiding arm of organizing drives and elections. Its chief concern is to provide an atmosphere that permits employees to make a clear choice. The

Decertification   The process, guided by the NLRB, that results in voting out a union that has been representing employees.

employer and union are not permitted to use threats, promises, or any means of influencing each person's free choice in the process.

Just as unions can be voted in and become the representative of employees, the same employees can also vote them out. The law that grants employees the right to organize also allows them to terminate the union's right to represent them. The process of voting out a union is called **decertification.** A petition must be submitted showing 30 percent employee support for the action. If there is support, the NLRB will conduct a secret ballot election to determine whether a majority of employees in the unit wish to decertify.

Employers use "union busting" consultants to help keep unions out in the first place or to decertify them when they are the representatives of employees. The consultants help managers comply with the law and use persuasive procedures to communicate better with employees. Programs developed by such consultants are usually designed to win the attention and loyalty of employees.

12-7 COLLECTIVE BARGAINING

A union certified by the NLRB becomes the *collective bargaining* representative of the employees. According to the Wagner Act, it is an unfair labor practice for the employer to refuse to bargain collectively with chosen representatives of a duly certified labor union. The Taft-Hartley Act states that it is an unfair practice for the representatives of a labor union to not bargain in good faith with an employer. The current national policy, then, is that employees and employers must bargain in good faith to work out employment issues and disputes.

Collective Bargaining
Negotiation of a labor contract by union and management.

Collective bargaining is a process by which the representatives of the firm meet and attempt to work out a contract with union representatives. Through this process, contractual agreements are established, managed, and enforced. *Collective* means only that representatives join in the attempt to negotiate an agreement. *Bargaining* is the process of cajoling, debating, discussing, and threatening to bring about a favorable agreement for those being represented.

Bargaining in Good Faith
Both sides in labor-management relations must communicate and negotiate.

Bargaining in good faith is the cornerstone of effective labor-management relations. It means that both sides must communicate and negotiate. Proposals are matched with counterproposals, and reasonable efforts are made to reach an agreement. The collective bargaining process and the final agreement reached are influenced by many variables. Exhibit 12-10 identifies some of the variables influencing union and management representatives. For example, the state of the economy affects collective bargaining. The firm's representative must consider whether, based on current and expected economic conditions, the company can pay an increased wage.

The actual process of collective bargaining involves a number of steps:

1. Prenegotiation
2. Selecting negotiators
3. Developing a bargaining strategy
4. Using the best tactics
5. Reaching a formal contractual agreement

Collective bargaining is not always favorable for workers, however. Collective bargaining can make it difficult for the union to reach a compromise with management, even if the compromise would benefit both sides.

12-8 THE UNION-MANAGEMENT CONTRACT

Union-Management Contract
An agreement that designates the formal terms reached in collective bargaining

The **union-management contract** designates the formal terms of agreement reached in collective bargaining. The average contract is good for two to three years and varies in length from a few pages to well over 100 pages, depending on the issues covered, the size of the organization, and the union. It must be in compliance with federal, state, and local laws.

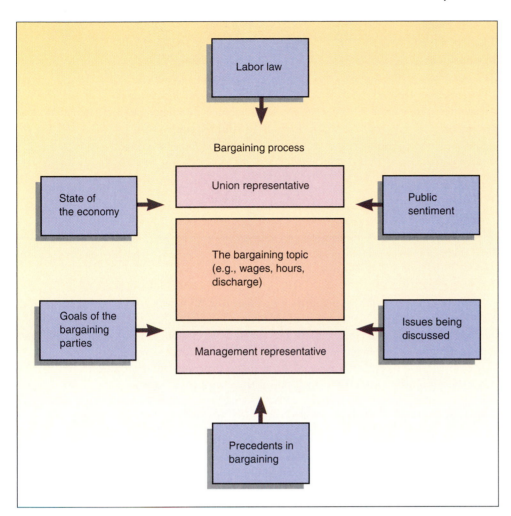

EXHIBIT 12-10

Forces Influencing the Collective Bargaining Process

The labor contract is divided into sections and appendixes. The sections covered in some labor agreements are listed in Exhibit 12-11. A major part of the contract is concerned with such employment issues as wages, hours, fringe benefits, and overtime.

A major task of labor and management is to jointly administer the contract. Contracts are difficult to administer perfectly because contract language requires interpretation—it is not perfect. Day-to-day compliance with contract provisions becomes an important responsibility of the first-line manager, who works closely with union members. As the representative of management, the first-line manager must discipline workers, handle grievances, and prepare for such actions as strikes.

12-8a Discipline

Most contracts state that management has a right to discipline workers. But any discipline in a unionized firm must follow legal due process. If an employee or a union challenges a disciplinary action, the burden of proof rests on the company. Often management will lose a case that is arbitrated (settled by an impartial third party), because improper disciplinary procedures have been followed.

Contracts usually specify the types of discipline and the offenses for which corrective action will be taken. Some of the infractions typically spelled out include the following:

- *Incompetence*—failure to perform the assigned job
- *Misconduct*—insubordination, dishonesty, or violating a rule such as smoking in a restricted area
- *Violations of the contract*—initiating a strike, for example, when there is a no-strike clause

EXHIBIT 12-11

Major Sections Found in Typical Labor-Management Contracts

Purpose and intent of the parties	Seniority
Scope of the agreement	Safety and health
Management	Military service
Responsibilities of the parties	Severance allowance
Union membership and checkoff*	Savings and vacation plan
Adjustment of grievance	Supplemental unemployment benefits
Arbitration	(SUB) program
Suspension and discharge cases	SUB and insurance grievances
Rate of pay	Prior agreements
Hours of work	Termination date
Overtime—holidays	Appendixes
Vacations	

*In a check-off arrangement, the employer deducts monthly union dues from the employee's pay. The dues are then transmitted to the union.

The contract should list penalties for infractions. Violators must be disciplined similarly, but inconsistent application of discipline is sometimes a problem. When one employee is reprimanded for regularly arriving at work late but another with a similar tardiness problem is discharged, discipline is being applied inconsistently.

Consistent, prompt, and reasonable discipline programs are what union and management representatives attempt to spell out in the contract. One strategy is to use progressive disciplinary actions in which repeated or serious violations result in penalties of increasing severity. The sequence of progressive discipline might be as follows:

1. An oral caution and a note in the personnel file of the employee
2. A written reprimand that becomes a part of the file
3. A short, two-day to one-week suspension
4. Demotion to the next-lower job position
5. A long, one- to three-month suspension
6. Discharge

The emphasis in a progressive discipline approach should be on developing within the total workforce a willingness to obey and follow rules and regulations. The goal is to encourage employees to follow rules because they want to, not because they are afraid of the progressively severe penalties. In one classic example of progressive discipline, an employee had broken many rules, but none so serious as to justify her discharge. This technology operator was finally fired by an Illinois firm for a hostile work attitude. Her record contained frequent notations for absenteeism, insubordination, smoking at her desk, and being absent from her workstation. A third-party judge acting as an arbitrator ruled that the firing violated a progressive discipline program. The employer cannot abruptly discharge the worker for a minor fault unless preliminary steps, such as reprimands and suspensions, have been administered in a timely manner.[10]

12-8b Grievances

A complaint about a job that creates dissatisfaction or discomfort, whether it is valid or not, is a **grievance.** The complaint can be made by a single employee or by the union. All grievances should be handled correctly. Even if a complaint seems absolutely without support, management should still handle it according to formal contractual provisions.

Grievance procedures are usually followed in unionized companies, but they are also important channels of communication in nonunionized organizations. In the unionized organization, the contract contains a clause covering the steps to be followed and how

Grievance   Complaint made by an employee or the union about a job, person, or condition that creates dissatisfaction or discomfort.

10. "Why America Needs Unions But Not the Kind It Has Now," *Business Week*, May 23, 1994, pp. 70–82.

EXHIBIT 12-12

Steps in a Grievance Process

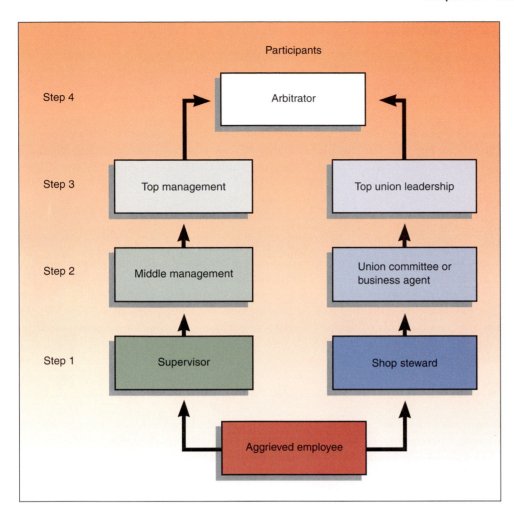

the grievance will be handled. The number of steps varies from contract to contract. Exhibit 12-12 illustrates a four-step grievance procedure used in a unionized company.

1. The employee meets with the supervisor and the union steward and presents the grievance. Many grievances are settled at this point.
2. If the grievance is not settled at step 1, a conference takes place between middle management and union officials (a business agent or union committee).
3. If the grievance cannot be settled at step 2, then a top management representative and top union officials attempt to settle the grievance.
4. If the grievance cannot be settled at step 3, both parties (union and management) turn the grievance over to an arbitrator, who makes a decision. Arbitration is usually handled by a mutually agreed upon individual or a panel of an odd number.

To ensure grievances are handled properly, managers should follow the following five principles with each instance:

1. Take every grievance seriously.
2. Work with the union representative.
3. Gather all information available on the grievance.
4. After weighing all the facts, provide an answer to the employee voicing the grievance.
5. After the grievance is settled, attempt to move on to other matters.

Occasionally, employees will file lawsuits against their firm and/or their managers when grievances don't turn out as they prefer. Following the grievance procedure and the five principles listed here will help managers protect themselves from liability in such situations.

12-8c Strikes

Strike An effort to withhold employee services so that the employer will make greater concessions at the bargaining table.

A **strike** is an effort to withhold employee services so that the employer will make greater concessions at the bargaining table. The strike, or a threatened one, is a major bargaining tool used by the unions.

A union planning to strike needs to consider the legality of striking, the members' willingness to endure the hardships of a long strike, and the employer's ability to operate the organization without union members. The greater the employer's ability to operate the organization, the less chance the union will have of gaining its demands.

When a strike occurs, management must be able to function during the work stoppage and protect the company from strike sabotage. Employers sometimes bring in strike replacement employees to keep the firm operating.

Management should also be aware of picketing procedures. Hoping to shut down the company during a strike, the union may place members at plant entrances to advertise the dispute and discourage people from entering or leaving. Peaceful persuasion through the formation of a picket line is legal, but violence is not. Picketing may also take place without a strike to publicize union viewpoints about an employer.

The number of days idle and the percentage of estimated working time lost because of strikes and lockouts were at historic lows in 2001, according to the U.S. Department of Labor's Bureau of Labor Statistics. Twenty-nine major work stoppages began during the year, idling 99,000 workers and resulting in 1.2 million workdays of idleness (less than 1 out of every 10,000 available workdays). Comparable figures for 2000 were thirty-nine stoppages, 394,000 workers idled, and 20.4 million days of idleness. Of the twenty-nine major work stoppages beginning in 2001, twenty-four were in the private sector; the remainder occurred in state and local government. In the private sector, thirteen stoppages occurred in goods-producing industries, including eight in construction. Eleven stoppages occurred in service-producing industries, including six in the health care services industry. Of the five stoppages in the public sector, four were in education.

The average length of work stoppages beginning in 2001 was twenty-two days, and a majority of the work stoppages (86 percent) lasted thirty days or less. Only 10 percent of stoppages extended more than fifty days. Work stoppages were concentrated in the eleven- to twenty-day and twenty-one- to thirty-day ranges. The longest stoppage beginning in 2001 was the dispute between Midwest Generation and the Electrical Workers, where 1,100 workers were on strike for 111 days. The dispute was also the longest stoppage in effect in 2001. Exhibit 12-13 highlights the number of work stoppages in the U.S. since 1970.

EXHIBIT 12-13 **Work Stoppages Involving 1,000 Workers or More, 1970–2001**

Year	Number of Strikes	Workers Involved	Year	Number of Strikes	Workers Involved
1970	381	2,468,000	1986	69	533,000
1971	298	2,516,000	1987	46	174,000
1972	250	975,000	1988	40	118,000
1973	317	1,400,000	1989	51	452,000
1974	424	1,796,000	1990	44	185,000
1975	235	965,000	1991	40	392,000
1976	231	1,519,000	1992	35	364,000
1977	298	1,212,000	1993	35	182,000
1978	219	1,006,000	1994	45	322,000
1979	235	1,021,000	1995	31	192,000
1980	187	795,000	1996	37	273,000
1981	145	729,000	1997	29	339,000
1982	96	956,000	1998	34	387,000
1983	81	909,000	1999	17	73,000
1984	62	376,000	2000	39	394,000
1985	54	324,000	2001	29	99,000

Source: U.S. Bureau of Labor Statistics.

FOCUS ON TECHNOLOGY

Internet Voting System Helps Resolve Labor Disputes

Hailing it as an Internet first, Boeing and its employees, represented by the Society of Professional Engineering Employees in Aerospace (SPEEA) union, resolved a labor dispute with a vote conducted over the Internet, the world's largest aerospace company.

SPEEA members, who had been on strike for the previous forty days, voted to accept a Boeing settlement by way of a secure Internet voting system, Boeing said in a statement. The SPEEA engineers and technical workers union hired 19 ☞ VoteHere to conduct the vote over its VoteHere website, Boeing said.

Seventy percent of those voting over the Internet voted to accept the contract offer and, as a result, returned back to work. The Internet system allowed for an immediate tally of the vote, avoiding the traditional delay caused by waiting for ballots from out-of-state members to be returned by post. Voting was closed at 4 P.M. on a Friday, and results were available minutes thereafter. Union officials and VoteHere worked together to ensure that only valid, out-of-area SPEEA members had access to the Internet voting system.

Source: Adapted from Laura Rhode, "Net Voting Helped Solve Labor Dispute at Boeing," *InfoWorld*, March 20, 2000.

Another type of union pressure is the **boycott.** In a primary boycott, union members do not patronize the boycotted firm. A secondary boycott occurs when a supplier of a boycotted firm is threatened with a union strike unless it stops doing business with the boycotted company. According to a 1988 Supreme Court decision, secondary boycotts are legal if they do not involve coercive tactics or picketing by the union. A special type of boycott is the **hot-cargo agreement.** Under this agreement, the employer permits union members to avoid working with materials that come from employers who have been struck by a union. This type of boycott is illegal except in the construction and clothing industries.

Management's response to these union pressures may be to continue operations with a skeleton crew of managerial personnel, to shut down the plant, or to lock the employees out. **Lockouts** are used by management to keep employees from their jobs, prevent union work slowdowns, prevent damage to property, or eliminate violence related to a labor dispute. Many states allow locked-out employees to draw unemployment benefits, thereby weakening the lockout. In practice, lockouts are more often threatened than used. The Focus on Technology box, "Internet Voting System Helps Resolve Labor Disputes," describes how Boeing used an online voting system to conduct a vote among striking mechanics to settle a labor dispute.

The **Racketeer Influenced and Corrupt Organizations Act (RICO)** was intended to be used to help keep organized crime out of labor-management business. However, a number of firms have attempted to use RICO as the basis of lawsuits to prevent or stop some union activities.[11] RICO-based suits by management usually result in lengthy litigation that would seem to favor companies.

Occasionally, serious disputes between union and management do not reach the strike or lockout stages. Instead a third party becomes involved. The third party may be a fact-finding group appointed by the government or the two parties. A fact-finding group investigates the issues and makes a public report; the public statement often causes the parties to become less antagonistic or extreme. Or the third party may be a mediator or an arbitrator.

Boycott   A bargaining tactic in which the union refuses to do business with a firm or attempts to get people or other organizations to refuse to deal with the firm.

Hot-Cargo Agreement A boycott agreement between management and union that workers may avoid working with materials that come from employers that have been struck by a union.

Lockouts   Management pressure tactic that involves denying employees access to their jobs.

Racketeer Influenced and Corrupt Organizations Act (RICO)   An act intended to be used to help keep organized crime out of labor-management business.

---

11. "Getting Their Dues," *The Economist*, March 25, 1995, pp. 68–74.

20 ☞

A **mediator** tries to get the two parties to reason and works at improving communication between them. Typically, mediators are full-time employees of the Federal Mediation and Conciliation Service (FMCS), a division of the U.S. Department of Labor. Under the Taft-Hartley Act, employers are required to notify the FMCS thirty days before the expiration of a contract or when new negotiating has begun. The FMCS provides experienced mediators at no cost to help the parties reach a contract agreement. The mediator does not make a decision but attempts to stimulate the parties to reach an agreement. Mediators have no power to impose a solution to the bargaining impasse.

An **arbitrator** is a third party who collects information, listens to the positions taken, and (unlike the mediator) makes a binding decision. Union and management must comply with the decision. Most labor contracts provide for use of an arbitrator in grievance procedures, as shown in Exhibit 12-12. In arbitration, each party tries to persuade the arbitrator that its position is ethical, fair, accurate, and in the best interest of everyone involved. Following an arbitration hearing, the arbitrator considers the evidence and renders a decision on the case that is legally binding unless one or both parties decide to appeal the arbitrator's decision in a court of law. This rarely occurs.

The written contract usually specifies the arbitrator's selection method and scope of authority. Most contracts state that the parties shall select a mutually acceptable arbitrator from a list of available arbitrators provided by either the American Arbitration Association (AAA) or the FMCS, or from both lists.

Mediator Third party to a labor dispute who tries to get union and management to reason and works at improving communication between them.

Arbitrator Third party to a labor dispute who makes the final, binding decision about some disputed issue.

21 ☞

12-8d National Emergencies

A widespread strike or lockout or one that occurs in a crucial industry could pose a threat to the nation's economy and security. For example, if the airline, trucking, or rail industries were shut down for any length of time, such vital services as food distribution, the movement of medical supplies, or the delivery of military repair parts could be threatened.

The president of the United States can take action to resolve such strikes and lockouts. The Railway Labor Act and the Taft-Hartley Act provide the mechanisms employed in national emergency situations. For example, if there is no contract agreement and a strike or lockout could threaten the nation's welfare or security, the president can (1) direct the attorney general to obtain a court order (an injunction) preventing the strike or lockout for eighty days, (2) appoint a board of inquiry to study the impasse and make recommendations, and (3) order the FMCS to attempt to mediate the dispute.

If the impasse is still not settled by the sixtieth day, the inquiry board is reconvened. After the board reports the employer's final offer, the NLRB conducts a secret ballot election among the employees. If the employees vote not to accept the offer, the attorney general must ask the federal court to dissolve the injunction. The union has a legal right to strike after this eighty-day cooling-off period.

By 1995 the national emergency provisions of the law had been invoked thirty-five times (only twice, however, since 1972). Thirty injunctions have been issued.

12-9 NONUNION ORGANIZATIONS

Most business firms in the United States are nonunion, or unorganized. One of the largest union-free firms is IBM. In most cases, union-free firms are small and are found in right-to-work states. Union penetration is highest in the Northeast and Midwest and lowest in the South and in rural areas.

An increasing number of firms have specific union-avoidance policies and, to support these goals, develop employee relations practices: participation programs, profit-sharing plans, formal grievance systems, and all-salaried (that is, everyone is paid a salary instead of hourly wages) compensation systems.[12]

A study of nonunion organizations concluded that two types of firms—doctrinaire and philosophy-laden—can operate effectively without unions.[13] The **doctrinaire firm**

Doctrinaire Firm A firm that wants to continue to be nonunion.

12. Micheline Maynard, "Enthusiasm Drives Saturn Workers," *USA Today*, August 31, 1990, p. 2B.

13. Brian Dumaine, "Why Do We Work?" *Fortune*, December 26, 1994, pp. 196–204.

wants to continue to be nonunion. It develops policies that mimic what unions have won in similar organizations. The belief is that, since the firm has good human resource policies, employees will resist union organizing efforts. The **philosophy-laden firm** has no unions because its climate of labor-management relations is excellent. Management has adopted policies on compensation, staffing, grievance handling, and discipline that it believes are correct and equitable.

Philosophy-Laden Firm
A firm that has no unions because its climate of labor-management relations is excellent.

12-10 LABOR DAY

Labor Day, the first Monday in September, is a creation of the labor movement and is dedicated to the social and economic achievements of American workers. It constitutes a yearly national tribute to the contributions workers have made to the strength, prosperity, and well-being of America. "Labor Day differs in every essential way from the other holidays of the year in any country," said Samuel Gompers, founder and longtime president of the American Federation of Labor. "All other holidays are in a more or less degree connected with conflicts and battles of man's prowess over man, of strife and discord for greed and power, of glories achieved by one nation over another. Labor Day . . . is devoted to no man, living or dead, to no sect, race, or nation."

More than 100 years after the first Labor Day observance, there is still some doubt as to who first proposed the holiday for workers. Some records show that Peter J. McGuire, general secretary of the Brotherhood of Carpenters and Joiners and a cofounder of the American Federation of Labor, was first in suggesting a day to honor those "who from rude nature have delved and carved all the grandeur we behold." But Peter McGuire's place in Labor Day history has not gone unchallenged. Many believe that Matthew Maguire, a machinist, not Peter McGuire, founded the holiday. Recent research seems to support the contention that Matthew Maguire, later the secretary of Local 344 of the International Association of Machinists in Paterson, New Jersey, proposed the holiday in 1882 while serving as secretary of the Central Labor Union in New York. What is clear is that the Central Labor Union adopted a Labor Day proposal and appointed a committee to plan a demonstration and picnic.

☞ 22

The first Labor Day holiday was celebrated on Tuesday, September 5, 1882, in New York City, in accordance with the plans of the Central Labor Union. The Central Labor Union held its second Labor Day holiday just a year later, on September 5, 1883.

☞ 23

In 1884 the first Monday in September was selected as the holiday, as originally proposed, and the Central Labor Union urged similar organizations in other cities to follow the example of New York and celebrate a "workingmen's holiday" on that date. The idea spread with the growth of labor organizations, and in 1885 Labor Day was celebrated in many industrial centers of the country.

Through the years the nation gave increasing emphasis to Labor Day. The first governmental recognition came through municipal ordinances passed during 1885 and 1886. From them developed the movement to secure state legislation. The first state bill was introduced into the New York legislature, but the first to become law was passed by Oregon on February 21, 1887. During the year four more states—Colorado, Massachusetts, New Jersey, and New York—created the Labor Day holiday by legislative enactment. By the end of the decade Connecticut, Nebraska, and Pennsylvania had followed suit. By 1894, twenty-three other states had adopted the holiday in honor of workers, and on June 28 of that year, Congress passed an act making the first Monday in September of each year a legal holiday in the District of Columbia and the territories.

The character of the Labor Day celebration has undergone a change in recent years, especially in large industrial centers where mass displays and huge parades have proved a problem. This change, however, is more a shift in emphasis and medium of expression. Labor Day addresses by leading union officials, industrialists, educators, clerics, and government officials are given wide coverage in newspapers, radio, and television.

INTERNET EXERCISE

Exploring *Norma Rae*

Activity

This Internet Exercise may better be classified as a "multimedia" exercise. It is designed to expose students to the 1979 film *Norma Rae* starring Sally Field. This classic union-organizer film is a great introduction to the stresses, conflicts, and emotions inherent in labor-management relations. The Norma Rae character was based loosely on Crystal Lee Sutton, who succeeded in unionizing a textile mill in North Dakota. The project was rejected by several major studios before it was picked up by Twentieth-Century Fox, assuming everyone would work for a reduced salary. Execs were no doubt surprised when the gritty drama became a box office success.

Directions

1. Students should view the following websites to get some background on *Norma Rae*, including the sociohistorical context in which the movie was made. They should also be encouraged to search other sites using popular search engines to learn more about the film.
http://www.mtholyoke.edu/courses/sgabriel/filmcourse_files/sarah.htm

http://www.classicsondvd.com/norma.htm
http://www.fromscript2screen.com/vault/normarae_1979.html
http://www.rottentomatoes.com/m/NormaRae-1015244/about.php
http://www.dvdfile.com/software/review/dvd-video_3/normarae.html

2. Students should rent the video from a local video store and view it after having visited the above websites.
3. While viewing the video, students should keep the following questions in mind.

Questions for Discussion

1. What explains the hostility of the textile workers to the union and its organizers? What *attitudes* are crucial?
2. What is the role of personal contacts in expanding union membership? Compare the methods of Norma Rae and the professional union organizer.
3. How is solidarity created among union members? What aspects of working-class culture help to create solidarity?
4. How do tensions develop within the union movement? For example, between the most committed (like Norma Rae) and others? Between the volunteers and the paid staff? Between blacks and whites?

EXPERIENTIAL EXERCISE

Reviewing the Advantages and Disadvantages of Union Representation

Activity

Students will individually analyze the advantages and disadvantages of having union representation and then share their findings with the class. About fifty minutes of class time will be needed.

Directions

1. Ask each class member to make a list of the advantages of having a union to represent workers, and then a list of the disadvantages of union representation. Allow about five minutes for each list.

2. Ask each student to identify at least two situations at work where it would be good to have a union representing a worker. Allow five minutes.
3. Calling on several individual students to share the advantages list, the instructor should write down the responses on the chalkboard. Do the same for the disadvantages list.
4. The instructor will summarize the advantages and disadvantages on the chalkboard.
5. The instructor should now call on several students to the situations where it would be good to have union representation for the worker. The instructor should encourage class discussion.

BUSINESS APPLICATION

The Right to Strike

Activity

Students will participate in small-group discussions reviewing the issue of public employees having the right to strike. Allocate about fifty minutes of class time for this activity.

Directions

1. Divide the class into groups of five to seven students, with each group electing a spokesperson/recorder.
2. Provide background information to the class that includes the following:
   - Historically, one of the most potent weapons of a union has been either to strike or threaten to strike.
   - Public employees, such as police officers and garbage collectors, have often been prohibited from striking. When the air traffic controllers went on strike during the early 1980s President Reagan fired the striking workers for breaking regulations prohibiting their going on strike.
   - If public employees are prohibited by law from striking, such laws significantly weaken the power of a union to acquire wage increases for its workers.

3. Ask each group to discuss the issue of public employees having the right to strike with each group taking a yes or no position on the issue. (Allow about ten minutes for this part of the exercise.)
4. Each group's spokesperson is to report the group's decision, with the instructor noting the voting decisions on the chalkboard.
5. Following the reporting of each group's vote, the instructor should ask various group members to clarify their thoughts and feelings about the issue and why the group voted yes or no.
6. The instructor will summarize the group's voting positions and underlying rationale.

13

Marketing Strategy

Photo: comstock.com

Botox Parties: A New "Wrinkle" in Marketing

Almost nothing incurs greater wrath among aging baby boomers than the appearance of wrinkles on skin that was supposed to stay young looking forever. As many marketers have learned over the past half century, the wave of people born during the post–World War II years is an extremely lucrative target market. The so-called baby boomers, those born roughly between 1946 and 1964 have been a driving force for a wide range of consumer goods. Now that this group is discovering the joys and pains of middle age, a new generation of products designed to preserve youth are finding a receptive audience. One product that has been well received by aging boomers is the wrinkle-eliminating protein called Botox.

1 ☞

2 ☞ Botox, made by Allergan, Inc., is the commercial name for botulinum toxin type A—a purified protein derived from bacteria that, when ingested, can cause botulism. Botox, when injected in the face, temporarily erases the signs of aging. Doctors who prescribe Botox market the product to middle-age individuals, primarily women, through "Botox parties," gatherings where the drug and its benefits are introduced and injections are administered.

In one typical Botox party, Dr. David Stephens, a Bellevue, Washington, plastic surgeon, presented a talk on Botox to a group of women at the home of the female host. After a fifteen-minute talk on how the procedure works and a bit of history about the drug, each woman signed a consent form and the lineup to receive injections began. With soft jazz playing in the background, the partyers slipped away one by one into the formal dining room for the quick procedure.

Each time a patient emerged with her new face the others offered a round of applause. The party's host went last, receiving five injections in her face: three between the eyebrows and one on each temple.

Dr. Stephens provided the champagne and snacks for the party and was responsible for recruiting the host, who already was a patient. Stephens now conducts regular Botox parties, which yield five to ten new patients per party. For patients, mixing cocktails with cosmetic injections takes some of the anxiety out of the procedure. And for doctors, providing Botox to as many as ten patients in less than sixty minutes offers a financial boon. The treatment costs between $250 and $1,000 and must be repeated every six months.

For its part, Allergan does not endorse the Botox party phenomenon, but it doesn't condemn them either. Taking a more-or-less hands-off approach, the company line is that it won't dictate how doctors run their practices. Some physicians, feeling the sting of professional disapproval of the party approach, opt instead to have wine and cheese gatherings in their clinical offices. Although the venue is different in such cases, the intent is the same—to help women feel comfortable about the procedure and to gain new customers. With baby boomers continuing to age and wanting to fight wrinkles at nearly any price, Botox parties are likely here to stay.

Sources: Adapted from Rachel Zimmerman, "Botox Gives Special Lift to These Soirees," *The Wall Street Journal*, April 16, 2002, pp. B1, B3; and Rhonda L. Rundle and Sarah Lueck, "FDA Clears Botox for Cosmetic Use," *The Wall Street Journal*, April 16, 2002, p. D6.

Botox parties are a prime example of how creative marketing can help achieve business goals. Effective marketing strategy contributes greatly to success; the lack of it can doom a business to failure. Marketing closely links the company to customers, their needs, and their desires. Medical procedures involving some type of body invasion, such as injections, can be intimidating for many people. Providing a setting in which the procedure is a sideshow helps diffuse the anxiety and increases sales. Although some controversy surrounds the Botox party approach, there is no denying its effectiveness in helping physicians gain new clients.

In this chapter we provide an overview of basic marketing concepts. First, we define marketing and discuss the benefits and costs of marketing activities. After briefly tracing the evolution of marketing, we introduce the marketing concept. Next we explain the steps involved in developing a marketing strategy: (1) selecting a target market and (2) designing a marketing mix (product, price, promotion, distribution) that will satisfy the needs of the target market. We also discuss the impotance of understanding buyer behavior and the value of marketing research. Finally, we look at what the future holds for marketing.

13-1 AN OVERVIEW OF MARKETING

Each of you has been involved in marketing activities at one time or another. Perhaps you have tried to sell a used textbook back to the campus bookstore or to convince your parents to finance a spring vacation. You may not have known it at the time, but you were performing marketing activities.

13-1a What Is Marketing?

When people hear the term **marketing,** many think of advertising or selling. Although those are part of marketing, and the part we see most, marketing is much more. As the American Marketing Association defines it, "Marketing is the process of planning and executing the conception, pricing, promotion, and distribution of ideas, goods, and services to create exchanges that satisfy individual and organizational objectives."[1] This definition emphasizes the diverse activities marketers perform: deciding what products to offer, setting prices, developing sales promotions and advertising campaigns, and making products readily available to customers. Exhibit 13-1 lists several activities of the marketing team.

Marketing activities are required for many different kinds of products. The term **product** often brings to mind tangible goods—those that can be held or touched, such as compact disc players or soft drinks. From the perspective of marketing, the term *product* also refers to services or ideas. For example, the health care services offered by hospitals are packaged, marketed, and sold as discrete products. The American Cancer Society markets an idea, quitting smoking, as a product. Similarly to firms that produce tangible goods, nonprofit and service organizations and even individuals rely heavily on marketing. The American Red Cross, for example, used a number of marketing techniques to raise money to aid the victims of the September 11, 2001, terrorist attacks on the United States. The organization's efforts were so successful that it ended up taking in more money than it could effectively distribute.[2]

Ultimately the purpose of marketing activities is to bring about exchanges between buyers and sellers. **Exchange** consists of one party providing something of value to another party, who gives something in return.[3] Just as the "something of value" is not

> **Marketing**   The process of planning and executing the conception, pricing, promotion, and distribution of ideas, goods, and services to create exchanges that satisfy individual and organizational objectives.

3

> **Product**   A good, service, or idea, including all the tangibles and intangibles provided in an exchange between buyer and seller.

> **Exchange**   The process by which parties provide something of value to one another to satisfy the needs of each.

EXHIBIT 13-1

Typical Marketing Activities

Product	Pricing	Promotion	Distribution
Develop new products.	Establish price objectives.	Determine type of promotion (advertising, personal selling, sales promotion, publicity).	Select wholesalers and retailers.
Modify existing products.	Conduct cost analysis.	Design the advertising message.	Establish procedures for hand ling and moving products (transportation, storage, inventory control).
Test-market products.	Analyze competitors.	Select the advertising media (print, radio, television, billboard, specialty items).	Find the best locations for plants, warehouses, and retail outlets.
Select brand names.	Set actual prices.	Schedule the advertisements.	
Package products.			

1. "AMA Board Approves New Marketing Definition," *Marketing News*, March 1, 1985, p. 1.

2. Alex Phillipidis, "Red Cross Rethinks September 11 Benefit Payout," *Westchester County Business Journal*, November 26, 2001, p. 3.

3. Philip Kotler, *Marketing Management: Analysis, Planning and Control*, 5th ed. (Englewood Cliffs, NJ: Prentice Hall, 1984), p. 8.

The Exchange Process

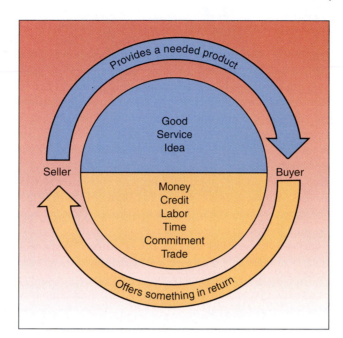

always a physical good, the "something in return" is not always money, as Exhibit 13-2 shows. The American Cancer Society's notion of quitting smoking to live a longer, healthier life is an intangible product, one that cannot be physically touched. For smokers who "buy" that idea, the price is the effort required to break a habit that they have found pleasurable.

13-1b Marketing Adds Value

Through activities that enable exchanges to take place, marketing adds value to products. This value is **utility,** the ability of a product to satisfy a consumer need. Utility is created when a firm's production function yields a product. For example, through the use of raw materials, labor, and other inputs, publishers produce newspapers and magazines. Marketing indirectly affects utility, since an organization may depend on its marketing people to find out which products consumers would welcome in the marketplace.

Marketing directly creates utility in other ways. By making products available when consumers want and need them, marketing creates utility. Publishing companies print and distribute morning newspapers early so readers can read them at breakfast or while commuting to work. Making products available where consumers need or want to obtain them also creates utility. Newspapers are delivered to homes and businesses; sold in vending machines, supermarkets, convenience marts, drugstores, and bookstores; and placed in libraries. Marketing again creates utility when the ownership of a product is transferred from seller to buyer. To obtain newspapers, customers pay the publishing company for home delivery, drop money into vending machines, or pay clerks in stores.

Consumers make buying decisions based on how well a product is perceived to meet their needs. Consumer choice has been extensively studied by market research specialists. They typically boil consumer choice down to two types of goods: utilitarian and hedonic. Utilitarian goods are those that meet a consumer need, while hedonic goods appeal more to consumer emotions. As an example, the individual out to purchase a new car may be interested in the good gas mileage from the utilitarian perspective. The sporty design of the vehicle may be appealing from a hedonic perspective. Marketers must tailor their message to appeal appropriately to different markets at different times.[4]

> **Utility**   The ability of a product to satisfy consumers' needs.

---

4. Ravi Dhar and Klaus Wertenbroch, "Consumer Choice Between Hedonic and Utilitarian Goods," *Journal of Marketing Research*, February 2000, pp. 60–71.

13-1c Marketing Affects Everyone

Marketing is important to businesses and consumers alike. Marketing is important to consumers because, through the price they pay for their purchases, each consumer indirectly supports the costs of marketing. By estimate, nearly half of every dollar spent on goods and services pays for marketing activities. Most people would agree that marketing costs are worth it because the many and varied marketing activities enable us to identify and find goods and services that satisfy our needs and wants. To review earlier discussions, a *need* is something required for human survival, such as food, water, shelter, and clothing; a *want* is something desired but not necessary for basic survival. Without marketing, many needs and wants would go unsatisfied because exchanges would be much harder to accomplish.

Marketing critics contend that marketing activities are often designed to stimulate the worst instincts and desires in people. The critics say that marketing is unethical because it appeals to these basic human emotions. Cigarette advertising was banned from television in the 1960s because it was believed that the ads appealed to youths who were unable to rationally deal with the appealing images used.

On the other hand, marketing advocates argue that market forces reflecting the needs of society drive marketing activities. Thus, marketing is not inherently unethical, because it satisfies consumer demands.[5] Perhaps it is difficult for you to come to grips with this issue, but we touch on it several times throughout the book. Exhibit 13-3 allows you to explore your attitudes toward marketing.

13-2 HOW MARKETING EVOLVED

When organizations and individuals conduct marketing activities today, they usually have consumers' needs and desires clearly in mind. But that has not always been true. Beginning with the Industrial Revolution in the nineteenth century and the capability of mass production that resulted, most businesses had a *production orientation*. Demand for new manufactured goods was so great that producers were concerned primarily with increased production and operating efficiency rather than with consumer preferences. As goods rolled off the production line, marketing consisted of taking orders and shipping products.

By the mid-1920s manufacturers discovered that supplies of basic consumer goods had caught up to demand. They were now producing an abundance and, in some cases, an overabundance, of goods. Needing to sell their products to markets that had increasing choices and decreasing demand, firms had to switch from a production orientation to a *sales orientation*. Firms began to emphasize advertising and sales. Companies started using sophisticated sales techniques to increase demand for existing products, but they still did not look to the marketplace to ensure that consumers' needs and desires were met.

Not until the early 1950s did firms begin to develop a *consumer orientation*. With soldiers returning from World War II, reentering the workplace, and starting families, demand for consumer goods and services surged. Competition among firms striving to meet that demand also surged. Somewhere during this postwar industrial boom, marketers realized that the way to sell products was to focus on satisfying customers. One of the first companies to state a policy of customer satisfaction was General Electric. GE said that a focus on customer satisfaction should be integrated into each phase of business. The policy of customer satisfaction has become known as the *marketing concept*.

13-2a The Marketing Concept

During the "customer satisfaction revolution," many adaptations in industrial practices were initiated. For example, at Whirlpool, the marketing department conducted a survey that showed that customers wanted a cooking range that was easy to clean.

---

5. Robert E. Pitts and Robert Allan Cooke, "A Realistic View of Marketing Ethics," *Journal of Business Ethics*, April 1991, pp. 243–244.

EXHIBIT 13-3

How Do You Feel about Marketing Activities?

Directions: Circle the number that represents your level of agreement with each statement.

	Strongly Agree					Strongly Disagree
1. Marketing helps improve the quality of goods and services.	1	2	3	4	5	6
2. The number of commercials on TV is about right.	1	2	3	4	5	6
3. I would be proud to have a marketing job.	1	2	3	4	5	6
4. Marketing people are concerned with product safety.	1	2	3	4	5	6
5. Most marketing activities are conducted ethically.	1	2	3	4	5	6
6. Advertisements portray women and minorities realistically, without stereotypes.	1	2	3	4	5	6
7. The benefits of marketing justify the costs.	1	2	3	4	5	6
8. Marketing doesn't increase materialism in our society.	1	2	3	4	5	6
9. Marketing doesn't encourage people to buy things they don't really need.	1	2	3	4	5	6
10. Marketing doesn't make people too concerned with how they look and dress.	1	2	3	4	5	6

Feedback: Now let's assess your attitudes toward marketing. Items circled 1 or 2 show a positive attitude; 3 or 4 suggest a middle-of-the road or neutral position; and 5 or 6 identify a negative feeling.

Anyone considering a marketing career would want to feel positive about the different activities marketers perform. But, like consumers in general, students usually have mixed feelings about marketing. It is the most visible side of business and often one of the most controversial. Why? Are consumers generally skeptical of the purpose, methods, and results of marketing activities? Are they unfamiliar with the benefits marketing brings? To build positive attitudes toward marketing, do marketers and their organizations need to make changes in the ways goods, services, and ideas are developed, promoted, and sold?

Engineers then designed a range with electronic touch pad controls, which could be cleaned with the sweep of a cloth or sponge. Industry wisdom suggested touch pads would fail, because earlier models with push buttons failed. Marketing, design, and engineering worked closely together to test consumer reactions every step of the way, and the new range succeeded where the old push-button design had failed.[6]

The **marketing concept** is a management philosophy stating that an organization should strive to satisfy the needs of consumers through a coordinated set of activities that also allows the organization to achieve its objectives.[7] Thus, customer satisfaction is the major force underlying the marketing concept and driving the entire company. The marketing concept calls for all departments and all employees to be committed to satisfying customers. The firm must determine consumer needs and wants, develop quality products that satisfy them, make products readily available at prices acceptable to buyers (and that

Marketing Concept
A managerial philosophy of customer orientation with the goal of achieving long-term success.

6. Sally Solo, "How to Listen to Consumers," *Fortune*, January 11, 1993, pp. 77–79.

7. Lynne W. McGee and Rosann L. Spiro, "The Marketing Concept in Perspective," *Business Horizons*, May–June 1988, pp. 40–45.

allow a reasonable profit), and provide service and after-sales support.[8] If a firm can answer yes to the following questions, it is customer oriented:

- Are we easy for customers to do business with?
- Do we keep our promises?
- Do we meet the standards we set?
- Are we responsive to customer needs?[9]

Firms benefit from practicing the marketing concept. They do not waste money on products in which customers are not interested. Also, customers pay more for products they believe will provide greater value and satisfaction, and if they are pleased with their purchase they come back and they refer business. Repeat business lowers sales costs and boosts profits; holding on to current customers is about one-fifth the cost of acquiring new ones.[10] Some marketers say the marketing concept helps set up a cycle of success: Customer satisfaction leads to loyal customers, which produces higher profits that make employees want to stay with the firm, which in turn makes for better customer service and satisfaction.

Focusing on the customer sounds like an obvious, commonsense way to run a successful business, but not all firms gear their marketing activities closely to the customer. The marketing concept is not always easy to put into practice. Top-level managers must be committed to it and must gain the commitment of other members of the organization. An organization may need to restructure departments or functions to better coordinate activities. Often a firm must be willing to forgo short-term profits for long-term customer satisfaction. And because consumer tastes and preferences constantly change, the firm must continually obtain information about customers and their needs and tailor its products to meet changing consumer preferences.

13-2b Beyond the Marketing Concept

Does giving consumers what they want and need serve the long-term interests of society? In addition to satisfying customers to meet company goals, many firms today also take into consideration how marketing affects society. The broader *societal orientation* means that firms are concerned with the welfare of society as well as their own interests and those of consumers.

Many firms and nonprofit organizations take active roles in dealing with issues such as scarce resources, environmental destruction, hunger, housing shortages, and illiteracy. Forward-thinking firms and their employees are involved in programs to work on such problems, as well as to help their communities, improve education, support the arts, and provide job training and opportunities for disadvantaged children and adults.

The marketing activities we discuss throughout this chapter focus on satisfying consumer needs and wants. In the next section, we look at how firms can design marketing strategies to satisfy consumers.

13-3 DEVELOPING A MARKETING STRATEGY

To put the marketing concept into action, a firm must decide on the appropriate marketing activities to satisfy customer needs and achieve its goals. A **marketing strategy** is an overall plan for conducting marketing activities that enables an organization to use its

Marketing Strategy   A plan for selecting and analyzing a target market and developing and maintaining a marketing mix that will satisfy this target market.

8. Milind M. Lele and Jagdish N. Sheth, "The Four Fundamentals of Customer Satisfaction," *Business Marketing*, June 1988, pp. 80–94.

9. Benson P. Shapiro, "What the Hell Is 'Market Oriented'?" *Harvard Business Review*, November–December 1988, pp. 119–124.

10. Sharyn Hunt and Ernest F. Cooke, "It's Basic But Necessary: Listen to the Customer," *Marketing News*, March 5, 1990, pp. 22–23.

resources and strengths to meet the needs of the marketplace. Firms developing a marketing strategy follow two basic steps: (1) Select a target market and (2) design a marketing mix (a combination of product, price, promotion, and distribution) that will satisfy the needs of the target market.

13-3a Selecting a Target Market

Organizations gear their marketing activities to reach certain customers—a market. A **market** is a group of people who need and want a product and have the ability, willingness, and authority to purchase it. Markets are divided into two broad categories: consumer and industrial. **Consumer markets** are made up of individuals who purchase products for personal use. **Industrial markets** consist of individuals or organizations that purchase goods and services so they can produce products to supply to others. Examples include manufacturers, governments, hospitals, nonprofit organizations, and stores.

Firms often sell products to both types of markets. Rossi Pasta, for example, is a family-owned business in Ohio that sells hand-rolled pasta through catalogs mailed to households (consumer) and also supplies the pasta to restaurants, supermarkets, and businesses (industrial).

Consumer or industrial, most markets include numerous customers with many different needs. Businesses are rarely able to satisfy the needs of all customers in a market, so they divide a market into **market segments,** groups of individuals with one or more similar product needs. Then they decide which segment or segments to serve. Coke, for example, has a number of products designed to satisfy the refreshment needs of multiple market segments. Regular Coke targets a youthful audience that isn't concerned about calories. Diet Coke generally appeals to middle-age people and others concerned about caloric intake. Although these two products alone provide broad market coverage, Coke continues to invest in research and development to create new beverage products to meet ever-changing consumer tastes.

A **target market** is a group of customers—consumers or other businesses—to which a business directs a marketing campaign. The organization focuses its marketing efforts on this group, trying to address its specific needs and preferences. When analyzing potential target markets, marketing managers must determine whether the organization has the resources to produce a marketing mix that meets the needs of the target market and whether satisfying those needs is consistent with the firm's overall objectives. Managers must also evaluate possible markets to see how entering them would affect the firm's sales, costs, and profits. Finally, managers must consider the size and number of competitors already in that market.

A more modern approach to market segmentation is targeting market niches. A **market niche** is a small, somewhat unique part of a market segment. By targeting marketing activities at a market niche, referred to as *niche marketing,* organizations can match customer needs even more precisely. For example, there is a large market for small car buyers in the United States. Automakers such as Toyota have been building cars for this market, aiming at serving particular lifestyle needs. Toyotas are popular, in particular, with college students, young couples, and others who are concerned about gas mileage and low-priced, high-quality vehicles. One niche market within this segment is individuals who are also environmentally conscious. For this group, Toyota has developed a hybrid vehicle—the Prius—that uses both electricity and gas. This is a niche market in which Toyota has invested millions of dollars to develop the Prius product and marketing campaign. Why would Toyota invest so much for such a small market? Perhaps the company sees growth potential. Or perhaps it believes people will visit dealers to look at the Prius and wind up purchasing another Toyota vehicle. The Focus on Diversity box, **"EthnicGrocer.com Markets to Diverse Customers,"** examines how one dot-com company uses a unique approach to attract diverse customers.

☞ 6

☞ 7

Market   People with the authority, financial ability, and willingness to purchase a product.

Consumer Markets   People who purchase products for personal use.

Industrial Markets   Those who purchase products to use in the production of other products or to resell.

Market Segments   Groups of individuals with one or more similar product needs.

Target Market   A group to which a firm directs its marketing activities.

Market Niche   A small, somewhat unique part of a market segment.

FOCUS ON DIVERSITY

EthnicGrocer. com Markets to Diverse Customers

8 ☞

Market niches can provide a unique advantage to companies that learn how to serve them. Niches can come in a wide variety of forms. Some are based on age groups: Florida, for example, markets its senior lifestyle communities and moderate climate to retirees. Some are based on lifestyle: Harley-Davidson markets its motorcycles to individuals who have a free-spirited, adventurous side.

One surviving dot-com company that has made the most of niche marketing is EthnicGrocer.com. This company caters to multiple niche markets—people of a diverse range of ethnic backgrounds who want to eat traditional ethnic foods. Rather than being stuck in a single niche market, as many other dot-com companies found themselves, EthnicGrocer.com uniquely serves a number of niche markets. This enables the firm to cater to special tastes, without limiting its potential market size. Imagine if the firm catered only to ethnic Chinese or Indian tastes. Would the market be large enough to sustain the website, food inventory, and other overhead costs?

13-3b Market Demographics

Marketers must be concerned about demographics. *Demographics* refers to the makeup of a population—racial, age range, ethnic, economic, and other factors. The demographics of the United States are rapidly shifting. Throughout history, the age picture of any population has been a pyramid, with a wide base representing a large share of babies born; a narrowing midsection because many died in early childhood and others died (at a lower rate) as they aged; rising to a pinnacle depicting the few who survived to old age. In this world, half the population was children, and many died before they had children of their own. The few elderly, along with the children, could be cared for by the people in the middle. This is the population the nation's communities and housing were designed for, and this was very much the U.S. population as recently as 1970.

Exhibit 13-4 shows two age pictures for the United States: 1970 and 2020, as projected by the U.S. Census Bureau. The age picture for 1970 is still the traditional population pyramid, but for 2020 it is more of a population "pillar," because each age group is roughly the same size, except for the oldest ones. This is not because people are having fewer children. For over a decade now, U.S. fertility rates have steadily reflected American families' long-standing preference for two children, and more babies have been born each year than the year before. But with fewer people dying before old age, the bars toward the top are becoming much wider. This pillar is the graphic display of what is probably the biggest success story of the twentieth century. At the century's end, the death of a child was a tragedy, not a routine event as it was at its beginning. Americans now take it for granted that women will survive childbirth and that children will live to have children of their own. And adults, far better educated on average than ever before, have translated new health knowledge and resources into practices that make a full lifetime a reasonable expectation for virtually everyone.[11]

Selecting a target market is crucial to developing an effective marketing strategy. Trying to sell a product to a group of customers who do not want or need it is bound to fail.

---

11. Martha Fransworth Riche, *The Implications of Changing U.S. Demographics for Housing Choice and Location in Cities*, prepared for The Brookings Institution Center on Urban and Metropolitan Policy, March 2001, 41 pp.

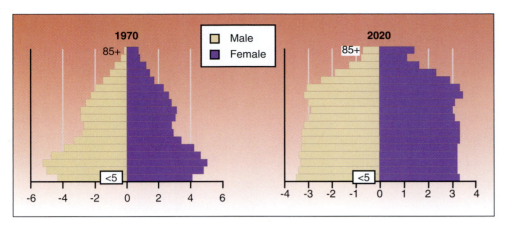

To select a target market, firms use either the total market (or undifferentiated) approach or the market segmentation approach.

13-3c Total Market Approach

A firm using the **total market** (or undifferentiated) **approach** develops one marketing mix for the total market for a product. It offers one type of product with little or no variation, sets one price, establishes one distribution system, and conducts one promotional program. Producers commonly use this approach to sell staple food items like salt or sugar, many fruits and vegetables, and other products that most customers consider similar from brand to brand.

Two conditions must exist for the total market approach to be effective. A large proportion of customers in the total market must have a similar need for the product, and the company must have the resources and skills to fill that need. If customers' needs are dissimilar or if the organization is unable to develop and maintain a satisfying marketing mix, then this approach will not be effective.

One example of a total market approach is heavy trucks. Builders of heavy trucks generally appeal to an undifferentiated, industrial market. The point of a marketing campaign for heavy trucks is to emphasize the ruggedness and reliability of the equipment. There's very little styling or other innovation that can be aimed at some particular niche or segment of the total market. In the United States, large trucks are built by companies such as Kenworth and Peterbilt. The challenge for their marketing divisions is to create some sense of differentiation that provides buyers of heavy trucks with a compelling reason to choose one company over another. Can you think of ways that heavy trucks can be differentiated from one another?

☞ 9, 10

Total Market Approach
The tactic of developing one marketing mix for the total market for a product. Also called undifferentiated approach.

13-3d Market Segmentation Approach

Customers in a market may have many different needs that cannot be satisfied by a single marketing mix. Then a **market segmentation approach** proves crucial. The firm divides the total market into segments and creates a marketing mix for one smaller market segment rather than for the total market (see Exhibit 13-5).

Segmenting enables a firm to apply its strengths and resources to satisfy the needs and wants of consumers. For instance, to sell cars with an undifferentiated approach—one type of vehicle for all drivers—would be difficult if not impossible. Some drivers want luxury vehicles, others prefer economy models; some crave sports cars, and others can get by only with a station wagon or minivan. As a result, automakers divide the total vehicle market into several segments.

Firms segment markets in one of two ways. An auto company could specialize in vehicles for one group of consumers with the concentration approach, as Rolls-Royce Motor Cars does with its top-of-the-line luxury vehicles. The **concentration approach** allows a

Market Segmentation Approach
The division of the total market into segments, with a marketing mix directed to one of the segments.

Concentration Approach
A marketing approach that allows a firm to use all its knowledge, experience, and resources to meet the needs of a distinct customer group.

☞ 11

Approaches to Selecting a Target Market

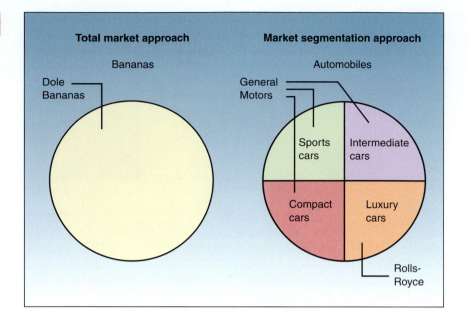

firm to use all its knowledge, experience, and resources to meet the needs of a distinct customer group. In this way, firms with limited resources often can compete with larger firms. However, a company using this approach is dependent on a single market segment, with sales and profits tied closely to that segment's demand for the product. A drop in demand will cause a drop in sales and profits.

A firm with considerable resources and expertise may use a **multisegment approach,** directing its efforts at two or more groups by developing a marketing mix for each. General Motors produces a wide range of different vehicles intended for different groups of customers. The multisegment approach can help an organization reach more customers and increase sales in the total market. But it also can push up a company's costs, since the firm often must use more production processes, materials, and labor, as well as several different promotion, pricing, or distribution methods for each model.

To divide a market into segments, marketers use **segmentation bases** to define characteristics of individuals or groups of customers. Marketers can segment consumer markets according to geographic, demographic, psychographic, or product-related bases.

Geographic segmentation bases include city, state, region, and zip code areas as well as characteristics such as climate, terrain, and population density. A heating and air-conditioning manufacturer marketing to the entire United States, for instance, could divide the country into several regions: northeast, southeast, midwest, north, northwest, southwest, and west. Property owners living in different regions—and climates—may require different heating and cooling systems.

Demographic segmentation bases divide a market in terms of personal characteristics such as age, income, education, occupation, sex, race, social class, marital status, or family size. Such vital statistics determine in large part a person's product needs. For instance, the distribution of age groups in the United States is changing, and marketers need to understand how these changes will influence various markets. The median age of the U.S. population was 35.7 years in 2000, up from 32.8 in 1990; over 37 million people fell in the 45- to 54-year-old age group. Demographers project that the U.S. population will increase steadily from 225 million in 1992 to about 383 million by 2050. As baby boomers born between 1946 and 1964 age over this period, more than 43 percent of the population will be over 45 years old; more than 20 percent will be over 65. This increase will present some major opportunities for organizations that market products for these age groups. For instance, people in their forties and fifties tend to focus on personal finances, which provides opportunities for financial services firms. In addition, music tastes vary strongly by age, education, race, and gender. Smart companies find ways to deliver differ-

12 ☞

Multisegment Approach A marketing approach in which a firm directs its efforts at two or more groups by developing a marketing mix for each.

Segmentation Base The individual or group characteristics that marketing managers use to divide a total market into segments.

entiated products directly to market segments to maximize their overall market coverage. Some firms will even use different **brands** in different markets to create an appearance of a complete market focus on that particular segment. For example, GM has a variety of automobile brands that identify with different segments. Cadillac and Buick appeal to mature and relatively affluent individuals. In contrast, Saturn and Chevrolet vehicles are built for a different market segment and are marketed as such.

Psychographic segmentation bases are a person's attitudes, personality, opinions, lifestyle, interests, and motives. In recent years, many consumers have grown more health conscious and fitness oriented. Products from athletic footwear and clothing to exercise equipment and "light foods" have cropped up to appeal to those leading active or health-conscious lifestyles. Many entrepreneurs have realized that they can convert their own personal lifestyle preferences into business opportunities. Paragon Guides is a firm that takes people on mountaineering adventures. Its founders were individuals who enjoyed mountaineering and decided to convert this love into a business by helping others who have similar psychographic characteristics.

Product-related segmentation bases divide the total market according to aspects of product use, including volume of use (heavy or light, frequent or infrequent), brand loyalty, and expected benefits. For instance, bankers have segmented customers according to the benefits they're looking for. There are loan seekers, one-stop customers wanting convenience, value seekers searching for the lowest loan interest rates and no-charge checking accounts, and major investors who bank only at big-name institutions.

Many marketers believe that segmentation will become increasingly important as firms attempt to identify and reach their markets. For many products, the U.S. market, once considered fairly uniform, is slowly breaking up along regional and demographic lines, such as location, ethnic heritage, or age. Firms also segment industrial markets. Common bases include geographic location, size of customer firms, type of organization, and product usage.

13-3e Global Marketing Strategies

The world economy is becoming increasingly integrated. Transportation and telecommunications have linked nations around the globe. Just as foreign firms like Toyota and Sony market products in America, U.S. firms like Microsoft, Nike, and Cisco, as well as smaller firms, market products throughout the world. This global boom is opening new opportunities, and many companies are developing global marketing strategies to capitalize on them. By developing marketing mixes for target markets throughout the world—or parts of the world—firms can satisfy more consumers and increase sales.

The global boom is also touching parts of the world previously closed to foreign countries. Only a few years ago it would have been hard to imagine a McDonald's or Pizza Hut restaurant in Moscow. But the former Soviet Union, Eastern Europe, Chile, and several Third World nations have abandoned communism and are welcoming free enterprise. For an example of how these famous U.S. brands are marketed internationally, go to the following links to view the Pizza Hut websites that have been created for Poland and China, respectively:

- http://www.pizzahut.com.pl/
- http://www.pizzahut.com.cn/

13-3f Designing a Marketing Mix

Once a firm has selected a target market, it must decide how to satisfy the needs of the target through a **marketing mix,** the combination of four elements: product, price, promotion, and distribution (see Exhibit 13-6). The marketing mix of Curtis Mathes, for example, consists of state-of-the-art television sets priced higher than most other brands, available through selected dealers, and promoted through print and television

Brand   A name, sign, symbol, or design a company uses to distinguish its product from others.

☞ 13

☞ 14, 15, 16

☞ 17, 18

Marketing Mix
The combination of four elements—product, price, promotion, and distribution—used to satisfy the needs of the target market.

☞ 19

The Marketing Mix and the Marketing Environment

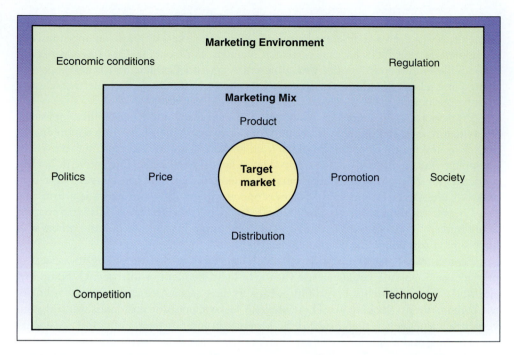

advertisements emphasizing the product's quality and dependability. Curtis Mathes targets its televisions to consumers who are willing and able to pay extra for a television and who want a strong warranty. Now let's look more closely at the marketing mix elements.

Product

As we said earlier, a product can be a good, a service, or an idea. Manufacturing a product (creating utility) is a production function. But marketing managers have the responsibility to inform the production people about products consumers would find appealing and about existing products that need to be changed or that are no longer needed. Marketers also develop brand names, packaging, and warranties. You'll read more about developing products in Chapter 14.

Price

Once a firm develops a product, it must set a price. Pricing requires crucial decision making because price is very visible to the consumer and is closely tied to a company's profit. Customers may not accept products priced too high; a firm may not recover its costs when products are priced too low. Chapter 14 discusses price in more detail.

Distribution

Even a terrific product that is priced right can fail if it is not available where and when the customer wants it. Distribution of products, a complex process, involves decisions about transportation, storage, and store selection. Chapter 15 gives a detailed look at distribution.

Promotion

Before they can purchase a product, consumers must know about its availability, its characteristics or benefits, and where it can be purchased. Promotion, consisting of advertising, personal selling, sales promotion, and publicity, informs or reminds the target market about a product and tries to persuade consumers to buy or adopt it. We examine aspects of promotion in Chapter 16.

13-3g The Marketing Environment and Marketing Strategy

Marketing does not take place in a vacuum. Several key forces outside the firm influence its marketing decisions. Economic conditions, regulation by government and industries, politics, and attitudes of society, technology, and competition from other firms combine to form the **marketing environment** (see Exhibit 13-6). These forces continually change. An organization often must adjust its marketing mix or focus on a new target market to meet changes in the marketing environment.

Economic Conditions

Economic forces in the United States and throughout the world can fluctuate rapidly and greatly influence marketing activities. Periods of slow economic growth, inflation, high interest rates for borrowers, or high unemployment may decrease consumers' ability or willingness to spend. Depending on their products and target markets, some organizations are more vulnerable than others to changes in economic conditions. During the 1990s, the United States experienced tremendous growth in technology companies, focusing in particular on the so-called dot-com companies. The explosive growth of dot-coms began with the 1995 initial public offering of Netscape, an early and popular web browser. The rapid rise in value of the stock for that company led many to believe that other dot-coms would experience the same phenomenon. Money poured into these firms from venture capitalists, angel investors, and others who wanted to get in early. This once-in-a-lifetime availability of capital created a market environment where the focus was on hype, promise, and grand visions of creating a "new economy." Of course, that bubble burst in early 2000, and technology companies had a much harder time finding needed capital after that. Many simply vanished; others survived by focusing on traditional sources of value and providing utility to customers.

Marketing Environment
All the forces outside an organization that directly or indirectly influence its marketing activities.

Regulation

As Chapter 5 discussed, laws and regulatory agencies bear directly on marketing decisions. Numerous federal, state, and local laws have been enacted to preserve competition and protect consumers. In addition to government agencies that enforce laws, industry associations impose self-regulation. The National Restaurant Association, for example, sets policies regarding food safety that it expects member restaurants to comply with. Consumer groups like Consumers Union also serve as watchdogs, testing products, publishing ratings, and providing other information to potential customers.

☞ 20

☞ 21

Politics

Elected officials, who can create legislation having a favorable or an unfavorable impact on for-profit and nonprofit organizations alike, determine laws and government policies. Organizations and entire industries often use a strategy known as *lobbying* to inform politicians and elected officials about issues of concern and to obtain support for favorable legislation. Legislators or federal officials who believe automobile manufacturers are trying to comply with pollution standards, for example, are less likely to impose additional restrictions. Lobbying is a common practice that is highly political in nature, and sometimes results in illicit activities such as bribery or special gifts. The U.S. government carefully monitors lobbying activities, and places limits on the gifts that politicians are allowed to accept. Can you see the danger of unregulated lobbying activity? What if there were no restrictions? Who would benefit the most from unrestricted lobbying activities?

Society

Individuals and groups in our society raise questions about business practices that they believe go against the wishes of society, as we discussed in Chapter 4. When marketing activities have the potential to harm society, special-interest groups may raise objections through publicity, consumer protests, or boycotts—refusals to buy certain products. In recent years, consumer groups who object to certain television programs have boycotted products of firms that advertise on those shows; in response, some companies have pulled their advertising from the programs in question. In 2002, controversy erupted over a decision by Seagrams to begin hard-liquor advertising on television. Prior to that, the industry had policed itself and had refused to advertise hard liquor on television, although there is no legal ban against it. Why do you think the industry imposed this ban on itself? What

☞ 22

FOCUS ON GLOBALIZATION

Ford Launches Global "Rebranding" Campaign

23 ☞ **F**ord Motor Company **has a sophisticated marketing infrastructure that includes a number of specialized units aimed at niche consumer segments. For example, Ford has had marketing units dedicated to "women" and "diversity." In recent years, the firm has consolidated many of these units under a more general "Global Marketing" rubric.**

Ford underwent a major restructuring beginning in 2002 with the ascendance of Henry Ford's great-grandson, Bill Ford, to the CEO role. The latter Mr. Ford took over when the board of directors appointed him in response to lackluster global sales. Bill Ford's challenge is to reinvigorate the "Ford" brand on a worldwide scale. To that end, he has developed a global trademark initiative, which encompasses all Ford brands.

Ford plans to achieve its aims by returning to symbols of its more glorious past. In 2000, the company had dropped its familiar blue oval logo in favor of a script-design nameplate. The global marketing effort being led by Bill Ford returns to the blue oval, in an effort to regain consumer trust and confidence. "The blue oval is one of the most valuable and most widely recognized brand icons in the world," Mr. Ford. "We need to get it shining brightly again because the oval is our core high-volume nameplate. It's also our identity."

Sources: Adapted from Julie Cantwell, "Ford Alters Marketing Structure," *Automotive News,* December 17, 2001, p. 6; and Tanya Irwin, "Ford Seeking to Restore Image," *Adweek,* January 21, 2002, p. 2.

does Seagrams stand to gain by going against the industry? What does the company stand to lose?

Competition

The actions of competitors have a big impact on a firm's marketing activities. When one organization identifies a target market and introduces a successful product, others often follow with similar offerings. Similarly, when a competing firm raises or lowers prices, improves packaging, launches innovative promotional programs, or rewrites service policies, others evaluate and often adjust their marketing strategies. Competition forces escalating innovation in the marketing wars. Pepsi and Coke have been battling the so-called cola wars for decades. Each has a subset of brand loyalists whom they can count on. Each also wants to win market share in both domestic and international markets. Coke suffered a major black eye internationally when it was reported in Belgium that bottles of its beverage had been contaminated with a noxious substance. Coke's slow response to the allegation—subsequently determined to be a problem with a Belgian bottler—cost it from both a reputation and market share perspective. In fact, the Coke CEO at the time, Douglas Ivester, eventually resigned based in part on what was perceived to be his lack of concern for the health impact of the event. The Focus on Globalization box, "Ford Launches Global 'Rebranding' Campaign," examines how Ford is rebranding itself to compete more effectively in international markets.

Technology

The explosion of technological innovations has deeply affected marketing mix decisions for many organizations. Dramatic developments such as the microchip, robotics, laser technology, and satellite communications offer great potential for the design, production, distribution, and promotion of products. Marketers are still trying to figure out the most effective way to use the Internet as a marketing medium. Innovations are constantly appearing. In 2001, a new form of advertising known as the "pop under" ad propelled a small web-cam company into international prominence. Known as much for their annoying pattern of popping up under the main browser window as for their content, these ads created a buzz for the company that, despite the almost universal distaste for the ad campaign, resulted in remarkable sales growth.[12]

Although they cannot control these environmental forces, marketers can influence them. They can shape the political environment to some extent through lobbying, as mentioned earlier. They can use a strong promotional program of advertising, news coverage, or sponsoring a sports event to color society's attitude toward a firm or product or to minimize a controversy. A firm that can anticipate and quickly respond to the actions of society, competitors, or other environmental forces can more effectively control its destiny.

13-4 UNDERSTANDING BUYER BEHAVIOR

What makes consumers choose one brand of soft drink over another? Why do some shoppers looking for video recorders consult *Consumer Reports* and poll all their friends, while others simply go to an electronics store and pick one out? Marketing managers study consumer behavior and consult with experts to answer such questions. Understanding buyer behavior helps firms bring about satisfying exchanges. Since purchase decisions in consumer markets differ from those in industrial markets, we discuss those two types of buying decisions separately.

✍ 24

13-4a Consumer Buying Behavior

The actions and decisions of individuals who purchase products for their personal use constitute **consumer buying behavior.**[13] The process involved in purchasing products can differ from buyer to buyer and from product to product. Exhibit 13-7 shows a decision-making continuum. Product cost and frequency of purchase influence consumer decisions. Choosing low-cost, often-used products requires little thought and quickly becomes *routine decision making*. Buyers often use *limited decision making* for products they purchase occasionally that require some consideration. To choose expensive, infrequently purchased products that involve complex thought, consumers use *extensive decision making*.

After buying a product, especially something expensive, consumers sometimes worry that they bought the wrong brand or that they should not have bought the product at all. The conflict buyers experience when they have doubts about a purchase is called *cognitive dissonance*, also known by some as *buyer's remorse*. Consumers ask themselves whether the product should have been purchased at all or whether a different brand should have been purchased, or whether they could have gotten a better price. Often firms try to reduce

> **Consumer Buying Behavior**
> The decisions and actions of individuals who purchase products for personal use.

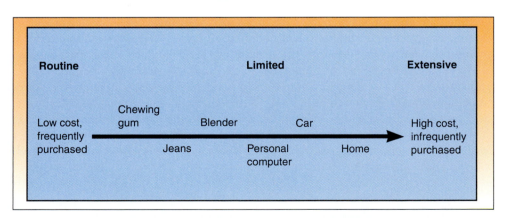

Routine	Limited	Extensive

Chewing gum — Blender — Car

Low cost, frequently purchased → High cost, infrequently purchased

Jeans — Personal computer — Home

Types of Consumer Decision Making

---

12. "Tech Enthusiasts Giddy Over X-10's Pan'n Tilt Wireless Camera," *Business Wire*, April 8, 2002.

13. Leah Rickard, "Minorities Show Brand Loyalty," *Advertising Age*, May 9, 1994, p. 29.

Consumption Chain
An analysis of all of the steps
involved in a consumer's
purchasing decision.

buyers' doubts through advertising or by providing follow-up information or service, because such doubts can decrease satisfaction and goodwill after the sale.

Several factors, some within individuals and some external, affect the buying decisions of consumers. People are influenced by social factors (e.g., family members, peers), psychological factors (attitudes, personality), personal characteristics (age, education), and specific conditions that exist at the time of a purchase decision. Exhibit 13-8 explains and gives examples of factors influencing buyer behavior.

Consumer attitudes toward a firm and its products certainly affect the success or failure of its marketing strategy. For some luxury products, premium brands, and stylish services, consumer attitudes are more important—for marketing purposes—than demographics like age and income.[14] If enough consumers have strong negative attitudes toward some part of a firm's marketing mix, the firm may try to change consumer attitudes to make them more favorable. Changing negative consumer attitudes to positive ones is usually a long, difficult, and expensive task.

13-4b The Consumption Chain

Organizations seeking to gain competitive advantage often can use an analysis of the **consumption chain** to identify opportunities.[15] The consumption chain is an analysis of all of the steps involved in a consumer's purchasing decision. A standard consumption chain commonly has fourteen links or stages, but there can be more or less depending on how detailed is the analysis. The consumption chain presented in Exhibit 13-9, on page 346, is a standard breakdown of the stages that consumers might use in the purchase of a product.

As you can see from the illustration, the consumption chain begins with the consumer's awareness of his or her need for a product or service. This is followed by the decision to search for a product or service that meets that need and goes through twelve additional stages ending up with final disposal of the product. Marketers who recognize these various stages of consumer behavior can develop a market advantage around any single stage. For example, some firms emphasize their flexible financing programs to help people purchase their products. Others emphasize their delivery or service functions. Typically, firms must pay attention to each stage of the consumption chain. However, in cases where consumers are particularly perturbed about one stage because no existing firm gets it right, a chance for a competitor to enter the market by effectively handling that stage opens up. Dell Computer, for example, entered a crowded market space in computer manufacturing, but excelled in the "selection" and "order and purchase" stages to create a huge advantage that no competitor has been able to match.

25 ☞

Organizational Buying Behavior
The decisions and actions of
buyers in organizations.

13-4c Organizational Buying Behavior

The purchase decision making of organizations such as manufacturers, service providers, government agencies, institutions, and nonprofit groups is referred to as **organizational buying behavior.** Buying decisions by organizations typically differ from consumer purchases in several ways. First, organizational transactions are usually much larger and less frequent than typical consumer purchases. Organizational buyers, who must meet exact product specifications, tend to be more concerned than consumers about quality and service. Buyers usually seek more information and base decisions less on emotional factors than consumers do. In small companies, one person (usually the owner) is responsible for purchase decisions; in large firms, the responsibility for buying rests with several individuals who make up a buyer center.

14. Judith Waldrop, "Markets with Attitude," *American Demographics*, July 1994, pp. 22–33.

15. Rita Gunther McGrath and Ian MacMillan, *The Entrepreneurial Mindset* (Cambridge, MA: Harvard University Press, 2000), pp. 57–78.

Influence	Examples

EXHIBIT 13-8
Influences on Consumer Purchase Decisions

Social

Family: parents, siblings, children, grandparents.

A woman buys the same brand of dishwasher her mother always had.

Roles: as parents, spouse, child, student, employee, club member.

A young man orders flowers to send his mother on Mother's Day.

Reference groups: people such as coworkers or friends with whom a person identifies and shares attitudes and behaviors.

An accountant chooses the same kind of computer her associates use.

Social class: group of people with similar values, lifestyles, and behaviors, often classified by income, occupation, education, religion, or ethnic background.

Wealthy art lovers from all over the world come to auctions at Sotheby's in New York.

Culture: values, behaviors, and ways of doing things shared by a society and passed down from generation to generation.

Americans like soft drinks colder than Europeans do.

Subculture: group that shares values and behaviors different from those of the broader culture to which it belongs.

An American woman of Oriental background shops at a specialty food store.

Psychological

Motive: reason or internal force that drives a person toward a goal.

A student gets a haircut before a job interview.

Perception: the way people select, organize, and give meaning to the things they see, hear, taste, smell, and touch.

A mall shopper smells cookies and stops at the cookie shop to buy some.

Attitude: a person's overall feeling about something.

A family donates money to an animal rights organization.

Learning: changes in an individual's behavior caused by experiences and information.

After a high cholesterol reading, a man cuts down on the amount of meat and fats he eats.

Personality: traits, experiences, and behaviors that make up a person.

An outgoing young woman with many friends racks up huge long-distance phone bills.

Demographic

Personal characteristics such as age, sex, marital status, family size, race, income, education, and occupation.

A working couple take their young children to a daycare center.

Situational

Conditions that exist when a person is making a purchase decision, such as unexpected circumstances, amount of time for the decision, or expectations for future employment.

A man who is laid off from his job puts off buying a new car.

13-5 MARKETING RESEARCH

Throughout this chapter, we have emphasized that marketing activities should focus on customer satisfaction. No matter what its size or objectives, a firm cannot implement the marketing concept without information about customer needs. Are customers' lifestyles or preferences changing? Do some market segments still need to be reached? Who are the competitors? What product, price, distribution system, and promotional activities would enable satisfying exchanges to take place with people in the target market? To answer

EXHIBIT 13-9

The Consumption Chain

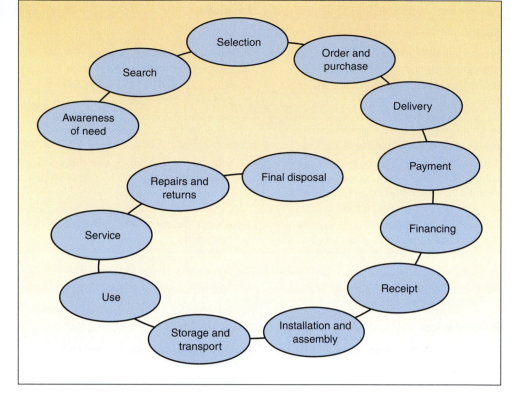

such critical questions, marketers must continually look at buying trends, talk to customers, and establish ways to receive feedback. Much of this communication with consumers takes place through marketing research. **Marketing research** is the systematic gathering, recording, and analyzing of information relating to the marketing of goods and services.[16]

13-5a The Need for Marketing Research

Years ago, the attitudes of many businesspeople toward marketing research could be summarized as "If it's not broken, don't fix it." Firms conducted research in response to problems such as decreasing profits, failure to reach sales quotas, or customers lost to a competitor. But many firms today realize that research should be ongoing. Successful firms, regardless of size, continually talk to customers and study the market. As Exhibit 13-10 shows, marketing research can be proactive to prevent "breakdowns" or reactive to respond to a problem. Unfortunately, marketing research conducted after serious problems emerge may be too late. Forward-looking companies take a proactive stand to keep ahead of the competition.

13-5b The Research Process

The **marketing research process** consists of six steps: problem definition, research design, data collection, data analysis, interpretation, and conclusions.

Problem Definition

Trying to identify the nature and boundaries of a problem is the first step toward solving a marketing problem through a research study. The first sign of a problem is often a devi-

Marketing Research
The systematic gathering, recording, and analyzing of information for guiding marketing decisions.

Marketing Research Process
Series of steps consisting of problem definition, research design, data collection, data analysis, interpretation, and conclusions.

16. *Report of the Definitions Committee of the American Marketing Association* (Chicago: American Marketing Association, 1961).

Proactive	Reactive
Are we attracting new customers?	Why are we losing customers?
How do we maintain and increase sales?	Who has surpassed us in our sales?
Are we satisfying our current customers?	How do we get lost customers back?
What new products are needed by our target market?	Can we develop a new product to keep up with our major competitor?

EXHIBIT 13-10

Proactive and Reactive Research Questions

ation from normal operations, such as a failure to attain objectives. For example, if an organization's objective is to increase its share of a particular market to 15 percent but it has captured only 10 percent of the market, the organization should recognize that a problem exists. Decision makers should realize that something inside or outside the organization has blocked the achievement of the desired objective or that the objective may be unrealistic. Decreasing sales, increasing expenses, and decreasing profits are all broad indications of problems. Whatever the problem, researchers and decision makers should remain in the problem definition state until they have established precisely what they want from the research and how they will use it.

Whether research is conducted on an ongoing basis or after a problem occurs, it is critical for the marketing researcher to work closely with the marketing manager in the problem definition stage. If together they can clearly define a problem, the researcher can conduct research that will provide information the manager requires to make marketing decisions.

Research Design

After defining the research question, marketers formulate a plan for collecting information essential to the study. Depending on the type and amount of information already available, the researcher will choose one of several alternative designs.

If little is known about the question being investigated, marketers engage in *exploratory research*. They may look at company records and government or industry publications or talk to knowledgeable people inside or outside their organization. Focus group interviews, in which a researcher informally discusses an idea or issue with a small group of employees, consumers, or others, can provide helpful insights.

Sometimes organizations conduct *experimental research* to determine whether one event, circumstance, or situation causes another. For example, a publisher may distribute an issue of a magazine with different covers in different parts of the country. After a trial period, researchers investigate which cover resulted in the highest sales.

Marketers often want to know the age, sex, education, income, lifestyle, buying habits, or buying intentions of consumers. To obtain such information, they conduct *descriptive research*. Descriptive research produces reports that give business managers an idea of the makeup of their target markets. This can be extremely useful information when crafting a marketing campaign. It would be inefficient, for example, to develop a campaign aimed at a geographic market and using tactics designed for young people if the market is composed primarily of seniors. Imagine, for example, McDonald's using Ronald McDonald to market products to a senior community in Arizona.

Data Collection

After settling on a research design, marketers accumulate the information that will answer the research question. Researchers sometimes rely on *secondary data*—published information available inside the firm or from government, industry, or other sources. Secondary data offer tremendous advantages. They usually can be obtained quickly at relatively little cost, which may be especially important to small firms and nonprofit organizations. Marketers generally start all research projects by looking for secondary data. Exhibit 13-11 lists common sources of secondary data.

**Sources of
Secondary Data**

Internal Sources

Company reports   Reports from the sales staff
Sales and cost data from accounting   Cash register receipts

External Sources

Private publications   Census data
  Editor and Publisher Market Guide   Census of Population
  Guide to Consumer Markets   Census of Retail Trade
  Moody's manuals   Census of Service Industries
  Poor's registers
  Sales & Marketing Management Survey   Government publications
  of Buying Power   County and city statistics
  Chamber of Commerce publications   *Economic Indicators*
  Industry reports and publications   *Statistical Abstract of the United States*
  Computer databases available through   *Survey of Current Business*
  industry associations of research
  organizations
  University business and economic
  research centers

Often secondary data are unavailable or inadequate. In such cases, marketers obtain *primary data*—information collected for the first time and specific to the study. Researchers use experiments, observation, or surveys to collect primary data.

Researchers conduct experiments either in a controlled, isolated setting (laboratory experiments) or in actual marketplace settings such as a store (field experiments). *Observation* involves watching a situation and recording relevant facts. A marketer may observe supermarket shoppers and record the purchases made. Through *surveys* or *polls*, researchers question respondents to obtain needed information. Mail, telephone, and in-person surveys are becoming more and more common. You probably have taken part in a consumer survey over the phone or at the shopping mall. Many restaurants, for example, place consumer feedback forms on the table to collect immediate information from customers about their dining experience.

Another popular form of collecting data about an organization is to use a technique known as *mystery shopping*. Under this approach, a firm will hire a mystery shopping consultant to actually patronize its establishments. The mystery shopper does not identify himself or herself as a researcher but merely behaves as a typical customer. This technique, though sometimes considered deceptive, can produce valuable data about a firm's ability to deal with consumer issues. For example, if the mystery shopper finds that employees are surly or unhelpful, correcting that problem can have a dramatic impact on consumer attitudes and sales.

Because reaching all consumers in the target market (e.g., all television viewers) is often impossible or impractical, researchers collect data from a sample. A *sample* is a portion of a larger group and accurately represents the characteristics of the larger group. Companies that provide ratings for television shows may survey 1,200 viewers throughout the United States. With a sufficient sample, the researcher can use the data collected to infer important facts about the larger group. The Internet has enabled companies to collect customer information in myriad new ways, including online surveys. The Focus on Technology box, "E-Surveys Help Companies Gauge Customer Satisfaction," examines how such surveys can be used to assess customer satisfaction.

Data Analysis

To determine what all the information means, researchers analyze the data they collect. Usually they enter the data into a computer and run sophisticated statistical programs to find the frequency of responses and how different items of information are related.

FOCUS ON TECHNOLOGY

E-Surveys Help Companies Gauge Customer Satisfaction

26 ☞ **H**alogen Software designs and develops web-based survey software that enables companies to gauge customer and employee satisfaction. The firm markets two product lines: eSurveyor, an electronic survey tool that allows companies to solicit feedback from employees and consumers on topics including workforce climate, benefits packages, new products and customer support; and e360, an on-line questionnaire that asks employees to assess coworkers' communication skills, leadership qualities, and customer commitment.

Both products allow for completely anonymous responses. Surveys are accessed by clicking on a hyperlink within an e-mail message, while a built-in reporting function enables companies to generate customized reports. Halogen's prices begin at $15,000 for an annual license, and maintenance fees typically amount to 22 percent of total licensing costs.

By soliciting customer feedback, Halogen president Paul Loucks says, companies are able to spot emerging trends, cater to customer preferences, address product shortcomings, and strengthen communication channels. And it is precisely this ability to gather timely consumer data that makes Halogen's software a valuable weapon in today's battle for consumer dollars. According to research from the *Harvard Business Review* magazine, it is six to ten times cheaper to keep a current customer than to add a new one.

Source: Adapted from Cindy Waxer, "Tough Times Help, Hurt e-Survey Firm," *Toronto Globe and Mail*, February 14, 2002.

Although it is extremely valuable, computer analysis is costly because of the equipment, programs, and skills required. Businesses often hire marketing research consulting firms to conduct the data analysis.

Interpretation and Conclusions

Data analysis isn't worth much unless it provides a workable answer to the research question. In the final research step, marketers determine what the information means, draw conclusions, and recommend actions. Business owners and managers concern themselves most with this part of the study; they use the interpretations and conclusions as the yardstick for measuring the value of the research.

Firms of all types and sizes use research to tackle marketing challenges or problems. Some have their own marketing research departments, while others use outside consultants or research firms from time to time. Either way, marketing research often requires considerable time and money, as well as a commitment to act on the findings.

13-6 MARKETING IN THE FUTURE

Through the 2000s and beyond, marketing will no doubt undergo many changes. It is already well into a new era marked by intense global competition. This does not mean marketers will abandon the marketing concept. Satisfying customers will be even more important than before, as will developing sound marketing strategies. What the changes do mean is that, as the sizes of many markets remain constant or even decrease, competition will grow fiercer; firms will have to develop products that can compete in the global economy.

Different Ways Organizations Define Quality

Organization	Definition of Quality
IBM	". . . meeting the requirements of our customers, both inside and outside the organization, for defect-free products, services, and business processes."
Boeing	". . . it (quality) means providing a product that satisfies the needs of the customer; translated . . . 'conformance to requirements' . . . makes the customer's needs paramount. Now, the key to this?. . . 'Customer' means Boeing internal customer, also."
Corning	"Quality is knowing what needs to be done, having the tools to do it right, then doing it right—the first time."
Xerox	"At Xerox quality means meeting customer requirements . . . You have to understand exactly what the customer requires for every bit of the work that you do for him."

Quality   The totality of features and characteristics of a good or service that bear on the ability to satisfy stated or implied needs.

Perhaps no greater challenge has grown out of the global economy than the need to produce high-quality goods and services at low cost. As you can see in Exhibit 13-12 there are many different ways to define quality, but all the definitions say one thing: The customer is the focal point of quality requirements and standards. In the case of IBM and Boeing, "customer" refers to the individuals and organizations outside the firm that purchase or influence the firm's products, and also to "internal customers"—other employees or departments within the organization. In essence, **quality** is the totality of features and characteristics of a good or service that bear on the ability to satisfy stated or implied needs. The challenge managers face in this environment is to manage in such a way that the outcome is a quality product.

The quality of many products made in the United States has improved in a wide variety of industries ranging from computer chips to toilet paper made from recycled paper. Unfortunately, competitors throughout the world have also been improving product quality, in some cases at a faster pace than U.S. firms.[17] One outcome of the global economy is a change in the competitive structure within industries. Firms no longer compete on a local, regional, or national basis; they compete on a global basis.

The field of marketing promises to be challenging and exciting as businesses strive to deliver quality products to consumers in the midst of tremendous worldwide competition. In the next three chapters, we take a closer look at how companies can develop a marketing mix that will enable them to withstand fierce competition.

17. Andrew Kupfer, "How American Industry Stacks Up," *Fortune*, March 9, 1992, pp. 30–46.

SUGGESTED WEBSITES

Note: These websites were functional when we went to press. Please access the online text for the most up-to-date URLs.

1. www.botox.com
2. www.allergan.com
3. www.ama.org
4. www.ge.com
5. www.whirlpool.com
6. www.rossipasta.com
7. www.coke.com
8. www.ethnicgrocer.com
9. www.kenworth.com
10. www.peterbilt.com
11. www.rollsroyce.com
12. www.gm.com
13. www.paragonguides.com
14. www.microsoft.com
15. www.nike.com
16. www.cisco.com
17. www.mcdonalds.com
18. www.pizzahut.com
19. www.curtismathes.com
20. www.restaurant.org
21. www.consumersunion.org
22. www.seagrams.com
23. www.ford.com
24. www.consumerreports.org
25. www.dell.com
26. www.halogensoftware.com

SUMMARY OF LEARNING OBJECTIVES

1. *Explain the purpose and importance of marketing.* Through marketing, firms plan and execute decisions on what products to offer, how to price them, how to distribute them, and how to inform customers about them. Marketing enables firms to create exchanges that satisfy consumer needs and organizational objectives. Marketing is valuable because it creates or enhances utility.

2. *Trace the evolution of marketing.* Marketing's emphasis on satisfying customers is a relatively recent occurrence. Beginning with the Industrial Revolution, most firms focused solely on producing enough needed consumer goods. With basic goods available in sufficient quantities in the 1920s, firms began concentrating on selling more products. Only in the early 1950s did companies embrace the marketing concept, a philosophy that they can achieve their goals by satisfying customers. Many firms today also consider society's welfare.

3. *Define the term* market *and distinguish between the two major types of markets.* Firms decide to offer products to a *market*, a group of people who need a product and who have the ability to purchase it. *Consumer markets* consist of individuals who purchase products for personal use. *Industrial markets* include buyers who purchase products in order to make other products.

4. *Describe the steps involved in developing a marketing strategy.* To develop a marketing strategy, a firm (1) selects a target market and (2) designs a marketing mix to meet the needs of that group of people. Depending on the product and the firm's goals and resources, a firm may sell to the total market for a product or divide the total market into segments based on customers' geographic area, demographic characteristics, or psychographic aspects (such as attitudes), or on product characteristics.

5. *Identify the four elements of the marketing mix.* *Product* decisions require marketers to determine what would satisfy customers' needs and wants. *Price* affects a customer's purchase decision and the seller's profits. *Promotion* communicates product information to the target market. *Distribution* makes products available when and where people in the target market want them.

6. *Define the term* marketing environment *and list the environmental forces.* The marketing environment is the combined outside forces that influence business firms' marketing decisions. Economic conditions, regulation by government and industry, societal attitudes, political policies, actions of competitors, and technological advancements have tremendous impact on marketing activities.

7. *Describe how consumers make purchase decisions and compare consumer buying behavior to industrial buying behavior.* Considering buyer behavior helps firms conduct activities that will bring about more exchanges. Consumers go through a decision-making process of recognizing a need, seeking information about a product, comparing alternatives, deciding on a product, and evaluating the product. Purchase decisions for industrial markets differ from consumer decisions because transactions are larger and less frequent and require more information.

8. *Explain the value of marketing research and outline the research process.* Ongoing, systematic research gives firms information they need to satisfy customers and achieve their objectives. To conduct effective and accurate studies, marketers (1) define the specific purpose of the research, (2) design a plan to collect information, (3) gather needed information, (4) analyze the information, usually by computer, and (5) interpret the information and draw conclusions to use in marketing decisions.

KEY TERMS

brands (p. 339)
concentration approach (p. 337)
consumer buying behavior (p. 343)
consumer markets (p. 335)
consumption chain (p. 344)
exchange (p. 330)
industrial markets (p. 335)
market (p. 335)
market niche (p. 335)

market segmentation approach (p. 337)
market segments (p. 335)
marketing (p. 330)
marketing concept (p. 333)
marketing environment (p. 341)
marketing mix (p. 339)
marketing research (p. 346)
marketing research process (p. 346)
marketing strategy (p. 334)

multisegment approach (p. 338)
organizational buying behavior (p. 344)
product (p. 330)
quality (p. 350)
segmentation base (p. 338)
target market (p. 335)
total market approach (p. 337)
utility (p. 331)

QUESTIONS FOR DISCUSSION AND REVIEW

1. What are some typical activities performed by marketers? How do these activities add value to products? Would consumers be better or worse off if these activities were not performed?

2. In today's business environment, why is it essential for companies to practice the marketing concept? Identify a firm that you feel has adopted the marketing concept, and explain why. If possible, identify one that has not.

3. It has been reported that McDonald's has lost market share to its competitors. What role can marketing play in helping the firm regain market share?

4. Give an example of a firm using the total market approach for a product and one using the market segmentation approach. Why do you think these approaches were selected?

5. Think of a product you have purchased recently. Describe the marketing mix for the product, and compare it with the marketing mixes used for competing products. Why did this product, and specifically its marketing mix, appeal to you?

6. What is the marketing environment? How does it affect the following: environmental legislation, national health insurance, new product introductions, and global competition?

7. What is the consumption chain? Can you name a product or service that you have purchased that focuses particularly on one or two stages of the consumption chain? What stages are they? Why does the firm focus on these stages?

8. In terms of automobiles, what psychographic group do you fall under? What product features and benefits are most appealing to you? Compare your answers with those of your professor or those of your parents. How are they different?

9. What are some of the differences between consumer purchases and industrial purchases? Why do we even need to make a distinction between the two for marketing reasons?

10. Explain how you think an individual or organization could benefit from using marketing research.

END-OF-CHAPTER QUESTIONS

1. Making products available where consumers need or want to obtain them creates *utility*.   **T** or **F**

2. Hedonic goods appeal more to consumer emotions than do utilitarian goods.   **T** or **F**

3. A firm using the *total market approach* develops multiple marketing mixes, which it delivers to the market simultaneously.   **T** or **F**

4. The *concentration approach* allows a firm to use all its knowledge, experience, and resources to meet the needs of a distinct customer group.   **T** or **F**

5. Lobbying is highly political in nature and sometimes results in illicit activities, such as bribery or special gifts.   **T** or **F**

6. The consumption chain begins with the consumer's awareness of his or her need for a product or service.   **T** or **F**

7. Polling is the systematic gathering, recording, and analyzing of information relating to the marketing of goods and services.   **T** or **F**

8. Trying to identify the nature and boundaries of a problem is the first step toward solving a marketing problem through a research study.   **T** or **F**

9. A survey involves watching a situation and recording relevant facts.   **T** or **F**

10. Marketers are not concerned with the distribution of products.   **T** or **F**

11. Companies use an influence strategy known as _____ to get politicians to look favorably on the issues affecting them.
    a. bribery
    b. advertising
    c. public relations
    d. lobbying

12. A _____ is a small, somewhat unique part of a market segment.
    a. niche market
    b. target market
    c. market campaign
    d. consumer market

13. Distribution of products involves decisions about transportation, storage, and _____.
    a. publicity
    b. advertising
    c. price
    d. store selection

14. A product can be a _____.
    a. good
    b. service
    c. idea
    d. all of the above

15. _____ segmentation bases divide a market in terms of personal characteristics, such as age, income, education, occupation, sex, race, social class, marital status, or family size.
    a. Geographic
    b. Demographic
    c. Psychographic
    d. Product-related

INTERNET EXERCISE

Learning More about Demographics

Marketers are constantly looking at demographic trends and statistics in order to build better and more effective marketing campaigns. There are any number of ways marketers can stay in touch with what's happening demographically. Many are involved in regular and ongoing primary research. However, that can be time-consuming and expensive. Another effective technique is to keep up with secondary research—research that others conduct.

One good source of secondary research is the following website:

http://www.inside.com/default.asp?entity=AmericanDemo

Students should visit this website outside of class and consider the following questions. They should be prepared to discuss these questions during the next class.

Questions for Discussion

1. What are the main demographic trends that you read about at the American Demographics website?
2. What do these trends suggest to marketing professionals in the following industries?
   Automobile
   Clothing
   Grocery
   Home products
   Music
3. Think of a major consumer products company from which you have recently purchased a product. Do you think the marketing of the product you purchased is in line with the demographic trends you identified? Explain.

EXPERIENTIAL EXERCISE

The Marketing Database

Activity

In this activity, students will select an organization in the area, find out who is responsible for marketing information, and phone that person to request a brief interview. A fifteen- to twenty-minute telephone interview is sufficient.

Directions

1. Find out what information the organization compiles in its marketing databank. How is it used?
2. Compare the information from the organization you selected with the information gathered by other members of your class.

BUSINESS APPLICATION

Developing a Marketing Plan

Professional Management Consultants (PMC) is in the process of developing a marketing plan and is not sure just where to start the process. PMC is composed of three consultants and one clerical staff member. The company provides consulting services in the area of human resources management, assisting clients with management expertise in hiring, training, and developing employees.

PMC is concerned about a continuous decline in business and the arrival of competing consulting companies in its city. The company has limited its advertising efforts to a small ad in the yellow pages of the local telephone book. If business continues to decline at the current pace, PMC will have to cut back on its number of employees.

Questions for Discussion

1. What should be among the first steps PMC needs to take in developing a marketing plan?
2. How should PMC go about market segmentation?
3. Spending capital on expensive advertising during a time of declining business is a controversial strategy for a small organization like PMC. What type of advertising do you think should be included in a marketing plan for PMC?

Case

Kimberly-Clark Struggles with Marketing of "Sensitive" Product

Seeking to wipe out potty discomfort, Kimberly-Clark Corp. plunged into the market with a new product: moistened toilet paper on a roll. The maker of Kleenex, Huggies, and Kotex believed its latest creation could be the biggest advancement in toilet paper in a century. The Irving, Texas–based company spent $40 million marketing Fresh Rollwipes under the Cottonelle brand name, one of its biggest product introductions ever. Company officials predicted annual sales could hit $150 million within a year and $500 million in six years.

"Using a moist product cleans and freshens better than dry toilet paper alone," said Peggy Nabbefeldt, a Kimberly-Clark marketing director. "They have to realize this should be a normal part of a universal task."

Unfortunately, less than one year after the product was introduced, analysts wonder if Rollwipes will find its place in the market. The product, which consists of a roll of moist wipes in a plastic dispenser that clips onto a regular toilet-paper holder, has not been accepted in its test markets. The company argues that its market research indicated Americans were willing to spend more on Rollwipes, which would be used in addition to regular toilet paper. Early skeptics were brushed aside by company officials who pointed to their market research indicating that 63 percent of adults were already in the habit of wetting toilet paper or using a wipe.

Ultimately, the company spent more than $100 million to develop the roll and the dispenser, which it guards with more than thirty patents. Part of the problem for the product's poor showing lies with marketing mistakes. Hobbled by a product that few can discuss without blushing, the ads designed for the product never showed consumers what the product does. For instance, one advertising agency hired to promote the product decided to depict a "fun" image with shots of people from behind splashing in the water. The ads, which cost $35 million to produce, carried the slogan "Sometimes wetter is better." A print ad created by the same firm was an extreme close-up of a sumo wrestler's behind.

Analysts criticized the ads for not clearly explaining the product—or helping create demand. And in another marketing mistake, Kimberly-Clark didn't design Rollwipes in small trial sizes, which meant it couldn't distribute free samples. Instead, it had scheduled a van outfitted with a mobile restroom and Rollwipes to stop at public places in the Southeast in mid-September, 2001. That road trip was put on hold after the September 11 terrorist attacks in the United States.

Finally, Rollwipes, unlike other wipes that come in boxes, come in a plastic contraption that is immediately visible in a bathroom. This visibility was another obstacle for people already bashful about buying the product. A starter kit, which has an $8.99 retail price, includes a beige plastic dispenser that clips onto the spindle of the regular toilet tissue, but is about the size of two rolls on top of each other. Tom Vierhile, a marketing critic from Marketing Intelligence Service, Ltd., a research firm that tracks new product introductions, said "You do not want to have to ask someone to redecorate their bathroom."

At the core, the failure of Rollwipes to catch on shows how hard it is for marketers to invent—or reinvent—household staples. Consumers' closets are already stuffed full of laundry detergents, fabric softeners, special liquid soaps, and even soap-coated wipes.

When the product was introduced to analysts in January 2001, Kimberly-Clark couldn't have been more optimistic. The new product was introduced to major news outlets, and the company held a special conference call for analysts and investors to brief them on their sales forecasts. Kimberly-Clark opted for a high-profile product launch, hoping that the hype would create demand from consumers and persuade retailers to make room on their shelves.

In what many perceive as another marketing gaffe, the product was not ready to ship to stores until June 2001—six months after the product was announced. Kimberly-Clark blamed the delay on the late arrival of manufacturing equipment. By July 2001, most shoppers had forgotten about the publicity surrounding the product launch.

In contrast, Procter & Gamble, seeing the buzz created by Rollwipes, bought out a Boston inventor who had created "Moist Mates," a simpler version of baby wipes on a roll. P&G repackaged the product under the name Charmin Fresh Mates and shipped the product to the same test markets as Kimberly-Clark. P&G also started TV advertising the same day as Kimberly-Clark. P&G is satisfied that the product is performing adequately, although it has no immediate plans for expanding its market reach.

In the end, it may happen that Kimberly-Clark's marketing team will not be able to generate sufficient demand to offset the huge up-front investment in Rollwipes. On the other hand, P&G's efforts with a similar, yet simpler product have been successful. This case stands as a lesson in matching the marketing campaign, and budget, to real market needs and adoption patterns.

Questions for Discussion

1. Do you think Kimberly-Clark can salvage the future of Rollwipes by creating more clever advertising? How would you describe this product on television?
2. What role does packaging play in the successful marketing of this product? Do you think Kimberly-Clark needs to change its packaging?
3. Do you believe it's acceptable to distribute this product through standard retail stores? Is there another distribution channel that may prove more effective?

Sources: Adapted from David Koenig, "Paper Company Cleans Up with Brand," *Marketing News*, February 12, 2001, p. 8; "A New Twist to TP," *DSN Retailing Today*, March 5, 2001, p. 17; and Emily Nelson, "Is Wet TP All Dried Up?," *The Wall Street Journal*, April 15, 2002, pp. B1, B3.

14

Product, Pricing, and Promotion Strategies

Photo: comstock.com

Micropayment Pricing Model

Instead of subscribing to a newspaper, magazine, or business journal, imagine what it would be like to order each article à la carte for delivery via the Internet. A main story might cost $.60. Shorter pieces might sell for $.20. Pricing could be tied to how many pages you wanted. Keep reading and you keep getting charged. Stop reading and no more payments.

The Internet economy introduced the possibility of micropricing. Why pay $16.99 for a whole compact disc when you could pay $1.50 for your favorite song. Website guru Jakob Nielsen suggested in 1998 that online micropayments would become commonplace in five years. This prediction never caught on like Nielsen and many others predicted.

This pricing approach was analyzed and experts found that three factors in the mind of consumers play a vital role in pricing Internet available goods. First, most people believe that the Internet is free. Even a $.20 charge to read an article is resisted. Second, consumers often don't believe that the content is worth what the providers charge. Third, people don't want to deal with the hassles of micropayment transactions. They would rather take the subscription to the *Wall Street Journal* than make payments each time they want to read something.

The micropayment pricing model applied to the Internet simply seems to annoy most people. Convenience, timeliness, and value are all considerations that users of the Internet weigh in making purchases. As prices become so small, such as $.50 for a 500-word *Wall Street Journal* article, purchasers don't believe it is worth their precious time to just buy the one piece. Thus, what Jakob Nielsen believed would be welcomed by consumers, micropayment pricing, is still not catching on. Consumers value their time and convenience perhaps more so than making micropayment after micropayment.

Source: George Anders, "Nickeled-and-Dimed to Death," *Fast Company*, November 2001, pp. 204–205.

14-1 WHAT ARE PRODUCTS?

A **product** consists of all the tangible and intangible characteristics provided in an exchange between a seller and a buyer. People buy a product for the benefits and satisfaction it gives. A product's characteristics include not only its physical aspect but also its function, brand name, image, packaging, warranty, and price, as well as the provider's reputation and customer service policy.

As we noted in Chapter 13, a product can be a good (an actual physical entity such as a drill bit), a service (your checking account at the bank), or an idea (the American Heart Association's advice to follow a diet low in fat and cholesterol). Sometimes a product is a blend of all three. Dinner at a fine restaurant, for example, consists not only of the tangible items, food and beverages, but also preparation, service, and the appeal of dining in that special setting.

Products are often a firm's most important link with customers and are critical to the achievement of organizational objectives.[1] Because different products are designed for different target markets, they require various pricing, distribution, and promotion decisions. To help plan effective marketing strategies, marketers classify goods and services according to the manner in which they are purchased and used. Marketers generally divide products into two broad categories: consumer and industrial products.

> **Product** A good, service, or idea, including all the tangibles and intangibles provided in an exchange between buyer and seller.

14-1a Consumer Products

Products used by individuals for personal and family consumption are **consumer products.** Marketers classify consumer products according to customers' buying behavior.

Convenience Products. Inexpensive goods and services that consumers buy often, without much thought or effort, are **convenience products.** Milk, bread, magazines, soft drinks, and gasoline are examples. So are the routine services offered by dry cleaners and automatic teller machines. People make such purchases or go to such service providers because of habit and closeness of the outlet: They've always bought that brand; the store is nearby.

> **Consumer Products** Goods or services used for personal or family consumption.
>
> **Convenience Products** Frequently purchased, inexpensive items that buyers spend little effort to find and purchase.

---

1. Paul Belleveau, Abbie Griffin, and Stephen Somermeyer, eds., *The PDMA Toolbook for New Product Development* (New York: Wiley, 2002).

Shopping Products Items that buyers will expend time and effort to find and purchase.

Specialty Products Products with one or more unique features that a group of buyers will spend considerable time and effort to purchase.

Industrial Products Goods or services used by an organization in producing other goods or services or in carrying out its operations.

Shopping Products. Consumers will expend time, effort, and energy to find and obtain some goods and services. Buyers comparison shop for these; thus they are known as **shopping products.** Consumers gather information about different brands and styles, visit different stores, note prices, read advertisements and consumer guides, and consult family or friends. This category includes goods such as DVDs, major appliances, and furniture and services such as dental care, legal advice, and tax preparation.

Specialty Products. Goods and services that have specific attributes desired by a particular group of consumers are known as **specialty products.** Buyers go to considerable trouble to obtain a specialty product, no matter what the price or location, and will rarely accept a substitute. Specialty products can be expensive and unique, such as a Rolex watch, Dolce and Gabanna designer dress, or less costly but still fairly uncommon, such as a certain breed of dog or tickets to a Broadway show.[2]

Because consumers differ in their purchasing behaviors, the convenience-shopping-specialty distinction is not absolute.[3] One customer may order food from a pizza parlor strictly because of its delivery service (convenience). Another may choose to eat there after comparing the pizza and prices all over town (shopping). Other customers may go out of their way for the super deluxe, ten-topping pan pizza available only at that restaurant (specialty). Since marketers classify products according to the buying patterns of the majority of consumers, pizza thus would fall in the convenience category, based on the shopping patterns of most consumers.

14-1b Industrial Products

Products used by organizations in producing goods and services or in carrying out their operations are **industrial products.**[4] Manufacturers, contractors, mining companies, utilities, government agencies, wholesalers, retailers, and institutions such as hospitals and schools buy and use a great array of goods and services to carry out their operations and produce products of their own. Industrial products often require substantial investment but have a long, useful life span, such as a robotics system in an automobile plant or a computer network for the government. Other industrial products cost much less and are purchased regularly, such as office equipment or the printing of an annual report.

Marketers sometimes find it useful to categorize industrial products into more specific classifications, including the following:

- Installations, such as large storage and distribution centers or factories
- Major equipment, including machinery and large tools essential to the production process
- Accessory equipment, such as forklifts and small tools or office equipment and furniture
- Component parts, usually prefinished items put into a physical product, such as cassette players installed in autos
- Raw materials, such as minerals, sand, coal, and petroleum, which become part of physical products
- Supplies, such as pens and paper and cleaners, which do not become part of the item produced
- Services, either provided in-house or hired from outside the organization, such as accounting, advertising, printing, legal, and janitorial

2. Scott Bedbury and Stephen Fenuhell, *A New Brand World: Eight Principles for Achieving Brand Leadership in the Twenty-First Century* (New York: Viking, 2002).

3. Ibid.

4. Jakki J. Mohr, *Marketing of High-Technology Products and Innovations* (Upper Saddle River, NJ: Prentice-Hall, 2001).

14-1c Classifying Services

While services are classified as consumer or industrial, other classifications are also important because of the unique characteristics of many services. Exhibit 14-1 shows the classifications marketers use for services. Marketers often find it useful to categorize services by degree of *labor intensiveness*. Services such as hair styling, education, and health care require a great amount of human labor while others, such as automatic car washes, rely heavily on machines and equipment. Labor-intensive services are especially difficult to standardize.

Another way to classify services is by degree of *customer contact*. High-contact services, such as real estate agencies, involve frequent interactions with customers. The consumer must be present for such services to be performed. Low-contact services involve much less participation on the part of the customer. The consumer may need to be present only to initiate the contact but not for the service to be performed. A customer goes to the dry cleaner to drop off clothes, for example, but does not have to stay while they are being cleaned.

A fourth way to classify services is by *skill of the service provider*. Some services require professionals, such as lawyers, physicians, or accountants. Other services can be offered by

Classification of Services

Category	Examples
Type of market	
Consumer	Life insurance, car repairs
Industrial	Lawn care, management consulting
Degree of labor intensiveness	
Labor based	Repairs, executive recruiting
Equipment based	Public transportation, air travel
Degree of customer contact	
High contact	Hotels, health care
Low contact	Dry cleaning, motion pictures
Skill of the service provider	
Professional	Legal counsel, accounting services
Nonprofessional	Taxi, janitorial
Goal of the service provider	
Profit	Financial services, overnight delivery
Nonprofit	Government, education

individuals with lower levels of skills. Consumers are more selective when choosing providers for services that require higher levels of skills.

Finally, services can be classified by the *goal of the service provider.* Not all service organizations are profit oriented. Universities, charities, libraries, and some clinics are a few examples of nonprofit service organizations.

14-2 PRODUCT LINE AND PRODUCT MIX

Decisions concerning what products to offer—the type, number, and variety—are fundamental to any organization. Often firms manufacture and sell goods or offer services that are similar in design, production, or use and are targeted to similar market segments. A group of related goods or services marketed by a firm is called a **product line.** A firm's product line can be shallow, with only one or two products, or deep, including many products. Midas Muffler's product line is shallow, with a few types of car mufflers. Toyota has a deep product line, with a wide range of autos, trucks, and SUVs.

Firms realize distinct advantages in offering related products and introducing new products within an established product line: They can use their know-how, resources, and experience to effectively produce and market new products. Similar products help promote each other. Marketers can stretch advertising dollars by emphasizing an entire product line in an advertising campaign.

Although many firms expand existing product lines by introducing new, similar items, others decide to add completely different product lines. The collection of items and services a firm offers for sale make up its **product mix.** Marketers refer to product mixes as narrow or wide, depending on how many product lines are carried.

Some companies opt for a narrow product mix, such as Mita, which has advertised that it makes only photocopiers. Others develop several product lines targeted to the same or similar markets. Fisher-Price, known for years for its popular toys, added a line of baby furniture and equipment including high chairs, portable cribs, and car seats. Still other firms develop an extremely wide product mix consisting of multiple product lines aimed at different markets. Procter & Gamble has more than twenty lines, including detergents, cleaners, analgesics, cosmetics, diapers, fragrances, paper products, and foods and beverages.[5] Kraft Foods' many and diverse product offerings, shown in Exhibit 14-2, illustrate a wide product mix.

Product Line A group of related products that are considered a unit because of marketing, technical, or use similarities.

Product Mix The total group of products a firm offers for sale, or all of the firm's product lines.

1 ☞

2 ☞

EXHIBIT 14-2

Kraft Foods' Product Mix

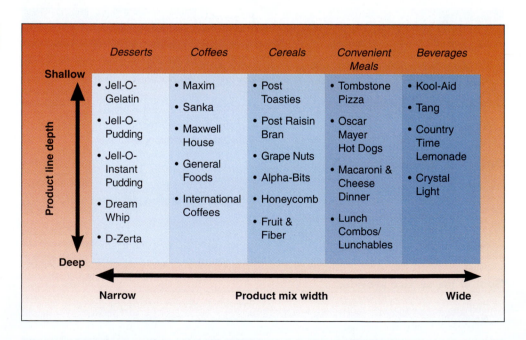

5. *Procter & Gamble, Wet Feet Insider Guide* (New York: Wet Feet Press, 2002).

The decision to offer a single line of related products or many and varied product lines depends on an organization's knowledge, goals, and resources. Developing new product lines often allows a company to expand into different markets, achieve growth, and increase stability. Firms with multiple product lines often find themselves in a better position to adapt to changes in economic conditions, technology, or consumer needs.

14-3   MANAGING THE PRODUCT MIX

Whether they offer a few similar products or many diverse ones, firms face numerous decisions in developing and managing their products. They must determine which to offer and must continue to develop new ones. They may need to modify products in response to competition and changing consumer preferences. Firms also must determine when to stop offering certain products.

14-3a   Developing New Products

Firms spend billions of dollars each year developing new products. Boeing spent over $5 billion designing the 777. The 777, like the 747, is still a profitable machine and will be for years to come.[6] But many of the more than 10,000 new products introduced each year fail.[7] According to a survey of new-product managers conducted by Group EFO, a Connecticut-based consulting firm, 8 percent of their new products survived to reach the market. Once there, 83 percent of these new products failed, which overall resulted in a 99 percent failure rate.[8] Beech Aircraft invested over $350 million in its innovative new airplane, Starship, only to stop producing the plane a few years after its introduction. The performance of the plane did not live up to expectations.[9]

Many reasons account for the high failure rate of new products. The most common reasons are lack of research, design problems, and poor timing of the product's introduction.[10] The most successful new products are superior to competitors' offerings, have been developed to meet well-defined consumer wants and needs, and enable customers to perform a unique task.[11]

Although it is risky to introduce new products, an organization cannot afford *not* to do so. New products are critical to a firm's growth for several reasons. As products age, profits decrease and their expected life span becomes shorter.[12] About 15 percent of a corporation's sales is based on new products.[13] Without new product development, even the best of organizations risk decline. For instance, the railroad industry, in recent years, has experienced an unanticipated rapid decline. By failing to explore new transportation alternatives that would better satisfy customer needs, it became vulnerable to competition from trucking and air transportation. Conversely, by developing the minivan, Chrysler beat competitors to this growing market. Combined sales of Chrysler's minivans hit a record 140,773 in the first quarter of 1994, outselling every passenger car on the road.[14] One study reported that internationally developed new products and services are expected to increase dramatically in the next five years.[15]

6. Robert Redding and Bell Yenne, *Boeing: Peacemaker to the World* (New York: Thunder Bay Press, 1997).

7. Jim Betts, *The Million Dollar Deal* (Point Pleasant, NJ: Point, 1985), p. 7.

8. Cyndee Miller, "Survey: New Product Failure Is Management's Fault," *Marketing News*, February 1, 1993, p. 2.

9. Alan Farnham, "It's A Bird! It's A Plane! It's A Flop," *Fortune*, May 2, 1994, pp. 56–66.

10. Linda Gorchels, *The Product Manager's Handbook* (New York: McGraw-Hill, 2000).

11. Torsten H. Nilson, *Competitive Branding: Winning in the Market Place with Value-Added Branding* (New York: Wiley, 1999).

12. Doug Hall, *Jump Start Your Business Brain* (New York: F&W Publications, 2002).

13. Robert Gravlin Cooper, *Winning At New Products* (Cambridge, MA: Perseus Publishing, 2001).

14. Accessed at www.daimlerchrysler.com/history/epochen-e.htm, April 30, 2002.

15. "Launching New Products Is Worth the Risk," *Marketing News*, January 20, 1992, p. 2.

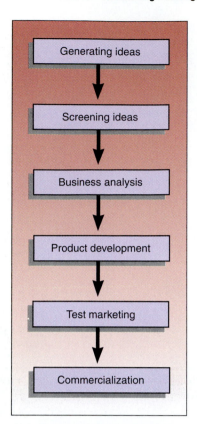

**The New-Product
Development Process**

Companies that fail to introduce new products risk even greater losses than those firms that do. In fact, as numerous firms are cutting staff and reducing operating costs, they are at the same time increasing budgets to launch new products.[16] Investing in new products during an economic downturn is a good opportunity to get ahead of competitors who are cutting back on new products. Firms cannot eliminate the risks inherent in introducing new products, but they can reduce risks through a well-planned, thorough product development process (see Exhibit 14-3). Let's examine how a firm uses a six-step process to develop new products. The process is expensive and time-consuming, but it is helpful in avoiding costly mistakes.

Generating Ideas

The road to a new product begins with finding ideas that fit with the organization's goals and objectives. Ideas emerge from within the firm through engineers and researchers or from outside sources such as customers, competitors, or consultants. Fewer than 10 percent of all new ideas make it into the later stages of product development.[17]

Screening Ideas

The many ideas born in the initial step must be screened to select the ones the firm will pursue. An idea may not match a firm's objectives. Others may require resources and knowledge that the firm does not have and cannot easily obtain. Such ideas will be rejected, while others are evaluated further.

Business Analysis

During this phase, the firm estimates the market potential of the product: What are the expected costs, sales, and profits? If management believes the product will make enough profit to justify the costs, the idea will advance to the product development phase.

Product Development

Here firms develop a working model of the product. In this way, they can examine the feasibility of making and offering the product on a large scale. Some ideas are rejected at this stage because the production costs are too high to bring the product to market.

Test Marketing

Before full-scale introduction of a new product, a firm introduces it in selected areas chosen to represent the entire market. Test marketing can be used to monitor consumer reaction to the product and to refine the marketing mix if needed. Sometimes test marketing uncovers a weakness in the product, price, promotion, or distribution that can be adjusted before introduction to the entire market. Marketers carefully select locations to test market a product.

Commercialization

When a product shows promise in test marketing, the firm generally begins the process of production and distribution to the entire market. In some cases, the firm introduces the product in a selected geographic region (e.g., Cajun-style foods in the Southwest) and eventually moves it into other regions. Because the firm has invested so much money in its development, failure of a new product at this stage costs dearly. Thus, marketers monitor commercialization carefully and attempt to make any necessary adjustments in the product itself, the price, advertising or other promotional methods, or distribution system. The commercialization of a new product begins its life cycle.

A firm that can bring out a product faster than its competitors can enjoy a huge advantage. Several companies have taken steps to speed up the new product development

16. Kurt T. Ulrich and Steven Eppinger, *Product Design and Development* (New York: McGraw-Hill, 1999).

17. J. Paul Peter and Jerry C. Olson, *Consumer Behavior* (New York: McGraw-Hill, 2001).

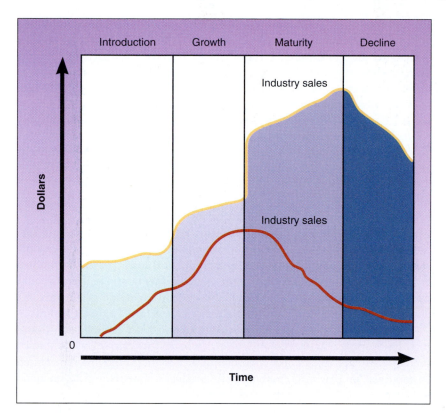

Stages in the Product Life Cycle

process. For instance, Japanese producers of projection televisions developed a new television in one-third the time required by U.S. firms.[18] It is becoming increasingly important that firms get it right the first time when developing products.

14-3b The Product Life Cycle

Like living things, products go through several stages, known as the **product life cycle.**[19] New products enter the market during the introduction stage, they gain momentum and begin to bring a profit during the growth stage, they stabilize during the maturity stage, and finally they fade away in the decline stage. Exhibit 14-4 illustrates the four stages of the product life cycle.

Products pass through these stages over time. For some products, the life cycle may be very short. Fad items such as cartoon-cat Garfield stick-ons for cars lasted for only a few years. Other products, such as black-and-white television sets and microwave ovens, enjoy a life cycle of several decades. Let's examine what generally occurs at each stage of the product life cycle.

Introduction Stage

In the first stage of the product life cycle, a firm makes the new product available to customers, who gradually become aware of it. Profits for a newly introduced product are negative because initial sales are low during this stage and the firm must recover its research and development expenses while it is spending large sums for promotion and distribution. Notice in Exhibit 14-4 that sales move upward from zero, but profits move from below zero. An example of a product currently in the introduction stage is the liquid crystal television.

> **Product Life Cycle**
> The theoretical life of a product, consisting of four stages: introduction, growth, maturity, and decline.

---

18. *Made in Japan: Revitalizing Japanese Manufacturing for Economic Growth* (Tokyo: Japanese Commission on Industrial Performance, 1997).

19. Paolo Frankl and Frieder Rubik, *Life Cycle: Assessment in Industry and Business: Adoption, Patterns, Applications, and Implications* (New York: Spring-Verlag, 2000).

Marketers face several challenges during a product's introduction. They must develop and carry out promotional programs to inform potential customers about the product's availability and its features. Hybrid (gas and electric) vehicles, for instance, cost more than gasoline-powered ones. Marketers face a challenge in convincing car buyers to purchase hybrid cars, and must pick their target markets carefully.[20] Marketing managers must monitor sales, which may be slow, and make early adjustments in the product or in promotional efforts if needed. Many products don't survive the introduction stage. Have you ever heard of Campbell's Red Kettle Soups, Listerine Toothpaste, or Scott's Baby Scott Diapers? How about a graphics compact-disc player? All were brought to the marketplace, but none made it past the first stage of the product life cycle.

Growth Stage

Sales increase more rapidly during the growth stage, and the product begins to generate a profit. Competitors, seeing an opportunity, are likely to enter the market with similar products during this stage. The firm that originated the product may reduce its price as a result of new competition and decreased production costs. For instance, the prices of such growth products as compact-disc players, video cameras, and personal computers fell after manufacturers recovered their initial development costs and other firms began to introduce competing products. As prices fall, profits peak and begin to decline.

A product in the growth stage usually faces intense competition from similar offerings. Firms must rely heavily on repeat purchases for continued sales growth. Marketers therefore attempt to establish consumer loyalty to their products. They often create fresh promotional programs to emphasize the product's benefits and to encourage loyal customers to continue buying the same brand. Current growth stage products include cellular phones and facsimile (fax) machines.

Maturity Stage

During the maturity stage of the product life cycle, sales peak as profits continue to decline. As other products are introduced with new features and improvements, the product may become somewhat outdated. Color television sets and video recorders are examples of products in the maturity stage.

Intense competition from many different firms forces some products out of the market. Companies may cut prices further and increase their promotion budgets to compete for customers. They also may try product improvements, new package designs, and changes in style to encourage consumers to keep buying the product.

Decline Stage

Sales fall rapidly during the decline stage of the product life cycle. Profits also continue to fall, and sometimes additional price-cutting leads to losses. Consumers often prefer new products in earlier stages of their life cycles that provide greater satisfaction or meet different needs or wants. Electric typewriters, for example, are in decline as people increasingly use personal computers. Rotary-dial telephones are also in the decline stage.

Managers must decide at which point to eliminate a product nearing the end of its life cycle. Some products in the decline stage, such as black-and-white televisions, are not immediately eliminated. Sometimes firms generate a profit from decline-stage products by reducing promotional costs and selling to only the most profitable markets.

14-3c Extending the Product Life Cycle

Ideally firms would like their products to remain forever in the growth stage, when profits are highest. Although products eventually reach the decline stage, that some survive for decades is no accident. Firms can extend the life cycle of a product in several ways.

20. Jim Motavalli, *Forward Drive: The Race to Build the Car of the Future* (New York: Sierra Club Books, 2000).

Increasing the Frequency of Use

Marketers commonly try to keep their product sales growing by encouraging consumers to use their goods and services more. Telephone companies, for example, run advertisements using emotional appeals to spur people to call relatives and friends more often. In some markets, Coca-Cola promotes Coke as a morning drink to replace coffee or tea. Toothbrush ads, citing dentists' recommendations, advise consumers to buy a new toothbrush more often, every two or three months.

Identifying New Users

Another way to extend a product's growth stage is to identify new target markets and promote the product to them. Oreo cookies and Frosted Flakes cereal, usually kids' fare, have been targeted to adults. Nintendo has promoted its video system to adults to expand beyond its major category of users, teenage boys.

Finding New Uses

Marketers sometimes maintain and increase sales by showing consumers other ways to use the product. For instance, Kraft has run television commercials explaining how to create a Mexican dip by pouring salsa over Velveeta cheese and putting it in a microwave.[21]

Product Modification

As products encounter fierce competition and reach the maturity stage, firms may need to modify products to compete more effectively. **Product modification** is a life-cycle extension strategy that involves changing a product's quality, features, or style to attract new users or increase usage.

Quality modification means altering the materials used to make the product or changing the production process. Adding longer life to a battery is a quality modification. *Functional modification* is achieved by redesigning a product to provide additional features or benefits. With microcomputer technology, Toshiba enabled its microwave oven to select a power level for cooking based on the weight and density of the food. In an effort to attract new users, Arm & Hammer has expanded its original baking soda into products ranging from kitty litter to deodorant. Changing how a product looks, sounds, smells, or feels results in a *style modification*. Denim jeans have been prewashed, stonewashed, and acid-washed to alter color and reduce their characteristic stiffness.[22]

> **Product Modification**
> The changing of one or more of a product's features as a strategy to extend its life cycle.

14-3d Deleting Products

Products in the decline stage of the product life cycle may become too costly for a firm to continue offering. A company may decide the money would be better spent on developing new products or modifying existing ones that are still profitable. For example, as consumers moved to buying cassettes and compact discs, many music companies stopped making vinyl records.

A firm can delete a product in one of several ways. A *phaseout* approach gradually eliminates the product without any change in the marketing strategy. When using a *runout* strategy, firms may increase distribution and promotion and try to exploit any strengths left in the product. If a product is very unprofitable, a firm often makes an *immediate-drop* decision.

14-4 CREATING PRODUCT IDENTIFICATION

Firms could not succeed in developing and managing products without effectively identifying their products. Consumers must be able to distinguish one product from another. Organizations identify their offerings in three important ways: branding, packaging, and labeling.

---

21. "Kraft Foods, Inc. Reports 2001 Results," www.businesswire.com, accessed January 29, 2002.
22. "Denim Blue Jean Discounters," www.evertize.com/jeans/catalog.htm, accessed October 10, 2002.

14-4a Branding

Brand   A name, sign, symbol, or design a company uses to distinguish its product from others.

Brand Name   The part of a product's brand that can be verbalized in the spoken or written word.

A name, sign, symbol, design, or combination of these used to identify a product and distinguish it from competitors' offerings is called a **brand.** The part of the brand that can be spoken is the **brand name.** The AT&T brand includes the brand name and a design, its stylized globe. Exhibit 14-5 shows some examples of brands.

Firms usually want exclusive use of their brands and take steps to prevent others from using them. A brand registered with the U.S. Patent and Trademark Office is called a *trademark*. A trademark, legally protected, can be used only by its owner. People sometimes identify a brand so closely with a product that they use it for the product itself. Xerox Corporation has run advertisements pointing out that the name Xerox refers only to its products, not to all copy machines. Many brand names, including aspirin, celluloid, lanolin, zipper, and escalator, have become generic terms because their owners failed to protect them.

Firms are acutely aware of the importance of brand names. Good names sell products. Firms often search for short names that are easy to pronounce and easy to remember, such as Sprite, Tide, or Suave. Names can suggest the product's function (L'Eggs pantyhose) or its performance (SupraLife, Energizer, and Duracell batteries). Brand names must also fit the image the company desires for its product, like the Jaguar car or Joy perfume.

Types of Brands

Brands are classified as manufacturer, private, or generic. A *manufacturer* (or producer) brand is owned and used by the manufacturer or service provider. Firms often use manufacturer brands to market products throughout the United States and abroad in many stores and outlets. Such brands identify who makes the products and provide the consumer with a nationally known, uniform, and widely available product such as Butternut bread, Lee jeans, or Chevrolet trucks.

A *private* (or store) *brand* is owned by a wholesaler or retailer. Examples of private brands include Sears' Die Hard and A & P's Master Choice. A firm offering private brands often can sell them at lower prices, achieve higher profits, and encourage customer loyalty. Most products sold under private brands are produced by companies that also market products under manufacturer brands. These firms find this practice profitable because they can use any excess production capacity and greatly reduce their marketing costs. For example, Whirlpool makes the refrigerators Sears sells under its Kenmore brand. The number of private label brands is growing in response to value-conscious consumers who demand higher-level quality at a reasonable price.[23] Private label brands now account for about 12 percent of supermarket spending, the top products being milk and bread.[24]

Some products have no brand name at all. These are *generic products*, usually sold in simple, no-frill packages that identify only the contents. Many grocery items such as canned vegetables, cereals, crackers, and paper goods are available as generics. Generic products offer consumers an alternative to manufacturer and private brands. By using plain packages and keeping advertising to a minimum, producers and stores can sell generics at reduced prices. Sometimes, but not always, products sold as generics are not uniform in size or appearance or are of lower quality than branded goods.

Today even people are thought of in terms of being a brand. Tavis Smiley's story in the Focus on Careers box, "Be Your Own Brand," illustrates how he branded himself.

Brand Loyalty

Consumers frequently buy only their favorite brands of certain products. They will not switch brands even if an alternative is offered at a lower price. *Brand loyalty* is the extent to which a consumer prefers a particular brand.

EXHIBIT 14-5

Product Identity: Brands

Sources: Mr. DJ logo reproduced with permission of Mr. DJ; AT&T logo reproduced with permission of AT&T Corp.; and YAHOO! logo reproduced with permission of Yahoo!, Inc. © 2003 by Yahoo! Inc. YAHOO! and the YAHOO! logo are trademarks of Yahoo! Inc.

23. Arthur C. Martinez and Charles Madigan, *The Hard Road to the Softer Side: Lessons from The Transformation of Sears* (New York: Crown Business Publications, 2001).

24. Marcia Mogelonsky, "When Stores Become Brands," *American Demographics*, February 1995, pp. 32–38.

FOCUS ON CAREERS

Be Your Own Brand

Tavis Smiley was fired as the host and executive producer of Black Entertainment Television (BET) with Tavis Smiley. Within weeks after leaving BET, Smiley closed a number of deals as a correspondent for ABC's Good Morning America and CNN's Primetime Live. He believes that he "branded and promoted" himself to find his new work pattern. He made his name, experience, and skills work for him. He is a firm believer in "personal branding."

Smiley recommends a number of "personal branding" action steps that can work for anyone:

1. *Find your niche*—Who are you? What are you? You have to find your niche, which is a natural extension of yourself. Don't use your job to describe yourself.

2. *Determine if your brand is marketable*—Examine the market, the environment, and the demand. You must do your own homework, listen to feedback, and not try to appeal to everyone. Focus on a niche market and think in a way to narrow it down.

   When martial arts expert Bill Blanks decided he wanted to create a new form of exercise called Tae Bo (a combination of aerobics, martial arts, and boxing), he tried it first on a target market. He listened to feedback and fine-tuned his exercise. He found his narrow niche.

3. *Seek professional help*—Find the best professional to coach, guide, and support you.

4. *Promotion, promotion, promotion*—Test your ideas and get feedback. Speak for free just to sell yourself. You have to be a self-promoter.

5. *Network your brand*—Think in terms of making and using strategic alliances. Use all your network sources to keep yourself and the brand you are creating visible.

6. *Going beyond the brand*—Even if you can't be there, audiotapes, videotapes, books, and printed speeches can be there. You can be all over by going beyond physically being somewhere in person.

Whether you are a manager, owner, or worker you can gain stature, power, and prestige by branding yourself.

Source: Ann Brown, "Brand Yourself," *Black Enterprise*, March 2002, pp. 74–79.

Marketers measure consumers' brand loyalty at three stages. The first, *brand recognition*, means consumers are familiar with a manufacturer's product. Buyers are more likely to choose a brand they recognize than an unfamiliar one. At the second stage of brand loyalty, *brand preference*, consumers will buy the product if it is available. At the third stage, *brand insistence*, buyers will not accept a substitute for their favorite brand.

The degree of brand loyalty varies from customer to customer and from product to product. A study by J. D. Powers & Associates found that older car buyers are twice as loyal to a particular make as younger customers. [25] Firms attempt to establish brand loyalty through the product's performance, packaging, price, and advertising and other promotional efforts. Loyalty keeps consumers coming back for more. Are you a brand-loyal consumer? The values and attitudes quiz in Exhibit 14-6 will help you find out.

25. William R. Diem, "Bond Stronger with Age," *Advertising Age*, March 28, 1994, pp. 5–6, 42–43.

Are You a Brand-Loyal Consumer?

Directions: Test your brand loyalty to the toothpaste you use. Answer the following questions; then discuss your classmates' responses.

1. The last time you bought toothpaste, what brand did you buy?

   _____

2. Was price a major factor in your most recent toothpaste purchase?

   _____ Yes _____ No

3. Do you ever buy other brands of toothpaste?

   _____ Yes _____ No

4. Would you switch brands for a lower price?

   _____ Yes _____ No

5. If the store were out of the brand you bought most recently, would you buy a different brand?

   _____ Yes _____ No

6. Would you consider buying a new brand of toothpaste being introduced to the market?

   _____ Yes _____ No

Feedback: Although the quiz considered only one product, it should help you see how brand loyalty pertains to one consumer—you. If you said yes to all the questions, you are not at all brand loyal about toothpaste. If you answered no every time, you are extremely loyal. You would insist on one brand whenever you buy toothpaste. If you answered some questions yes and others no, you prefer one brand but would consider switching. You would be the target of competitors looking for customers!

Discuss with your classmates how they answered the quiz. Give possible reasons why some people are brand loyal to toothpaste while others are not. How important are differences between individuals, such as when and where they shop, financial situations, interest in finding a bargain, family shopping patterns, or willingness to try new things? Answer the questions again for other products—soft drinks, shampoo, fast food, shoes. You may find your brand loyalty varies from one product to another.

Brand Strategies

A company can use either individual branding or family branding when developing brands for its products. *Individual branding* requires creating a different brand for every product. It establishes separate identities for different products and thus helps target products to different market segments. Also, with individual branding, problems with one product seldom influence the success of other products in the line.

With *family branding*, a firm uses the same brand for most or all of its products. Many companies adopt this strategy to develop a product mix with a recognized brand name. Pepperidge Farm, for example, employs family branding. All of its breads, cookies, crackers, and desserts bear the Pepperidge Farm brand name. A company using the same brand for most or all of its products often uses similar packaging for all the products, too.

An interesting case of a branding strategy has been employed by a Chinese painter, Chen Yifei. His story is described in the Focus on Business box, "From Communism to Capitalism."

14-4b Packaging

Packaging The development of a container and a graphic design for a product.

Packaging involves designing a product container that will identify the product, protect it, and attract the attention of buyers. It is important to both consumers and manufacturers. Packaging can make a product easier to use, safer, and more versatile. It can also affect consumers' attitudes toward a product, which in turn affect their purchase decisions.

Originally, packages were designed mostly for their functional value; they protected products from damage or spoilage. Today packaging also has significance as a marketing tool. To develop an appealing package that will catch the buyer's eye, marketers consider not only function but also shape, color, size, and graphic design.

FOCUS ON BUSINESS

From Communism to Capitalism

The times have changed. Chen Yifei painted some of the most inspiring propaganda canvases glorifying the communist dream of the cultural revolution in China. Chen now has become one of China's boldest entrepreneurs. Just as Martha Stewart did in the United States, Chen has built a lifestyle brand around his own personality. During the Cultural Revolution, Chen was painting workers, soldiers, and peasants expressing communism. Today he's designing logos and brands to further his latest cause—creating a luxury label made in China.

"Luxury" and "brand" are not words usually associated with China, one of the cheaper manufacturers in the world. The country's most popular brand of consumer goods-makers, Haier and Konka and PC Maker Legend, use a simple strategy: to turn a profit, sell as much as possible at low prices.

Yifei is working to turn the profit-at-low-prices formula on it head. With its Layefe fashion label and just-launched *Vision Magazine*, the company is eyeing a newly emerging market of young, upper-middle class professionals who demand chic designs and high quality. It is a niche market that is expanding rapidly.

Chen has become quite an entrepreneur. He has taken money earned from the sale of signature portraits he paints to fund his business ventures. He has started eight companies under the Yifei group since 1996 without taking on debt. "If I need more money, I'll just sell a few more paintings," says Chen.

Chen's fashion company, Layefe, recorded a profit of $3.6 million in 2001, on sales of $36 million. One reason for its success is the label's unique market position as a local Chinese brand with international flair.

Source: Suh-kyung Yoon, "Shanghai Chic," *Far Eastern Economic Review,* March 21, 2002, pp. 3436–3438.

Firms work to create innovative packages to meet the needs of the consumers they want to reach. For example, after a scientific study reported that taking an aspirin a day can ward off first heart attacks, Bayer promptly designed "calendar paks." These packages contain 28 aspirins in separate blister compartments, to help buyers keep track of whether they took their daily aspirin tablet. Other innovations are Clorox's no-splash spouts on bleach containers, Armour's Golden Star Fresh Packs with deli meats individually wrapped in two-slice servings, and Wella's So Fine Shampoo Mist in a self-pressurized spray applicator that eliminates spills.

The trend toward clear bottles illustrates the many uses of packaging. Clear bottles can create an image of a product that is purer, milder, and lighter. They can be made of recycled plastic and can contain less material than thicker, opaque bottles, and they let customers see how much the package contains. A host of products are packaged in clear packages, including beverages, dish detergents, and deodorants.[26]

Packaging has become an important aspect of product safety. Since 1982, when eight Chicago-area people died from Tylenol capsules injected with cyanide, manufacturers have developed tamper-proof packages for products such as medicines, foods (peanut butter, catsup), and personal care items (toothpaste). Products available in safety-sealed packages satisfy an additional consumer need.

The impact of packaging on the environment has become another critical issue many manufacturers are facing. Packages from foods and consumer goods make up much of the

26. See www.d2products.com/BRYAN.htm, accessed April 26, 2002.

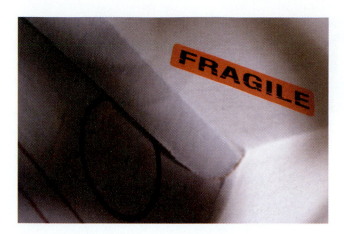

tons of waste dumped into landfills each day in the United States. In response, some firms are changing packaging and products. Kellogg Company puts its cereals into boxes made from recycled paper, and manufacturers now make disposable diapers such as Pampers and Luvs with half the amount of material as before. In spite of such efforts, groups such as the Environmental Action Foundation and the U.S. Public Interest Research Group continue to criticize companies for developing wasteful packages.

14-4c Labeling

> **Labeling**   The display of important information on a product package.

Manufacturers communicate with buyers through **labeling.** The label is the part of the package that identifies the brand and provides essential product information regarding contents, size, weight, quantity, ingredients, directions for use, shelf life, and any health hazards or dangers of improper use.

Labels also provide the means for automatic checkout and inventory monitoring. The universal product code (UPC), an electronic bar code on labels that identifies manufacturers and products, enables supermarkets and other stores to use computerized scanners at the checkout counter. Not only do scanners save time and help keep down costs, they also compile complete sales records valuable to both stores and manufacturers.

The Consumer Product Safety Commission and the Food and Drug Administration require that labels indicate warnings, instructions, and manufacturer's identification. Federal laws mandate that labels include content information and potential hazards. Manufacturers are required to be truthful in listing product ingredients on labels. Ingredients must be listed in order, beginning with the ingredient that constitutes the largest percentage of the product down to the ingredient that makes up the smallest percentage. Snack chips that contain more vegetable oil than potatoes, for example, must be labeled to show oils as the first ingredient.

14-5 PRICING

The price of a product is one of its most important aspects for both sellers and buyers. The opening vignette on micropricing illustrates the role the Internet was expected to play in micropricing. Many terms are used to represent price: taxi *fare*, insurance *premium*, *micropayment*, parking *fine*, apartment *rent*, and, let's not forget, income *tax*. No matter how it is expressed, **price** represents the value consumers exchange in a marketing transaction.

> **Price**   The value that buyers exchange for a product in the marketing transaction.

Money usually is the commodity exchanged for a product that satisfies a consumer need. But sometimes money isn't involved at all; the parties exchange goods or services instead. Children trade baseball cards. Teenagers may do yard work to earn use of the family car. A retail store and a radio station may work out a deal to trade merchandise for free radio ads. Such trading, called *barter*, is the oldest form of exchange used in all societies.

The pricing decision is crucial for marketers because price is highly visible to consumers and greatly affects purchase decisions. After noticing a product, buyers generally look at the price tag. Prices that consumers perceive as too high will deter them from buying. The opening story focused on the use of "micropayments" and their use on the Internet. The failure of this approach indicates that consumers are conscious of "how" they are to make payments as much as they care about "how much."

14-6 PRICING OBJECTIVES

Before establishing prices, marketing managers must decide their pricing objectives. Survival is the most fundamental one; firms will tolerate financial losses and other difficulties if needed for survival. Besides survival, firms use price to increase sales and market share, boost profits, achieve a return on their investment, and maintain their present position in the industry.

14-6a Market Share

A firm's *market share* is its percentage of the total industry sales in the geographical area where it sells its products. Maintaining or increasing market share is a common pricing objective. Many firms use market share figures to assess their performance. An increase in sales may help a company reduce production costs and achieve higher profits since it is cheaper on a per unit basis to produce more goods or offer more services. Firms sometimes lower prices to try to capture a larger share of the market. Canon, for instance, attempted to increase market share by offering basic copiers in the $1,000 to $1,200 range when the low-end copier on the market was priced around $2,000.

14-6b Profit

Of course the objective of many companies is to maximize profit. But in practice, defining "maximum profit" is difficult. No matter how profitable a firm becomes, it still may not have reached a point of maximum profit. Most firms express this pricing objective as a percentage increase over current profits; for example, a company's pricing objective may be to increase profit by 10 percent in one year.

14-6c Return on Investment

Return on investment (ROI) is the amount of profit earned, expressed as a percentage of the total investment. ROI is sometimes more desirable as a pricing objective than is profit maximization, because it is a better measure of a firm's operating performance. For instance, the typical ROI in the automobile industry is 20 percent per year.

14-6d Status Quo

Firms wishing to maintain their present situation in the industry may establish status quo pricing objectives. A company that wants to meet (but not beat) competitors' prices, develop a favorable public image, or maintain its market share would favor status quo pricing objectives. By maintaining price stability, a firm reduces the risk it could face in a climate of price competition. For instance, when several airlines planned price hikes in the late 1980s, a few airlines lowered their airfares. Most competitors then matched the price cuts, and all the airlines lost revenues from the resulting lack of price stability.

14-7 FACTORS IN PRICING DECISIONS

A firm cannot determine a product's price without considering several factors that affect price. Managers must take into account the use of price and nonprice competition, supply and demand, and consumer perceptions of price.

14-7a Price and Nonprice Competition

The pricing decision is influenced by the extent to which firms decide to use price as a competitive tool. Some rely heavily on price competition while others compete on aspects other than price. Firms competing on **price competition** generally set prices equal to or lower than competitors' prices. Car rental companies often compete based on price competition by emphasizing economy rates.

> **Price Competition**   A policy of using price to differentiate a product in the marketplace.

A firm competing based on price must be prepared to change prices quickly and frequently in response to competitors' price changes. One drawback to this strategy is that competitors can easily reduce their prices to counter it. Price competition is practiced by firms in many different industries, such as hotels, electronics component manufacturers, and automakers.

> **Nonprice Competition**   A policy of emphasizing aspects other than price, such as quality, service, or promotion, to sell products.

Nonprice competition involves competing based on factors other than price, such as quality or service. This strategy is useful in building brand loyalty. Customers who prefer a brand for reasons other than price are less likely to switch to a brand that costs less. For instance, consumers who pay thousands of dollars for a Rolex watch are not likely to switch brands because of a lower price. Several firms in the athletic shoe industry use nonprice competition and emphasize the benefits and styling of their brands.

14-7b Supply and Demand

The economic forces of supply and demand also influence the price of a product. The penny you pull out of your pocket is worth just that—a penny. But a coin collector may pay a great deal for a rare penny. That's the principle of supply and demand at work. **Supply** refers to the quantity of a product that producers will sell at various prices. The **demand** for a product is the quantity that consumers will purchase at different prices. For most products, quantity demanded goes up as the price goes down; quantity demanded goes down as the price goes up.

> **Supply**   The quantity of a product that producers will sell at various prices.
>
> **Demand**   The quantity of a product that consumers will purchase at various prices.

Exhibit 14-7 shows a supply and demand curve for video recorders. The curve marked S is a typical supply curve. The supply curve slopes upward to the right, which means manufacturers are willing to offer more DVDs for sale when they can receive higher prices. The number of items supplied increases as price increases. The demand curve, labeled D, slopes downward to the right. This means that consumers are willing to buy more DVDs at lower prices; the number of items demanded goes up as price goes down.

The point at which the two curves intersect is called the equilibrium point, E on the graph. At this point, the quantity supplied equals the quantity demanded. In our example, a manufacturer is willing to supply 20,000 DVDs at a price of $200, and consumers will buy 20,000 DVDs at $200 each. If the manufacturer makes more than 20,000 DVDs, or prices them higher than $200, not all DVDs will be sold.

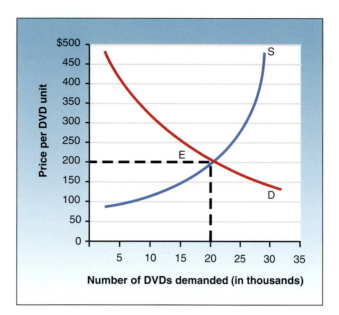

EXHIBIT 14-7

Supply and Demand Curve: DVDs

14-7c Consumer Perceptions of Price

Pricing decisions also require firms to consider consumers' perceptions of price. Price may be the top consideration in the buying decision of some consumers, while to others it may be much less important. The importance of price varies a great deal for different products and different target markets.

Buyers generally believe price is closely related to quality. For products such as wine, jewelry, and perfume, a higher price signals higher quality to the target market. In such cases, firms can use price to establish an image of product superiority. A person shopping for a diamond ring may expect a high price and be skeptical of lower-priced gems.

14-8 PRICING METHODS

After establishing pricing objectives and considering various factors that influence price, a firm decides on a **pricing method,** a procedure used to determine prices on a regular basis. When selecting a pricing method, a company takes into account the product, the market, and sales volume. The method used to price products in a hardware store carrying thousands of items must be fairly simple. On the other hand, calculating the price of a bridge or a dam would be complex. In this section, we examine three common pricing methods: cost-oriented, demand-oriented, and competition-oriented pricing.

> **Pricing Method**   A systematic procedure for determining prices on a regular basis; considers costs, product demand, or competitors' prices.

14-8a Cost-Oriented Pricing

Firms such as supermarkets, department stores, and discount stores that sell numerous products often use a **cost-oriented pricing** method. They calculate prices by determining a product's total cost and adding on a percentage called the **markup.** The markup covers additional expenses incurred in marketing a product and allows the store to make a profit.

The percentage of the markup varies substantially from one product category to another but is often standardized across an industry. For instance, the markup for hardware is around 35 percent, while the markup for greeting cards is about 100 percent. How would you determine the price of a greeting card? Suppose that the total cost of producing one greeting card is 50 cents and the markup is 100 percent above costs. The price of the greeting card would be $1 (50 cents + 100 percent of 50 cents).

> **Cost-Oriented Pricing**   A method whereby a firm determines a product's total cost, then adds a markup to that cost to achieve the desired profit margin.
>
> **Markup**   In cost-oriented pricing, a percentage added to the total cost of the product to cover marketing expenses and allow a profit.

The major difficulty in using a cost-oriented pricing method is determining the actual markup percentage. If a firm uses a markup percentage that is too low, it underprices the product and loses potential profit. If the markup percentage is too high, the product is overpriced, and the firm may not sell enough units to cover costs.

14-8b Demand-Oriented Pricing

Demand-Oriented Pricing
A method based on the level of demand for the product.

Breakeven Analysis
A determination of how many product units must be sold at various prices for a firm to recover costs and begin making a profit.

Breakeven Quantity   The point at which the cost of making a product equals the revenue made from selling the product.

Incorporating the level of demand for the product into the pricing decision is **demand-oriented pricing.** A strong level of demand means that prices can be high. Where demand is weak, prices must be lower. The price of houses, for example, fluctuates with demand (as well as interest rates). Home prices in the San Francisco Bay area are extremely high because of the great demand for houses in a relatively small area.

In using demand-oriented pricing, firms estimate the quantities of a product that consumers will demand at various prices. A technique called **breakeven analysis** can help a manager determine how many product units must be sold at various prices for a firm to break even—to recover the costs of production and marketing and to begin making a profit. The **breakeven quantity,** the quantity beyond which profits occur, is reached when the total revenue for all units sold is equal to the total cost of all units sold. Total revenue, or all income from product sales, is obtained by multiplying the number of units sold by the selling price.

Besides total revenue, marketers must consider various business costs to calculate the breakeven quantity. *Fixed costs* are expenses that remain constant regardless of the number of units produced. Insurance, rent, and equipment are fixed costs. *Variable costs* are those that change depending on the number of units produced. Costs for raw materials and labor, for example, rise when more units are produced and fall when fewer units are produced. Fixed costs plus variable costs equal the total cost of producing a specific number of units.

Exhibit 14-8 shows how the breakeven quantity is calculated for college textbooks. A publishing company has fixed production costs of $100,000. The variable costs are $20 per book, meaning the company incurs a cost of $20 for every book produced. Suppose the textbook sells for $40. The breakeven quantity is calculated as follows:

$$\text{Breakeven quantity} = \frac{\text{Fixed costs}}{\text{Price} - \text{Variable costs}}$$

In our example, the breakeven quantity is:

$$\frac{\$100{,}000}{\$40 - \$20} = \frac{\$100{,}000}{\$20} = 5{,}000 \text{ textbooks}$$

If 5,000 textbooks are sold, the publisher's total costs (both fixed and variable) will be recovered. Take another look at the graph in Exhibit 14-8. The breakeven quantity can be found where the total revenue line and the total cost line intersect. If more than 5,000 books are sold at $40, the publisher will generate a profit. Sales below 5,000 books will result in a loss.

A firm can use breakeven analysis to figure the profits and losses that would result from several different possible prices by calculating the breakeven quantity for each price. In our example, if the publishing firm reduces the price to $32, it would need to sell 8,333 books to break even. Raising the price to $48 would lower the breakeven quantity to 3,571 books. Marketers must rely on their research and experience to estimate how many units can be sold at each potential price. Then they can compare their estimated sales with the breakeven quantities to find the most appropriate price, the one at which sales will exceed the breakeven quantity and result in a profitable venture.

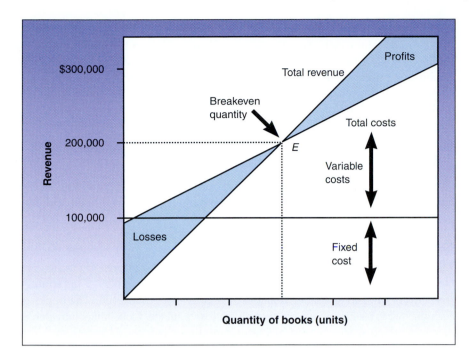

EXHIBIT 14-8

**Breakeven Analysis
for Textbooks**

14-8c Competition-Oriented Pricing

In the two pricing methods we have discussed, costs and demand are the major considerations in setting a price. In **competition-oriented pricing,** firms consider the prices charged by competitors as the major factor in setting their own prices. Competition-oriented pricing is appealing, especially to retailers, because it is simple. It involves no complex calculations; prices are simply set close to (preferably below) competitors' prices. This method is useful when a firm's pricing objective is to increase sales or market share.

Firms find competition-based pricing especially important when fierce price competition exists in the market or when competing products are very similar. Customers often use price to select a service provider, especially when services are quite comparable. If students perceive all copy shops to do work of similar quality, they are likely to select the one that charges the lowest price per copy. Likewise, if customers view all banks as similar, they will probably select the one that charges the lowest checking account fee.

> **Competition-Oriented Pricing**
> A method whereby a firm sets prices on the basis of its competitors' prices rather than its own costs and revenues.

14-9 PRICING STRATEGIES

Once a firm selects a pricing method, it develops a strategy for setting and adjusting prices. We will examine four common pricing strategies: pioneer pricing, psychological pricing, professional pricing, and price discounting.

14-9a Pioneer Pricing

A firm setting a price for a new product may use **pioneer pricing.** There are two pioneer pricing strategies: price skimming and penetration pricing.

> **Pioneer Pricing**   New-product pricing strategy of charging the highest possible price to regain costs quickly (price skimming) or setting the price below competitors' prices to build sales quickly (penetration pricing).

Price Skimming

Firms using *price skimming* charge the highest price possible during the introduction stage of the product life cycle. The purpose of this strategy is to "skim" the best buyers from the top of the market—those willing to pay a high price. When manufacturers introduced compact-disc players, they priced them fairly high. However, prices of personal computers have dropped substantially since their introduction. Price skimming helps firms recover development costs more quickly and also may help to keep the quantity demanded down during product introduction, when production capacities may be limited.

Penetration Pricing

Some firms prefer to set prices low when offering a product for the first time. *Penetration pricing*, used to generate a large sales volume and gain a substantial market share quickly, establishes prices for new products below what competitors charge. Firms introducing consumer goods such as cosmetics, soups, or cleansers often use this strategy. One drawback is less flexibility than price skimming; raising a penetration price is more difficult than lowering a skimming price.

14-9b Psychological Pricing

Psychological Pricing   A policy that encourages purchase decisions based on emotion rather than reason; includes odd-even pricing, customary pricing, prestige pricing, and price lining.

Psychological pricing strategies encourage consumers to make purchase decisions on an emotional rather than a rational basis. Such strategies include odd-even pricing, customary pricing, prestige pricing, and price lining.

Odd-Even Pricing

Marketers sometimes try to influence buyers' perceptions of price by using certain numbers. In *odd pricing,* prices end with odd numbers, such as $98.99. This strategy assumes that buyers will perceive the product as a bargain—less than $100. The opposite strategy, *even pricing,* is used to give a product an exclusive image. Consumers may perceive a pair of slacks priced at $98 to be of higher quality than a pair priced at $97.95.

Customary Pricing

When firms price products based on tradition, they use *customary pricing.* Products such as candy bars, gum, magazines, and mass transit are priced according to this strategy. A company introducing a new candy bar probably would charge the same price that consumers already pay for other candy bars.

Prestige Pricing

An organization that sets an unusually high price to provide a quality image for a product uses *prestige pricing.* This strategy is most useful when buyers perceive a relationship between the item's price and its quality; indeed, they may have second thoughts about purchasing the product if it does not cost enough. Prestige pricing is used for products such as furs, jewelry, and perfume.

Price Lining

In *price lining,* sellers set a limited number of prices for selected lines of merchandise. These prices reflect various ranges in which consumers concentrate their purchases. For instance, a clothing store may sell a line of men's shirts for $22, $30, and $36. By holding prices constant within a certain range, price lining simplifies pricing decisions of sellers and purchasing decisions of consumers.

14-9c Professional Pricing

Professional Pricing   A policy—practiced by doctors, lawyers, and others with skills or experience in a particular field—of charging a standard fee for a particular service.

People with great amounts of training and skill in different fields use **professional pricing.** Doctors, lawyers, accountants, and many other professionals charge standard fees that reflect the expertise required to perform their jobs. For instance, a doctor may charge $30 for an office visit and $100 for a physical examination.

14-9d Price Discounting

Price Discounting   A policy of offering buyers deductions from the price of a product.

Many sellers engage in **price discounting,** offering customers deductions from the price of a product. Sellers often give cash discounts for prompt payment. A seller may specify a *cash discount* of "2/10 net 30," which means that a 2 percent discount is offered if the account is paid in ten days and that the full balance is due in thirty days. *Quantity discounts* are provided to customers who buy on a large basis. Producers offer *trade discounts* to other sellers for performing various functions such as transporting, storing, and selling goods.

Discounts during times of lower demand are common. Because of the perishable nature of services (unused capacity cannot be stored), service providers often use price to increase demand during slow periods. Movie theaters, for instance, charge less for morning and afternoon shows than for evening shows. Some health clubs drop prices during the summer. Telephone companies reduce rates for late night or weekend long-distance calls.

Another pricing practice growing among service firms is *bundling,* which involves selling two or more services in one package for a special price.[27] An example of bundling is an airline package that includes air travel, car rental, and hotel accommodations.

14-10 THE ROLE OF PROMOTION

Promotion, an important element in the marketing mix, supports products, pricing, and distribution decisions. It is critical to the success of any firm. Before deciding what type of promotional program to conduct, a firm needs to establish its objectives.

> **Promotion**
> The communication of favorable, persuasive information about a firm or product in order to influence potential buyers.

14-10a Promotional Objectives

Firms set promotional objectives that will help meet their broader marketing and organizational objectives. Promotional programs can be built around a single objective or multiple objectives.

Informing

The basic objective underlying all promotion is providing information. Firms want to tell potential customers about themselves as well as what products are available, where they can be purchased, and for what price. A new restaurant, for example, may advertise in local newspapers or magazines and on radio and television stations, distribute coupons in the mail, invite the newspaper restaurant critic to review and publicize it, rent billboards, and buy a listing in the telephone directory.

Increasing Sales

Aside from providing information, encouraging prospective customers to purchase products is the most common promotional objective, since sales mean survival and success for firms. Using advertisements, coupons, and other promotional methods, firms attempt to persuade customers to buy new products, remind them of the benefits of products that have been on the market awhile, and reinforce their choice of particular brands.

Stabilizing Sales

Firms also rely on promotional activities to reduce or eliminate substantial variations in demand throughout the year. Companies marketing seasonal products may step up promotional efforts during slow times of the year to use production facilities and distribution systems most effectively.

Positioning the Product

Often a firm uses promotion to position a product as different or superior to competing products. *Positioning* means emphasizing certain product features to create a specific image for the product and add to its appeal. Firms often rely on advertising to position products.

Building a Public Image

Sometimes a company wants to develop a certain image through promotion. Publicity and, to a lesser extent, advertising provide effective vehicles for image building. Mobil, for example, sponsors programs on public television stations to provide quality entertainment for viewers and to foster goodwill toward the corporation.

---

27. "Jet Fax Announces Bundling Agreement with Hewlett-Packard," *Business Wire,* February 23, 1998, pp. 1–3.

14-10b The Promotion Mix

To inform, influence, and remind customers in their target markets or the general public, firms use personal selling (person-to-person approach) and advertising, sales promotion, and publicity (nonpersonal approaches). How these four elements are combined to promote specific products is called the **promotion mix.**

A promotion mix may contain any or all of the four elements, depending on the firm's objectives, promotional strategy, product characteristics, and target market characteristics. As you read further it will become clear that technology has changed the impact of the promotion mix on consumers' purchasing decisions.

> **Promotion Mix**
> The combination of advertising, personal selling, sales promotion, and publicity used to promote a specific product.

14-11 ADVERTISING

Any paid form of nonpersonal communication to a target audience through a mass medium such as television, newspapers, or magazines is **advertising.** Of all promotional activities, consumers are most familiar with advertising. We see and hear many advertisements every day. Organizations and individuals spend over $240 billion on advertising in the United States each year.[28] Exhibit 14-9 will give you an idea of how much money ten large companies can spend to advertise their products to consumers.

Advertising can be quite expensive, especially using national media with immense audiences. For instance, the cost of a thirty-second commercial during the 2002 Super Bowl was over $2 million.[29] Since some 50 million American households watch the game each year, advertisers such as PepsiCo, Anheuser-Busch, Nike, and other companies believe the exposure their products receive from these advertisements makes the cost worthwhile. The average cost of making a national television commercial is $350,000.[30] Firms often find advertising to be cost-effective, however. It can reach a vast number of people at a low cost per person. It is also quite flexible, since advertisers can choose outlets to reach audiences of any size or demographic makeup. Ads can be repeated as often as sponsors wish.

> **Advertising** A paid form of nonpersonal communication to a target audience through a mass medium such as television, newspapers, or magazines.

14-11a Types of Advertising

An advertiser can use any of several different types of advertising, depending on its promotional objectives. Companies advertise brands, industries advertise products, and firms or individuals advertise themselves, their activities, and their beliefs. We examine three major categories of advertising: primary-demand, selective (brand), and institutional.

Primary-Demand Advertising

At times organizations want to create or increase demand for all products in a product group. In this case, they use **primary-demand advertising.** The Florida Department of Citrus, for instance, sponsors advertisements to persuade consumers to buy and drink more orange juice. Their advertisements promote orange juice without mentioning any particular brand or producer.

> **Primary-Demand Advertising**
> Advertising used to create demand for all products in a product group.

Selective Advertising

Most often a firm wants to create selective demand, or demand for a specific brand of product rather than for other, competing products. **Selective (brand) advertising** makes up the majority of advertising; marketers of virtually all goods and services use it in their promotion mixes. Over $15 billion is spent each year to advertise automobiles, $14 billion to advertise food, and over $22 billion to advertise financial and insurance services.[31]

> **Selective (Brand) Advertising**
> Advertising used to sell a specific product or brand.

28. David A. Aaker, V. Kumar, George S. Day, and George Day, *Marketing Research* (New York: Wiley, 2000).

29. "Super Bowl XXXVI Preview: By the Numbers," www.cnnsi.com, accessed January 31, 2002.

30. Ariane Herra, "AAAA TV Production Survey Show Largest Cost in 13 Years," *New Release,* November 20, 2000.

31. "100 Leading National Advertisers," *Advertising Age,* August 2001, p. 80.

	Company	Annual Advertising Expenditures ($ in millions)
1	General Motors	$3,935
2	Philip Morris	2,603
3	Proctor & Gamble	2,364
4	Ford Motor Company	2,345
5	Pfizer	2,265
6	PepsiCo	2,101
7	DaimlerChrysler	1,984
8	AOL-Time Warner	1,770
9	Walt Disney	1,757
10	Verizon Communications	1,613

EXHIBIT 14-9

Expenditures by Leading U.S. Advertisers

Source: "U.S. Leading Advertisers," *Advertising Age*, 2001, pp. 50–52.

Sometimes a firm compares its brand of product to another in advertisements. *Comparative advertising* identifies competitors and claims the superiority of the sponsor's brand. Selective advertising has grown in popularity during the last decade. A study conducted by Research Systems Corporation found comparative advertising most effective when it involved indirect comparative claims made by new products.[32]

Institutional Advertising

When an organization desires primarily to build goodwill and create a favorable public image rather than promote a specific product, it employs **institutional advertising.** Philip Morris continues to advertise the fact that it is engaged in cleaning up and protecting the environment. This promotion is a form of goodwill that shows the firm is doing much more than produce cigarettes.

> **Institutional Advertising**
> Advertising used to build goodwill and create a favorable public image.

14-11b Advertising Media

The different outlets that present advertisements are called **advertising media.** The most commonly used are newspapers, television, direct mail, radio, magazines, and the yellow pages. Advertising on the Internet is a new phenomenon that constitutes less than 2 percent of all advertising expenditure.[33]

To obtain the greatest benefit from these media expenditures, advertisers must develop an effective **media plan** that selects the specific media (particular newspapers, radio and television stations, etc.) to be used and the dates and times that advertisements will appear. The marketer or skilled media planner developing the media plan tries to communicate with the largest number of persons in the target market per dollar spent on media.

In developing the media plan, the planner must decide which kinds of media to use. The strengths and weaknesses of the major advertising media, shown in Exhibit 14-10, influence this decision.

> **Advertising Media** Advertising outlets, including newspapers, television, direct mail, radio, magazines, and outdoor displays.

> **Media Plan** Selection of specific media in which advertisements will be run and when they will be run to reach the target markets.

14-11c Developing Advertising Campaigns

Firms go to considerable effort and expense to design, create, and evaluate advertisements that will accomplish their promotional goals. For example, to lure overseas business, American Express launched a $100 million campaign that featured sixty advertisements seen in nearly thirty nations.[34] Developing an effective advertising campaign generally takes these steps:

32. Leah Rickard, "New Ammo for Comparative Ads," *Advertising Age*, February 14, 1994, p. 26.

33. Beth Snyder Bulik, "Digital Marketing Hits the Mainstream," *Business 2.0*, March 12, 2001, pp. 30–34.

34. Jon Berry, "Don't Leave Home Without It, Wherever You Live," *Business Week*, February 21, 1994, pp. 76–77.

**Strengths and Weaknesses
of Advertising Media**

Medium	Types	Strengths	Weaknesses
Newspapers	Daily Weekly Special	Accessible to almost everyone; national geographic flexibility; short lead time; frequent publication; favorable for cooperative advertising; merchandising services	Not selective for socioeconomic groups; short life; limited reproduction capabilities; large advertising volume limits exposure to any one advertisement
Magazines	Consumer Business National Local Regional	Socioeconomic selectivity; good reproduction; long life; prestige; geographic selectivity when regional issues are available; read in leisurely manner	High absolute dollar cost; long lead time
Television	Network Local CATV	Reaches large audience; low cost per exposure; uses audio and video; highly visible; high prestige; geographic and socioeconomic selectivity	High dollar cost; short life of message; size of audience not guaranteed; amount of prime time limited
Radio	AM FM	Highly mobile; lost-cost broadcast medium; message can be quickly changed; can reach a large audience; geographic selectivity; socioeconomic selectivity	Provides only audio message; has lost prestige; short life of message; listeners' attention limited because of other activities while listening
Direct mail	Letters Flyers Catalogs Samples Coupons Price lists	Little wasted circulation; controlled by advertiser; few distractions; personal; stimulates actions; use of novelty; relatively easy-to-measure performance hidden from competitors	Expensive; no editorial matter to attract readers; considered junk mail by many; criticized as invasion of privacy
Outdoor displays	Painted buildings and vehicles Posters Billboards Electric spectaculars	Allows for repetition; low cost; message can be placed close to the point of sale; geographic selectivity; operable 24 hours a day	Message must be short and simple; no socioeconomic selectivity; seldom attracts readers' full attention; criticized for being traffic hazard and blight on countryside
Transit	Buses Taxicabs Subways	Low cost; frequency of message; "captive" audience; geographic selectivity	Limited audience; low impact; does not secure quick results
Internet	Ticker tapes Flashing Interactive Banners	Inexpensive; global reach	Inaccessible, difficult to assess effectiveness, disrupts flow of content.

- Identify the target audience of the advertisements.
- State the objectives to be accomplished (increase sales, build awareness, etc.).
- Determine how much money to spend.
- Develop an *advertising platform* consisting of the points to be emphasized to consumers (such as Maytag's dependability, Dell Computers hassle-free customized shopping experience).
- Outline a media plan, indicating specific media in which advertisements will be run and when they will be run to reach the target markets.
- Create the actual advertisement.
- Place the advertisements with the media.
- Through sales or research, evaluate the effectiveness of the ads (see if the objectives were met).

Some firms handle their own advertising through in-house staff that plan, design, and create advertisements and place them with the media. Others use specialists outside the organization. An *advertising agency* is a business that specializes in planning, producing, and placing advertising and offers other promotional services for clients. Agencies, ranging from small firms handling local and regional advertising to large firms with national and international clients, can offer expertise and production facilities unavailable in many firms. Newspaper, radio, and television companies also offer advertising assistance, as do freelance writers, artists, and producers. Small firms often find that these sources can provide needed assistance at a reasonable cost.

14-12 PERSONAL SELLING

Advertising acquaints potential customers with a product or service and makes the personal selling experience more pleasant and possible. **Personal selling** is communicating person-to-person with one or more prospective customers to make a sale.[35] At one time or another, all of us have encountered personal selling. Has a car salesperson ever taken you on a test drive? Or maybe a salesperson helped you during a recent clothing purchase. These activities are highly visible because they are aimed at consumers. Yet they represent only a fraction of the situations involving personal selling. More than four times as many personal selling activities are directed toward industrial customers than toward consumers.

For many firms, personal selling is a critical element in the promotion mix. In the United States, companies spend more each year on personal selling than they spend on any other promotional method. Personal selling is also the most costly component of the promotion mix. The average cost of making a sales call on an organizational customer is over $250, about $220 for service customers, and $210 for consumer-goods customers.[36] Approximately 7 million people are employed in personal selling in the United States, compared with half a million in advertising.[37]

Salespeople play an important role in the success of many firms. The best are highly trained professionals who before and after the sale help buyers satisfy their wants and needs. They know the product and effectively communicate their knowledge to buyers face-to-face. They also keep track of new products and competitors' activities. At IBM, salespeople are not only expected to bring in more revenue and profit, they are expected

> **Personal Selling** Person-to-person communication with one or more prospective customers in order to make a sale.

35. Thomas N. Ingram, LaForgi Williams, Avila Schwepker, Charles H. Schwepker, and Raymond W. LaForgi, *Professional Selling* (Cincinnati, OH: South-Western, 2000).

36. Erin Strout, "Salespeople Ripping You Off," *Sales & Marketing Management*, February 2001, pp. 57–62.

37. Thomas W. Leigh, Ellen Bolman Pullins, and Lucette B. Comer, "The Top Ten Sales Articles of the 20th Century," *Journal of Personal Selling & Sales Management*, Summer 2001, pp. 217–227.

to act as sophisticated consultants selling both IBM and non-IBM technology to solve business problems.[38] Sales representatives often can reap substantial financial rewards; a highly skilled salesperson can earn more than $100,000 a year.

14-12a Types of Salespeople

Firms employ different types of salespeople for various selling situations, depending on such factors as type of product, price, number of customers, and channels of distribution used. We examine three common types of salespeople: order getters, order takers, and support salespeople.

Order Getters

> **Order Getter** A salesperson who recruits new customers and increases sales to current customers.

A salesperson responsible for selling products to new customers and increasing sales to current customers is an **order getter.** Order getters engage in *creative selling*. They size up a customer's needs and convey product information in a thorough and persuasive manner. Creative selling is especially important when customers are carefully weighing alternatives in making their purchase, when they are not aware of product features and benefits, or when the product is a new one. Many industries, including insurance, computers, appliances, and heavy machinery, employ order getters.

Order Takers

> **Order Taker** A salesperson who processes repeat sales and maintains positive relationships with customers.

The person who receives and processes orders for repeat sales, with the objective of maintaining positive relationships with customers, is an **order taker.** The major function of order takers is to ensure that customers have the right amount of products they need when and where they need them. Order takers include salespeople who handle telephone and mail orders in a sales office and salespeople in retail stores. Other order takers handle routine sales of products such as milk, potato chips, bread, and beverages. They call on stores to check stock, inform managers of inventories, and make deliveries.

Support Personnel

> **Support Salespeople** Salespeople who assist in selling by locating potential customers, educating them about products, building goodwill, and providing after-sales service.

Firms commonly employ **support salespeople** to assist in selling, primarily to locate potential customers, educate them about products, build goodwill, and provide service after sales. Support people must often help sell industrial products.

Producers of technical industrial products such as computers, chemicals, steel, and heavy equipment rely on *technical salespeople* to provide information and service to current customers. Technical salespeople usually need formal education in engineering or science because they instruct customers in how a product is designed or made, how to install it, or how to use it.

38. David Kirkpatrick, "The Future of IBM," *Business*, February 18, 2002, p. 27.

Directions: Circle the number that represents your level of agreement with each statement.

EXHIBIT 14-11

Do You Have What It Takes for Sales?

	Strongly Agree					Strongly Disagree
1. If I didn't have direct supervision in my job, I would work just as hard anyway.	1	2	3	4	5	6
2. I am willing to work long hours.	1	2	3	4	5	6
3. I enjoy trying hard to please people.	1	2	3	4	5	6
4. I am organized and plan my daily schedule to make the most of my time.	1	2	3	4	5	6
5. I can be flexible if the situation requires it.	1	2	3	4	5	6
6. When under pressure, I try to remain calm and solve the problem.	1	2	3	4	5	6
7. I can speak to groups of people.	1	2	3	4	5	6
8. I don't think being late for appointments is a good idea.	1	2	3	4	5	6
9. I listen carefully to others in conversations and ask them questions about themselves.	1	2	3	4	5	6
10. I think solving a problem or completing a task I'm interested in is exciting.	1	2	3	4	5	6

Feedback: Pinpointing the sort of person who is destined for success in sales is impossible; after all, there are as many styles of selling as there are products to be sold. But those who succeed in the field share certain characteristics. If you think those qualities include being pushy, manipulative, or sneaky, think again. In fact these stereotypes generally come from salespeople who are failing.

Sales achievement requires three basic qualities. The first is *ego drive*, the desire to succeed, to win a yes, that keeps people doing the hard work required to get there. Ego drive also helps salespeople, who are largely independent, motivated, and manage themselves. The second quality is *empathy*, the ability to listen and understand what someone else is thinking and feeling. Top salespeople know what questions to ask and how to interpret answers. Third, salespeople need to possess *ego strength*, the ability to take rejection and to persevere during slumps. If you find it painful when someone tells you no, don't go into sales!

How you answered the quiz questions should give you an idea of whether you have the qualities needed by effective salespeople. If you circled 5 or 6 to most of the questions, you probably don't have the interest or characteristics for sales. If you circled 3s or 4s, you might make a good salesperson if you really want to work at it and learn. If you circled 1 or 2 to most questions, you have many of the qualities shared by successful salespeople. You are hardworking, emotionally mature, dependable, independent, and knowledgeable.

Manufacturers often employ *missionary salespeople* to encourage retailers and other sellers to purchase their products. Missionary salespeople commonly represent pharmaceutical and medical supply companies to promote their products to physicians, hospitals, clinics, and pharmacies.

Trade salespeople help customers, especially retail stores, promote products to their own customers. They may set up displays of a manufacturer's product, demonstrate products to customers, give out samples, and restock shelves. Trade salespeople often work for food producers.

Chances are good that some of you reading this book will become salespeople. In the United States, roughly one of every nineteen workers performs a sales-related job. Did you ever wonder what makes a successful salesperson and whether you might share some of those characteristics? The values and attitudes quiz in Exhibit 14-11 can help you find out whether you have what it takes to sell.

14-12b Sales Positions and Relationships

As we have noted, the nature of personal selling is changing. The major thrust of this change is focusing on the customer as many firms are recognizing that the key element to improving quality is continual focus on the customer. As a result, salespeople are being asked to do a great deal more listening and questioning of the customer.[39] Many salespeople are selling to diverse racial and ethnic groups, and understanding differences and similarities is vital for success.[40] The resulting relationships between salespeople and their customers take many forms; salespeople may act as partners, consultants, advisers, or problem solvers. We refer to this emerging trend in general as *smart selling*.

Having a successful sales career today depends on a salesperson's ability to build a relationship with the customer. Additionally, successful salespeople have to be willing to work with others to satisfy customer problems. Eastman Kodak has begun to evaluate its sales representatives on how well they coordinate with coworkers to help a customer.[41]

Selling involves convincing customers that a firm can give them the most value for the least money. This approach requires a sincere and concentrated focus on the customer. The successful salesperson must concentrate on contributing to the success of the customer.

14-12c The Selling Process

> **Selling Process** A series of steps salespeople perform, consisting of prospecting, preparing, approaching, presenting, answering objections, closing, and following up.

A salesperson's work is outlined in the steps that take place in the **selling process** (see Exhibit 14-12). Of course, not all salespeople perform their jobs in exactly the same way, and an individual salesperson may alter tactics for different situations. But the ultimate goal of the selling process is a long-term relationship with the customer. In the current highly competitive business environment, many firms are discovering that keeping current customers is more economical than finding new ones.[42] Customer loyalty is invaluable to a firm's long-range success.

Prospecting

Locating potential customers is called prospecting. Salespeople find prospects through many sources, including current customers, trade directories, business associates, telephone directories, newspaper or magazine articles, or public records. At this stage in the selling process, the salesperson tries to identify as possible customers those who have a need for a product and the financial ability and authority to purchase it.

Preparing

Sales calls require some preparatory research. A salesperson attempts to find out about the prospect's needs, attitudes about available products and brands, and personal characteristics, as well as the products and brands currently used. Knowing as much as possible about the prospect allows a salesperson to tailor the approach and presentation specifically for that prospect and that situation.

Approaching

The third step involves making the initial contact with, or approaching, a prospect. A salesperson's approach makes the all-important first impression with a potential customer. Adequate preparation and knowledge increase a salesperson's chances of making a good first impression. In approaching the prospect, a salesperson may mention a referral from an

39. Harvey Thompson, *The Customer-Centered Enterprise: How IBM and Other World-Class Companies Achieve Extraordinary Results By Putting Customers First* (New York: McGraw-Hill, 1999).

40. Marilyn Halter, *Shopping for Identity: The Marketing of Ethnicity* (New York: Schocken Books, 2000).

41. Thompson, *The Customer-Centered Enterprise*.

42. Jill Griffin, Michael W. Lowenstein, Dom Peppers, Marilyn Rogers, and Martha Rogers, *Customer Winback—And Keep Them Loyal* (San Francisco: Jossey-Bass, 2001).

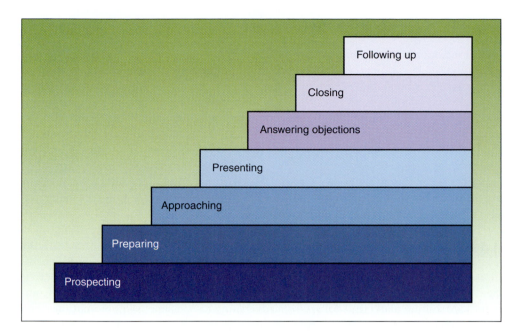

Steps in the Selling Process

acquaintance or business associate or remind the prospect of a previous meeting. Salespeople may make the call "cold"—without the prospect's prior knowledge or an appointment.

Presenting

The next step is actually presenting the promotional message to the potential customer. During the presentation, a salesperson points out the product's features and benefits and emphasizes any advantages the product offers over competitor's products. When possible, salespeople encourage potential customers to hold, touch, or use products to experience them personally and reinforce significant points of the presentation. A salesperson also needs to ask the client questions and listen carefully to determine the client's needs and focus the presentation on those needs.

Answering Objections

After presenting, the salesperson gives a prospect sufficient opportunity to ask questions or raise objections. By answering objections, the salesperson increases the likelihood of a sale. This step gives the salesperson a second chance to tell the major benefits of the product or service and point out additional features, guarantees, service, and so forth.

Closing

In closing the sale, the salesperson asks the prospect to buy the product. Some salespeople ask directly if the prospect is ready to make a purchase. Others use trial closing to imply that the customer will buy the product. A salesperson can ask questions such as Would you like us to finance the car for you? or When would you like delivery? to encourage customers to finalize the purchase. Sometimes salespeople offer prospects a chance to try the product for a period of time with no obligation to buy.

Following Up

A salesperson would make a critical mistake to assume that the selling process ends after the sale. To follow up, a salesperson contacts the customer to make sure that the product was delivered and installed properly (if needed) and to ask if it is performing as expected. When a problem exists, an effective salesperson assists the customer in resolving it. Providing service after a purchase encourages future sales and helps build a long-term relationship.

14-13 SALES PROMOTION

Sales Promotion An activity that offers customers or marketing intermediaries direct incentives for purchasing a product.

Sales promotion is a paid form of nonpersonal communication that provides direct incentives to customers, salespeople, and marketing intermediaries for purchasing a product. Methods such as coupons, contests, and displays can get consumers excited about a product, motivate salespeople to be enthusiastic, and stimulate dealers to be interested and involved in distributing it. Sales promotion activities, generally short-term, offer the advantage of immediacy; firms can implement them and obtain results quickly. Firms use sales promotions occasionally or year-round to support their personal selling, advertising, and publicity programs.

Sales promotion is big business in the United States. More than 300 billion coupons are distributed in the United States each year.[43] In this section, we examine the major categories of sales promotion: consumer and trade.

14-13a Consumer Sales Promotion

Consumer Sales Promotion Activities—including coupons, rebates, samples, gifts, premiums, trading stamps, contests, and sweepstakes—directed to consumers to increase sales.

Firms that market consumer products frequently use **consumer sales promotion,** activities that encourage customers to buy certain brands or to shop at a particular store. Companies are shifting marketing dollars from advertising to consumer sales promotions. The most common consumer sales promotion methods are coupons, rebates, samples, gifts, premiums, trading stamps, contests, and sweepstakes. Firms may use one or more of these methods in a promotional campaign.

Coupons

Coupon A sales promotion technique that reduces the price of a product by a stated amount at the time of purchase.

Manufacturers and retailers provide special price reductions for consumers through **coupons.** The reduction may be a specified amount ranging from a few cents to several dollars, or a certain percentage to be deducted from the price of a product. Manufacturers and retailers often use coupons to encourage consumers to try new products. Some try coupons to reverse a decline in sales of a product. Sometimes a firm will distribute coupons as a defensive tactic when a competitor introduces a new product or begins a new sales promotion program. Firms distribute more than 400 billion coupons every year in the United States through newspapers, magazines, direct mail, store displays, and other methods; customers redeem about 5 percent of these. However, about 30 percent of online shoppers use online coupons.

Rebates

Rebate An extra discount or refund given to consumers who buy a product and supply proofs of purchase.

Firms may offer customers who buy a product and send in proof of their purchase an extra discount or refund in the form of a **rebate.** Rebates range from a small percentage of the purchase price to the full purchase price. Firms typically use rebates both to motivate consumers to try new products and to provide incentives for purchasing established products. Manufacturers offer rebates for all types of products, from convenience items such as toothpaste to big-ticket goods such as cars.

Free Samples

Free Sample A free package or container of a product given as a sales promotion technique.

Premium A fee paid to the insurance company for protection; also refers to a gift given to customers for purchasing a certain product.

An effective way to encourage consumers to get familiar with a product is to provide them with a **free sample** of the merchandise. Companies may mail or deliver samples to homes, give them out in stores, or distribute coupons for free products. Although providing samples is the most expensive method of consumer sales promotion, it generally works the best to induce buyers to try new products.

Premiums and Trading Stamps

Many firms offer a **premium,** or gift, to customers as a bonus for purchasing a certain product. Banks, for example, often offer household items to customers who open new

43. Bill Carmody, *Online Promotions: Winning Strategies and Practices* (New York: Wiley, 2001).

accounts. To attract customers to a particular store, retailers sometimes give customers **trading stamps** based on the dollar amount spent. Customers can save the stamps and exchange them for merchandise. Trading stamps such as S&H Green Stamps were once widely distributed by grocery stores but have lost their popularity in recent years.

Contests and Sweepstakes

Contests and sweepstakes probably generate more excitement than do other promotional methods. To stimulate sales, firms offer consumers the chance to win free trips, vacation dream houses, cars, cash, and merchandise. In a **contest,** consumers compete for prizes based on some skill. Food manufacturers, for example, often sponsor cooking contests in which contestants use certain products to create new recipes. In a **sweepstakes,** consumers send in their names to enter a drawing for prizes. Sweepstakes cost considerably less than contests and attract many more participants.

14-13b Trade Sales Promotion

A manufacturer often uses **trade sales promotion** activities to encourage wholesalers and retailers to stock and promote its products or salespeople to increase sales. Common methods of trade sales promotion are point-of-purchase displays, trade shows, trade allowances, premium or push money, and sales contests.

Point-of-Purchase Displays

Manufacturers or wholesalers provide and set up signs, posters, freestanding shelves, and other specialized materials to use as **point-of-purchase displays** in retail stores. For example, a large, inflatable plastic Green Giant may stand atop the frozen vegetable case in a supermarket to grab attention and promote that brand. A display may contain the product being promoted. For example, PepsiCo has supplied refrigerators bearing the Pepsi name to retailers carrying its products. Displays can be very effective in increasing sales, as many buying decisions (two-thirds by some estimates) are made in the store.[44]

Video players with videotapes provided by manufacturers are among the newest point-of-purchase displays. Department stores, for instance, play videos on how to tie scarves and how to put together clothing separates for a complete outfit.

Trade Shows

Sellers in an industry gather at **trade shows** to exhibit their merchandise. Their manufacturers display and demonstrate products to potential customers and gather names of prospects. Industries representing food, fashion, furniture, computers, toys, and many other products hold trade shows each year, usually in large cities. Although manufacturers conduct most trade shows for retailers, some also are designed for a consumer audience, such as shows featuring home building and interior decorating products, or boats and recreational vehicles.

Trade Allowances

A manufacturer may give retailers and wholesalers a **trade allowance,** a discount for performing certain functions or for making purchases during a specified time period. For instance, a firm could offer price reductions to retailers to encourage them to stock a product and pass the savings on to consumers. A retailer also may earn a discount for setting up a special display to promote a manufacturer's products.

Premium or Push Money

Firms often conduct sales promotion activities for their own salespeople and those representing distributors and other sellers. To encourage salespeople to push a product, a firm

Trading Stamps Tokens given out by retailers based on the amount of purchase; redeemable for gifts.

Contest A sales promotion method in which consumers compete for prizes on the basis of some skill.

Sweepstakes A sales promotion method in which consumers enter a drawing for prizes.

Trade Sales Promotion Activities a firm directs to wholesalers, retailers, or salespeople to encourage them to stock or sell its products.

Point-of-Purchase Displays Promotional materials such as signs, posters, and freestanding shelves used in retail stores.

Trade Shows Temporary exhibits where manufacturers display products to potential customers and gather names for a list of prospects.

Trade Allowances Discounts a manufacturer gives for performing certain functions or making purchases during a specified time period.

44. Sharon Clark, *The Co-Marketing Solution: Strategic Marketing Through Better Branding, Improved Trade Relationships, Super Promotions, Effective Selling* (New York: McGraw-Hill, 2000).

Premium or Push Money
Additional compensation
provided to salespeople to
encourage them to sell a product.

may provide additional compensation in the form of **premium or push money.** Although expensive, using premium or push money can boost commitment from salespeople when personal selling is a major part of the promotion mix.

Sales Contests

Conducting a contest for the people who sell and distribute its products is another method a firm could use to increase involvement and create excitement. In a **sales contest,** a firm may offer prizes to salespeople, distributors, and retailers who meet certain sales goals in a specific time period. A sales contest with a desirable prize, such as a trip to an exotic vacation spot, can increase participation and sales throughout the channel of distribution. The results may be only temporary, however, and the cost of prizes may be high.

Sales Contest   A competition
designed to stimulate sales efforts
by salespeople, distributors, or
retailers.

14-14 PUBLICITY

Publicity   A nonpersonal form
of communication transmitted in
news story form and not paid for
directly by a sponsor.

Public Relations   A set of
communications activities
designed to create and maintain
a favorable public image for
a firm.

Like advertising and sales promotion, **publicity** is a nonpersonal form of communication. But it is transmitted by a mass medium in news story form and is not paid for directly by a sponsor. Publicity is actually part of **public relations,** a set of communications activities designed to create and maintain a favorable public image for a firm. Superman generated a great deal of publicity when he was killed off by his editor at Time Warner's DC Comics in 1992, selling 3.5 million copies at $1.25 each—one of the best-selling comic books ever.[45] Many organizations, industries, and individuals conduct ongoing public relations campaigns to demonstrate social responsibility.

14-14a Publicity Approaches

Firms attempt to gain publicity for several purposes. They may want to increase awareness of their products, to build a positive image with the general public, to gain recognition for employees and their accomplishments, to encourage others to participate in community projects, or at times to counter negative events or news stories.

Companies use several vehicles to obtain publicity. The *news release* is a brief report—a page or two—that announces an organization's national, regional, or local events. Firms distribute news releases widely and include the names of people within the firm for media representatives to contact for more information. A *feature article* is a longer, more detailed story about a firm, its products, or its people. It may run as long as 3,000 words and include photographs or illustrations. Firms usually submit a feature article to a specific magazine or newspaper. A *captioned photograph*, a picture along with a short explanation, can be effective in informing consumers about new products or stores. Another option is sending an *editorial* or tape to broadcast media for inclusion in news programs. To release important or timely news, a firm may invite media representatives to a *news conference* to make announcements, hand out supplemental materials, and answer questions.

Another approach gaining use is *sponsorship* of events, programs, people (such as Nike's sponsorship of golfer Tiger Woods), and sports stadiums (e.g., Coors Field). Besides publicity, sponsorship can involve advertising and sales promotion activities such as samples and contests. Each year thousands of firms sponsor sporting events, arts festivals, public radio and television programs, and public interest advertisements. Companies paid as much as $15 million to be major sponsors of the 1994 World Cup soccer tournament.[46] At least 400 large U.S. corporations have developed event marketing departments with separate budgets; others hire consultants to manage sponsorship for them. Smaller firms often work with local government and community organizations to sponsor events.

45. Robert Calvin, *Sales Management* (New York: McGraw-Hill, 2001).

46. Ronald Grover and Greg Burns, "The World Cup of Ambush Marketing," *Business Week,* May 2, 1994, p. 37.

14-14b Using Publicity Effectively

Positive publicity provides many benefits for an organization. A newspaper or magazine article or television or radio broadcast can reach large and diverse audiences at no direct cost to the firm. News and feature stories can reach people who pay no attention to advertisements. Since publicity is provided by independent media, it has a great deal of credibility. Are you not more likely to believe a news story about a new product than an advertisement paid for by the seller?

Publicity also poses several limitations. A firm exerts little or no control over a message—its content, placement, timing, or whether the media transmits it at all. News editors may have different ideas of what is news than do members of an organization seeking publicity. A news story may run on the late news show and reach only a fraction of potential viewers. Or it may be cut to a line or two in a newspaper column full of corporate news. Publicity does not always enhance a firm's image. At times the media people report negative events and criticize a firm's activities, policies, or products.

To foster positive and effective publicity, a firm must conduct well-planned, regular efforts. Many firms employ individuals or departments to handle ongoing publicity efforts, while others rely on advertising or public relations firms or freelance writers or consultants. Personnel trained in communications can supply the media with newsworthy, well-written publicity releases, handle media requests, and build cooperative relationships with reporters, editor, news directors, and other media "gatekeepers."

14-15 THE INTERNET AND PROMOTION

The Internet economy has only begun to take off.[47] Consider these facts:

- In 2002, about 60 percent of U.S. households had a personal computer.

- Spending on the Web was about $220 billion in 2002 and is expected to double in five years.

- The Internet is growing faster than any other medium in history. It took radio about thirty-eight years to acquire 50 million listeners. Television took thirteen years to reach 50 million viewers. The Internet achieved 50 million users in just four years.

- Citibank works with car dealerships to approve or deny car loans within ninety seconds of a loan application being submitted.

- Papa John's offers takeout pizza delivery online.

Over a period of time companies learn who is buying what, when, and how often. This database allows them to develop a promotional strategy that meets the needs and preferences of their customers. Long Island–based 1-800-Flowers has been able to grow into the world's largest florist as a result of the effective use of technology and e-commerce (see the Focus on Technology box, "1-800-Flowers").

Viral marketing is a concept that ranges from paying people to say positive things on the Internet to setting up multilevel selling approaches for directing people to specific websites.[48] Spreading positive words about a product or service is creating publicity. Amazon.com asks customers before they check out if they want to send some "love" to a friend. That is, send a gift of a book, CD, or other merchandise to a friend. Amazon wants to spread the word about its products.

One of the main users of viral marketing was Hotmail.com. The strategy used by Hotmail.com was to give away free e-mail addresses and services, attaching a tag at the bottom

Viral Marketing A concept that ranges from paying people to say positive things on the Internet to setting up multilevel selling approaches for directing people to specific websites.

47. Rosabeth Moss Kanter, *Evolve! Succeeding in the Digital Culture of Tomorrow* (Cambridge, MA: Harvard Business School Press, 2001).

48. Jupiter Media Matrix, *Viral Marketing—Message Ultimately Trumps Media* (New York: MarketingResearch.com, 2001).

FOCUS ON TECHNOLOGY

1-800-Flowers

The company grew from a stand-alone ship to a chain of twelve flower shops in the New York area. In 1987, owner Jim McCann acquired the 1-800-Flowers number. Today, in addition to its 150 company-owned and franchised outlets, 1-800-Flowers partners with more than 2,500 florists.

The company decided to hire technology, marketing, and e-commerce experts in the mid-1990s. This allowed 1-800-Flowers to serve customers by phone, fax, in person, and on the Internet. On its Internet site, 1-800-Flowers receives over 100,000 unique visitors during busy times, such as Mother's Day. Of the potential buyers who visit the site about 20 percent order flowers or other products such as baskets of gourmet foods, chocolate-covered strawberries, and champagne pearl bracelets. The Internet customer orders by making selections on-line.

When customers order they're asked if they would like to receive marketing offers via e-mail. About 20 percent of all callers provide their e-mail addresses.

1-800-Flowers has approximately 40,000 affiliate marketing and distribution partners. An affiliate can earn a commission by promoting 1-800-Flowers products from its site using banner advertisements provided by 1-800-Flowers. Each time a visitor clicks from an affiliate's site to 1-800-Flowers.com to purchase items, the affiliate earns a commission of up to 8 percent with a ten-day cookie for return visitors.

The use of technology, marketing savvy, promotion, and affiliate programs has resulted in on-line sales of over $18 million for 1-800-Flowers and a total sales of about $442 million in 2001. 1-800-Flowers is currently increasing its affiliate program, providing state-of-the-art capability for its florist partners to communicate offering training courses via e-learning.

Sources: 1-800-Flowers.com, Annual Report 200; and Mark Del Franco, "The Popcorn Factory Sold to 1-800-Flowers.com," *Catalog Age,* June 1, 2002, p. 87.

of every free message: "Get your private, free e-mail at http://www.hotmail.com." The firm then waited as people passed along messages to their friends and associates who read the "free" tag, which many then proceeded to sign up for and become a user of Hotmail.com.

Off-the-Internet viral marketing is called word-of-mouth" or "creating a buzz" that gets people to talk about your product. Although the term *viral* is not very attractive, it has become a part of the promotion literature.

Viral marketing can have negative impact if something is wrong with the product or service. Negative chatroom discussions, on-line forums, bulletin boards, and word-of-mouth can spread quickly. Taking care of customers quickly, fairly, and respectfully is very significant in an era in which viral marketing exists

14-16 DEVELOPING THE PROMOTION MIX

A firm marketing several products often uses several promotion mixes simultaneously. When designing the promotion mix for a product, marketers first consider their promotional objectives (discussed earlier in the chapter). They also consider promotional techniques known as push and pull strategies, as well as product characteristics, including type of product, stage of product life cycle, and target market characteristics.

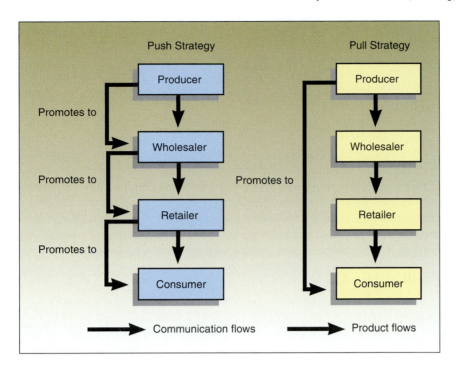

EXHIBIT 14-13

Push and Pull Strategies

14-16a Promotional Strategies

In developing promotional programs, marketers decide whether they want to use a push strategy or a pull strategy. With a **push strategy,** the firm promotes a product to wholesalers or retailers in the marketing channel, who in turn promote the product to consumers (see Exhibit 14-13). Personal selling often is used with this strategy to "push" the product to wholesalers and retailers.

In the **pull strategy** (also shown in Exhibit 14-13), by contrast, a firm promotes a product directly to consumers so that they will seek the product in retail stores and ask managers to stock it. In effect, customer demand "pulls" the product into stores. To implement a pull strategy, marketers usually use advertising and sales promotion to stimulate consumer demand for the product. While a firm often focuses on either a push or pull strategy, it could use both at the same time.

14-16b Product Characteristics

Various aspects of a product influence a firm's selection of promotion mix elements. Consumer and industrial products require different promotion mixes to meet the needs of those markets. Services often require unique considerations. For all products, firms must take into account the current product life-cycle stage and numerous characteristics of the targeted customers.

Type of Product

Firms selling industrial products generally emphasize personal selling techniques in their promotion mix, adding advertising, sales promotion, and publicity to support the personal selling efforts. For consumer products, advertising is the primary element. Firms offering consumer convenience products promote them heavily with advertising and sales promotion. Those selling consumer shopping and specialty products add personal selling to the mix so that salespeople can provide information and advice about high-priced or unfamiliar products such as appliances, cars, or computers.

Marketers of services face specific considerations when planning promotional activities. As intangible products, services cannot generally be defined in terms of physical attributes. Therefore, when service firms advertise, they use cues that provide physical

Push Strategy   Promotion of a product to wholesalers or retailers in the marketing channel, who in turn promote the product to consumers.

Pull Strategy   Promotion of a product directly to consumers to stimulate strong consumer demand.

representation of the service offered. Common cues are the physical facility or the employees. For example, Carnival Cruise Lines portrays its ships as resorts on water, complete with pools, casinos, and restaurants.

Services also are based on human performances—as in rock concerts, legal advice, or dental care—which are even more difficult to define in tangible terms. Marketers need to emphasize not only the actual service but all the benefits the customer is buying.[49] For many services, personal selling becomes especially useful; it provides the interaction between service personnel and consumers that is so valuable in marketing intangible products.

Publicity, with its lower cost and generally higher credibility compared to advertising, is an important promotion element for service firms. Health providers often receive publicity by sponsoring fairs in which medical personnel perform cholesterol screening, blood pressure checks, and vision and hearing tests free for the public. Service firms may also use sales promotion, such as coupons, rebates, and free first-time visits. Some sales promotion activities are not feasible for service providers; many services cannot be displayed, and providing a free sample requires giving away the entire product.

Product Life Cycle

A firm introducing a new product, either industrial or consumer, usually advertises heavily to make potential customers aware of it and encourage them to try it. Personal selling and sales promotion also prove valuable for many products in the introduction stage. For consumer convenience products in the growth and maturity stages, advertising usually continues to dominate the promotion mix. For industrial products in the growth and maturity stages, however, firms often concentrate on personal selling supported by sales promotion activities. When a product reaches the decline stage, marketers cut back on promotion, especially advertising. Instead they rely on personal selling and sales promotion to obtain a few more sales.

Target Markets

The size, geographic distribution, and demographic characteristics of a firm's target market greatly influence the choice of promotion elements. Personal selling will likely be an important element for the target market that has a limited number of potential customers, whereas advertising and sales promotion usually dominate the promotion mix designed to reach millions of people at a low cost per person. Similarly, personal selling is generally more practical when a firm's customers are concentrated in a small area; advertising and sales promotion, which are much more flexible, can be easily geared to markets in any geographic region whether small and precisely defined or large.

A target market's demographics—age, income, education, social class, occupation— also influence the promotion mix. A firm marketing to teenagers would emphasize advertising, especially on television, but rely less on personal selling, sales promotion, or publicity. A firm targeting educated, financially well-off consumers aged 35 and older would use personal selling, advertising, and perhaps publicity but not consumer sales promotion activities, since coupons, refund, and sweepstakes are more important to lower- and middle-income families.

SUGGESTED WEBSITES

Note: These websites were functional when we went to press. Please access the online text for the most up-to-date URLs.

1. www.fisherprice.com
2. www.pg.com
3. www.citigroup.com
4. www.papajohns.com
5. www.1800flowers.com
6. www.oceanspray.com

49. Robert G. Cooper and Scott J. Edgett, *Product Development for the Service Sector: Lessons from Market Leaders* (Cambridge, MA: Perseus, 1999).

SUMMARY OF LEARNING OBJECTIVES

1. *Define the term* product *and distinguish between consumer and industrial products.*   A product consists of all the tangible and intangible characteristics provided in an exchange between a seller and buyer. The products people use for personal or family use are consumer products, classified as convenience, shopping, or specialty products. Organizations use industrial products in producing goods and services and in carrying out their operations.

2. *Differentiate between product line and product mix.*   Firms often market a group of related products and services known as a product line. A product line of only one or two products is shallow; a deep product line contains many items. A firm's product mix is the entire collection of products it offers. Product mix width (narrow or wide) refers to the number of product lines a firm carries.

3. *Trace the process of developing new products.*   To be successful, firms try to develop new products to satisfy consumers. New-product development consists of (a) generating ideas that fit a firm's objectives; (b) screening ideas to determine which are feasible to pursue; (c) analyzing the costs, sales, and profits of the proposed product; (d) developing a working model of the product; (e) test marketing the product; and (f) distributing the new product to the entire market during commercialization.

4. *Describe the stages of the product life cycle and explain how firms can extend it.*   A product enters the market during the *introduction* stage, in which sales rise slowly and profits are low. In the *growth* stage, sales increase rapidly and the product begins to generate a profit. In the *maturity* stage, sales peak as profits decline. Sales volume falls rapidly during a product's *decline* stage. To extend a product's life cycle, a firm can modify the product's quality, functions, or style. It can find new uses for the product, identify new users, or encourage more frequent use. A product that becomes too costly for a firm is deleted from the product mix.

5. *Explain the purposes of branding, packaging, and labeling.*   Firms identify their products through branding, packaging, and labeling. In *branding*, products are named and sometimes represented with a design called a brand. Unbranded products, called generics, are often available. *Packaging* protects products, adds to their functions, helps ensure product safety, and attracts consumer attention. *Labeling* identifies the product and brand and provides information about contents and use.

6. *List four pricing objectives and identify three factors to consider when making pricing decisions.*   Price, the value consumers exchange for a product in a marketing transaction, is important to both buyers and sellers. Besides mere survival, a firm can use price to increase market share, increase profit, increase return on investment, or maintain the industry status quo. When making pricing decisions, a firm determines whether to compete based on price and nonprice competition and considers the forces of supply and demand and consumer perceptions of price.

7. *Distinguish between cost-oriented, demand-oriented, and competition-oriented pricing methods.*   A firm can use any of several methods to set prices. *Cost-oriented* pricing bases price on total cost of a product plus a predetermined percentage amount called the markup. *Demand-oriented* pricing, using breakeven analysis, considers the level of demand for the product at various possible prices in order to find out how many products must be sold for the firm to recover its costs. *Competition-oriented* pricing uses prices charged by competitors as the major factor in selecting prices.

8. *List and explain four pricing strategies.*   Various pricing strategies enable a firm to adjust the price of a product at certain times. *Pioneer pricing,* used in pricing new products, can mean setting the price high during a product's introduction to recover costs quickly (price skimming) or setting the price low during introduction to build sales and market share quickly (penetration pricing). A firm may use *psychological pricing* (odd-even pricing, customary pricing, prestige pricing, or price lining) to encourage consumers to make purchase decisions on some emotional basis. People with great amounts of training and skill use *professional pricing* to set standard fees. *Price discounting* means offering customers reductions from a product's price.

9. *Explain the role of promotion in marketing and list five promotional objectives.*   Organizations use promotion to communicate favorable, persuasive information about themselves or their products, to influence buyers to make a purchase, or to foster goodwill. Promotional objectives may include informing, increasing sales, stabilizing sales, product positioning, or building a public image. To meet these objectives, a firm develops a combination of advertising, personal selling, sales promotion, and publicity—called the promotion mix.

10. *Outline the personal selling process and describe each step.*   Salespeople perform a series of steps in the selling process: prospecting (locating potential customers); preparing (learning about prospects and their needs); approaching (making the first contact and a good first impression); presenting (explaining product benefits and demonstrating the product); answering objections (encouraging questions and emphasizing product benefits); closing the sale (asking the prospect to buy); and following up (finding out if the product satisfies the customer's needs and providing service).

11. *Describe how firms use publicity.*   Publicity can increase awareness of products and help build a positive image with target markets or the general public. Sponsors do not pay directly for publicity, which is transmitted through mass media. News releases, feature articles, captioned photographs, editorial films or tapes, and press conferences facilitate publicity. Many firms sponsor events, programs, and public interest advertising to gain recognition, target specific markets, and increase sales.

KEY TERMS

advertising (p. 378)
advertising media (p. 379)
brand (p. 366)
brand name (p. 366)
breakeven analysis (p. 374)
breakeven quantity (p. 374)
competition-oriented pricing (p. 375)
consumer products (p. 357)
consumer sales promotion (p. 386)
contest (p. 387)
convenience products (p. 357)
cost-oriented pricing (p. 373)
coupon (p. 386)
demand (p. 372)
demand-oriented pricing (p. 374)
free sample (p. 386)
industrial products (p. 358)
institutional advertising (p. 379)
labeling (p. 370)
markup (p. 373)
media plan (p. 379)

nonprice competition (p. 372)
order getter (p. 382)
order taker (p. 382)
packaging (p. 368)
personal selling (p. 381)
pioneer pricing (p. 375)
point-of-purchase displays (p. 387)
premium (p. 386)
premium or push money (p. 388)
price (p. 370)
price competition (p. 372)
price discounting (p. 376)
pricing method (p. 373)
primary-demand advertising (p. 378)
product (p. 357)
product life cycle (p. 363)
product line (p. 360)
product mix (p. 360)
product modification (p. 365)
professional pricing (p. 376)
promotion (p. 377)

promotion mix (p. 378)
psychological pricing (p. 376)
public relations (p. 388)
publicity (p. 388)
pull strategy (p. 391)
push strategy (p. 391)
rebate (p. 386)
sales contest (p. 388)
sales promotion (p. 386)
selective (brand) advertising (p. 378)
selling process (p. 384)
shopping products (p. 358)
specialty products (p. 358)
supply (p. 372)
support salespeople (p. 382)
sweepstakes (p. 387)
trade allowances (p. 387)
trade sales promotion (p. 387)
trade shows (p. 387)
trading stamps (p. 387)
viral marketing (p. 389)

QUESTIONS FOR DISCUSSION AND REVIEW

1. What do marketers mean when they refer to a convenience product? A shopping product? A specialty product? Name a product for each category.

2. Are the following product lines shallow or deep—Dr Pepper soft drinks, Levi's jeans, Reebok athletic shoes? Discuss. Would you consider the following companies to have a narrow or wide product mix? McDonald's, Rolls-Royce, IBM.

3. Identify two strengths and two weaknesses of each major advertising medium: newspapers, television, direct mail, radio, magazines, and outdoor displays and the Internet.

4. Why do many new products fail? Can you name a consumer product that failed? What are some possible reasons for its failure?

5. Products we see and use every day are in different phases of the product life cycle. Name two products in each phase.

6. Name the different types of salespeople. Give examples of situations in which you have interacted with each of these types of salespeople, and why they were effective.

7. Distinguish between manufacturer brands, private brands, and generic brands. Why would consumers select one versus the other?

8. A clothing store uses a 50 percent markup to price most of its items. What pricing method is the store using? Explain what 50 percent markup means.

9. Describe some of the advantages and disadvantages of publicity. Give a recent example of a firm receiving favorable publicity and an example of one receiving unfavorable publicity.

10. Which pioneer pricing strategy is a firm likely to use when introducing an innovative new medication that stops heart attacks instantly? Why?

END-OF-CHAPTER QUESTIONS

1. Marketers generally divide products into two broad categories: consumer and industrial. **T** or **F**
2. DVDs, major appliances, furniture, and services such as dental care and legal advice are considered *convenience products.* **T** or **F**
3. According to a survey of new-product managers, only 8 percent of their new products actually made it to market. **T** or **F**
4. New products stabilize during the *growth* stage of the product life cycle. **T** or **F**
5. *Quality modification* is achieved by redesigning a product to provide additional features or benefits. **T** or **F**
6. With individual branding, a firm uses the same brand for most or all of its products. **T** or **F**
7. If a potato chip snack product contains more vegetable oil than potatoes, oil must be the first ingredient listed on the product label. **T** or **F**
8. Penetration pricing means setting prices low when offering a product for the first time. **T** or **F**
9. *Promoting* a product means emphasizing certain product features to create a specific image for the product and to add to its appeal. **T** or **F**
10. When an organization wants to build goodwill and create a favorable public image rather than promote a specific product, it employs *institutional advertising.* **T** or **F**
11. Manufacturers often employ *missionary salespeople* to encourage retailers and other sellers to purchase their products. **T** or **F**
    a. bribery
    b. advertising
    c. public relations
    d. lobbying
12. With a *pull strategy*, a firm promotes a product to wholesalers or retailers in the marketing channel, who in turn promote the product to consumers. **T** or **F**
13. A very expensive Rolex diamond watch would be classified as a _____ product.
    a. service
    b. shopping
    c. convenient
    d. specialty
14. The concept of paying people to say positive things on the Internet in order to direct people to specific websites is called _____ marketing.
    a. virus
    b. viral
    c. spiral
    d. promotional
15. Which of the follow brand names have become generic terms because their owners failed to protect them?
    a. Aspirin
    b. Celluloid
    c. Zipper
    d. All of the above

INTERNET EXERCISE

World-Class Brands and Pricing

World-class brands exist and consumers are traditionally attracted to them for many different reasons such as price, quality, and value. The world-class brands sell for above or below the local prices for them. That is, a sixteen-ounce Coca-Cola drink in the United States sells at a local price, while the same Coca-Cola drink sells for a greater or lesser price in Zurich or Tokyo.

Using the Internet, find in current American currency ($) what the price would be for the following world-class brands:

	U.S.	Zurich	Tokyo
16-ounce Coca-Cola	_____	_____	_____
Toyota Highlander SUV	_____	_____	_____
Gillette Razor	_____	_____	_____
Estée Lauder Lipstick	_____	_____	_____
Nestle Chocolate Bar	_____	_____	_____
McDonald's Big Mac	_____	_____	_____
Chicco D'Oro Swiss Coffee	_____	_____	_____
Sony Network Walkman	_____	_____	_____

EXPERIENTIAL EXERCISE

Identifying Examples of Product Differentiation

Activity

Students will visit a grocery store and analyze the characteristics of similar products to determine examples of product differentiation.

Directions

1. Review the concept of product differentiation whereby a company tries to emphasize how its product is different from a competitor's product.
2. Assign each student the task of visiting a local grocery store to identify examples of product differentiation. The following aspects of the assignment may be used:

- Students should stay within the same type of products for the comparison. For example, one brand name of mustard should only be compared with a competitor's brand name of mustard; one brand of ice cream should be compared with a competitor's brand of ice cream, etc.
- Students should write down the product characteristics identified in the wording on the package. Also, students should write down the nonverbal characteristics, such as the shapes, sizes, and colors of packages.
- Students should then develop a list of common characteristics and list of differentiation characteristics.
- Each student should examine at least three competitors' products during the comparison.

3. On the due date of the assignment the instructor should call on as many students as possible to share the findings with the class.

BUSINESS APPLICATION

Reduce the Price or Increase the Promotion?

Judith Hardin, a 27-year-old manager of a local fast-food restaurant, has been asked by the owner to make a recommendation on possible price changes. The restaurant currently charges a slightly higher price for its food than does the competition. For example, Hardin's restaurant charges $3.00 for its quarter-pound hamburger while the competition charges $2.50 for the same menu item.

During the past two years the restaurant has been barely breaking even in its operations while the competition has done significantly better. Hardin has studied the competition's products and has been unable to determine any significant difference in actual quality, taste, or appearance between her store's food and the competition's offerings. She is now contemplating her recommendation.

Questions for Discussion

1. Before considering the option of lowering prices, what other avenues might Judith Hardin explore?
2. Do you think if Hardin recommends lowering the prices to that of the competition, then the restaurant will become as profitable as the competition?
3. What other factors besides price might be contributing to the success of the competitor's restaurant?

Case

Ocean Spray Is Extending Its Product

6 ☞ Over the years Ocean Spray Cranberries, Inc., in Lakerville, Massachusetts, has encouraged customers to "crave the wave." Posted prominently on the bottles of Ocean Spray products, the blue wave has come to represent the dominant shelf-table juice manufacturer as it secures a high portion of the grocery store juice aisle. It traditionally offered products red in color. Ocean Spray has also launched a line of white cranberry juice cocktails. Ocean Spray has grown from a $100 million company a few years ago to one that now has annual sales of over $1.3 billion.

A high shift in interest in cranberry juice has been attributed to a Harvard Medical School study in the mid-1990s. The research suggested that consuming cranberry juice has healthful benefits. Specifically, more consumption of cranberry juice was associated with less urinary tract infection problems. This resulted in many new growers coming into the industry. Suddenly there was an abundance of cranberries and prices plummeted.

Ocean Spray weathered the abundance storm. The firm realizes that getting more people to eat or drink more cranberries is how the business can grow. In 2002 Ocean Spray had a market share of about 55 percent. The firm isn't looking to cannibalize the red cranberry juice business. The strategy has been to grow a white cranberry (simply harvesting cranberries a few weeks earlier than cranberries). The white cranberries have resulted in a new line of products that are sweeter, less tart, and milder than the traditional juice. The line includes white cranberry juice cocktail, white cranberry and peach, and white cranberry and strawberry.

Ocean Spray's innovators are not sitting still and are working on new cranberry and grapefruit juice options. There are also juice spritzers and lemonade combinations. Different consumers have a range of tastes that Ocean Spray wants to attract to its product lines.

Ocean Spray has taken its traditional product and leveraged it to appeal to new as well as traditional consumers. Consumers differ in their tastes, needs, and purchasing patterns. Ocean Spray wants to continue providing taste satisfaction and pleasure to consumers.

Questions for Discussion

1. Is Ocean Spray jeopardizing its traditional red cranberry juice business by innovating a new line of white cranberry products?
2. What new target markets is Ocean Spray attempting to attract to its new product line?
3. How should Ocean Spray measure the success of its new cranberry juice product line?

Source: Jill Bruss, "Red, White, and Blue," *Beverage Industry,* February 2002, pp. 20–24.

15

Distribution and Supply Chain Management

Chapter Objectives

After completing this chapter, you should be able to

Photo: comstock.com

1 **Define** the term *marketing channel* and identify the two major types of marketing intermediaries.

2 **Explain** how marketing channels are integrated vertically.

3 **Define** *wholesaling* and describe the functions whole-salers perform.

4 **Define** *retailing* and outline the activities retailers perform.

5 **Describe** various forms of nonstore retailing.

6 **Explain** the benefits and possible problems of using a supply chain management approach.

7 **Explain** the role of physical distribution and identify its components.

Online Shopping

A U.S. Department of Commerce Survey has found that more than half the U.S. population is now connected to the Internet. In addition, about 39 percent of Internet users are making purchases directly online. Buying online is still not something people do regularly. It takes most people about two years of surfing and looking to take the plunge and make a purchase.

The cohort that is most attracted to online purchasing is web users ages 25 to 45. Also, individuals making more than U.S. $75,000 annually are buyers. About 49 percent of the $75,000 and up earners purchase online, compared with just 26 percent of those with an annual income of less than $15,000.

For all of 2001, e-commerce purchases accounted for just over 1 percent of all retail sales in the United States. This means about $32 billion of retail sales are made on the Internet. Within the next few years that figure is expected to reach about 5 percent of all retail sales. A big reason for the expected increase is that online auto sales are expected to grow. Purchasing a few $30,000 cars will have a bigger impact than purchasing a few $15.00 CDs.

Another expected growth area in online shopping involves global sales. With overseas competitors still gently moving into online selling, U.S. firms have been capturing market share. Expedia is building an overseas base one country at a time. The firm builds a team that established an in-country network. Expedia is moving into Europe because the rate of technology adoption is moving at a good pace.

Online shopping is still not as popular as sending and receiving e-mail, looking up information on products, playing games, or checking news. It is, however, here to stay and very likely to become more popular around the world.

Sources: Elaine X. Grant, "Report: The State of U.S. Online Shopping," *E-Commerce Times*, February 8, 2002; Keith Regan, "E-Commerce Goes Global for Growth," *E-Commerce Times*, February 5, 2002, pp. 1–3; and Keith Regan, "U.S.: E-Commerce Tops $32 B in 2001," *E-Commerce Times*, February 21, 2002, pp. 1–2.

15-1 MARKETING CHANNELS

A **marketing channel (channel of distribution)** is a group of interrelated organizations that directs the flow of products to ultimate customers.[1] The channel organization that provides the link between the producer and the consumer is called a **marketing intermediary.**

The two major categories of marketing intermediaries are wholesalers and retailers. Wholesalers, which sell primarily to other sellers or industrial users, generally involve large quantities of goods. Retailers specialize in selling products to consumers. They generally resell products that they obtain from wholesalers. We discuss wholesalers and retailers later in the chapter.

> **Marketing Channel (Channel of Distribution)** A group of interrelated organizations that directs the flow of products to ultimate consumers.
>
> **Marketing Intermediary** An individual or organization in a marketing channel that provides a link between producers, other channel members, and final consumers of products.

15-1a Functions of Marketing Intermediaries

Consumers often wonder whether products would cost less if one or more marketing intermediaries could be eliminated from the distribution system. Would cars be less expensive if customers could simply buy them straight from the manufacturer? Perhaps, but think about the practical aspects involved. How many consumers would be willing or able to go to Detroit, or maybe Japan, to buy a car? Even if manufacturers offered cars for sale by mail order, few consumers would buy a car without seeing and test driving it. Selling vehicles directly to buyers from around the United States or around the world would be impossible.

Marketing intermediaries ensure that products are available on a timely basis where they are needed.[2] Eliminating intermediaries does not eliminate the need for their services, such as storage, record keeping, delivery, and providing a product assortment. Either

---

1. David R. Bell and Xavier Dreze, "Changing the Channel: A Better Way to Do Trade Promotions," *MIT Sloan Management Review*, Winter 2002, pp. 42–49.

2. Gregory L. White, "General Motors to Take Nationwide Test Drive on Web," *Wall Street Journal*, September 28, 1998, p. B4.

Functions of Marketing Intermediaries

Function	Description
Buying	Purchasing a broad assortment of goods from producers
Carrying inventory	Assuming the risks associated with purchasing and holding an inventory
Selling	Performing activities required to sell goods to consumers
Transporting	Arranging for the shipment of goods
Financing	Providing funds required to cover the cost of channel activities
Promoting	Contributing to national and local advertising, and engaging in personal selling efforts
Negotiating	Attempting to determine the final price of goods
Marketing research	Providing information regarding the needs of customers
Servicing	Providing a variety of services, such as credit, delivery, and returns

the manufacturer, the consumer, or some other organization has to perform these essential services. Without intermediaries, most consumer purchases would be much less efficient. Products probably would cost more, not less. Some specific functions of marketing intermediaries are summarized in Exhibit 15-1.

15-1b Types of Marketing Channels

Thousands of marketing intermediaries move goods from producers to consumers. Clothes, food, appliances, shoes, CDs, DVDs, and automobiles are moved from producers through a series of intermediaries such as retail stores, wholesale centers, brokers, and others. Depending on the needs of the target market, firms utilize many different types of marketing channels to distribute products. Generally, channels for consumer products are different from channels for industrial products.

Consumer Products

The six most commonly used channels for consumer products are shown in Exhibit 15-2.[3] Channel A, the direct channel, shows the movement of products from producer to consumer. Some services are distributed through this channel, such as hair styling, dental work, and auto repair, while real estate, stocks, and bonds are distributed through Channel E.

Channel B reflects the movement of products from producer to retailer to consumer. This channel is commonly used for large, bulky items like automobiles and furniture, as well as perishable goods like fresh seafood. Bringing in another intermediary, such as a wholesaler, would add delays or unnecessary costs to the distribution of these products.

Channel C, producer to wholesaler to retailer to consumer, is the traditional marketing channel. A wide range of products, including appliances, beverages, tobacco, and most convenience goods, is distributed through this channel.

The final channel (D) for consumer products, producer to agent/broker to wholesaler to retailer to consumer, is used to distribute small, inexpensive products purchased frequently. Several wholesalers are involved in the distribution of items such as gum and candy bars that are purchased daily by millions of consumers at thousands of outlets. Channel F is a channel used by museums, government services, and charities.

Industrial Products

The common channels employed to distribute industrial products also appear in Exhibit 15-2. These channels are much shorter than the consumer channels. Most industrial products are distributed through the direct channel, producer to industrial user (Channel G).

3. Scott C. Friend and Patricia H. Walker, "Welcome to the New World of Merchandising," *Harvard Business Review*, November 2001, pp. 5–11.

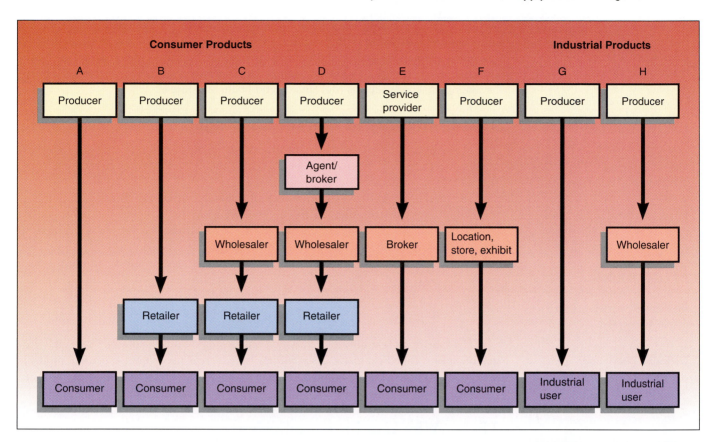

Typical Marketing Channels

For industrial products such as heavy equipment and machinery, the producer can communicate directly with the customer and provide needed and timely services such as training and repairs.

Some industrial products are distributed to customers through wholesalers (Channel F). This channel is most common for accessory (smaller) equipment and supplies that are produced in large quantities but sold in small quantities. Tools and automotive parts, for instance, are sold to industrial users through wholesalers.

15-1c Vertical Integration

When one organization in the marketing channel assumes control of another, **vertical integration** takes place. For instance, movie production companies like Twentieth-Century Fox Film Corporation began purchasing television stations to gain increased control over the outlets available for its products: movies and television programs. Total vertical integration occurs when one organization controls all of the channel functions, from producer to consumer. Some oil companies, for example, own the oil wells, refineries, terminals, trucks and tankers, and service stations.

Traditionally, marketing intermediaries have operated independently. However, vertical integration has led to the concept of a planned marketing channel. A **vertical marketing system (VMS)** is a planned marketing channel in which a single channel member manages the different intermediaries to improve distribution efficiency. Vertical marketing systems have become increasingly popular in recent years.

Vertical marketing systems can be one of three types: corporate, administered, or contractual. Under a **corporate VMS**, one organization owns the marketing intermediaries. The Sherwin-Williams Company, which makes paint and sells it in its own retail stores, uses a corporate VMS. In an **administered VMS**, channel organizations remain independent, but one member dominates the others. This organization, usually large and powerful, greatly influences the decisions of all organizations in the channel. Manufacturers

Vertical Integration
The combining of two or more functions of a marketing channel under one management.

Vertical Marketing System (VMS) A marketing channel in which the different intermediaries are coordinated through management to improve distribution.

Corporate VMS A marketing channel in which one organization owns successive stages of the channel.

Administered VMS
A marketing channel in which independent intermediaries use informal coordination; usually dominated by one channel organization.

such as Campbell Soup Company and Kellogg Company, for example, have extensive influence in distributing their products, including the ability to obtain adequate shelf space in supermarkets and promotional cooperation. The third type, **contractual VMS,** ties channel organizations together through legal agreements. This arrangement is popular among franchises such as McDonald's and Hallmark stores.

15-1d Intensity of Market Coverage

The characteristics of the product and the needs of the target market determine how many outlets a manufacturer will employ to cover the market. **Market coverage** refers to the number of outlets in which a product is sold.

The level of market coverage that uses all available outlets for distributing a product is called **intensive distribution.** Many convenience goods such as gum, candy bars, newspapers, bread, and soft drinks are distributed in a wide variety of locations convenient to consumers. Availability is a major factor in the sale of these items.

In **selective distribution,** only some of the available outlets are used to distribute a product. Goods such as furniture and electrical appliances are distributed selectively. Because these products are much more expensive and are purchased much less frequently than convenience goods, consumers will spend more time and will travel greater distances to shop for them.

The type of market coverage in which only a single outlet is used in a specific geographic area is called **exclusive distribution.** Infrequently purchased, expensive products are often distributed in this manner. Consumers wishing to buy a Rolls Royce, for example, would find only one dealership selling the car in their area.

15-1e Why Use Intermediaries?

A producer or service provider doesn't always need intermediaries to sell its goods or services. As Exhibit 15-2 shows, Channels A and G are direct links between producers and consumers. The Internet is also used to circumvent intermediaries. Dell Computer sells directly to a customer by using an efficient online connection and transaction system. However, in many cases intermediaries are needed to transport, sort, store, and advertise the product at a favorable cost. That is, instead of mailing a product to a consumer, FedEx, Airborne, UPS, or the U.S. mail can perform the necessary intermediary task at a cheaper cost per unit than the producer.

Wholesalers, brokers, and agents are also used in selling insurance, produce, real estate, stocks, bonds, and mutual funds. Their intermediaries bring producers and buyers together so that a sale occurs. Intermediaries such as a real estate agent never own the property or assume any risk; rather, they facilitate the exchange between a buyer and a seller.

15-2 WHOLESALING

Wholesaling involves the activities of marketing intermediaries—called *wholesalers*—who sell to retailers, other wholesalers, or industrial users. (Wholesalers generally do not sell directly to consumers.) Wholesaling is a major segment of the economy. Nearly 478,000 wholesaling establishments conduct business in the United States, with annual sales totaling over $2.5 trillion. About 6,219,000 people are employed in wholesaling.[4] It provides several essential services in the distribution of goods and services.

15-2a Services Wholesalers Perform

2, 3, 4 ☞

Wholesalers such as Sam's Club, Costco, and Staples are more than just conduits of merchandise. These and other wholesalers sell goods and services to wholesalers (other

---

4. Annual Benchmark Report FOW Wholesale, U.S. Census Bureau, February 2002.

Contractual VMS A marketing channel in which intermediaries are independent but have relationships formalized through legal agreements.

Market Coverage The number of outlets in which a product is sold.

Intensive Distribution Market coverage in which all available outlets are used for distributing a product.

Selective Distribution Market coverage in which only some of the available outlets are used for distributing a product.

Exclusive Distribution Market coverage in which one outlet is used in a specific geographic area for distributing a product.

Wholesaling The marketing activities of intermediaries who sell to retailers, industrial users, and other organizational customers.

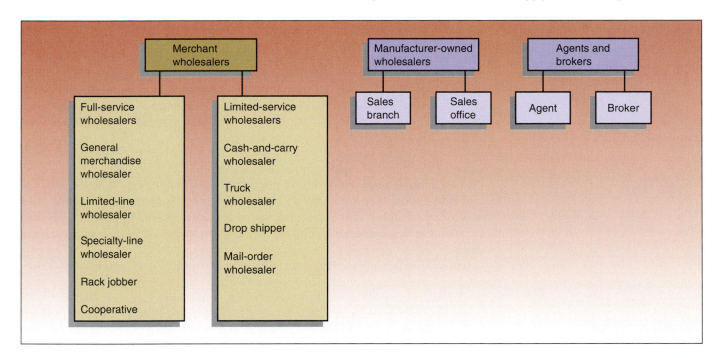

Types of Wholesalers

businesses) as well as regular customers. They provide a unique set of services of value to both their suppliers and their customers (retailers and others).

- *Ownership.* By purchasing large amounts of goods, taking title to them, and storing them for resale, wholesalers absorb inventory costs for manufacturers.
- *Financing.* Wholesalers invest large amounts of money in inventory, extend credit to retailers, and collect payment from retailers.
- *Risk assumption.* Wholesalers take possession and ownership of products that may become obsolete or deteriorate before they are sold. In that way, wholesalers assume a great deal of risk. They also face the risk of nonpayment from retailers.
- *Promotional assistance.* Wholesalers often help promote the products they sell. They may provide retailers with displays or ideas for special promotions.
- *Information.* Wholesalers commonly employ their own sales forces, publish catalogs, and sponsor trade journals. By those means, they provide both retailers and producers with valuable information about product demand, buying trends, and prices.
- *Product assortment.* Because wholesalers usually carry an assortment of products, customers can order from a single source.
- *Transportation.* Wholesalers generally arrange local and long-distance shipments to customers.

15-2b Types of Wholesalers

Many different types of wholesalers offer numerous channel alternatives. Wholesalers commonly are grouped into three categories: merchant wholesalers, manufacturer-owned wholesalers, and agents and brokers (refer to Exhibit 15-3).

Merchant Wholesalers

A wholesaler who takes title to products and resells them to retailers, other wholesalers, or industrial users is a **merchant wholesaler.** Most wholesalers fall into this category. They account for nearly 80 percent of total U.S. wholesale sales.[5] Merchant wholesalers can be either full-service wholesalers or limited-service wholesalers.

Merchant Wholesaler
Marketing intermediary that takes ownership of goods and the risks associated with ownership.

5. Ibid.

As their name implies, full-service wholesalers provide the widest range of services that wholesalers can offer, such as ownership, financing, and risk assumption. Full-service wholesalers who carry a very wide product mix are called *general merchandise wholesalers*. Those who carry only a few product lines are called *limited-line wholesalers*. For example, a general merchandise wholesaler may supply a supermarket with cosmetics, hardware, drugs, and tobacco and food items. A limited-line wholesaler may carry only a few product lines, such as tools and lighting fixtures. A *specialty-line wholesaler* usually carries a single product line, such as exotic flowers or fresh seafood. A *rack jobber* provides display units and places products on shelves. Rack jobbers serve a certain section of a store, such as bakery products, magazines, hardware, or cosmetics.

A *cooperative* is a full-service wholesaler that is owned and operated by its members. Co-ops are especially popular in the agricultural industry, where they are established by farmers to buy fertilizer in large quantities and to get better prices for their harvests than they could by selling individually. The profits earned by the co-op are divided among the members.

Limited-service wholesalers provide only a few of the services offered by wholesalers. Thus, they leave some of the functions for producers or retailers to perform. *Cash-and-carry wholesalers* sell products such as construction materials to customers for cash, with customers providing transportation of the goods. *Truck wholesalers* deliver products directly to customers but offer limited services and require cash payments. They often handle perishable items like fresh fruit and vegetables. *Drop shippers* do not physically handle products but simply take title and negotiate sales. They commonly work in the lumber and coal industries. *Mail-order wholesalers* use catalogs to sell products such as jewelry or automobile parts to retailers and industrial customers.

Manufacturer-Owned Wholesalers

In some cases, the manufacturer owns the wholesale business. There are about 36,000 manufacturer-owned wholesalers, accounting for over 30 percent of total wholesale sales.[6] These manufacturer-owned intermediaries are either sales branches or sales offices. Except that the manufacturer owns them, a **sales branch** resembles a merchant wholesaler, taking title to products and reselling them. Sales branches provide services such as carrying inventory, extending credit, providing delivery, and assisting with promotion. They commonly are found in the chemical and electrical supplies industries.

A **sales office** is basically a sales force owned by the manufacturer. Although they do not maintain inventories, sales offices sell the manufacturer's products. Sales offices also may sell other products that complement the manufacturer's product line.

Sales Branch Manufacturer-owned wholesaler that takes title to products, assumes the risks of ownership, and provides services.

Sales Office Manufacturer-owned sales force that sells products without maintaining an inventory.

Agents and Brokers

Agents and brokers negotiate purchases for a commission but do not purchase products outright. There are fewer agents and brokers, about 42,000, than merchant wholesalers. Agents and brokers account for over 10 percent of the total sales volume of wholesalers.[7]

A wholesaler hired permanently on a commission basis by a buyer or a seller is an **agent.** Agents can take possession of goods, but they do not accept legal title. By concentrating on a few products, they can provide a high level of selling effort. The major types of agents are commission merchants, manufacturers' agents, and selling agents.

A *commission merchant* receives goods from local sellers, establishes prices, and negotiates sales. For instance, in the agricultural industry, a commission merchant may take possession of a truckload of fertilizer and transport it to a central market for sale. A *manufacturers' agent* represents one or more manufacturers on a commission basis and offers noncompeting lines of products to customers. The relationship between the agent and the manufacturer is formalized by a written agreement. A *selling agent* is an independent wholesaler that sells a manufacturer's product for a commission, or fee. Manufacturers rely on selling agents to distribute canned foods, clothing, and furniture.

Agent A person hired by a buyer or seller on a permanent basis and paid commissions.

6. *Census of Wholesale Trade* (Washington, DC: U. S. Census, 1996), pp. 4–8.

7. George S. Day, *The Market Driven Organization* (New York: Free Press, 1999).

A **broker** is a wholesaler who brings together buyers and sellers on a temporary basis. Brokers are similar to agents, but they concentrate on specific commodities, such as insurance or real estate. A food broker, for example, markets food items to grocery chains, food processors, or other wholesalers. Brokers are paid a commission by the party that engages their services, such as a food manufacturer.

Broker Wholesaler who brings together buyers and sellers on a temporary basis.

15-2c Business-to-Business Wholesaling

A growing number of companies are going the **business-to-business** (also referred to as B2B) supply chain route. B2B e-commerce involves all the steps in the buying process from product information to order, invoicing, fulfilling, paying, and providing customer service. The Web provides purchasing managers with sources to transact business. Yahoo's site for B2B business is referred to as the Business-to-Business Marketplace. Wholesaling and retailing transactions using a B2B approach are used by such firms as Ford Motors, CSX Corporation, IBM, General Motors, and Cisco Systems.

B2B firms are using extranets or private networks that use Internet technology and a browser interface. Only authorized members of the extranet can utilize this approach to conduct business because a valid user name and password must be entered. Many of the B2B transactions can be smoothly conducted through the extranet.

Business-to-Business Commerce that involves all the steps in the buying process from product information to ordering, invoicing, fulfilling, paying, and providing customer service; also referred to as B2B.

15-3 RETAILING

The side of distribution most familiar to consumers is retailing; most of us come in contact with retail stores almost daily. The marketing activity of **retailing** focuses on the sale of goods and services to the ultimate consumer for personal or household use.[8] Retailers, an essential link in the marketing channel, are often the only intermediary that deals directly with consumers. Retailers also are customers themselves, since they buy from producers and wholesalers.

Retailing is a significant part of the U.S. economy. Over 2.5 million retailers provide a wide assortment of products to consumers and employ approximately 20 million people, with annual sales exceeding $3 trillion.[9] Many retailers, including two of the largest U.S. retailers, Wal-Mart and Home Depot, are also expanding globally from South and Central America to South China, where markets number in the billions of dollars.[10] Exhibit 15-4 shows retail sales for major store types in the United States.

Retailing The marketing activities involved in selling products to final consumers for personal or household use.

15-3a Types of Retail Stores

Most retail sales take place within stores. The diverse types of retail stores include department stores, discount stores, specialty stores, supermarkets, superstores, convenience stores, warehouse showrooms, catalog showrooms, and warehouse clubs.

Department Stores

Retail stores such as Nordstrom's, Hudson's, and Macy's carry a wide variety of products. These **department stores** are organized into separate departments for such items as apparel, housewares, furniture, sporting goods, and appliances. Department stores generally offer a full line of services, including credit, delivery, and personal assistance. Department stores have for a number of years lost market share to discount stores, specialty stores, and mail-order catalogs.

Discount Stores

Stores like Wal-Mart and Target that offer general merchandise at low prices are called **discount stores.** They carry a wide assortment of products but keep services to a mini-

Department Stores Large retailers offering a wide product mix, organized into separate departments and offering a full line of services.

Discount Stores Retailers offering a wide variety of general merchandise at low prices.

8. Karen J. Sack, "Retailing Specialty," accessed January 3, 2003, from http://icg.Harvard.edu/~ext12115/Home Depot/HD.pdf.

9. Ibid.

10. Cait Murphy, "Introduction: Wal-Mart Rules," *Fortune*, April 15, 2002, pp. 6–7.

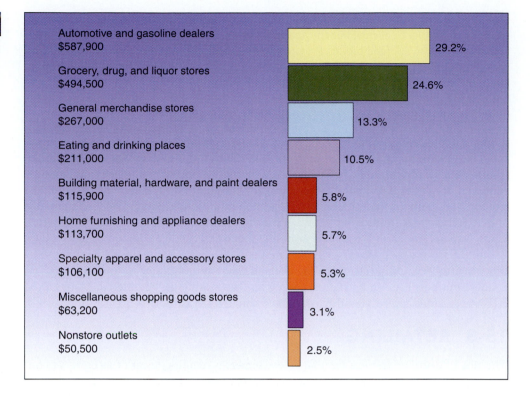

EXHIBIT 15-4

Retail Sales for Major Store Types ($ in Millions)

Source: Statistical Abstract of the United States (1994), p. 786.

Store type	Sales	Percent
Automotive and gasoline dealers	$587,900	29.2%
Grocery, drug, and liquor stores	$494,500	24.6%
General merchandise stores	$267,000	13.3%
Eating and drinking places	$211,000	10.5%
Building material, hardware, and paint dealers	$115,900	5.8%
Home furnishing and appliance dealers	$113,700	5.7%
Specialty apparel and accessory stores	$106,100	5.3%
Miscellaneous shopping goods stores	$63,200	3.1%
Nonstore outlets	$50,500	2.5%

mum. For example, Home Depot, the largest home-repair chain in the United States, stocks 30,000 separate items; its prices are 30 percent below those of a typical hardware store.[11]

Specialty Stores

Specialty Stores Retailers that offer a narrow mix of products with deep product lines.

5, 6 ☞
7 ☞

8 ☞
9 ☞

Retailers that offer a narrow mix of products with deep product lines are called **specialty stores.** The Foot Locker, for example, offers athletic shoes, and Talbots specializes in traditional clothing and accessories for women. The Gap, specializing in selling basic apparel, tries to limit the number of styles, thereby reducing inventory and the risk of picking the wrong styles.[12] Toys "R" Us has over 500 specialty stores around the world. Each carry over 18,000 different toys. Blockbuster is a service retail specialty store that provides rental videos and DVDs to customers.

As illustrated in the Focus on Innovation box, "Using Multiple Channels," Talbots, Circuit City, and Avon are attempting to use multiple channels to satisfy customer needs and preferences.

Supermarkets

Supermarkets Large, self-service retailers that stock a wide variety of groceries and a limited assortment of nonfood products.

Superstore A giant retail outlet that stocks food and nonfood items as well as most products purchased on a routine basis.

Known for their large size, self-service, wide variety of food products, and limited assortment of household goods, **supermarkets** usually offer convenient locations, adequate parking, and lower prices than those at neighborhood grocery stores. Kroger, Winn-Dixie, and A&P are large supermarket chains.

Superstores and Hypermarkets

A giant retail outlet that carries food and nonfood items plus a wide assortment of other routinely purchased products is a **superstore.** With about 30,000 square feet, superstores

11. Chris Roush, *Inside Home Depot* (New York: McGraw-Hill, 1999).

12. "Industry Environment and Analysis," *U.S. Business Reporter,* accessed January 10, 2002, from http://www.active-media-guide.com/specialtyretailing_industry.htm.

FOCUS ON INNOVATION

Using Multiple Channels

Suppose you want to purchase a new television set. Circuit City uses its stores and online selling to provide customers with freedom to look over the product before a purchase is made. Customers can browse Circuit City's website, purchase it on-line, and then go to a store to pick it up. Surveys suggest that shoppers like to use the catalog or website and then go to the store to finalize the sale.

The Circuit City multiple channel approach takes into consideration customer preferences. Regardless of customers' preferences—store, website, or some combination—it is important that the product be translated consistently across channels.

Talbots specialty retailer understands its target customers, women aged 35–55, very well. Talbots knows that customer service for any channel—store, website, or catalog is essential. Telemarketers are available twenty-four hours daily to provide the service online, and well-trained in-store sales personnel are a part of the personal service provided.

Multichannel retailing requires careful attention for Avon as it transforms its door-to-door method. Avon has moved into selling Avon in stores and into "e" space selling through kiosks and Internet selling. Avon has opened 500- to 1,000-square-foot stores inside JCPenney stores. The centers are staffed with "lifestyle" consultants who will provide personalized attention.

Source: "Integrating Multiple Channels," *Chain Store Age*, August 2001, pp. 24A–25A.

are much larger than supermarkets (about 18,000 square feet). They emphasize low prices and one-stop shopping. After losing market share to such high-volume, low-margin, low-price stores, many supermarket chains are switching to this format.

An even larger retail store is the *hypermarket*, which combines the one-stop supermarket and the discount store. Hypermarkets offer more than 50,000 items, including groceries, clothing, building materials and furniture. Retail giants such as Wal-Mart are still using the hypermarket concept. The hypermarket concept generally has not caught on in the United States, however; many shoppers think such stores are too big and too remote.

Convenience Stores

Small retail stores characterized by convenient locations and long hours open for business are called **convenience stores.** Convenient Food Mart and 7-Eleven fall into this category. At convenience stores, the variety of food and nonfood items is limited, with prices generally higher than at supermarkets.

Warehouse Showrooms

Retail stores with sizable inventories housed in large buildings, **warehouse showrooms** deal in volume and provide limited service. Warehouse showrooms commonly are operated by large furniture retailers.

Catalog Showrooms

A combination of catalog shopping and a warehouse showroom is found in the **catalog showroom.** Catalogs are sent to customers' homes and are also available in the store. Sample items are displayed in the store, with the merchandise kept in the warehouse.

Convenience Stores Small retail stores with a convenient location and open for long hours.

Warehouse Showrooms Retail stores carrying large inventories that deal in volume and provide limited services.

Catalog Showroom A form of warehouse showroom where customers select products from catalogs sent to customers' homes or available in the store.

10, 11 ☞

Customers can examine display items, then place orders with clerks. Customers are responsible for transporting their purchases. Service Merchandise, Zales, and Best Products are well-known catalog showrooms.

Warehouse Clubs

Warehouse Clubs Large discount retail stores offering members a broad range of name-brand merchandise at low prices.

Among the newest retail stores are **warehouse clubs,** large-scale, discount operations open to members only. Membership fees typically are around $25. These huge outlets, often located in industrial districts, carry a broad range of brand-name merchandise including appliances, tires, clothing, food, and beverages. Warehouse clubs usually sell items at 20 to 40 percent below prices at supermarkets and other discount stores. Prices are held down by keeping services to a minimum. Costco and Sam's Wholesale Club are warehouse clubs.[13] As their share of retail sales grow, and with over 600 warehouse clubs open in the United States, they are becoming the number one challenge for conventional supermarkets. Some successful retailers have expanded and diversified by opening warehouse clubs in addition to their existing store types.

With retailing making up a major part of the U.S. economy, business students frequently pursue careers in the retailing sector. Many Americans dream of one day owning and running their own retail store; some make it a reality. Use the values and attitudes quiz in Exhibit 15-5 to help you assess your potential as a retailer.

E-Tailing

E-tailing Companies sell goods and services to customers over the Internet.

Companies sell goods and services to customers over the Internet, which is called **e-tailing.** Amazon.com, Barnes & Noble, Wal-Mart, and other firms have invested millions in developing its e-tailing store image. Amazon.com has no brick-and-mortar store, while Barnes & Noble has stores and an e-tailing presence.

E-tailing shoppers purchase books, music, entertainment, computers, gifts, apparel, and numerous other goods and services online. As an early adopter in 1994 of e-tailing, Amazon.com continued to struggle in 2002 to make a profit. Although Amazon.com provides convenience, a wide selection, and discounts, its costs of conducting business (i.e., advertising, shipping, maintaining a top-level website) have been significant.

An important area to pay attention to in e-tailing is providing customer service. The technology occasionally fails, the product is delivered late, or there is no one responding to complaints. Each of these and other service problems need attention before concluding that e-tailing is the direction to take a business.

There is also still a reluctance on the part of many consumers to order and pay for goods and services over the Web. Many people resist providing their credit card numbers. Privacy and security issues should be given top priority if e-tailing is being evaluated as a method for conducting business. Companies such as Disney and Microsoft spell out clearly on their websites the company's position on privacy and security. This is an attempt to reduce consumers' fears that information or data concerning them will be released or provided to anyone.

12, 13 ☞

15-3b Nonstore Retailing

Nonstore Retailing Retailing that takes place outside of stores; includes in-store selling, direct marketing, and vending machines.
In-Home Selling Nonstore retailing activities that involve personal contacts with consumers in their homes.

As you know if you have ever bought merchandise from a catalog and had it delivered to your home or ordered items from a television shopping program, not all retailing takes place within stores. **Nonstore retailing** includes in-home selling, direct marketing, and vending machines.

In-Home Selling

Personal contact with consumers in their homes is the essence of **in-home selling.** Salespeople may go door-to-door or telephone potential customers in advance and make appointments. Avon, Fuller Brush, and Encyclopedia Britannica are a few of the firms that sell products to consumers in their homes. As its traditional U.S. market has decreased,

---

13. Bob Ortega, *In Sam We Trust* (New York: Time Books, 1999).

Retail Aptitude

Directions: Circle the number that represents your level of agreement with each statement.

	Strongly Agree					Strongly Disagree
1. I am a self-starter who doesn't need a lot of guidance in getting the job done.	1	2	3	4	5	6
2. I wouldn't mind working long hours, even weekends, as long as I'm working for myself.	1	2	3	4	5	6
3. I like making my own decisions.	1	2	3	4	5	6
4. I would be willing to take a risk for the right opportunity.	1	2	3	4	5	6
5. I like to set my own schedule on a job and be my own boss.	1	2	3	4	5	6
6. I like to perform a variety of tasks, the small stuff as well as the most visible duties.	1	2	3	4	5	6
7. I would enjoy being a leader and managing other people.	1	2	3	4	5	6
8. The potential for a high salary is important to me.	1	2	3	4	5	6
9. I like working with the public.	1	2	3	4	5	6
10. I am willing to stick with a job for several years if that's what it takes to succeed.	1	2	3	4	5	6

Feedback: Your answers should give you some feel for your potential as a retail store owner and operator. If you circled 5 or 6 for most items, you probably have little interest in owning a retail business. If you circled 1 or 2 to most statements, you just may possess many of the characteristics and skills needed to be a successful retailer. Retailing is a demanding field with no guarantees. The hours are long, the responsibilities great, and problems with employees or customers inevitable. But owning your own retail store also can be rewarding both personally and financially.

Avon has moved its door-to-door selling approach to emerging markets in China, Argentina, Poland, and Mexico, which are producing $1.3 billion in annual sales.[14] Sales representatives of firms such as Tupperware or Mary Kay Cosmetics sell products at demonstrations given in homes or offices.

Another method of in-home selling is television home shopping, which has grown into a billion-dollar industry. Televised home shopping services, such as the Home Shopping Network, are available twenty-four hours a day on some cable stations. They potentially can reach every home with a television and a cable hookup. In some instances, television shopping services employ as many as 400 to 500 operators in a room taking orders around the clock from a loyal following.

Direct Marketing

Many firms promote products directly to buyers through a variety of techniques referred to as **direct marketing.** This type of nonstore retailing includes catalog sales, direct mail, telephone soliciting, and television or radio ads that include telephone numbers and instructions for ordering the items offered. Direct marketing is useful in reaching potential members of a target market. For example, some retailers, like J C Penney, mail catalogs directly to elderly consumers. The catalogs feature products targeted at those 65 and older and offer services that this age group prefers, such as easy returns and toll-free telephone numbers.[15]

Direct Marketing Nonstore retailing that uses nonpersonal media to introduce products to consumers, who then purchase the products by mail, telephone, or computer.

14. Alison J. Clarke, *Tupperware: The Promise of Plastic in 1950s America* (Washington, DC: Smithsonian Institution Press, 2001).

15. Bob Stone, Ron Jacobs, and H. Robert Wientzen, *Successful Direct Marketing Methods* (New York: McGraw-Hill, 2001).

Direct marketing is one of the fastest-growing forms of retailing, with yearly sales in excess of $200 billion. Many firms generate telephone orders for their products by advertising them on cable television and including toll-free numbers. Thousands of firms use catalogs to sell a huge variety of items. L.L. Bean and Best Buy exemplify firms that operate large mail-order businesses throughout the United States. Lands' End, a mail-order clothing company based in Wisconsin, has distinguished itself by providing services that range from helping callers determine sizes to an unconditional guarantee that customers can return any purchases. As competition among firms in the industry intensifies, catalog companies are becoming more specialized, are increasing their efficiency, and emphasizing service.[16]

14, 15 ☞
16 ☞

Vending Machines

Candy, gum, snacks, soft drinks, coffee, newspapers, and other convenience goods are familiar items available in the self-service dispensers known as *vending machines*. In Japan even items like french fries and shrimp are sold in vending machines. Firms place vending machines in high-traffic areas of office and classroom buildings, service stations, and shopping malls. Vending machines offer the advantages of twenty-four-hour-a-day operation with no sales staff. Their main drawbacks include the costs of frequent servicing and needed repairs, as well as the threat of vandalism. Vending machines account for less than 2 percent of all retail sales.

15-3c The Wheel of Retailing

Wheel of Retailing   The idea that retailers enter the market as low-priced, low-status businesses, evolve into high-cost establishments, and become vulnerable to new competitors entering the market.

As they strive to succeed, retailers face constant changes as new stores replace established ones. A popular explanation for how retail stores originate and develop is called the **wheel of retailing,** illustrated in Exhibit 15-6. This theoretical depiction suggests that a retail business enters the market as a low-priced, low-profit, low-status store. Gradually it moves up by improving facilities and adding new services, thus increasing business costs. Over time it becomes a high-cost establishment that is vulnerable to new competitors entering the market—and the wheel turns.

17 ☞
18 ☞

The wheel of retailing can be illustrated by off-price retail chains such as T. J. Maxx and Clothestime. They attract customers by offering brand-name merchandise discounted as much as 60 percent below department store prices. In the past, the outlets were plain and offered limited services. Spurred by weak performance, department stores began to discount their prices up to 50 percent and started taking business from the off-price stores. Now some off-price retailers are imitating department stores—redesigning stores to be more attractive, conducting advertising campaigns that emphasize quality, and promoting specific products rather than focusing on discount prices.

15-3d Technology in Retailing

Advances in technology have affected retailing. Cable television and video ordering systems are changing the retail environment. Antishoplifting tags attached to merchandise reduce thefts. Computerized checking systems speed up check-outs, reduce cashier errors, and provide valuable data for inventory planning. New developments in computerized site selection programs enable firms to make better location decisions. Such technological advances help retailers improve efficiency, reduce labor costs, minimize losses, and obtain accurate and timely information.

15-4 SUPPLY CHAIN MANAGEMENT

Companies searching for ways to increase their profit markets and market share and, at the same time, gain competitive advantage have adopted supply chain management.

---

16. Annual Catalog Conference Proceedings, Chicago, IL, June 10–13, 2002.

EXHIBIT 15-6

The Wheel of Retailing

Source: Lewiston, Dale M. Retailing, 5e, © 1994, p. 94. Reprinted by permission of Prentice Hall, Upper Saddle River, New Jersey.

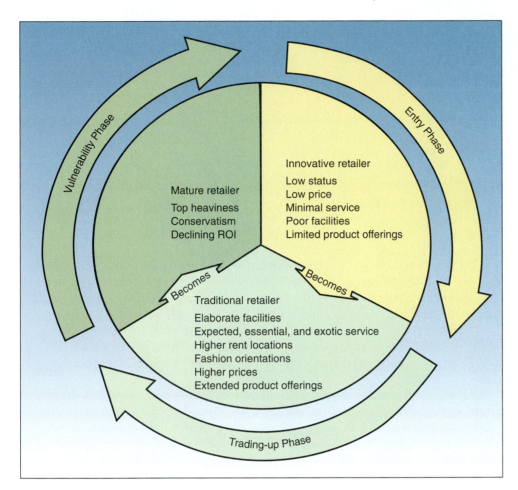

Managing, coordinating, and leading the supply chain is the core of the business approach used by firms because of its usefulness, efficiency, and focus.

Supply chain management is the process of managing the flow of materials, parts, work in progress, finished goods, the return of goods, and information by coordinating activities of all the organizations in the chain.[17] It is an example of cross-functional business process management. The visual image of a "chain" of people both within and between companies cooperating to pass materials/products from the point of origin to the point of need helps depict the supply chain.

Chrysler has created a collaborative initiative in its supply chain to the point where the firms in the "chain" are viewed as a family. Chrysler claims that through supply chain management it enjoys lower costs, improved quality, and shorter product development cycles. Firms such as SAP and PeopleSoft have developed software that Chrysler utilizes to coordinate the movement of goods, schedules, and costs in its family of suppliers. An example of the value of software is specified in the Focus on Technology box, "Supply Chain Management Software."

Harley-Davidson has evolved into a worldwide force in the motorcycle business. The company offers twenty-four models of custom and touring bikes through a worldwide network of dealers. It also provides branded clothing and financial services to dealers and consumers. When declining sales caused Harley-Davidson to put the company up for sale, and no buyer emerged, the firm decided to restructure and employ a supply chain process. The use of supply chain management has helped Harley-Davidson achieve its successful market share position.

Harley-Davidson's comeback is largely due to its focused attention on developing trust and deep relationships with 125 suppliers. These suppliers are integrated fully into

Supply Chain Management
The process of managing the flow of materials, parts, work in progress, finished goods, the return of goods, and information by coordinating activities of all the organizations in the chain.

17. Richard Karpinski, "Firms Ready Summer Test of CPFR, *Internet Week*, May 1, 2002, p. 1.

FOCUS ON TECHNOLOGY

Supply Chain Management Software

There are five basic components for supply chain management:

1. Plan
2. Source—Choose the Suppliers
3. Make—The Manufacturing Step
4. Deliver
5. Return

Each of these five steps is composed of dozens of specific steps. Software vendors have attempted to assemble many of these different steps under one roof. Supply chain software (SCS) uses fancy math algorithms to help a firm improve the efficiency of the supply chain and reduce inventory. SCS depends on information for the accuracy. If a manufacturer of consumer package goods is using SCS, it will need accurate, up-to-date information about customer orders, sales data from retailer customers' stores, manufacturing capacity and capability, and delivery capability.

Before the Internet, supply chain software developers were limited to improving to predict demand from customers and make their supply chains run more smoothly. With the Internet a firm's supply chain can now be connected with the supply chains of suppliers and customers in a network that optimizes costs and opportunities. This is one of reasons for the business-to-business explosion—everyone is now able to be connected together, sharing real-time information.

Two firms that have effectively used SCS to connect everyone are Wal-Mart and Procter & Gamble (P&G). The two giants built software that connected P&G to Wal-Mart's distribution centers. When P&G's products run low at the distribution centers, the system sends an automatic alert to P&G to ship more products. P&G is also able to monitor the shelves in Wal-Mart stores through real-time satellite linkups that send messages to the factory whenever a P&G item is scanned at the register. With this kind of minute-to-minute information, P&G knows when to make, ship, and display more products at the Wal-Mart stores. There is no need to keep products piled up in inventory in warehouses awaiting Wal-Mart's call. Invoicing and payments also happen automatically.

Source: Christopher Koch, "The ABCs of Supply Chain Management," *Supply Chain Management Research Center,* March 2002, pp. 1–7.

the development of products offered by Harley-Davidson. Each supplier is held up to a performance review process similar to employee performance reviews to make sure that they are maintaining the highest-level of Harley-Davidson standards.[18]

In 1994 Dell Computer was a struggling second-tier PC maker. Like many of its competitors, Dell ordered its components in advance and manufactured to inventory. Then Dell converted its operations to a build-to-order process, eliminated its inventories through a just-in-time system, and sold its products directly to consumers. By using supply chain principles Dell became a supply chain expert in scheduling and delivering what each customer preferred.

18. Peter Henshaw, *The Legend of Harley-Davidson* (New York: Stoeger, 2001).

Today's consumers expect far more than previous generations did in terms of instant and universal product delivery. If we can have a variety of ready-to-eat meals delivered to our homes or place of work in a few minutes, why do we need to travel long distances and wait longer for other items? Consumers' expectations require that supply chains respond quickly. Companies like Dell Computers will seek to gain and retain competitive advantage by providing their products in a timelier and more affordable manner than their competitors.

15-5 PHYSICAL DISTRIBUTION

Physical distribution includes the activities that enable the movement of products through marketing channels from manufacturer to customer. Physical distribution activities, which are essential marketing functions providing customers with the goods they want, as well as where and when they want them, include establishing customer service standards, selecting transportation modes, designing and operating warehouse facilities, handling products, and managing inventory. These activities are becoming more critical than ever in this era of total quality management; goods that move are better than goods that sit, and constantly moving goods have become a competitive advantage for modern firms.[19] These activities are strongly interrelated. For instance, a modern warehouse facility may reduce handling costs. However, if it is not properly located, it can increase transportation costs. Firms thus need to plan and integrate their physical distribution activities.

> **Physical Distribution**   Those activities that involve the movement of products through marketing channels from manufacturer to consumer.

Physical distribution begins with a consideration of customers' needs. Improving customer service is a major priority. Some marketers examine the activities performed by competing firms and develop service standards that meet or exceed those of competitors. **Service standards** are specific, measurable goals relating to physical distribution activities. Because on-time delivery is important to customers, for example, a company may set a service standard to "deliver all orders within 24 hours." When a firm such as Federal Express guarantees overnight delivery, it must develop physical distribution activities that will achieve this service standard. Federal Express transports packages via airplane in most cases, since shipping by truck or railroad could not meet the overnight deadline.

> **Service Standards**   Specific, measurable goals relating to physical distribution activities.

15-5a Transportation

Transportation, shipping goods to customers, is a critical physical distribution activity. To ship goods, firms generally choose one of the five major modes of transportation: rail, air, truck, water, and pipeline. Firms that transport products, through any means, are called *carriers*.

When selecting a transportation mode for products, marketing managers look at important factors such as cost, delivery speed, number of locations served, reliability, range of products carried, loss and damage records, and fuel efficiency. Exhibit 15-7 ranks

> **Transportation**   Shipping goods to customers by railways, airlines, trucks, waterways, and pipelines.

	1*	2	3	4	5
Lowest cost	Water	Pipeline	Rail	Truck	Air
Delivery speed	Air	Truck	Rail	Water	Pipeline
Number of locations served	Truck	Rail	Air	Water	Pipeline
Dependability	Pipeline	Truck	Air	Rail	Water
Range of products carried	Rail	Truck	Water	Air	Pipeline
Losses and damages	Pipeline	Water	Air	Truck	Rail
Fuel efficiency	Pipeline	Water	Rail	Truck	Air

*1 = highest ranking

EXHIBIT 15-7

Ranking the Transportation Mode

---

19. "Community on the Move," *Distribution*, October 2001, pp. 7–9.

EXHIBIT 15-8

Shipping Mileage and Revenue of Transportation Modes

Source: Statistical Abstract of the United States (1994), p. 627.

INTERACTIVE EXHIBIT

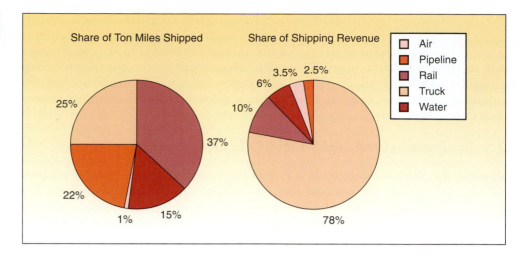

Share of Ton Miles Shipped   Share of Shipping Revenue

Legend:
- Air
- Pipeline
- Rail
- Truck
- Water

Share of Ton Miles Shipped: 25%, 37%, 15%, 1%, 22%

Share of Shipping Revenue: 3.5%, 2.5%, 6%, 10%, 78%

the different transportation modes according to these factors. Exhibit 15-8 compares the share of shipping mileage and shipping revenue for each transportation mode.

Rail

Railroads carry about 38 percent of all products and account for 10 percent of shipping revenue. Railroads are fairly cost- and fuel-efficient and can reach a large number of locations. A wide range of products such as coal, grain, chemicals, lumber, and automobiles can be transported by rail.

Air

Air transport, the most expensive means of transportation, accounts for only 1 percent of all products transported. Yet the use of air transit is growing rapidly. The need to deliver some items quickly, such as fresh flowers, perishable foods, technical instruments, and emergency parts, justifies the high cost.

Trucks

Trucking dominates the transportation industry, with a 78 percent share of shipping revenue. Although trucks account for only a 25 percent share of ton miles shipped, they often carry the most profitable products, such as clothing, paper goods, computers, fresh fruit and vegetables, and livestock. Trucks are the most flexible mode of transportation. They can travel anywhere there are roads and can provide door-to-door service.

The technology now available to truckers is so specific that what roads to travel, schedules, and where to purchase diesel fuel are spelled out. The following Focus on Technology box, "The Modern Trucker," illustrates the role technology plays in attempts to save money and speed deliveries.

Water

Barges and cargo ships are the least costly means of transportation; they also are among the slowest and least dependable. Another limitation is, of course, that only cities with ports can be served. In spite of these drawbacks, water transport accounts for about 15 percent of ton miles shipped. Products commonly transported on waterways include petroleum, chemicals, and iron ore.

Pipeline

The major products shipped via pipelines are oil, processed coal, and natural gas. Pipelines have increased in importance as the demand for oil and natural gas has increased. Pipelines account for 21 percent of ton miles shipped and 2.5 percent of shipping revenues.

FOCUS ON TECHNOLOGY

The Modern Trucker

19 ☞ Orlando Mitchell is a trucker and an employee of Marten Transport, a $260 million national carrier. He regularly hauls 42,000 pounds of batter from Cleveland to Gloucester, Massachusetts. His routing is handled by satellites and software. He uses his own "Qualcomm," a laptop-sized device that serves as a satellite link to Marten's headquarters in Mondovi, Wisconsin.

When a red light appears on the dashboard, Mitchell pulls over to check his message. It informs him that after he drops the batter at 10:00 A.M. in a warehouse grafted onto the offices of seafood firm Gorton's of Gloucester, he is to adjust the refrigeration unit. He is instructed to adjust refrigeration to minus 10 degrees Fahrenheit and wait for a load of fish sticks at 2:30 P.M., which he will haul to a warehouse in Lithia Springs, Georgia. He is also instructed to fill up in Raphine, Virginia, and is advised about how much fuel to get (63.8 gallons of diesel) and what it will cost.

Truckers like Mitchell are tethered electronically. Marten is squeezing every penny of savings possible, just as other firms are with their 2.5 million class 8 trucks driving on American highways. Transportation is the largest component of logistics costs. Modern truckers use software from Logistics.com, Manugistics, and i² Transportation for route planning, carrier bidding, scheduling, and mapping. Finding the best routes, at the lowest costs, and with the fewest delays is how technology can help carriers become more efficient. By studying the economics of transportation and using technology, firms such as Marten can make more informed and less costly decisions.

Sources: Adapted from David Diamond, "The Trucker and the Professor," *Wired,* December 2001, pp. 70–74; and *Statistical Abstract of the United States* (Washington, DC: U.S. Government), pp. 590–598.

15-5b Warehousing

Another important aspect of distribution is the design and operation of storage facilities. **Warehousing** includes various responsibilities involved in receiving, storing, and shipping goods. Warehouses accept delivered goods, record the quantities received, store them, coordinate shipments, and dispatch orders.

Private warehouses are owned and operated by firms who wish to distribute their own products. Usually they are companies that carry large inventories. For example, Spec's Music, a Miami-based firm with music and video outlets throughout Florida, has its own

> **Warehousing** The physical distribution activities involved in receiving, storing, and shipping goods.

warehouses. It carries huge inventories and can quickly process orders and deliver fast-selling items to the stores. *Public warehouses* provide storage on a rental basis. Firms that do not wish to own warehouses or that need extra space on a temporary basis often use public warehouses.

15-5c Order Processing

Order Processing   The receipt and preparation of an order for shipment.

Order processing refers to the receipt and preparation of an order for shipment. Efficient order processing procedures can reduce the time needed for delivery and thus help firms satisfy their customers.

Processing begins when a customer places an order by mail, telephone, or computer. Typically the order is forwarded to the warehouse and the credit department. Clerks can fill an order quickly if the item is in stock and the customer's credit rating is approved. For items not in stock, an order is placed at the factory. Finally, the product is packaged and shipped.

15-5d Materials Handling

Materials Handling
The physical handling of products during transportation and warehousing.

The physical handling of a product during transportation and while it is in the warehouse is termed **materials handling.** Firms institute materials handling procedures that make maximum use of warehouse space, minimize the number of times a product is handled, and reduce damage to merchandise.

The use of containerization and freight forwarders has improved the ability of organizations to handle materials. *Containerization* is packing goods within a strong container that is easy to transfer between train, truck, ship, and airplane. Containerization reduces damage, theft, insurance costs, and materials handling time, thereby reducing the cost of distribution. *Freight forwarders* combine small shipments from several firms. They arrange for the merchandise to be picked up from the shipper and delivered to the buyer.

15-5e Inventory Management

Inventory Management
The process of developing and maintaining stocks of products that customers need and want.

Inventory management is the process of developing and maintaining products that are in demand by customers. Efficient inventory management, an important aspect of physical distribution, can help a firm achieve its profit goals. A business should design its inventory system so that the number of products sold and the number of products in stock can be determined at specified checkpoints. One method could involve tearing off a code number from each product sold so that the correct sizes, colors, and models can be tabulated and reordered. In many larger stores, such as Toys "R" Us and Wal-Mart, checkout terminals or cash registers are connected to central computer systems to allow instantaneous updating of inventory and sales records.

Good inventory management balances the cost of holding a large inventory with the cost of losing sales because of shortages, or stock-outs, of certain products. One inventory management technique used to achieve this balance is *just-in-time (JIT) inventory*, popularized in Japan. Companies using JIT maintain smaller inventories by ordering more often and in smaller quantities, just in time for production. The results, when JIT is used properly, include better-quality products, quicker production time, and reduced operating costs, all of which increase competitiveness.

15-5f Distributing Services

Service firms are generally limited in their channels of distribution since services are produced and consumed at the same time and the customer is present to initiate the contact. Through employees, service providers usually perform services directly for customers with no use of intermediaries. Health care professionals at clinics, for instance, perform physical examinations and medical tests for clients.

Distribution can separate a service from the seller, however. Bank credit cards allow the intangible service of credit to be separated from the financial institution. Through bank credit cards, organizations such as restaurants, gas stations, retailers, supermarkets, and even fast-food outlets can distribute credit to consumers. Some service businesses have developed innovative methods of distribution. The communications industry offers cellular phones for cars, insurance companies sell policies through vending machines at airports, entertainment firms sell tickets to concerts through computers in stores, and banks allow customers to have paychecks deposited directly in accounts and to pay bills by automatic withdrawal.

SUGGESTED WEBSITES

Note: These websites were functional when we went to press. Please access the online text for the most up-to-date URLs.

1. www.expedia.com
2. www.samsclub.com
3. www.costco.com
4. www.staples.com
5. www.footlocker.com
6. www.talbots.com
7. www.gap.com
8. www.toysrus.com
9. www.blockbuster.com
10. www.servicemerchandise.com
11. www.zales.com
12. www.disney.com
13. www.microsoft.com
14. www.llbean.com
15. www.bestbuy.com
16. www.landsend.com
17. www.tjmaxx.com
18. www.clothestime.com
19. www.marten.com

SUMMARY OF LEARNING OBJECTIVES

1. *Define the term* marketing channel *and identify the two major types of marketing intermediaries.*   A marketing channel is a group of interrelated organizations that directs the flow of goods from producer to consumer. Marketing intermediaries, organizations that provide the link between producers and consumers, are vital because they create place, time, and possession utility. The major types of intermediaries are *wholesalers and retailers*.

2. *Explain how marketing channels are integrated vertically.*   Vertical integration occurs when one organization takes control of another member of the marketing channel, often by purchasing it. Distribution efficiency may be improved with a vertical marketing system (VMS), a planned marketing channel in which one channel member manages all intermediaries. The three types of vertical marketing systems are corporate, administered, and contractual.

3. *Define* wholesaling *and describe the functions wholesalers perform.*   Wholesaling consists of the activities of marketing intermediaries who sell to retailers, other wholesalers, or industrial users. Wholesalers provide several services, including ownership, financing, risk assumption, promotional assistance, information, product assortment, and transportation. The major types of wholesalers are merchant wholesalers, manufacturer-owned wholesalers, and agents and brokers.

4. *Define* retailing *and outline the activities retailers perform.*   Retailing activities consist of the sales of goods and services to consumers for personal or household use. Retailing activities can take place in stores or through the nonstore retailing methods of in-home selling, direct marketing and vending machines.

5. *Describe various forms of nonstore retailing.*   Nonstore retailing involves retailing activities that take place outside traditional store settings. A number of forms of nonstore retailing include in-home selling, direct marketing, e-tailing, and vending.

6. *Explain the benefits and possible problems of using a supply chain management approach.*   Supply chain management is the process of efficiently moving the flow of materials, parts, work in progress, finished goods, the return and recycling of goods and information through coordinating the activities of all the firms in the "chain."

7. *Explain the role of physical distribution and identify its components.*   Physical distribution activities accomplish the physical movement of products though marketing channels from manufacture to customer. Physical distribution activities include establishing customer service standards, selecting transportation modes, designing and operating warehouse facilities, handling products, and managing inventory.

KEY TERMS

administered VMS (p. 401)
agent (p. 404)
broker (p. 405)
business-to-business (p. 405)
catalog showroom (p. 407)
contractual VMS (p. 402)
convenience stores (p. 407)
corporate VMS (p. 401)
department stores (p. 405)
direct marketing (p. 409)
discount stores (p. 405)
e-tailing (p. 408)
exclusive distribution (p. 402)
in-home selling (p. 408)

intensive distribution (p. 402)
inventory management (p. 416)
market coverage (p. 402)
marketing channel (channel of distribution) (p. 399)
marketing intermediary (p. 399)
materials handling (p. 416)
merchant wholesaler (p. 403)
nonstore retailing (p. 408)
order processing (p. 416)
physical distribution (p. 413)
retailing (p. 405)
sales branch (p. 404)
sales office (p. 404)

selective distribution (p. 402)
service standards (p. 413)
specialty stores (p. 406)
supermarkets (p. 406)
superstore (p. 406)
supply chain management (p. 411)
transportation (p. 413)
vertical integration (p. 401)
vertical marketing system (VMS) (p. 401)
warehouse clubs (p. 408)
warehouse showrooms (p. 407)
warehousing (p. 415)
wheel of retailing (p. 410)
wholesaling (p. 402)

QUESTIONS FOR DISCUSSION AND REVIEW

1. Is it possible—or desirable—to eliminate the intermediary in the distribution of goods to consumers? Explain your answer.
2. What types of marketing channels are used to distribute consumer products? To distribute industrial products?
3. Have you ever purchased a product directly from a producer (Channel A)? Name some products that manufacturers or producers sell directly to consumers.
4. Distinguish between intensive, selective, and exclusive distribution. Give examples of products distributed by each method.
5. Wholesalers perform a variety of services in product distribution. What are those services? Whom do they benefit?

6. How do full-service wholesalers and limited-service wholesalers differ? Give two examples of each type.
7. What would be some of the possible difficulties of coordinating the scheduling and quality work of members of a supply chain?
8. Why do (don't) you purchase products online? Explain.
9. What can the wheel of retailing teach someone who is starting a retail business?
10. List the various forms of transportation and the advantages and disadvantages of each.

END-OF-CHAPTER QUESTIONS

1. For all of 2001, e-commerce purchases accounted for just over *1 percent* of all retail sales in the United States. **T** or **F**
2. The common channels employed to distribute industrial products are much shorter than the consumer channels. **T** or **F**
3. *Truck wholesalers* sell products such as construction materials to customers for cash, with customers providing transportation of the goods. **T** or **F**
4. *Order processing* is the process of developing and maintaining products that are in demand by customers. **T** or **F**
5. Wal-Mart and Target are classified as what type of retail establishment?
   a. Supermarket
   b. Discount
   c. Specialty
   d. Showroom
6. Which of the following generates the largest retail sales?
   a. Automobile and gas dealers
   b. Grocery, drug, and liquor stores
   c. Eating and drinking establishments
   d. Home furnishing and appliance stores
7. Market coverage that uses all available outlets is called _____.
   a. selective distribution
   b. intensive distribution
   c. corporate directorship
   d. market density

8. When an organization in the marketing channel assumes control of another firm, it is called _____.
   a. channel inversion
   b. producer catalyst
   c. vertical integration
   d. systems integration
9. Providing a variety of services, such as credit, delivery, and returns is called _____.
   a. carrying inventory
   b. selling
   c. promoting
   d. servicing
10. Which of the following transport methods carries the most product overall?
    a. Air
    b. Rail
    c. Pipeline
    d. Trucks
11. Firms that transport products, through any means, are called _____.
    a. transporters
    b. shippers
    c. handlers
    d. carriers
12. Vending machines account for approximately _____ of all retail sales.
    a. 2 percent
    b. 5 percent
    c. 10 percent
    d. 20 percent

END-OF-CHAPTER QUESTIONS

13. Superstores have approximately _____ of retail space.
   a. 18,000 square feet   b. 30,000 square feet
   c. 50,000 square feet
14. A rack jobber provides _____ and places products on shelves.
   a. display units   c. magazines
   b. bakery products   d. cosmetics

15. Contractual VMS ties channel organizations together through legal agreements. This arrangement is popular with which of the following?
   a. Campbell Soup Company   c. Sherwin-Williams Company
   b. Kellogg Company   d. McDonald's

INTERNET EXERCISE

The Category Killer Store

Category "killer" stores are large stores such as "Toys "R" Us," "Pets-Mart," "Virgin Records," "Barnes & Noble," and "Sportsmart." Visit the Internet and determine approximately how many items each of these six category killer stores offer. Who is the main competition (retailers, wholesalers) that competes head-on with these six category killer stores?

1. Have you purchased products at any of these six stores?
2. Do you find the best prices at category killer stores or stores like Wal-Mart that sell products at discount prices?
3. Is there a category killer in the field of education? Explain.

EXPERIENTIAL EXERCISE

Channels for Organizational Markets

Marketing channels for organizational markets are not readily visible to consumers. To learn more about the channels that organizational buyers use to obtain products, choose a firm located near you and find out some of the main products it uses. (You could choose your college or university and select some of the products that it purchases.)

Contact a purchasing agent for the organization. Ask him or her to outline the marketing channels through which the products flow and to name all the intermediaries, from the producer to the buyer's organization.

BUSINESS APPLICATION

From the Chicken House to the Dairy Aisle

Chuck Jennings has been the owner and operator of a chicken farm in rural Florida for the past eight years. He inherited the farm from his father and has worked in the chicken and egg business for many years. The vast majority of the income generated by the chicken farm comes from the sale of eggs to various intermediaries. The remaining income comes from the sale of the chickens themselves.

Jennings has been examining options for expanding the business and is considering the possibility of performing some of the intermediary, or middleman, functions. He thinks he may be able to increase his company's overall profits from egg sales by providing transportation of the eggs from the farm to supermarkets and convenience stores. Jennings has started making a list of tasks he will have to do in order to assume the role of intermediary.

Questions for Discussion

1. What are five things Chuck Jennings must be able to do in order to expand into the intermediary role?
2. What are some of the risks that might be associated with such a change?
3. If he decides to assume the intermediary role, how might the company gradually phase in the expansion?

Case

Corporate Express Promotional Marketing Uses Supply Chain Management

From the time a customer places an order, through shipping and billing, Corporate Express Promotional Marketing (CEPM) visualized a supply chain that allowed seamless operations and increased inventory control and order trading throughout the fulfillment process. CEPM selected Frontstep to help them build a real-time, automated, and synchronized supply chain. Frontstep bills itself as an experienced supply chain solution provider.

CEPM is a leading provider of centrally managed merchandise-based brand and corporate identity programs. It specializes in the assembly and distribution of promotional and advertising specialty items with company logos affixed to them. Most of CEPM's programs are centered on a core promotional merchandise catalog. Items can be selected from a 10,000-item catalog for promotions. CEPM's customers include AT&T, Bank One, Honda, and Pfizer. CEPM's customers can enter an order and search for order status information. Frontstep helps CEPM improve and expedite this kind of information.

The promotional items industry is a high-volume, low-transaction custom-driven market. Each order is unique because corporate identity specifications need to be adhered to when affixing a logo to any promotional item (e.g., hat, sweater, golf balls, luggage, clock, wrist watch). CEPM's customers want a timely, cost-effective promotion. Frontstep allows electronic communication of documents such as purchase orders, order acknowledgments, and advance shipping notifications.

CEPM also wanted a system that reduces telephone calls per transaction. It was taking five to ten telephone calls to perform price checks, locate inventory, and review order status. Frontstep software enabled CEPM's customers to check these types of issues online.

Frontstep software thus has allowed CEPM to take a manual step-by-step process that is inefficient and automate it to be quicker, more accurate, more cost-effective, and more customer-friendly. What CEPM believes is that the more customer-friendly approach will result in more repeat sales, more word-of-mouth goodwill, and increased loyalty toward CEPM products and services.

Questions for Discussion

1. Why would CEPM customers be interested in order tracking and inventory visibility?
2. Would you refer to CEPM's approach as interactive? Why?
3. Why is CEPM's business referred to as being custom-driven?

Source: "Corporate Express Promotional Marketing," www.frontstep.com/case-studies, accessed April 10, 2002.

part 5

Managing Information

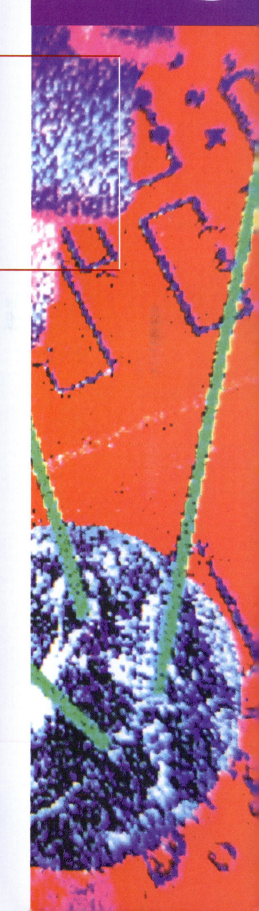

Managing Information Technology

Chapter Objectives

Photo: comstock.com

After completing this chapter, you should be able to:

1 **Explain** how businesses can benefit from information technology (IT).

2 **Trace** the evolution of computing.

3 **Explain** how businesses can take advantage of the Internet.

4 **Identify** the different types of computers.

5 **Understand** the basic components of a computer.

6 **Identify** and understand common business IT applications.

7 **Define** *management information system (MIS)* and explain how an MIS is used.

8 **List** trends in computer development and use and in information technology.

Nordstrom Bolsters Website to Enhance Sales

Nordstrom Inc., an upscale department store based in Seattle that targets female shoppers, had a problem. All its major competitors offered some high-value services on their websites that Nordstrom's website, Nordstrom.com, couldn't. Competitors' online customers could purchase a wide range of cosmetics and order gift cards by simply clicking on a link.

Lacking such services put Nordstrom at a "significant competitive disadvantage," says Paul Onnen, Nordstrom's former chief technology officer and now an independent consultant. But putting together the technology to offer and accept gift cards on the Web is a complex process. Using a gift card on the website would require a link to Nordstrom's bank so that the card number could be validated and the amount of the purchase deleted from the card's dollar value. The transaction would also have to link to Nordstrom's inventory control system on its corporate mainframes, which would deduct the items purchased from the company's inventory list. And if the purchase were executed through the store's catalog rather than its website, mail-order software on yet another system also had to be linked to the transaction to make sure the product got to the customer.

Nordstrom.com considered, but quickly rejected, the prospect of developing custom software. It could have been done, Onnen said, but it would have been far too expensive, and it would have taken close to a year to test and deploy. Instead, Nordstrom opted for web services development software from IONA Technologies PLC. The entire project

1 ☞

was completed in less than three months. The web-based application, which translates the gift card transaction data so that each system could process it through its respective firewall, worked correctly from the outset, said Onnen, allowing Nordstrom.com to provide not only gift cards, but cosmetics order fulfillment as well—and all in time for the holiday rush.

Cosmetics represented 10 percent to 15 percent of Nordstrom's total revenue in 2000, and sales from Nordstrom.com represented 7 percent to 10 percent of the company's overall sales. Had the cosmetics product category been available for the entire year, given Nordstrom's $6 billion in revenue for the fiscal year that ended January 2002, cosmetics revenue from Nordstrom.com could have reached $90 million.

But Nordstrom isn't stopping with cosmetics and gift certificates. Nordstrom is currently testing what Onnen calls a "perpetual inventory system" in the shoe department of some of its stores in the Pacific Northwest. Salespeople can go to a special version of the Nordstrom.com website to order out-of-stock shoes. The customer pays no shipping charges, the store is credited with a sale, and the salesperson gets the commission—a transaction that would not have been possible without web services, says Onnen.

Sources: Adapted from Stephen Lawton, "Custom Services: Putting Web Services to Work," *CIO Insight*, April 15, 2002; and Amy Cortese, "Price Flexing: How the Web Adds New Twists," *CIO Insight*, March 1, 2002.

Computers and other forms of information technology (IT) are by now firmly entrenched in our society, particularly in the workplace. IT performs tasks from the most mundane to the most complex. IT is used to store libraries of information. By quickly transmitting and analyzing important information, IT can help business managers make complicated decisions. And unlike humans, IT systems can work twenty-four hours a day, seven days a week. Computers never complain, take vacations, or ask for a raise (although they do break down occasionally).

In the opening vignette, you were introduced to Nordstrom.com, an e-commerce website that helps the giant retailer serve unique customer needs. When the Internet revolution was in full fury during the mid to late 1990s, online retailing was considered to be the heart of the "new economy." People would be able to shop and order goods with the click of a mouse. Many giant brick-and-mortar retailers shuddered as tiny start-ups swept ahead of them in technology and dramatically challenged them on the pricing front. But, as we all know by now, the online retailers (also called e-tailers) found it very difficult to survive when the venture capital ran out. Troubles with shipping, returned merchandise, and lack of profit margins caused many of them to go bankrupt. What survives today are the major retailers who had the cash to wait out the e-tailing revolution, and who now have the resources to convert to a clicks-and-mortar operation. That is, firms like Nordstrom are able to serve customers with traditional retail stores as well as with highly functional websites.

Hardware   The physical devices that make up a computer system.

Software   A sequence of instructions that a computer can carry out.

Almost every business today has some form of information technology at its core. Even the simplest of sole proprietorship operations usually have an IT system to keep track of business. As IT has pushed forward, businesses constantly strive to find ways to use IT for competitive advantage—whether through lower costs, improved communication, or faster cycle times. IT actually refers to two different types of product: hardware and software. **Hardware** is the physical equipment that lies at the heart of the information society—the computers, PDAs, routers, telecommunications equipment, and other devices. **Software** is the programming that makes these devices perform the processing and analyzing that leads to useful output. Word processing, spreadsheets, Internet browsers, e-mail organizers, and other applications enable us to work smarter and with greater efficiency.

In this chapter, we introduce the role of IT in the modern business and explore management information systems. First we look at how the information explosion has increased the importance of IT in business. Then we examine the evolution of computers and explain the different types of information technology. Next we investigate the many uses of computers in business. A discussion of management information systems follows. Finally we examine the future of computers and management information systems.

16-1   THE AGE OF INFORMATION

Businesses today have access to and create more information than ever before. The abundance of websites, newspapers, journals, magazines, television and radio networks, business and government reports, and educational alternatives has led many commentators to label this the *information age*. But the sheer volume of information available presents a real challenge to business managers. Obviously managers cannot use all the information that is available in their day-to-day business decisions. The challenges for any business are to collect, store, process, report, and apply the most relevant information that enables effective decisions.

Data   Facts, figures, and statistics concerning people, objects, events, and ideas.

Information   Data with meaning attached.

Information technology helps firms meet this challenge. IT assists managers in converting **data**—facts, figures, and statistics concerning people, objects, events, and ideas—into useful information. Thus **information** is data with meaning attached. The figure 1,000,000 is a piece of data, but if the term *sales* and a dollar sign are attached—sales = $1,000,000—it becomes a piece of information. Employees at all levels of the organization must then take information that is distilled from raw data and convert it into *knowledge* that can be used to help the business grow and prosper. The Focus on Diversity box, "MetLife Uses Passive Recruiting to Ensure IT Worker Diversity," highlights the efforts being made by firms in the insurance industry to ensure that their workforce is not only knowledgeable about IT, but also diverse.

IT is both the idol of those who think technology will help businesses achieve ever greater levels of efficiency and effectiveness, and the bane of those who have been victims of its occasional mishaps. Who among us hasn't from time to time been the victim of a dreaded "computer error"? Reliance on technology has helped many businesses emerge from also-ran to global competitor. However, overreliance on IT can alienate customers and lead to unforeseen problems. Telephone systems are a great example of how IT can go awry if carried too far. In the past few decades, telecommunications systems have grown increasingly sophisticated. Answering systems that ask callers to push certain buttons to route calls to appropriate individuals within a business are commonplace. You've probably experienced them: "If you want customer service, push 6." Unfortunately, overdependence on such systems has led to customer frustration and backlash. According to research by the Public Agenda, a New York nonprofit research group, 94 percent of consumers surveyed in 2002 say it's frustrating to "call a company and get a recording instead of a human

2 ☞

FOCUS ON DIVERSITY

MetLife Uses Passive Recruiting to Ensure IT Worker Diversity

Insurance companies are pulling out all the stops when it comes to recruiting IT help. In fact, some carriers are starting passive recruitment efforts years before they intend to hire prospects. Facing a large audience of 10- to 15-year-old girls, Peggy Fechtmann, chief information officer, client services group, MetLife recently concluded her remarks saying, "We hope when you leave high school you consider joining MetLife."

The event, held in observance of the annual Ms. Foundation–sponsored "Take Our Daughters To Work Day," was dedicated to recognizing young women's "ability to meet the information technology (IT) divide between men and women in the workforce," according to MetLife. And while the attendees were not of hiring age, Fechtmann says, the event represented a larger strategy of getting a message out to potential employees who may not be looking to work in the IT department of an insurance company.

As long as IT employment remains a seller's market, Fechtmann says, prospective hires of whatever background will need to be persuaded that the insurance industry is a viable destination for their IT career ambitions. Facing the challenge of recruiting for a diverse workforce is even greater, she says. Even at a carrier such as MetLife where, "diversity is in our DNA," Fechtmann adds, "we have to ask 'How do we make sure we catch a broader audience, and how do we communicate that having an inclusive environment is part of our core values?'"

Source: Adapted from Anthony O'Donnell, "Reaching Out for Diversity," *Insurance & Technology,* July 2001, p. 65.

being."[1] In 2002, U.S. companies will spend more than $7 billion on telephone answering technology. The reason for this spending is largely economic. In 2001, U.S. companies spent more than $150 billion to maintain call center operations staffed by live operators.[2]

Another major concern of many is the use of cell phones while driving. Granted, not all cell phone use is business oriented, but many of today's mobile professionals use their cell phones while driving. Exhibit 16-1 highlights some of the major gripes people have regarding cell phone use in vehicles.

Despite these drawbacks to IT use in business and community life, there is little doubt that IT has provided tremendous productivity gains. Nations that lead in IT development and implementation are far ahead in per capita GDP over less technologically developed nations. In fact, IT deployment and usage creates a **positive feedback loop.** More IT requires more highly educated workers to operate and maintain it. More highly educated workers create opportunities for more and better IT innovations.[3] Although some interest groups are opposed to IT in general, a few would prefer to live in a world without IT.

Positive Feedback Loop
A systematic interaction that results in the amplification of a process.

1. "Aggravating Circumstances: A Status Report on Rudeness in America," Public Agenda, April 2002.

2. Jane Spencer, "In Search of the Operator," *The Wall Street Journal,* May 8, 2002, pp. D1–D2.

3. Bill Gates, *The Road Ahead* (New York: Viking, 1995).

Major Complaints about Cell Phone Use

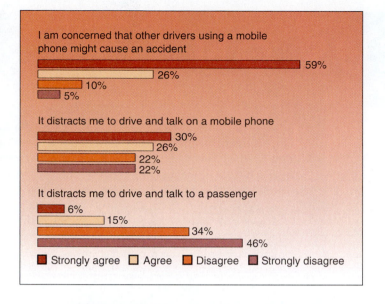

I am concerned that other drivers using a mobile phone might cause an accident
- 59%
- 26%
- 10%
- 5%

It distracts me to drive and talk on a mobile phone
- 30%
- 26%
- 22%
- 22%

It distracts me to drive and talk to a passenger
- 6%
- 15%
- 34%
- 46%

■ Strongly agree □ Agree ■ Disagree ■ Strongly disagree

16-2 BACKGROUND ON INFORMATION TECHNOLOGY

Computer   An electronic device used to input, store, and process data and to output them as useful information.

A **computer** is defined as an electronic device used to input, store, and process data and to output data as useful information. Universities, for instance, can enter into a computer the grade reports on thousands of students from hundreds of courses, store the information, process grades in a matter of seconds, and print out individual student grade reports ready to mail or put the grade reports in a secure online location for students to view immediately. Before computers, the process usually took weeks to complete.

Many of us are now in a position where we have grown up with computers and IT and take it for granted. Of course, universities process student records using sophisticated IT systems, we think. But it wasn't always that way. To understand the limited place of IT in business, we have to try to recall when IT was not as pervasive at it is today. It's important to remember that businesses exist to please customers, not to find and experiment with new IT systems. IT is a business enabler. Businesses that run into trouble with IT conceive it as an end in itself, rather than as a means to an end.

16-2a The Evolution of Computers

Electronic computers have evolved through five generations. The first generation (1945–1958) began with the introduction of the ENIAC (electronic numerical integrator and calculator). This massive computer, weighing more than thirty tons, operated with 19,000 glass vacuum tubes.[4] Primitive by today's standards, these tubes were extremely hot and burned out frequently—an average of one every seven seconds. Computer operators stood by with baskets of replacement tubes to keep the system working. During this early period, computers were used primarily for scientific and government purposes—the first ENIAC was used by the U.S. military to calculate trajectories of ballistic artillery. However, business firms also began to realize the value of computers in processing data. The ENIAC, despite all its limitations, was a major start for the electronic computer era.

The second generation of computers (1959–1964) was characterized by the use of the **transistor,** a small switch that controls electrical current. Transistors were much faster than vacuum tubes and produced less heat. With transistors, smaller, more powerful computers could be built at less cost than the first-generation computers. Businesses, even medium-sized and small ones, began using the computer to process an increasing number

Transistor   A small switch that controls electrical current; characterized second-generation computers.

4. "Soldiering into the Modern Computer Era, 1943," *The Wall Street Journal,* June 16, 1989, p. B1.

of business applications. The transistor was discovered in the Bell Telephones laboratory led by William Shockley in 1947. At first, no one understood the strange electrical effects that made the transistor possible. Shockley advanced understanding of the quantum effects apparent in the transistor and won a Nobel prize for his work in 1956. The first transistor was fabricated in his laboratory in 1951. Shockley left Bell shortly after that and established a private company in California, producing the first silicon-based transistor in 1956. Silicon Valley was born.

The third generation (1965–1977) began with the introduction of **integrated circuits,** small silicon chips containing dozens of tiny transistors and connections. Integrated circuitry resulted in much faster, smaller, and more reliable computers. Faster input and output methods and increased data storage facilities were developed during the third generation. More and more business firms began to rely heavily on computers. Remote terminals, typewriter-like machines located away from the computer but connected to it by telephone lines, made access to the computer possible from separate offices or even distant cities.

The fourth generation (1971 to present) started with **large-scale integrated (LSI) circuits.** These superchips, a mere cubic inch in size, contain thousands of small transistors. LSI technology enabled the development of personal computers, which are so common and so valuable today. Mass production of computer chips led to lower prices for small home and business computers. Increased storage capabilities in these small computers gave business firms the means of storing vast amounts of data.

Computer technology is now entering a fifth generation, as a result of **very large-scale integration (VLSI).** VLSI circuitry consists of a superchip created from extremely compact transistors and circuits assembled on a single silicon chip. This technology has led to advances such as **artificial intelligence** and expert systems, enabling computers to solve problems involving imagination, abstract reasoning, and common sense. Today, computer scientists are trying to empower computers to behave as though they could think, by perceiving and absorbing data, learning, reasoning, and communicating in ways similar to human behavior.

16-2b Types of Computers

Depending on their needs and resources, organizations use one of three types of computers: **mainframes, minicomputers,** or **microcomputers.** The largest and fastest computer, with the greatest storage capacity, is the mainframe. Large businesses and government units use mainframes to process and store vast amounts of data. Most mainframes today can be used by many people in several different locations at the same time. Because of their incredible speed and capacity to serve many users, mainframe computers are very expensive.

Some large businesses and government agencies connect multiple mainframes together to form **supercomputers,** the fastest computers available. Like nearly all computer hardware, supercomputers have decreased dramatically in size and price over time; simultaneously, their power has increased. Today's supercomputers are used to calculate exceedingly complicated processes, such as the effects of a nuclear explosion, or the intricacies of heart arrhythmias. Business applications are numerous, including calculating materials strength and the effects of forces on buildings and other structures, the effects of equity derivatives on securities prices worldwide, and other uses both practical and theoretical.

A *server* is a smaller version of the mainframe. Many small- to medium-sized firms rely heavily on servers that cost much less than mainframes. Most servers are the size of a desktop computer or smaller. Servers have decreased dramatically in cost, and now perform most of the same functions of a mainframe except they don't have the same data storage capacity. Servers are networked with a firm's desktop personal computers (see later) in what is known as a *client/server* configuration. This configuration provides the same functionality as a mainframe-based system that larger, Fortune 500–type firms might use. Many firms use multiple servers stored on racks to perform a variety of discrete functions, including networking, storage, e-mail, and video. Firms that elect not to administer their

☞ 3

Integrated Circuits Small silicon chips containing dozens of tiny transistors and connections; used in third-generation computers.

Large-Scale Integrated (LSI) Circuits Superchips that contain thousands of small transistors; fourth-generation innovation that made personal computers possible.

Very Large-Scale Integration (VLSI) Superchip circuitry, resulting from extremely compact transistors and circuits assembled on a single silicon chip; marked start of fifth generation of computers.

Artificial Intelligence A technology that allows computers to solve problems involving imagination, abstract reasoning, and common sense.

Mainframe The largest and fastest type of computer, with the greatest storage capacity.

Minicomputers Smaller, slower versions of the mainframe computer.

Microcomputers Personal computers, including a cathode ray tube and a keyboard.

Supercomputers Computers formed by connecting multiple mainframes.

4 ☞ own servers and other IT systems can purchase services from other firms that will administer their IT on an *outsourcing* basis. Firms such as EDS will, for a fee, take over another firm's *data center* and manage its needs, either on-site or remotely.

A *personal computer* (PC) is smaller, less powerful, and less costly than a server. PCs include a monitor, keyboard, and mouse or other cursor control device. A PC is a general-purpose information-processing device. It can take information from a person (through the keyboard and mouse), from a device (like a floppy disk or CD) or from the network (through a modem or a network card) and process it. Once processed, the information is shown to the user (on the monitor), stored on a device (like a hard disk) or sent somewhere else on the network (back through the modem or network card). Designed for use by one person, PCs are self-contained units that usually fit on a desk or table. Powerful PCs can be purchased for $1,000 or less. PCs are popular for use in homes and professional offices as well as in corporations of all sizes. Computer makers now ship an average of approximately 35 million PCs per quarter around the world.[5]

5 ☞ *Laptop* and *notebook* computers are even smaller versions of PCs. As the name implies, these devices fit on a person's lap and are convenient for use while traveling. These computers have become increasingly powerful over time. Miniaturization with increasing power is a function of a phenomenon known as *Moore's Law*. Gordon Moore, one of the cofounders of semiconductor powerhouse Intel, stated that computer chip speeds would double roughly every eighteen months. Moore's prophetic remark has held true, and today's smallest computers rival the speed and sheer processing power of the mammoth ENIAC. Laptop and the even smaller notebook computers are the computer industry's fastest-selling machines. Many business users have a *docking station* at the office that enables them to use their laptop on the road, and then quickly plug it into the organization's network when back in the office.

6 ☞ *Personal Digital Assistants (PDAs)* and other *handheld computers* are increasingly common for field service personnel, and are becoming handy tools for managers, executives, and other professionals. Handheld computing began with the Apple Newton and has evolved through several stages over the past fifteen years. Although the Newton no longer exists, thanks in part to its difficult-to-master stylus-based data input process, other handheld devices have come into prominence. With advances in chip design and miniaturization, the PDAs available today are more powerful than the first PCs of a decade ago. IT manufacturers are shipping over 3 million units per quarter worldwide, with major growth expected in the coming years.[6] Exhibit 16-2 shows the estimated growth of PDA usage over the coming years.

EXHIBIT 16-2

Estimated PDA Market

	2000	2001	2002	2003	2004	2005
ABN AMRO	10.7	11.9	15.0	21.3	29.2	–
CSFB Technology Group	9.4	12.2	17.7	24.4	31.8	–
eTForecasts	12.2	–	22.4	–	35.6	–
Gartner Dataquest	10.9	12.3	16.0	23.1	31.6	39.2
International Data Corporation (IDC)	13.6	–	–	–	–	70.9
USB Warburg	10.3	17.7	25.9	–	53.7	–
Aberdeen Group	9.0	11.8	16.8	23.1	30.7	39.3

5. "Gartner DataQuest Says Worldwide PC Market Experienced Flat Growth in First Quarter 2002," *Business Wire*, April 18, 2002.

6. IDC, "Worldwide Smart Handheld Shipments Declined 12.1% in First Quarter 2002," *IDC*, accessed April 2002 at http://www.idc.com/getdoc.jhtml?containerId=pr2002_04_22_114258.

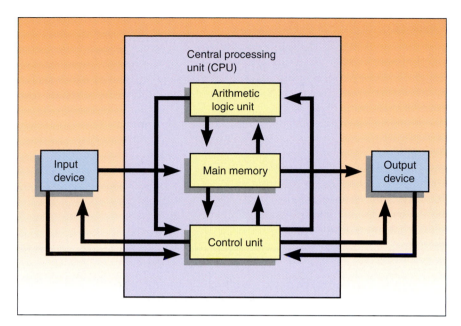

EXHIBIT 16-3

**Main Components
of a Computer**

16-2c Computer Structure

As mentioned, the physical devices that make up a computer system are called *hardware*. Exhibit 16-3 diagrams the basic structure of a computer, including the input device, the central processing unit, and the output device.

Through an **input device,** a user enters data into a computer and makes requests of the computer. The most common input device is a keyboard for typing data or requests. Other input devices are disks, magnetic tapes, punch cards, optical scanners such as those that read universal product codes in supermarkets, the movable mouse, and voice recognition devices.

The **central processing unit (CPU),** the heart of the computer, controls the entire computer system. The CPU includes the electronic hardware that performs the computer operations and consists of three components. **Main memory** stores data, instructions, and other information the computer needs to operate. If something is not in a computer's main memory, the CPU cannot process it. Memory is measured in *bytes;* one byte is the equivalent of one character—a numeral or letter of the alphabet. For example, computers containing 1 GB (gigabyte) of main memory have the capacity to store 1,000,000 characters. Exhibit 16-4 provides definitions of computer memory terminology.

The **arithmetic-logic unit** performs the computations. Data that need to be added, subtracted, multiplied, or divided are moved from the main memory to the arithmetic-logic unit. After the calculations have been performed, the resulting data are moved back into main memory. The **control unit** guides the operations of a computer. It directs the sequence of operations, interprets coded instructions, and sends needed data and instructions to the other units.

The **output device** is the hardware that displays the computer's requests or processed data. The most commonly used output devices are the display screen and the printer, which produces a paper printout (called hard copy). Other output devices include disks, magnetic tapes, graphic plotters, and even the spoken word.

16-2d Computer Software

Computers cannot think. They can operate and perform calculations only by following precise instructions devised by people. *Software* is the term for the instructions that tell the computer hardware what to do.

Input Device   The hardware used to enter data into and make requests of the computer.

Central Processing Unit (CPU)   The electronic hardware that performs the computer operations and controls the entire system.

Main Memory   The part of the computer central processing unit that stores data and instructions.

Arithmetic-Logic Unit   The part of a computer's central processing unit that performs computations.

Control Unit   The part of a computer's central processing unit that guides the operations of the computer.

Output Device   The hardware that displays the computer's requests or processed data.

Computer Memory Terminology

Term/Byte	Abbreviation	Value
Kilo	K, KB	1,024 bytes
Mega	M, MB, Meg	1,048,576 bytes (Million)
Giga	G, GB, Giga	1,073,741,824 bytes (Billion)
Tera	T, TB, Tera	1,099,511,628,000 bytes (Trillion)

Here is another way of looking at the measurement of memory:

Measuring Bytes

8 bits = 1 byte
1000 bytes = 1 kilobyte
1000 kilobytes = 1 megabyte
1000 megabytes = 1 gigabyte
1000 gigabytes = 1 terabyte

Computer Program   A detailed set of instructions written in a computer language.

Software can be broken down into three categories: operating systems, programming languages, and applications. The operating system allows the user to communicate with the system. It serves as an interface between the person using the computer and the computer. Two well-known operating systems are MS Windows® and the Apple OS®. Programming languages consist of a set of codes that the computer interprets as instructions. When a collection of instructions are linked together logically, they form a **computer program.** Widely employed programming languages for business include Visual Basic and C++. Application software includes such programs as spreadsheets, word processing, and graphics and is addressed in detail in the next section.

Businesses sometimes develop their own computer applications for specific tasks. For instance, many firms employ computer programmers to write special programs for payroll, billing, inventory control, and other functions. The programmer must analyze the business process and outline a series of logical steps that will result in a useful application that makes the process easier and/or less costly. Developing software can be both time-consuming and expensive and often is not practical for small firms, which generally do not have programmers on staff. Therefore many firms purchase ready-made software, available from a multitude of companies. Ready-made, or *commercial off-the-shelf,* software can handle a variety of business applications and often costs less than developing computer programs from scratch. Ready-made software is also instantly available, whereas developing a computer program can take months or even years.

Much of today's computer software is "user friendly," meaning that people can use it without a great deal of technical training. User-friendly software communicates by using menus and a *graphical user interface* (GUI). A menu lists a number of commands that usually can be executed with the assistance of a mouse or by typing in the first letter of the command.

A GUI is just an interface that allows people to navigate around and use an application using intuition and common sense. For example, Steve Jobs and Apple revolutionized computing in the 1980s with the first Apple operating system that introduced the notion of a desktop. Using icons and simple, intuitive graphics (such as a trash can for discarding files) Apple converted a complicated and imposing medium into an everyday device that even children could use and master. The Apple operating system launched the true era of home and small-business computing.

16-3 INFORMATION TECHNOLOGY AND BUSINESS

Information technology is a valuable asset to and often a necessity for business firms. As one firm adopts and diffuses a useful IT tool to its employees, it gains productivity and efficiency advantages over its rivals. To keep up, the rivals soon also adopt the technology, fueling a seemingly never-ending spiral of capital spending for IT. Many firms have created organizational structures that account for IT spending, embodying authority over IT in the role of *chief information officer* (CIO) or *IT director*. These titles are increasingly common in the organizational charts of large firms and are creeping into small- to medium-sized firms' organizational charts as well, as IT decision making gets more complex. CIOs and IT directors help firms manage their existing IT assets as well as plan future expenditures. In this section, we examine various capabilities of IT and common business applications.

16-3a Computer Capabilities

Computers possess virtually unlimited capabilities. Computer technology changes so rapidly that new uses for computers are being discovered every day. Computer hardware and software today can satisfy almost any business need. Let's look at some of the ways firms commonly use computers.

Word Processing

Personal computers have revolutionized **word processing,** which consists of creating documents such as letters, reports newsletters, memos, and books. Through the computer keyboard, an individual enters documents and instructions into computer memory to be stored on magnetic disk. Material stored on disk can be accessed and altered easily and kept for later use. For instance, a manager can write memos, letters, and reports; store them on disk; and print them when needed. Many word-processing programs (e.g., MS Word®, Word-Perfect®) perform functions such as checking spelling and grammar, suggesting alternate words, and inserting graphics such as lines, boxes, diagrams, and illustrations.

Word Processing   Creating written documents with a computer.

Spreadsheets

Many firms use computer software to generate electronic accounting ledgers known as **spreadsheets.** A manager or accountant can use computerized spreadsheets to organize data into rows and columns and to perform mathematical calculations. Popular spreadsheet software such as Lotus®, and MS Excel® are used to generate balance sheets, develop sales projections, and estimate profits. The use of computer-based spreadsheets has introduced many people in business to the world of accounting and finance. Spreadsheets enable people to ask real-time "what if?" questions. Changing a single entry on a spreadsheet, such as average price of a product, creates an instant cascade of changes to the rest of the spreadsheet, providing a glimpse at the implications of a price change without having to actually carry it out in the real world. Spreadsheet applications have made this sophisticated type of decision support available to anyone within the firm who has a basic understanding of computers.

Spreadsheets   Electronic accounting ledgers generated by computer software.

Computer Graphics

Computer programs can also translate data into graphs, figures, and designs. Computer graphics are useful to display financial information and to make comparisons between companies or performance in different years. Figures, pictures, and other computer art can add clarity and emphasis to documents and reports and oral presentations. For example, Exhibit 16-5 shows the performance of the Dow Jones Industrial Average from 1950 to 2001. The same data are displayed graphically and in text format. Which of these displays do you think is more instructive?

Desktop Publishing

The computer can also be used to produce high-quality printed materials. With **desktop publishing** software, such as PageMaker and Ventura Publisher, the user can design page layouts and formats comparable to magazines and books, and insert graphics, including illustrations, wherever needed. Desktop publishing enables individuals and firms of any size to produce high-quality reports, brochures, and newsletters at much less than the

Desktop Publishing   Producing printed materials using computer software that can do page layouts and formats, insert graphics, and print with high quality.

The Dow Jones Industrial Average 1950–2001 in Graphic and Text Format

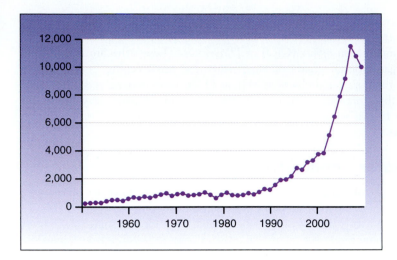

price charged by a printer. Desktop publishing is done using powerful color laser printers, now available for less than $1,000. New packages now also integrate the Internet, providing simple tools for nonprogrammers to create hyperlinks and other Internet-related programming.[7]

Presentation Applications

Using presentation graphics software, such as PowerPoint and Freelance Graphics, the personal computer can produce full-color text and graphic screens for overhead projection. Using LCD technology, the computer can be used to display dynamic presentations that incorporate audio, video, text, and animations.

16-3b Business Applications

Firms use computers to perform a variety of tasks quickly, efficiently, and accurately. The most common business applications of computers are payroll, record keeping, inventory control, scheduling, order processing, and **electronic mail.**

Electronic Mail   A computer network used to relay messages from one user to another instantly.

Payroll

Many companies generate their payroll with computers. For most, calculating employees' pay is complicated. They must make deductions for taxes, insurance, profit-sharing programs, and even parking fees and contributions to charity. Employee pay can be calculated in several ways, including salary, sales, bonus, commission, and hourly wages plus overtime. Computers can make the many calculations required to meet a payroll in a matter of seconds.

Record Keeping

Computers are valuable for maintaining and updating records such as payroll and personnel files, customer lists, accounts receivable, and accounts payable. Business owners and managers can easily maintain accounting and financial records and generate financial statements on demand.

Inventory Control

Another common application of computers in business is inventory control. Many firms use programs to keep track of inventory and place orders when inventory drops to a certain level. These programs can also tell a manager the quantity and dollar amount of inventory at any time.

7. Luisa Simone, "New Desktop Publishing Packages Heat Up the Rivalry," *PC Magazine*, April 9, 2002, pp. 32–33.

Scheduling

Computers can be used to schedule a variety of activities. Manufacturing companies rely on computers to construct production schedules, while a number of businesses use them to schedule personnel activities such as work schedules, employee breaks, and vacation time. Recent technology is seeking to replace personal organizers that have become so popular in today's society.

Order Processing

Firms of all types and sizes use computers to process orders. Supermarket checkout lanes have computerized registers. Large manufacturing firms use computers to place orders at a warehouse, check customer credit and inventory levels, and print invoices. Many catalog retailers use computers to fill mail and telephone orders.

Collaboration

Many companies today foster employee collaboration through *corporate portals* or other collaboration tools such as Lotus Notes. These applications enable workers dispersed throughout the company, and maybe dispersed throughout the world, to work together in real time on documents, projects, and innovations. Using secure systems such as *virtual private networks* (VPN), firms can allow access to key proprietary information only to individuals with proper security clearance. George Gualda, CIO at Link Staffing Inc., wanted to securely connect forty-nine branch offices in twenty-three states to his company's Houston headquarters. Gualda decided he needed a VPN to tie the far-flung parts of Link Staffing together. He used a commercial system called OpenReach to achieve his goal.[8] An extreme form of collaboration is presented in the Focus on Globalization box, "Telemedicine Changes Meaning of 'House Call'." Telemedicine is an emerging technology that enables medical specialists from around the globe to collaborate on complex procedures.

Computer-Aided Design

Computer-aided design (CAD) has revolutionized production planning for everything from fabricated metals, valves, and fittings to aircraft. Boeing, for example, designed the entire Boeing 777 aircraft on a CAD system—consisting of more than 1 million parts—before the first rivet was driven. One CAD developer, SolidWorks, is distributing its software to universities in China for free to instruct a new generation of designers who will take their skills into that country's manufacturing and machine shops.[9]

Computer-Aided Manufacturing

Computer-aided manufacturing (CAM) has transformed the factory floor. Years ago, workers could report to the factory with little more than manual labor skills to offer. Today, workers must be able to manage computer systems that keep track of process flow, complex robotics, and working capital. CAM has become a "must have" in nearly every manufacturing setting as it is a source of distinct competitive advantage for those who use it wisely.

Supply Chain Management

Businesses, especially those involved in manufacturing, often must coordinate processes with suppliers to ensure smooth process flow. Doing so requires applications that enable one firm's IT systems to talk to another's. Sophisticated new supply chain management (SCM) systems are designed to help firms manage these interrelationships. SCM applications allow firms to handle procurement, inventory tracking, invoice management, and a host of other supply-oriented functions through a single interface. Increased process-flow efficiency and reduced costs are just some of the benefits of SCM software. Some firms,

8. James Cope, "Outsourcing VPNs: Privacy for Hire," *ComputerWorld*, February 11, 2002, pp. 36–37.

9. Katharine A. Kelley, "MMS Shop Talk," *Modern Machine Shop*, April 2002, pp. 42–43.

FOCUS ON GLOBALIZATION

Telemedicine Changes Meaning of "House Call"

You think sending critical files over telecommunications networks is difficult? In late 2001, New York doctors removed a gall bladder from a 68-year-old woman 4,000 miles away in Strasbourg, France, via a high-speed network and surgical robots. The implications are astounding, say analysts: Doctors can now collaborate on medical procedures, and medical experts can perform surgery on patients in remote parts of the world. It presents a slew of new applications for advanced network technology. "I felt as comfortable operating on my patient as if I had been in the room," said one of the doctors who performed the surgery. France Telecom S.A. and Equant N.V. (Amsterdam) provided an end-to-end high-speed fiber optic service that let the surgeon work with virtually no time delay. It was imperative that a time delay of less than 200 milliseconds be maintained between the time the doctor manipulated the robot controls in New York and when he saw the results in France.

Source: Adapted from "Who Says Doctors Don't Make House Calls?," *tele.com*, October 1, 2001.

7 ☞ such as Dow Chemical, outsource their SCM functions to logistics firms that specialize in the practice. This helps reduce Dow's operating costs.[10]

Customer Relationship Management

Many businesses are using IT to improve relationships with customers. *Customer relationship management* (CRM) applications empower customers to purchase goods and services, track an order, or even lodge a complaint. In addition, CRM applications track customer activity and provide reports to managers. Many use complicated *online analytical processing* (OLAP) to provide real-time information about customer activity and sales performance. CRM software is used by firms such as Cisco, to help route incoming customer calls, manage customer relations, and provide data to managers and executives regarding customer satisfaction and other key indicators of performance.[11]

Project Management

Project management is the process of setting goals, allocating resources, taking action, and achieving milestones on the way to a completed project. Software that assists managers in project management collects information from individuals involved in a project and records progress. Many project management applications include colorful graphical displays to keep everyone on the project team informed about progress, or its lack.

Enterprise Resource Planning

The "be all, end all" of business computing are the so-called enterprise resource planning (ERP) systems that attempt to encompass and integrate all of a business's processes in one interface. Imagine a system that handles payroll, procurement, supply chain management, project management, e-mail, and every other business process. That is the goal of ERP systems. ERP systems originated to serve the information needs of manufacturing companies. Over time, though, they have grown to serve other industries, including health care, financial services, the aerospace industry, and the consumer goods sector. With this

---

10. "One Giant Step for BDP," *Traffic World*, March 4, 2002, pp. 13–14.

11. Jennifer Maselli, "It's Still About Keeping Customers Happy," *Information Week*, April 8, 2002, p. 22.

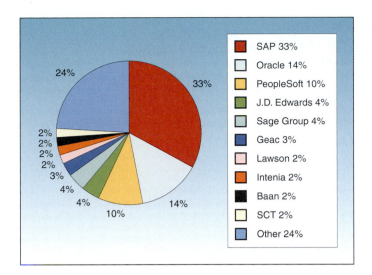

EXHIBIT 16-6
Major ERP Vendors

growth, ERP systems, which first ran on mainframes before migrating to client/server systems, are now migrating to the Web and include numerous applications.[12]

To date, it's not clear that such systems can be successful. After early excitement, systems such as Germany's SAP have met with mixed reviews. ERP systems are very complicated, require massive investments of time and capital, and often require extensive organizational culture change. The culture change is due to the need for individuals to have to change their practices to fit the software. ERP software typically is so comprehensive that customizing it for an individual workplace to adapt to its existing processes has ripple effects on the system that create other costs. Exhibit 16-6 shows the major ERP vendors.

16-4 MANAGEMENT INFORMATION SYSTEMS

Because of the information explosion, managers making decisions must regularly confront an abundance of facts and figures and determine which information is most useful. Many organizations design management information systems to provide managers with the necessary information to make intelligent decisions. A **management information system (MIS)** combines computers and regular, organized procedures to provide the information managers use in making decisions.

Management Information System (MIS) A combination of computers and procedures for providing information that managers use in making decisions.

16-4a MIS Functions

An MIS is used to collect, store, and process data and present analyzed information to managers (see Exhibit 16-7). This section discusses each of these functions.

Collect Data

We have emphasized the massive amount of information available to organizations—personnel records, information about competitors, sales data, accounting data, information about customers, and so on. The first function of an MIS is to determine the information needed to make decisions and to organize it into a database. A **database** is an integrated collection of data stored in one place for efficient access and information processing.

Data can be obtained from sources within and outside the organization. Generally most data collected for an MIS come from internal sources, such as company records or reports and information supplied by employees and by managers. External sources include trade publications, customers, vendors, suppliers, and consultants.

Database An integrated collection of data stored in one place for easy access and information processing.

12. Adrian Mello, "ERP Fundamentals: Benefits and Applications," *ZDNet Tech Update*, accessed February 7, 2002, at http://techupdate.zdnet.com/techupdate/stories/main/0,14179,2844319-2,00.html.

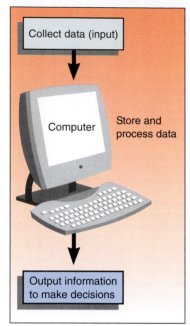

EXHIBIT 16-7

Functions of an MIS

Collect data (input)

Computer — Store and process data

Output information to make decisions

INTERACTIVE EXHIBIT

Data Processing Mechanically transferring raw data into some specific form of information.

Database Management Systems (DBMS) Computer software that helps firms manage various data files.

Computer Network A collection of computers connected so that they can function individually and communicate with one another.

Store Data

Once created, a database must be stored in a form useful to managers. Data are generally stored on magnetic tape or hard disks when mainframe computers are used and on hard disks or floppy disks when minicomputers or microcomputers are used. The data can be loaded into the computer in seconds for easy access by the user.

Data for an MIS must be current, which requires periodic updating of the database. A computer operator or programmer can update the database manually. More likely, each employee on the system will have some responsibility to upload data regarding their work activity and results. Systems also are available to automatically update data. In this case, the database is permanently connected to the MIS, and the computer automatically makes changes as new data become available.

Process Data

Once data are stored in the MIS, managers can use the data for decision making. Some data can be used in the form in which they are stored. But more often, data must be processed to meet specific information needs of managers. **Data processing** involves electronically transferring raw data into some specific form of information. Business firms process both text, such as reports, and numerical data, such as sales figures. The MIS provides data and information necessary to help managers make decisions.

Management information systems are developed by following a set of steps known as the *systems development life cycle (SDLC)*. The steps or phases include planning, analysis, design, and implementation. Planning consists of examining the MIS and the overall and system goals of the organization to make sure they are in congruence with one another. The analysis phase explores the strengths and weaknesses of the current system. Users are interviewed to gather their viewpoints and suggestions for improvements in the system. With this feedback from the analysis phase, a new system can be designed that corrects the problems of the old system. Next, the new system must be implemented and placed into operation.[13]

A **database management system (DBMS)** is a computer software program that helps firms manage their data files. Such programs change information stored in data files, add new information, and delete information no longer needed. DBMS software can also be used to sort and merge files, process data, and print reports. Some database programs used frequently are Oracle and Microsoft SQL.[14]

Present Information to Managers

Processed data must be put in a form useful to managers. Verbal information can be presented in text format in the form of reports, outlines, lists, articles, or books. Numerical information can be presented in table or graph format. As noted earlier, computer programs can offer numerous graphic options. The most commonly used graphic information displays for managers are bar charts, pie charts, and graphs. A *bar chart* uses vertical or horizontal bars to represent values, with longer bars representing greater values. A *pie chart* is a circle divided into portions, or "slices," each representing a different item. The size of each slice shows the proportion of that item to the total. Bar charts and pie charts help visualize the relative size or importance of various bits of information. A *graph* is used to plot data, illustrating how information changes over time.

16-4b Computer Networks

An MIS can include multiple computers connected to one another. A **computer network** is a collection of computers connected in a manner that allows them to function individually and communicate with each other. Computer networks usually include a mainframe or server connected to personal computers as the foundation of the system. Other main-

13. Douglas Tudhope, "Prototyping Praxis: Constructing Computer Systems and Building Belief," *Human-Computer Interaction*, December 2000, pp. 353–383.

14. Even Koblentz, "New DBMS Tools Reduce Complexity," *eWeek*, March 4, 2002, pp. 9–10.

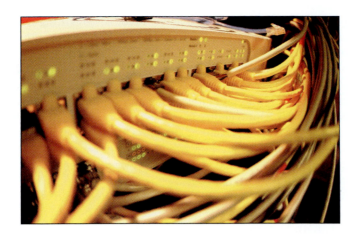

frames, and personal computers on the network can communicate with each other. Networks link computers within an office, across the country, or even worldwide—in which case the computers are linked by telephone lines or satellites.

16-4c The Internet

No discussion of computer networks would be complete without a thorough review of the Internet and its implications. The Internet or "World Wide Web" is a global computer network that grew out of university research laboratories in the 1960s. In 1973, the U.S. Defense Advanced Research Projects Agency (DARPA) initiated a research program to investigate techniques and technologies for interlinking *packet networks* of various kinds. The objective was to develop communication protocols that would allow networked computers to communicate transparently across multiple, linked packet networks. This was called the *Internetting project,* and the system of networks that emerged from the research was known as the "Internet." The system of protocols developed over the course of this research effort became known as the TCP/IP Protocol Suite, after the two initial protocols developed: *Transmission Control Protocol (TCP)* and *Internet Protocol (IP)*.

🖙 10

The Internet grew slowly during the 1970s and 1980s, confined primarily to use by university researchers, government agencies, and a few in-the-know high-tech aficionados. The major use of the Internet during this time was file sharing and e-mail, as all early "browsers" were text only. There was little thought of expanding into commercial applications. It wasn't until the early 1990s, with the advent of the first graphically oriented browser, developed by Marc Andreessen and some of his college friends at the University of Illinois at Urbana-Champaign, that the commercial Internet took off. The graphical browser, called "Mosaic," offered a new range of possibilities that led to the Internet boom of the 1990s.[15] Andreessen and several of his fellow Mosaic programmers eventually founded Netscape, rocketing themselves to wealth and stardom when the company went public in 1995. Today's leading browsers are Microsoft's Internet Explorer and Netscape.[16]

🖙 11

Today, Internet usage and Internet browsing are commonplace all over the world and in nearly every demographic group. A U.S. Department of Commerce report notes that about 54 percent of the population—143 million Americans—were online as of September 2001. That represents a nearly 23 percent increase over the 116.5 million found to be online in August 2000.

🖙 12

The growth amounts to about 2 million new Internet users per month. And the study also reports that expansion of the Net population happened across all social and demographic sectors. Internet use among individuals in the highest household income brackets—$75,000 or more per year—has grown only 11 percent annually between

15. A good overview of the history of the Internet is available at the website http://www.let.leidenuniv.nl/history/ivh/chap2.htm.

16. "Browsers," *PC World,* February 2002, pp. 82–83.

December 1998 and September 2001. But among households earning less than $15,000 annually, Internet use increased 25 percent annually. Rural areas also experienced a higher Internet surge. Over the 1998 to 2001 period, growth of Internet usage by individuals in nonurban areas grew at an annual average rate of 24 percent. The number of users located in central cities grew only 18 percent.

The report also notes that Internet use among racial groups still varies widely. Adoption of the Internet among whites and Asian-Americans hovered around 60 percent. But only 40 percent of blacks and 32 percent of Hispanics claim to use the Internet. Still, the report notes that both demographics show a much faster growth rate in terms of Internet use than others. Internet usage among blacks and Hispanics grew at an annual average rate of 31 percent and 26 percent, respectively.

And while not every home may have a computer, schools and other public institutions have stepped in to fill the gap. The report states that 90 percent of children between the ages of 5 to 17 have access to a computer. And 75 percent of kids ages 14–17 years old and 65 percent of 10- to 13-year-olds use the Internet.

Some researchers doubt that the growth of the Internet will continue at current rates. "We're deeply penetrated among those that have some interest in adopting the [Internet]," says Lee Rainie, director of research for the Pew Internet and American Life Project. "After that, it will probably be tougher to get the last cohorts online." And according to Rainie, there are a number of reasons why the Net won't become as ubiquitous as the telephone or TV in the American household.

Still, with 90 percent of today's kids growing up with computers or some form of Internet technology; some say it will be inevitable that the Internet will become as common as the TV in American homes. It will just take longer than expected. "It's a normal tech adoption story that will play out like other technologies," says Rainie. "If you hold out the telephone or TV as the high standard [of adoption] where it's in 98 percent of the homes, it will take another 10 years to get to that level with the Net."[17]

16-4d Decision Support Systems

Decision Support System (DSS) A system that enables managers to instantly access information on past and current performance.

A **decision support system (DSS)** is an interactive information system that enables managers to gain instant access to information in a less structured format than an MIS. DSS software combines corporate information on past performance with what is currently taking place, allowing managers to work with large amounts of data not available otherwise.[18] Through a DSS, managers can obtain information about the firm, competitors, and the business environment. One DSS available over the Web helps divorce lawyers in their decision-making processes.[19]

Executive Information System (EIS) A user-friendly decision support system designed for executives that requires little computer knowledge and provides instant high-quality displays.

An **executive information system (EIS)** is a user-friendly DSS designed specifically for executives to assist them in making business decisions. An EIS is easy to use and requires no knowledge of the computer. By moving a mouse or merely touching the screen, the user directs the computer to provide information. Executive information systems use big-screen, high-quality monitors and produce full-color displays. An EIS allows top-level managers to ask questions and receive immediate answers in the form of graphs, charts, and reports. EIS systems are increasingly being used for strategic decision making in organizations of all sizes. One of the more common uses of an EIS is continuous monitoring of the firm's financial performance.[20]

17. Paul Eng, "A Nation of Surfers," *ABCNews.com*, February 6, 2002.

18. Sandy Butters and Sean Eom, "Decision Support Systems in the Healthcare Industry," *Journal of Systems Management*, June 1992, pp. 28–31.

19. John Kingston, "A Web-Based Decision Support System for Divorce Lawyers," *International Review of Law*, November 2001, pp. 265–279.

20. Sanjay K. Singh, Hugh J. Watson, and Richard T. Watson, "EIS Support for the Strategic Management Process," *Decision Support Systems*, May 2002, pp. 71–85.

16-5 TRENDS IN INFORMATION SYSTEMS

The amount of information available to managers will continue to increase dramatically in the future. The ever-growing volume of information will make computers even more crucial to firms. The business sector's use of computers to process information is expected to grow rapidly as new hardware and software create new competitive advantages. Virtually no business firm, regardless of size, will be able to function efficiently without IT systems.

Smaller, portable computers such as laptops and PDAs are changing the way people in business use computers. Laptops now are as essential as a briefcase or suitcase for many business travelers. Salespeople, reporters, writers, managers, and others use the small computers to work on airplanes and commuter trains and in hotels and to communicate with coworkers in other places. Salespeople often have computers in their cars for quick access to information from their managers. Computers in Federal Express vans and trucks help couriers keep track of letters and packages being shipped.

A major IT trend is the migration to *wireless networks*. Many firms have distributed workforces that are away from their offices and desks for much of their work time. Oil field workers, sales professionals, and others who spend time away from the office can benefit from staying connected to their firm's IT network. Wireless systems enable these workers to stay connected from nearly anywhere. A wireless network is literally what it says, a network that doesn't require that workers plug their computers to the wall to be able to access their firm's network. Using radio-frequency signals, wireless networks are increasingly fast and reliable. It's likely that wireless technologies will provide competitive advantages to those firms that use them wisely, and they will spur others firms to jump into wireless technology to keep up.[21] This type of *positive feedback loop* is what propels an IT innovation into a transformative technology. Wireless networks and wireless computing have the potential to transform the workplace, enabling people to work nearly anywhere while retaining connection to vital business data and the ability to communicate and collaborate with coworkers.

Because of the ever-increasing power of computers, management information systems are also becoming more sophisticated. **Expert systems** are computer programs that imitate human thinking and offer advice or solutions to complex problems in much the same way that a human expert does.[22] For instance, people use expert systems to plan shipping schedules, provide financial advice to investors, and help managers respond to the actions of competing firms. Accountants are using expert systems to solve tax return problems.

Expert Systems   Computer software that imitates human thinking.

A number of other trends in computers and MIS have evolved over time. As companies have become more decentralized, with managers rather than executives making decisions, computing has moved away from the mainframe environment and into distributed data processing, where each department within the organization is now able to process its own data. Because of this decentralization, users are beginning to develop their own programs and systems to provide information they need for decision making.

Another trend increasing in popularity is *outsourcing* of computing activities. Activities such as payroll are now commonly being outsourced to companies that specialize in them. By allowing another entity to perform these rather simple computing tasks, the company is able to focus on processing activities more likely to lead to the generation of profits. Some firms even outsource the maintenance of their software administration, preferring to lease software from other firms who specialize in maintaining and upgrading business applications. This form of "pay-as-you-go" software usage is handled through firms known as "Application Service Providers," or "ASPs."

Computers have increasing significance in our lives, not only for work but also for personal and family use and for play. Eventually they may be as common in homes as

21. Marshall Breeding, "The Benefits of Wireless Technologies," *Information Today*, March 2002, pp. 42–43.

22. Justin Kestelyn, "The New Expert Systems," *Intelligent Enterprise*, September 18, 2001, p. 6.

FOCUS ON CAREERS

IT Being Used in Job Interview Process

14 ☞ Today, more organizations are conducting interviews with technology, including the use of teleconferencing and streaming video for interviewing candidates from afar. Interviews by video conference are on the rise, says Andrew Davis of Wainhouse Research, which specializes in teleconferencing. With job candidates and recruiters less inclined to travel after September 11, employers and professional recruiters are investing in video technology, says 15 ☞ Jennifer Sigmund of Polycom, a leading provider of video-conferencing equipment. After so many layoffs, "there are more candidates available to be interviewed," says Davis. At the same time, companies keeping a close eye on travel budgets are less willing to whisk job seekers off to corporate headquarters for a first or second interview.

Sources: Adapted from Carrie Picardi, "Making a Good First Impression," *Network Computing,* July 9, 2001, p. 82; and "Smile for the Boss," *Kiplinger's Personal Finance,* January 2002, p. 26.

microwave ovens. The profusion of computers will enable business firms to explore still more computer applications, such as placing orders, paying bills, and performing bank transactions through personal computers in homes or offices.

The growth of computer technology has drawbacks. Computer crime, for instance, has gained much attention in recent years. People have used access to computer records to steal money and tamper with records in business firms and government agencies. Another serious threat to computer users is the *computer virus,* a computer program that copies itself endlessly to other programs and destroys stored data in the process.

Improper use of the computer's tremendous capability to compile information can violate people's right to privacy. Some businesses have been accused of keeping large data files on individuals and then releasing the data unethically. For example, firms sometimes sell their customer database to others who may use it to solicit business. Selling customer lists has led to an increase in junk mail and telephone solicitations. In many cases, computers actually make telephone calls and play recordings to try to sell products or solicit donations.

The most likely scenario is that IT will continue to evolve and create dramatic changes in the workplace. Businesses will constantly experiment with new forms of IT in a never-ending quest for competitive advantage. Issues that must be addressed as IT forges ahead include reliability, security, and ease of use. Over time, IT systems have grown increasingly reliable, but they still fail all too often. Computer security is an ongoing concern as the arms race between security experts and "hackers" creates a need for ever-more sophisticated defense mechanisms. Finally, despite tremendous advances in GUIs and networking connectivity, computers are still too difficult to use. It is possible that advances in voice activation and speech recognition will lead to computers that respond to spoken commands. These and other advances will likely make IT an important part of business for many years to come. In fact, it's possible that you may encounter advances in IT as you graduate and move into the job search process. The Focus on Careers box, "IT Being Used in Job Interview Process," highlights how firms are using IT to reduce the costs of the recruitment and hiring process.

SUGGESTED WEBSITES

Note: These websites were functional when we went to press. Please access the online text for the most up-to-date URLs.

1. www.iona.com
2. www.publicagenda.com
3. www.belllabs.com
4. www.eds.com
5. www.intel.com
6. www.apple.com
7. www.dow.com
8. www.cisco.com
9. www.sap.com

10. www.darpa.mil
11. www.archive.ncsa.uiuc.edu
12. www.doc.gov
13. www.pewinternet.org
14. www.wainhouse.com
15. www.polycom.com
16. www.pg.com
17. www.askme.com

SUMMARY OF LEARNING OBJECTIVES

1. *Explain how businesses can benefit from information technology (IT).*   Managers today have access to more statistics, facts, and predictions than ever before. Computers enable businesses to convert all these data into useful information. With computers readily available and affordable, business firms are taking advantage of their capabilities and becoming increasingly dependent on them.

2. *Trace the evolution of computing.*   Through an evolution of five generations, computers have become smaller, faster, less costly, and capable of more functions and greater storage. The first generation consisted of enormous computers operating with vacuum tubes. The second was marked by transistors. The third began with integrated circuits. The fourth generation resulted from large-scale integrated (LSI) circuits contained on tiny superchips. The fifth and current generation is developing through very large-scale integration (VLSI) and the study of artificial intelligence.

3. *Explain how businesses can take advantage of the Internet.*   Businesses can use the Internet to supplement and complement their offline business. Innovations in collaboration software, project management, and others can be combined into a virtual private network enabling people to work together from anywhere in the world, as long as they are able to gain access to the Web.

4. *Identify the different types of computers.*   Three different types of computers can meet the needs and resources of firms. The largest and fastest, *mainframes*, are also the most expensive. *Servers* are smaller, somewhat slower, less costly versions of the mainframe. *Personal computers (PCs)*, which include a display screen and keyboard, are adaptable, affordable, and adequate for use in homes and businesses.

5. *Understand the basic components of a computer.*   All computers consist of physical devices called *hardware*, including an input device, central processing unit (CPU), and output *device*. *Software*, sets of instructions called computer programs, is needed to tell the computer exactly what to do.

6. *Identify and understand common business IT applications.*   Common business IT applications include such things as word processing, spreadsheets, and computer graphics. More complex applications include computer-aided design, computer-aided manufacturing, supply chain management, and enterprise resource planning.

7. *Define* management information system (MIS) *and explain how an MIS is used.*   An MIS is a combination of computers and procedures for providing regular, timely information that managers use in making decisions. Through an MIS, a firm can collect data from internal and external sources, store and process data, and present information in a form useful to managers.

8. *List trends in computer development and use and in information technology.*   The continuing information explosion will prompt business firms to make even greater use of computers and MISs. Computers will become faster, smaller, and more portable; MISs will become increasingly sophisticated to further aid decision making. As more and more personal computers enter homes, they will increase in importance for personal and family use as well as for work. Along with the growth of computers has come a trend toward more computer crime, including invasion of privacy.

KEY TERMS

arithmetic-logic unit (p.429)
artificial intelligence (p. 427)
central processing unit (CPU) (p. 429)
computer (p. 426)
computer network (p. 436)
computer program (p. 430)
control unit (p. 429)
data (p. 424)
data processing (p. 436)
database (p. 435)
database management system
    (DBMS) (p. 436)

decision support system (DSS) (p. 438)
desktop publishing (p. 431)
electronic mail (p. 432)
executive information system (EIS) (p. 438)
expert systems (p. 439)
hardware (p. 424)
information (p. 424)
input device (p. 429)
integrated circuits (p. 427)
large-scale integrated (LSI) circuits (p. 427)
main memory (p. 429)
mainframe (p. 427)

management information system
    (MIS) (p. 435)
microcomputers (p. 427)
minicomputers (p. 427)
output device (p. 429)
positive feedback loop (p. 425)
software (p. 424)
spreadsheets (p. 431)
supercomputers (p. 427)
transistor (p. 426)
very large-scale integration (VLSI) (p. 427)
word processing (p. 431)

QUESTIONS FOR DISCUSSION AND REVIEW

1. An abundance of information can be beneficial to managers who are trying to make decisions. Is it possible to have too much information? Why or why not? What can be done to deal with "information overload?"

2. Through the evolution of several generations of development, computers have become more powerful and smaller. What new developments in computing will the next generation hold?

3. Software and hardware develop together to help push the evolution of information technology. Do you think it's possible that IT development will slow down in the near future? What might be some factors that could slow it down?

4. A number of security concerns are involved with any IT system and/or network. Discuss some of these concerns. What is being done to alleviate these concerns?

5. In terms of computers, small businesses have different needs than large corporations. What are some IT applications that small businesses might use uniquely?

6. Management information systems provide all types of information that managers may need for decision making, while accounting information systems provide financial information for every category of decision maker. Is there any overlap in the contents of these two information systems? Explain.

7. The systems development life cycle (SDLC) is a technique for helping firms develop effective management information systems. What features might be included in an effective MIS? Discuss.

8. What advantages does a firm gain by utilizing internal computer networks? What advantages can a firm develop by making wise use of the Internet?

9. Expert systems can provide assistance in making decisions by simulating the decision processes of experts. Can you think of ways that expert systems could be developed to help in medicine? Insurance? Banking? Manufacturing? Others? Discuss.

10. There are many business benefits to be gained from a computer's ability to process data. What are some of the most important benefits? What are some potential drawbacks of data processing for business?

END-OF-CHAPTER QUESTIONS

1. According to research by Public Agenda, *94 percent* of consumers surveyed in 2002 said it's frustrating to "call a company and get a recording instead of a human being." **T** or **F**
2. Nations that lead in IT development and implementation are far ahead in per capital GDP over less technologically developed countries. **T** or **F**
3. The first computer weighed more than thirty tons. **T** or **F**
4. The largest and fastest computer, with the greatest storage capacity, is the *server*. **T** or **F**
5. Computer makers now ship approximately 35 million PCs per quarter around the world. **T** or **F**
6. Gordon Moore, one of the cofounders of Intel, stated that computer chip speeds would double roughly every eighteen months. **T** or **F**
7. Computers can think. **T** or **F**
8. Telemedicine is an emerging technology. **T** or **F**
9. The goal of an ERP system is to place a common interface on each separate application in order to make them easier to learn and use. **T** or **F**
10. Expert systems are computer programs that imitate human thinking. **T** or **F**
11. In late 2001, doctors in New York removed a gall bladder from a woman 4,000 miles away via surgical robots and a high-speed network. **T** or **F**
12. Many firms use computer software to generate electronic accounting ledgers known as spreadsheets. **T** or **F**
13. Which of the following represents the smallest amount of memory?
    a. Kilobyte
    b. Megabyte
    c. Gigabyte
    d. Terabyte
14. A U.S. Department of Commerce report states that _____ of children, ages 5 to 17, have access to a computer.
    a. 25 percent
    b. 50 percent
    c. 70 percent
    d. 90 percent
15. A U.S. Department of Commerce report notes that about _____ of the population was online as of September 2001.
    a. 10 percent
    b. 27 percent
    c. 54 percent
    d. 76 percent

INTERNET EXERCISE

Comparing the Early Days of Computing with Today

In the fast-paced world of information technology, leading hardware and software systems are changing daily. Business leaders are bewildered by choices among ERP, SCM, CRM, and other enterprise-wide software packages. They are equally bewildered by hardware choices, from network computing to wireless PDAs. The decisions are complicated and fraught with implications, as hardware and software choices made today will impact the firm for years to come.

In the early days of computing, there wasn't as much choice. Computers were cumbersome, difficult to access, and limited in their functionality. Students should visit the following websites to get an idea of the early days of computing and then consider the questions that follow.

http://ftp.arl.mil/~mike/comphist/eniac-story.html
http://ei.cs.vt.edu/~history/ENIAC.Richey.HTML
http://www.inventorsmuseum.com/eniac.htm

Questions for Discussion

1. What do you notice about the pictures of the ENIAC computer? Do you think it's possible that, in the late 1940s, ENIAC's inventors could have envisioned desktop computers as we have them today? Explain your answer.
2. What were the primary uses for ENIAC? Were there any *economic* reasons to build the ENIAC computer? Explain.
3. Do you think the creators of ENIAC were thinking about business applications when they were building it? What do you think were the early business uses of computing power? What are the business uses of computing today? Are there some business processes that cannot benefit from computing? Explain.
4. In the late 1950s the space race began with the launch of Sputnik by the Soviet Union. Today, there is a race for ever-faster computers. Do you think there are *business* reasons for running this race? What are they?

EXPERIENTIAL EXERCISE

Using Information Systems in Business Operations

Activity

This project entails learning about information systems actually in use in real-world businesses.

Directions

1. After students are placed into groups of five to six, each group should identify and interview the person or people in charge of a computerized information system in a local business (i.e., retailing, manufacturing, or service).

   Here is a list of sample questions concerning information systems that might be used in the interview:

   - Who are the users of the information produced by the information system?
   - What type of hardware does the information system consist of? Who was the vendor? Were there any problems with the selection of the hardware?
   - What type of software does the information system consist of? Who was the vendor? Were there any problems with the selection of the software?

- What were the steps involved in developing the information system? Did the company use the systems development life cycle (SDLC)? Why or why not? Were there any problems with the implementation of the information system?
- For what types of applications is the information system used?
- Does the information system employ networks? In what capacity?
- Do decision support systems help managers make decisions? How?
- What security features are in place to protect the information system?
- What types of new technology are currently employed in the information system?
- In terms of information requirements, what does the future hold?

   Do not feel that these are the only questions that need to be asked. These questions are meant to serve as a starting point for group members.

2. Once the interview has been completed, the group should use the notes taken during the interview to prepare a presentation of ten to fifteen minutes (suggested) for the class.

BUSINESS APPLICATION

Information Systems Applications

For this class assignment students will work in pairs. Students are asked to identify computerized information systems applications in particular businesses. The instructor should assign different types of retail (e.g., clothing, sporting goods, hardware, toy, and grocery), manufacturing (e.g., automobiles, chemicals, plastics, pharmaceuticals, and office equipment), and service (e.g., law firm, hospital, bank, hotel, and insurance company) companies to the pairs of students.

Students should be given approximately fifteen minutes to record different examples of computerized applications that may be used in their particular business. Remember first to focus on the main goal of the organization in order to identify applications for the business.

As the students share their applications, the instructor will record the information on the blackboard for further discussion. Recording the information on the blackboard will help summarize the different kinds of applications that may be used in a particular line of business.

Case

Procter & Gamble Uses Employee Portal to Increase Innovation

Any company's greatest asset is its employees, but tapping their store of knowledge can present a challenge to large, geographically dispersed enterprises. Aware that its success hinges largely on the knowledge locked in the minds of its nearly 110,000 employees around the world, consumer-products giant Procter & Gamble turned to knowledge-sharing software to transform departmental experts into tangible information resources for the whole company.

From improving the blend of ingredients in toothpaste to manufacturing diapers, P&G's scientists and researchers depend on information exchange among workers in multiple, distributed departments to develop and market about 300 of the world's most recognizable brands of products. In 1997 P&G established an online employee portal to facilitate collaboration among workers involved in product development.

Employee portals are company specific "entry points" to the Internet that allow employees to access and share information they need to do their jobs. Many portals provide access to benefits and compensation information, corporate news, and other items pertinent to individual employees. In addition, employees can customize the portal interface to present them with external news that they would like to track as part of their workday. Some portals also have online employee directories that enable people to locate relevant expertise within the company. Finally, many companies use portals to track employee productivity and performance. This feature requires that employee upload information about the work they are doing, which is then analyzed and presented to managers through their customized portal.

Dubbed Innovation Net, the P&G portal is used by about 18,000 workers around the world in the areas of R&D, engineering, purchasing, and marketing, said Mike Telljohann, associate director at P&G's technical center in Cincinnati. The portal was successful in providing workers with browser-based access to published information such as documents, reports, and data from a variety of disparate sources. But the intranet was limited because it could not extract one of the company's most valued resources: employee knowledge. "[Innovation Net] was doing a good job connecting people to knowledge that is documented and articulated, but not as good a job in connecting them to experts," Telljohann says. "Because we are a global company, people are building products all over the world. People often didn't know where to go with questions or issues. They suspected, given the size of the company, that there was more out there that they just didn't get to leverage," he says.

This feedback prompted P&G to seek out tools for tapping the knowledge of its many experts. Enter AskMe Enterprise knowledge-sharing software, which P&G deployed on a trial basis in 2001 to about 1,000 Innovation Net users. AskMe Enterprise is designed to be integrated into corporate intranets and portals to add qualified experts to the pool of information resources. Based on how much particular workers are involved in certain subjects, the system forms a directory listing of individuals noted as subject-matter experts who can be called upon to lend advice or collaboration for problem solving and product development.

What attracted Telljohann to Bellevue, Washington–based AskMe, apart from the software's scalability—a key issue for P&G's large number of employees and locations—was the software's method of rewarding workers most active in their field with distinguished rankings. "We found that the way the experts were highlighted within the project was an implicit reward system. It made experts want to participate," he says. "The more active you are in a particular area, AskMe highlights you as a featured expert. People in the innovation area enjoy being seen as an expert. I think it gives a lot of personal satisfaction."

The technology deployment went off without a hitch, but Telljohann says one of the biggest challenges was integrating the system into the day-to-day business process of workers. "People are very busy. Anything new tends to be seen on the surface as a distraction. Getting people to listen as to why this is valuable is a bit of a struggle," he says.

Telljohann says he and his team spent a lot of time on marketing, conversations, and meetings to evangelize about how the product could help workers. The tangible return-on-investment (ROI) results of the pilot deployment were enough to persuade management to invest in a larger rollout to all 18,000 Innovation Net users, which P&G is in the process of completing. "The quality of conversations going on was very high and could be tied to people moving projects forward. It was clear this would be a pretty good investment," he says.

Another benefit that users appreciated was the efficiency that resulted from establishing a single knowledge base in the company. "Experts see great value in being able to see a question once and refer repeat questions to those answers," Telljohann says.

Users liked the ease with which they could locate experts and the fact that the system was integrated with e-mail so questions or feedback could be sent immediately. The software gave P&G employees a place to go to ask questions and to share their knowledge. "I think the experts feel like they can make more of an impact. They typically have close circles they share experiences and knowledge with; this broadens their ability to share what they know, and the people with questions have a place to go."

Questions for Discussion

1. What are the advantages firms can realize by linking employees together online via an employee portal? What are some potential disadvantages of employee portals?
2. What are the challenges that firms must face when introducing a workforce to a new employee portal? How can these challenges be managed?
3. What kinds of web services do you think an employee portal must have? What are some services that should be avoided? Explain your responses.

Sources: Adapted from Cathleen Moore, "Tapping Knowledge," *InfoWorld*, October 15, 2001, p. 38; Jim Kerstetter et al., "The Web at Your Service," *Business Week*, March 18, 2002, pp. EB12–EB16; Roberto Michel, "Portal Power," *Manufacturing Systems*, April 2000, pp. 40–45; and David Meuse, "How to Create a Successful Employee Portal," *Employee Benefit News*, February 2002, pp. 27–28.

17

Accounting Practices and Principles

Photo: comstock.com

After completing this chapter, you should be able to:

1 **Explain** the purpose of accounting and its importance to a firm's managers, creditors, and investors.

2 **Distinguish** between financial and managerial accounting.

3 **List** the steps in the accounting cycle.

4 **Explain** the accounting equation, define its elements, and describe its relationship to double-entry bookkeeping.

5 **Explain** the purpose of the balance sheet and identify its major elements.

6 **Explain** the purpose of the income statement and identify its major elements.

7 **Explain** the purpose of ratio analysis and list the major financial ratios.

Qwestionable Accounting

1 ☞ **Q**west Communications International, Inc., and Joseph P. Nacchio, its chief executive, had it rough during Spring 2002. On March 11, the telecom company said that the Securities & Exchange Com-

2 ☞ mission (SEC) had launched an inquiry into certain accounting practices. On April 1, Qwest said it would have to take a charge of $20 billion to $30 billion to write off goodwill and that the SEC had launched a second inquiry into its accounting. Then, in an April 9 securities offering document, the Denver-based firm said the probes could require it to make a "material" restatement to its earnings. All this dropped Qwest's stock price more than 50 percent.

The chairman of the company's audit committee, which is responsible for overseeing its accounting practices, had a potential conflict of interest that was never disclosed in Qwest's financial documents. W. Thomas Stephens is the

3 ☞ former chairman and now a director of Mail-Well, Inc., an Englewood, Colorado, printing company that got a multimillion-dollar contract from Qwest in December 2001. Such payment raises concerns that Stephens may not have been as critical of Qwest's accounting as a more independent director.

Stephens and Qwest deny there's any conflict. A spokesman for Qwest says the payments to Mail-Well do not

4 ☞ need to be disclosed under SEC and New York Stock Exchange rules because Stephens is no longer an executive at Mail-Well and owns much less than 10 percent of its stock. But experts say such guidelines are not always clear. "Generally, the SEC reserves the right to define something as material," says Theodore Sonde, a former SEC enforcement attorney. Stephens says he was unaware of the con-

tract. The chairman also contends that the audit board has been tough, pushing Qwest to make big changes in its accounting. In 2001, for example, it asked the company to disclose more information about how much of its revenues came from sales of network capacity to other telcos. And in March, it banned troubled accountant Arthur Andersen from doing new nonaudit work. In 2001, Qwest paid Andersen $1.4 million for auditing services and $10.5 million for other services.

The SEC investigation is focusing on whether Qwest used aggressive accounting practices in 2000 and 2001 to keep its stock flying high while Nacchio and Qwest founder Philip Anschutz sold stock. Qwest has denied that it did anything improper. The importance of Qwest's payments to Mail-Well is unclear. The printing company reported revenues of $1.6 billion for 2001, while one insider at Qwest said its contract was worth about $3 million over three years. Still, those payments are a substantial part of the revenues of Mail-Well 1-2-1, the subsidiary that received the contract. "It's our biggest customer," says Bob Hicks, Mail-Well 1-2-1's general manager.

Stephens is not the only audit committee member with a possible conflict. Linda G. Alvarado, another member, is president of Alvarado Construction, Inc., which received ☜ 5 $1.3 million from Qwest for construction services in 2000. The accounting problems for Qwest don't seem to be anywhere close to resolution.

Sources: Adapted from Peter Elstrom, "A Case of Conflicts at Qwest," *Business Week,* April 22, 2002, p. 37; and Shawn Young and Deborah Solomon, "Probe of Qwest by SEC Is Now Formal Inquiry," *Wall Street Journal-Eastern Edition,* April 5, 2002, p. A3.

17-1 INTRODUCTION

Accounting is an old profession. Business transactions have been recorded and analyzed for centuries. But only in the last seventy-five years or so has accounting been given the importance and respect accorded other professions. As the opening vignette highlights, accounting practices are essential to business confidence. When corporate directors and officers abuse the system, their corporate reputation and stock price can be negatively affected. In the case of Qwest Communications, several members of the company's board, including its founder, have been scrutinized for questionable accounting practices. The firm's investors paid a heavy price as the stock lost more than 50 percent of its value.[1] Accounting matters, and businesses must be concerned with practicing accounting in a fair, objective, ethical, and professional manner.

Accounting is sometimes derided by busy entrepreneurs and aggressive businesspeople as little more than "bean counting." However, as most *successful* entrepreneurs and businesspeople will attest, a basic understanding of accounting principles is an essential

1. Christopher Palmeri, "Qwest: A New Stink Bomb," *Business Week,* May 27, 2002, pp. 90–91.

Generally Accepted Accounting Principles (GAAP)   Rules developed by the Financial Accounting Standards Board to which accounting practitioners adhere.

6 ☞

Financial Accounting Standards Board (FASB)   An entity that consists of seven board members who issue statements and guidelines regarding accounting practices.

Accounting   The process of identifying, measuring, and communicating economic information to permit informed decisions by users of the information.

business tool. In a word, accounting is the language of business.[2] Anyone who aspires to a business career must, to some degree, speak that language. Corporations run on their numbers, and accounting plays an important role in generating and validating the numbers that drive business decisions.

Over the years, accounting has become increasingly standardized, but there are always new and unexpected transaction types that must be understood in accounting terms. It's important for business people to realize that accounting, although based on rules, is an evolving discipline. In general, accounting practitioners adhere to what is known as **generally accepted accounting principles,** or **GAAP.** The Financial Accounting Standards Board, or FASB, developed the principles in GAAP. FASB consists of seven board members who issue statements and guidelines regarding accounting practices. As new financial reporting and measurement systems arise, FASB board members consider how business transactions should be recorded. For example, during the dot-com revolution of the 1990s, many start-ups were eager to show profits, and projected revenues based on "clicks per thousand" and the "stickiness" of their websites.[3] As it turned out, website traffic did not translate readily into sales and many revenue projections were overstated. This led to major accounting errors and led many companies to restate their projected revenues and earnings. Investors who believed the accounting forecasts would get hurt by these disclosures. FASB needed to step in and study how best to book revenues and profits in the new dot-com businesses.[4]

In this chapter, we examine how businesses use accounting information. We first define accounting and discuss the various uses and users of accounting information. We describe the professional certifications that accountants may attain and differentiate between public and private accountants. We then explain the accounting cycle, the accounting equation, and double-entry bookkeeping. Next we present the basic financial statements and their components. Finally we show how business firms interpret the financial statements through the use of ratio analysis. First, the Focus on Technology box, "Software Does the Accounting for You," discusses advances in accounting software that have made it far easier for nonaccountants to keep track of their business.

17-2   WHAT IS ACCOUNTING?

7 ☞

The American Accounting Association defines **accounting** as "the process of identifying, measuring, and communicating economic information to permit informed judgments and decisions by users of information."

Accounting can be divided into two categories: financial accounting and managerial accounting. These categories differ according to the people they are designed to serve. *Financial accounting* is intended primarily for use by external decision makers (such as

8 ☞

investors, creditors, and the Internal Revenue Service). *Managerial accounting* is mainly used by internal decision makers such as company managers.

Accounting information is useful to investors, creditors, managers, unions, governmental organizations, and others (see Exhibit 17-1). Current investors use it to review the past performance of the company in which they have interest and to determine whether to maintain, increase, or liquidate their investment. Potential investors use accounting

9 ☞

information to help them make investment decisions. When General Electric reported in the spring of 2002 that it had used "aggressive" accounting practices in its reporting of quarterly earnings, investors battered its stock.[5] An analyst report that GE had achieved its remarkable 15 percent annual profit growth based to great extent on debt financing

---

2. Sidney Davidson, Clyde P. Stickney, and Roman L. Weil, *Accounting: The Language of Business* (Sun Lakes, AZ: Thomas Horton & Daughters, 1982).

3. Karen J. Bannan, "Measure for Measure," *CFO*, July 2001, pp. 58–59.

4. Christopher Farrell, "Needed: 21st Century Accounting Rules," *Business Week Online*, March 22, 2002.

5. Diane Brady, "GE: More Disclosure Please," *Business Week*, February 18, 2002, p. 34.

FOCUS ON TECHNOLOGY

Software Does the Accounting for You

Many business owners and managers shy away from doing their own accounting because it can be time-consuming, often confusing, and usually tedious. The good news is that numerous powerful and intuitive software packages are available that can make the accounting process easier for do-it-yourselfers. Most of these packages are very familiar to public accountants and integrate well with their more sophisticated systems. Thus, managers of small businesses can save money by doing their own accounting, and then uploading data to a public accountant for review and verification. A good place to review the available accounting software packages is at the following website:

http://www.2020software.com/acct.htm

sent the stock price into a nosedive. The analyst said that GE's management had not been forthcoming about the debt accumulation in its accounting statements.[6]

Creditors use financial information to evaluate credit applications and to make decisions about worthy candidates for loans. In most cases when making a loan decision, creditors will look at a firm's historical financial records (usually, at least three years). Most lenders focus on cash flow when making a loan decision to ensure that the firm has sufficient liquidity to make interest payments. Depending on the size of the loan application, the lender may also audit a firm's current assets to validate the balance sheet information (more information on balance sheets is provided later in this chapter).

Managers are the most frequent users of a firm's accounting information. They must have reliable information to make decisions about allocating company resources through the use of budgets. Managers also use accounting information to forecast the consequences

EXHIBIT 17-1

Users of Accounting Information

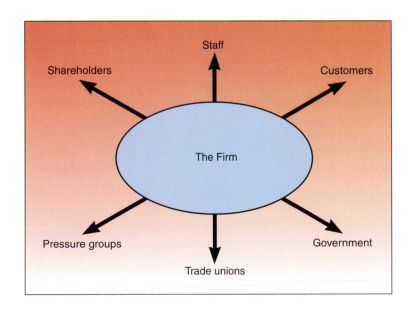

Users and Uses of Accounting Information

User	Typical Uses
Current investors	Evaluate the income generated by a company and its components. Evaluate the cash flow generated by a company. Evaluate management's performance.
Potential investors	In addition to the above, determine a company's future growth potential and the risk of investing in the company.
Creditors	Evaluate a prospective borrower's ability to make principal and interest payments.
Managers	Make resource allocation decisions.
Unions	Review a company's financial condition before negotiating wages and benefits.
Government agencies	Determine a company's tax liability.

10

Securities Act of 1933   The federal law that covers the new issue of securities. The Act also requires full disclosure of information relating to the new issues and contains many antifraud provisions. It regulates the primary market to prevent fraud on the sale of securities, and it provides purchasers of new issues information.

Securities Exchange Act of 1934   Another "full disclosure law" that requires public corporations to provide annual financial reports to shareholders.

of alternative business strategies.[7] In addition, managers use accounting information to compare actual financial results with expectations. For example, Cisco CEO John Chambers had been lauded as a super-manager for managing to hit quarterly earnings estimates for seven straight years. When Cisco reported that it missed its earnings estimates in the second quarter of 2000, its stock was hit hard, going from a high near $80 to a low of $10 per share.[8] Today, most managers live or die by the numbers on the quarterly reports. By reviewing accounting information regularly, management can act swiftly when results deviate too much from expectations.

Unions review company accounting information to help determine reasonable wage and benefit demands in salary negotiations. Governmental organizations rely on accounting information when establishing a company's tax liability. Exhibit 17-2 lists the various users of accounting information and some of the purposes for which the information is used.

17-2a Federal Oversight

The last decade has been one of furious corporate activity, with many new companies being formed, hundreds of them going public, and many declining into bankruptcy court. Federal oversight of business accounting practices has been common since the 1929 stock market crash. Many people believe that one cause of the collapse was a lack of sufficient publicly available information about corporate accounting practices and activities.[9]

In response to these concerns, the U.S. Congress passed the **Securities Act of 1933.** This legislation required most corporations to file registration statements before selling stock to investors.[10] As part of these statements, corporations were also required to provide financial reports containing balance sheets and income statements. Additional legislation, the **Securities Exchange Act of 1934,** required public corporations to provide annual financial reports to stockholders. The legislation also required that independent

7. Sunil Dutta and Frank Gigler, "The Effect of Earnings Forecasts on Earnings Management," *Journal of Accounting Research*, June 2002, pp. 631–655.

8. John T. Mulqueen, "Cisco Earnings Disappoint, Weak in Optical Products," *Interactive Week*, February 12, 2001, p. 21.

9. Anita Dennis, "Taking Account: Key Dates for the Profession," *Journal of Accountancy*, October 2000, pp. 97–106.

10. Samuel L. Hayes, III, "The Transformation of Investment Banking," *Harvard Business Review*, Jan./Feb. 1979, pp. 153–170.

FOCUS ON GLOBALIZATION

U.S. Resists International Accounting Standards

Credibility in America matters to the International Accounting Standards Board (IASB), a London-based private body that is responsible for devising international accounting standards. If it can't get the world's biggest capital market to respect its rules, companies will be less inclined to follow them. Although the IASB may lay down any rules it likes, it has no power to enforce them.

The United States' Financial Accounting Standards Board (FASB), the GAAP standard setter, argues that international standards are less comprehensive than GAAP. America relies less on broad principles than on detailed and prescriptive rules. The IASB inherited its standards from the IASC, a body set up in 1973 that had to take into account all the views of the many countries represented on its board. Because the IASC could not get everybody to agree, many standards allow different accounting treatments.

The IASB believes that the furor surrounding the bankruptcy of Enron should give it more of a hearing in America. International rules would have forced it to report more about its special-purpose vehicles, and Harvey Pitt, the head of the SEC, has criticized the FASB for taking too long over its decisions. That all European-listed companies will have to use international accounting standards by 2005 is another boost. The IASB has begun the process of improving its standards, some of which it admits are flawed. For its part, FASB is not interested in abandoning the hard work that has gone into GAAP. It recognizes the need for international accounting standards and believes that GAAP can provide those standards.

Sources: Adapted from "The Impossible Dream," *The Economist*, March 2, 2002, p. 69; and Brian J. Farrell and Deirdre M. Cobbin, "Global Harmonization of the Professional Behavior of Accountants," *Business Ethics: A European Review*, July 2001, pp. 257–266.

---

accountants audit these reports. The 1934 Act also created the Securities and Exchange Commission (SEC), a federal agency reporting to Congress. The SEC was given responsibility for overseeing external financial reporting by publicly traded corporations.[11]

Currently, the SEC requires publicly traded corporations to publish annual and quarterly financial reports. In addition, annual and quarterly registration statements must be filed by corporations with the SEC. Annual registration statements filed by corporations are known as **Form 10-K reports.** They are required by Section 10-K of the 1934 Act. Quarterly statements are known as 10-Qs.

In the increasingly global economy, there is also a drive to establish international accounting and reporting standards.[12] This drive is being led by the U.K.-based International Accounting Standards Board. However, as the Focus on Globalization box, "U.S. Resists International Accounting Standards," discusses, the United States is not ready to adopt the international standards, arguing that in fact GAAP is more stringent and better evolved than the proposed international standards.

✒ 11

Securities and Exchange Commission (SEC) The federal body that governs the issuance and sale of equity securities (stocks).

Form 10-K Reports Annual registration statements filed by corporations, which are required by Section 10-K of the Securities Exchange Act of 1934.

✒ 12

11. Mark Morgan and Gary John Previts, "The SEC and the Profession 1934–1984: The Realities of Self Regulation," *Journal of Accountancy*, July 1984, pp. 68–77.

12. Patrick Casabona and Victoria Shoaf, "International Financial Reporting Standards: Significance, Acceptance, and New Developments," *Review of Business*, Winter 2002, pp. 16–20.

Certified Public Accountants (CPAs) Accountants who have their own businesses or who work for public accounting firms. They perform a broad range of accounting, auditing, tax, and consulting activities for their clients, who may be corporations, governments, nonprofit organizations, or individuals.

13 ☞

14 ☞

Certified Management Accountants (CMAs) Financial management professionals who combine accounting knowledge and professional management skills to provide employers with a variety of leadership and decision-making services.

15, 16, 17, 18 ☞

Audit An examination of a company's financial statements to determine the fairness of the statements in accordance with generally accepted accounting principles.

17-3 TYPES OF ACCOUNTANTS

Accountants and auditors held about 976,000 jobs in 2000. They worked throughout private industry and government, but almost 1 out of 4 salaried accountants worked for accounting, auditing, and bookkeeping firms. Approximately 3 out of 25 accountants or auditors were self-employed.[13] Accountants can be classified by the type of certification they achieve, as either a certified public accountant (CPA) or a certified management accountant (CMA). They are also classified as public or private accountants.

Certified public accountants (CPAs) are licensed by the state in which they practice. Licensing requirements vary by state, but generally a CPA must meet certain educational requirements and pass a rigorous, four-part examination developed by the American Institute of Certified Public Accountants (AICPA). In most states, two years of accounting experience are required.

Certified management accountants (CMAs) must meet educational and experience requirements similar to those for a CPA. They take a five-part examination developed by the National Society of Accountants. Both CPAs and CMAs are employed in public accounting; however, only a CPA can conduct an audit as to the fairness of a company's financial statements.

17-3a Public Accountants

A public accountant typically works for a firm that provides accounting services to other companies, organizations, and the general public on a fee-for-service basis. Public accounting firms vary in size from the very largest, to sole-practitioner firms. The largest firms have thousands of employees and offices throughout the world. Public accounting firms typically provide three areas of service: auditing, tax consulting, and management consulting. In the mid-1990s, it was common to refer to the "Big Six" accounting firms. However, following a period of consolidation in the industry, that terminology no longer applies as many have joined forces, creating tongue-twisting corporate names such as PriceWaterhouseCoopers. Other majors include Ernst & Young, KPMG, and Deloitte & Touche.

Auditing, the oldest area of practice, remains the largest for many firms. An **audit** is a CPA's examination of a company's financial statements in order to express an opinion about the fairness of those statements in accordance with GAAP. When a company wants to borrow funds from a bank or have its stock listed on a stock exchange, it must present statements regarding its financial affairs. Because these statements are prepared by inde-

13. *Occupational Outlook Handbook*, 2002–2003 edition, accessed at http://www.bls.gov/oco/ocos001.htm.

pendent auditors, those interested in the information can reasonably assume that it has been presented fairly and accurately. An auditing firm's reputation depends on its strict adherence to GAAP and to guidelines put forth by the SEC.

When energy trading giant Enron collapsed in the fall of 2001, many questions were raised about the firm's accounting practices. How could such a large company fall into bankruptcy so quickly? Searching for answers, employees, investors, and government officials alike focused on management and accounting. Managers were scrutinized for their lack of oversight into questionable business deals and transactions. Enron's accounting firm, Arthur Andersen, was deeply scrutinized and heavily criticized for not raising questions about Enron's dealings.[14]

An increasingly common area of practice for major public accounting firms is *tax consulting and preparation*. Public accounting firms help devise strategies to minimize the tax liabilities of their client companies. In many instances, the accounting firm will also prepare and review the company's tax returns. Effective tax consulting firms can save large amounts of money for client firms simply by knowing the ever-changing tax code inside and out. Business managers who attempt to manage their own tax accounting are at a disadvantage in that they cannot possibly keep up with the complex and evolving tax law in the United States. For example, there were 440 tax law changes in 2001.[15]

The third major area of practice for public accounting firms is *management consulting*. Activities in this area typically vary from one firm to another. Some examples include computer systems analysis, design, and implementation; employee benefits and compensation consulting; risk management services; and litigation support. To provide an example of the amount of new business that management consulting can add to a major accounting firm, consider that Cap Gemini bought Ernst & Young's management consulting practice in 2001. At the time of the purchase, E&Y's management consulting practice consisted of over 20,000 employees and $4 billion in annual revenue.[16]

✍ 19

17-3b Private Accountants

The title **private accountant** includes all positions not in public accounting. Private accounting can be divided into management accounting, government accounting, and academia. Management accounting describes accounting positions within a company. The private accountant is employed by a single business, whereas a public accountant may have many clients. Government accounting positions can be at the federal, state, or local level. Accountants in academia teach and conduct research at the college and university level.

In this discussion, we mention only some of the career opportunities available to those interested in accounting as a profession. How much do you know about the accounting field? Exhibit 17-3 will help you assess your knowledge and perceptions of accounting.

Private Accountant
Accountant in any position not included in public accounting; may work in management accounting, government accounting, or academia.

17-4 THE ACCOUNTING CYCLE

A primary purpose of accounting is to communicate the results of business transactions. The **accounting cycle** is the sequence of six steps used to keep track of what has happened in the business and to report the financial effect of those events.[17] The steps in the accounting cycle are depicted in Exhibit 17-4 on page 455.

Accounting Cycle   The steps—analyzing, recording, posting, and preparing reports—by which the results of business transactions are communicated.

14. Cathy Booth Thomas and Deborah Fowler, "Will Enron's Auditor Sing?," *Time*, May 20, 2002, p. 44.

15. Thomas Pack, "Coping with Tax Law Changes," *Link Up*, March/April 2002, p. 12.

16. Chris Gonsalves and John Madden, "Cap Gemini Buys E&Y Consultancy," *PC Week*, March 6, 2000, p. 14.

17. James Edwards, Roger Hermanson, and Roland Salmonson, *The Basic Accounting Cycle* (New York: Richard D. Irwin, 1975).

**Are You Up
on Accounting?**

Directions: Below are some statements about job opportunities in accounting and the different types of accountants. Circle the number that represents how strongly you agree or disagree with each statement.

	Strongly Disagree				Strongly Agree
1. Accountants tend to be employed in very boring jobs.	1	2	3	4	5
2. There is little opportunity to move out of accounting because other departments do not want "bean counters."	1	2	3	4	5
3. Accountants do not make enough money.	1	2	3	4	5
4. Because accountants deal primarily with numbers, they do not need good people skills.	1	2	3	4	5
5. The opportunities for women in accounting are not as good as those for men.	1	2	3	4	5
6. The only accountants with professional certifications are CPAs.	1	2	3	4	5
7. A CPA is independent with respect to his/her client.	1	2	3	4	5
8. A CMA is independent with respect to his/her client.	1	2	3	4	5
9. CPAs are limited to jobs in public accounting.	1	2	3	4	5
10. CMAs in public accounting can express an independent audit opinion on a company's financial statements.	1	2	3	4	5

Feedback: If you tended to agree with the first four statements, you need to learn some basic facts about the accounting profession. Whether it is auditing a multinational company such as IBM or working for the FBI as an agent, opportunities abound for accountants to move out of the accounting area and into other departments. Most departments view the financial training accountants receive as an excellent background for all areas of business. Also, opportunities for women within the accounting profession today are every bit as good as they are for men. Most larger CPA firms actively recruit, hire, and promote qualified accountants who happen to be women. Women make up more than 50 percent of the enrollment in many accounting programs in schools around the country.

The last five questions deal with types of accountants. CPAs are entrusted with the public welfare when they undertake audits of financial statements; the primary responsibility of CMAs is to their employers. CPAs are extensively employed outside of public accounting. More AICPA members are engaged in private practice than in public accounting. Another fundamental difference between CPAs and CMAs is that only a CPA can express an audit opinion on a company's financial statements.

The accountant first analyzes business transactions to determine which should be recorded and at what amount. Typically accountants only record transactions that can be measured and verified with some degree of precision. For example, the purchase of a truck for the logistics department can be accurately measured and easily verified. However, an event like the resignation of a key employee, also a business transaction, would not be recorded. Although such an event may represent an economic loss to a company, it is difficult to determine accurately what the amount of the loss would be.

Accounting transactions are recorded chronologically in a **journal.** A journal may be either a book (in a manual accounting system) or an electronic file (in a computerized accounting system). Each entry contains the date of the transaction, its description, and debit and credit columns. Transactions are recorded in the firm's general journal or in specialized journals. A *general journal* is a book or file in which transactions are

Journal   A book or computer file in which business transactions are recorded chronologically.

EXHIBIT 17-4

The Financial Accounting Cycle

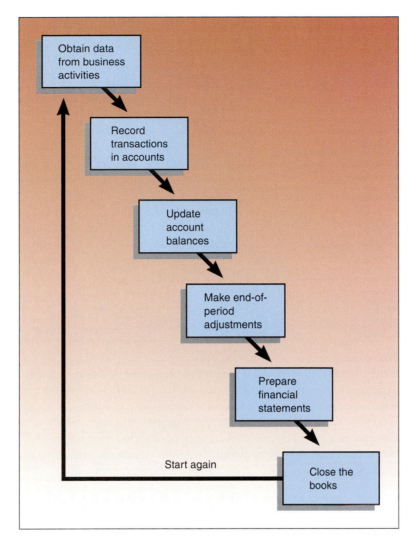

recorded in the order they occur. As businesses expand, they may adopt *specialized journals* to record particular types of business transactions (for example, credit sales or cash disbursements).

Businesses need to know the balances of various financial statement elements (assets, liabilities, owners' equity, revenues, and expenses) at any point in time. **Accounts** are used to summarize all transactions that affect a particular financial statement component. A business maintains separate accounts for each of its assets, liabilities, equities, revenues, and expenses. All transactions affecting an account are **posted** (recorded) from the general journal or specialized journals to the account. All the accounts of a business are summarized in the **general ledger.**

The final steps of the accounting process involve preparing financial statements. **Financial statements** present a company's financial position, results of operations, and flow of cash during a particular period of time. The financial statements that are prepared include the income statement, balance sheet, statement of cash flows, and statement of retained earnings. They can be prepared for any time interval, but they are always prepared annually. Investors, creditors, company managers, and others interested in a firm's financial position all rely heavily on financial statements. In preparing these statements, accountants check the balance sheet to determine whether their entries balance (see section 17-7a for more on balance sheets). If not, adjustments are made to how the numbers have been entered until a balance is achieved and the books can be closed.

Accounts Record of all transactions affecting a particular financial statement element.

Posted Refers to transactions being recorded from the general journal or specialized journals to an account.

General Ledger A book or computer file summarizing all accounts of the business.

Financial Statements Documents presenting a company's financial position, results of operations, and cash flow during a stated period of time.

17-5 THE ACCOUNTING EQUATION

Accounting Equation
Assets = Liabilities + Owners' Equity, indicating a company's financial position at any point in time.

The **accounting equation** indicates a company's financial position at any point in time. On its framework rests the entire accounting process. According to the accounting equation, a company's assets equal its liabilities plus owners' equity, thus:

$$\text{Assets} = \text{Liabilities} + \text{Owners' Equity}$$

Any recorded business transaction can be analyzed in terms of its effect on the accounting equation. Also, business transactions must be recorded to maintain the equality of this equation. This equality is reflected in the balance sheet, one of the financial statements a firm is required to prepare.

Assets Anything of value owned by the business and used in its operation.

Liabilities Debts owed by a business to its creditors.

Owners' Equity Claims of owners, partners, and shareholders against the firm's assets; the excess of assets over liabilities.

Revenues Inflows of assets resulting from the ongoing operation of the business.

Expenses Costs incurred to produce revenues.

Net Income The excess of revenues over expenses; also called the bottom line.

Assets are anything of value owned by the business and used in conducting its operations. Examples include cash, investments, inventory, accounts receivable, and furniture and fixtures. **Liabilities** are debts owed by the business to its creditors, including obligations to perform services in the future. Liabilities include accounts payable and notes payable (for example, when a firm uses credit to purchase machinery or inventory), wages payable to employees, and taxes payable. **Owners' equity** represents the claims of the owners, partners, and shareholders against the firm's assets. It is the owners' claim on the firm's assets, or the excess of assets over all liabilities.

Revenues are inflows of assets resulting from the ongoing operation of a business. Businesses generate revenues by sales of goods and services, interest earned on investments, rents, royalties, and dividends. **Expenses** are costs incurred to produce revenues. Expenses include the costs of goods sold (the goods or services that the firm used to generate revenues), salaries, utilities, taxes, marketing, and interest payments. Revenues and expenses are components of owners' equity. Revenues result in an increase, while expenses result in a decrease in owners' equity. **Net income,** or the bottom line, is the excess of revenues over expenses. Investors, creditors, and company managers closely watch net income, a chief barometer of business performance.

17-6 DOUBLE-ENTRY BOOKKEEPING

Debits Entries that record an increase in assets, a decrease in liabilities, or a decrease in owners' equity; recorded on the left side of a journal or ledger entry.

Credits Entries that record a decrease in an asset, an increase in a liability, or an increase in owners' equity; recorded on the right side of a journal or ledger entry.

Double-Entry Bookkeeping A method of recording business transactions in which offsetting debits and credits keep the accounting equation in balance.

Every business transaction is analyzed to determine whether it increases or decreases a firm's assets, liabilities, owners' equity, revenues, and expenses. Debits and credits are bookkeeping entries that reflect business transactions. **Debits** are used to record increases in assets, decreases in liabilities, or decreases in owners' equity. Debits are recorded on the left side of an entry in the journal or ledger. **Credits** are used to record decreases in assets, increases in liabilities, or increases in owners' equity. Credits are recorded on the right side of entries made in the journal and ledger.

The terms *debit* and *credit* can be confusing. Whether debits and credits *increase* or *decrease* accounts depends on the type of account being debited or credited. The important point to remember is that debit means left side of a journal or ledger entry, and credit means right side.

Double-entry bookkeeping enables the firm to keep the accounting equation in balance. In **double-entry bookkeeping,** each business transaction is recorded with two or more offsetting entries in which the total amount of debits must equal the total amount of credits. Exhibit 17-5 shows an example of journal and ledger entries for the Music Box, a hypothetical retail establishment specializing in CD players and other stereo equipment.

The Music Box's books are kept by Laura Baker, the owner. The accounts shown on the journal page in the upper portion of Exhibit 17-5 represent the company's sources and uses of funds. These accounts are then summarized in the ledger accounts, which are shown in the lower portion of the figure.

On September 1, Laura Baker contributed $40,000 cash in return for capital stock to get the company started. This transaction increased the firm's assets and the owners' equity. The Cash account is debited (to show an increase in assets), and the Capital Stock account is credited (to show an increase in owners' equity).

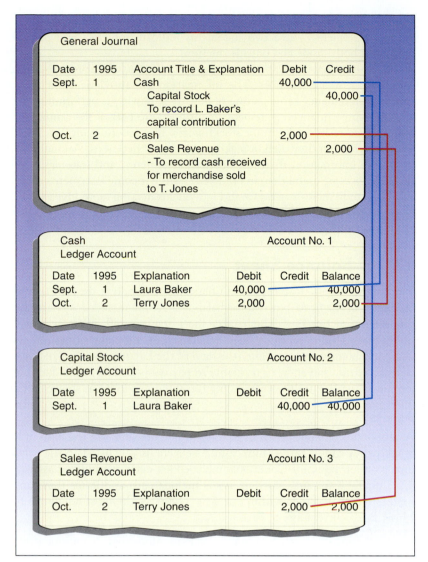

$$\text{Assets} = \text{Liabilities} + \text{Owners' Equity}$$
$$\$40{,}000 = \$0 + \$40{,}000$$
$$(\text{Cash}) \quad (\text{Capital Stock})$$

On October 2, a sale was made. A customer paid $2,000 cash for a CD player/stereo system. The journal entry records a debit (to show the increase in cash) and a credit (sales increase equities, and credits are used to show increases in owners' equity).

$$\text{Assets} = \text{Liabilities} + \text{Owners' Equity}$$
$$\$\,2{,}000 = \$0 + \$2{,}000$$
$$(\text{Cash}) \quad (\text{Sales Revenue})$$

As you can see, double-entry bookkeeping keeps the accounting equation in balance.

17-7 FINANCIAL STATEMENTS

We already know that one accounting cycle step is to summarize a firm's transactions in various financial statements. Every business prepares a balance sheet and an income statement. Most businesses also prepare a statement of cash flows.

The numbers and accounts appearing in the financial statements are drawn from the general ledger. The elements of the accounting equation (assets, liabilities, and owners' equity) are reflected in the balance sheet. Revenues and expenses are shown on the income statement. These two statements indicate solvency and profitability for those interested both inside and outside the firm.

Solvency relates to a firm's ability to pay its debts, while profitability describes a firm's ability to generate revenues. The information presented is meant to give users of the financial statements a true picture of how the company is performing.

The three financial statements mentioned are part of the annual report, which is a main source of information for stockholders. In a recent study, stockholders were asked what information they used in making investment decisions. Annual reports, which contain more information than just financial statements, and statements of cash flow were found to be more useful than in prior years, while income statements were seen as less useful. This study shows a trend toward individuals making more investment decisions based on company information provided mainly by financial statements and annual reports and relying less on the advice of stockbrokers.

17-7a Balance Sheet

The **balance sheet,** or statement of financial position, lists the assets, liabilities, and owners' equity of the firm. Items on the balance sheet are recorded at their historical costs, the original transaction cost. The balance sheet does not reflect accounts at their liquidation or fair market value, today's values. A balance sheet indicates the firm's financial position at a particular moment in time (the date of the balance sheet). This financial statement reflects a firm's solvency, or its ability to pay debts as they come due. The balance sheet for the Music Box for the year ending December 31, 2002, is shown in Exhibit 17-6.

Assets

Assets (items of value to the company) can be classified on the basis of liquidity, or how quickly they can be turned into cash. Assets are usually listed on the balance sheet in the order of their liquidity. Commonly included are current and fixed assets.

Usually listed first, **current assets** include cash and items that can or will be converted to cash and used within one year. These are the most liquid of a firm's assets. The Music Box's current assets are as follows:

1. *Cash* ($62,000)—cash on hand and bank funds that management has immediate access to when needed.
    Accounts receivable ($50,000)—amounts owed to the store by customers who made purchases on credit. Because the manager believes that not all of this amount will be collected, an allowance for doubtful accounts is included to reflect this possibility ($53,000 – $3,000).
2. *Inventory* ($85,000)—merchandise (CD players, stereos, speakers, etc.) on hand for sale to customers.

Relatively permanent assets that a firm expects to use for periods longer than one year are called **plant assets.** Long-term assets include such items as land, buildings, machinery, vehicles, and furniture and fixtures. Except for land, all these assets are considered depreciable because they wear out and must be replaced. **Depreciation** amortizes the cost of a plant asset over the course of its useful life. This procedure gives a more accurate idea of the total cost involved in a firm's operations. The Music Box's plant assets include the following:

1. *Store equipment* ($25,000)—office computers, display models. This amount was obtained by deducting accumulated depreciation from the assets' cost ($30,000 – $5,000).
2. *Furniture and fixtures* ($60,000)—office furniture, display cases, cabinetry, and lighting. Again, the cost of these items was reduced to reflect accumulated depreciation ($70,000 – $10,000).

Balance Sheet A financial statement that indicates a firm's financial position at a particular point in time; reflects a firm's solvency, or its ability to pay its debts as they come due. Also called the statement of financial position.

Current Assets Cash plus items that can or will be converted to cash and used within one year.

Plant Assets Relatively permanent assets that a firm expects to use for more than one year.

Depreciation Procedures for spreading the cost of a plant asset out over the course of its useful life.

Assets

Current assets
Cash		$ 62,000
Accounts receivable	$53,000	
Less: Allowance for doubtful accounts	3,000	50,000
Inventory		85,000
Total current assets			$197,000

Plant assets:
Store equipment	30,000	
Less: Accumulated depreciation	5,000	25,000
Furniture and fixtures	70,000	
Less: Accumulated depreciation	10,000	60,000
Total plant assets			85,000
Total assets			$282,000

Liabilities

Current liabilities:
Accounts payable	$ 50,000

Long-term liabilities:
Notes payable in 2000	150,000
Total liabilities		$200,000

Owners' Equity

Capital stock	$ 40,000	
Retained earnings	42,000	
Total owners' equity		82,000
Total liabilities and owners' equity		$282,000

EXHIBIT 17-6

The Music Box Balance Sheet at December 31, 2002

Liabilities

As we have already noted, liabilities are debts the business owes to its creditors. Businesses list liabilities on the balance sheet in the order in which they are due to be paid. Two types of liabilities show on the balance sheet: current and long term.

Financial obligations of the firm that will be repaid within one year are classed as **current liabilities.** Current liabilities for the Music Box include accounts payable ($50,000). These accounts reflect the portions of inventory and supplies that were purchased on credit.

Because current liabilities must be repaid within one year, they could create a financial crunch for a firm with inadequate cash reserves or other liquid assets. So firms pay close attention to the relationship between current assets and current liabilities. **Working capital,** the difference between current assets and current liabilities, reflects the firm's ability to meet its short-term obligations. For the Music Box, working capital amounts to $147,000 ($197,000 – $50,000).

Amounts owed that must be repaid more than one year from the balance sheet date are called **long-term liabilities.** For the Music Box, long-term liabilities include notes payable ($150,000) in 2000. Notes payable are debts owed to banks that are usually the primary lenders of money.

Owners' Equity

Owners' equity represents the claims of the owners, partners, and shareholders against the firm's assets. It is the excess of assets over liabilities and includes both capital stock and retained earnings. One of the ways that businesses raise capital to operate is by issuing

Current Liabilities   Financial obligations of a firm that will be repaid within one year.

Working Capital   Capital Measure of a firm's ability to meet short-term obligation; computed as current assets minus current liabilities.

Long-Term Liabilities Amounts owed by a business that must be repaid more than one year from the balance sheet date.

capital stock and selling shares of ownership to stockholders. Laura Baker invested $40,000 to get the Music Box off and running, so this amount becomes the capital stock entry on the balance sheet.

A firm's profits can either be distributed as dividends to shareholders or retained and reinvested in the firm. **Retained earnings** are a firm's accumulated net income minus dividends to shareholders. They help a firm grow and expand by providing the means to invest in land or buildings or expand the items carried in inventory. The Music Box has retained earnings of $42,000.

As you can see in Exhibit 17-6, the balance sheet illustrates the accounting equation in that assets ($282,000) equal liabilities ($200,000) plus owners' equity ($82,000).

17-7b Income Statement

The **income statement** (sometimes called an earnings statement or profit and loss [P&L] statement) lists a firm's revenue, expenses, and net income over some *period* of time, typically a year. (Recall that the balance sheet indicates the firm's financial position as of a particular *moment* in time, the balance sheet date.) The firm's profitability, its ability to generate income, is determined by comparing revenues with the expenses incurred in producing these revenues.

In addition to indicating a firm's profitability (or unprofitability), the income statement focuses on overall revenues and costs, giving managers the big picture of the firm's operations. It also provides data for the ratio analyses used by managers to get a handle on day-to-day operational performance. (Ratio analysis is discussed later in the chapter.)

The income statement for the Music Box for the year ending December 31, 2002, appears in Exhibit 17-7.

On the income statement, all expenses are deducted from revenues to determine net profit (or loss), the net income. For the Music Box:

$$\text{Revenues} - \text{Expenses} = \text{Net Income}$$
$$\$720{,}000 - \$712{,}000 = \$8{,}000$$

Revenues

As mentioned earlier, sales of products or services, interest, rents, royalties, and dividends generate revenues. The Music Box earned a gross revenue of $740,000 on the sale of compact-disc players, stereos, CDs, and other merchandise during the year. This figure minus returned and defective merchandise yielded a net revenue (also called net sales) of $720,000.

Cost of Goods Sold

This section of the income statement itemizes the cost of the goods or services that generate revenues for the firm. Here's how the Music Box determines cost of sales. Inventory on hand at the beginning of the year was $70,000. To this amount is added the cost of new inventory purchased during the year ($605,000). This calculation results in the firm's cost of goods available for sale, $675,000. The ending (unsold) inventory amount ($85,000) as of the income statement date is deducted from this figure. The resulting amount, $590,000, represents the cost of sales for the Music Box.

Firms determine gross profit by subtracting the cost of sales from net revenue. The Music Box had a gross profit of $130,000 ($720,000 - $590,000).

Operating Expenses

A firm's **operating expenses** include all the costs of doing business except the cost of goods sold. **Selling expenses** are the costs incurred in marketing and distributing the firm's goods or services. For the Music Box, selling expenses include salespeople's salaries ($35,000) and advertising ($83,000). **General and administrative expenses** arise from the overall management of the business. For the Music Box, they include Laura Baker's salary

Retained Earnings   A firm's accumulated net income minus dividends to shareholders.

Income Statement   A financial statement showing a firm's revenues, expenses, and net income over a period of time; indicates profitability, the ability to generate income. Also called earnings statement or statement of profit and loss.

Operating Expenses   All costs of doing business except the cost of goods sold.

Selling Expenses   Costs incurred in marketing and distributing a firm's goods and services.

General and Administrative Expenses   Costs incurred in the overall management of the business.

Revenues

Gross revenue		$740,000
Less: Sales returns and allowance		20,000
Net revenue		$720,000
Cost of goods sold:		
Beginning inventory		70,000
Purchases during year		605,000
Cost of goods available for sale		675,000
Less: Ending inventory		85,000
Cost of goods sold		590,000
Gross profit		130,000
Operating expenses:		
Selling expenses:		
Sales salaries	$35,000	
Advertising	3,000	
Total selling expenses		38,000
General and administrative expenses:		
Advertising salaries	35,000	
Rent	10,000	
Utilities	2,500	
Insurance	2,000	
Depreciation—equipment	15,000	
Total general expenses		64,500
Total operating expenses		102,500
Income from operations		27,500
Interest expense		15,000
Income before taxes		12,500
Income tax expense (at 36 percent)		4,500
Net income		$ 8,000

EXHIBIT 17-7

The Music Box Income Statement for the Year Ending December 31, 2002

($35,000), rent ($10,000), utilities ($2,500), insurance ($2,000), and depreciation on equipment ($15,000), for a total of $64,500.

Net Income or Loss

Net income (or net loss) is the bottom line—the firm's profit or loss over a period of time. It is, literally, the bottom line of the income statement. Net income (or loss) is determined by subtracting all expenses from revenues.

Income from operations is determined by deducting total operating expense from gross profit. In our example, $130,000 minus $102,500 yields income from operations of $27,500. We must then deduct interest expense ($15,000) and income taxes ($4,500) to arrive at the bottom line, a net income of $8,000 for the Music Box.

17-7c Statement of Cash Flows

The last financial statement to be presented in this chapter is the statement of cash flows. In November 1987, the FASB made the statement of cash flows a requirement (as are the balance sheet and income statement) for all companies listed on an organized stock exchange.[18] The statement of cash flows is the most complicated of the primary financial statements, and we will not give a detailed analysis here.

18. John J. MaHoney, Mark V. Sever, and John A. Theis, "Cash Flow: FASB Opens the Floodgates," *Journal of Accountancy,* May 1988, pp. 26–34.

Statement of Cash Flows
Financial statement showing the flow of cash into and out of a business during a period of time.

Operating Activities A firm's primary revenue-generating activities.

Investing Activities Activities that include buying fixed assets, buying stock in other companies, and selling stock held as an investment in another company.

Financing Activities Include issuing new stock, paying dividends to shareholders, borrowing from banks, and repaying amounts borrowed.

The **statement of cash flows** shows the flow of cash into and out of a business during a period of time. This statement indicates net cash flow (either inflow or outflow) from operating, investing, and financing activities. Cash flow from **operating activities** measures the cash results of the firm's primary revenue-generating activities. (In the case of the Music Box, cash flow from operations represents net cash flow from merchandising activities.) **Investing activities** include buying fixed assets, buying stock in other companies, and selling stock held as an investment in another company. **Financing activities** include issuing new stock, paying dividends to shareholders, borrowing from banks, and repaying amounts borrowed. The statement of cash flows also shows the net change in cash for the period.

As a summary of the effects on cash of all the firm's operating, financing, and investing activities, the statement of cash flows allows managers to see the results of past decisions. The statement may, for example, indicate a great enough cash flow to allow the firm to finance projected needs itself rather than borrow funds from a bank. Or management can examine the statement to determine why the firm has a cash shortage, if that is the case. Investors and creditors can use the statement of cash flows to assess the firm's abilities to generate future cash flows, to pay dividends, and to pay its debts when due, as well as its potential need to borrow funds.

17-8 ANALYZING FINANCIAL STATEMENTS

Once financial statements have been prepared, managers, creditors, and investors are interested in interpreting them. Managers' analyses of the financial statements primarily pertain to *parts* of the company, allowing them to plan, control, and evaluate company operations. Creditors and investors focus on the company as a *whole* to decide whether the company is a good credit or investment candidate.

Financial statement analysis compares (or finds relationships in) accounting information to make the data more useful or practical. For example, knowing that a company's net income was $50,000 is somewhat useful. Knowing also that the prior year's net income was $100,000 is more useful. Knowing the amounts of the company's assets and sales is better yet. To this end, several types of financial statement analysis have been developed. In this chapter, we discuss the technique of ratio analysis.

17-8a Ratio Analysis

Ratio Analysis Method of analyzing financial information by comparing logical relationships between various financial statement items.

Ratio analysis examines the logical relationships between various financial statement items. Items may come from the same financial statement or from different statements. The only requirement is that a logical relationship exist between the items. Ratios are very important to investors and other stakeholders in evaluating the financial health of the firm.[19]

The dollar amounts of the related items are set up as fractions and called *ratios*. Comparing company ratios to industry standards can indicate areas in which the company is successful—and those in which the company is below standard. Trends in a company's performance are also easily spotted by comparing ratios from the current period with ratios from earlier periods. Industry standards on certain key financial ratios can be found for most industries through trade associations, investment analyst reports, or from leading business publications.

Credit managers, bankers, and financial and investment analysts use several hundreds of different ratios. Only a handful of these ratios are useful in interpreting a company's financial standing, and many more may give misleading information. The ratios presented in this chapter—liquidity, activity, profitability, and debt—are some of the so-called key ratios that are in common use.

19. "Taking the Measure," *The Economist*, November 24, 2001, p. 72.

	2002	2001
Revenues		
Current assets:		
Cash	$ 40,000	$ 62,000
Accounts receivable	70,000	50,000
Inventory	110,000	85,000
Total current assets	220,000	197,000
Plant assets:		
Store equipment	25,000	25,000
(net of accumulated depreciation)		
Furniture and fixtures	50,000	60,000
(net of accumulated depreciation)		
Total plant assets	75,000	85,000
Total assets	295,000	282,000
Liabilities		
Current liabilities:		
Accounts payable	$ 55,000	$ 50,000
Long-term liabilities:		
Notes payable	150,000	150,000
Total liabilities	205,000	200,000
Owners' Equity		
Capital stock	40,000	$ 40,000
Retained earnings	50,000	42,000
Total owners' equity	90,000	82,000
Total liabilities and owners' equity	205,000	200,000

EXHIBIT 17-8

The Music Box Comparative Balance Sheet December 31, 2001 and 2002

It is important to note that different industries have distinct standards for ratio adequacy. What is an adequate ratio for a company in one industry may not be adequate for a different company in another industry. Beware of judging a ratio solely on the basis of a universal standard; ratios should be viewed against industry norms. For instance, the banking industry and manufacturing industry would differ significantly in terms of current assets. Banks carry an enormous amount of liquid current assets, while manufacturing firms have a much more even division of current and long-term assets. So a comparison of a bank and a manufacturing firm in terms of any ratio that contains current assets would not be realistic. Exhibits 17-8 and 17-9 present the figures that are used in this section to compute ratios.

17-8b Liquidity Ratios

A firm's ability to pay its short-term debts as they come due is measured by **liquidity ratios.** (Recall that liquidity is a measure of how quickly an asset can be converted to cash.) Highly liquid firms can more easily convert assets to cash when needed to repay loans. Less liquid firms may have trouble meeting their obligations or obtaining loans at low cost. Two common liquidity ratios are the current ratio and the quick (acid-test) ratio.

We have already said that working capital is the excess of current assets over current liabilities. The **current ratio,** which is current assets divided by current liabilities (two balance sheet items), indicates a firm's ability to pay its current liabilities from its current assets. Thus the ratio shows the strength of a company's working capital.

Liquidity Ratios Measure of a firm's ability to pay its short-term debts as they come due.

Current Ratio The measure of a firm's ability to pay its current liabilities from its current assets; computed by dividing current assets by current liabilities.

EXHIBIT 17-9

**The Music Box
Comparative Income
Statement December 31,
2001 and 2002**

	2002	2001
Net revenue	$800,000	$720,000
Cost of goods sold	640,000	590,000
Gross profit	160,000	130,000
Operating expenses		
Selling expenses		
Sales salaries	39,500	35,000
Advertising	4,000	3,000
Total selling expenses	43,500	38,000
General and administrative expenses		
Administrative salaries	39,500	35,000
Rent	15,000	10,000
Utilities	6,000	2,500
Insurance	2,000	2,000
Depreciation	15,000	15,000
Total general expenses	77,500	64,500
Total operating expenses	121,000	102,000
Income from operations	39,000	27,500
Interest expenses	15,000	15,000
Income before taxes	24,000	12,500
Income tax expenses (at 40 percent)	8,640	4,500
Net income	15,360	8,000

$$\text{Current Ratio} = \frac{\text{Current Assets}}{\text{Current Liabilities}}$$

Current ratios for the Music Box for 2001 and 2002 are computed as follows:

$$2001: \frac{197,000}{50,000} = 3.94 \text{ to } 1$$

$$2002: \frac{220,000}{55,000} = 4 \text{ to } 1$$

The current ratio is excellent in both years. Generally a ratio in excess of 2 to 1 is considered favorable. In 2002 the Music Box's current ratio increased slightly to 4 to 1, meaning it had $4 of current assets for every $1 of current liabilities.

The **quick ratio,** also called the acid-test ratio, divides quick assets by current liabilities. It measures more immediate liquidity by comparing two balance sheet items. Quick assets do not include inventory because to convert inventory to cash, merchandise must be sold and a receivable collected. **Quick assets** are cash or those assets the firm expects to convert to cash in the near future. For the Music Box, the quick ratio is computed as follows:

Quick Ratio The measure of a firm's immediate liquidity; computed by dividing quick assets by current liabilities. Also called acid-test ratio.

Quick Assets Cash or those assets the firm expects to convert to cash in the near future.

$$\text{Quick Ratio} = \frac{\text{Quick Assets}}{\text{Current Liabilities}}$$

$$2001: \frac{112,000}{50,000} = 2.24 \text{ to } 1$$

$$2002: \frac{110,000}{55,000} = 2 \text{ to } 1$$

The Music Box's quick ratio has deteriorated slightly.

17-8c Activity Ratios

How efficiently the firm uses its assets to generate revenues is measured by **activity ratios.** These ratios indicate how efficiently a firm uses its resources. A common activity ratio is accounts receivable turnover. **Accounts receivable turnover** is the number of times per year that the average accounts receivable is turned over (collected). An income statement item (net sales) is compared with a balance sheet item (accounts receivable). We calculate this ratio by dividing net sales by average net accounts receivable.

The allowance for doubtful accounts is first deducted to arrive at net accounts receivable. Average net accounts receivable is computed by adding the accounts receivable amounts at the beginning and end of the year, then dividing by two. For the Music Box, we determine this figure for 2002 by adding the beginning amount (which is 2000's ending amount, $50,000) to the ending amount ($70,000) and dividing by two to reach $60,000.

Accounts receivable turnover for the Music Box is computed as follows:

$$\text{Accounts Receivable Turnover} = \frac{\text{Net Sales}}{\text{Average Net Accounts Receivable}}$$

$$2002: \frac{800,000}{60,000} = 13.3$$

The Music Box, then, is collecting its accounts receivable thirteen times per year on average.

We can also look at accounts receivable turnover by computing the number of days it takes for each credit sale to be converted to cash. In other words, how many days does it take credit customers to pay their bills? This measure, referred to as the number of days sales in receivables, is computed as follows:

$$\text{Number of Days Sales in Receivables} = \frac{\text{Number of Days in Year}}{\text{Accounts Receivable Turnover}}$$

$$2002: \frac{365}{13.3} = 27.4$$

This means that the Music Box's accounts receivable are collected in twenty-seven days on average. Because the Music Box's credit terms for its customers are for payment to be made within thirty days, this ratio indicates that customers are indeed paying for their credit purchases within the required time. Thus the company's accounts receivable policies are considered to be of good quality.

A larger ratio, say fifty or sixty days, would indicate that credit customers are slow in paying their bills; thus, they would be using the Music Box as a source of interest-free credit (the company does not charge interest on past-due accounts).

17-8d Profitability Ratios

A company's overall operating success—its financial performance—is measured by **profitability ratios.** These ratios measure a firm's success in terms of earnings compared with sales or investments. Over time these ratios can indicate how successfully or unsuccessfully management operates the business. Two common profitability ratios are return on sales and return on equity.

Return on sales measures a firm's profitability by comparing net income and net sales, both income statement items. It is computed by dividing net income by net sales.

Activity Ratios Measure of how efficiently assets are being used to generate revenues.

Accounts Receivable Turnover The number of times per year that the average accounts receivable is collected; computed by dividing net sales by average net accounts receivable.

Profitability Ratios Ratios that measure a firm's financial performance by comparing earnings to sales or investment.

Return on Sales Measure of a firm's profitability, or its ability to generate income; computed by dividing net income by net sales.

For the Music Box:

$$\text{Return on Sales} = \frac{\text{Net Income}}{\text{Net Sales}}$$

$$2001: \frac{8,000}{720,000} = 1.1 \text{ percent}$$

$$2002: \frac{15,360}{800,000} = 1.9 \text{ percent}$$

These ratios show a quite low profit per dollar of sales. Retail establishments average around 5 percent. However, return on sales did increase from 1.1 percent in 2000 to 1.9 percent in 2001. This trend may mean the company is becoming more profitable.

Return on equity measures the return the company earns on every dollar of shareholders' (and owners') investment. Investors are very interested in this ratio; it indicates how well their investment is doing. We compute return on equity by dividing net income (an income statement item) by equity (a balance sheet item). For the Music Box:

Return on Equity Measure of the return the company earns on every dollar of owners' and shareholders' investments; computed by dividing net income by equity.

$$\text{Return on Equity} = \frac{\text{Net Income}}{\text{Equity}}$$

$$2001: \frac{8,000}{82,000} \quad 9.8 \text{ percent}$$

$$2002: \frac{15,360}{90,000} = 17.1 \text{ percent}$$

For every dollar invested in 2000, the Music Box earned nearly 10 cents. This return on equity is not good. A return of 9.8 percent is not much better than what can be earned on a bank certificate of deposit. Stock investments carry more risk, so they should offer higher returns. The 17 percent return on equity in 2001, a substantial improvement, is a better return for the risk assumed by investing in stocks.

17-8e Debt Ratios

Debt Ratios Measure of a company's ability to pay its long-term debts.

Companies measure their ability to pay long-term debts by **debt ratios.** These ratios try to answer questions such as (1) Is the company financed mainly by debt or equity? and (2) Does the company make enough to pay the interest on its loans when due? Potential investors and lenders are very interested in the answers to such questions. Two ways to answer them are the debt-to-equity ratio and the times-interest-earned ratio.

The **debt-to-equity ratio** measures a firm's leverage as the ratio of funds provided by the owners to funds provided by creditors, both balance sheet items. For the Music Box:

Debt-to-Equity Ratio A measure of a firm's leverage; computed by dividing total debt by owners' equity.

$$\text{Debt to Equity} = \frac{\text{Total Debt}}{\text{Equity}}$$

$$2001: \frac{200,000}{82,000} = 2.44$$

$$2002: \frac{205,000}{90,000} = 2.28$$

Total debt includes current liabilities and long-term liabilities. The debt-to-equity ratio demonstrates the risk incurred by the owners of the firm. The higher the debt-to-equity ratio is, the greater the chance that the firm will be unable to meet its obligations. The Music Box's ratio seems high, but there is no ideal debt-to-equity ratio. Examining other firms in the Music Box's industry should give a better picture of how the Music Box stands with regard to debt to equity.

Creditors need to know whether a borrower can meet interest payments when they come due. The **times-interest-earned ratio** compares cash received from operations with cash paid for interest payments. It measures how many times the firm earns the amount of interest it must pay during the year. This ratio is calculated by dividing income before interest and taxes ("Income from operations" in Exhibit 17-9) by interest expense on the income statement. For the Music Box:

$$\text{Times Interest Earned} = \frac{\text{Income Before Interest and Taxes}}{\text{Interest Expense}}$$

$$2001: \frac{27,500}{15,000} = 1.83$$

$$2002: \frac{39,000}{15,000} = 2.6$$

These ratios for the Music Box are improving. The higher the ratio, the more likely that interest payments will be made. Low ratios mean a company may have trouble making its interest payments to its creditors. The Music Box's ratios would probably be considered unsatisfactory.

17-9 WORKING WITH ACCOUNTANTS

Unless you are an entrepreneur bent on going it alone, most business managers will work with professional accountants to manage the financial condition of their firms. Working with accountants can mean interfacing either with employees who have been assigned to work in the accounting department, or with external consultants. We've already identified several of the major accounting firms and reviewed some of the services they provide to businesses. Although the major firms have name recognition—in addition to thousands of CPAs and accountants—there are a large number of smaller, or "boutique," public accounting firms that businesses can use. Most will assign a lead accountant to a client. The lead accountant will be the person who the business manager can contact with questions about accounting, taxes, or financial statements. The lead accountant may not work on each aspect of a client's account, but he or she will be responsible for interfacing with the client.

As many businesses have painfully learned, it is not necessarily prudent to leave all of the tax and accounting decision making to an outside consultant. Although most accounting firms will stand behind their work, simply allowing them to work without scrutiny is not in the best interests of the business. At the same time, managers hire consultants precisely because they are expert at what they do and the manager needs to focus on other issues.

Proper management of the external accountant, then, requires a balance between strict oversight and complete disinterest. What is that balance? Unfortunately, there is no absolute formula to use when attempting to answer this question. Working with external consultants requires that managers have some knowledge of the work they do and how to determine its quality. When Enron's executives and board of directors allowed Andersen Consulting to legitimize its questionable energy trading activities, the company ended up paying a heavy price. Although several insiders had raised questions about some of Enron's trading practices, the firm's executives and board decided that sign-off from Andersen would be enough to legitimize their decisions and continued with business as usual. This type of benign neglect on the part of managers can be counterproductive or worse. Managers should never completely turn over the reins of accounting and financial decision making to outside consultants. It's always wise to maintain some oversight over their actions and decisions.

Times-Interest-Earned Ratio
The measure of how many times during the year a business earns the amount of interest it must pay; computed by dividing income before interest and taxes by interest expense.

Most major accounting firms, and the smaller ones as well, will welcome input from managers on their performance. Managers of public companies should ensure at a minimum that they have expertise on their board of directors who can review the accounting firm's work and make a judgment about its effectiveness. Smaller firms may want to use third-party advisers or legal counsel to help them determine if their accounting firm is serving their best interests.

20 ☞   When selecting an accounting firm that is not one of the majors, such as PriceWaterhouseCoopers, a business can assess a few things to ensure that they are working with a quality firm.[20] One of the things to look for is the number of CPAs in the firm who are accredited by the American Institute of Certified Public Accountants (AICPA). The AICPA is the leading national accounting professional association in the United States. Its mission is to provide members with the resources, information, and leadership that enable them to provide services in the highest professional manner. In fulfilling its mission, the AICPA works with state CPA organizations and gives priority to those areas where public reliance on CPA skills is most significant. Each state has established policies for accrediting accountants, and most require ongoing continuing education to maintain that accreditation (see the end-of-chapter Internet Exercise).

Another thing that businesses can look for when seeking a qualified public accounting firm is references. Most firms have a list of clients for whom they have worked and will provide a contact with those clients who can speak to the professionalism of the accounting firm. Business owners and managers should not hesitate to request references and should beware any accounting firms that are reluctant to provide them.

In choosing a public accounting firm to assist in financial reporting and decision making, there are really only a few qualities to keep in mind:

- Reputation
- Professionalism
- Ethics
- Reliability

If a firm can demonstrate that it scores high on each of these criteria, then it should be able to help business owners and managers deal effectively with their accounting and financial obligations.

SUGGESTED WEBSITES

Note: These websites were functional when we went to press. Please access the online text for the most up-to-date URLs.

1. www.qwest.com
2. www.sec.gov
3. www.mail-well.com
4. www.nyse.com
5. www.alvarado.emergingsolutions.com
6. www.fasb.org
7. www.accounting.rutgers.edu/raw/aaa
8. www.irs.gov
9. www.ge.com
10. www.cisco.com
11. www.sec.gov
12. www.iasc.org.uk/cmt/0001.asp
13. www.aicpa.org
14. www.nsacct.org
15. www. pwcglobal.com
16. www.ey.com
17. www.kpmg.com
18. www.deloitte.com/vs/0,1010,sid=2000,00.html
19. www.cgey.com
20. www.aicpa.org

20. Elizabeth Stanny, Sherri Anderson, and Linda Nowak, "Contributing Factors in the Selection and Retention of Local Accounting Firms," *National Public Accountant*, June 2001, pp. 19–21.

INTERNET EXERCISE

Basic Accounting 101

Most states require about forty hours a year of continuing professional education for accountants in approved subjects. Besides accounting, auditing, consulting, and taxation, topics can include personal development, industry-related studies, information systems, management practices, general business (such as economics, business law, production or operational systems, marketing, and finance), and others. Many professional accountants are satisfying their ongoing training needs through a variety of e-learning opportunities.

For this exercise, students should explore the following e-learning websites to determine their educational offerings and value. In some cases, the links will take students directly to an accounting demo course. In other cases, the students may have to explore a bit to locate a free accounting course. Students should review a few sample courses and then respond to the following discussion items in class.

www.magellan.edu
www.learning.net
http://www.emind.com/htm/index.cfm?section=2&name=catacc#
http://www.pay-as-you-learn.com/e-accounting/default.html

Questions for Discussion

1. What are your impressions of the quality of the accounting e-learning that you examined?
2. Do you think these courses are sufficient to ensure that accounting professionals maintain a necessary level of expertise? Explain.
3. What do you think of the policy requiring accounting professionals to routinely participate in continuing education? What do you think is the best way to provide this ongoing training? What do you think accountants prefer?
4. In light of what we have learned about accounting and its importance to sound business practices in this chapter, do you think states should allow accountants to fulfill their continuing education using e-learning? Explain.

EXPERIENTIAL EXERCISE

Sources of Information for Decision Makers

Activity

Firms listed on any major stock exchange, such as the New York and American, generally prepare an annual report for investors and potential investors. The annual report contains a set of audited financial statements along with other pieces of financial and operating information that can be used to make investment and/or credit decisions.

In this chapter, we have examined the process of accounting that leads to the identification, measurement, and communication of financial information. This project attempts to show that the information on the face of the financial statements is only a portion of the accounting information available to decision makers. A significant amount of financial and operational information is contained in other locations within the annual report and in the notes to the financial statements.

Directions

1. To complete this project, you or your group need to obtain a recent copy of an annual report. Annual reports may be acquired easily in a variety of ways. First, companies of interest can be phoned or written directly (phone numbers and addresses of most public companies can be obtained from business directories located in your local or school library). Second, some libraries may actually have original or microfilmed copies of annual reports on hand. In this case, copies can be made at little expense. Third, your local stockbroker may have access to annual reports or may be willing to direct you on how to obtain one.
2. Once you have obtained the annual report, examine it carefully and become familiar with it. Then answer the following questions:

With regard to the balance sheet:

1. For which year(s) is(are) the balance sheet(s) prepared?
2. What items are listed as current assets? What are their amounts?
3. What cost allocation methods are used on inventories?
4. Are fixed assets aggregated (listed together) or listed separately? What items are listed as fixed assets? What are their amounts?
5. What depreciation methods are used to allocate costs on fixed assets?
6. What other assets are listed on the balance sheets? What are their amounts?
7. If intangible assets are present, for how many years are they amortized?
8. What items are listed as current liabilities? What are their amounts?
9. What is the amount of long-term debt (or liabilities)?
10. What additional information is present for debt or liabilities?
11. How many different types of stock are present on the balance sheet? How many shares of each have been issued?
12. What other information is present in the annual report pertaining to stock?
13. Do Assets = Liabilities + Stockholders' (Owners') Equity? What is the amount of each?

SUMMARY OF LEARNING OBJECTIVES

1. *Explain the purpose of accounting and its importance to a firm's managers, creditors, and investors.* Accounting identifies, measures, and communicates financial information about a company to its managers and outside parties to improve their decisions about allocating company resources and to evaluate the results of those decisions. Creditors examine a company's financial records to decide whether a firm is a good credit risk. Investors need to know whether a firm is a good investment candidate and, if so, how their investment is doing.

2. *Distinguish between financial and managerial accounting.* Financial and managerial accounting are the two categories of accounting. They are defined according to the users of the accounting information. Financial accounting is intended primarily for use by external decision makers (i.e., investors and creditors), while managerial accounting is mainly used by internal decision makers (i.e., managers).

3. *List the steps in the accounting cycle.* The accounting cycle is the way accountants communicate the results of financial transactions. First they *analyze* business transactions to determine which can be measured and verified with some precision. These transactions are then *recorded* chronologically in a journal. Next these journal entries are *posted* in the general ledger, which summarizes all the company's accounts. In the final step, the accountant *prepares* financial statements.

4. *Explain the accounting equation, define its elements, and describe its relationship to double-entry bookkeeping.* The accounting equation states that assets equal liabilities plus owners' equity. Assets are anything of value owned by the company and used in the process of conducting business. Liabilities are creditors' claims against a company's assets. Owners' equity is the owners' claim against the company's assets. This equation is always kept in balance. Double-entry bookkeeping uses two entries (a debit and a credit) to record each transaction, thus keeping the accounting equation in balance.

5. *Explain the purpose of the balance sheet and identify its major elements.* The balance sheet indicates a firm's financial position at a particular *moment* in time and reflects a firm's solvency, or its ability to pay debts as they come due. The major elements of the balance sheet are those of the accounting equation—assets, liabilities, and owners' equity.

6. *Explain the purpose of the income statement and identify its major elements.* The income statement reflects a firm's profitability, or its ability to generate income. It indicates a firm's financial position over a *period* of time. All expenses are deducted from net revenue, thus giving the bottom line: the firm's profit or loss for the period of time covered by the income statement.

7. *Explain the purpose of ratio analysis and list the major financial ratios.* Accountants use ratio analysis as another method of interpreting a company's financial information. Ratio analysis examines the logical relationships between various financial statement items. Comparing a company's ratios with those of other companies in the same industry gives an indication of how well the firm is doing according to industry standards. Comparing the company's ratios for the current period with those of previous periods may indicate trends (positive or negative) in the company's performance. The major categories of financial ratios are liquidity, activity, profitability, and debt.

KEY TERMS

accounting (p. 448)
accounting cycle (p. 453)
accounting equation (p. 456)
accounts (p. 455)
accounts receivable turnover (p. 465)
activity ratios (p. 465)
assets (p. 456)
audit (p. 452)
balance sheet (p. 458)
certified management accountants (CMAs) (p. 452)
certified public accountants (CPAs) (p. 452)
credits (p. 456)
current assets (p. 458)
current liabilities (p. 459)
current ratio (p. 463)
debits (p. 456)
debt ratios (p. 466)
debt-to-equity ratio (p. 466)
depreciation (p. 458)

double-entry bookkeeping (p. 456)
expenses (p. 456)
Financial Accounting Standards Board (FASB) (p. 448)
financial statements (p. 455)
financing activities (p. 462)
Form 10-K reports (p. 451)
general and administrative expenses (p. 460)
general ledger (p. 455)
generally accepted accounting principles (GAAP) (p. 448)
income statement (p. 460)
investing activities (p. 462)
journal (p. 454)
liabilities (p. 456)
liquidity ratios (p. 463)
long-term liabilities (p. 459)
net income (p. 456)
operating activities (p. 462)
operating expenses (p. 460)

owners' equity (p. 456)
plant assets (p. 458)
posted (p. 455)
private accountant (p. 453)
profitability ratio (p. 465)
quick assets (p. 464)
quick ratio (p. 464)
ratio analysis (p. 462)
retained earnings (p. 460)
return on equity (p. 466)
return on sales (p. 465)
revenues (p. 456)
Securities Act of 1933 (p. 450)
Securities and Exchange Commission (SEC) (p. 451)
Securities Exchange Act of 1934 (p. 450)
selling expenses (p. 460)
statement of cash flows (p. 462)
times-interest-earned ratio (p. 467)
working capital (p. 459)

QUESTIONS FOR DISCUSSION AND REVIEW

1. Accounting is the process of identifying, measuring, and communicating financial information. How does this differ from strictly recording business transactions (the purpose of bookkeeping)? Explain.
2. What different types of financial information about a company would external decision makers versus internal decision makers need? Why?
3. How does a public accountant's job differ from a private accountant's? Explain the differences.
4. If the primary objective of accounting is to communicate financial information to those who need to make decisions, how does the accounting cycle help to achieve this purpose?
5. How might accounting information be useful in planning business strategy? Provide details.

6. How does the fundamental accounting equation reflect double-entry bookkeeping?
7. The balance sheet reveals how well a business is doing at a certain point in time. How does this differ from the statement of cash flows? From the income statement?
8. How would the statement of cash flows help users of financial statements assess the liquidity of a company? Explain.
9. What types of ratios would be common in analyzing the financial statements of banks? Manufacturers? Why?
10. There has been a great deal of discussion about how much control companies should cede to public accounting firms. How can firms maintain a balance between letting public accountants do their jobs unimpeded, and providing analytical oversight?

END-OF-CHAPTER QUESTIONS

1. Projected earnings during the dot-com revolution of the 1990s were often based on "clicks per thousand" and website "stickiness."   **T** or **F**
2. Managerial accounting is intended primarily for use by external decision makers, such as investors, creditors, and the Internal Revenue Service.   **T** or **F**
3. The SEC requires publicly traded corporations to publish annual and quarterly financial reports.   **T** or **F**
4. After attaining certain educational requirements and passing a rigorous examination, certified public accountants are licensed to practice in all fifty states.   **T** or **F**
5. A *reconciliation* is a CPA's examination of a company's financial statements in order to express an opinion about the fairness of those statements in accordance with generally accepted accounting principles.   **T** or **F**
6. According to the accounting equation, a company's assets equal its liabilities plus the owners' equity.   **T** or **F**
7. *Liabilities* are the costs incurred in order to produce revenues.   **T** or **F**
8. *Solvency* describes a firm's ability to generate revenues.   **T** or **F**

9. Businesses list liabilities on the balance sheet in *smallest to largest* order.   **T** or **F**
10. Amounts owed that must be paid within one year from the balance sheet date are called *long-term liabilities*.   **T** or **F**
11. A firm's ability to pay its short-term debts as they come due is measured by liquidity ratios.   **T** or **F**
12. Companies measure their ability to pay long-term debts by _____.
    a. debt ratios   c. equity ratios
    b. profitability ratios   d. return on sales
13. Assets are usually listed on the balance sheet in the order of their liquidity. Which of the following would be listed first?
    a. Inventory   b. Cash   c. Accounts receivable
14. There were over _____ tax law changes in 2001.
    a. 50   c. 200
    b. 100   d. 400
15. In most cases, loan decision makers want to review _____ year(s) of a firm's historical financial records.
    a. ten   c. three
    b. five   d. one

Photo: comstock.com

18 Financial Management

Chapter Objectives

After completing this chapter, you should be able to:

1 **Define** *finance* and explain its role within a firm.

2 **Identify** the reasons firms need cash and why financial management is important.

3 **Discuss** the different sources of funds available to a firm.

4 **Compare** the different types of short- and long-term financing.

5 **Identify** the specific duties of a financial manager.

6 **Explain** the role of working capital management and capital budgeting in the ongoing success of a firm.

Computer Associates Runs into Cash Flow Problems

Computer Associates International Inc., (CA), Islandia, New York, maker of software for managing computer networks, had a tough winter. Then, on February 5, smack in the middle of CA's sale of $1 billion in bonds, Moody's Investors Service said it was concerned about weakening cash flow and would review CA's credit rating. CA's stock dropped 13.5 percent the next day. It canceled the offering.

The Moody's news came at a crucial point in CA's twenty-five-year history. CEO Sanjay Kumar was trying to shake off a series of blows that pounded the company's stock down 62 percent from a peak of $75. First came a blizzard of customer complaints about inattentive salespeople and overly rigid contract terms. Then there was confusion over the company's pro forma earnings. The capper came in the summer of 2001 when Texas entrepreneur Sam Wyly staged an unsuccessful proxy battle to take control of CA's board.

Add it all up, and Kumar will be hard-pressed to get the world's fourth-largest software company out of its rut. The Sri Lanka native and fourteen-year CA veteran was appointed CEO in August 2000, when combative chairman Charles B. Wang gave up daily operations. Kumar has vowed to forego the acquisitions that CA relied on to boost revenues, but he has not proven it can grow rapidly without them. Even analysts who rate the stock a buy say CA will grow only by single digits for years to come, versus 30 percent growth in the late 1990s.

Moody's was concerned about CA's ability to repay its $3.6 billion in debt. The agency forecasts operating cash flow will probably be $1 billion in FY2002, ending in March, down from $1.3 billion in 2001 and $1.5 billion in 2000. That would leave CA with a debt-to-cash-flow ratio of three to one. That ratio is on the high side.

Kumar rejects the cash-flow worries. The company paid down its debt by $850 million in FY2002. Kumar blames the decline in cash flow from $462 million in the third quarter of fiscal 2001 to $354 million in fiscal 2002 on an unusual $200 million up-front payment made a year ago by a big customer. Typically, customers pay for products in installments over the life of multiyear contracts and pay finance charges on the unpaid balance. This customer chose to pay up front and avoid the finance charges.

The cash-flow debate is a piece of something larger: CA's switchover in its basic business model. Starting in October 2000, CA added a clause to new contracts allowing it to recognize revenue in equal increments over time. The goal is to smooth out wild ups and downs in earnings. But the company got into hot water. Last April, it reported pro forma fourth-quarter profits of $274 million, while under generally accepted accounting principles it suffered a loss of $410 million because more revenue was deferred. CA prepared the pro forma numbers by recalculating past and current results as if CA had always deferred revenues. Analysts didn't entirely trust the results.

Sources: Adapted from Steve Hamm, "A Long Climb Out of a Deep Rut," *Business Week*, February 25, 2002, pp. 124–125; Dan Golden and Jerry Guidera, "Moody's Lowers CA Bond Rating on Cash Flow Slide, Pending Probe," *The Wall Street Journal*, March 4, 2002, p. B5; and Savita Iyer, "CA Shelves Plans After Downgrade Warning," *Bank Loan Report*, February 11, 2002, p. 2.

Every business needs capital to start, operate, maintain itself, and grow. Money fuels business. If businesses are successful, they will make more money than they need to operate. Businesses need money to purchase or lease equipment, build up inventory, and to pay the utilities, employees' wages, taxes, and rent. Without cash a business cannot survive. A well-funded business can lose money for a long time while it builds a customer base and moves toward profitability; but without the cash needed to pay its creditors, it cannot last. It will be forced into bankruptcy.

The opening vignette highlights the case of Computer Associates, Inc. (CA), a software company that ran into financial difficulties when its debt rating was lowered. CA is a large company with many assets, and yet it has to manage its financial affairs carefully to survive day to day. No business, no matter how large or how small, is immune from the need for sound financial management. Often, when firms get large and they lose track of their financial condition, they run into large problems that may take months or even years to fix. Some never get fixed. The bankruptcy of large companies such as Kmart, Enron, and Global Crossing has placed a new emphasis on financial control and reporting.

In this chapter, we define finance and the role of the financial manager. Then we look at the uses of money for a firm—what the specific costs of running a firm are. Next we discuss the sources of money—where firms can go to get the funds they will use. Finally we examine the management of a firm's finances, including the management of working capital, capital budgeting, and the use of financial controls.

18-1 DEFINING FINANCE

Since a firm must have a sufficient supply of cash, the area of cash management requires special attention. Management must determine the firm's cash needs for both the short and the long term and then find sources to provide the necessary cash. Cash management within the firm is its finance responsibility.

As a discipline in a business school, **finance** is the study of how to manage money within the firm. Within the business itself, *finance* is the functional area with the responsibility for finding funds for the firm, managing those funds, and determining their best uses. The **financial manager** is the individual responsible for the firm's finance function. It has become increasingly common for large firms to use the title of **chief financial officer (CFO)** to refer to the person in charge of a firm's financial affairs. Some firms do not formally appoint a financial manager, but the financial management tasks must still be performed, and one of the managers or owners will handle these tasks. In this text, when we refer to the financial manager, we are referring to the individual who is responsible for the finance function, regardless of the person's title.

To be effective, the financial manager has to develop and follow a financial plan. A number of tasks must be performed:

1. Project the month-by-month flow of funds out of the business.
2. Project the month-by-month flow of funds into the business.
3. Compare the monthly inflows to the monthly outflows.
4. If excess funds exist, find ways to generate revenue from these excess funds.
5. If funds are short, adjust inflows or outflows if possible and/or look for other sources of funding.
6. If other funding sources are needed, analyze the alternatives to find the most efficient source.
7. Establish a system to monitor and evaluate the results of this process.

An additional responsibility that has gained in stature for financial managers is that of maintaining the ethical integrity of the business. The financial manager in many companies has the responsibility of collecting, interpreting, and presenting financial information to a firm's executive team and governing board.[1] Not only is it important for financial managers to maintain the ethical integrity of the company, but they must maintain their own integrity as well. They can develop a reputation for integrity among their peers through the fine art of networking. The Focus on Careers box, "Financial Managers Network for Success," talks about the importance of networking in the career of a financial manager.

The importance of effective financial management to all businesses makes finance a crucial subject for all business students. Exhibit 18-1 on page 480 will help you determine how effective you might be as a financial manager.

18-2 PLANNING FOR CASH FLOW

One common mistake made by new businesses is the failure to plan for sufficient start-up capital (the money needed to start a business). As a result, many businesses get started with little real chance of success. Insufficient capital is not only a problem for small firms. It can also be a problem for long-established firms. Cash needs change over time, and having sufficient capital for continued operations is a concern even for these firms. For example, Chrysler Corporation had to seek federal loan guarantees in 1979 to stay in

Finance The study of money within the firm; the business function responsible for finding funds, managing them, and determining their best use.

Financial Manager The individual responsible for a firm's finance function.

Chief Financial Officer (CFO) The title of the person in charge of a firm's financial affairs.

5 ☞

---

1. Richard J. Henley, "Ensuring Ethical Governance in Your Organization," *HealthCare Financial Management*, January 2000, p. 14.

FOCUS ON CAREERS

Financial Managers Network for Success

Much has been said about the value of networking in increasing job effectiveness and promoting career development. Yet many financial managers still seem to pay scant attention to developing and maintaining collegial networks. Some managers may think the challenges they face are unique to their situations and, therefore, that solutions must be formulated individually. Others may be satisfied with the way their careers are going and simply feel no need to begin or continue networking with colleagues. No matter what the rationale, networking often is seen as a goal that would be "nice" to achieve, once other, more pressing matters have been attended to.

However, career experts contend that networking should be a high priority and ongoing effort for finance professionals. Things can change quickly, and organizations that are sound one day may be distressed the next. A professional network can offer financial managers looking for solutions the informed opinions and guidance they need to point them in the right direction.

Organizations need to explore new ways to keep pace with changing opportunities. The executives charged with strategically positioning their organizations to respond to market changes understandably rely on secondary sources, such as case studies published in books and magazines, for ideas and strategic models. Executives who have a well-developed network of contacts within their industry, however, can do more than "read between the lines" of a chapter for real-world insights into how a particular strategy might play out. They can discuss events with those who participated in them directly.

Finally, when contemplating a career change or conducting a job search, financial managers who have developed and maintained a network of professional contacts are able to make their own career choices and opportunities more easily. After their first entry-level position, many financial managers change jobs primarily through referrals and contacts made through networking.

Sources: Adapted from Richard J. Henley, "Enhancing What You Know Through Who You Know," *Healthcare Financial Management,* December 1999, p. 14.

EXHIBIT 18-1

Your Attitudes toward Financial Management

Look Before Leaping

Directions: Assume that you are interested in buying a business. You believe that you have the intelligence, energy, and skills to be successful. Review the following list of points. Then write down what things you will do to be sure that the business is right for you.

- Profits
- Cash flow
- Business records
- Financial statements
- Industry trends
- Inventories
- Supplier relationships
- Employees
- Customers

Check your steps or ideas with the feedback report, which just wants you to be cautious. The list, compiled by Western States Business Consultants, is not intended to be negative; it encourages caution. How many points that you raised correlate with the feedback pointers?

Feedback: When Buying a Small Business

1. *Determine exactly why the company is for sale.* People sell businesses for a lot of reasons, many of them good. But if you are buying, you need to know why they are selling. Avoid getting stuck with someone else's lemon.
2. *Ensure that a seller hasn't made a business look more attractive than it is.* You not only want to know what the owner says profits and cash flow are like, but you should also take the time to do estimates of these yourself. Survey the area, look at competition, check payroll and expense numbers, and talk to suppliers. Be happy with your project—not the seller's.
3. *Hire an experienced lawyer to review all business records.* You can't do it all. An experienced lawyer can review records, check on unusual liabilities, and advise you on how to write the sales contract to protect yourself against past or hidden costs or liabilities.
4. *Tie financial statements to historical tax returns to spot deviations.* This is another opportunity to check what is being said against reality. If an individual will not give you tax records for the business, be suspicious.
5. *Analyze major developments and trends within the company and the industry.* This serves two purposes: It helps you make some kind of long-term forecast for the business and forces you to familiarize yourself with the nature of the business and competition. If long-range prospects are not good or you cannot understand the nature of the business, back out.
6. *Verify inventories and supplier relationships.* Take a physical inventory of goods and make sure it matches reported inventories. Spot-check invoices to verify costs. Call some suppliers, at random, to determine potential credit problems or past-due bills.
7. *Check key personnel to determine if the sale will trigger employee benefits or loss of major customers or contracts.* In a lot of selling firms, the customers are loyal to the salesperson they work with rather than to the company they are buying from. If a key salesperson would leave because of the sale, you may lose significant accounts. Also, severance agreements, golden parachutes, and the like may be activated by the sale. Explicitly inquire about these.

---

business.[2] Kmart declared Chapter 11 bankruptcy in 2002, asking for court protections from the creditors it was unable to pay due to insufficient funds.[3]

To avoid problems, a firm must plan its cash flow; it has to know what its cash needs will be. By developing a detailed financial plan, management helps ensure the long-run success of the firm. We discuss details of the financial planning framework in this section.

---

2. "Lessons from the Chrysler Bailout," *California Management Review*, Summer 1985, pp. 157–183.

3. Bill Saporito, Bernard Baumohl, and Joseph R. Szczesny, "K-Mart's Blue Period," *Time*, January 14, 2002, p. 45.

18-2a Projecting Month-by-Month Outward Flow of Funds

The month-by-month flow of funds out of the business represents the firm's use of funds. A financial manager sitting down to project the firm's use of funds needs to consider such areas as the cost of daily operations, the cost of the firm's credit service, the purchase of inventory, the purchase of major assets, debt repayment, and dividend payments.

Cost of Daily Operations

When a new business is formed, the owners generally have considered the cost of leasing office space, purchasing or leasing office equipment, purchasing stationery and business cards, and payroll and benefits. However, many of the costs of daily operation are not considered start-up costs. The costs of payroll, utilities, rent, taxes, and interest on loans all have to be paid as part of normal operations no matter the stage of the company's growth. In a new business, which has little if any revenue at first, these costs have to be paid out of a **cash reserve.** If this cash reserve, needed to cover daily expenses until revenues are sufficient to cover them, is not figured into the start-up capital, the firm will run out of funds. For example, the Internet music firm Musicbank had to shut down before it even launched due to inadequate start-up capital.[4] Firms must plan to have sufficient cash reserves to pay rent, utilities, wages, interest expense, taxes, and the other short-term expenses of doing business until sufficient revenue can be generated to cover these costs.

> **Cash Reserve** The inventory of uncommitted cash that a company has and can use for investing purposes.

Cost of Credit Service

Most firms cannot do business on a strictly cash basis. Typically they provide customers with some form of credit to gain new customers and to encourage larger purchases. A firm that provides credit must maintain **accounts receivable** (the amount of money owed to a business from customers who purchased its goods or services). As long as the credit remains outstanding, as long as the receivable has not been collected, it cannot be counted as part of the firm's cash flow. The firm does not have the use of those funds to purchase the goods and services it needs to remain in business.

> **Accounts Receivable** The amount of money owed to a business from customers who purchased its goods or services.

Since much of a firm's assets can be tied up in accounts receivable at any given time, customers who are slow to pay greatly affect the short-term cash needs of the firm. For this reason, most firms "date" their accounts receivable; that is, they keep track of how many days receivables have been outstanding. Accounts that have been outstanding for the longest period of time get special attention from the financial manager.

The financial manager may follow a policy of sending a friendly reminder to customers whose accounts are over thirty days past due and a more stern reminder to customers whose accounts are over sixty days past due. Finally, a strong reminder with a threat of ending all credit privileges may be sent to accounts over ninety days past due.

Such measures may seem harsh, but if the firm does not receive the money customers owe, it may have to go to outside sources for its cash needs. These outside sources will charge interest for the money lent. Therefore, the firm loses in two ways: It has to pay interest for the funds it needs, plus it cannot earn the interest it might have if timely payment of the receivables had generated excess funds. Many of these problems can be avoided if the firm performs careful credit checks prior to granting customers credit. For example, TransUnion is a firm that provides quick credit checks for businesses to determine if customers are reliable in their bill payments. Exhibit 18-2 shows common tactics firms use to improve their collection of accounts receivable.

☞ 6

Cost of Inventory

A firm that hopes to survive in a competitive environment has to provide for its customers' needs. It cannot afford to be out of products that its customers demand. If it does not maintain sufficient inventory, it may irritate customers and force them to go

---

4. "Web Music Start Up Shuts Before Launch Date Due to Lack of Funds," *The Wall Street Journal, Eastern Edition,* April 12, 2001, p. B11.

EXHIBIT 18-2 Techniques for Improving Credit and Collections

Most Successful Techniques to Improve Management and Control the Cost of Credit and Collections, by Number of Employees					
	Up to 249	250 to 500	501 to 1,500	Over 1,500	Overall
Improved management of bad debt/collectible accounts	65.4%	63.5%	53.7%	45.1%	63.0%
Reduced numbers of customers paying late	60.7	59.5	63.4	39.2	61.9
Improved relations with the sales department	44.9	54.1	48.8	56.9	54.6
Improved staff productivity	35.5	39.2	53.7	72.5	49.8
Worked with management to tighten credit standards	42.1	51.4	39.0	43.1	48.4
Tightened controls on sales staff selling to those who don't meet credit standards	54.2	48.6	31.7	31.4	48.0
Increased use of Internet for the credit department	33.6	39.2	53.7	39.2	42.5
Used new computer technology, software, automation	38.3	28.4	34.1	51.0	42.1
Focused on customers taking unauthorized deductions	29.9	33.8	48.8	41.2	38.1
Streamlined approval of credit for new customers	29.9	25.7	24.4	25.5	28.9
Focused on customers taking unearned discounts	17.8	17.6	19.5	15.7	19.0
Cutback on staff or bonus	7.5	6.8	9.8	13.7	10.3
Worked with management. to loosen credit standards	6.5	5.4	2.4	2.0	4.8
Other	16.8	6.8	7.3	15.7	13.9

Source: The Institute of Management and Administration (IOMA) cited in How to Raise Your Credit and Collections Department Effectiveness, *Financial Executive's News*, May 2002, p. 15.

elsewhere to meet their needs. Maintaining sufficient inventory to satisfy customers' needs requires considerable expenditure of funds.

7 ☞ Inventory needs are further complicated by the fluctuations in demand that occur in various businesses. A retail business such as Wal-Mart will have to build up its inventory for the Christmas season, when sales are brisk, and then hold down inventory levels in January and February, when sales are slower.[5] A farmer must purchase his inventory of seed and fertilizer all at one time but can expect no income from his crops until they are harvested. While a vegetable canner will have to purchase the vegetables for canning when the vegetables are harvested, that is, all at one time of the year, sales of that inventory will be stretched over the entire year. A detergent manufacturer, on the other hand, will experience a relatively stable product demand and material supply and therefore will experience much less fluctuation in inventory needs than the other firms mentioned. Exhibit 18-3 shows the different demand cycles just discussed and their effect on cash flow.

Purchase of Major Assets

While major assets such as land, buildings, and equipment often have to be purchased by a firm at start-up, these same assets must be periodically replaced and upgraded. And as business increases, additional assets may be required. A firm may need to open a second plant, purchase another delivery truck, or buy additional machinery. The company may also want to plan for the future by purchasing land for future expansion when the real estate market is most favorable. All of these represent major expenditures and therefore major uses of company funds. If these expenditures are not planned for, the company may have to borrow unnecessarily or at high interest rates. Or the firm may have to forgo the purchase of new equipment, expansion of the plant, or purchase of delivery equipment.

One factor cited when businesses from Japan and other nations took over so much of the United States' steel business was the failure of U.S. steel corporations to recapitalize.[6]

5. Brian Garrity, "Holiday Season Opens Big at Retail," *Billboard,* December 8, 2001, p. 10.

6. J. Kendall Middaugh, II and Scott S. Cowen, "Five Flaws in Evaluating Capital Expenditures," *Business Horizons*, March/April 1987, pp. 59–67.

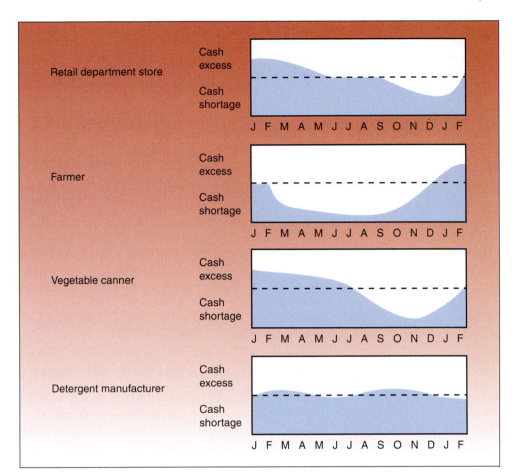

EXHIBIT 18-3

Effect of Varying Demand Cycles on Cash Flow

That is, they did not upgrade their plants and machinery, and the older equipment became obsolete and inefficient. With new plants and equipment, manufacturers from other countries were able to produce steel more efficiently and therefore sell it at lower prices than U.S. steel manufacturers. Obviously it is important for companies to plan for the replacement of equipment as better equipment becomes available and to plan for growth.

Payment for Debt

Most firms need to borrow money at some time or another. They may borrow to make major purchases or to get over a particularly tight cash period during the year; however, the financial manager has to consider the payment of interest and principal on any outstanding debt as a use of funds and needs to add this debt service into the calculation for funds usage. The use of debt is discussed in Section 18-4.

Payment of Dividends

Dividends are payments made to the firm's shareholders as a form of earnings on their stocks. Although stock usually does not require the payment of dividends, most firms pay dividends to keep their stock attractive to potential investors and to show that the firm is financially sound. As a use of funds, the payment of dividends must be planned for. Dividend payment has been less fashionable for companies in the last few decades. In 1970, fully 98 percent of S&P 500 companies paid dividends. In 2001, only 70 percent did so. In the wake of the accounting scandals and the collapse of the Internet bubble, the importance of dividends to investors is likely to rise.[7]

7. Kenneth Klee, "Paying Dividends," *Inc.*, June 2002, pp. 52–53.

Businesses need funds for many reasons. Fortunately, a business is able to acquire funds from many different sources. Some of these sources are internal and therefore have no interest cost or repayment. Others are external and therefore cost interest and require repayment. In Section 18-3, we examine where a firm can get money and look at the advantages and disadvantages of the various sources of funds.

18-2b Projecting Month-by-Month Flow of Funds into the Business

The finance function in a business is responsible for acquiring the funds the business needs. Sound financial management involves determining how much money is needed for various time periods and the most appropriate sources of these funds. Obviously the most appropriate place to get funds for the daily running of the business—that is, for expenses such as payroll, taxes, utilities, and rent—is from the revenue generated by the business. To determine the amount of outside financing needed, financial managers project the internal revenues the firm can expect on a month-to-month basis. They do this by estimating sales volume. If credit sales are involved, then the rate of payment on accounts receivable must also be estimated, since the company will not receive the cash from a credit sale until the receivable is paid. Managers should also consider any interest income expected from the investment of cash reserves and other excess funds.

18-2c Comparing Monthly Inflows to Monthly Outflows

Comparing expected income to expected expenditures yields three possible outcomes. First, the two can match perfectly, and no action need be taken (highly unlikely). Second, expected expenditures for the month can exceed expected income, and additional funds must be found to cover the shortfall (discussed in Section 18-3). Third, expected income for the month can exceed expected expenditures, and the company will have excess funds. Section 18-3 examines how firms generate revenue from excess funds.

18-3 GENERATING REVENUE FROM EXCESS FUNDS

If expected income for the month exceeds expected expenditures, the firm must decide how to use the extra funds. Firms may decide to expand the business, or they may use the funds to make highly liquid investments.

18-3a Expansion

A company with substantial excess funds may want to consider expansion of current operations through an increase in production capacity, the addition of new sales outlets, or some other form of expansion. The firm might want to look at acquiring another firm. As Exhibit 18-4 shows, U.S. and U.S. cross-border Mergers & Acquisitions (M&A) activity peaked in 2000 as the Internet bubble was bursting and has fallen off since then. Despite the decreased M&A activity, it still represents an excellent opportunity for a business to grow without having to develop new product lines or add staff. By acquiring another firm, a business can simply add products, clients, and key talent to its asset base. Especially in times of business recession, firms with a healthy balance sheet can acquire other firms without using up any cash—a firm with great products but little revenue might be interested in being acquired for stock.

18-3b High-Liquidity Investments

To protect liquidity, a company has alternatives that will produce interest income and still allow the firm access to its cash almost immediately. The first of these is an interest-bearing checking account. Although this does give some interest income, the yield is typically low compared with other liquid market alternatives.

Year	Deals	Value($bil)	Year	Deals	Value($bil)
2002	2,895	$147.1	1991	1,877	$71.2
2001	8,423	$704.0	1990	2,074	$108.2
2000	10,952	$1,284.8	1989	2,366	$221.1
1999	9,614	$1,425.9	1988	2,258	$246.9
1998	7,809	$1,192.9	1987	2,032	$163.7
1997	7,800	$657.1	1986	3,336	$173.1
1996	5,848	$495.0	1985	3,001	$179.8
1995	3,510	$356.0	1984	2,543	$122.2
1994	2,997	$226.7	1983	2,543	$73.1
1993	2,663	$176.4	1982	2,533	$53.8
1992	2,574	$96.7	1981	2,395	$82.6

EXHIBIT 18-4

Global M&A Activity 1981–2002

The most popular placement for excess funds is in marketable securities. These securities can easily be converted into cash, giving a high level of liquidity. They pay relatively high rates of interest for a liquid investment. The three most commonly used marketable securities are U.S. Treasury bills, commercial paper, and certificates of deposit.

Treasury bills are, in essence, short-term loans to the U.S. Treasury and have maturity dates of one year or less. They are sold each week by the Treasury to the highest bidder. The maturity date is the date on which the principal must be repaid to the purchaser. Treasury bills (often called T-bills) are considered to be virtually risk free and therefore are one of the most popular marketable securities. However, since they are only issued in minimum amounts of $10,000 or more, they are not for the small investor. Beyond the minimum, T-bills can be sold in $1,000 increments; for instance, you could buy an $11,000 T-bill.

Commercial paper is a short-term note that represents a loan to a major corporation with a good credit standing. The maturity date on commercial paper may run from three days to nine months. Although commercial paper carries more risk than T-bills and is not as liquid, it does pay the purchaser a higher rate of interest. Commercial paper is normally issued in amounts of $25,000 to $100,000. Companies use commercial paper for everything from purchasing assets and inventory to acquiring companies. In 2002 Eastman Chemical acquired a competitor's resin business for $244 million and financed the deal with commercial paper—thirty-day renewable notes with a mere 2.5 percent interest rate.[8]

Certificates of deposit (CDs) are notes issued by a commercial bank or brokerage firm. The size of a CD runs from $100 to $100,000. The smaller CDs are usually available with very long maturity dates (generally 10 years); the larger CDs ($100,000) can be purchased for periods as short as 24 hours. The more common CDs are issued for 7 to 31 days, 3 months, 6 months, 18 months, and 42 months. CDs issued by banks can be redeemed early; however, early redemption results in a substantial interest penalty. Typically, large banks offer CDs since they are purchased by institutional investors who want to purchase large issues. However, as the Focus on Technology box, "Web Enables Small Banks to Sell CDs to Institutions," shows, the Internet now enables small community banks to play in this market.

Treasury Bill A loan to the U.S. Treasury that typically has a maturity date of three or six months; often called a T-bill.

Commercial Paper A short-term loan to a major corporation with a high credit standing.

Certificates of Deposit (CDs) Interest-bearing note issued by a commercial bank or brokerage firm.

18-4 SOURCES OF FUNDS

Often a firm will find that projected expenditures exceed projected revenues for a given period, making it necessary to seek funds from other sources. The financial manager must determine the most efficient source, given the firm's needs at that time. Generally managers match the source of funds to the type of need. That is, for a short-term need, short-term sources should be used. If the need is long term, then long-term sources should be used.

8. Dean Foust, Margaret Popper, Amy Barrett, and Peter Elstrom, "There Goes the Cheap Money," *Business Week*, April 15, 2002, pp. 44–45.

FOCUS ON TECHNOLOGY

Web Enables Small Banks to Sell CDs to Institutions

9 ☞ Institutional investors looking to round out their portfolios with large CDs usually turn to large banks, but a new online service is offering community banks a chance to compete for that business. FinancialOxygen, Inc., of Walnut Creek, California, and Web CD Exchange, Inc., of Miami, Florida, announced that they have teamed up to bundle CDs issued by community banks into portfolios of up to $25 million, in order to sell them to institutional investors at attractive rates.

Through FinancialOxygen's trading website, www.bankoxygen.com, a community bank can offer CDs in increments of $100,000 to be pooled with those from other community banks. Web CD bundles the CDs into large portfolios and sells them to institutional investors.

Robert Oxenburgh, FinancialOxygen's chief executive officer, said the bundling effort—which he called the first of its kind—should open the institutional market to many small and midsize banks, which historically have been ignored by large investors because their CDs have been too small. Since community banks can offer larger volumes to institutional investors through these new pools, they can pay lower rates, he said. "These CDs will be about 15 to 20 basis points cheaper than brokered CDs issued to individual investors," he said.

Source: Adapted from Katie Kuehne-Hebert, "Bundling Small Banks' CDs for Institutional Investors," American Banker, April 26, 2002, p. 4.

Debt Capital   Funds obtained through borrowing.

Equity Capital   Funds provided in exchange for some ownership in the firm.

Retained Earnings   A firm's accumulated net income minus dividends to shareholders.

The two major sources of funds for a business are debt capital and equity capital. **Debt capital** is simply funds obtained through borrowing. **Equity capital,** on the other hand, does not require repayment. These funds come from the current owners of the firm or from outsiders who provide capital in exchange for some other ownership in the firm. Sources of equity capital include **retained earnings,** or earnings that the owners do not pay to themselves but rather leave in the firm as an additional investment; additional contributions of the owners, additional money from the owners' personal sources; investments by outsiders in a privately owned firm, adding new partners to bring in new capital; and stock issues to the general public, stock sold to the public for capital. Exhibit 18-5 compares debt and equity capital.

EXHIBIT 18-5

Characteristics of Debt and Equity Capital

Debt Capital	Equity Capital
Repayment is designated.	No repayment required.
Interest is an expense.	Dividends can be an expense but are optional.
Interest paid may be deductible.	Dividends are not a deductible expense.
Can place claim against firm's assets.	Has only secondary claim against assets.
Does not directly affect management power.	Can challenge corporate control.
Lenders may constrain management.	Shareholders typically will not block management.

18-4a Short-Term Financing: Debt Capital

Short-term financing is used to obtain money to finance current operations, with required repayment within one year. The finance manager spends the most time obtaining short-term financing, generally when funds needed for day-to-day operations are not sufficient. Short-term financing can come from several different sources: trade credit, family and friends, commercial banks, commercial paper, and internal funds management.

Trade Credit

The most widely used source of short-term financing for large industrial and retail firms is trade credit. **Trade credit** is credit given to a firm by the trade—that is, by the suppliers the company deals with. For example, when Kroger purchases a carload of green beans from Del Monte, Kroger does not pay for the green beans at the time that it receives them. Del Monte gives the beans to Kroger on credit, with the understanding that Kroger will pay for the beans according to the terms of the invoice.

Invoice terms are usually stated in numbers, such as "2/10 net 30." Interpretation: The buyer can take a 2 percent discount if the invoice is paid within ten days; if the discount is not taken, the full bill is due in thirty days. The financial manager pays close attention to such discount terms, as they represent considerable savings.

You might see 2 percent as a not very large discount, but think about it. If the firm pays the bill twenty days before the bill is due, it saves 2 percent of its cost. Twenty days is about one-eighteenth of a year (365 ÷ 20). If the buyer firm were to save 2 percent every twenty days, it would save 2 percent about eighteen times a year, for an annual return of just over 36 percent. Thus, if necessary, borrowing money for twenty days in order to pay the bill and gain the discount would be a wise decision as long as the annual interest rate on the loan is less than 36 percent.

Family and Friends

When funds are only needed for a short time, friends and family will often help a small business. However, such borrowed funds bring an extra risk; if things do not work out and the business goes sour, not only the business may be lost but the friend or the family relationship as well. If money is borrowed from family or friends, it should be handled the same as any other loan. An agreement should be prepared specifying the agreed-upon terms of interest and payment and then paid back just as if it were a bank loan.

Commercial Banks

As an alternative source of short-term funds, commercial banks generally make more sense than relatives or friends. The commercial banker can better help with any cash flow

> **Trade Credit** Credit given by suppliers for the purchases the firm makes from these suppliers.

📖 10
📖 11

Unsecured Loans   Loans issued on the good credit of the borrower and requiring no collateral.

Personal Guarantee   Means that the owners of a company would be personally liable for a debt should the business fail to make scheduled interest payments.

Secured Loans   Loans backed with some form of collateral.

12 ☞

Pledging   Using accounts receivable as collateral for a loan.

Line of Credit   A preapproved amount the holder may borrow in whole or in part, provided that the bank has sufficient funds.

Revolving Credit Agreement   A line of credit guaranteed by the bank.

13 ☞

Factoring   The sale of accounts receivable to a bank or other lender, generally at a considerable discount.

Floor Planning   The term used to refer to financing a company receives that is secured by the work in process. For example, a car manufacturer may receive a loan from a bank that is secured against the inventory of cars currently under production.

problems and give sound advice. Developing a close relationship with a local banker is a good idea. Once you select one, send him or her your financial statements and meet regularly to discuss your business. Establishing a close and open relationship with the bank will pay off in the long run because the banker will pay closer attention to your business and alert you to potential problems. Also, when you need emergency funds, the banker will be more willing to help out, since you have developed a trusting relationship.

Bank loans come in many different forms. **Unsecured loans** are loans based solely on the good credit of the borrower. They require no collateral. New businesses have great difficulty getting unsecured loans. Generally banks require some form of collateral to guarantee the loan. Often, the owners of a new business are asked to provide a **personal guarantee** in order for a bank to release loan funds. This means that the owners would be personally liable for the debt should the business fail to make scheduled interest payments.[9]

Secured loans are backed by collateral, by something valuable. For example, Chase Bank offers car loans for as little as 6 to 8 percent when the automobile is used as collateral. The collateral reduces the risk for the banker. If the borrower fails to repay the loan, the lender may take possession of the collateral. Other types of collateral include a business's property, equipment, inventory, or accounts receivable. Using accounts receivable as collateral for a loan is called **pledging.** The cash received for the accounts receivable goes to the banker instead of being retained in the company.

A borrower who has a good relationship with the bank may be able to open a **line of credit.** This means the bank preapproves the borrower for a specified amount of credit, usually unsecured. Provided the bank has the funds available, the borrower may borrow up to that amount without having to apply for a loan each time funds are needed. As the customer's credit record with the bank lengthens and the business matures, this line of credit is often increased. However, a line of credit does not guarantee that the loan will be available. A **revolving credit agreement** guarantees that the bank will honor a line of credit up to the stated amount. A revolving credit agreement generally requires payment of a fee. For example, Bayou Steel of Louisiana acquired a $50 million revolving credit agreement with Congress Financial Corporation that is secured by accounts receivable and inventory.[10]

A relatively expensive form of short-term credit is **factoring.** Rather than pledging its accounts receivable to a financial institution as collateral, a firm actually sells the accounts receivable to the factoring company—at a discount. The seller receives less than the full value of the accounts receivable. For example, a factor may only pay $7 for each $10 of receivables. This protects the factoring firm from any uncollectible accounts and allows it to make a profit for its services. Firms do not generally like to use factoring; it is expensive and sends a message to suppliers and creditors that the company may be in financial trouble. According to the International Factoring Association, this form of financing is one of the fastest-growing and most profitable financial services sectors for community banks and commercial lenders.[11]

Floor planning is another option in bank financing. In some industries, such as automobiles and major appliances, borrowers assign the title to their inventory to the bank as collateral for short-term loans. As the inventory is sold, borrowers pay off the loan, plus interest, to the lender. This type of financing has become less common in recent years as advances in technology have enabled firms to manage their inventory more effectively, resulting is less inventory on the shop floor.[12]

Internal Funds Management

Whenever possible, a firm should attempt to get its needed funds from internal sources. Frequently a close review of the balance sheet and accounting ratios will reveal possible

9. Jeff Meltzer, "Borrowing Money. The Hidden Dangers," *NZ Business*, May 2001, pp. 28–29.

10. "Bayou Steel Secures $50M Revolving Credit Agreement," *American Metal Market*, April 23, 2001, p. 4.

11. "In Brief," *Bank Marketing*, March 2002, p. 9.

12. Sidney Rutberg, "Floor Planning: An Anachronism or a Vital, Growing Financing Field," *Secured Lender*, October 2000, pp. 18–22.

sources of funds that have been overlooked. For example, overdue accounts receivable can be collected more quickly, or a discount can be offered for earlier payment. Inventory can be reduced, since every dollar of excess inventory that is reduced represents one less dollar needed from outside sources. (Of course, the manager always has to remember the need to provide adequate inventory for customer demand.) Costs can also be cut and expenses reduced to free up more dollars. A good financial manager will work hand in hand with accountants to ensure that funds are not tied up in noncash assets.[13]

18-4b Long-Term Financing

A firm planning its finances should plan for long-term needs as well as short-term needs. Successful companies constantly refocus on their long-term goals and objectives. If the firm has an objective to maintain a certain level of growth, it must provide the funds to pay for that growth.

If a company knows its objectives, it needs to look at possible sources of long-term capital to help it accomplish those objectives. The principal questions are What sources of capital are available? and What sources best fit the company's needs?

Because they involve the purchase of fixed assets and the expansion of the organization, decisions involving long-term financing usually take place at the highest company levels. In large firms, this may involve the chief executive officer (CEO) and the financial vice president as well as the board of directors. In smaller firms, it generally involves the owners.

Debt Capital

Debt capital can be used for long-term financing as well as for short-term financing. The interest rates are generally higher than for short-term financing because the lender has to incur the risk of loss for a longer period of time.

SBA Loans

Long-term debt financing can often be used once a firm has established a rapport with a bank or other financial institutions, such as an insurance company or pension fund. For a smaller business, the U.S. Small Business Administration (SBA) can often be a good source of loans. Congress created the SBA in 1953 to help entrepreneurs form successful small enterprises. Today, SBA offices in every state, the District of Columbia, the Virgin Islands, and Puerto Rico offer financing, training, and advocacy for small firms.

By guaranteeing major portions of loans made to small businesses, the SBA enables its lending partners to provide financing to small businesses when funding is otherwise unavailable on reasonable terms. The agency does not have funding for direct loans nor does it provide grants or low-interest rate loans for business start-up or expansion. Fleet Financial was the leading provider of SBA loans in 2001, providing nearly 3,000 loans of which 80 percent were for $50,000 or less.[14]

The eligibility requirements and credit criteria of the program are very broad to accommodate a wide range of financing needs. When a small business applies to a lending partner for a loan, the lender reviews the application and decides if it merits a loan on its own or if it requires additional support in the form of an SBA guaranty. The lender then requests SBA backing on the loan. In guaranteeing the loan, the SBA assures the lender that, in the event the borrower does not repay the loan, the government will reimburse the lending partner for a portion of its loss.

To qualify for an SBA guaranty, a small business must meet the SBA's criteria, and the lender must certify that it could not provide funding on reasonable terms without an SBA guaranty. The SBA can guarantee as much as 85 percent on loans of up to $150,000

☞ 14

---

13. Guy G. Stevens, "Internal Funds and Investment Function," *Southern Economic Journal*, January 1994, pp. 551–563.

14. Veronica Agosta, "Fleet Is Tops in Number of SBA Loans," *American Banker*, October 9, 2001, p. 31.

and 75 percent on loans of more than $150,000. In most cases, the maximum guaranty is $1 million. There are higher loan limits for International Trade, defense-dependent small firms affected by defense reductions, and certified development company loans.

Term Loans

Most long-term loans have three- to seven-year terms, though some may extend to fifteen or twenty years. For these loans, the business signs a **term loan agreement**. This agreement is a **promissory note,** which requires the borrower to repay the loan according to a schedule of specified installments at either a fixed (remains constant) or flexible (changes as market conditions change) rate of interest.

Most long-term loans require some form of collateral, such as real estate, machinery, equipment, or stock. Typically, when determining the interest rate for such loans, the bank looks at the length of time the loan is for, the type of collateral, the firm's credit rating, and the general level of market interest.

Bonds

Another form of long-term debt financing is a **bond.** This IOU is usually held by an investor and stipulates periodic interest payments (usually every six months) and payment of the principal at maturity (usually ten years or more). Bonds almost always are issued in $1,000 amounts or multiples. The details are spelled out in an agreement called an **indenture.**

Bonds, just like loans, can be secured or unsecured. A **secured bond** is backed by some form of collateral—specific property such as real estate, inventory, or long-term assets that would pass to the bondholders should the company not live up to the terms of the agreement. Unsecured bonds, or **debenture bonds,** are backed by the good name of the issuing company. Holders can make claims against the assets of a failed company only after the creditors with specific collateral have been paid. For example, American International Group, Inc. (AIG) issued zero coupon debentures due 2031 with a principal amount at maturity of nearly $1.52 billion. AIG is offering the funds at an initial price of $658.01 per $1,000 principal amount at maturity.[15]

Bonds pay interest to the bondholders, at specified intervals or on specified dates. For example, the holder of a $1,000 bond that pays 10 percent interest due April 1 and October 1 could expect to receive $50 on each of these two dates.

Generally, the lower the quality of the bonds (higher risk of loss due to the heavy debt of the issuing corporation or a poor credit record), the higher the interest paid to the bondholders. This only makes sense, since no one would buy a low-quality bond without receiving a sufficient premium over the normal amount paid on higher-quality bonds. The

Term Loan Agreement A promissory note that requires a borrower to repay a loan according to a schedule of specified installments at either a fixed or flexible rate of interest.

Promissory Note A legally binding promise of payment that spells out the terms of the loan agreement.

Bond An agreement between a firm and an investor with specific terms spelled out in an indenture.

Indenture The agreement that spells out the maturity date and interest payments for a corporate bond.

Secured Bond A bond backed by some form of collateral—specific property such as real estate, inventory, or long-term assets that would pass to the bondholders should the company not live up to the terms of the agreement.

Debenture Bonds Unsecured bonds backed by the good name of the issuing company.

15. "AIG Announces Zero Coupon Convertible Debt Offering," *Insurance Advocate*, November 10, 2001, p. 38.

term **junk bond** designates a low-grade bond issued by financially weak companies with no solid collateral, to fund internal expansion or corporate acquisitions and buyouts. In 2002, former high-flying technology firms such as Lucent and Juniper Networks were selling junk bonds with yields in the range of 10 to 12 percent.[16]

A firm that sells bonds must repay its debt to the bondholders. The point at which payment is due is known as maturity. The amount due at maturity can be huge, since bonds usually fund major expansions or asset purchases. To ease their payment burden, companies sometimes issue **serial bonds,** which mature at different intervals from the date of issue. This way, the company pays off the debt in portions. A **sinking fund** may also be used. The sinking fund requires that the company set aside a certain sum of money each year to "sink" the bond debt. The company may then pay off a portion of the bonds each year or accumulate the funds until the bonds mature.

Two special types of bonds sometimes issued by corporations are callable bonds and convertible bonds. **Callable bonds** give the company the right to purchase back its bonds early. This might be desirable if the interest rates have fallen since the bonds were issued and the company wants to issue new bonds at a lower rate of interest. Callable bonds generally carry a slightly higher rate of interest than **noncallable bonds,** and the company usually pays a premium (an amount over the normal interest rate) to the holder when the bonds are called.

Convertible bonds may be paid off with the stock in the company. The amount of stock is indicated in the indenture terms. The decision to accept stock or money is left up to the individual bondholder. As the Focus on Innovation box, "Credit Derivatives Help Firms Manage Risk," illustrates, financial instruments are getting increasingly complex in an effort to provide risk protection to companies.

Leverage

The use of long-term debt to raise needed cash is sometimes referred to as **leverage.** The borrowed cash acts like a lever to increase the purchasing power of the owner's investment. Exhibit 18-6 on page 493 shows the different rate of return on the owner's investment generated when leverage is used versus when leverage is not used. Bill's Inc. used a $50,000 owner's investment and a $50,000 bond issue to raise $100,000. Jane's Inc. sold 10,000 shares of common stock at $10 per share to raise $100,000. Both companies earned $20,000 before interest and taxes. After Bill's pays the $5,000 in interest on the bond issue, it makes a 30 percent return (15,000 ÷ 50,000) on the investment of $50,000. Jane's, however, returns only 20 percent ($20,000 ÷ 100,000) to its stockholders.

Leverage works to maintain higher rates of return on owners' investments and allows the owners to create a larger firm for the same investment. As long as earnings exceed interest payments on the borrowed funds, the firm should be all right. However, leverage also means a continued obligation to service the debt, and any significant downturn in sales could threaten survival. The ability to generate additional cash through debt would be limited, leaving few outside sources of funds. The required interest payments would represent a larger percentage of total sales. Current creditors and suppliers may become worried if the balance sheet does not look healthy. Suppliers may demand cash payments for merchandise, increasing the size of any cash flow shortages. The judicious use of leverage can help increase owners' returns, but too much debt can create massive problems for a company.

Equity Capital

As we discussed earlier, equity capital is funds from the firm's owners. The funds can be contributed by current owners or by outsiders who receive some share of ownership in the company in return. The five forms of equity capital are retained earnings, additional contributions by the current owners, the sale of partnerships in privately held firms, venture capital, and the sale of stock issues to the general public.

16. Ilyana Polyak, "Queen of Junk," *Money*, May 2002, pp. 38–39.

Junk Bond   A low-grade bond that carries a very high risk.

Serial Bonds   Bonds that mature at different intervals from the date of issue to enable a company to pay off debt in portions.

Sinking Fund   A fund that requires that the company set aside a certain sum of money each year to "sink" the bond debt, so that the company may pay off a portion of a bond each year or accumulate funds until the bond matures.

Callable Bonds   Bonds that give a company the right to purchase back its bonds early.

Noncallable Bonds   Bonds issued to holders that cannot be redeemed by the issuing company prior to their expiration date.

Convertible Bonds   Bonds that may be paid off with the stock in the company.

Leverage   The use of long-term debt to raise needed cash.

FOCUS ON INNOVATION

Credit Derivatives Help Firms Manage Risk

Credit derivatives, once relegated to the fringes of the financial world, have exploded in use over the last two years. Banks are currently the biggest users of these products. Insurers and reinsurers, however, as the largest holders of credit risk, are increasingly using credit derivatives as an investment and risk management tool.

Market participants feel that over the next few years, the insurance industry will become the largest end user of credit derivatives. Although banks and securities firms were the first entrants into the credit derivatives market, as the utility of these instruments is realized, it is likely that insurance and reinsurance companies, as well as money managers will ultimately surpass them as the largest users of these products.

Credit derivatives are not difficult to understand and their utility, when used as an investment or risk management tool, is remarkable. The building block of credit derivatives is called the "credit default swap," and it is essentially a contract that transfers credit risk from one party to another. For example, an institution wishing to hedge credit risk it holds can do this by purchasing "protection"—a credit default swap contract. The seller of that protection can be an insurance company. If there is subsequently a credit event at the underlying company, the credit default swap contract is triggered, and the institution that purchased the protection can physically deliver the credit risk (usually bonds or loans) to the seller of protection in exchange for par value.

The cost of the protection is a number of basis points determined by the market of the notional value of the underlying credit. If the credit risk totals $10 million and the price of protection on the credit risk is 100 basis points, the cost of the protection per annum is $100,000. This is paid in premiums to the seller on a quarterly basis for a period of five years.

There is little doubt that as the largest holders of credit risk, insurers and reinsurers will continue to use credit derivatives to increase their exposure to these securities. It is likely, also, that as the comfort level with these types of products increases, the insurance industry as a whole will continue to find innovative ways to not only use credit derivatives as a mechanism for revenue enhancement, but also as a key element of their risk management strategy.

Source: Adapted from Michael Pohly and James Vore, "Insurers Eye Derivatives for Credit Risk," *National Underwriter*, April 15, 2002, pp. 38–39.

Retained Earnings

Retained earnings are profits the owners have chosen to leave in the company rather than pay out in the form of dividends to shareholders. Although this method of financing growth is extremely safe, it limits the amount of cash that will be available and may cause long delays before expansion can occur.

Contributions

The current owners of the firm can increase their contributions to the firm. This also tends to be a safe method for financing growth, but the funds of current owners are often limited, which means slower growth. Outside investors may have more funds to spend, but they may demand some control over the operations of the company.

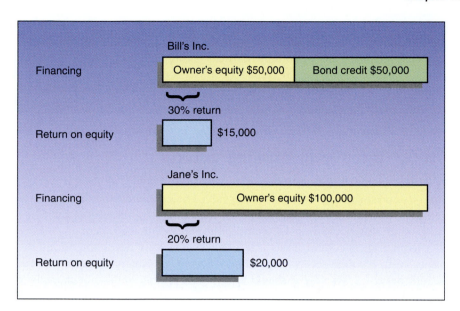

Example of Leverage

Sale of Partnerships

If the current owners of the firm do not have extra funds to contribute to the firm, additional partners can be sought. The additional partners contribute funds to the firm and in return receive a share of the ownership.

Venture Capital

One popular form of financing for new, small, or struggling businesses is **venture capital.** Venture capitalists provide funds for such a firm (provided they see potential for rapid growth) and in exchange receive a share of the ownership and frequently a share of control.

Public Sale of Stock

As a company grows, its need for funds also grows. Typically, at some point, debt financing, retained earnings, and owner contributions no longer meet these needs. Then the owners have to consider selling shares of ownership in their company. These shares of ownership are called *stocks*. As evidence of ownership, a shareholder receives a stock certificate. Each certificate shows the name of the shareholder, the number of shares of stock owned, and the special characteristics of the stock. Many stocks will also show a par value, a small, arbitrary value bearing no relation to the market value of the stock.

After making a request to the secretary of state of the state in which incorporation is sought (in some states, to the attorney general), the original incorporators and the board of directors of the corporation set a maximum number of shares into which the company can be divided. This represents all the shares of stock that can be sold at any time and is called the **authorized stock.** Typically a company does not place all the authorized stock up for sale at one time but rather sells only a portion of the shares. The shares sold are called **issued stock,** and unsold shares are **unissued stock**.

When a company sells stock, it gives a portion of the firm's ownership to outsiders. However, shareholders do not directly run a firm. They elect a board of directors to represent them. Each shareholder has a number of votes equal to the number of shares owned and uses these votes to elect the members to the board of directors. Shareholders may also vote on mergers, acquisitions, and takeovers.

The company also may pay **dividends** to shareholders. Dividends are a distributed portion of the firm's earnings. The company is not required to pay dividends; many do not, or they distribute only a small portion of the earnings in dividends in order to conserve cash for growth, research, and similar types of expenditures. Chapter 19 discusses stocks, as well as bonds and other investments, in greater detail.

Venture Capital   Funds provided by individuals or organizations to new firms with high potential for growth; the investor receives a share of the ownership and frequently a share of control.

Authorized Stock   All the shares of a firm's stock that can be sold or issued.

Issued Stock   The term used to refer to shares of a company's stock to which another person or company has taken title.

Unissued Stock   Shares that have been authorized by a company but that remain in its treasury to be issued at a future date.

Dividends   A distributed portion of the firm's earnings.

18-5 MANAGING THE FINANCES OF THE FIRM

Financial managers are responsible for maintaining the proper flow of funds. They help manage the use of funds and find the appropriate sources of funds. They also invest excess cash to earn additional income for the company. In performing these duties, the financial manager has to manage the company's working capital, develop capital budgets, and develop appropriate financial controls.

18-5a Managing Working Capital

If a firm's current liabilities (obligations that must be paid within a year) are subtracted from its current assets, the result is the value of working capital. Working capital represents the amount of capital available for the day-to-day running of the firm. Sufficient working capital is obviously important to the effective management of a firm's operations.

In managing current assets, the financial manager needs to concentrate on three assets: cash, accounts receivable, and inventory. The primary concern with cash is that it should never be left idle; it should always be working. Funds not immediately needed should be invested and earning interest. At the very least, an interest-earning checking account should be used. Investment possibilities were discussed earlier in this chapter.

Float is the amount of money that has not yet been withdrawn from the company's checking account even though the checks have been written. If you have a checking account, you may notice that when you balance it at the end of the month, some of the checks you have written have not yet cleared. Therefore, the balance on your statement is greater than the balance in your checkbook. The difference is float. The same is true for businesses. In a large company such as General Motors, this may represent billions of dollars and significant potential earnings. Actions taken by the Federal Reserve System and advances in electronic payment systems have resulted in float being less significant today than in the past. However, float still occurs, with three primary components (sources): mail float, processing float, and check-cleaning float.

Accounts receivable are really promises of cash from customers of the firm. Until this cash is in hand, the firm has only the promise. One task of the financial manager is to speed up the collection of accounts receivable as much as possible. This, of course, must be done without offending customers and with the understanding that, in many cases, providing credit is necessary to sales.

In managing accounts receivable, the financial manager needs to date accounts receivable so that overdue accounts are flagged immediately and appropriate letters are sent, or some other action is taken. The financial manager also wants to speed up the conversion of received payments into cash in the company's account. Once received at the office, they must be processed and then sent to the bank. This means that the cash may not be credited to the company's account for two more days. To speed this up, many companies have a lockbox, a post office box used as a mailing address. The bank collects payments directly from the lockbox several times a day and immediately starts to process and credit payments to the customers' account. The business receives a summary of payments and can then credit the customers' accounts.

Inventory is an investment in future sales. Until sold, however, it represents a cash use for the firm. The financial manager needs to continuously review inventory levels to pinpoint any excess inventory and work with production and marketing to alleviate the condition. Of course, understanding inventory's importance to sales, the financial manager also works with production and marketing to make sure sufficient inventory is available to satisfy customer needs.

Many inventory models use computer programs and company information to determine the best level of inventory for different levels of sales. These models also help determine the best time to order additional inventory and the amount of inventory to order. The auto industry has begun working more closely with its suppliers to reduce the lead

Float The amount of money not yet withdrawn from the company's checking account even though checks have been written.

Inventory The term used to refer to finished goods that a firm has stored in preparation for distribution to a customer, or to supplies that will be used in product assembly.

time needed for deliveries. The goal is to achieve just-in-time (JIT) deliveries, or deliveries of materials that arrive at the plant just when they are actually needed for production.

The management of current liabilities was covered earlier in this chapter. As we discussed, taking advantage of cash discounts offered by suppliers generally makes sense.

18-5b Developing Capital Budgets

Capital budgets represent the funds allocated for future investments of the firm's cash. These may be plant expansion, equipment improvement, acquisitions, or other major expenditures. The process of **capital budgeting** involves comparing and evaluating alternative investments.

Capital investments are generally long-term investments and therefore involve long-term sources of funds. When evaluating different capital projects, the financial manager looks not only at the amount of money required to do the project but also at the incremental cash flow the project will produce. These cash flows are looked at to determine when the project will have paid for itself (generated sufficient cash to pay for the initial investment) and what the long-term rate of return will be.

Determining the long-term rate of return can be difficult because it depends on factors such as customer response, competitive reactions, the state of the economy, and other environmental factors. Therefore, benefits are difficult to gauge in advance. Managers generally look at the most likely circumstances and try to estimate returns based on these. However, this does not always work.

> **Capital Budgeting**
> The budgeting of funds for future, generally major, investments of the firm's cash; investments are generally ranked on the basis of the return potential.

18-5c Financial Controls

Financial controls mean that once cash flow projections, capital budgets, and so on are established, they must be reviewed to make sure that the actual results match projected results. Without review, there is little reason to do the budgeting in the first place. If you set a budget for a particular capital project—for example, building an extension onto the current plant—the estimated returns for that project are based on the budgeted costs. If the project comes in over cost, then the returns will be less, and some other project may have proved to be a better investment. When comparing actual and projected results, the financial manager must look for deviations. If they occur, the reasons must be found and corrective action taken. Financial planning is only worthwhile if financial controls are put in place that ensure that the financial plan is followed.

This chapter has examined the basic elements of financial management for business. As we have stated, all businesses must be concerned with effective financial management, whether or not they have a dedicated financial manager. Effective planning, capital acquisition, cash management, and financial control are the key elements of an effective financial structure.

SUGGESTED WEBSITES

Note: These websites were functional when we went to press. Please access the online text for the most up-to-date URLs.

SUMMARY OF LEARNING OBJECTIVES

1. *Define* finance *and explain its role within a firm.*   Finance is the study of money within the firm. It is also the functional area with responsibility for managing corporate funds. To function, a firm must have adequate funding, and the finance department manages these funds by developing and monitoring the firm's financial plan. This plan should include balancing the monthly inflows and outflows of funds, determining liquid investments for excess funds, finding efficient outside sources for funds, and properly monitoring and controlling the process.

2. *Identify the reasons firms need cash and why financial management is important.*   Firms need cash to fund the cost of daily operations, to handle the cost of the firm's credit service, to handle the cost of the firm's inventory, to purchase major assets, to service the firm's debt, and to pay dividends. Financial management is important to this process because the financial manager not only determines the future uses of funds but also identifies the most efficient sources of these funds. The financial manager makes it possible for the firm to function uninterrupted and efficiently.

3. *Discuss the different sources of funds available to a firm.*   The firm has several sources of funds. The most obvious is the revenue generated from daily operations. When additional cash is needed, the firm should use short-term sources for short-term needs and long-term sources for long-term needs. Short-term sources of funds include debt capital, trade credit, family and friends, commercial bank loans (secured and unsecured), lines of credit, factoring of accounts receivable, and floor planning, commercial paper, and internal funds management. Long-term sources include long-term loans, bonds, and equity financing. Equity capital includes retained earnings, additional contributions of current owners, the sale of partnerships, venture capital, and the sale of public stock issues.

4. *Compare the different types of short- and long-term financing.*   For short-term financing, unsecured commercial bank loans may be preferred but are often difficult to get. Many businesses must secure the loan with some form of collateral, a situation that ties up the property used as collateral until the loan is paid off. Loans from family and friends can be a problem, unless they are handled as a legal loan obligation complete with written and agreed-upon terms. Trade credit should always be used if available, since this is like an interest-free loan. Commercial paper will generally only be available as an option to large companies. Factoring accounts receivable poses a danger because it is expensive and negatively impacts the reputation of the firm.

   For long-term sources, long-term loans are perhaps the easiest to execute, although they may require relatively high rates of interest. For small amounts, they make sense. Bonds are better for larger amounts, due to the more favorable terms, although only larger firms can issue these. The firm needs to prepare for the date the bonds come due. Long-term debt financing also provides leverage. Equity financing has the advantage of not requiring interest or repayment; however, it reduces the return of profits to current owners and may require some sharing of ownership responsibility.

5. *Identify the specific duties of a financial manager.*   The financial manager is responsible for maintaining the proper flow of funds. To accomplish this, he or she must manage uses of funds, help find sources of funds, find appropriate investments for excess cash, and manage the company's working capital and capital budgeting processes. The financial manager must also develop appropriate financial controls.

6. *Explain the role of working capital management and capital budgeting in the ongoing success of a firm.*   Working capital is the current assets minus the current liabilities of the firm. The current assets of cash, accounts receivable, and inventory must be managed. Cash must always be earning interest income, accounts receivable should be collected quickly, and inventory should be kept to the minimum needed to satisfy customer demand. Accounts payable should generally be paid in time to take advantage of cash discounts. Otherwise payment should not be made until the last possible day. Capital budgets represent the funds allocated for future investments of the firm's cash. These investments include plant expansion, equipment improvement, or other major expenditures. The capital budget has limited funds, so all proposed capital expenditures must be evaluated to determine which will provide the best return.

KEY TERMS

accounts receivable (p. 481)
authorized stock (p.493)
bond (p.490)
callable bonds (p. 491)
capital budgeting (p. 495)
cash reserve (p. 481)
certificates of deposit (CDs) (p. 485)
chief financial officer (CFO) (p. 478)
commercial paper (p. 485)
convertible bonds (p. 491)
debenture bonds (p. 490)
debt capital (p. 486)
dividends (p. 493)
equity capital (p. 486)

factoring (p. 488)
finance (p. 478)
financial manager (p. 478)
float (p. 494)
floor planning (p. 488)
indenture (p. 490)
inventory (p. 494)
issued stock (p. 493)
junk bond (p. 491)
leverage (p. 491)
line of credit (p. 488)
noncallable bonds (p. 491)
personal guarantee (p. 488)
pledging (p. 488)

promissory note (p. 490)
retained earnings (p. 486)
revolving credit agreement (p. 488)
secured bond (p.490)
secured loans (p. 488)
serial bonds (p. 491)
sinking fund (p. 491)
term loan agreement (p. 490)
trade credit (p. 487)
Treasury bill (p. 485)
unissued stock (p. 493)
unsecured loans (p. 488)
venture capital (p. 493)

QUESTIONS FOR DISCUSSION AND REVIEW

1. Why does a manager need to understand the concept of cash flow?
2. What is the difference between short-term and long-term financing?
3. What sources of funds would a new business owner count on to sustain the business?
4. If you were opening a new business, what should you consider relative to needed start-up capital? Be as specific as possible.
5. List the steps in the financial planning process. Explain why each of these steps is necessary.
6. Explain internal funds management. How can it be used to generate funds?
7. What is a corporate bond? What are the different types of bonds discussed in the text? Are there any concerns a firm should have when it issues bonds? If so, what are they?
8. What are the responsibilities of a firm's financial manager?
9. Name the different types of equity financing. What are the advantages or disadvantages of each?
10. Why would a lender decide to offer unsecured loans rather than demand collateral?

END-OF-CHAPTER QUESTIONS

1. Some firms do not formally appoint a financial manager. **T** or **F**
2. Dividend payment has been less fashionable for companies in the last few decades. **T** or **F**
3. Unsecured loans require no collateral. **T** or **F**
4. Interest rates are generally higher for short-term financing. **T** or **F**
5. *Debenture bonds* are backed by some form of collateral. **T** or **F**
6. Dividends are a distributed portion of the firm's earnings. **T** or **F**
7. *Float* is the amount of money that has not yet been withdrawn from the company's checking account, even though the checks have been written. **T** or **F**
8. One common mistake made by new businesses is the failure to plan for sufficient _____.
   a. meeting space   c. start-up capital
   b. computer equipment   d. vice president
9. The use of long-term debt to raise needed cash is sometimes referred to as _____.
   a. equity capital   c. a sinking fund
   b. indenture   d. leverage
10. Floor planning, another option in bank financing, is most common in which industry?
    a. Automobile manufacturing c. Agriculture
    b. Retail   d. Financial services
11. Using accounts receivable as collateral for a bank loan is called _____.
    a. pledging   c. an unsecured loan
    b. factoring   d. a line of credit
12. Which of the following is *not* one of the three most popular marketable securities into which companies place excess funds?
    a. Interest-bearing checking   c. U.S. Treasury bills
       accounts
    b. Commercial paper   d. CDs
13. Which of the following would have the least inventory fluctuation?
    a. A farmer   c. A detergent manufacturer
    b. A vegetable canner   d. Wal-Mart
14. Which of the following is *not* considered a start-up cost?
    a. Purchasing office   c. Utility and other service
       equipment   deposits
    b. Deposit on leased space d. Taxes
15. Kmart had to file bankruptcy because of _____.
    a. hostile takeover   c. employee strike
    b. merger   d. poor financial control

INTERNET EXERCISE

Calculating College Financing

One of the more effective applications of the Internet is the ability to enable live data input and analysis. Many financial sites have used this feature to enable visitors to use their own data to calculate a variety of financial information. For example, the following website can be used by businesses and individuals alike to determine their financial health:

www.financenter.com

For this exercise, students should go to the financenter.com website outside of class. There is a set of "Solution Centers" that provide insight into different areas of personal finance. Students should visit the College Planning Center to determine whether they have their college finances in good order. They should also be encouraged to visit some of the other centers and be prepared to discuss the following issues when they return to class.

Questions for Discussion

1. What is the value of financial planning for college living and education expenses? Do you think students should be involved in such planning? Explain.
2. Do you think that there should be more financing options for students, such as government loans or other credit agreements? Do you think most students would be capable of understanding such agreements? Explain.
3. One novel form of college financing that has been proposed is selling equity in the college student. Under this type of financing, the college student sells equity in his or her future cash flows. Investors are paid a portion of the student's future income for a period of time after graduation. What do you think of this form of financing a college education?

EXPERIENTIAL EXERCISE

Identifying Conditions for Borrowing

Activity

A business may be so new or so small that it cannot borrow money. Thus, the owner may have to borrow the needed money himself or herself. In this activity, students will develop a list of conditions for borrowing money through consumer loans or credit cards.

Directions

1. The instructor reviews the advantages and disadvantages of using credit to purchase items rather than using cash.
2. The instructor assigns each student the task of developing a list of conditions under which using credit might be considered.

The instructor might wish to prompt students with the following questions:

- How do you know whom to borrow from?
- How much debt is too much?
- What is a reasonable interest rate to pay?
- How long a repayment schedule is advisable?
- How much is a reasonable monthly payment?

3. The instructor might wish to take about twenty minutes of class time to have students share their lists of conditions with the class.

BUSINESS APPLICATION

Researching a Financial Management Topic

Activity

Each student will write a two- to three-page paper on a financial management topic. Five to six hours of homework time will be needed to prepare the paper.

Directions

1. After reviewing the financial management material from the textbook, the instructor assigns students the task of researching a particular aspect of financial management and writing a two- to three-page paper on the topic. Suggested topics might include the following:

- bond market operations
- factors involved in a line of credit
- the uses of common and preferred stock
- comparing debt capital with equity financing
- U.S. government-backed finance vehicles: CDs, T-bills, etc.

2. The students should be encouraged to research the topic from an application point of view. That is, how would utilizing the topic chosen impact a company's financing decisions?
3. The instructor collects the papers on the due date and grades accordingly.

Case

Eagletech and Others Burned by Convertible Preferred Financing

Rodney Young thought he'd hit the big time. For months he had been casting about for cash to save his young telecom-services business, Eagletech Communications. Then in March 2000 he sent a team of executives to New York to meet a group of potential investors at Salomon Smith Barney. Young had a patent, but no sales, and yet here were five Salomon officers and a group of investors offering to buy convertible preferred shares from Eagletech for up to $6 million. "I thought these people wanted to help us," he says.

15 ☞

16 ☞

He was soon disabused of that notion. Immediately after the meeting at Salomon, Eagletech's share price began to sink. By November it was down from $14 to 75 cents, erasing $113 million in stock market value. That seemed extreme even for a company that had only $300,000 in cash and was burning $100,000 a month.

Young now claims the wave of selling was led by the very investors at Salomon's table. In a suit filed in Florida, where Eagletech is based, Young alleges that Salomon, along with a group of conspirators, set him up for a fall with convertible-debenture financing, then shorted the common stock all the way down. Salomon has asked the court to throw out the complaint, claiming it did nothing to harm Eagletech.

Eagletech's suit is one of five similar actions. Each complaint has been filed on behalf of small companies against well-heeled financiers who allegedly offered desperately needed capital and then profited by short-selling of shares—all in the thinly regulated world of Bulletin Board stocks. One plaintiff, a legal-research outfit known as Internet Law Library, says it has identified more than 100 companies damaged in convertible-securities schemes, resulting in billions of dollars in lost market value.

17 ☞

The kind of financing at issue, since discredited, goes by the telling name of "death spiral preferred." It worked like traditional convertible securities, except that the conversion price was a movable goalpost. The more the stock went down, the more shares the owner of the convert could claim on converting.

In malevolent hands, this kind of convertible stock could produce a windfall for the owner of the preferred stock and disaster for the company that issued it. Suppose a company's common stock is trading at $10 and an investor provides $5 million in convertible financing. In a conventional convert deal, the preferred would be exchangeable for, say, 400,000 shares of common stock. In the death spiral variety, the holder of the convertible is entitled to $5 million worth of shares, whatever their price. So the investor might buy the convertible preferred and immediately short 500,000 shares of common stock. If the stock sinks, the investor could short more. In fact, the investor might run the stock down to $1, pocketing, say, $20 million on the short sale of 10 million shares. Now the investor converts his or her preferred shares, demanding the 10 million common shares he or she is entitled to and using them to cover short sales. The investor has shelled out $5 million and collected $20 million without taking any risk. Meanwhile, the firm's stock price has tanked, and those holding common stock have gotten burned.

Whether anything this blatant happened is a matter of dispute. What's certain: Plenty of companies with death spiral financing saw their common shares go into death spirals. Somebody was selling all the way down, and those sellers may have been in cahoots with convert holders.

The defendants say the allegations are completely unsubstantiated and have asked the courts to dismiss the cases.

Questions for Discussion

1. What is meant by the term *convertible preferred stock?* Why do investors want to have conversion rights on stock?
2. How could Rodney Young have prevented the slide in his company's stock price using careful financial management?
3. Do you think it is legal to invest in convertible preferred shares as they were structured in this case and then short-sell the stock? Do you think it is ethical? Explain the difference between these perspectives.

Sources: Adapted from Brandon Copple, "Sinking Fund," *Forbes,* June 10, 2002; Joseph McCafferty, "New Regs for Deadly Convertibles?," *CFO,* December 1998, p. 21; and Aaron Luchetti and Leslie Scism, "Unusual Convertible Preferred Raises Needed Cash—and Risks," *The Wall Street Journal—Eastern Edition,* September 28, 1998, p. C1.

19

Investments and Securities

Photo: comstock.com

Chapter Objectives

After completing this chapter, you should be able to:

1 **Differentiate** between *common stock* and *preferred stock*.

2 **Identify** the major types of investors.

3 **Discuss** five investment objectives and identify appropriate investments for each objective.

4 **Explain** various investment options.

5 **Describe** the investment exchanges.

6 **Explain** the investment process and the role of the stockbroker.

7 **Identify** the principal regulations dealing with investment markets.

1 ☞ **D**oral Financial Corporation was able to acquire a company and enter its local insurance market using proceeds from a successful public offering of preferred stock. Doral chairman and CEO, Solomon Levis said that the company successfully closed the sale of an underwritten public offering of 2 million shares of its 8.35 percent noncumulative monthly income Series B preferred stock.

Net proceeds to Doral Financial, after deducting expenses, were estimated at approximately $41.9 million. If the underwriters' overallotment option is exercised in full, net proceeds are estimated at $48.2 million. "We intend to use the net proceeds for general corporate purposes," said Levis. Capital contributions to its banking and nonbanking subsidiaries were mentioned.

Other uses include investing in mortgage servicing rights through the internal origination of mortgage loans; acquisition of mortgage loans with the related servicing rights; purchase of contracts to service loans; acquisition of mortgage banking and other financial institutions, including insurance companies; and increasing working capital. "We feel very positive about the outcome of the public offering," said Levis. "The excellent results show the strong confidence local investors have in our financial institution. We closed the sale in a record time of two days."

The sale was arranged through a group of underwriters led by Paine Webber Inc. of Puerto Rico and Popular ✉ Securities, Inc. at a price of $25 per share. Doral Financial **2, 3** Corp., a financial holding company with twenty-eight years of experience, specializes in providing selected consumer financial services through its subsidiaries, Doral Mortgage Corp., HF Mortgage Bankers, Doral Bank, Doral Securities, and Doral Bank New York. The company is headquartered in Hato Rey, Puerto Rico, and consists of twenty full-service branches with a support staff of 1,200.

Source: Jeffrey Mari-Valentin, "Doral Nets $42 Million in Preferred Stock Offering," *Caribbean Business,* September 14, 2000, p. 12.

19-1 INTRODUCTION

When people think of investments, they often think of stocks and the major stock markets. Today, the daily activities of the stock market are tracked by a large number of American households. Entire television networks, such as Bloomberg, CNBC, and CNNfn are ✉ **4, 5, 6** dedicated to continuous reporting and analysis on the ups and downs of the market. As Chapter 18 pointed out, corporations use stocks and bonds and other securities as a means to finance long-term capital expenditures. Understanding the workings of financial markets is important to businesses that may, at some point, depend on them for their capital needs. These markets are equally important to individuals, who may improve their own financial security through careful investment.

Even the most casual observer has become more familiar with the stock market in the last couple of years. The gyrations in the market over the last few years of the 1990s and early 2000s have put trading and securities regulation in a spotlight. Securities trading is regulated at the federal level by the U.S. Securities and Exchange Commission (SEC). The SEC sets rules for fair trading and enforces them through an investigatory arm. That arm is designed to ensure that the U.S. securities markets don't provide unfair advantages to anyone. For example, in 2002, ImClone CEO Dr. Samuel Waksal was unceremoniously ✉ **7** arrested for insider trading. He was charged with selling his shares in the company he founded after he learned that the U.S. Food and Drug Administration was not going to ✉ **8** review his firm's cancer drug. Trading on inside knowledge such as this is illegal.[1]

But the term *finance* means much more than the daily events on the major stock exchanges. Businesses use their knowledge of finance to acquire funding needed for operations and growth, to invest retained earnings and make nonoperating revenues, and to hedge risks and provide the greatest possible return to shareholders. The opening vignette describes how Puerto Rico–based Doral Financial Corporation issued preferred stock to

---

1. Geeta Anand, Jerry Markon, and Chris Adams, "ImClone's Ex-CEO Arrested, Charged with Insider Trading," *The Wall Street Journal,* June 13, 2002, pp. A1, A8.

raise money it needed to acquire a company and initiate several new business lines. The techniques and practice of tapping public markets for capital is an acquired skill that all growing businesses need to develop. The ability to acquire capital in this manner hinges on a number of factors, such as the firm's past financial performance, the firm's brand image and management integrity, the firm's past record of paying dividends and notes, and the firm's basic business ethics.[2]

We begin this chapter by reviewing the use of stocks and bonds as a source of long-term financing for corporations. Then we take a look at who invests in the market and the expanding role that institutional investors play. Next we discuss the varying objectives different investors may have. We examine the various investment options available, the exchanges on which investments take place, and the methods used to make investments. Finally, we identify the major regulations affecting the securities markets.

19-2   USE OF SECURITIES FOR LONG-TERM FUNDING

Securities   Documents that can be bought or sold and that reflect ownership or debt.

Debt Capital   Funds obtained through borrowing.

Equity Capital   Funds provided in exchange for some ownership in the firm.

In Chapter 18 we discussed the use of **securities** (instruments, such as stocks and bonds, that can be bought or sold and that reflect ownership or debt) as a means to provide long-term funding for the firm. A firm's use of securities for funding is generally referred to as either **debt capital** (bonds) or **equity capital** (stocks). In this chapter, we examine the use of securities markets in greater detail.

Firms can, of course, use the securities market to invest funds and thereby increase income by making money from the invested funds. However, companies also commonly use security markets as a means of obtaining cash when operating funds are short.

19-2a   Use of Bonds

Companies issue bonds to investors for several reasons. They may give a firm a favorable interest rate, permit a long period for payback, or allow a firm to borrow more than it could from traditional commercial sources. Regardless of the reasons, bonds are an extremely common method of long-term financing. Using bonds allows a firm to maintain complete management control, since bondholders have no vote in decision making. Also, interest paid to bondholders is a deductible expense. Managers must consider, however, that bonds increase a firm's debt, interest is a legal obligation, and the face value of the bonds must be repaid at maturity.

19-2b   Use of Stocks

The sale of stock means a company has decided to create needed funds by selling some ownership in the firm itself. Offering stock has advantages: Shareholders never have to be repaid, there is no legal obligation to pay dividends, and the sale of stock can improve the balance sheet. Of course, firms do give up some control to voting shareholders. They must pay dividends out of after-tax profits. And managers sometimes become so focused on shareholders that they change decisions to satisfy them.

A firm can issue two types of stock: preferred stock and common stock. In each case, the evidence of the purchase is called a stock certificate.

Preferred Stock

Preferred Stock   Stock that has preference over common stock in the payment of dividends and in claims against the assets of the firm but does not confer voting rights.

The fact that it has preference over common stock in the payment of dividends and in any claim against the firm's assets gives this stock its name: **preferred stock.** Preferred stock dividends must be paid before any common stock dividends can be paid. And if the firm is liquidated, the holders of preferred stock will have to be paid out of the proceeds of the sale of the firm's assets before any holders of common stock would be paid.

2. Knight Kiplinger, "Ethics on the Ropes," *Kiplinger's Personal Finance*, May 2002, pp. 66–67.

Payments would include both dividends owed and the value of the stock itself. Preferred stock is similar to bonds in that regular cash payments to the bearer of the security are required. However, preferred stock has an advantage over bonds in that missing a dividend payment doesn't constitute default, whereas missing a coupon payment on a bond places a firm in default.[3]

The dividend on preferred stock is often fixed. It is typically based on some percentage of the par, or face, value of the preferred stock. For example, if a share of preferred stock has a par value of $50 and pays a 6 percent dividend, the annual dividend would be $3 (.06 × $50).

Some preferred stock is **cumulative preferred stock.** It simply accumulates unpaid dividends until they are all paid. If a company decided not to pay dividends one year because of a cash crunch, preferred stock rights to dividends would accumulate until all dividends were paid in full. If an individual had one share of 8 percent, $100 par value, cumulative preferred stock and the company did not pay dividends one year, the individual would be entitled to $16 (2 × .08 × $100) the second year—assuming dividends were paid in the second year—and would be entitled to payment before any common stock dividends could be distributed. Preferred stock also is sometimes convertible; it can be converted to common stock at a price specified at the time the preferred stock is purchased. Because preferred stock offers these extra benefits, holders of such stock are typically not entitled to vote for the board of directors or on other corporate matters.

Common Stock

Why would anyone want to buy common stock when it offers no guarantees? Because **common stock** gives shareholders a vote in corporate matters, an opportunity to realize greater growth in the value of their investment, and the possibility of greater income return since the dividend rate is not fixed. Common stock does not guarantee any dividends or entitle holders to any share in the assets until all other creditors have been paid. Companies often use common stock in lieu of cash to pay for services or to reduce debt. Nextel, for example, in seeking to get out from under some of its debt, traded 21.6 million shares of common stock for $857 million in corporate bonds, saving the company nearly $25 million in quarterly interest payments.[4]

Common stock has two values: a market value and a book value. The **market value** of the stock is the price at which the stock is currently selling. The **book value** is the value of the stock relative to the value of the company. Book value is obtained by subtracting the value of all liabilities and preferred stock from the value of all assets and dividing the results by the number of shares of common stock outstanding. The market value of a stock may be more or less than the book value, based on investors' perceptions about the company's prospects for growth. During the Internet bubble of the 1990s, the book value of many dot-com stocks was literally near zero. However, their market value was high based on investors' beliefs that the dot-coms were going to some day enjoy significant profits.[5]

19-2c Making a Stock or Bond Offering

Stock and bond offerings appear daily in the form of simple announcements in business newspapers such as the *The Wall Street Journal*. Potential investors can find a stock offering price per share and where to obtain a copy of the **prospectus,** a statement containing information about the firm, its management, its operations, the purpose for the stock issue, and other information that might be helpful in making an investment decision. The bond-offering announcement gives similar information for bonds. It states the interest and due date and whether the bonds are convertible.

Cumulative Preferred Stock Preferred stock that pays a dividend to the bearer, which will accumulate and be payable at a future date if the company is unable to pay at the regularly scheduled distribution date.

Common Stock Stock that confers voting rights but not preferential rights of dividends or claims against the assets of the firm.

✎ 9

Market Value The price at which a share of common stock is currently selling.

Book Value The value of common stock relative to the value of the company.

✎ 10

Prospectus A statement used by potential investors that gives information about a firm, its management, its operations, the purpose for the stock issue, etc.

---

3. Richard Lehmann, "Yield Without Volatility," *Forbes*, March 19, 2001, p. 226.

4. Vincent Ryan, "Want to Reduce Debt? Try Buying It Back," *Telephony*, September 24, 2001, pp. 26–27.

5. Molly Williams, "Some Failed or Ailing Dot-Coms' Stocks May Be Worth More Dead Than Alive," *The Wall Street Journal*, July 13, 2001, p. B6.

Investment Bankers Financial specialists who handle the sale of new stock or bond offers.

11, 12, 13 ☞

14 ☞

Although a corporation can market its own bond or stock issue, **investment bankers** usually handle the sale of new stock or bond offers for large firms. Some better-known investment banks include Goldman Sachs, Lehman Brothers, and Merrill Lynch. The investment banker advises the issuer on the timing, pricing, and appropriate size for the offering and purchases the total issue from the company at a discount. For example, an investment bank may purchase a $10-per-share stock offering for $8.50 per share. The investment bank may then sell the shares to other underwriters, who will sell them to the public. This is a lucrative business for investment banks. For example New York–based Salomon Smith Barney raised $5.15 billion in seventeen IPOs during the first quarter of 2002. The firm takes a percentage of the money raised as its fee for services.[6] For offerings with more risk, an investment bank may not prepurchase shares but rather must sell them to the investing public on a "best efforts" basis.

19-3 WHO INVESTS IN THE SECURITIES MARKET?

The securities market sees two major types of investors: institutional and private. **Institutional investors** are professional investors who invest for large groups or organizations such as pension funds, insurance companies, mutual funds, and universities. Institutional investors have come to dominate the trading in marketable securities, holding over 50 percent of corporate equities.

Institutional Investors Professional investors who invest for large groups or organizations such as pension funds, insurance companies, mutual funds, and universities.

The securities market still has room for private investors, however, and many participate. More than 51 million people own corporate shares of stock representing 48 percent of all U.S. households, a 71 percent increase since 1989. U.S. households have also increased the overall percentage of assets held in stock to greater than 25 percent from less than 14 percent in 1989.[7]

The mix of investors is changing. In recent years, the number of women and men actively investing in stocks has become about equal. Additionally, the types of households that have at least some of their assets in securities crosses all racial and ethnic boundaries. Young and old alike invest in the stock market. The average age of traders has been constantly dropping, and the median age of shareholders is now 46, down from 53 in 1975.[8]

15 ☞

Some amateur investors do quite well in the market. The National Association of Investors Corporation (NAIC) claims that the nation's 32,000 plus investment clubs outperformed the Standard & Poor's 500 stock 12.2 percent to 9.2 percent for the five years ended December 31, 2001.

Many individuals invest in the market. What motivates them to purchase stocks and other securities? What are their reasons for making investments of any kind? Section 19-4 discusses some of the motivations individuals have for making investments.

19-4 WHY INDIVIDUALS INVEST IN SECURITIES

People invest in the stock market and other securities for a wide variety of reasons. Their objectives typically fall into one of five categories: growth, income, security, liquidity, and deferment of taxes.

19-4a Growth

Capital Gains Refers to the profit individuals make when they sell an investment for more than they paid for it.

Many people see the market as a way to increase their personal wealth. They are interested in getting capital gains from price appreciation. **Capital gains** are the profit individuals make when they sell an investment for more than they paid for it. If a person

---

6. Colleen Marie O'Connor, "Banks Are Still Booming," *Trader's Magazine*, May 2002, p. 48.

7. Paul Vogelheim et. al., "The Importance of Courting the Individual Investor," *Business Horizons*, January 2001/February 2001, pp. 69–76.

8. Mary Lowengard, "Individual Initiatives," *Institutional Investor*, July 1997, p. 38.

bought a stock for $5 and sold it a year later for $10, they would have realized a $5 profit, a $5 capital gain.

Investors who have gain as their objective will invest in growth stocks (young or rapidly expanding companies), real estate, precious metals, or, in some cases, collectibles. Collectibles are items that increase in value because they are rare, such as stamps, coins, baseball cards, or Elvis paraphernalia.[9] Growth stocks may not pay dividends, since fast-growing companies prefer to plow money back into the company to finance growth rather than pay dividends. However, because high-growth stocks are often young or rapidly expanding companies, they typically carry greater risk than other stocks. Such companies do not have the long record of success that more mature corporations have.

☞ 16

19-4b Income

Many individuals look to investments in securities as a means of producing additional income. They want to receive a steady, reasonably predictable flow of income. Investors desiring steady income may look at Treasury bills, corporate bonds, and some common stocks, such as utilities or blue-chip stocks. **Blue-chip stocks** are securities issued by large, well-capitalized firms such as Disney, Coca-Cola, and General Electric that pay consistent dividends. These stocks return fairly high levels of income for long-term holders. Obviously the opportunities for income vary greatly; a certificate of deposit insured by the federal government may pay 5 percent interest, whereas some highly speculative corporate bonds, such as so-called **junk bonds,** may return 12 percent or 15 percent interest. The factor that dictates the difference in return is the level of risk involved in investing in the various securities. The Focus on Ethics box, "Socially Responsible Investing," discusses an investing strategy that combines desire for income with a concern for social issues.

Blue-Chip Stocks Stocks issued by large, well-capitalized companies that consistently pay dividends.

☞ 17, 18, 19

Junk Bond A low-grade bond that carries a very high risk.

19-4c Security

The more concerned an individual is about losing money, the farther away that person should stay from speculative investments. Typically, the higher the risk of a security, the higher will be its rate of return. The **rate of return** is the dollar value of the interest earned or dividend received from a security, divided by the market value of the security. This concept is sometimes referred to as the risk/return trade-off. Investors must be willing to assume a certain level of risk to accomplish higher rates of return, either in growth or income. Those interested in security may invest in highly secure investments such as savings bonds, certificates of deposit, or Treasury bills.

Rate of Return The dollar value of the interest earned or dividend received divided by the market value of the security.

19-4d Liquidity

Some investors need to keep their money as liquid as possible; that is, they need to be able to get the cash out of their investment at any time. Those who desire **liquidity** will not want to choose an investment with a value that fluctuates very much in the short run. If an investor who chose such a stock needed to get the money out when the stock's value was low, the unfortunate timing of the need would mean the loss of a great deal of money. For example, an individual investing $10,000 in a stock selling for $10 at the time of purchase would own 1,000 shares of stock. If the price of the stock dropped to $9 and the investor had to sell it to get cash, the sale would bring only $9,000, for a $1,000 loss.

People who want liquidity need to invest in stable investments, those with little price fluctuation. As noted in Chapter 18, marketable securities such as blue-chip stocks and Treasury bills are excellent investments for liquidity and provide a reasonably high rate of return.

Liquidity A measure of how quickly an item can be converted to cash.

9. Debbie Galante Block, "Elvis: The King of Licensing," *Billboard*, June 15, 2002, p. 74.

FOCUS ON ETHICS

Socially Responsible Investing

20 ☞ Investors didn't quite know what to make of the Pax World Fund when it was launched in 1971, but with $1.1 billion in assets today, the fund has averaged 10.2 percent annual returns. Not bad for a do-gooding upstart.

Despite cynical observations to the contrary, investors are eager to do the right thing, economists have long argued. And now there are numbers to prove that doing the right thing can be profitable, too. Socially responsible investment (SRI) assets have grown five times faster than all other kinds of mutual funds in the thirty years since they hit the market.

It's been a long, but profitable ride, according to a report commissioned by Pax World Funds to mark the thirty-year anniversary. By mid-2001, there were 192 such funds with total assets of $103 billion, compared with a rate more than 13.5 times for assets of all other mutual funds, which rose from $50.1 billion in 1971 to $6.9 trillion as of mid-2001.

The Social Investment Forum indicated that performance has been better than average returns in the mutual fund universe. The ten-year average returns for the Calvert Social Investment Fund was 11.06 percent and for the Domini Social Equity Fund, 14.53 percent. The seven-year-old Citizens Emerging Growth chalked up 19.51 percent in average returns; the five-year-old Meyers Pride Value Fund reported 19.08 percent in returns; the eight-year-old Women's Equity Mutual Fund claimed 11.21 percent; the nine-year-old Green Century Equity Fund had 13.92 percent; and the six-year-old Flex Funds Total Returns Utilities Funds reported 16.23 percent.

In 1971, investors didn't quite know what to make of Pax World Fund, the first U.S. mutual fund to use broad-based social and financial criteria for screening purposes, which is now known as Pax World Balanced Fund. Today, SRI funds allow investors to invest according to their values and to challenge corporations to establish and live up to specific social and environmental responsibility. Since its inception the Balanced Pax Fund has averaged 10.2 percent annual returns, as of June 30, 2001.

Sources: Adapted from Karen Kresbach, "Socially Responsible Investing Is Making the World a Richer Place," Bank Investment Marketing, November 2001, p. 54; and Mike Kennedy, "Socially Screened Funds Hold Their Own," Pensions & Investments, November 12, 2001, p. 24.

19-4e Tax Deferment or Avoidance

Some investors may want to put off paying taxes on a portion of their income, and some investment vehicles do allow tax deferment. Other people want some of their income to be tax-free. Many municipal bonds and government securities are not taxed. Municipal bonds, for example, typically do not require the payment of any federal income tax on the income they provide. Some federal government securities do not require the payment of any state or local income tax on their income. However, the Supreme Court has given Congress the right to tax these if it chooses to do so. Because such securities are currently tax-free, they typically have a slightly lower rate of return than fully taxable investments.

19-5 CHOICES FOR INVESTMENT

The principal investment choices are stocks, bonds, government securities, certificates of deposit, money market funds, mutual funds, and commodities. Real estate and collectibles also are options, but here we concentrate on investing in the intangible property listed in Section 19-4.

19-5a   Stocks

Although, as explained in Section 19-2b, the two types of stocks are common stock and preferred stock, we focus here only on common stock. Stock investments are typically made through the stock exchanges (discussed in Section 19-6). As you know, stock prices change regularly. Today, it's not uncommon for even casual investors to have "real-time" streaming stock quotes via the Internet. Online trading firms, such as Datek, allow individual investors to track prices on major markets, make trades, and build a portfolio from their desktops.

🖎 21

Over time the market tends to rise and fall as the economy expands and contracts. During boom years, the market is usually bullish. In a **bull market,** share values are generally going up. During recessions the market typically becomes bearish. Share values generally decline in a **bear market.** Of course these are general trends. Some stocks may go down in a bull market either because of the nature of their industry, such as oil in the 1980s, or because the company's performance is questionable. Likewise some stocks can go up in price during a bear market. Investors must understand several terms referring to the purchase of stock; we discuss these terms now.

Lot Purchases

Institutional investors usually purchase stocks in quantities called **round lots,** which are 100-share lots of stock. An individual who wants to buy stock in a smaller quantity will be purchasing in **odd lots.** Odd lots are then distributed to the various odd-lot purchasers.

Margin Trading

When buying a stock, an investor can pay the full price for the stock at the time of purchase or can buy the stock on margin. **Margin trading** means that the investor does not pay the full price for the stock but rather puts down a portion of the price and borrows the remainder from the broker. The broker retains the stock as collateral and charges interest on the loan. Margin—the percentage of the purchase price required in cash—is under the control of the Federal Reserve Board and can change; the current margin rate of 50 percent has been in effect for a number of years.

Margin trading enables an individual to leverage a purchase. For example, a person investing \$1,000 could ordinarily buy 200 shares of a \$5 stock. With a 50 percent margin, that same \$1,000 investment can purchase 400 shares. If that person bought 400 shares on margin at \$5 and the price went up to \$6 after one year, he or she would make \$400 profit minus the interest paid on the margin loan. If the investor had not bought on margin, the profit would have been \$200 (see Exhibit 19-1). Investors must take care when buying on margin; if the stock value falls, the broker may require them to pay back the loan. The broker will issue a **margin call** if it is believed that the investor does not have sufficient assets in the brokerage account to cover the loan. In such a case, the investor may have to liquidate the stock purchase at the current price and add additional cash from some other account to cover the margin call.

Stock Options

If you see a car you think you might want to buy and you want to make sure it is not sold to someone else, you might put a \$100 deposit on the car. This deposit would give you the right to purchase the car at the specified price within some time period, say five days. If at the end of five days you decided you did want the car, you could get it for the price you originally offered, regardless of what other offers the dealer may have received or whether the price of identical cars had gone up. If after five days you decided not to purchase the car, you would lose the \$100 deposit.

Bull Market   A market state in which stock values are generally rising and investors are generally optimistic.

Bear Market   A market state in which stock values are generally declining and investors are generally pessimistic.

Round Lots   Stock purchases of 100 shares.

Odd Lots   Stock purchases of less than 100 shares.

Margin Trading   Purchasing more stock shares than a given amount of money would buy because a portion of the shares are bought on credit.

Margin Call   A request from a broker to an investor to place additional funds into the brokerage account because the investor has insufficient funds to cover the money borrowed to invest in securities that have dropped in value.

EXHIBIT 19-1

The Leverage in Margin Trading

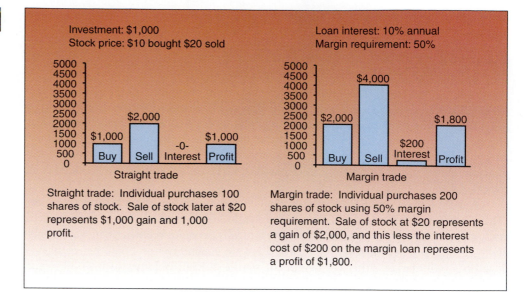

Investment: $1,000
Stock price: $10 bought $20 sold

Loan interest: 10% annual
Margin requirement: 50%

Straight trade: Individual purchases 100 shares of stock. Sale of stock later at $20 represents $1,000 gain and 1,000 profit.

Margin trade: Individual purchases 200 shares of stock using 50% margin requirement. Sale of stock at $20 represents a gain of $2,000, and this less the interest cost of $200 on the margin loan represents a profit of $1,800.

Stock Option   The purchased right to buy or sell shares of stock at a predetermined price within a specified time period.

Exercise   Refers to when an investor cashes out a stock option; the transaction is said to be an "exercise" of that option.

Strike Price   Refers to the price at which the holder of a stock option is able to purchase the underlying security.

Put Option   An option to buy stock shares at market price and sell at a specified price.

Call Option   An option to buy stock shares at a specified price and sell at market price.

Stock options work in the same way. A **stock option** is the purchased right (similar to the deposit on a car) to buy or sell shares of stock at a predetermined price, provided the purchaser does so within a specified time. If the stock goes up in price, the option holder may **exercise** his or her option and purchase the stock at the predetermined price. If the stock has gone below the option's **strike price,** the option holder may elect not to exercise the option. If the price rises above the strike price, the option holder may elect to exercise the options, purchase the stock at the strike price, and then sell the shares in the open market for a profit.

Two types of options are available: put options and call options. A **put option** allows an individual to sell shares at a predetermined price. If an investor bought put options for a stock at $10 and the price dropped to $8, the investor could purchase shares on the market at that price and sell them back to the firm that offered the put options at $10/share, netting a $2/share gain. This strategy is not without risk, however. For example, if the stock went to $12, the investor would have to purchase the stock at $12 to exercise the put at $10 and would lose $2 per share. Why would the investor purchase shares at a loss? Usually, it's to prevent further loss. For example, the put option holder may want to get out of the stock at the $2/share loss because he or she believes that the stock price is going to go even higher.

A **call option** allows an individual to purchase a stock at a predetermined price. For example, a person may hold call options on IBM to purchase common stock at $100/share. If the stock price rises above this amount, the individual may exercise the option at the $100/share price and sell them on the open market for a profit.

Options are issued by firms that are making a bet on the movement of a stock. They are usually time limited and are sold in blocks. For example, a call option on IBM stock may have an expiration date of September 30, 2004, and would allow the bearer to purchase 100 shares of IBM at $100/share. The price of the option might be $50. Thus, the purchaser would profit from the option unless IBM rose to at least $100.50/share during the period. If the investor chooses not to exercise the option by September 30, 2004, the option will expire and the investor loses the money paid for it ($50). In contrast, when people buy stock, they receive the stock and can wait an indefinite amount of time for the market to shift.

52 Weeks										
Ytd						Yld		Vol		Net
% Chg	Hi	Lo	Stock	Sym	Div	%	PE	100s	Close	Chg
-20.8	11.59	1.28	Aphton	APHT		...	dd	2420	3.05	0.35
8.5	15.60	7.57	Apogeetnt	APOG	.23	2.4	9	853	9.71	-0.29
22.3	45.95	21.66 +	AploGp A	UOPX s		...	62	3631	43.83	-1.03
22.1	56.06	30.60 +	ApolloGp A	APOL s		...	50	26115	53.74	-1.91
-6.2	25.98	12.72	AppleCptr	AAPL		...	dd	56821	13.44	-0.14
20.6	28.90	19.03	Applebee	APPB s	.06f	.2	19	3432	27.96	0.06
0.0	7.25	1.41	AppldExtr	AETC		...	dd	53	2	-0.18
4.0	26.55	7.41 +	AppldFilm	AFCO		...	dd	4519	20.79	0.87
-4.3	4.90	2.11	Appldinnovt	AINN		...	dd	397	2.90	...
15.5	27.72	10.26	AppldMatl	AMAT		...	((	240327	15.05	-0.52
12.2	7.75	2.45	AppldMicro	AMCC		...	dd	57499	4.14	0.08
46.8	7.48	1.81	AplMolcirEvol	AMEV		...	dd	609	3.01	-0.09
20.8	14.94	7.41 +	AppldSignal	APSG	.25	1.7	37	251	14.31	0.35
62.2	2.10	0.90 +	Applix	APLX		...	dd	266	1.80	0.02
44.9	2.52	1.05	AproprosTch	APRS		...	dd	387	1.97	-0.06
130.3	6.80	1.95	aQuantive	AQNT		...	dd	2766	6.68	0.11
-30.2	4.64	0.66	Aradigrm	ARDM		...	dd	2019	1.13	-0.09
5.6	10.35	6.93	Arcadis NV	ARCAF	.51e	5.8	8	9	8.85	0.35
11.4	36.82	22.85 +	ArchCapGp	ACGL		...	54	1008	34.71	-0.78
7.9	20.75	12.35	ArcticCat	ACAT	.24	1.4	12	213	17.27	0.01
2.6	9.48	5.20	ArenaPharm	ARNA		...	dd	z75955	6.68	-0.08

Labels on the exhibit (left): **Year to date percent change**; **High and low price for the year**; **Company name abbreviated**; **Company symbol**; **Annual dividend paid**.

Labels on the exhibit (right): **Change since last trading day**; **Last price for day**; **Number of shares traded in a day (in hundreds)**; **Price-earnings ratio**; **Yield = Dividend / Current price**.

Reading Stock Quotations

Exhibit 19-2 will help you understand how to read stock quotations. It reproduces a stock quotation from *The Wall Street Journal*. Other sources of stock quotations include *Investor's Business Daily*, *USA Today*, and most major daily newspapers.

Notice the shaded stock, Apple Computer, with the **ticker symbol** AAPL. This is the stock table from the Friday, April 25, 2003, *Wall Street Journal*. Starting from the left-hand column, the stocks year-to-date change in price on a percentage basis is listed (–6.2). The next two columns indicate the stock's fifty-two-week (one year) high and low prices ($25.98 and $12.72, respectively). These figures help potential investors to understand how the stock has performed over the trailing twelve months. If the stock paid a dividend, that would be listed next. In the case of Apple, there was no dividend. Many technology companies do not pay dividends, but rather reinvest all earnings into research and development. Tech investors understand this and are looking for growth rather than income. The next column tells us the company's divident (none), dividend yield (0%), and **price/earnings ratio (P/E).** In this case the term "dd" is entered which means the company lost money in the last quarter. The next column indicates the stock's trading volume for the previous day, in hundreds (56,821). The next two columns indicate the stock's closing price on the previous day ($13.44) and its percent change from the day before that (–14%).

19-5b Bonds

As Chapter 18 explained, bonds are debts owed by the issuer to purchasers of the bonds. They typically pay the holder a set rate of interest on a semiannual basis.

Corporate Bonds

Bonds are initially offered and sold at a specified price, typically $1,000 or multiples of $1,000. However, once a bond is on the market, the actual selling price may vary. Bondholders do not have to keep their bonds until maturity; in fact, very few do. As with

EXHIBIT 19-2

Reading Stock Quotations

👉 22, 23

Ticker Symbol The symbol by which a company is represented on a stock exchange.

Price/Earnings Ratio (P/E) The current market price of a stock divided by the annual earnings per share.

stocks, bonds can be sold to other investors. The difference is that the selling price of a bond results primarily from changes in the interest rate and the value of the corporation.

Assume you bought a $1,000 bond that would return an annual interest of 10 percent, or $100. Assume also that the interest rate on similar bonds goes up to 12.5 percent. Obviously investors will not want to buy your bond for $1,000 to earn a return of 10 percent when they can get similar bonds for $1,000 that will return 12.5 percent. You may be able to sell your bond for a price that would enable the buyer to in effect earn 12.5 percent. In this case, paying $800 for the $ 1,000 bond that yields 10 percent interest ($100) would produce the equivalent yield ($100 ÷ $800 = 12.5 percent). Therefore, your bond might sell for approximately $800, a price determined by interest rate changes.

24 ☞   The value of the corporation also affects the price. Bonds are rated on the likelihood that the corporation will be able to pay the interest and the principle as indicated. Very high quality bonds are rated AAA according to Standard & Poor's or Aaa according to Moody's, and very low quality bonds are rated C by both rating services. Bonds and preferred stock that are rated C are the lowest-rated class of bonds, and issues so rated can be regarded as having extremely poor prospects of ever attaining any real investment standing.

The amount of interest a bond must earn for the person holding it is dictated by the rating as well as the market interest rate. In our example, if the bond you held was B-rated, it might have to return a 15 percent rate to be acceptable. This means your bond would probably sell for $666.66 ($100 ÷ $666.66 = 15 percent).

Defaults on Bonds

> **Default** Failure to pay the interest on a debt instrument.

When a corporation falls to make an interest payment on a bond it has issued, it is said to have defaulted. Bonds in **default** are rated D, the lowest rating. Bonds in this rating are priced based on the likelihood that the company will be able to make future payments. If that is not likely, the price is based on the salvage value of the bond—its likely share from the sale of the firm's assets.

Reading Bond Quotes

25 ☞   Look at the bond quotation from the *Wall Street Journal* in Exhibit 19-3. Notice the shaded listing for Bausch & Lomb, a maker of contact lenses and lens maintenance supplies. The numbers next to "BauschL" read 6 1/2, which means that this bond was issued to pay an annual interest rate of 6 1/2 percent and has a maturity date of 2004. The next number, 6.5, is the current yield of the bond. In this case, the bond is actually paying 6.5 percent of its current selling price in interest. The next number indicates the volume of trading: 15 of these bonds were traded on this day. The close number, 103.25, represents the price these bonds were selling for at the end of the trading day. Bond prices are quoted in 100s, and bonds are issued in denominations of $1,000. Thus, the actual selling price for each bond is ten times the stated closing price; this bond was trading for $1032.50 at the close of the day. The final entry tells us that the current price is .63 percent higher than the previous day's closing price.

19-5c Government Securities

The U.S. government finances its projects primarily through taxes. However, just as in business, these funds do not always come in when needed, so borrowing becomes necessary. Another reason for government borrowing is to finance the deficit.

The government finances most of its borrowing with Treasury bills (T-bills). These mature in 91 to 364 days and do not pay interest but rather are sold at a discount and then redeemed at full face value at maturity. The return to the buyer is equal to the difference between the full face value and the discounted selling price.

The government also issues Treasury notes and Treasury bonds. These finance long-term debt. Treasury notes mature in one to ten years, and the bonds mature in thirty years. These securities pay a fixed amount of interest, generally about 1 percent less than the

EXHIBIT 19-3

Reading Bond Quotations

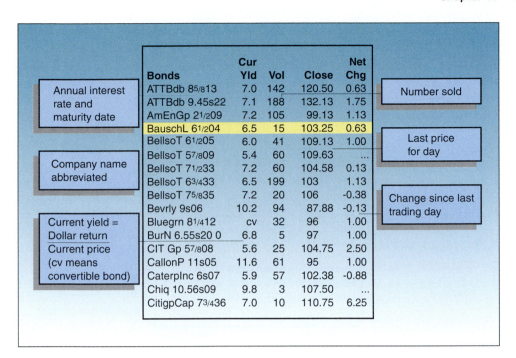

		Cur			Net	
Annual interest rate and maturity date	**Bonds**	**Yld**	**Vol**	**Close**	**Chg**	
	ATTBdb 85/813	7.0	142	120.50	0.63	**Number sold**
	ATTBdb 9.45s22	7.1	188	132.13	1.75	
	AmEnGp 21/209	7.2	105	99.13	1.13	
	BauschL 61/204	6.5	15	103.25	0.63	
Company name abbreviated	BellsoT 61/205	6.0	41	109.13	1.00	**Last price for day**
	BellsoT 57/809	5.4	60	109.63	...	
	BellsoT 71/233	7.2	60	104.58	0.13	
	BellsoT 63/433	6.5	199	103	1.13	
	BellsoT 75/835	7.2	20	106	-0.38	**Change since last trading day**
	Bevrly 9s06	10.2	94	87.88	-0.13	
Current yield = Dollar return / Current price (cv means convertible bond)	Bluegrn 81/412	cv	32	96	1.00	
	BurN 6.55s20 0	6.8	5	97	1.00	
	CIT Gp 57/808	5.6	25	104.75	2.50	
	CallonP 11s05	11.6	61	95	1.00	
	Caterplnc 6s07	5.9	57	102.38	-0.88	
	Chiq 10.56s09	9.8	3	107.50	...	
	CitigpCap 73/436	7.0	10	110.75	6.25	

rate of interest on high-quality corporate bonds. The interest on U.S. government securities is exempt from all state and local income taxes.

Many other agencies issue debt securities to finance their operations. Some of the better known include the Government National Mortgage Association (Ginnie Maes) and the Federal National Mortgage Association (Fannie Maes).

✉ 26
✉ 27

19-5d Municipal Bonds

Municipal bonds are issued by states, towns, and other municipalities to finance schools, hospitals, roads, and other civic projects. The interest earned on municipal bonds is exempt from federal income tax; in many cases, it is also free from state and local income taxes. Because of their tax-exempt status, municipal bonds pay a lower rate of interest than many other securities do.[10]

> **Municipal Bonds**   Bonds issued by states, towns, and other municipalities to finance schools, hospitals, roads, and other civic projects.

19-5e Certificates of Deposit

Certificates of deposit (CDs) are really time deposits that pay investors higher-than-average rates of interest (see Chapter 18). CDs, insured by the federal government, are very secure. But an investor can suffer a substantial interest penalty if the certificate is not held until its maturity date. A person who purchases CDs through brokers can sometimes avoid an interest penalty for early withdrawal because the CDs can be resold to other investors. In this case, they are treated in much the same way as bonds.

> **Certificates of Deposit (CDs)**   Interest-bearing note issued by a commercial bank or brokerage firm.

19-5f Mutual Funds

Individual investors sometimes find it difficult to participate in the market. The idea behind **mutual funds** is that a group of investors can pool their money and invest in securities. Formal organizations generally manage these funds, and a professional investment manager usually handles the investment. The fund may buy stocks, bonds, government securities, commodities, or other assets. The net asset value per share of a mutual fund is calculated by adding up the values of all the securities the fund holds and dividing the number of mutual fund shares outstanding.

> **Mutual Funds**   Funds formed by a group of individuals who pool their money to invest in securities, and usually handled by a professional investment manager.

10. Brian P. Knestout, "Fatten Your Yields," *Kiplinger's Personal Finance*, June 2002, pp. 82–83.

EXHIBIT 19-4

Reading Mutual Fund Quotations

INTERACTIVE EXHIBIT

Fidelity Advisor B

	Inv. Obj.	NAV	Offer Price	NAV Chg.
BalancB p	14.35	-0.08	5.1	-3.5
DivGthB t	9.28	-0.08	7.3	-5.2
EqGrB p	33.70	-0.33	4.5	-18.8
EqInB t	20.38	-0.23	1.2	-2.6
FltRateB t	9.70	...	2.1	NS
GovLnB t	10.30	0.04	0.8	8.3
GroIncB p	13.45	-0.15	5.4	-10.5
GrOppB	22.90	-0.22	5.4	-14.9
HiIncAdvB t	8.38	0.05	17.1	-0.1
IntBdB	11.34	0.04	1.7	8.4
MidCapB t	15.73	-0.15	4.0	-3.0
MortSecB t	11.28	0.02	1.0	7.8
MunIncB t	13.06	0.03	1.6	7.6
SmilCapB t	14.12	-0.12	0.6	-8.5
StrinB t	10.91	0.04	7.0	8.0
ValStraB t	19.78	-0.19	4.2	-1.4

Net asset value (NAV) per share =
$$\frac{\text{Net asset value of fund}}{\text{Number of shares}}$$

Name of fund abbreviated

Change in NAV since last trade day

Offer price = NAV + sales charge Or if no load it equals NAV

28 ☞

Mutual funds are sold by brokers, and many banks now also sell mutual funds. Because the fees earned on sales of mutual funds is a stable base of income compared with lending, banks are expected to continue selling mutual funds in the future. Some mutual funds may also be purchased directly from the managers of those funds.

Mutual fund quotes are provided in the *The Wall Street Journal* and many other newspapers. Exhibit 19-4 shows a portion of the *The Wall Street Journal's* quotations for mutual funds sold by Fidelity Investments. The highlighted fund is Fidelity's Growth & Income Fund B. The first number is the net asset value per share of the fund ($13.45). The second number is the change in the net asset value since the last trade day, down 15 cents ($0.15). The third number is the year-to-date percent return (5.4%), and the final number is the three-year-to-date return (-10.5%). In this case, the fund has not done very well for shareholders over the past three years.

19-5g Commodities

29 ☞

30 ☞

Commodities include raw materials, precious metals, and agricultural products such as wheat, corn, and cattle that can be traded in large volume at a commodities exchange. The major exchange is the Chicago Board of Trade (CBOT). Two types of trading occur at the exchange. The first is spot market trading, where actual merchandise is purchased at the time of the sale. The second is futures market trading, where the purchase is made for future delivery, sometimes up to a year or more. The Commodity Research Bureau develops indexes (CRB indexes) of spot market and futures prices.

Commodities trading is highly speculative. The market is driven by weather, rumor, political climate, the economy, and almost any other environmental condition you can think of.[11] Because the market is volatile—changing rapidly—getting caught in a shifting market and losing a great deal of money is not uncommon.

Exhibit 19-5 shows the quotation system for commodities from the *The Wall Street Journal*. The pricing method used and the size of a contract appear at the top of the quotation. In the case of corn, the price is in cents per bushel, and the purchase contract represents 5,000 bushels.

Commodities Large-volume items, such as raw materials, precious metals, and agricultural products, in which individuals can invest.

11. Susan Bisset, "Independent vs. Managed Trading," *Futures*, March 2002, pp. 68–70.

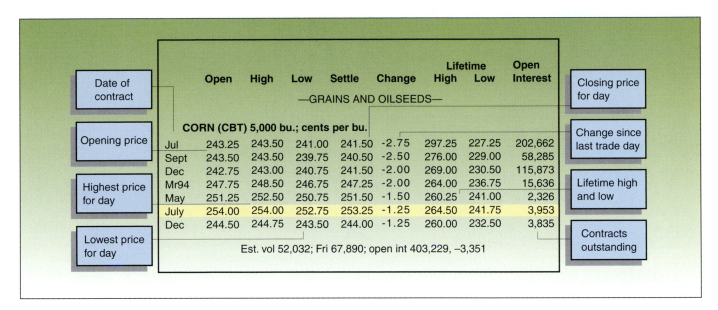

	Open	High	Low	Settle	Change	Lifetime High	Lifetime Low	Open Interest
Date of contract								Closing price for day
			—GRAINS AND OILSEEDS—					
CORN (CBT) 5,000 bu.; cents per bu.								Change since last trade day
Opening price — Jul	243.25	243.50	241.00	241.50	-2.75	297.25	227.25	202,662
Sept	243.50	243.50	239.75	240.50	-2.50	276.00	229.00	58,285
Dec	242.75	243.00	240.75	241.50	-2.00	269.00	230.50	115,873
Highest price for day — Mr94	247.75	248.50	246.75	247.25	-2.00	264.00	236.75	15,636
May	251.25	252.50	250.75	251.50	-1.50	260.25	241.00	2,326
July	254.00	254.00	252.75	253.25	-1.25	264.50	241.75	3,953
Dec	244.50	244.75	243.50	244.00	-1.25	260.00	232.50	3,835
Lowest price for day			Est. vol 52,032; Fri 67,890; open int 403,229, –3,351					Contracts outstanding

The date of the contract, in the first column, states the date when the actual product will be delivered. Then the quotation shows the open, high, low, and closing (settle) prices for the day. The final columns show the change in price since the last trade day, the life-time high and low, and the open interest in each contract—that is, the number of contracts outstanding. Notice that the closing price of corn for July delivery was 253.25; because corn is priced in cents per bushel, that translates to $2.5325 per bushel. Thus, the market value of a contract is $12,662.50, since each contract involves 5,000 bushels.

Commodities trading is extremely risky. It requires great expertise and should be conducted only by professionals.

19-5h Derivatives

Another avenue of trading is derivatives. **Derivatives** are financial securities whose value is derived from another "underlying" financial security. Options, futures, swaps, swaptions, and structured notes are all examples of derivative securities. Derivatives can be used for hedging, protecting against financial risk, or speculating on the movement of commodity or security prices, interest rates, or the levels of financial indices. These more recent innovations in financial instruments are designed to help firms manage financial risks. The Focus on Innovation box, "New Website Facilitates Securities Futures Trading," introduces you to a website where individual stock futures are sold. This derivative product enables investors to speculate on the movement of an individual stock without actually purchasing the stock.

One example of a derivative is weather futures. These instruments enable firms heavily dependent on the weather to lessen their exposure to this unpredictable variable. A ski resort, for example, might issue weather futures to hedge against a warm winter season with little snow. Investors who purchase the futures would profit from a good winter season, along with the ski resort. If the winter season brought little snow (and thus few skiers), the resort would reduce its financial losses because it had profited from the sale of the weather futures. The investors would lose money on the deal, but their losses might also be hedged by a diversified portfolio. Derivatives, essentially, distribute risk among a variety of investors and enable a more predictable cash flow for businesses. Without such instruments, the ski resort in our example might be forced to close down with one bad winter season.

Derivatives Financial securities whose value is derived from another "underlying" financial security.

FOCUS ON INNOVATION

New Website Facilitates Securities Futures Trading

31 ☞

OneChicago, LLC and IBM announced the launch of a new website, www.onechicago.com, designed to facilitate the introduction of security futures to the U.S. financial markets.

Security futures, the class of financial derivatives that includes futures on individual stocks and narrow-based stock indices, were approved for trading by the U.S. Congress in late 2000. When trading begins later this year, OneChicago will list futures contracts on more than eighty stocks and fifteen narrow-based indices. Trading at OneChicago will be entirely electronic.

William J. Rainer, OneChicago chairman and CEO, said, "Our objective for the Web site is to provide a complete resource regarding security futures. We are committed to offering market participants educational materials and research tools for these important new products, and this site will play a key role in that effort."

The new OneChicago website provides traders, brokers, money managers, and other investment professionals with detailed information about OneChicago's products and security futures trading. The site also will offer state-of-the-art analytic software for researching potential trades and access to a comprehensive database including historical prices for over 3,000 securities.

Sources: Adapted from "OneChicago and IBM Deliver Web Site for U.S. Launch of Securities Futures," *Business Wire News*, June 3, 2002; and Robert Sales, "The Hybrid Zone: Who Holds the Key to Trading Single-Stock Futures?," *Wall Street & Technology*, June 2002, pp. 20–22.

Stock Exchange
An organization of individuals who buy and sell securities to the public.

32 ☞
33 ☞

Over-the-Counter (OTC) Market An electronic network of several thousand brokers who communicate trades through NASDAQ.

34 ☞
35, 36 ☞

19-6 WHERE INVESTMENTS ARE HANDLED

For the most part, security transactions occur on or through an organized exchange. A **stock exchange** is simply an organization of individuals who buy and sell securities to the public. While this is usually a physical location, it does not have to be. The largest stock exchange in the United States is the New York Stock Exchange (NYSE). More than 75 percent of all trading is done at the NYSE. The American Stock Exchange (AMEX), also located in New York, is much smaller. Both are national exchanges that handle stocks for companies from all over the United States. Securities of international firms may be listed on foreign exchanges such as those in London, Paris, Frankfurt, and Tokyo. International exchanges, also known as "Bourses," have become more important to the U.S. economy in this age of globalization.

In addition to the national and foreign exchanges, regional exchanges include the Midwest, Philadelphia, Boston, Pacific, and Cincinnati.[12] Regional exchanges primarily list the stocks of firms within their own market area, although some national firms also list on regional exchanges.

Many stocks are not listed on any of the major or regional exchanges. These stocks are traded through the **over-the-counter (OTC) market** and handled through an electronic network of several thousand brokers who communicate trades through the National Association of Securities Dealers Automated Quotation System (NASDAQ). Besides stocks—some of which are very well known, such as Cisco and EBay—the OTC market handles most corporate and U.S. government bonds as well as many city and state government bonds. NASDAQ quotes are given in *The Wall Street Journal* on a daily basis.

12. Forbes Financial Glossary, accessed June 23, 2002, at http://www.forbes.com/tools/glossary/search.jhtml?term=stock_exchanges.

There are no trading floors with the NASDAQ, rather firms and individuals use telephones and computers to buy and sell stocks in their own accounts.

Commodity exchanges specialize in the buying and selling of commodities such as agricultural goods and precious metals. The Chicago Board of Trade is the largest commodity exchange; the Chicago Mercantile Exchange is the second largest. The exchanges operate similarly to stock exchanges. The trading is done in "pits" where commodity-specific transactions occur. The "corn pit," for example, may be active with traders one day because of a drought in the Midwest, while the "pork bellies" pit may be quiet due to little price movement. It is truly a wonder to behold the frenetic activity that begins each day with the ringing of the bell as traders shout orders to one another in a seemingly chaotic manner. However, the experienced traders on the floor execute transactions with little confusion as millions of commodity units are bought and sold each business day.

> **Commodity Exchanges**
> Organizations that specialize in buying and selling commodities.
>
> ☞ 37

19-7 THE INVESTMENT PROCESS

The investment process typically involves several steps. An investor usually works with a stockbroker to decide which stock to buy, the broker places the order, and the investor follows the movement of the purchased stock and the market in general by reading market indicators.

19-7a Contacting a Broker

A typical first step in investing in stocks or bonds is to contact a **stockbroker,** an individual licensed to act on an investor's behalf in buying and selling securities. The stockbroker acts as a financial intermediary and in many cases as an investment adviser. When dealing with stockbrokers, clients need to make their investment objectives known. Your broker needs to know whether you are looking for growth or income, the risk you are willing to take, the level of liquidity you want to maintain, and whether you are looking for tax deferment or tax avoidance. With this understanding, the stockbroker can recommend the types of securities you should consider and, for stocks and bonds, recommend specific company securities. The values and attitudes quiz in Exhibit 19-6 will help you prepare to meet with a stockbroker.

> **Stockbroker**   An individual licensed to act on behalf of an investor in the buying and selling of securities.

19-7b Ordering

Once you have decided to purchase a particular stock to meet your goals, your broker can place the order for you through the appropriate stock exchange. Let's say you want to purchase some General Electric stock, which is trading at around $30/share. You think the stock is going to go up, so you place a market order with your broker. A **market order** authorizes the broker to purchase at the current market price. If you want to make sure you do not pay more than a certain price, you can place a limit order. Under a **limit order,** the broker would purchase the stock only if the price were at or below the price you had specified as the limit. Another way to protect yourself from taking excessive losses is a **stop-loss order.** A stop-loss order tells your broker to sell a stock when its price hits a price on the downside. Selling after a stock price sinks registers a loss for an investor, but smart investors understand the virtue of limiting their losses and moving on. Remember, stock prices are never assured of going back up if they happen to go down.[13]

> **Market Order**   An order that authorizes a broker to purchase stock at the current market price.
>
> **Limit Order**   An order to purchase stock only if the price is at or below a specified limit.
>
> **Stop-Loss Order**   An order that tells your broker to sell a stock when its price hits a price on the downside.

To place the order, the stockbroker contacts the firm's member on the floor of the NYSE (General Electric is listed on the NYSE). The New York representative goes directly to the location on the floor of the exchange where GE is traded and attempts to make the purchase. Provided someone is offering (selling) at the time, the purchase will be made; otherwise the order will be held to wait for someone to offer to sell. The same process is followed if you decide to sell, except that you would place a sell order.

---

13. Lynette Khalfani, "Know When to Sell," *Personal Investor,* September 2001, pp. 30–31.

EXHIBIT 19-6

How Much Risk Are You Willing to Accept?

Directions: Circle the number that represents your level of agreement with each statement.

	Strongly Disagree				Strongly Agree
1. In making an investment, one of my major goals is to protect my initial principal.	1	2	3	4	5
2. Buying stock would worry me because the price could drop at any time.	1	2	3	4	5
3. The loss of money through an investment would be very upsetting to me.	1	2	3	4	5
4. I prefer investments that are insured, like savings accounts.	1	2	3	4	5
5. I don't consider myself much of a gambler.	1	2	3	4	5
6. I like a sure thing.	1	2	3	4	5

Feedback: In terms of investment decisions, do you consider yourself a risk taker or a risk averter? Items circled 1 or 2 suggest that you are a risk taker; 3 or 4 suggest a moderate risk position; and 5 suggests a risk averter.

Though this is a fairly simple exercise, anyone selecting a stockbroker should assess their risk position. The stockbroker should be specifically instructed as to how much risk an investor is willing to assume. This also means that you make yourself aware of the risk associated with different types of investments. Sometimes stockbrokers are blamed for problems that were a result of misconceptions of risk associated with various types of investments. Do you know what risk factors are associated with the various types of investments?

19-7c Online Trading

38 ☞

39 ☞

Brokerage Accounts An account an investor holds with a brokerage firm (such as Charles Schwab or Fidelity) that allows the investor to trade in stocks, bonds, options, and other securities.

Day Trading The practice of trading in major securities markets during the day from a desktop computer or workstation in a day trading center.

The advent of the Internet has made it possible for individual investors to track the market in real time and make their own trades via computer. Today, many investors use online brokerage firms such as E-Trade, Datek, and others to execute transactions in securities of all types. In fact, most of the major offline brokerage firms, such as Fidelity, Merrill Lynch, Charles Schwab, and others, have online trading options. For individuals with **brokerage accounts,** trading via computer has become fast and easy. Most online brokerages offer real-time streaming quotes to keep up with the ever changing prices, charts, news, and most of the other tools of the professional investor. Despite the ease of trading and the powerful tools available, it's generally not advisable for businesses or individuals to speculate too heavily in securities. Investment professionals who make a living by tracking and analyzing stocks, bonds, and other securities are generally able to provide better returns than an individual who merely dabbles in the markets.[14]

Day trading, a special form of online trading, reached its zenith during the 1990s when the Internet bubble was still expanding. Many individual investors leased a workstation at day trading firms across the country and bought and sold stocks all day long. During a rising market such as occurred in the mid to late 1990s, astute financial judgment wasn't necessarily needed to make a profit in day trading. However, during the post-2000 bear market, day trading became less widespread—mainly because it became less profitable. Nonetheless, with the sophistication of the technology that makes day trading possible continuing to move forward, a number of people still make their living buying and selling stocks all day as day traders.[15] Most day traders limit their buying and selling to only a few listed stocks. The trick is to buy shares when the price goes down

14. "Study: More Wealthy Investors Seeking Out Financial Advisors," *Best's Review*, September 2001, p. 125.

15. Gaston F. Ceron, "Day Traders Aren't Ready to Say Goodnight," *The Wall Street Journal—Eastern Edition*, March 6, 2002, p. B5A.

and sell them when the price rises again. It's easy to see why this is a risky way to make a living.

19-7d Reading the Market Indicators

Several indicators provide information on the condition and direction of the stock market. As we noted previously, investors can get current information on certain stocks in the stock listings of local newspapers or national newspapers such as *The Wall Street Journal* and *Investor's Business Daily*. These publications feature a number of articles every day concerning the financial markets. Investors should also watch what is happening to the economy in the United States and in the world and be aware of any special activity in any industry.

Indicators that are commonly tracked include inflation gauges such as the **consumer price index** (CPI) and **producer price index** (PPI), unemployment, interest rates, gross domestic product (GDP), and productivity. Some of the data that brokers and analysts track are called **leading indicators.** These figures are tracked to determine where the economy is headed.[16] Other data that brokers and analysts track are **lagging indicators.** These are figures that tell where the economy has been and can be used to develop trend lines.[17] Inside companies, these data are watched by the chief financial officer (CFO), financial analysts, and others involved in the financial affairs of the firm. The Focus on Careers box, "Careers in Corporate Finance," examines what a job in corporate finance might be like.

Broad indicators of stock market activity are also available. The most well known of these is the Dow Jones Industrial Average (DJIA). The DJIA was introduced in 1896, but it has undergone vast changes since then. Unlike almost all other indexes, which weight their stocks by market capitalization (price × shares outstanding), the Dow is unweighted. Its durability is due mainly to the fact that the thirty Dow industrial stocks represent every important sector (except transport). It is a highly respected barometer throughout the business world.[18]

The "Dow," as it is commonly called, includes old-guard industrial firms such as Caterpillar, International Paper, and ExxonMobil as well as newer technology firms such as Microsoft and IBM. Exhibit 19-7 on page 519 lists the stocks that currently make up the DJIA. The Dow is the most widely reported index of the stock market's activities. Many people believe the Dow is too narrowly defined since it represents a relatively small number of large blue-chip companies. Another index, the Standard & Poor's 500 (more commonly known as the S&P 500), is more broadly based, developed from the market performance of 400 industrial, 40 financial, 40 utility, and 20 transportation stocks.

19-8 REGULATION OF SECURITIES MARKETS

Both the issuance and trading of securities are regulated by state and federal laws. State laws, often called **blue-sky laws,** prevent corporations from issuing worthless securities to unsuspecting investors. These laws also require stockbrokers to be licensed and securities to be registered before they can be sold.

At the federal level, the most significant legislation is the **Securities Act of 1933.** This act protects the public from interstate sales of fraudulent securities. It requires a firm to provide full disclosure of information that might affect the value of its securities. This information is filed in a registration with the Securities and Exchange Commission (SEC). In addition, every prospective buyer of newly offered securities must be given a prospectus. As we noted earlier, the prospectus is a summary of the registration statement

---

Consumer Price Index (CPI)
A quarterly indicator of prices in the United States based on a standard "basket" of consumer goods.

Producer Price Index (PPI)
An index that measures the average change over time in the selling prices received by domestic producers for their output. The prices included in the PPI are from the first commercial transaction for many products and some services.

Leading Indicators Figures that are tracked to determine where the economy is headed.

Lagging Indicators Figures that tell where the economy has been and can be used to develop trend lines.

✍ 40, 41, 42
✍ 43, 44

✍ 45

Blue-Sky Laws State laws that prevent corporations from issuing worthless securities; also require stockbrokers to be licensed and securities to be registered.

Securities Act of 1933
The federal law that covers the new issue of securities. The Act also requires full disclosure of information relating to the new issues and contains many antifraud provisions. It regulates the primary market to prevent fraud on the sale of securities, and it provides purchasers of new issues information.

✍ 46

---

16. Maximo Camacho and Gabriel Perez-Quiros, "This Is What the Leading Indicators Lead," *Journal of Applied Econometrics,* January/February 2002, pp. 61–80.

17. Michael J. Mandel and Peter Coy, "Lagging Indicators," *Business Week,* June 23, 1997, p. 28.

18. "NASDAQ/Dow Jones Industrial Average," *The News,* May 30, 2001.

FOCUS ON CAREERS

Careers in Corporate Finance

A career in corporate finance means you would work for a company to help it find money to run the business, grow the business, make acquisitions, plan for its financial future, and manage any cash on hand. You might work for a large multinational company or a smaller player with high growth prospects. Responsibility can come fast and your problem-solving skills will get put to work quickly in corporate finance.

The job of the financial officer is to create value for a company. For example, the finance group at American Electric Power of Columbus, Ohio, has four main areas of concentration: liquidity, flexibility, compliance with laws, and regulatory support. The goals of the objective are met through four main activities carried out by AEP's Finance Department: (1) designing, implementing, and monitoring financial policies, (2) planning and executing the financing program, (3) managing cash resources, and (4) interfacing with the financial community and investors.

Jobs in corporate finance are also relatively stable while performance in these jobs counts. But it's not like your job is going to depend on whether you're selling enough this week or getting good deals finished this quarter. Rather, the key to performing well in corporate finance is to work with a long view of what is going to make your company successful. Many would argue that corporate finance jobs are the most desirable in the entire field of finance.

Some of the benefits of working in corporate finance are as follows:

1. You generally work in teams, which helps you work with people.
2. It's a lot of fun to tackle business problems that really matter.
3. You'll have many opportunities to travel and meet people.
4. The pay in corporate finance is generally quite good.

Source: Adapted from "Corporate Finance: Overview," *Careers-in-Finance.com,* http://www.careers-in-finance.com/cf.htm.

Securities Exchange Act of 1934   Another "full disclosure law" that requires public corporations to provide annual financial reports to shareholders.

Maloney Act   An amendment to the Securities Exchange Act that created the National Association of Securities Dealers (NASD) as a private trade organization to regulate the OTC market.

Investment Company Act of 1940   The act that brought mutual funds under the jurisdiction of the SEC.

filed with the SEC and contains information about the firm and any information that would be helpful to a potential investor. The SEC does not judge the merit of individual securities, however, so the buyer should pay careful attention to the information in the prospectus.

The SEC, a five-member commission appointed by the president with the consent of the Senate, was established by the **Securities Exchange Act of 1934.** Based on this act, all corporations whose securities are listed on national securities exchanges must file registration statements with the SEC. They must also update their registration statements with annual reports.

The **Maloney Act** (1938), an amendment to the Securities Exchange Act, created the National Association of Securities Dealers (NASD) as a private trade organization to regulate the OTC market. The SEC, however, does maintain final authority over the OTC market. Mutual funds were brought under the jurisdiction of the SEC by the **Investment Company Act of 1940.**

Company	Ticker	Primary Group
3M Co.	MMM	Industrial Diversified
Alcoa Inc.	AA	Aluminum
American Express Co.	AXP	Diversified Financial
AT&T Corp.	T	Fixed-Line Communications
Boeing Co.	BA	Aerospace
Caterpillar Inc.	CAT	Heavy Machinery
Citigroup Inc.	C	Diversified Financial
Coca-Cola Co.	KO	Soft Drinks
E.I. DuPont de Nemours & Co.	DD	Chemicals Commodity
Eastman Kodak Co.	EK	Recreational Products & Services
Exxon Mobil Corp.	XOM	Oil Companies Major
General Electric Co.	GE	Industrial Diversified
General Motors Corp.	GM	Automobile Manufacturers
Hewlett-Packard Co.	HPQ	Computers
Home Depot Inc.	HD	Retailers Specialty
Honeywell International Inc.	HON	Industrial Diversified
Intel Corp.	INTC	Semiconductors
International Business Machines Corp.	IBM	Computers
International Paper Co.	IP	Paper Products
J.P. Morgan Chase & Co.	JPM	Banks Ex-S&L
Johnson & Johnson	JNJ	Pharmaceuticals
McDonald's Corp.	MCD	Restaurants
Merck & Co. Inc.	MRK	Pharmaceuticals
Microsoft Corp.	MSFT	Software
Philip Morris Cos. Inc.	MO	Tobacco
Procter & Gamble Co.	PG	Household Products Nondurable
SBC Communications Inc.	SBC	Fixed-Line Communications
United Technologies Corp.	UTX	Aerospace
Wal-Mart Stores Inc.	WMT	Retailers Broadline
Walt Disney Co.	DIS	Broadcasting

Companies in the DJIA

Investors receive some protection through regulation, but they are not protected against losses caused by the failure of a company. An investor who purchases a stock takes on the risk of company failure. The situation may differ, however, when funds are left with a brokerage house. The **Securities Investor Protection Act of 1970** established the Securities Investor Protection Insurance Corporation. The corporation, which is not a government agency, provides insurance protection for investors who suffer losses resulting from fraud or from a broker going out of business while still owing investors money. Investors are protected for up to $100,000 in cash losses and up to $400,000 in losses of securities.

✎ 48

Securities Investor Protection Act of 1970   The act that established the Securities Investor Protection Insurance Corporation.

Securities Investor Protection Insurance Corporation
The corporation that provides insurance protection for investors who suffer losses resulting from fraud or from a broker going out of business while still owing investors money.

SUGGESTED WEBSITES

Note: These websites were functional when we went to press. Please access the online text for the most up-to-date URLs.

1. www.doralfinancial.com
2. www.ubspainewebber.com/Home
3. www.bancopopular.com/securities/pages/preng/secu-preng-home.jsp
4. www.bloomberg.com
5. www.cnbc.com
6. www.money.cnn.com/ontv/
7. www.imclone.com
8. www.fda.gov
9. www.nextel.com
10. www.wsj.com
11. www.goldmansachs.com
12. www.lehman.com
13. www.ml.com
14. www.salomon.com
15. www.better-investing.org
16. www.elvis.com
17. www.disney.com
18. www.coke.com
19. www.ge.com
20. www.paxfund.com
21. www.datek.com
22. www.ibd.com
23. www.usatoday.com
24. www.moodys.com
25. www.bausch.com
26. www.hud.gov/progdesc/gnmaindx.cfm
27. www.fanniemae.com
28. www.fidelity.com
29. www.cbot.com
30. www.crbtrader.com
31. www.onechicago.com
32. www.nyse.com
33. www.amex.com
34. www.nasdaq.com
35. www.cisco.com
36. www.ebay.com
37. www.cme.com
38. www.etrade.com
39. www.charlesschwab.com
40. www.caterpillar.com
41. www.internationalpaper.com
42. www.exxonmobil.com
43. www.microsoft.com
44. www.ibm.com
45. www.standardandpoors.com
46. www.sec.gov
47. www.aep.com
48. www.sec.gov/answers/sipc.htm
49. www.hewitt.com/hewitt
50. www.sageo.com

SUMMARY OF LEARNING OBJECTIVES

1. *Differentiate between* common stock *and* preferred stock. Preferred stock has preference over common stock in the payment of dividends and in claims against the firm's assets. Holders of preferred stock are generally not entitled to vote. Common stock is voting stock. The holders of common stock have no guarantees of return, and their rights to assets of the firm are subordinate to the rights of creditors and holders of preferred stock.

2. *Identify the major types of investors.* There are two major types of investors: institutional and private. Institutional investors are professionals who invest for large groups such as pension funds and insurance companies. Private investors are individuals who invest in the market on their own behalf.

3. *Discuss five investment objectives and identify appropriate investments for each objective.* Investor objectives include *growth*, which can be satisfied with high-growth stocks, real estate, precious metals, and collectibles; *income*, best gained with Treasury securities, bonds, utilities, and blue-chip stocks; *security*, best satisfied with nonspeculative investments such as savings bonds, certificates of deposit, or T-bills; *liquidity*, which requires the use of marketable securities such as T-bills and stocks; and *tax deferment or avoidance*, which means using government or municipal bonds.

4. *Explain various investment options.* Investment choices include *stocks* (including stock options, the purchased right to buy or sell stock at a fixed price); *bonds*, loans to corporations and governments; *government securities*, secure loans to the government; *mutual funds*, pooled funds for investment by many investors; *commodities*, items people will later purchase, such as gold, corn, and cattle; and derivatives, sophisticated instruments that refer to other securities.

5. *Describe the investment exchanges.* A stock exchange is an organization of individuals who buy and sell securities to the public. The largest is the New York Stock Exchange. Others include the American Stock Exchange and the regional exchanges at Chicago, Philadelphia, Boston, and Pacific. Over-the-counter (OTC) stocks are traded on the NASDAQ. Commodity exchanges are similar to stock exchanges but deal in commodities.

6. *Explain the investment process and the role of the stockbroker.* Stockbrokers are individuals licensed to act on investors' behalf in the buying and selling of securities. The stockbroker not only places trades but also advises on trades. The process of making a securities trade involves the investor discussing the trade with the broker, placing a market order or a limit order, and the broker relaying the order to the appropriate exchange. The broker's representative then goes to the appropriate area on the stock trading floor and places the order. Online trading enables individuals to access major stock exchanges from their desktops via the Internet.

7. *Identify the principal regulations dealing with investment markets.* The states have *blue-sky laws* that prevent corporations from issuing worthless stock. On the federal level, the most significant legislation is the *Securities Act of 1933*, which requires full disclosure of information about the firm to prospective buyers. The *Securities Exchange Act of 1934* established the Securities and Exchange Commission (SEC) and requires any corporation whose securities are listed on the national exchanges to file registration statements with the SEC. The National Association of Securities Dealers (NASD) was created by *the Maloney Act* in 1938; mutual funds were brought under the SEC's jurisdiction by the *Investment Company Act of 1940*.

KEY TERMS

bear market (p. 507)
blue-chip stocks (p. 505)
blue-sky laws (p. 517)
book value (p. 503)
brokerage accounts (p. 516)
bull market (p. 507)
call option (p. 508)
capital gains (p. 504)
certificates of deposit (CDs) (p. 511)
commodities (p. 512)
commodity exchanges (p. 515)
common stock (p. 503)
consumer price index (CPI) (p. 517)
cumulative preferred stock (p. 503)
day trading (p. 516)
debt capital (p. 502)
default (p. 510)
derivatives (p. 513)
equity capital (p. 502)

exercise (p. 508)
institutional investors (p. 504)
investment bankers (p. 504)
Investment Company Act of 1940 (p. 518)
junk bond (p. 505)
lagging indicators (p. 517)
leading indicators (p. 517)
limit order (p. 515)
liquidity (p. 505)
Maloney Act (p. 518)
margin call (p. 507)
margin trading (p. 507)
market order (p. 515)
market value (p. 503)
municipal bond (p. 511)
mutual fund (p. 511)
odd lots (p. 507)
over-the-counter (OTC) market (p. 514)
preferred stock (p. 502)

price/earnings ratio (P/E) (p. 509)
producer price index (PPI) (p. 517)
prospectus (p. 503)
put option (p. 508)
rate of return (p. 505)
round lot (p. 507)
securities (p. 502)
Securities Act of 1933 (p. 517)
Securities Exchange Act of 1934 (p. 518)
Security Investor Protection Act of 1970 (p. 519)
Security Investor Protection Insurance Corporation (p. 519)
stockbroker (p. 515)
stock exchange (p. 514)
stock option (p. 508)
stop-loss order (p. 515)
strike price (p. 508)
ticker symbol (p. 509)

QUESTIONS FOR DISCUSSION AND REVIEW

1. Why do companies use bonds to secure long-term financing? What are the advantages to using bonds as opposed to issuing stock?

2. If you had $1,000 to invest in stock, would you invest it in preferred stock or common stock? Why?

3. If you had $10,000 to invest in any single investment or combination you wanted, what would you choose? Why? Would any conditions, environmental or economic, change your decision?

4. Do you think the stock market is still a healthy place for small investors, or have the large investors made it too treacherous? Explain your answer.

5. If you have $5,000 to purchase stock shares and you buy 100 shares of Acme at $50 a share, how much money will you make on the sale of the stock if the stock price goes up to $60 in one year? How much money would you make if you used margin trading to increase your potential investment, if the cost of the margin loan were 10 percent per year?

6. What are stock options? What is the difference between a put option and a call option? If you buy stock options on a stock that is currently trading for $10 and that you expect to go up in value, should you buy put options or call options? Why?

7. In the stock quotation in Exhibit 19-3, what was the final selling price for the day for Arena Pharmaceuticals? What was the price/earnings ratio for Apropros Technology? If you had to choose one of the stocks on that page to purchase, which would you choose? Why?

8. Assume that you buy a $1,000 bond that will yield 8 percent for thirty years. A year later, when you want to sell that bond, similar bonds are yielding 10 percent. How much will you be able to sell your bond for? If similar bonds were yielding 6 percent, what would you be able to sell the bond for?

9. Describe the process you would go through to invest in the stock market. If you invested, would you place a market order or a limit order? Why?

10. Explain the concept of weather futures. How might a farmer benefit from this type of derivative security?

END-OF-CHAPTER QUESTIONS

1. Securities trading is regulated at the federal level.   **T** or **F**

2. The *book value* of a stock is the price at which the stock is currently selling.   **T** or **F**

3. More than 48 percent of all U.S. households own corporate shares of stock.   **T** or **F**

4. *Junk bonds* are securities issued by large, well-capitalized firms, such as Disney, Coca-Cola, and General Electric that pay consistent dividends.   **T** or **F**

5. Investors who desire liquidity should choose an investment with a value that is likely to fluctuate in the short run.   **T** or **F**

6. In a bear market, share values are generally going up.   **T** or **F**

7. Bondholders must keep their bonds until maturity.   **T** or **F**

8. Options, futures, swaps, and structured notes are all examples of derivative securities.   **T** or **F**

9. The DOW is developed from the market performance of 400 industrial, 40 financial, 40 utility, and 20 transportation stocks.   **T** or **F**

10. The SEC is a five-member commission appointed by the president with the consent of the Senate.   **T** or **F**

11. Interest paid to bondholders is a deductible expense for a business.   **T** or **F**

12. Capital gains are the profits individuals make when they sell an investment for more than they paid for it.   **T** or **F**

13. A _____ authorizes the broker to purchase at the current market price.
    a. limit order   b. market order   c. stop-loss order

14. The two types of options available are _____.
    a. puts and calls   c. shorts and longs
    b. pushes and pulls   d. round lots and odd lots

15. Instruments, such as stocks and bonds, that can be bought or sold and that reflect ownership or debt are called _____.
    a. debt capital   b. equity capital   c. securities

INTERNET EXERCISE

Visit BusinessFinance.com

Finding capital to finance a business venture is a never-ending obligation and challenge for business owners, CFOs, CEOs, and others. In good times, capital is relatively easy to come by as everyone wants to participate in bull markets. In bad times, however, it can be especially challenging to acquire the capital needed to keep a business running.

The website www.businessfinance.com is dedicated to identifying and linking to nearly 80,000 potential sources of capital for business. Although getting money via the Internet is highly unlikely, business owners and managers can identify likely targets for them to present their ideas and funding needs.

Students should visit the website outside of class and explore some of the financing options listed on the page. During the next class session, the following issues can be discussed:

1. What are the most likely sources of funding for a large company with significant assets? What are the most likely sources for an entrepreneur with a start-up venture? Are these funding sources different? Why?
2. What makes one lender different from another? Do lenders tend to specialize? In other words, are some lenders more adept at asset-based financing than others?
3. What do venture capitalists look for in their investments? Are they more likely to prefer debt or equity? What is the advantage of having venture capitalists involved in a business? What are some potential disadvantages?

EXPERIENTIAL EXERCISE

What Would You Do with $10,000?

Activity

This exercise will help students learn about the various ways individuals could invest $10,000.

Directions

1. The instructor opens the exercise by explaining that each student has won a moderate sum in a local lottery. There is enough money to pay the taxes and pay off any outstanding debts and future education expenses. Beyond that there is $10,000 available for investment purposes.
2. Each student should complete the values and attitudes quiz in Exhibit 19-7 and then contact a broker in person or by phone and discuss the investment possibilities for the money.
3. After talking with the broker, students should make notes as to the questions the broker asked and suggestions that were made.
4. Classroom discussion should lead to a list of guidelines for the new investor.

BUSINESS APPLICATION

Finding the Handle on Controlling Debt

Allan Chang is a 19-year-old college sophomore who is contemplating how to deal with his debt problems. Chang has run up a lot of credit purchases in the past two years, which have resulted in his not having enough money to pay his monthly bills.

During the past three months Chang has not paid his Visa bill or his car payment. When the letters from the Visa bank and the auto loan bank come in the mail each week Chang simply doesn't open them. The last two communications from these two banks have been discarded in the trash.

Chang is trying to stay in college but is finding this increasingly difficult to do with his mounting bills. He has contemplated taking another loan to "consolidate all his bills into one."

Questions

1. What will be the outcome of Chang not paying his Visa bill for the past three months?
2. What will be the outcome of Chang not paying his auto loan payment for the past three months?
3. Should Chang take out another loan to consolidate his bills?

Case

Hewitt Associates Plans $250 Million IPO

49 ☞ Hewitt Associates, Inc., the second-largest benefits consultant in the world and the biggest in the United States based on U.S. revenues, filed a registration statement with the U.S. Securities and Exchange Commission for a proposed $250 million initial public offering (IPO) of common stock. Hewitt intends to list the shares on the New York Stock Exchange under the symbol HEW.

According to the statement, Hewitt plans to use about $78 million of the proceeds to pay deferred tax obligations and about $68 million to repay debt from the distribution of accumulated earnings to its owners. The balance would be used for working capital and general corporate purposes.

Lincolnshire, Illinois–based Hewitt said it wants to go public to have access to additional capital for growth; to share ownership broadly with employees, who would hold a majority stake in the company; and to use publicly traded stock for strategic acquisitions and alliances. Currently, the firm is owned by an undisclosed number of employees. The announcement of the IPO, which Hewitt last year said it was considering, comes at a time when the company has been rapidly growing but also is facing significant challenges.

Hewitt, which was founded in 1940, has grown at a significantly faster rate than its major competitors over the past several years. Between 1997 and 2001, its revenues more than doubled to $1.48 billion from $686 million, powered mainly by internal growth. And revenue growth has been accompanied by a high level of profitability: Hewitt reported operating income of $197 million in 2001, up from $182 million in 2000 and $161 million in 1999.

A key factor in Hewitt's growth has been its benefit outsourcing business, which now makes up 64 percent of Hewitt's revenues. Outsourcing revenues leaped by about 50 percent between 1999 and 2001—rising to $939 million—both through the addition of new clients and the expansion of services provided to existing clients. For example, revenues generated by 60 of Hewitt's 100 largest outsourcing clients soared to $542 million in 2001, up from $223 million in 1997. In addition, the average number of outsourcing services provided per client increased to 1.6 in 2001, up from 1.2 in 1997, according to the registration statement.

Revenue growth from consulting services, though, has been more modest. Between 1999 and 2001, consulting revenues grew just 24 percent, to $540 million. Still, among its biggest consulting clients, Hewitt has enjoyed big revenue growth, with annual consulting revenues among its fifty biggest clients rising to an average of $3.1 million per client in 2001, up from $1.7 million in 1997.

Despite these successes, Hewitt faces considerable challenges. Although it is a leader in the benefits outsourcing field, the need to make enormous investments to keep technology up to date is constant. According to the company, that is a huge financial challenge for a privately owned company that, unlike some of its publicly held competitors, can't sell shares to raise capital.

In addition, one of Hewitt's recent efforts to provide cutting-edge services has generated large losses. In 2000, Hewitt launched a new unit called Sageo, an e-commerce service for the complete administration of health plans. Among other services, Sageo would allow employees and retirees of clients to use the Internet to compare and enroll in health plans. ☞ 50

Originally operated as a separate company, Hewitt last year integrated Sageo after it determined that the stand-alone costs for the company were likely to exceed revenues for an extended period of time. In fact, Sageo wracked up $73 million in losses in 2001, including a $26 million charge for the write-off of Hewitt's remaining investment in Sageo software. Sageo earned just $10.4 million in revenues in 2001.

Hewitt intends to offer 11,500,000 shares of Class A common stock at an estimated price of $18 to $21/share. Goldman Sachs & Company is acting as the lead underwriter for the proposed offering. Comanagers for the offering are Banc of America Securities LLC, JPMorgan, Salomon Smith Barney, UBS Warburg, and Wachovia Securities.

Questions for Discussion

1. What will Hewitt use the proceeds of the IPO for? Do you think investor interests are best served by these uses? Explain.
2. Hewitt estimates that it will offer its common stock at $18 to $21/share. Do you think the company will be able to sell its common stock at that price? Explain. What factors may affect the final IPO price? List at least five.
3. What advantages can Hewitt gain by becoming a public company? What are some possible disadvantages? Do you think the IPO is a good idea? Explain.

Sources: Adapted from Jerry Geisel, "Hewitt Forges Ahead on Planned IPO," *Business Insurance,* March 18, 2002, pp. 30–31.

FOCUS ON THE FUTURE

Credit Errors Can Be Corrected

Do you know who Fair, Isaac & Co. (NYSE: FIC) are? They (FICO) are the granddaddy of credit report and scoring verification companies. FICO scores are used by banks, employers, investment companies, and other lenders to determine a person's creditworthiness. The scores are based on statistical models that analyze the electronic credit files maintained on virtually all adults in the United States and other countries. The scores range from the 300s to around 850, with higher scores indicating lower risk.

Many lenders reserve their most favorable quotes of rates and fees for applicants (e.g., for house mortgage and car loans) in the upper FICO score ranges of 700 and above. Prior to July 1, 2001, when California passed a law to let people see their scores, FICO scores were kept secret from consumers.

If you're denied credit, insurance, or employment because of a consumer credit report, you should check your record. The three major credit bureaus that can provide a copy of your report are Equifax, Experian, and Trans Union. Under the Fair Credit Reporting Act, you have the right to correct inaccurate information. If something is inaccurate on a credit report, write a letter to the consumer reporting agency (e.g., Equifax), providing information supporting your claim. Include a copy of your report and circle the inaccuracies. Keep a copy of everything you send. The consumer reporting agency must reinvestigate the items you question, usually within thirty days. If the information is found to be in error, the consumer reporting agency (CRA) you contacted must correct it. The CRA must provide you with the written results of your claim. Also, if you request, the CRA must send notices of corrections to anyone who received your report in the past six months.

The review and maintenance of an accurate credit report is your responsibility. If you want free information on what to do, call 1-877-FTC-HELP.

Sources: Kenneth R. Harney, "Scorepower Opens Door to Once Secret Credit Results," *The Arizona Republic*, March 18, 2001, p. 18; and Jed Graham, "Fair, Isaac Makes More Use of Its Analytical Minds," *Investor's Business Daily*, February 12, 2001, pp. 21–22.

---

other financial institutions to issue credit cards. Visa and MasterCard are the two largest global cards with 323.3 and 204 million outstanding cards, respectively.[5]

Banks and other financial institutions want to issue credit cards because they are profitable. Credit card issuers earn money in three ways: fees charged to customers, interest from outstanding credit balances, and the "discount" charge assessed to merchants on each purchase. In many cases, cardholders pay an annual membership fee, and interest charges on unpaid balances can range from 6 to 20 percent annually.[6] As a result, credit cards generate more profits than other bank services. Cobranded cards, which are those issued jointly by businesses and credit card companies, are a growing trend in the credit card business. Some recent partnerships in cobranding include General Motors and Household International, Shell Oil and Chemical Bank, and Apple Computer and Citicorp.

It is very important to know and maintain an accurate credit rating. Often credit card inaccuracies tarnish a person's credit rating.[7] The Focus on the Future box, "Credit Errors Can Be Corrected," provides information on how to correct credit report inaccuracies.

5. Ibid.

6. Ibid.

7. See www.freecreditreport.com.

20-5 FINANCIAL INSTITUTIONS: THEIR ROLE IN BUSINESS

Financial institutions that serve business include banking institutions—commercial banks, thrifts, credit unions—and nonbanking institutions, such as insurance companies and commercial and consumer finance companies.

20-5a Banking Institutions

Before 1863 all commercial banks in the United States were chartered by banking commissions of the states in which they operated. To eliminate the abuses of some of the state-chartered banks, the National Banking Act of 1863 created a new banking system of federally chartered banks, supervised by the Office of the Comptroller of Currency, a department of the U.S. Treasury.[8] Today the United States has a dual banking system in which banks supervised by the federal government and by the states operate side by side. Insurance companies and consumer finance companies are regulated by the states in which they operate.

Commercial Banks

About 13,000 commercial banks do business in the United States.[9] A **commercial bank** is a profit-making institution that holds the deposits of individuals and businesses in checking and savings accounts and then uses these funds to make loans to individuals, businesses, and the government. Commercial banks in the United States are chartered by either the state or the federal government. Although bank charters issued by states and federal government do differ, the differences are not noticeable to the individual depositor. Exhibit 20-3 shows the top ten commercial banks in the United States, based on their annual revenue.

Commercial banks are sometimes called full-service banks. Certainly most offer an extensive range of services. In addition to checking and savings accounts and personal and business loans, commercial banks offer bank credit cards, safe-deposit boxes, discount brokerage services, wire transfers of funds between banks, financial advice, overdraft protection (for checking accounts), travelers' checks, and trusts.

Commercial Bank A profit-making institution that holds the deposits of individuals and businesses in checking and savings accounts and then uses these funds to make loans.

Thrifts and Credit Unions

Institutions other than commercial banks can accept deposits from customers or members and provide some form of checking account. These other banking institutions include thrifts (savings and loan associations and savings banks), and credit unions.

	Bank	Assets ($ in millions)
1	Bank of America Corp.	$52,641
2	J.P. Morgan Chase	50,429
3	Wells Fargo	26,891
4	Bank One Corp.	24,527
5	Wachovia Corp.	22,396
6	FleetBoston	19,190
7	U.S. Bancorp	16,443
8	MBNA	10,145
9	National City Corp	9,093
10	Sun Trust Banks	8,435

EXHIBIT 20-3

The Largest Ten U.S. Banks Based on Assets

Source: "The 2002 Fortune Ranking," www.fortune.com/lists/F500, May 6, 2002.

8. Accessed at www.ustreas.gov, May 21, 2002.

9. Rose and Rose, *Commercial Bank Management.*

Savings and Loan Association (S&Ls) Institutions that now offer both checking and savings accounts and use the majority of their funds to finance home mortgages; sometimes called thrifts.

Savings Banks Depositor-owned, banklike institutions that began in New England in the early nineteenth century with the purpose of paying interest on deposits.

Credit Unions Member-owned savings cooperatives, normally sponsored by a union, company, or professional or religious group; typically concentrate on small, short-term consumer loans.

Savings and loan associations (S&Ls) offer both savings and checking accounts and use the majority of their funds to make home mortgage loans to consumers. They were created with the primary purpose of encouraging family thrift. Individual households could regularly place small amounts of money in these institutions and earn higher interest on their savings than they could in banks. (With deregulation this is no longer true.) The S&Ls would in turn lend this money to individual households for the purchase of homes. At one time, over 60 percent of all residential mortgages were originated by thrifts.

Savings banks are also called mutual savings banks because they are depositor owned. They are almost identical to S&Ls in their operation and are chartered by the individual states. Although savings banks have existed for nearly 200 years in New England, they have not really caught on in other parts of the country. Today, savings banks are primarily concentrated in the New England states, New York, and New Jersey.

A form of savings cooperative because they are member owned, **credit unions** are typically sponsored by a union, company, or professional or religious group. Because credit unions are member owned, and thus not profit motivated, they typically offer no-fee or no-minimum-balance checking accounts, lower interest rates on loans, and higher interest rates on deposits.[10] While there are over 13,400 credit unions nationwide, individual credit unions tend to be rather small.[11] They have typically concentrated on savings and short-term consumer loans such as auto loans. However, with deregulation they have been able to expand their services and today offer share draft accounts (similar to checking accounts) and even provide some long-term mortgage loans.

20-5b Nonbanking Financial Institutions

Financial institutions act as sources and users of funds. Given this fact, many institutions that do not provide banking services qualify as financial institutions. These include insurance companies, pension funds, large brokerage houses, and commercial and consumer finance companies.

Insurance Companies

Insurance companies were originally created by groups (such as trade unions and religious groups) who pooled their resources to provide some financial protection for members and families should the member become disabled or die. The first life insurance company in the United States, Presbyterian Ministers' Fund in Philadelphia, was established in 1759.

Today insurance companies accept premium payments from policyholders and provide various types of protection. (Insurance is discussed in greater detail in Chapter 21.) Insurance companies use the funds generated through premium payments to provide long-term loans to corporations, to provide commercial real estate loans, and to purchase government bonds. Property and casualty insurance companies are regulated by states and operate in a similar fashion to life insurance companies.

Pension Funds

Pension funds can be set up by a company, union, or nonprofit organization to provide for the retirement needs of its members or employees. To meet these needs, the fund uses a pool of money created by contributions of the members, the employer, or both. They invest these funds in long-term mortgages on commercial property, business loans, government bonds, and common stock in major firms. In addition, company pension funds typically invest a portion of the fund in the company's own stock.

State, local, and federal governments have set up pension funds for their employees. A very important public pension plan is social security (Old Age and Survivors Insurance Fund), which covers virtually all individuals employed in the private sector. The fund was

10. Michael Mukian, "What Do Credit Unions Want?" *Credit Union Journal,* May 6, 2002, pp. 42–43.

11. Nicole Duran, "To Credit Union Advocate, Service Record Says It All," *American Banker,* May 3, 2002, p. 6.

originally set up to supplement individual savings and other pension funds as a means of support for retired persons. It is administered through the federal government, which collects social security funds from employers and deducts them from employee checks. These funds are used to pay benefits to the retired, the disabled, and young children of deceased parents.

However, many experts fear there will not be sufficient funds to pay future benefits. The reason for this concern is the change in the makeup of the American workforce. The average age of U.S. citizens (about 36 years) is increasing and, with the current low birth rate, will continue to increase. As a result, the number of people requiring benefits (especially retirement benefits) is increasing, while the number of people working and contributing to the fund is decreasing. This means that in the future fewer people will be paying into the social security fund and more people will be withdrawing funds from it. The result could be a serious shortfall.

Large Brokerage Houses

Brokerage firms buy and sell stocks, bonds, and other assets for their customers. They have also started to provide other financial services. Many brokerages have created accounts for their customers, such as Merrill Lynch's Cash Management Account and Paine Webber's Cash-Fund, which pay interest on deposits and allow clients to write checks, borrow money, and withdraw cash.

Commercial and Consumer Finance Companies

By issuing commercial paper (large corporate promissory notes) or stocks and bonds, **finance companies** acquire funds. They use the funds to make loans appropriate to consumer and business needs. Finance companies typically charge a higher rate of interest because of the higher risk of the loans that they make. These companies also frequently require some sort of collateral for loans. Businesses may be required to pledge their inventory as security for the loan, and an individual may have to put up an automobile or some interest in stocks as security. In recent years, finance companies such as Household Finance Corporation and General Motors Acceptance Corporation have become increasingly competitive with commercial banks. They are now often able to offer attractive loans with longer-term paybacks.

> **Finance Companies**
> Institutions that offer short-term loans, typically at a higher rate, to businesses and individuals unable to obtain loans elsewhere.

As you can see, consumers have more choices for financial services than ever, and the choices are harder to make. Test your choice of bank and banking services with the values and attitudes quiz in Exhibit 20-4.

20-6   GOVERNMENT INVOLVEMENT IN MONEY AND BANKING

The federal government is very involved in money and banking in this country. It insures deposits in commercial banks and other banking institutions, regulates commercial banks and other banking and financial institutions, and through the Federal Reserve System controls the money supply and the flow of money through the banking system.

20-6a   Insuring Bank Deposits

Before the creation of insurance funds, any bank failure resulted in almost all of the depositors losing whatever savings they had deposited with the bank. This problem was most apparent during the early years of the Depression. In 1933 nearly 4,000 banks collapsed, leaving hundreds of thousands of depositors without any way of recovering their savings. In many cases, this spelled financial ruin both for individuals and for businesses.

The Federal Deposit Insurance Corporation (FDIC) is responsible for protecting the deposits in banks. The FDIC provides $100,000 worth of insurance for depositor accounts and, perhaps more important, sets requirements for sound banking practices and regularly checks on banks to make sure these practices are being followed. Any commercial bank

EXHIBIT 20-4   Your Values and Attitudes

Directions: Assess your financial services by answering the following questions. If you cannot answer them, ask your banker. Then review the feedback to determine what changes you might make in your banking practices.

Checking account:

1. What are the fees?
2. Must you maintain a minimum balance to avoid fees or to qualify for free services?
3. What does the monthly statement look like?
4. What does the bank charge for money orders or certified checks?

Interest-paying accounts:

1. How is interest calculated?
2. Are there any restrictions on withdrawals, such as only a certain number allowed each month or a fee after a certain number?
3. Can you write checks on the account? How many per month?

Credit cards:

1. What are the annual percentage rate and the annual fee?
2. What is the grace period on the card?
3. Does the card also function as a debit card?

Feedback: After reviewing the information that follows, think about changes you might consider in your banking choices. How will these changes benefit you?

Checking accounts:

Fees vary. If no minimum balance is required, you should pay no more than 20 cents a check and $5 per month. With a required-minimum-balance account, first figure how much interest you would earn if the minimum balance were invested. If the interest you would earn is equal to or greater than the fees you would have to pay if you did not have the balance tied up, you may be better off paying the fees.

Balancing the checkbook at the end of every month is easier if the statement lists checks in numeric order rather than by date of receipt. Statements that summarize types of transactions are also helpful.

While the cost of money orders or certified checks may vary, money orders should not cost any more than you would have to pay at the currency exchange or the post office. Certified checks should run $3 to $6.

Interest-paying accounts:

For the saver, the best method for calculating interest is day of deposit to day of withdrawal. And the more often your interest is compounded, the higher the yield. Daily compounding is ideal.

Withdrawal restrictions can cause a problem for small savings accounts used as a backup to bill payments. Check for required minimum balances to avoid fees, and make sure the fees are reasonable.

Many savings or interest-bearing accounts give check-writing privileges. If the restrictions are not too great and your volume is not too high, many of these accounts make excellent alternatives to simple checking accounts.

Credit, debit, and smart cards:

If you use your card a great deal and let your unpaid balance build up, you need a card with a lower rate of interest and no transaction fees. If you pay off your card every month, look for minimum annual fees and don't worry about the interest rate. Most banks allow a 25-day grace period before any interest is changed. Some charge interest from the day of purchase on the card. If you pay off your balance every month, look for a card with a grace period.

Debit cards, similar to credit cards, deduct funds directly from the customer's account rather than creating a loan. The difference between a debit and a credit card is that a person can spend no more than is in his or her account with the debit card. The debit card is used at the point-of-sale purchase simply by inserting it into a terminal that signals the bank to make a funds transfer.

Smart cards are a combination credit, debit, phone, and Internet payment mega-card. The magnetic tape on any of these cards is replaced with a microprocessor. Visa USA introduced a VISA smart card in mid-2000. The card includes a chip that transmits information online via a card reader connected to the user's computer. Visa Buxx and Colbalt-card have smart cards for teenagers. The parents can deposit or withdraw funds from the child's account via the Internet or the telephone. This system allows parents to monitor and control their children's financial transactions.

Sources: Deanne Loonin and Robin Leonard, *Money Troubles: Legal Strategies to Cope with Your Debts* (Berkeley, CA: Nolo Press, 2001); www.scia.org/knowledgebase/default.htm; and Robert D. Minning, *Credit Card Nation: The Consequences of America's Addiction to Credit* (New York: Basic Books).

that is a member of the Federal Reserve System must also subscribe to the FDIC; most other banks have joined voluntarily. About 98 percent of all commercial banks are now insured by the FDIC. Up until 1989, similar protection was provided for depositors of most savings and loans by the Federal Savings and Loan Insurance Corporation (FSLIC). However, the responsibilities for protecting savings and loans have now passed to the FDIC. The National Credit Union Association (NCUA) insures deposits for federally chartered credit unions.

As mentioned, FDIC insurance is limited to $100,000 for any depositor. However, accounts in different banks are separately and fully protected; so the number of $100,000 deposits that can be fully protected in different banks is unlimited. Joint accounts opened by one person in combination with another person or persons are all eligible for insurance coverage, even when opened in the same bank.

20-6b Bank Supervision

In addition to providing insurance, the FDIC and NCUA also set requirements for sound banking practices. Compliance is controlled through the use of bank examiners. These trained representatives of the enforcement agency regularly inspect the financial records and management practices of the financial institutions. Inspections are unannounced and occur at least once a year. Examinations almost always take at least a week to complete and may take up to several months.

Examiners look at the ability of the bank's management, level of earnings, sources of earnings, adequacy of loan security, capital, and the current level of liquidity. A bank with serious problems in one or more of these areas will be included on a "problem list." These banks are seen as candidates for failure unless problems are corrected. Examiners discuss the nature of the problems and potential actions with the management of the bank, and more frequent examinations are scheduled to ensure compliance with the examiners' recommendations.

20-6c Deregulation of the Banking Industry

Prior to 1981, the banking industry was highly regulated. The role that each of the financial institutions played within the system was clearly defined. Commercial banks were the only institutions allowed to offer demand deposit accounts. Savings banks and savings and loan associations offered home mortgage loans, and credit unions offered their members savings accounts and short-term consumer loans. The government even regulated the amount of interest each institution could pay on savings accounts.

With the high inflation of the late 1970s, this system began to fall apart. Depositors, seeking higher interest rates, began to move their deposits to money market mutual funds and other higher-yielding investments. Since the government dictated interest rates, banks could not respond to this threat. Pressure brought by the banks and thrifts resulted in a deregulation of the banking industry, and, although this did increase the competition among different types of financial institutions, it also blurred the differences between them.

The primary deregulation legislation was the Depository Institution Deregulation and Monetary Control Act (DIDMCA) of 1980. It permitted all deposit institutions to offer checking accounts; expanded the lending powers of the thrifts to nonmortgage loans, increasing the competition between commercial banks and thrifts; allowed credit unions to make mortgage loans; and eliminated the interest ceilings on all types of deposits.

The intent of the DIDMCA was to increase competition among financial institutions. It did throw many of the small thrifts into a competitive environment. The number of savings and loans declined from 4,600 in 1980 to less than 2,000 in 2002.[12] DIDMCA also increased the amount of control the Federal Reserve System had over all financial institutions.

12. "Top 150 Bank & S&L Companies in Domestic Consumer Loans," *American Banker*, February 19, 2002, pp. 31–43.

The Twelve Federal Reserve Bank Districts

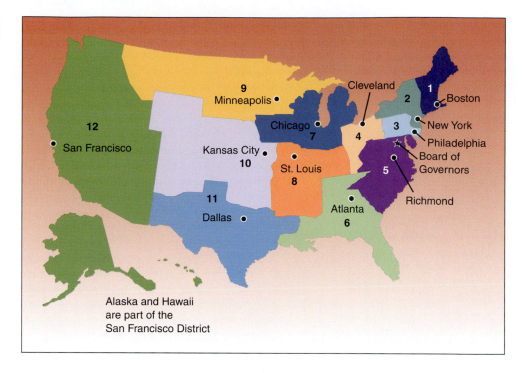

Alaska and Hawaii
are part of the
San Francisco District

20-6d Federal Reserve System

Federal Reserve System
The twelve Federal Reserve Banks that serve as the central bank of the United States. Generally referred to as the Fed.

The base of the commercial banking system in the United States is the **Federal Reserve System** (generally referred to as simply the Fed). The Federal Reserve System—the central bank of the United States—was established by Congress in the Federal Reserve Act of 1913 to control the nation's money supply.

The Fed was originally created to help eliminate the problems that bank panics brought to the economy.[13] Since banks do not hold the deposits of their customers but rather lend these deposits out to other customers of the bank in order to earn interest, the banks can give only a small percentage of their depositors the funds in their account at any given time. When a number of depositors demand their money at one time, it creates a problem for the bank. The bank has to borrow the needed funds from other banks.

If the bank cannot quickly raise the needed funds to handle depositors' withdrawals, a bank panic may result. That is, the bank would have to close its doors until the needed funds could be collected from the borrowers. Panics can result in the failure of commercial banks and can have devastating effects on the national economy. Between the Civil War and 1907, four economic depressions in the United States began with bank panics. After the depression of 1907, Congress appointed a commission to study the problems of the banking system and recommend changes. The result of this study was the foundation of the Federal Reserve System in 1913.

The Federal Reserve System is a network of twelve district banks (Exhibit 20-5) supervised by a board of governors. This board, the Federal Reserve Board, has seven members, appointed by the president of the United States with the advice and consent of the Senate. Because members serve fourteen-year terms, with one term expiring every two years, political control is minimized. Theoretically no president should control the appointment of more than a few members of the board (although retirements and deaths can change this). The president does, however, appoint the chairman of the Federal Reserve Board every four years. Therefore, the president controls the appointment of the most influential member of the board.

The organization of the Federal Reserve revolves around the twelve bank districts, each with a Federal Reserve Bank. These Reserve Banks are owned by the member commercial banks in that district. Each Reserve Bank has nine directors. Three are appointed

13. Rob Garver, "In Brief: Fed to Emphasize Bank Emergency Plans," *American Banker*, May 13, 2002, pp. 10–11.

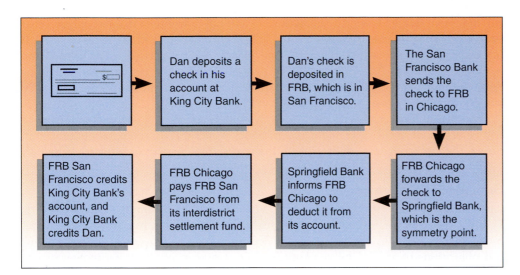

EXHIBIT 20-6

The Path of a Check in the Fed

by the board of governors; the member commercial banks elect three to represent banks and three to represent businesses. In addition to the board of governors, the Fed has a Federal Advisory Council. This council is comprised of twelve members, one from each of the Reserve Banks. The council advises the board of governors on policies of the Fed.

The Fed provides general direction to the twelve Reserve Banks, and it has the power to audit district bank books and coordinate their operations in the public interest. In addition, the Fed has considerable power to control the money supply. This power is discussed in the later section entitled "Monetary Policies."

The Federal Reserve performs several major functions: It manages regional and national check-clearing procedures; it controls the money supply through control of the reserve requirement, open market operations, and control of the discount rate; it regulates commercial banks; it supervises the federal deposit insurance of financial institutions belonging to the Federal Reserve System; and it provides services to the U.S. Treasury.

Check Clearing

The Federal Reserve provides national check clearing. The Federal Reserve clearinghouse handles almost all checks drawn on a bank in one city and presented for deposit to a bank in another city. Not all checks, however, are cleared through the Fed. Small banks in rural areas pay larger banks to provide the check-clearing service for them. Also, commercial banks have their own system for clearing checks written and deposited within the same city. However, checks that involve more than one Federal Reserve district are handled by the Fed. Exhibit 20-6 illustrates how a check is cleared through the Federal Reserve System.

Monetary Policies

The Fed controls the size of the money supply, both M1 (currency and demand deposits) and M2 (time deposits and money market accounts). Though the primary focus traditionally has been on M1, the Fed has recently found that the size of M2 and its effect on the money supply are more predictable. The tools the Fed uses to control the money supply include control of the reserve requirement, open market operations, and control of the discount rate.

Reserve Requirement

Each time you deposit money into your account at the bank, the bank is allowed to lend that money out to someone else. The amount lent out, however, does not equal the amount you deposited. The bank must keep a prescribed amount on hand or deposited at its Federal Reserve Bank as **reserve.** The Federal Reserve dictates the reserve requirement. Lowering or raising it can very significantly affect the money supply.

Let's say your grandmother deposits $100 of her social security benefit in her bank; this is new money into the system. If the reserve requirement is 10 percent, her bank holds

Reserve   The percentage of money from deposits that a bank must keep on hand or on deposit in the Federal Reserve Bank. Funds above this amount can be loaned out.

$10 in reserve and lends out the rest. If the $90 lent out is deposited in another bank, that bank keeps $9 as reserve and lends out $81. This continues until all the funds are used. If full expansion were reached, the $100 your grandmother deposited would expand the money supply by $1,000. We compute this effect by dividing new deposit dollars by reserve requirement. So, if the reserve requirement were 5 percent, a new deposit of $100 would expand the money supply by $2,000 ($100 ÷ 5 percent).

Because of its dramatic effect on the money supply and because such a dramatic move will be discussed in the news and may send shock waves through corporations and Wall Street, the Fed rarely uses adjustments in the reserve requirement to regulate the money supply.

Open Market Operations

Open market operations are conducted by the Federal Open Market Committee. The FOMC consists of the seven members of the board of governors, plus five Reserve Bank presidents. The FOMC uses savings bonds, Treasury notes, and Treasury bills—the financial obligations of the federal government—to expand or contract the money supply. Open market operations involve the sale or purchase of these securities.

If the FOMC decides to purchase Treasury bills, Treasury notes, or savings bonds on the open market, the cash used to pay for the purchases is a new infusion of cash; it expands the money supply. If the FOMC decides to sell these securities on the open market, the money used by individual investors to purchase these is removed from the money supply and held by the Fed. The actual buying and selling of securities takes place between the Federal Reserve Bank of New York, on behalf of the system, and a few dozen large dealers in bonds. Open market operations are the most widely and most regularly used of the three methods for controlling money supply.

Discount Rate

Discount Rate The rate of interest charged to member banks when they borrow money from the Fed.

If member banks need to borrow money to fulfill their reserve requirement, they may borrow it from the Fed. The rate of interest charged to member banks to borrow funds from the Fed is called the **discount rate.** Each Reserve Bank sets its own discount rate, with the approval of the board of governors. Raising the discount rate makes member banks less willing to borrow and causes them to increase the interest rate they charge their borrowers. This in turn reduces the tendency of bank customers to borrow and results in a reduction in the money supply. Lowering the discount rate has the opposite effect.

Perhaps the most important impact of the discount rate, however, is that changes in it gain a great deal of national attention. It signals how the Fed feels about the economy in general and what its future policy is likely to be relative to the money supply. The Federal Reserve increased the discount rate several times during 1994 and early 1995, and interest rates for mortgages and other types of loans also increased. Many businesspeople consider changes in the discount rate as strong indicators of economic conditions.

Supervising Banks

The Fed is responsible for regulating commercial banks. It approves requests to open a branch or merge with another bank, enforces regulations, and admits banks to membership within the system. Each of the twelve Reserve Banks examines member banks in its district.

Depository Insurance

The Federal Reserve Board also supervises the two federal depository insurance agencies: the Federal Deposit Insurance Corporation and the National Credit Union Administration. As indicated earlier in Section 20-6a, recent occurrences in the savings and loan industry have made this an extremely important function of the Fed.

Services to the Treasury

The Fed is really the U.S. government bank. In addition to its other functions, it provides a number of services to the U.S. Treasury and to the public:

- The Federal Reserve Banks physically house much of the coins and paper money in circulation. They provide for the movement of paper money and coins throughout the nation and also remove worn and damaged currency from the system.

- The Fed takes care of all paperwork involved when the government sells securities such as savings bonds, Treasury bills, and other government securities.

- The Fed holds the legally required reserve accounts of member banks and acts generally as a bank for banks.

- The Fed makes sure that state member banks comply with consumer protection regulations.

20-7 TECHNOLOGY IN BANKING

The future of banking will develop around three important areas: (1) technological innovation and its impact on banking, (2) the further development of interstate, regional, and possibly national banks in this country, and (3) the changing impact of the world banking community.

20-7a Technological Impacts: Electronic Funds Transfer

The impact of technology on banking will be far-reaching. Some key areas developing very rapidly involve electronic funds transfer. **Electronic funds transfer (EFT)** is the transfer of funds by means of an electronic terminal, telephone, computer, or magnetic tape that orders a bank or other financial institution to debit (reduce) or credit (increase) an account. Areas showing the most promise for EFT use include automated teller machines (ATMs), automated clearinghouses (ACHs), point-of-sale (POS) systems with the use of debit cards, and in-home banking.

Automated teller machines (ATMs) allow depositors to access their accounts and make payments, deposits, and cash withdrawals twenty-four hours a day. Yet they were relatively slow to catch on. Early ATMs broke down frequently, and customers were reluctant to trust the machines. They worried that their account would get charged but the money wouldn't come out, or that a deposit they made wouldn't get credited. However, because of their convenience and improved reliability and because younger consumers are growing more accustomed to dealing with machines, ATMs have become extremely popular. There are almost 100,000 ATMs in the United States.[14] Nearly half of U.S. residents aged 18 to 34 use automated banking, while only 8 percent of the more reluctant over-65 group uses ATMs.[15]

With expansion of ATM networks, customers of member banks can use ATMs nationwide, always having access to their bank funds. To use an ATM, the customer inserts a plastic card supplied by the bank and then punches in a personal identification number. To access the account, the customer needs both the card and the identification number. This helps protect the accounts of customer who lose their cards.

ATMs help reduce transaction costs for banks as well as providing convenience for bank customers. Each teller transaction costs a bank an estimated $2 to $3; each ATM transaction only costs about $1 to $1.50.[16] It may cost an extra $1 to $2 to make a transaction at another bank's ATM.[17] ATMs are now available in shopping malls, supermarkets, student centers, airports, and just about every other public place.

Automated clearinghouses (ACHs) allow payments or withdrawals to and from a bank account by magnetic computer tape. Employers use ACHs to make payroll account

Electronic Funds Transfer (EFT)   The transfer of funds by means of an electronic terminal, telephone, computer, or magnetic tape that orders a bank or other financial institution to debit or credit an account.

Automated Teller Machines (ATMs)   Machine that dispenses cash from a customer's account, accepts deposits to the account, or performs other banking functions.

Automated Clearinghouses (ACHs)   Allows payments or withdrawals to and from a bank account by magnetic computer tape.

---

14. Galina Diker Pildush, *Cisco ATM Solutions* (New York: Alpha 2000).

15. Brian O'Connell, "Next Generation ATMs Proliferate: Got Fees? Big Banks See Web-Enabled ATMs As Cash Cows," *Bank Technology News*, April 1, 2002, pp. 1–3.

16. Ibid.

17. Edward F. Mrkvicka, Jr., *Your Bank Is Ripping You Off* (New York: St Martin's Press, 1997).

withdrawals and transfer employees' pay directly to employee accounts. ACHs are also becoming popular with utilities such as telephone and electric companies, who sign customers up to have their bills deducted directly from their checking accounts. The federal government is the largest ACH system user; over 50 percent of all social security payments are made through this system. Also, almost all payments for interest on Treasury notes and bills are deposited directly into the holders' accounts. However, ACH systems are expensive to implement and therefore are only efficient for large batch processing.

Point-of-sale (POS) systems, along with electronic fund transfers, allow merchants to draw money directly from a customer's bank account at the time a purchase is made. These systems work through the use of a debit card. Recall that the **debit card** is similar to a credit card except that the card does not create a loan but rather transfers funds from the customer's account to the merchant's account. Both the customer and the retail store must belong to the same bank or bank network, and the retailer must have a POS terminal.

When the customer makes a purchase using this system, the cashier enters the debit card on the POS terminal. If sufficient funds are in the customer's account, the money automatically transfers to the retailer's account through an EFT. The transaction is then complete. POS systems help reduce check processing costs and the problem of bad checks. They also help with security, since fewer funds need to be kept on hand in the store.

The Fedwire system utilized by the Federal Reserve Bank uses extensively EFT as described in the Focus on Technology box, "Transferring Funds Electronically."

20-7b Interstate Banking

The 1927 Pepper-McFadden Act prohibited banks from having offices in more than one state unless authorized by state law. It also required that banks adhere to the branch banking laws of the states in which they operate. Since some states do not even permit branch banking within the same city, this law greatly restricted bank growth.

In June 1985, the U.S. Supreme Court ruled that interstate banking within regions (e.g., New England, the Southeast) should be allowed. This would be controlled by the states themselves, which would have to make mutually acceptable agreements that would allow banks in each region to merge across state lines. Today, all fifty states, plus the District of Columbia, permit some form of interstate banking.[18] Furthermore, the problems faced by banks in certain economically depressed areas have caused the FDIC to allow banks from other regions to buy weakened banks to protect the troubled banks' depositors.

---

18. Robert X. Cringely, "Meet Your New Banker," *Worth*, December/January 2001, pp. 51–52.

Point-of-Sale (POS) Systems Systems, along with EFT, that allow merchants to draw money directly from a customer's bank account at the time a purchase is made.

Debit Card   A plastic card, similar to a credit card, that deducts funds directly from the customer's account rather than creating a loan.

FOCUS ON TECHNOLOGY

Transferring Funds Electronically

Fedwire is an electronic transfer system developed and maintained by the Federal Reserve System that enables financial institutions to transfer funds and book-entry securities. The system connects Federal Reserve Banks and branches, the Treasury and other government agencies, and more than 9,000 online and offline depository institutions.

In 2000, some 108 million funds transfers with a total value of $380 trillion were made over Fedwire—an average of $3.5 million per transaction.

The Federal Reserve has been moving funds electronically since 1918. In conjunction with the change from weekly to daily settlement, the Reserve Banks installed a private telegraph system for themselves and began to process transfers of funds.

Until 1980 Fedwire services were offered without cost to Federal Reserve member commercial banks. However, the Depository Institutions Deregulation and Monetary Control Act of 1980 required the pricing of Fed services, including funds and securities transfers, and gave nonmember depository institutions direct access to the transfer system.

Transfers over Fedwire require relatively few bookkeeping entries. For example, suppose an individual or a private of government organization asks a bank to transfer funds. If the banks of the sender and receiver are in different Federal Reserve districts, the sending bank debits the sender's account and its local Reserve Bank serving the receiver's bank. The two Reserve Banks settle with each other through the Interdistrict Settlement Fund, a bookkeeping system that records Federal Reserve interdistrict transactions. Finally, the receiving bank notifies the recipient of the transfer and credits its account. When the transfer is received, it is final and the receiver may use the funds immediately.

If the sending and receiving banks are in the same Federal Reserve district, the transaction is similar, but all of the processing and accounting are done by one Reserve Bank.

Source: "Fedwire," Federal Reserve Bank of New York, Fedpoint 43, May 2002.

As a result, a number of *superregionals* have developed in different regions of the country. Banks such as Bank of America and Wachovia, both of North Carolina, Bank One of Chicago, and PNC Financial in Pennsylvania are operating across state lines. Bank of America (formerly NationsBank) has acquired a reputation as a growth-oriented superregional.

3, 4
5, 6

With regional banking possible, national commercial banking may not be too far in the future. A number of factors point to this. First, firms such as American Express and Merrill Lynch are not subject to the same restrictions as the commercial banks. Since deregulation has enabled these companies to offer checking accounts and banking services on a nationwide basis, we currently have the equivalent of national banking. Second, as a nation, we are still very mobile. On average, one out of every six families will move in any year. National banking would provide greater convenience to these customers. Finally, the disasters in the banking industry in Texas and Oklahoma brought about by the drop in the oil business indicate the need to have banks less concentrated in areas where a single industry dominates. A broader base would have helped many of the Texas and Oklahoma banks.

Rank	Bank and Head Office	Country	Assets (US$ millions)
1	USB AG	Switzerland	757,879
2	Deutsche Bank AG	Germany	735,789
3	The Bank of Tokyo-Mitsubishi Ltd.	Japan	666,085
4	Bayerische Hypo-und Vereinsbank AG	Germany	514,018
5	ABM AMRO Holding NV	Netherlands	507,372
6	The Sumitomo Bank, Ltd.	Japan	493,878
7	Dresdner Bank AG	Germany	429,159
8	Credit Agricole	France	418,033
9	Westdeutshe	Germany	416,082
10	The Dai-Ichi Kangyo Bank Ltd.	Japan	412,770

Source: "Largest International Banks," *Industry Week,* www.industryweek.com/iwiprint/data/chart2-4.html, May 6, 2002.

20-7c World Banking Community

Exhibit 20-7 presents the ten largest banks in the world based on value of the bank's assets. Four are German, three are Japanese, and none are American. The largest bank in the United States, Citibank, ranks twenty-first worldwide with $300,895 million in total assets.[19] Although our focus has been on banking in this country, banking and finance obviously are global, not local, issues.

Any decisions made within the U.S. economy have an impact on the world economy. If the Fed decides to lower the interest rate, foreign investors can withdraw their money and invest it in banks in other countries with higher rates. Bankers look for the maximum return on their money. For this reason, they do not tend to be nationalistic in their business decisions, and the banking market becomes more and more global.

Many of the financial difficulties faced by major U.S. banks arose in part from international circumstances. First, their large investments in Third World economies for the development of oil and natural resources went sour because the market price for oil fell and many of the nations were unable to repay the loans. Second, aggressive foreign lenders have lured away many U.S. corporate borrowers; foreign sources now lend about $4 to U.S. companies for every $10 lent by U.S. banks.

Certainly, as economic stability and growth continue and as previously unopened markets such as Russia, China, and Eastern Europe remain open, global financing will expand even more. The 1992 formalization and lifting of trade restrictions within the European Union and the creation of euro currency have led to more intense competition. The world economy is now financed by international banks. U.S. banks are just one more player in this arena—an important player, but one that must more completely understand its role in a world economy and the importance of consumers. American bankers need to compete with international banks and to win more business with smarter marketing, packages of products, and service.

SUGGESTED WEBSITES

Note: These websites were functional when we went to press. Please access the online text for the most up-to-date URLs.

1. www.visa.com
2. www.mastercard.com
3. www.bankofamerica.com
4. www.wachovia.com
5. www.bankone.com
6. www.pnc.com

19. "Largest International Banks," *Industry Week,* accessed at www.industryweek.com/iwiprint/data/chart2-4.html,may6,2002.

SUMMARY OF LEARNING OBJECTIVES

1. *Define* money *and state its functions and characteristics.*   Money is anything that is commonly accepted as a means of paying for the goods and services individuals need and want. The three basic functions of money are that it serves as a medium of exchange, making it possible for two individuals to exchange without having to barter; as a measure of relative value, allowing two dissimilar items to be purchased on a similar basis; and as a store of value, making it possible for us to hold the value over time. The desirable characteristics of money are acceptance, divisibility, portability, durability, stability, and scarcity.

2. *Identify the elements that make up both the M1 and M2 money supplies.*   The M1 money supply consists of the most liquid forms of money. M1 includes currency (including cashier's checks, travelers' checks, and money orders) and demand deposits. The M2 money supply consists of all the elements of M1 plus time deposits and money market accounts.

3. *Compare the different types of financial institutions.*   The primary types of financial institutions are banking institutions, consisting of commercial banks, savings and loans, savings banks, and credit unions, and nonbanking institutions, such as insurance companies, pension funds, brokerage houses, and commercial and consumer finance companies. Before deregulation, the differences between the banking institutions were clear and their functions distinct; now the differences are not as significant. All of them offer some type of demand deposits, and all can handle most types of loans. Nonbanking institutions, while acting as sources and users of funds, do not perform major banking services.

4. *Explain how the federal government is involved in money and banking in the United States.*   The federal government insures bank deposits for up to $100,000 through the Federal Deposit Insurance Corporation; the National Credit Union Association insures deposits for federally chartered credit unions. The federal government had also regulated the types of accounts financial institutions could offer and the amount of interest institutions could pay in savings accounts. Deregulation has eliminated the interest ceilings on all types of deposits and has permitted all deposit institutions to offer checking accounts. Finally, the Federal Reserve System was established by Congress in 1913 to manage regional and national check-clearing procedures, to control the money supply with monetary policy, to regulate commercial banks, to supervise the federal deposit insurance for banks belonging to the Federal Reserve System, and to provide services for the U.S. Treasury.

5. *Discuss how the Federal Reserve System controls the supply of money and credit.*   The Fed controls the money supply and credit primarily through open market operations and through control of the reserve requirement and the discount rate. The reserve requirement is the percentage of deposits a bank must keep on hand. Due to the deposit multiplier effect, changes in the reserve requirement can have extreme effects on the money supply; therefore, the Fed rarely uses this tool. It does use open market operations—that is, buying or selling government securities on the open market—to expand or contract the money supply. The final tool of the Fed is the discount rate, the rate banks must pay to borrow money from the Fed. By raising the discount rate, the Fed can discourage banks from borrowing and therefore from lending money, thus slowing the rate of expansion. By lowering the discount rate, the Fed can have the opposite effect.

6. *Identify the major changes occurring in banking and the impact of technology.*   Deregulation has enabled a broad range of financial institutions to provide banking services. Technology is impacting banking through electronic funds transfers in the form of automatic teller machines, automated clearinghouses, point-of-sale systems, and in-home banking. Banks have been given the right to expand across state borders within regions, and national banking may occur in the near future. Finally, the role of foreign banks is becoming more significant, not only on the world market but also on the domestic market in the United States.

KEY TERMS

automated clearinghouses (ACHs) (p. 543)
automated teller machines (ATMs) (p. 543)
commercial bank (p. 535)
credit unions (p. 536)
currency (p. 532)
debit card (p. 544)
demand deposits (p. 532)
discount rate (p. 542)

electronic funds transfer (EFT) (p. 543)
Federal Reserve System (p. 540)
finance companies (p. 537)
liquidity (p. 532)
M1 (p. 532)
M2 (p. 533)
money (p. 528)
money market accounts (p. 533)

point-of-sale (POS) systems (p. 544)
reserve (p. 541)
savings and loans associations (S&Ls) (p. 536)
savings banks (p. 536)
time deposits (p. 533)

QUESTIONS FOR DISCUSSION AND REVIEW

1. What is money? Why is it important for an efficient economic system? Give an example of how exchanges would occur if money were not available.

2. Why is it important for each person to maintain an accurate credit report rating?

3. What is the difference between demand deposits and time deposits? Why are checks the most used method of paying for exchanges? Do you think they will remain as the most useful and frequently used method of payment?

4. Explain how the various deposit insurance funds work. If a bank were in trouble, would the Fed immediately go to payment out of the insurance funds? If not, what steps would the Fed first take?

5. Do you properly manage the use of personal credit cards? How? What steps do you take to protect yourself from identity theft (someone using your name, social security number, and other personal data) to make fraudulent purchases?

6. List the desirable characteristics of money. Why is each important to the usefulness of money within an economic system?

7. Many small governments have been overturned because they were unable to maintain a stable value for their money. Why is stable value so important? How could the lack of stability cause a revolt?

8. You have been elected chairman of the Federal Reserve board of governors. Recently you have noticed that inflation is rising; you fear that the money supply might be expanding too fast. What actions might you take to alleviate this problem? Which actions would be most appropriate to take first?

9. Identify the major changes occurring in banking at this time. How will these changes affect the future of banking? How do you think a bank will operate in 2023? Do you think that U.S. banks need to become more active in the world financial market?

10. Why should you determine whether your savings deposits in a bank are protected by the Federal Deposit Insurance Corporation?

END-OF-CHAPTER QUESTIONS

1. Money has not always been coins and paper bills.   **T** or **F**

2. Money makes it possible for us to hold onto value over time.
   T or **F**

3. If money grew on trees, and everyone had all they wanted, money would have little value.   **T** or **F**

4. Cashier's checks, money orders, and travelers' checks are considered currency.   **T** or **F**

5. FDIC insurance is limited to $100,000 for any depositor.
   T or **F**

6. The number of savings and loans is increasing.   **T** or **F**

7. ATMs caught on relatively quickly.   **T** or **F**

8. Deregulation has enabled American Express to offer checking accounts on a nationwide basis.   **T** or **F**

9. Of the ten largest banks in the world, based on the value of the bank's assets, only four are American.   **T** or **F**

10. Money has three basic functions: (1) as a store of value, (2) as a measure of relative value, and (3) as _____.
    a. a competitive marker
    b. a foreign debt/credit item
    c. a medium of exchange
    d. government note

11. The _____ were the first to use paper money.
    a. Romans
    b. Egyptians
    c. Chinese
    d. French

12. The M1 money supply consists of _____.
    a. currency and demand deposits
    b. time deposits and money market accounts
    c. international funds available
    d. money deposits

13. Four economic depressions in the United States began with _____.
    a. wars
    b. stock market crashes
    c. presidential elections
    d. bank panics

14. The two largest global credit cards are _____.
    a. Visa and Mastercard
    b. Discover and Mastercard
    c. Discover and Visa
    d. Visa and American Express

15. The average dollar bill is in circulation for _____.
    a. six months
    b. twelve months
    c. eighteen months
    d. two years

INTERNET EXERCISE

Analysis of a Bank

Exhibit 20-3 presents the names of the ten largest banks in the United States and Exhibit 20-7 presents the names of the world's ten largest banks. Select one name from each exhibit and use the Internet to determine the following:

- A history summary of each
- The employment opportunities available in each bank for a person with your experience and educational background
- The type of technology used in each bank
- The biggest foreign customers of each bank
- What each bank reports to be their future strategy to remain successful

EXPERIENTIAL EXERCISE

Interviewing Managers of Financial Institutions

Activity

Student groups will interview managers of various types of financial institutions and report findings to the class. Approximately one hour of homework/interview time, forty minutes of classroom time for reporting, and ten minutes of initial class time for organizing the group effort will be needed.

Directions

1. The instructor should provide students with a brief overview of the following types of financial institutions: commercial banks, savings and loans, credit unions, and finance companies.
2. The instructor should divide the class into four small groups, with each group electing a recorder/spokesperson. Each group is to interview the manager of a financial institution as follows:
   Group 1 — Manager of a commercial bank
   Group 2 — Manager of an S&L
   Group 3 — Manager of a credit union
   Group 4 — Manager of a finance company

3. The interviews should include the following types of questions:
4. What types of loans does your institution emphasize or specialize in? Provide some degree of proportion, such as 20 percent of loans in autos, 40 percent in residential mortgages, and so on.
5. What types of investments or savings vehicles does your institution provide? What interest rate is your institution currently paying for each of the vehicles?
6. How does your institution determine the credit rating of an applicant for a loan?
7. Who is your institution's typical customer?
8. Why should a customer borrow from your institution? Why should a customer open a savings account with your institution?
9. The students should report their findings in class.

BUSINESS APPLICATION

Securing a Loan

Activity

Experience the process of learning about varying interest rates on loans by contacting several lending institutions. Because students are not in the position to seek a business loan, they can gain experience by seeking an auto loan.

Directions

1. The instructor should explain to students that interest rates on loans may vary from financial institution to institution. Not only will the institutions themselves have varying rates, but the way each institution sees a loan applicant tends to vary. For example, one bank may be willing to make a $10,000 auto loan to an 18-year-old with a part-time job, while another institution may insist on the addition of a cosigning parent or other adult before making the loan.

2. Assign each student the task of contacting several financial institutions about their conditions on making an auto loan. The following factors should be used by all students:
   - The loan is to be used for an auto loan on a three-year-old car with 40,000 miles on the odometer.
   - The auto is to be purchased for $12,500 with $2,500 to be paid up front by the buyer as a down payment and the remaining borrowed from the institution.
   - The loan may be either a four-year or a five-year loan.
   - Each student should use his/her actual age and employment status.
   - The information being sought from each financial institution should include the actual interest rate and actual monthly payments to be made for the $10,000 loan.
3. Students are to write their findings in a short homework-type paper to be turned in at the next class meeting.

Case

Protect Your Identity At All Times

The following case illustrates the problems that identity theft can cause for banks. U.S. Attorney Katrina Plummer is involved in a case involving John Viking (name changed since example is only for illustrative purposes). According to court records:

a. In 1999 and 2000, Viking and another person executed a scheme to defraud two banks.

b. Viking fraudulently obtained moneys by withdrawing cash and wire transferring money from the savings account of a victim of identity theft.

c. Viking utilized the name, date of birth, social security number, and savings account without the victim's consent or knowledge.

d. Viking's accomplice obtained a western state driver's license bearing the name and date of birth of the victim, but showing the accomplice's picture on the face of the license.

e. Viking opened an account at a bank in the southeast. Viking then fraudulently caused a western state bank to wire transfer $15,000 from the victim's savings account to the southeast bank as a deposit into a newly opened account.

f. Unbeknownst to the victim, Viking opened an account in an investment company in the victim's name. Viking deposited a counterfeit check into the investment account in the amount of $99,979.35.

g. Viking later caused the investment company to issue two checks from the account. Both checks were issued from an account that actually had no funds.

h. The first check was made payable in the name of the victim for $49,990 and mailed to an address associated with Viking. Viking's accomplice presented the check and used the state driver's license (with the victim's name) and other information to cash the check.

i. The second check was made payable to the victim for $40,000. The checks were then cashed.

This is a "true" case that illustrates how identity theft can be used fraudulently.

Questions for Discussion

1. What steps can a person take to prevent identity theft?
2. Should the banks, drivers license bureau, or investment company be held responsible for any of these fraudulent activities? Why?
3. If found guilty, what type of sentence would you recommend for Viking and his accomplice? Why?

Source: U.S. Department of Justice, Seattle, Washington District, April 13, 2001.

21

Financial Planning

Photo: comstock.com

After completing this chapter, you should be able to:

1 **Explain** the six steps in the personal finance planning process.

2 **Describe** the advantages and the disadvantages of leasing a car.

3 **Identify** the types of life, health, and home protection insurance policies that are available.

4 **Explain** how a Keogh plan differs from a personal savings account.

5 **Define** the meaning of fee-for-service health insurance.

6 **Describe** why the careful monitoring of your cash inflow and cash outflow is an important responsibility.

7 **Provide** an analysis of retirement planning and the role that you must play in preparing to retire.

Your Financial Future Is in Your Hands

There are a few smart actions that anyone can take to create more wealth. These actions are based on common sense, are legal, and are used by many educated men and women who create more wealth each day and hour, 24/7. While the smart person is asleep his or her wealth is growing.

A few simple steps are these:

1. Spend less than you earn—cut back or hold your standard of living in check. Looking for sales, spending less on extravagant items (e.g., gold Rolex watches), and careful budgeting can result in spending less (less outflow) than you earn (inflow).

2. Have your money work for you—finding compound interest savings accounts is a starting point. Examine IRAs, traditional or Roth. Finding deals on savings and using a plan can result in more money, called a nest egg, down the road.

3. Create responsible savings and investment goals—set a goal, stick with it, and watch your money grow. The key here is to set reasonable goals such as: 10 percent or 20 percent of inflow will be saved. A person with a family who sets unrealistic goals such as saving 80 percent of all inflow each month is going to become disappointed.

4. Manage your investments—instead of doing a once-a-year peek at your investments, use a software program such as Microsoft Money or Quicken to keep you up-to-date. Reviewing investments once in a while is not sufficient for creating more wealth.

These are four simple steps that anyone with a minimum understanding of financial planning can immediately take. As this chapter illustrates, awareness, involvement, and planning are necessary to enjoy the benefits of working hard. No financial planner can correct laziness or a lack of understanding of how wealth can and is created in a free enterprise, capitalistic society.

Source: Terry Savage, "The Basics," *MoneyCentral,* May 23, 2002.

At each stage of life, beginning with high school, through college, and into a career, money and handling finances are major issues. Personal financial planning is the process of properly managing your money to achieve personal and economic satisfaction. A sound understanding of how to manage and handle money can lead to making more efficient decisions that result in improving one's quality of life. In more concrete terms, sound personal financial planning results in the following:

- Growing and protecting your financial resources
- Having available the financial resources needed to enjoy life
- Avoiding unnecessary and excessive debt
- Independence to conduct your life and career in a manner that fits your needs

This chapter explores steps to take and decisions you can make that achieve these four results. Without a plan, an approach, or an understanding of how to handle your money and finances there will likely be embarrassments, shortfalls, and perhaps even bankruptcies. An estimated 1 million Americans declared personal bankruptcy in 2001.[1] That is, individuals used a legal process because they were unable to meet their financial obligations. In a bankruptcy the court divides up assets among creditors.

The Web provides many calculators to help you keep track of your financial situation. The Focus on the Future box, "Planned Calculators Are Great!," presents a few of the available calculators.

21-1 A PERSONAL FINANCE PLANNING PROCESS

A logical six-step process is a concise way to begin your journey of managing your personal finances. Each step should be carefully thought through and completed.

1. Roland Gary Jones, *They Went Broke: Bankruptcies and Money Disasters of the Rich and Famous* (New York: Gramercy, 2002).

FOCUS ON THE FUTURE

Planned Calculators Are Great!

The Web makes many of our daily tasks easier. We receive up-to-the-minute stock market news, information about weather in every part of the world, and breaking news reports. Another online aid comes in the form of financial planning calculators. Whatever you need—from saving money to paying off debt to determining your net worth—there are calculators available.

A few of the wonderfully quick and easy calculators are as follows:

Debt Planner—You enter the balance on each of your credit cards, the interest rate, and the minimum pay; the results will tell you how long it would take to pay off the balance if you make just the minimum payment. (www.cgi.money.cnn.com/tools/debtplanner/debtplanner.jsp)

Net Worth—The calculator will figure out what you're worth by reconciling your debts and your assets. (http://financialplan.about.com/gi/dynamic/offsite.htm?site=http://www.bygpub.com/finance/NetWorthCalc.htm)

Retirement—You enter some basic information and this calculator will estimate how well your current savings program will prepare you for retirement. (http://financialplan.about.com/gi/dynamic/offsite.htm?site=http://cgi.money.cnn.com/tools/retirementplanner/retirementplanner.jsp)

Credit Card Chooser—This calculator lets you see how your decisions will affect interest charges and your credit card balance. (http://creditcardmenu.com/s/s.ccm?_ust_todo_=64417&_rid_=5&_xid_=g.zFR4DHH1OCs2-1023285925&)

Instead of fumbling around with numbers and guesses, the use of calculators is easy, quick, and accurate. Try out a few and use the ones you need and like.

Source: Deborah Fowles, "Financial Planning," www.financialplan.about.com/library/weekly/aa072700a.htm.

21-1a Step 1: Inventory of Current Situation

A needed first step is to determine your present financial situation in terms of income, savings, living expenses, and debts. Prepare your own personal balance sheet of Assets = Liabilities + Equity.

For example, Hunter Zacha is ready to graduate from the University of Texas. He has worked for four summers and saved $6,800. He has no debts and is ready to begin his career in banking.

21-1b Step 2: Develop Your Financial Goals

You should regularly analyze your financial values and goals. This means you must ask yourself "How do I feel about money? What are my tastes in clothes, living conditions, food products, leisure and recreation, and hobbies? Which of these tastes are needs and wants?"

Hunter wants to return to school for a law degree, but he currently doesn't have the money to spend three more years in college.

21-1c Step 3: Identify Various Courses of Action

Developing a set of possible actions and evaluating each one is recommended. You can continue doing what has become your routine or you can change your course. For example, you may be saving $100 from each paycheck but decide that now is the time to save

$200 from each check. Being alert to opportunities and willing to take a different course requires flexibility and knowledge. Flexibility allows you to change, while knowledge results in making better decisions.

Hunter has a number of options. He can take one of the five job offers he has secured. He could take out loans to go to law school full- or part-time, or he could sit and live off the savings he accumulated for at least a short period of time.

21-1d Step 4: Evaluate the Courses of Action

You will need to evaluate how each course of action matches up with your goals. For example, if you decide to buy a new car, you cannot invest in the new start-up business you and a friend have discussed. Each course of action has some risk associated with it. There is risk in any financially based decision. For example, some investments have the potential for high earnings, but there is the risk of a wipeout. No investment is risk-free. Likewise no career decision is risk-free. Changing environmental factors, needs, desires, and goals will require you to pay close attention to risk factors over time.

As Hunter evaluates his alternative courses of action, he must consider how he wants to live in the short and long run. He also needs to consider market conditions and the demand for lawyers.

21-1e Step 5: Create and Execute Your Financial Plan

This is the "can do" action step in the process. What action must you now take to achieve your goals? Financial planning experts, courses, newsletters, books, and software programs are available that can help you in this action phase. Although these services and materials will not provide a perfectly clear picture on what action you should take, they will provide helpful guidance so that the actions taken will be grounded and based on pertinent data, information, and knowledge.

Hunter has decided to take a job offer in San Diego with an international consulting firm. He plans to work for three years, save 25 percent annually of his salary, take a few courses each year via e-learning so he stays academically sharp, and read at least ten hours per week in his favorite law field, intellectual property and rights.

21-1f Step 6: Monitor and Reevaluate Your Plan

Regularly checking on your financial and career decisions is a wise course of action. Your entire financial condition in terms of assets, liabilities, and equities should be completed at least once per year. Assessing what events have transpired during the year that impact your financial resources, goals, and situation is a way to make modifications quickly when they are necessary.

After being on the job for about six months Hunter should examine where he is in terms of his financial goals, career plans, and personal circumstances. Is he on the right course for his present goals? This is a question we all need to continually ask and honestly answer.

The six-step financial planning approach is presented in a graphical portrayal in Exhibit 21-1. You can create your own personal representation to use and modify as you review, take action, and monitor financial and career decisions.

21-2 MANAGING YOUR CASH

Every day some financial event or situation can effect your net worth. Your *net worth* is your financial condition at a specific moment—your assets minus your liabilities.[2] When you receive an income or a wage and pay for rent, electricity, groceries, gasoline, clothing, and highway tolls, an inflow (money) and an outflow (money) process is occurring. This is referred to as your *cash flow*. A cash flow statement is a summary picture or snapshot of the inflow (wage or salary) and outflow (paying expenses). The cash flow snapshot is

---

2. John Hagel and Marc Singer, *Networth* (Cambridge, MA: Harvard University Press, 1999).

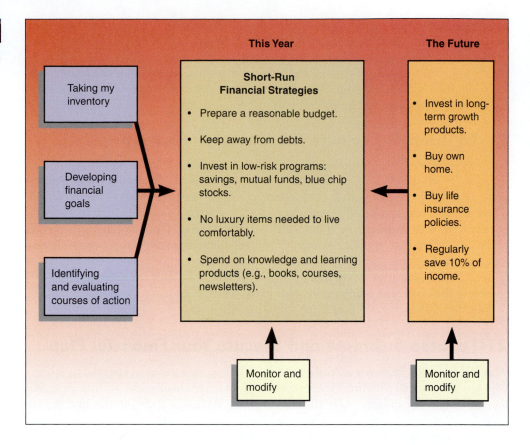

Total Money Received − Total Money Outgoing = Money Surplus/Deficit
(Inflow)   (Outflow)

A summary cash flow statement for Hailey Murphy is presented in Exhibit 21-2.

Hailey's month of August inflows exceed her outflows by $1,040. She allocates this surplus three different ways—donation, savings, and stock. The amount Hailey has remaining after inflows and outflows are examined allows her to make some financial decisions. These decisions can have long- and short-term consequences.

If the cash flow statement indicates a deficit, Hailey would have to dip into her savings account, cash out some of her stock investment, or secure a loan. This suggests that keeping some money in savings is smart because of the need for cash to make up for a deficit.

Hailey's maneuvering room is primarily in the variable outflow area. These expenses fluctuate because of economic conditions, time of the year, preferences, and a variety of other reasons. For example, Hailey could eliminate her golfing for a period of time or cut back in some other variable expense area.

A typical after-tax budget allocation profile for different categories is spelled out in Exhibit 21-3 on page 558. Hailey as a working single with no dependents can compare her cash flow patterns with the average person in her category. Where a person lives geographically, as well as inflation, will influence his or her cash flow and budgeting.

21-3 THE SAVING DECISION

When compared with individuals in other developed nations, the typical American generally saves less.[3] This means that if an emergency occurs, there may not be enough money available. The savings plan you adopt can make facing emergencies much easier.

3. Joel Bessis, *Risk Management in Banking* (New York: John Wiley, 2002).

EXHIBIT 21-2

Hailey Murphy Cash Flow for the Month: August

Inflow of Money

Salary (net after subtraction of federal and state income tax and social security deductions)	$4,200.00	
Interest from savings account	150.00	
Earnings from stock investment	60.00	
Total Inflow		$4,410.00

Outflow of Money

Fixed

Loft rent	$1,700.00	
Toll road fees	65.00	
Life insurance	45.00	
Apartment insurance	40.00	
Jewelry insurance	20.00	
Total	$1,870.00	

Variable

Groceries	320.00	
Meals at restaurants	350.00	
Clothing	310.00	
Telephone	65.00	
Beauty care/products	100.00	
Entertainment	100.00	
Painting/art supplies	80.00	
Golf	175.00	
Total	$1,500.00	

Total Outflow		$3,370.00
Surplus (+) / Deficit (−)		$1,040.00

Uses of Surplus

Salvation Army donation		200.00
Savings		500.00
Stock investments		340.00

One approach is to direct savings as a fixed expense in your cash flow analysis. That is, take 10 percent of your inflow (money) and establish a fixed savings amount.

You can choose from a variety of savings plans when making a decision. Exhibit 21-4 examines the benefits and drawbacks of six savings opportunities. Each of these options may fit your needs at a particular moment in time.

Regular **savings accounts** usually are easy to open, but they have low interest returns (e.g., in 2002 some were as low as 1%). You can withdraw your money easily and will receive a summary of transactions statement monthly or quarterly.

Certificates of deposit (CDs) pay higher interest rates than savings accounts, but you must leave your money on deposit for a specified period of time. Most financial institutions impose a penalty for early withdrawal of CD funds. Some individuals prefer to create a CD portfolio with CDs maturing at different times, $2,000 in a three-month CD, $4,000 in an eighteen-month CD, and $3,000 in a two-year CD. This provides you with more flexibility.

Interest-earning checking accounts, sometimes called NOW accounts (negotiable order of withdrawal), usually require a minimum balance. If the balance dips below this amount, you may not earn interest and will likely have to pay a fee. Examine the restrictions, frequency of interest payments, and fees for having a NOW account.

Savings Accounts Accounts that are easy to open but low interest returns; money can be withdrawn easily and account holders receive a summary of transactions statement monthly or quarterly.

Certificates of Deposit (CDs) Interest-bearing note issued by a commercial bank or brokerage firm.

Interest-Earning Checking Accounts Sometimes called NOW accounts (negotiable order of withdrawal), accounts that usually require a minimum balance. If the balance dips below this amount, you may not earn interest and will likely have to pay a fee.

After-Tax Budget Allocations for Different Life Situations

Budget Category	Student	Working Single (no children)	Couple (children under 18)	Single Parent (young children)	Parents (children over 18 in college)	Couple (over 55, no dependent children)
Housing (rent or mortgage payment: utilities; furnishings; and appliances	0–25%	30–35%	25–35%	20–30%	25–30%	25–35%
Transportation	5–10	15–20	15–20	10–18	12–18	10–18
Food (at home and away from home)	15–20	15–25	15–25	13–20	15–20	18–25
Clothing	5–12	5–15	5–10	5–10	4–8	4–8
Personal and health care (including child care)	3–5	3–5	4–10	8–12	4–6	6–12
Entertainment and recreation	5–10	5–10	4–8	4–8	6–10	5–8
Reading and education	10–30	2–4	3–5	3–5	6–12	2–4
Personal insurance and pension payments	0–5	4–8	5–9	5–9	4–7	6–8
Gifts, donations, and contributions	4–6	5–8	3–5	3–5	4–8	3–5
Savings	0–10	4–15	5–10	5–8	2–4	3–5

Sources: Bureau of Labor Statistics (http://stats.bls.gov); American Demographics: Money; and The Wall Street Journal.

EXHIBIT 21-4

Savings Alternatives

Type of Account	Benefits	Drawbacks
Regular savings accounts/passbook accounts/share accounts	Low minimum balance Ease of withdrawal Insured	Low rate of return
Certificates of deposit (CDs)	Guaranteed rate of return for time of CD Insured	Possible penalty for early withdrawal Minimum deposit
Interest-earning checking accounts	Checking privileges Interest earned Insured	Service charge for going below minimum balance Cost for printing check; other fees may apply
Money market accounts	Favorable rate of return (based on current interest rates Allows some check writing Insured	Higher minimum balance than regular saving accounts No interest or service charge if below a certain balance
Money market funds	Favorable rate of return (based on current interest rates) Some check writing	Minimum balance Not insured
U.S. savings bonds	Fairly good rate of return (varies with current interest rates) Low minimum deposit Government guaranteed Exempt from state and local income taxes	Lower rate when redeemed before five years

	Compounding Method			
End of Year	**Daily**	**Monthly**	**Quarterly**	**Annually**
1	$10,832.78	$10,830.00	$10,824.32	$10,800.00
2	11,743.91	11,728.88	11,716.59	11,664.00
3	12,712.17	12,702.37	12,682.41	12,597.12
4	13,770.82	13,756.66	13,727.85	13,604.89
5	14,917.62	14,898.46	14,859.46	14,693.28
Annual yield	8.33%	8.30%	8.24%	8.00%

EXHIBIT 21-5

Compounding Example

Money market accounts are savings accounts that require a minimum balance and have earnings based on market interest rates. These accounts allow you to write a limited number of checks or to transfer money to other accounts. Money market accounts at banks and savings and loan associations are covered by federal deposit insurance. This is not true of money market funds, which are issued by investment and insurance companies.

U.S. savings bonds are issued by the U.S. Treasury Department. These bonds are inflation indexed, which can guarantee that a saver's return will exceed inflation. Series EE bonds may be purchased for amounts ranging from $25 to $5,000 (face values of $50 to $30,000). You must hold the bonds at least five years to earn the stated rate. If redeemed within the five-year period, the bondholder receives a lower rate of return. The Series EE bonds' interest is exempt from state and local taxes. You do not pay federal income tax until the bonds are redeemed.

The savings plan or combination you select should be evaluated on the basis of yield or rate of return, compounding inflation, and tax considerations. The **rate of return** is the percentage of increase in the value of your savings from earned interest. **Compounding** refers to interest earned on previously earned interest. Each time interest is added to your savings total, the new interest is computed on this total amount. The more frequent the compounding, the higher the rate of return. Exhibit 21-5 illustrates this principle with daily, monthly, quarterly, and annual compounding. The daily compounding yield is 8.33 percent, while the annual compounding yield is 8 percent.

The rate of return you earn on the money you save should be compared with the inflation rate. If your savings account is earning 2 percent and inflation is 3.5 percent, you will experience a loss of buying power.

Taxes will also reduce the money you earn on savings. If you are in the 28 percent tax bracket, your after-tax return yield will be lower. For example, subtract your tax rate from 1.0, or 1.0 − .28 = .72. Suppose your savings account yield is 4 percent. In real terms, your after-tax return is .72 × .04, or 2.88 percent. Consider your after-tax real return yield in evaluating savings proposals.

Growing your own wealth is an exciting and challenging endeavor. The rule of "72," as explained in the Focus on the Future box, "The Rule of '72'," outlines a quick rule of thumb for estimating the rate of wealth growth.

21-4   BUYING/LEASING AND OPERATING A CAR

After purchasing a home, the most expensive expenditures you will make involve automobiles/SUVs/trucks.[4] Used cars, new cars, and leased cars all involve a process of making financial decisions. We will focus on new or leased cars in our discussion. The first necessary step in this process is to acquire new car information. *Edmunds New Car Prices* is a book that provides information on a dealer's cost. *Consumer Reports* also provides valuable new cost data.

Of course you want to get the best deal possible. Some experts believe that the best time to purchase a new car is at the end of the month in the winter or spring when auto

Money Market Accounts
Deposits that pay interest rates very competitive with those paid on other short-term investments; some allow a limited number of checks to be written in amounts over $500.

U.S. Savings Bonds   Bonds issued by the U.S. government. The money paid for the bond helps pay to finance the United States borrowing needs.

Rate of Return   The dollar value of the interest earned or dividend received divided by the market value of the security.

Compounding   Refers to a type of ever-increasing interest payment; that is, money invested in interest-bearing accounts or other instruments earns a specific amount (interest). If that interest is reinvested rather than removed from the account, subsequent interest payments are higher.

4. Remar Sutton, *Don't Get Taken Every Time* (New York: Penguin, 2001).

FOCUS ON THE FUTURE

The Rule of "72"

Growing money fast and faster—this sounds like a great idea. The rule of "72" is a quick tip formula that will help you learn about money growth. Using it, you can figure out how many years it will take for a sum of money to double its value using compound interest. It works for accruing interest, debts, and savings plans.

Suppose you had $40,000 and placed it in a savings account earning 4 percent compound interest. Divide 72 by 4, and you find out that it will take eighteen years to grow your $40,00 to $80,000. Suppose you found an account that paid 6 percent compound interest. In this case you would have your $80,00 in twelve years. Of course, we are assuming you never added a penny to the original $40,000.

sales are typically slow (see the Focus on Technology box, "Internet Resources," for informative websites regarding vehicles).

21-4a The Price Decision

Price bargaining is still the preferred method of many buyers. If this is what you prefer, gather as much information as possible. The closer your final drive-out price is to the dealer's cost, the better the deal you have negotiated. Don't focus at all on sticker price. It is the dealer's cost number that you must research.

To prevent excessive haggling, do not mention a trade-in vehicle until you have focused on the cost or you are asked. Then determine how much you can receive for your trade-in vehicle. Do not answer the sales technique question: "How much do you want to pay?" You can't provide a proper answer.

A growing number of new car dealers use no bargaining sales techniques; that is, the price is presented to the customer for a yes or no decision. This eliminates the back-and-forth haggling. There are also car buying firms. These firms charge a fee and can help you purchase a new car for a small amount, $100 to $300, over the dealer's cost.

21-4b Leasing a Car

About 20 percent of all new cars are leased. Federal tax laws eliminated deductions for consumer loan interest and sales tax, which immediately made leasing more attractive. **Leasing** is a contractual agreement that requires monthly payments for the use of the car over a set period of generally three or four years. At the end of the lease period, the car is usually returned to the leasing company.

Leasing A cost-effective technique whereby companies pay monthly for assets used in business without taking ownership of those assets.

Advantages

Leasing includes the following advantages:

- Individuals who lease make only a small cash deposit, which is about two or three monthly payments.
- Monthly lease payments are usually lower than monthly financing payments.
- Lease records and amounts are kept up to date for tax reporting purposes.

FOCUS ON TECHNOLOGY

Internet Resources

The Internet has a wealth of information on car specifications, prices, financing, and leasing programs. Some of the exceptional websites include:

www.caranddriver.com
www.kbb.com
www.carfinance.com
www.leasesource.com
www.carsafety.com

Disadvantages

The disadvantages of leasing include the following:

- Individuals who lease pay additional costs for extra mileage, repairs, or returning a car before the lease term ends.
- The vehicle is not owned.
- You must qualify to become a lessee.
- Lease agreements are not typically consumer friendly and need to be closely examined.

21-4c Financial Factors of Leasing

A recommended guideline for evaluating the lease versus buy decision is referred to as the "2 percent rule." A three-year, no-money-down lease may be a good deal if the monthly payment is 2 percent or less of the new car's retail price. This and other aspects of the lease agreement should be carefully reviewed.

The lease versus buy worksheet shown in Exhibit 21-6 needs to be completed to examine the financial aspects closely.

When examining the lease versus buy worksheet data and the lease agreement, be sure to know the full cost of the obligation. Compare the monthly payments and other terms of at least three leasing companies. After choosing the leasing company you prefer, compare the buying versus the leasing costs one last time by using the financial calculation form displayed in Exhibit 21-7 on page 563.

21-4d Car Costs

You need to consider a number of outflow items when examining new car purchases or leasing. These costs can be fixed, such as depreciation, the interest on a loan, insurance, taxes fees, and license charges. For example, a new car depreciates about 50 percent during the first two years of an expected five-year life.

There are also variable operating costs for gasoline and oil, tires, maintenance and repairs, and parking and toll fees. How much, where, and how you drive will impact these costs. It would be wise to keep good records of your fixed and variable costs so that in the future when car decisions are being made, you have an ability to include them in the decision-making process.

EXHIBIT 21-6

Lease versus Buy Worksheet

Cost to Purchase

Cost of Vehicle and Extras

a. Purchase price	$_____	
b. License and fees	$_____	
c. Options	$_____	
d. Sales tax	$_____	
e. Total cost of vehicle (add a–d)		$_____

Down Payment

f. Cash down	$_____	
g. Rebate (if any)	$_____	
h. Net trade-in value	$_____	
i. Total down payment (add f–h)		$_____

Terms of Financing

j. Term of loan in months _____ × monthly payment

Total cost to purchase (e + i + j) $_____

Cost to Lease

Cost of Vehicle and Extras

a. Capitalized cost of vehicle	$_____	
b. License and fees	$_____	
c. Options	$_____	
d. Upfront sales tax	$_____	
e. Total cost of vehicle (add a–d)		$_____

Down Payment

f. Cash down	$_____	
g. Rebate	$_____	
h. Net trade-in (if any)	$_____	
i. Upfront sales tax	$_____	
j. Security deposit (may be refundable)	$_____	
k. First/last monthly payment	$_____	
l. Total down payment (add f–k)		$_____

Lease Terms

m. Term of lease in months _____ × monthly payment (including tax)		$_____
n. Residual purchase payment		$_____
o. Sales tax exemption on trade-in		($_____)
Total cost to lease (e + l + m + n − o)		$_____

Source: Washington State Attorney General at http://www.wa.gov/ago/CPD/WRKSHEET.html.

21-5 INSURANCE

The word *insurance* triggers some confusion in many individuals. Insurance is something that can provide protection and is a part of risk management. There are many different kinds of insurance, and they cost money. We are subject to risks in life, in the home, and in our automobiles. Evaluating the alternative ways to cope with these risks is complicated and time-consuming.[5]

5. Michael Crouhy, Robert Mark, and Dan Galai, *Risk Management* (New York: McGraw-Hill, 2000).

EXHIBIT 21-7   **Financial Calculation: Buying versus Leasing an Automobile**

Purchase Costs	Example	Your Figures	Leasing Costs	Example	Your Figures
Total vehicle cost, including sales tax ($20,000)			Security deposit ($300)		
Down payment (or full amount if paying cash)	$7,000	$_____	Monthly lease payments: $300 x 48-month length of lease	$14,400	$_____
Monthly loan payment: $336 x 48-month length of financing (this item is zero if vehicle is not financed)	16,128	_____	Opportunity cost of security deposit: $300 security deposit x 4 years x 6 percent	72	_____
Opportunity cost of down payment (or total cost of the vehicle if it is bought for cash): $2,000 x 4 years of financing/ownership x 6 percent	480	_____	End-of-lease charges (if applicable)*	1,500	_____
			Total cost of lease	$15,972	_____
Less: Estimated value of vehicle at end of loan term/ownership period	23,000	_____	* With a closed-end lease, charges for extra mileage or excessive wear and tear; with an open-end lease, end-of-lease payment if appraised value is less than estimated ending value.		
Total cost to buy	$15,608	_____			

For commercial property and casualty insurers, the World Trade Center attack on September 11, 2001, is called an "extreme event." Insured losses are expected to be between $30 billion to $70 billion. The entire commercial property and casualty insurance industry has only about $300 billion in capital.[6] After September 11, the premiums that insurers could charge skyrocketed. The fact that terrorism and fear are a part of the insurance equation is and has been a reality. Since risks have increased, insurance companies can demand higher prices for protection. This is how insurance protection and payments work in all segments of the industry.

21-5a   Insurance Terminology

A *speculative* risk is an uncertain situation in which you are faced with a gain or a loss. You cannot obtain insurance for this type of risk. For example, the baseball you caught at a New York Mets game might increase or decrease in value over the years. You can only buy insurance for a *nonspeculative* risk situation. That is, an owner can insure her New Orleans home against the possibility of loss from a flood.

Insurance policies use the words *risk, peril,* and *hazard*. **Risk** is the uncertainty of loss you may incur due to a peril. A **peril** is anything that can cause a loss, such as a flood or fire. A **hazard** increases the probability that a peril will result in a loss. You would be creating a hazard if you stored filled gasoline cans next to a hot water heater in your attic.

Underwriting is the process of evaluating the risks involved and determining the price of coverage the insurance company is willing to provide. Insurance companies are not required to insure you.

The premium is the periodic payment you make to purchase and maintain insurance. You and others pay premiums to transfer the risk of uncertain loss to the insurance company.

21-5b   Buying Insurance

Agents represent insurance companies and sell policies—independent agents often represent several companies, while exclusive agents represent a single company. Brokers

Risk   The possibility of suffering an injury or loss.

Peril   Describes a specific contingency that may cause a loss.

Hazard   A condition that exists that either increases the chance for loss from particular perils or tends to make the loss more severe once the peril has occurred.

Underwriting   Includes all activities necessary to select risks offered to the insurer in such a manner that general company objectives are fulfilled; the main objective is to see that the applicant accepted will not have a loss experience that is very different from that assumed when the rates were formulated.

6. Carol J. Loomis, "Insurance After 9/11," *Fortune*, June 10, 2002, pp. 160–163.

represent the buyers of insurance. A broker evaluates several policies to find the best for the client.

Agents are licensed by the state. They must pass exams regularly. Two of the more rigorous set of credentials are the Chartered Life Underwriters (CLU) and the Chartered Property and Casualty Underwriter (CPCU). The CLU specializes in life insurance and must pass a number of examinations. The CPCU is credentialed to sell property and casualty insurance.

21-5c Life Insurance

Life insurance is designed to protect someone who depends on you from financial losses caused by your death. It could be a spouse, child, or relative. The proceeds received from life insurance are used to:

- Provide financial resources to support children
- Provide a retirement income
- Pay off a home mortgage at the time of death
- Provide savings surplus
- Provide an education fund for survivors

If your death would cause financial stress for someone or your family, you need to consider purchasing life insurance. What type of life insurance policy is needed depends on how much you can pay, what income you or your spouse need at retirement, and how much money you believe your dependents should have if you die.

One method to estimate your insurance needs is to assume your family will need 70 percent of your salary for at least seven years. Thus, an example of insurance need estimating would be:

$$\$40,000 \times 7 = \$280,000 \times .7 = \$196,000.$$

You may need more than $196,000 if you have a large family or number of dependents.

21-5d Types of Life Insurance

Term Insurance Life insurance that covers an individual for a specified number of years but has no value when the term is over.

Whole Life Insurance Provides a combination of insurance and savings and stays in force for the life of the insured.

Term insurance is protection for a specified period of time, such as ten, fifteen, or twenty years. A term policy pays a benefit only if you die during the period it covers. It is also referred to as temporary life insurance.

The most common type of permanent life insurance is the **whole life insurance** policy or straight life policy. You pay a premium each year as long as you live. In return, the insurance company pays a specific amount to the beneficiary when you die. The amount of your premium depends primarily on the age at which you purchase the policy.

Whole life policies have what is called cash value. This is an amount that increases over the years, which you receive if you give up the insurance.

A type of whole life policy is the *limited payment* policy. You would pay premiums for a set period of time, such as twenty years. The policy becomes "paid up," and you are insured for life. At the time of death, the insurance company would pay the face value of the policy. Since the payment period is more limited than it is in the typical whole life policy, the annual premium is higher.

The *adjustable life* insurance policy is one that can be adjusted as needs change. This type of policy combines the concepts of term insurance and investment.

A comparison of the features of a number of temporary and permanent insurance coverages is presented in Exhibit 21-8.

Before purchasing life insurance check with a number of companies and perform your own comparative analysis.[7] Find the policy that fits your needs.

---

7. Ben G. Baldwin, *New Life Insurance Investment Advisor: Achieving Financial Security for You and Your Family Through Today's Insurance Products* (New York: McGraw-Hill, 2001).

EXHIBIT 21-8   **Comparison of Term, Whole Life, Universal Life, and Variable Life Insurance**

	Type of Policy	Period Covered	Cash Value	Insurance Protection	Premium	Coverage	Comments
Temporary	**Term**						
	Level	For a stated number of years, such as 1, 5, 20	None	High	Stays the same with renewal	Stays the same	Pure insurance coverage
	Decreasing	For a stated number of years, such as 1, 5, 20	None	High	Stays the same	Decreases	Least expensive type of insurance
Permanent	**Whole Life**						Part insurance, part savings
	Straight	Whole life	Low	Moderate	Stays the same	Stays the same	
	Limited Payment	Whole life	Low	Moderate	Stays the same	Stays the same	Paid up after a certain number of years
	Universal Life	Varies	Low to high	Low to high	Varies	Varies	Combines renewable term insurance with a savings account paying market interest rates
	Variable Life	Varies	Low to high	Low to high	Varies	Varies	Part insurance, part investments in stock, bond, or money market funds

21-5e Health Insurance

The costs of health care and medical insurance are annually increasing. Visiting a doctor is now a $50 to $100 expenditure. The daily rate for hospital care is generally more than $800 per day. As medical costs increase insurance premiums have kept pace.

Fee-For-Service

An insurance contract between an insurance company and you enables you to obtain medical care for illnesses and injury. **Fee-for-service health insurance** in the form of an indemnity policy will pay a fixed sum for services. You would submit claims to the insurance company requesting payment and receive a fixed sum for the treatment received.

Standard fee-for-service coverage includes basic coverage for hospital stays, physician visits, and surgical expenses. Some plans also include, for a higher premium, major medical coverage for extraordinary expenses for serious medical problems. Typically, there is a deductible threshold or an amount you would pay before the insurance company begins to pay. For example, a $400 deductible means that you would pay the first $500 in a calendar year and then the insurance company would pay.

Often fee-for-service health insurance has a stop-loss cap or a limit that you would pay in a year. The level may be $5,000 or $10,000. Once you have incurred the stop-loss cap, the insurance company would cover any additional costs.

Fee-for-Service Health Insurance   Reimbursement for physicians for the amount of services provided.

Managed Care Insurance

Managed care insurance is between the insured and the organization of health care providers.[8] **Health maintenance organizations (HMOs)** are a group of health care providers such as the Kaiser Foundation, which owns hospitals, clinics, and other care facilities. An HMO subscriber pays a monthly premium and receives all required care at no cost or only a minimal additional cost.

A **preferred provider organization (PPO)** is a managed care organization that provides a degree of freedom of choice. The PPO contracts with hospitals and physicians to provide health care to PPO subscribers. The care providers agree to the PPO set fees for services.

2 ☞

Managed Care Insurance
Provisions made to control costs of health care, making high-quality health care available at an affordable price.

Health Maintenance Organizations (HMOs)
Organizations that provide extensive medical care and services for members, based on a prepared monthly fee.

Preferred Provider Organization (PPO) A form of health care coverage that offers employers reduced premiums; employees must choose physicians and hospitals from the PPO's list of approved providers.

21-5f Home and Personal Property Insurance

Your home and personal belongings make up most of your financial assets. Thus, property insurance that covers the building, living expenses (e.g., in case of fire), and personal property are important. Keeping an inventory list of property items in each room is important. Videos and photographs are also valuable to show the value of property items.

A home owner also faces the possible financial loss due to injuries to others or damage to property for which you are responsible. For example, a house guest may fall and break a leg in your foyer or a spark from your lawn mower may set a neighbor's yard, fence, and, eventually, roof on fire. A home owner's policy can provide personal liability coverage and you can, for a higher premium, receive extended medical and liability coverage.

Determination of the amount of home owner's insurance to have should include consideration of the replacement cost of the house, the value of the contents, the liability coverage, and protection for special items such as antiques, jewelry, and art work.

21-5g Automobile Insurance

Automobile insurance varies from state to state. There are, however, a number of common forms of coverage: bodily, injury liability, property damage liability, medical payments, uninsured or underinsured motorist, collision, comprehensive, and miscellaneous. Most states require that you have some level of bodily injury liability and property damage liability protection. Since the state requirements are usually low, you are still exposed to risk if you are in an accident.

Difficulties and the excessive costs of settling claims for medical expenses and personal injuries resulted in no-fault insurance. Under this type of insurance, the driver in an accident collects medical expenses, lost wages, and other expenses from his or her own insurance company. Some no-fault states set a limit on the amount that can be collected.

Rates and service vary among companies providing automobile insurance. Examine www.insuremarket.com to compare rates. This website allows you to receive premium and coverage quotes for automobile, term, home owner's, renter's, and health insurance.

21-6 RETIREMENT PLANNING

Why should I even think about retirement? is a common question asked by people of all ages that is usually laughed at and answered, "No reason to think about it now; I'll think about it later!" The earlier you start retirement planning, however, the better off you will be. Retirement is a concept that means different things to different people.[9] Whatever it means, it will somehow involve financial resources, financial decisions, and quality of life.

Most people use a combination of financial resources to maintain a desired standard of living when they retire (work part-time, quit working completely, work on a contract/project basis, become a volunteer).

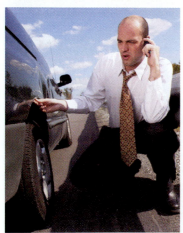

8. William M. Shernoff, *Fight Back and Win: How to Get HMOs and Health Insurance to Pay Up* (New York: Boardman Books, 1999).

9. Henry K. Hebeler, *J.K. Lasser's Your Winning Retirement Plan* (New York: John Wiley, 2001).

21-6a Social Security

The Social Security Act was passed in 1930. You qualify to receive social security benefits by working for at least forty calendar quarters earning at least $600 per quarter. A nonworking spouse of a covered worker can receive benefits equal to 50 percent of the working spouse's benefit.

The amount you receive is based on how old you are. If a person was born before 1937, his or her retirement age is 65. Those born after 1937, say in 1944, have a retirement age of 66, since retirement age is increasing in two-month increments. Individuals can receive social security benefits at the age of 62, but they will forfeit some benefits.

A retiree who continues to work while drawing social security benefits may find the benefits reduced. An early retiree loses $1 in benefits for every $2 earned over the 2002 base amount of $30,000. For those age 70 or over, there is no reduction; you can earn any amount and still collect social security benefits.

You can check your social security account by contacting the Social Security Administration and asking for a Request for Earnings and Benefit Estimate Statement. The report will show the monthly benefit you can expect at the early retirement age of 62, your normal retirement age, and at age 70.

21-6b Medicare

As you age, Medicare will become a part of your life. Part A is the basic hospital coverage for up to 150 days. If you are 65 but are not drawing social security benefits, you will pay a monthly insurance premium.

Medicare Part B is supplementary insurance that pays for doctors, medical equipment, and outpatient services. It's optional for those who are eligible for Part A, but the covered individual must pay the monthly premium regardless of social security status. There is a yearly deductible of $100 and then Medicare pays 80 percent of the Medicare approved amount.

21-6c Employer Pension Plans

Most organizations have a pension plan. The employer contributes to the plan, and under some plans you will also make contributions. The majority of these plans are *defined contribution plans*. Under such a plan each person has an individual account. The plan specifies what the employer will contribute, but it does not promise a particular benefit amount.

In a *defined benefit plan*, a specific amount is promised to you at the normal retirement age. The employer's contribution is managed so that the funds promised will be available.

Some pension plans allow you to carry earned benefits from one employer's pension plan to another's when you change jobs. Determining whether your plan is portable is an important factor when considering job changes.

21-6d Individual Retirement Accounts

Individual Retirement Accounts (IRAs) Accounts that establish a trust or custodial account, which is a retirement savings plan; if you are under age 50 and have earned income, you can contribute up to $3,000 annually to an IRA; if you are under age 70.5 years old but over 50 and have earned income, you can contribute up to $3,500 annually.

Individual retirement accounts (IRAs) establish a trust or custodial account, which is a retirement savings plan.[10] If you are under age 50 years old and have earned income, you can contribute up to $3,000 annually to an IRA; if you are over 50 but under 70.5 and have earned income, you can contribute up to $3,500. Whether the contribution is tax deductible depends on your tax filing status, your income, and your participation in an employer-provided retirement plan.

The Roth IRA allows for a $3,500 annual contribution (reduced by the amount contributed to the traditional IRA) if you are over 50; $3,000 if you are under 50. Contributions are not tax deductible, but earnings accumulate tax-free.

A spousal IRA allows you to contribute up to $3,000 amount (for those under 50; $3,500, over 50) on behalf of your nonworking spouse if you file a joint tax return.

The education IRA allows individuals under certain income levels to contribute up to $500 per child under age 18. The contributions are not tax deductible, but they do provide tax-free distribution for education expenses.

When you retire, you can withdraw your IRA in a lump sum, withdraw it in installments over your life expectancy, or place it in an annuity that guarantees payments over your lifetime. An annuity is a financial contract written by an insurance company that provides you with a regular income. Generally, you receive the income monthly, often with payments designed to continue for as long as you live. The annuity can be immediate or deferred for a later date.

21-6e Salary Reduction Plans: 401(k) and 403(b)

401(k) A retirement investment account that allows tax-free gains offered by for-profit organizations.

403(b) A retirement investment account that allows tax-free gains offered by not-for-profit organizations.

Salary reduction plans include **401(k),** established by private employers, and **403(b),** established by educational, religious, or charitable organizations. You would have your salary reduced by the amount you contribute. You can contribute up to $11,000 in a 401(k) plan and the lesser of 25 percent of compensation or $9,500 in a 403(b) plan.[11]

The money is deposited into a tax-deferred account and invested by the employer. Employers can provide a number of investment options for the employee to choose. Some employers have a range of investment choices, such as money market funds, income mutual funds, annuity contracts, and stocks. Each individual controls the investment decision making. You have the responsibility for growing your own nest egg.

Sometimes employees make poor investment choices and end up with no nest egg or less money than they had hoped to accumulate for retirement. Employers can protect themselves from distraught and legally inclined employees by complying with Section 404(c) of the Employee Income Security Act (ERISA). By providing at least three investment choices and investment education for employees, there is a lesser chance that an employee can sue and win because he or she lost money in the salary reduction plan.

21-6f Keogh Plans

Keogh Plans Self-employment retirement plans that allow the business owner to invest money and enjoy tax-free gains until retirement.

Keogh plans allow self-employed individuals to make tax-deductible contributions to a retirement plan. Anyone who has self-employed income qualifies for a Keogh plan. This plan is a defined contribution plan. It allows a maximum contribution of 15 percent of profits, but not exceeding $30,000.

Any bank, brokerage firm, or mutual fund company will allow you to set up a Keogh fund. These institutions have an already approved IRS model to use.

---

10. Neil Drowning, *The New IRAs and How to Make Them Work for You* (Chicago: Dearborn Trade, 2002).

11. Steven J. Franz, Joan C. McDonagh, and John Michael Maier, *401(K) Answer Book: 2002* (New York: Aspen Publishers, 2001).

FOCUS ON CAREERS

Certified Financial Planner

Have you considered a career in financial planning? Financial planners are trained and can be licensed as certified financial planners (CFP) to analyze and provide advice to clients on income tax management, employee benefits, retirement planning, and estate planning.

Certified financial planner licensees must meet the initial certification and relicensing requirements. Course examinations, experience, and complying with a code of ethics must be met. Also, prior to certification, a candidate for the CFP designation must show evidence of having worked for three years in a financial-planning-related position for compensation. Not all individuals who call themselves CFPs are CFP licensees.

According to surveys, the average earnings of a CFP licensee are about $67,000 per year. Some successful CFPs earn well in excess of $100,000 annually. CFPs can be paid fees, fees and commissions, commissions, or salaries. However earnings are made, CFPs must disclose to their clients how they are paid.

After completing the CFP certification process, you must continue to comply with the CFP board's ethical standards. You must also fulfill a continuing education requirement every two years.

3 ☞ The place to receive more information about a career as a CFP is the Certified Financial Planner Board of Standards in Denver. If you are not interested in a career but would like to consider hiring a CFP, this Board of Standards is an excellent place to start.

21-7 FINAL MESSAGE

Your financial health and well-being is up to you. If there is a major message to learn from this chapter's discussion, it is to "spend less than you earn and start planning now for your retirement." Although this is a simple message, most people do not spend less, and they put off retirement planning until much later than they should.

We humbly recommend three action steps:

1. Determine where you are financially and keep track of your inflow and outflow.
2. Reduce or eliminate all of your debt and do not incur debt.
3. Take control of your retirement planning immediately.

Even if you are fortunate to have a financial planning support system (e.g., experts in financial planning), you are the responsible party. The expert will not have to face financial circumstances that have your name attached. By staying involved in all personal finance matters, you can very likely enjoy a positive quality of life in terms of financial decisions and consequences. The Focus on Careers box, "Certified Financial Planner," discusses the financial planner's work and career.

SUGGESTED WEBSITES

Note: These websites were functional when we went to press. Please access the online text for the most up-to-date URLs.

1. www.consumerreports.org
2. www.kaiserpermanente.org
3. www.cfg-board.org
4. www.microsoft.com/money
5. www.quicken.com

SUMMARY OF LEARNING OBJECTIVES

1. *Explain the six steps in a personal finance planning process.*   The six-step approach starts with taking an inventory of your current situation—inflow and outflow of money. Next you need to establish realistic and meaningful financial goals. Then you must identify possible courses of action or next steps. Next each course of action and possible consequences should be evaluated. Step 5 involves creating and executing a well-designed and achievable financial plan. Last, but certainly important, is the monitoring and evaluation step. Each step fits into a plan to help you create personal wealth.

2. *Describe the advantages and disadvantages of leasing a car.* Car leasing is growing in popularity. The reasons for its growth include only having to make a small cash deposit, having monthly lease payments that are usually lower than monthly financing payments, and having accurate records of all transactions for tax reporting purposes. A few disadvantages of leasing include additional costs for extra mileage, repairs, or returning the car before the lease term expires.

3. *Identify the type of life, health, and home protection insurance policies that are available.*   Exhibit 21-8 presents a concise picture of the different types of life insurance polices such as term, whole life, universal life, and variable life. Health insurance can be fee-for-service or managed care. Home and personal property insurance coverage are available.

4. *Explain how a Keogh plan differs from a personal savings account.* A Keogh plan is available to self-employed individuals who make tax-deductible contributions to this type of retirement plan. It allows a maximum contribution of 15 percent of profits, but not exceeding $30,000. A personal savings account can be set up by any individual and has no limit. Accounts of $100,000 or less are insured by the Federal Deposit Insurance Corporation.

5. *Define the meaning of fee-for-service health insurance.*   This is an insurance contract between an insurance company and a person that pays a fixed sum for each medical service. Coverage includes basic coverage for hospital stays, physician visits, and surgical expenses. Often this type of insurance has a stop-loss cap or a limit that a person would pay in a year. Once the limit is reached the insurance company covers any additional health care costs.

6. *Describe why the careful monitoring of your cash inflow and cash out-flow is an important responsibility.*   Knowing, controlling, and planning for inflows and outflows is a personal responsibility. Allowing outflows to exceed inflows can result in debt, bankruptcy, or poor credit ratings. Each person is responsible for his or her state of financial affairs. The start of this responsibility is in the inflow versus outflow equation.

7. *Provide an analysis of retirement planning and the role you must play in preparing to retire.*   It's never too soon to start preparing for retirement. Social security payments to retirees are not sufficient to cover total living expenses. Pensions, investments, and other inflows of money need to be entered into the retirement plan. Even if you use a financial planner you must be involved in the process. Your needs, wants, nest egg, and quality of life are each impacted by your plan.

KEY TERMS

certificates of deposit (CDs) (p. 557)
compounding (p. 559)
fee-for-service health insurance (p. 565)
401(k) (p. 568)
403(b) (p. 568)
hazard (p. 563)
health maintenance organizations
   (HMOs) (p. 566)
individual retirement accounts (IRAs) (p. 568)

interest-earning checking accounts (p. 557)
Keogh plans (p. 568)
leasing (p. 560)
managed care insurance (p. 566)
money market accounts (p. 559)
peril (p. 563)
preferred provider organization
   (PPO) (p. 566)
rate of return (p. 559)

risk (p. 563)
savings accounts (p. 557)
term insurance (p. 564)
underwriting (p. 563)
U.S. savings bonds (p. 559)
whole life insurance (p. 564)

QUESTIONS FOR DISCUSSION AND REVIEW

1. Explain the difference between a personal finance budget and a personal cash flow statement.

2. How well do you really know your financial spending patterns? Prepare a monthly spending profile based on only your memory. Next prepare an actual monthly spending profile based on receipts and records. How accurate is your memory?

3. What market factors and conditions influence the price of homes, apartments, lofts, and condos in your area?

4. Why was the Federal Deposit Insurance Corporation (FDIC) created?

5. What risks do you face if you do not have any health insurance coverage?

6. Why should you comparison shop when evaluating what type of life insurance policy to purchase?

7. Why is it difficult to get people to think about retirement planning?

8. Does a Keogh plan differ from an IRA account? How?

9. Establish three specific and realistic financial goals for yourself for the next six-month period. How will you monitor your progress in accomplishing these three goals?

10. Microsoft Money and Quicken offer financial planning soft-ware. What value could you receive from using a software program such as these? Visit the Internet locations of these two software packages before responding.   4, 5

END-OF-CHAPTER QUESTIONS

1. Regular savings accounts are generally easy to open but have low interest returns.   **T** or **F**
2. About 50 percent of all new cars are leased.   **T** or **F**
3. One method of estimating your life insurance needs is to assume that your family will need 70 percent of your salary for at least seven years.   **T** or **F**
4. Under no-fault insurance, the driver in an accident collects medical expenses, lost wages, and other expenses from his or her own insurance company.   **T** or **F**
5. If you choose to begin collecting social security benefits at the age of 62 rather than 65, you will forfeit some benefits.   **T** or **F**
6. When you retire, you can withdraw your IRA in a lump sum.   **T** or **F**
7. The *rule of 52* provides a quick way to figure out how many years it will take for a sum of money to double using compound interest.   **T** or **F**
8. Insurance companies are required by law to insure you.   **T** or **F**
9. Health maintenance organizations are _____ providers.
   a. company-sponsored
   b. a group of health care
   c. tax-deductible
   d. nonprofit government
10. _____ refers to interest earned on previously earned interest.
   a. Rate of return
   b. Compounding
   c. Money market
   d. Negotiable orders
11. A _____ is anything that can cause a loss, such as a flood or fire.
   a. risk
   b. peril
   c. hazard
12. A new car depreciates about _____ during the first two years of an expected five-year life.
   a. 20 percent
   b. 30 percent
   c. 50 percent
   d. 75 percent
13. After purchasing a home, the most expensive expenditure generally made involves _____.
   a. automobiles/SUVs/trucks
   b. furniture
   c. electronic equipment
   d. travel
14. A _____ is a savings account that requires a minimum balance and has earnings based on market interest rates.
   a. CD
   b. regular savings account
   c. savings bond
   d. money market account
15. The first step in managing your personal finances is to _____ .
   a. determine your present financial situation
   b. analyze your financial values and goals
   c. develop a set of possible actions
   d. evaluate each course of action

INTERNET EXERCISE

Financial Planning

The importance of planning your financial future should never be underestimated. Time moves quickly, and putting off correct and smart planning is difficult to make up.

The following websites are just a few of the numerous helpful financial-planning help sites:

www.personalwealth.com
www.financecenter.com
www.qfn.com
www.moneycentral.msn.com
www.kiplinger.com
www.bls.gov
www.moneyadvisor.com/calc

Visit these seven sites and become familiar with the data and information they have available. Based on what they have available and your understanding of the knowledge presented in this chapter, address the following:

1. Prepare your ten-year financial plan.
2. Prepare ten-year savings and investment strategy.
3. How will you monitor the progress you are making in your ten-year plan?

EXPERIENTIAL EXERCISE

Assessing Online Insurance Quotes

Activity

Students will visit three online quote services.

Directions

1. Review quotes for life, health, and home protection policies from the three insurance quote services.
2. How much difference is there in the lowest and highest quotes?
3. Why would there be differences in the quotes?
4. Prepare a two-page paper on your search and findings.
5. Submit the paper to the instructor for a review.

The instructor may call on you and others to present what was found.

BUSINESS APPLICATION

Growing a Nest Egg

Mike is a 29-year-old college grad who is worried about his financial solvency. His good friend Katie asked him what he was doing about planning for retirement. In a quick response Mike stated, "Nothing." Katie encouraged him to look at the type of nest egg he could build if he started at 29 to plan for retirement rather than waiting until he was 50.

Set up a 29-year-old versus a 50-year-old initiation of a retirement plan. What could the 29-year-old nest egg be like at 65, and what could the 50-year-old nest egg be? Use a contribution of $8,000 per year for both individuals.

Case

Banking Is Religiously Influenced in the Middle East

Banks in Canada, the United States, Spain, and Brazil pay interest on savings accounts. In the Middle East, however, banks provide a different concept of banking. Shamil Bank in Bahrain keeps the savings of customers but pays no interest. In Muslim states such as Bahrain the Koran dictates how banking is conducted. The Koran bans receiving or giving interest. Chapter 2, verse 278 of the Koran states: "O you who believe! Have fear of Allah and give up what remains of what is due to you of usury. . . . If you do not, then take notice of war from Allah and Messenger."

Customers in Bahrain, Saudi Arabia, and Quatar do not want to behave in a way that is contrary to the Koran. Shamil does not have what are referred to in this chapter as savings accounts. It has what is called a *mudarabah account*. Instead of earning fixed interest, savings are invested directly in a range of ventures such as real estate and construction. In Islam, money that is working provides profits that must be shared. In the Muslim world's financial systems, interest does not exist.

Spread across the Middle East are over 200 Islamic financial institutions: banks, mutual funds, mortgage companies, insurance companies, for which the Koran provides guidance.

Shamil Bank helps customers buy a car through a transaction known as *murabaha*, which is more distinct than mudarabah. A customer (Abdullah) identifies, say, a Toyota Corolla as the car of choice. Abdullah asks the bank to buy the car from a dealer for 3,600 dinar (about $9,500). At the same time he agrees to buy the car from Shamil for 4,000 dinar, to be paid in monthly installments over three years.

This transaction looks a lot like interest. The markup Shamil charges is very close to prevailing interest rates. But it is not according to bank officials. For example, any late fees Shamil collects must be donated to charity, and the bank cannot penalize a borrower who is genuinely out of money or broke.

Mortgages are out of reach for Abdullah. He started a house four years ago and it is unfinished. He stops construction until he is able to accumulate enough money.

The interest concept and how to deal with it were presented fourteen centuries ago. Stock options, junk bonds, futures contracts, credit cards and other modern-day concepts were unheard of. The golden era of the Islamic world was superceded by the domination of Western-style banking.

Questions for Discussion

1. Do you believe that the Islamic concept of interest is better than the traditional type of interest-producing accounts you probably use or search for when starting a savings account?
2. Is the Koran's teachings on interest compatible with the dominant economic systems of the world?
3. Is Abdullah's car dealing with the bank that different from taking out a bank loan to make a car purchase in the United States?

Source: Jerry Useem, "Banking on Allah," *Fortune*, June 10, 2002, pp. 23–24.

Appendix I
How to Prepare a Business Plan

A business plan is a formal document that helps a business leader determine the best way to achieve success. Every business should have a plan. Sometimes entrepreneurs will get by without a formal, written plan for a while. Things change fast, and individuals have to be nimble and responsive to the changing business environment. Nonetheless, most business-people will affirm the value of a written plan. Such a document not only provides strategic guidance as the business evolves, it also provides a point of measurement to determine whether it is growing and changing in a methodical way.

Most business plans contain sections that are fairly standard and cover the range of challenges a business faces. They also contain descriptive sections that help people outside the business understand the firm's products and services. Often, especially when fund-raising, businesses distribute their plans to outsiders. Since it's not always obvious when or if a business will need to seek external funds, it's a good idea for companies to maintain a current business plan. Although there are no hard and fast rules, it's generally a good idea for a business to revise its plan—or at least update it—every six months or so.

This brief introduction to the business plan provides an overview of the standard sections of a plan and the contents of each. It also provides some hints about how to obtain the research data needed to credibly write each section. The following business plan sections are standard, but they are not necessarily always arranged in the order that we have placed them. The exception is the Executive Summary, which is always the first section of the business plan.

SECTION 1 EXECUTIVE SUMMARY

It's often stated that the Executive Summary is the most important part of a business plan. This statement is made because investors who receive business plans get so many that they don't read past this section if it doesn't get them excited about the business. To make it even more challenging, the Executive Summary should generally be no longer than one or two pages. Therefore, the business plan author must include an entire plan's worth of content into a small space, and the business story must be told in an exciting and compelling manner. The Executive Summary should refer to the following:

- The products/services offered by the business
- The differentiating features of those products/services
- The size of the market in which the business participates
- The expertise of the management team

- The investment opportunity being offered
- The milestones already achieved
- The expected profitability of the company
- The anticipated exit strategy for investors

You may think of other things that should be included in the Executive Summary. Just remember, busy investors will rarely read more than a few pages of your plan, and they will not read past the Executive Summary if you don't get their attention.

SECTION 2 PRODUCT/SERVICE DESCRIPTION

This section should be descriptive of the products/services offered by the business. The description should include a thorough discussion of the features associated with the product/service and be appropriately technical. That is, the product description should convey relevant details about the product but shouldn't overwhelm the reader with technical jargon. However, if part of the firm's competitive advantage lies in a technical innovation, this should be described in appropriate detail without giving away trade secrets. If your business is primarily a service, the unique features of the service should be highlighted.

This section may also contain a comparative analysis of competitor products and their related feature sets. Of course, such an analysis should demonstrate clearly how your product/service is unique. Relevant information that might also be provided in this section includes:

- Product/service pricing
- Product lead times and life cycle
- How the product/service is used
- Materials in the product
- How product/service is delivered
- Product/service life cycle (i.e., how it is consumed)
- Possible substitutes in the market

SECTION 3 MARKET ANALYSIS

This section looks at the market in which the product or service will be sold. The primary issue to be addressed is the size of the target market, a figure that is often difficult to obtain. However, market size can be extrapolated from related information that is fairly easy to obtain. For example, if your product is a new type of automobile tire and your market is confined to the United States, you could obtain market size information by examining the sales of the major tire manufacturers. Firms such as Goodyear and Cooper Tire & Rubber are public companies and must file quarterly and annual reports. These reports are available on the Internet either from the firm's website or from www.Edgar-online.com. If you know a firm's sales, and you have information about its relative market share (which also may be included in the quarterly or annual filing), you can extrapolate the size of the market for tires.

The market analysis should also include information about the characteristics of the target market. This may include items such as:

- Buying habits of the customer
- Customer demand
- Degree to which customers must be educated about product/service
- Techniques for reaching the market
- Market life cycle (growing, shrinking, or flat)
- Geographic location of market
- Market demographics and psychographics

The market analysis tells potential investors the size of the market you are seeking and how your product/service meets the customer need. The analysis may also contain brief analyses of secondary markets. It also should elucidate whether customers are aware of their need, or whether the product/service will have to be pushed into the marketplace. Finally, the unique features of your product/service should be included in this section to build the perception that the business has competitive advantages.

SECTION 4   INDUSTRY ANALYSIS

This section is often confused with a market analysis by first-time business plan writers. The main difference in these sections centers on the drivers of change. In the market analysis, the main drivers of change are connected to customers, their tastes, and their buying habits. In the industry analysis, the main drivers are connected to other companies in the industry, government regulation, and foreign competition. For example, the tire industry has several major players in the United States and is subject to major foreign competition. Anyone interested in entering this market must understand the competitive forces within the industry itself, and the potential competitive reaction that may arise if and when

existing firms learn about your offering. Industry analyses generally include:

- Discussion of the major players in the industry
- Description of the various niches that are addressed
- Regulatory issues
- Sociological forces
- Technological forces
- Economic forces
- Political forces

In fact, a good memory device that is often used is that this section of the business plan is a STEP analysis (for Sociological, Technological, Economic, and Political forces).

SECTION 5   COMPETITIVE ANALYSIS

Although the competitors were mentioned in Section 4, they should be investigated more thoroughly in this section. This section should define direct and indirect competitors. Direct competitors are those firms in your industry that will be attempting to sell products/services to your target market. Indirect competitors are those firms who do not currently sell to your target market, but who may do so or who may have some part of your target market due to their brand recognition or quality. For example, a local upscale restaurant doesn't compete directly with McDonald's, but it may siphon off some of the business of a McDonald's without directly targeting the same market.

The leading direct competitors in the industry should be described independently with respect to the following:

- Relative market share
- Product/service features
- Strategies (niche, pricing, marketing)
- Possible response to competitive threats

In addition to direct competitors, indirect competitors should be listed and their possible incursions into your target market discussed. In general, less discussion of indirect competitors is necessary than of direct competitors. This discussion is primarily to assure investors that you are aware of potential market erosion by indirect competitors and have given some thought to their possible strategies and your responses.

SECTION 6   MARKETING STRATEGY

This section provides an outline for how your firm will market your product/service. Any product needs marketing to reach its customers. Often, entrepreneurs underestimate the difficulties and costs associated with building a brand and acquiring customers. Many of the dot-com companies of the 1990s underestimated their customer acquisition costs and soon used up all their venture money on glitzy and very expensive advertising and marketing campaigns. Companies can begin to get a handle on the possible costs of customer acquisition through test marketing, focus groups, and other techniques. Investors will be looking for any primary data that you may be able to provide that will confirm your assumptions about marketing techniques and costs. The business plan section on marketing strategy should include the following:

- Advertising strategies and likely media to be used
- Marketing budget
- Value proposition
- Warranties and/or guarantees
- Market entry strategies (e.g., free giveaways, discounts)

The marketing strategy will tell investors that you are aware of the challenges that you will face in creating awareness of your products/services and your brand. Every new business faces the difficult prospect of entering a marketplace awash with existing and competing brands. How consumers will come to be aware of your unique value proposition and associate it with your brand should be described in detail in this section.

SECTION 7 OPERATING PLAN

The operating plan should explain how the business functions. Every business has certain operations that are established to create value. The manner in which products/services are designed, delivered, and continuously improved should be the focus of this section. In addition, this section should focus on how the business will use information technology to manage and control the operation. Many business plans use a basic "value chain" to structure the operating plan discussion. The value chain provides a basic outline of both the direct operational and supporting divisions of the organization. Support divisions include such things as human resources, accounting, finance, and sales. Operational divisions include incoming logistics, manufacturing, warehousing, and so on. The operating plan should especially highlight any operational innovations that give the firm a competitive edge over the competition. Some items to include in the operating plan are as follows:

- A flow chart of how the products/services are provided

- An overview of any operational advantages that your firm has over competitors
- A description of suppliers and the nature of the relationship with them
- A description of alternative suppliers
- An overview of information technology that will be used to manage operations
- An overview of personnel policies

The operations plan should give investors confidence that you have thought through the details of providing your product/service and are prepared to deliver it consistently and reliably to customers.

SECTION 8 MANAGEMENT TEAM

This section highlights the management team and its qualifications for operating the venture. The section should clearly outline the roles various individuals will play in the organization. It should also clearly state the gaps that exist in the current management team and the plans that are in place for filling those gaps. A minor debate in business plan writing centers on whether a firm should reveal management gaps or keep them quiet. In general, most agree that it's better to acknowledge management gaps and demonstrate to potential investors that the firm is aware of its weaknesses. The argument is that it is better to acknowledge any weakness and outline a strategy for addressing it than it is to ignore it. Savvy investors will recognize a gap whether or not it's mentioned. They will be far more concerned about that gap if they believe that the firm is not aware of it. This section should highlight key managers, including:

- Their experience in the industry
- Their length of service in the industry
- Their experience in related industries/businesses
- Their educational background
- Other items that will highlight their business acumen, integrity, and stewardship of shareholder value

In addition, if external consultants and/or professional services are needed or used this should be specified in this section.

SECTION 9 FINANCIAL PRO FORMAS

This section of the business plan provides the financial details of many of the claims made in other sections of the business plan. References to market size, potential sales, costs, gross and net margins, and operational controls must be consistent with the data provided in the financial pro formas. In general, this section should include three to five years worth of financial pro formas, and any "actual" financial statements from existing operations (not more than the last two years). The financial statements to include in this section include:

- Personnel forecast
- Sales forecast
- Income statement
- Cash flow statement
- Balance sheet
- Capital expenditure budget

The details about how to prepare these various statements is beyond the scope of this appendix. However, they are essential elements of the business plan, and all managers should learn the techniques involved in preparing them. Anyone involved in running and managing a business or a business division should have an understanding of how these statements are derived and how they affect business decision making.

SAMPLE BUSINESS PLAN SECTIONS

Following are the Market Analysis, Industry Analysis, and Competitive Analysis sections of an actual business plan. The plan was written for a friendly corporate turnaround that took place in the summer of 2002. The name of the company for which the plan was written has been changed to a fictitious name; the names of the competitor companies, however, are actual.

MARKET ANALYSIS

Specialty Towers is involved in the design and manufacture of tubular steel towers for use in the transmission of electric energy and in telecommunications. With the build-out of telecommunications wireless networks during the 1990s, the demand for new tower construction in the telecommunications market has dropped significantly. Consequently, about 70 percent of Specialty's business in the near-term future will focus on the design and manufacture of transmission towers for the electric utility industry.

Specialty manufactures standard design SPC poles for transmission, subtransmission, and distribution of electric power. Specialty also manufactures substation dead-end structures designed and fabricated from tubular or rolled structural shapes. Specialty's tubular steel transmission towers are primarily used in urban areas. The tubular steel towers are considered aesthetically superior to the lattice steel towers, which are less expensive and predominate in rural areas. Thus, tubular steel transmission towers typically comprise only a fraction of the tower needs for most transmission projects. Tubular steel is also commonly used for short-run transmission projects, such as those that connect power generation or substation facilities to the grid.

This market analysis examines the near-term potential for sales in Specialty's two major markets: electric transmission towers, and telecommunication towers.

Electric Transmission Tower Market

In North America, the utility products sector experienced a lull in activity during the first quarter of 2002 as most utilities were awaiting the release of the U.S. government's energy bill in order to analyze and prioritize their investment schedules over the next year. At the end of the quarter, there was a strong increase in transmission project design and quotation activity. Although a solid increase in annual "replacement" market growth in steel distribution poles has developed, it is clear that the majority of utility investment in new overhead power lines will be in the light duty, H-frame, and custom, heavy-duty transmission product sectors.

Exhibit I-1 below shows the rolling nine-year forecast for transmission line expansion in the United States. With an estimated six to eight towers per transmission mile, the market for new transmission towers in the 2000–2009 period is from 45,000 to 61,000 units. Of these, approximately 20 percent will be tubular steel, making the market for new tubular towers between 9,000 and 12,200 units. Assuming a stable average price of $12,500 per tower, the dollar value of this market over the period is $113 million to $150 million. Thus, the annual new tubular steel market is between $9 and $12 million.

In addition to new transmission construction, analysts estimate that the pole replacement market for light duty and H-frame in North America will exceed $100 million annually for the next five to ten years. Given the hundreds of thousands of circuit miles of U.S. light duty/H-frame transmission, which exist today on wooden structures more than forty

EXHIBIT I-1　　**Rolling Nine-Year Forecast for Transmission Line Expansion—U.S.**

Period	Existing Transmission Circuit Miles	Planned Additions Circuit Miles	Planned Additions Existing Transmission %
1994–2003	150,093	10,400	7%
1995–2004	150,286	8,851	6%
1996–2005	153,782	6,818	4%
1997–2005	151,510	5,834	4%
1998–2007	150,225	5,587	4%
1999–2008	155,691	5,817	4%
2000–2009	157,810	7,572	5%

Source: David K. Owens, "Transmission: The Vital Link," Edison Electric Institute, International Financial Conference, February 27, 2001.

years old, and the virtual absence of tenders calling for wood replacements, analysts expect to see a very high conversion rate to steel.

Finally, Specialty also participates in markets for subtransmission and substation tubular steel poles and structures. Given the emphasis on new power generation and the constant development of new distribution markets, the demand for subtransmission and substation work is strong and should continue to be strong into the near future. Market size estimates for these types of specialized projects is in the $100–$150 million annual range.

In summary, Specialty participates in three highly related markets in the electric transmission space:

New tower market:	$113–150 million
Replacement tower market:	$100 million
Subtransmission and substation:	$100 million
Total	$313–350 million

Transmission Infrastructure Outlook

Between 1979 and 1989, transmission capacity increased slightly faster than did summer peak demand. However, during the subsequent decade, utilities added transmission capacity at a much lower rate than loads grew. The trends established during the 1990s are expected to persist through the next decade. According to one analyst, maintaining transmission adequacy at its current level might require an investment of about $56 billion during the present decade, roughly half that needed for new generation during the same period.[1]

The decline in construction of new transmission capacity has not yet caused major reliability problems because the industry has, for the time being at least, found substitutes. System operators are using improved data collection, communications, and computing systems to enable operation of the transmission network closer to its physical limits. Many new gas-fired generating units are being located close to load centers, reducing the need for new transmission. Finally, small-scale transmission investments (e.g., capacitor banks and line upgrades) provide sufficient capacity for a few more years.

The key obstacles to building new transmission lines are local opposition and the associated local and state regulatory/ approval processes. Although transmission increasingly serves regional needs, decisions on whether and where to site new facilities remain a state and local responsibility.

Another barrier to new transmission is the uncertainty facing utilities about the future returns on their investments. Responsibility for transmission is shifting from state regulators to the U.S. Federal Energy Regulatory Commission (FERC). Whether FERC will allow an adequate return on equity for transmission investments and whether it will approve pricing systems that provide financial incentives for efficient operation and expansion of transmission systems are not yet clear. As a consequence, many utilities are reluctant to invest in facilities with lifetimes of several decades when they do not know what the regulatory environment will be in a few years.

Although the nation faces a serious transmission-adequacy problem, possible solutions are at hand. Formation of large regional transmission organizations (RTOs), as proposed by FERC, would help rationalize transmission planning and investment. The large regional scope of an RTO and its clear separation from the financial interests of bulk-power market participants would strengthen the substance and credibility of its transmission plans.

Increased funding commitments by governments and utilities to both renew and/or develop their power line infrastructure systems has resulted in a major increase in the percentage of tenders for steel structures of light duty transmission and H-frame products. The market is clearly indicating preference for engineered material-based structures as well as a higher level of environmental consciousness.

---

1. E. Hirst and B. Kirby, Transmission Planning for a Restructuring U.S. Electricity Industry (Washington, DC: Edison Electric Institute, 2001).

INDUSTRY ANALYSIS

The United States does not have a national transmission grid. Instead, there are four integrated transmission grids serving North America: the Western Interconnection, the Eastern Interconnection, the Electric Reliability of Council of Texas, and the Province of Quebec. These regional grids themselves are international, encompassing the United States, Canada, and part of Mexico. Transactions among the four integrated transmission grids are very limited because they are interconnected at only a few locations through interties, so for all practical purposes they can be viewed as separate transmission grids. The four integrated transmission grids break down into a series of smaller regions, largely defined by transmission constraints.

Altogether, 204,000 miles of transmission lines in North America move power from the point of generation to where electricity is needed. There are 157,810 miles of transmission lines in the United States. Transmission grid expansions are expected to be slow over the next ten years, with additions totaling 7,000 miles.

Federal Oversight of Electricity Transmission

The Bush administration's National Energy Policy (NEP)[2] recognizes that the transmission system in the United States faces numerous problems, few of which have any short-term solutions. A lack of sufficient investment in new transmission projects has resulted in insufficient transmission capacity in a growing number of regions. The gap between demand for electricity and the investment in transmission is clear. As a result of these problems, the NEP specifically identifies certain areas of the country that may suffer from transmission-related price and reliability pressures. These regions include California, Long Island, the Great Lakes, the Southeast, and New England. To address these problems the NEP recommends that

- The secretary of energy develop legislation providing reliability enforcement by a self-regulatory organization, subject to FERC oversight;
- The secretary of energy work in a collaborative effort with federal, state, and local authorities to develop legislation to grant federal authority to obtain transmission right-of-ways;
- The secretary of energy identify transmission bottlenecks and measures to remove these bottlenecks, as well as to examine the benefits of establishing a national transmission grid;
- Federal utilities determine whether they can undertake necessary transmission expansions to relieve congestion, with particular emphasis on BPA, and, if additional financing is needed for BPA to undertake necessary transmission investment, that the administration seek an increase in BPA's borrowing authority.

The most significant recommendation regarding transmission involves the siting of new high voltage lines. The siting of natural gas pipelines and other interstate systems, such as highways and railroads, is a federal responsibility. Transmission siting, on the other hand, remains largely under state and local jurisdiction. Since the benefits of new transmission investments often accrue over a large region, state and local authorities often have little incentive to support such initiatives. The NEP recommends that federal authority over siting interstate transmission rights-of-way be granted through legislation. If enacted, federal siting authority may go a long way toward removing some of the most significant barriers facing new transmission investment.

Passing legislation that reduces states rights, in favor of greater federal authority over an issue as sensitive and visible as transmission may be difficult, due to state, as well as local, NIMBY sentiments. However, momentum has been building on this issue for some time, and should the initiative be proposed by a Republican president, a Republican Congress could be responsive. In terms of providing financial incentives for greater transmission investment, it is interesting that, for a Republican administration, the NEP relies heavily on government intervention and investment. For example, BPA and WAPA are directed to examine the use of federal funds to resolve transmission constraints in the west. In view of the current lack of federal transmission siting authority, this may have been viewed as the most expedient way in which to deal with the need for greater transmission investment, particularly in the west. However, more

---

2. Report of the National Energy Policy Group, May 2001.

support could have been given to the private sector to spur investment in the transmission system. For example, the NEP acknowledges FERC's willingness to consider innovative rates, and directs the secretary of energy to work with FERC to encourage the use of incentive rate-making proposals. But there are no general statements about the importance of private sector investment in creating a healthy transmission infrastructure; nor are there any tax breaks or other incentives (other than those related to rate making) to address the need for more investment. Indeed, the focus on the use of federal funds by federal power authorities to resolve transmission investment issues, in the west and elsewhere, may remove opportunities for private sector firms that also wish to invest in these markets.

Additional federal ownership of transmission lines may also present a greater barrier to the further development of large, regional for-profit transcos, which would act as regional transmission organizations (RTOs) in the west and elsewhere. The NEP encourages the Department of Energy (DOE) to expand its R&D budget, to identify research in select transmission-related fields, but again without any discussion of the need for private sector initiatives or incentives. To the extent that some technologies have already been identified but require additional work to be commercialized, tax incentives for private firms pursuing this work may be beneficial. The recommendation to allow greater access to federal lands to alleviate right-of-way issues surrounding some transmission constraint solutions is a step in the right direction, though it will only affect some transmission constrained areas. However, the achievement of this initiative may be hampered by environmental concerns over public land use issues.

Reliability of the electric grid is currently managed through the voluntary reliability standards, represented by participation in NERC and its regional councils. The NEP says there is consensus to change this approach and recommends that a self-regulatory organization with enforcement authority and FERC oversight be created. NERC and its expanding circle of stakeholders are close to agreement and implementation of the industry-enforcing system that is recommended. Thus, the recommendation to create a reliability organization under the jurisdiction of FERC is welcomed by many and may be achievable in the near term. Finally, while the policy contains significant federal government initiatives to address problems in the transmission sector and also alludes to market design problems in some regions, the NEP does not recommend that the FERC take any actions to standardize power market rules or RTO structures. Identifying industry best practices in these areas could be accomplished through the appointment of a bipartisan blue ribbon panel headed by a FERC commissioner. Such a mandate would refocus the FERC's role from that of a price regulator to that of a market manager, much like the SEC's role in financial markets. However, there are no such bold statements with regard to the role of the FERC.

COMPETITIVE ANALYSIS

There are a number of competitors in the steel pole industry. Many of these have migrated to steel pole products from related product lines, such as irrigation and steel tubing. Three or four main players must be considered leaders in the steel pole industry in North America:

- Valmont Industries, Inc., Valley, Nebraska
- Thomas & Betts, Inc., Memphis, Tennessee
- International Utility Structures, Inc., Calgary, Alberta
- Dis-Tran Steel

Each of these firms has diversified product lines, with significant market share in the steel utility tower industry. A number of other competitors have small shares of local or niche markets. These include:

- Newmark Infrastructure Solutions
- Summit Tower

Each of the preceding companies are examined briefly next:

Valmont Industries

Valmont began manufacturing steel pipe and tubing for irrigation purposes in 1959. From that beginning, the company saw an opportunity to not only manufacture pipe for its irrigation systems, but also to develop markets throughout the United States for original equipment manufactures (OEMs), steel service centers, and for use in both private and public projects.

In the 1960s, Valmont's development and use of high-speed, resistance welding for tubular products led directly to the manufacture of tapered tubes for outdoor lighting, traffic signals, and other applications. A production line was designed that continually cut, formed, and welded at high speeds and with very low labor requirements. Valmont expanded into the manufacture of large tubular structures for the electrical utility industry during the 1970s.

Net sales in the Poles segment increased 16 percent to $38 million for the first quarter 2002 from $32 million for the same period in 2001. The sales increase was attributable to continued strong sales in North America. Strong order flow from utility alliance partners, partly due to replace storm-damaged poles, and a strong sales backlog at the beginning of the year resulted in record quarterly sales of utility structures.

Thomas & Betts

Thomas & Betts Corporation is a manufacturer of connectors and components primarily for worldwide electrical markets. The company classifies its products into business segments that are organized around the market channels through which its products are sold: electrical, steel structures, communications and heating, ventilation, and air conditioning (HVAC). The majority of the corporation's products, especially those sold in the electrical segment, has region-specific standards and is sold mostly in North America or in other regions sharing North American electrical codes.

Sales for the Steel Structures segment increased to $140.6 million in 2001 from $121.9 million in 2000. Earnings for the Steel Structures segment increased from $10.2 million in 2000 to $18.2 million in 2001. Higher sales volumes for 2001 are due to added capacity and strong demand for infrastructure to support power grids. The 2000 earnings were significantly impacted by charges taken in that year while favorable product mix in 2001 boosted segment earnings.

Sales for the Communications segment decreased to $108.1 million in 2001 from $178.4 million in 2000 largely as a result of the depressed domestic market conditions in the cable TV (CATV) and telecom markets. Segment loss for 2001 was $10.2 million as compared to $25.6 million for 2000. The 2000 results were significantly impacted by charges taken in that year while 2001 segment results were positively affected by efforts made to reduce manufacturing and SG&A expenses to better match current demand levels.

Sales in the Steel Structures segment were $35.1 million for the first quarter, compared to $33.4 million in the year-ago period. Earnings in this segment were $3.9 million, up from the $3.5 million recorded in the first quarter 2001. Earnings for the first quarter 2002 were positively impacted by the absence of goodwill amortization. On a comparable basis as if goodwill amortization had not been recorded in the prior year, earnings of $3.9 million for the first quarter 2002 would have been relatively flat with $4.1 million in the prior year period.[3]

International Utility Structures, Inc. (IUSI)

IUSI commenced business in 1991 and continues to focus on the use and benefits of steel distribution poles as a viable alternative to historically dominating wood and concrete. In 1998, IUSI expanded its markets for steel distribution poles by acquiring Petitjean Industries, located in Troyes, France, for its strong global presence and reputation for quality. Petitjean is an international leader in the manufacture of lighting, transmission, and cellular structures and now includes distribution poles.

In the utility structure sector, global growth in distribution, transmission, and land-line telecommunications structures has resulted in an improved order book. IUSI's international Distripole backlog is now over 50,000 poles, all slated for delivery in the second half of calendar 2002. IUSI received orders for approximately $15 million of transmission products during the first quarter, also scheduled for delivery in calendar 2002, which represents a major increase over previous years' performances. Current utility projects under negotiation are expected to further increase IUSI's utility product shipment requirements over the balance of this calendar year.

For the second quarter of fiscal 2002, January 1, 2002, to March 31, 2002, IUSI reported sales of $20.0 million compared to $25.0 million for the same period last year, which included $3.6 million of sales from the Stainton Metal Company subsidiary ("Stainton"), which was sold in October 2001. For the six months ended March 31, 2002, IUSI reported sales of $42.5 million compared to $45.5 million for the same period last year, which included $6.4 million from Stainton. On a comparative basis, not including Stainton, IUSI increased its year to date sales compared to last year by 9 percent. This increase was primarily in the North American utility markets.

Dis-Tran Steel Pole, LLC

This Pineville, Louisiana, company is a secondary supplier and a direct competitor in the steel transmission pole market with Specialty. The firm specializes in engineering and manufacturing of tapered tubular steel substation structures and tapered transmission and communication poles. Dis-Tran Steel Pole is one of a number of companies in the Dis-Tran family, which includes:

- Dis-Tran Packaged Substations, LLC
- Dis-Tran Steel Fabrication, LLC
- Dis-Tran Wood Products, LLC
- Mid-State Supply Company
- Beta Engineering, LLC

Together, this family of companies provides a comprehensive set of products and services to the electric utility and telecommunications industries. Dis-Tran also maintains electrical, civil, and mechanical engineering capability for extended scope projects involving substation arrangement, grounding, surge protection, relaying and control, HVAC, station service, site planning, site drainage, outline plan and profile, line loadings, sag/tension, and so on.

3. Thomas & Betts, Form 10-Q, March 31, 2002.

Newmark Infrastructure Solutions

Newmark, formerly known as Sherman Utility Structures, has increased its offerings to become the only provider of spun concrete, tubular steel, and fiberglass-reinforced composite (FRC) poles. Since its beginning in 1983 Newmark has been delivering infrastructure solutions to the power delivery, wireless communications, lighting, and other industries.

Summit Manufacturing, LLC

Since 1988 Summit Manufacturing, based in West Hazelton, Pennsylvania, and Bessemer, Alabama, has provided the nation's communication, utility, lighting, and transportation industries with quality monopoles. Summit offers a broad range of products to meet changing demands. It uses an integrated approach—from quotation to design to manufacturing to delivery—to give customers a reliable turnkey source for their monopole needs. Summit's team of responsive, expert personnel is committed to offering unparalleled customer service, quality control, and comprehensive pricing. Summit Manufacturing designs and fabricates:

- Custom tubular steel poles
- Top-mount and colocate platforms and arms for monopoles, utility towers, and self-support towers
- Patented raise/lower systems for antennas, base stations, and other pole-mounted RF equipment
- Site concealment solutions

In August 2001, Summit announced a 20 percent reduction in force due to weakness in the telecommunications sector.

Appendix II

Career Planning and Management

Career planning and management is an individualized process. Each of us has a unique set of values, interests, and work and personal experiences. Understanding how this unique set of factors blends is an important part of career planning. But understanding the requirements of various jobs is also necessary so that your own personality and intellectual abilities can be matched with the job. Your career decisions will shape your lifestyle.

College students eventually have to find out how they fit into the spectrum of career choices available. The purpose of this appendix is to provide

- A few career basics and hints on self-assessment.
- Information on the mechanics of getting a job.

In his best-selling book *What Color Is Your Parachute?* (this is an excellent reference on careers that is updated annually by Ten Speed Press in Berkeley, California), Richard Bolles presents a clear and accurate picture of how employers prefer to fill job vacancies. The most- to the least-preferred methods are (1) hire from within, (2) hire a job candidate who offers proof, (3) use a search firm for higher-level jobs, (4) use an employment agency for lower-level jobs, (5) peruse resumes, and (6) look at candidates who come in through newspaper ads. Bolles states that typical job candidates complete the search cycle in reverse. That is, they start with numbers 6 and 5—the ads trigger the sending of a resume.

Since employers have mountains of unsolicited mail and e-mails, they use a winnowing process. Resumes are screened and the vast majority are eliminated. Even though this is how the process unfolds, most people still prepare a resume. If and when you do, make sure it is accurate, concise, clearly written, and designed properly. An example of an acceptable resume is presented later.

CAREER BASICS AND SELF-ANALYSIS

First, before thinking about specific career areas, sit back and spend time mulling over those things that you want from a career. Here are a few questions to consider:

- Do you want a job or a career? Do you want it to be personally satisfying, or are the financial rewards enough? How important is career advancement?
- Are the status and prestige associated with a career important to you?
- What about financial rewards?
- Do you have geographical preferences? What about living in a large versus a small city?
- What size employer would you prefer? Might this preference change later on?

Now, think about yourself for a minute.

- What education, experience, and skills do you have to offer?
- Are you quantitatively ("thing") oriented or qualitatively ("people") oriented, or do you enjoy both? Organizations have places for both types.
- What are your weak and strong points? How will they relate to your performance on the job?
- What kind of work is interesting to you?
- What kind of work do you like?
- What kind of work will make you feel worthwhile?

A personal evaluation of these and similar questions is a worthwhile exercise. These questions may help you develop a job or career identity.

You must take control of your self-analysis. Think in terms of what you can offer an employer. What skills do you have that can make a contribution to the employer that is noticed and measurable?

PROFESSIONAL HELP FOR SELF-ASSESSMENT

Professional counselors can help you decide which career path to take. Most high schools and colleges provide free counseling services in which trained professionals help students perform a realistic self-assessment.

Vocational tests are often used to verify one's self-analysis and to reveal any hidden personal characteristics. This information is then explained and interpreted by professional counselors. No one test or battery of tests can make a career choice for you. But tests can supplement the information you are reviewing as you consider career opportunities and personal characteristics. Your college placement office has counselors who can recommend which tests are most appropriate.

In addition, the counselor can help you with your self-assessment by providing publications discussing career opportunities. Some widely publicized and frequently used publications include

- College Placement Annual, College Placement Council, Inc., 62 Highland Avenue, Bethlehem, PA 18017 (215) 868-1421. Published annually. Provides information on current job openings in companies, as well as suggestions on preparing resumes and interviewing for jobs.

- Occupational Outlook Handbook, U.S. Department of Labor, Government Printing Office, Washington, DC (202) 783-3238. Published annually. Lists all major companies, with a brief description of job requirements, opportunities available, and future job prospects.

Self-assessment, help from a professional counselor, and career publications can provide the background information necessary to properly plan your career. But in the final analysis, you alone must make the career decision and seek appropriate job opportunities. A counselor, parent, or firm cannot make a career decision for you.

THE JOB SEARCH: A PLAN

In school, you prepare for examinations by organizing your notes and planning. In searching for a job, you also need to organize and plan. The first job after college can affect your entire career, so a plan is a must. Without a plan, you will lose valuable time and experience unnecessary frustration. There is no single best job-search plan, but there are some basic principles. Because your time is limited, you should use a systematic procedure to narrow the number of job possibilities.

When evaluating any particular career, you should consider some specific issues. As you think over the broad career options available, examine them with the following areas in mind:

- What are the qualifications for the job? Will you need more education or more experience?

- What is the financial situation? Is the salary reasonable? How are the benefits? What salary is likely in three to five years? Is there going to be a conflict between the value you place on money and your returns from this job?

- What are the opportunities for advancement? Do these appear to agree with your aspirations?

- What is the present supply and demand for this field and what might it be in the future?

- Will the job involve much travel? Is that desirable or undesirable? How mobile are you?

- What is the atmosphere associated with the job? Is it pressure-filled and demanding? Cooperative? Tranquil? Creative?

- Is this job something that you will be proud of? Does it fit your self-image?

- Is it work that you will enjoy? Is it in line with your goals and ethics? Will you be happy?

Within any given career choice, one faces a number of prospective employers. Each company offers different conditions, opportunities, and rewards to its employees. Here are some important questions to ask about the firms you are considering:

- Does the company have opportunities for a person with my skills, aptitudes, and goals?

- What are the promotion opportunities in the company?

- Does the company usually promote from within?

- What type of professional development is available for new employees?

- What kind of working environment exists within the company?

- What is the future growth potential for the company and the industry?

Answers to these kinds of questions will enable you to narrow the available job opportunities. Answers can be found in such sources as company annual reports, Standard and Poor's Corporation Records, and Dun and Bradstreet's Reference Book of Manufacturers. Another source is the company's employees. If you know some employees, ask them for firsthand information.

Most companies furnish brochures on career opportunities. These sources are impressive, but they often give a totally positive picture of the company. Consult your school's placement officer to learn more about each company and to determine the accuracy of the brochures.

Professional magazines, such as *HR Managing, Training and Industry, Human Resource Management,* and *Nation's Business,* often list vacancies. These advertisements are for recent graduates or people with work experience. If you are interested in a particular occupation, consulting the professional magazines in that functional area can be helpful. Specialized trade journals are also good sources for job leads. Even the yellow pages in phone directories are a helpful guide to companies operating in a particular area. Talk to family, friends, faculty members, and others who may know of job leads or people with pertinent information.

UTILIZING THE WEB

A large number of business, government, and nonprofit organizations are utilizing the Web to recruit employees. In addition, information about pursuing a career and searching for employment can be found on the Web.

Employer Sites

Are you interested in obtaining a position with a particular employer? Thousands of private, public, and nonprofit organizations utilize a portion of their websites to recruit employees. The "career," "employment," or "job" links located in the firm's site map and the director or home page of an organization's website can be used to learn about positions that the employers want to fill. The use of the Internet is increasing each year. Over 3 million job candidates are online each month searching, posting resumes, or chatting about careers, companies, and job vacancies. What is known now about the Internet and job searching is that it is a process that is slow and perhaps not as productive as the hype surrounding its value to job candidates. Thus, although the Internet is another dimension or technique for finding a job, do not rely solely on the Internet and do not be impressed with the numbers of resumes or job listings on any site. Some sites to visit include

www.tenspeed.com/parachute   www.espan. com
www.monster.com   www.jobweb.org
www.careermosaic.com   www.jobtrak.com
www.careerbuilder.com   www.jobengine.com.

In addition to providing the titles and brief descriptions of positions that they want to fill, the websites of employers can be an important resource in other ways. Such sites usually contain information about an organization's products or services, human resource policies, benefit programs, and recruitment contacts. Much of this information can be of help in determining whether you would want to apply for a position with an organization.

Job Listings

You don't have to limit your search to the sites of individual employers to find job openings on the Web. A great many business, government, and nonprofit organizations list positions that they want to fill on one or more of the many compilations of employment opportunities that are on the Web. America's Job Bank identifies about *one million openings* posted with state employment agencies. More than a quarter million job openings can be found on CareerPath and the Job Factory.

Management Recruiters

Many executive search firms have established websites. Some provide information about the managerial and professional positions that they are attempting to fill and/or solicit resumes from experience executives. Furtherestep, LAIcompass.com, and LeadersOnline are among the subsidiaries that management recruiters have established for the purpose of recruiting on the Web. You can obtain information about, as well as links to, executive search firms on such sites as the Recruiters Online Network and SearchBase

Resume Posting

You can make your qualifications known to a great many organizations by posting your resume on websites such as Career Mart (www.careermart.com) and JobOptions (www.joboptions.com). Employers and recruiters search electronically through such extensive compilations of resumes for "key words" that indicate that the qualifications of an individual may match the requirements for a position.

E-Mail Communications

E-mail can be used to inquire about employment opportunities, submit cover letters with resume attachments, and conduct follow-up correspondence with prospective employers. You also can use e-mail to supplement telephoning, meetings, and letter writing as means of establishing and maintaining networking contacts.

Search Assistance

A wealth of information and practical advice about searching for employment can be obtained on sites such as The Riley Guide (www.rileyguide.com) and *The Wall Street Journal* (www.wsj.com). This can include suggestions about finding job openings, networking techniques, preparing paper and electronic resumes, corresponding with employers, answering interview questions, and negotiating job offers.

Career Advice

Several websites furnish an extensive amount of career advice. This can include information about assessing personal aptitudes and interests, prerequisites for various careers, and the employment outlook and salary ranges for many occupations. Sites such as What Color Is Your Parachute? (www.jobhuntersbible.com) will furnish suggestions about searching for employment as well as links to other career and employment-related websites.

PERSONALIZING THROUGH A RESUME

You were cautioned earlier about placing total confidence in a resume as the way to get a job. Millions of resumes are floating around, so it is likely that even your best attempt will just be one more in a pile. That said, you will likely want to work up the best resume possible.

A *resume* is a written summary of who you are. It is a concise picture of you and your credentials for a job. A resume should highlight your qualifications, achievements, and career objectives. It should be designed to present you as an attractive candidate for a job.

There is no generally accepted format for a resume. Its purpose is to introduce you to the employer and to get you an interview. Few, if any, employers hire college graduates solely on the contents of a resume. In most cases, you can attract attention with a one-page resume. Longer resumes are for people who have had extensive professional experience.

Employers like resumes that read well and look attractive. Resumes read well if they are concise, grammatically correct, and easy to follow. Resumes look more inviting if they are reproduced on a laser printer on high-quality paper. Some companies prepare professional resumes for a fee; the yellow pages in the telephone directory can provide names of firms that sell this service.

Other elements found in good resumes are job objectives, educational background, college activities, work experiences, and references. The arrangement of these elements is a personal decision. But keep the resume uncluttered and neatly blocked to create an attractive and informative resume with eye appeal. Exhibit II-1 presents an example of an effective resume.

It may be necessary to prepare a different resume for each employer so that your credentials can be slanted for the job openings. Whether you think a different resume for each company can do the job is a decision that only you can make.

Just as important as the points to include are some points to avoid in preparing your resume:

- Don't state what salary you want.
- Don't send a resume with false information.
- Don't send a resume that is sloppy and contains typographical or grammatical errors.
- Don't clutter your resume with unnecessary information.
- Don't inform employers that you will accept only a certain kind of position.
- Don't use fancy colors or gimmicks to sell yourself.

A cover letter should accompany the resume. The objective of the cover letter is to introduce you. It can also encourage the employer to read your resume and meet with you. The cover letter should not duplicate the more detailed resume. Instead, it should add to what is presented in the resume and show that you are really interested in working for the company. The cover letter also reveals how well you can communicate. This clue is often used by employers to put prospective employees into one of two categories: a good communicator and a poor communicator.

Employers receive cover letters and resumes from many more job applicants than they could ever hire or even interview. Therefore, they screen whatever letters and resumes they receive. Screening is often accomplished rather quickly, so it is better to present your story and objectives concisely and neatly.

The number of letters and resumes you send depends on your strategy. Some people narrow down their list of organizations to the ones they really would like to work for and prepare a personal cover letter to accompany the resume. Other candidates use a "shotgun" approach. They mail numerous letters and resumes to any company with an opening in a particular area of interest. Newspapers, professional magazines, listings in the placement office, telephone directories, directories of organizations, and tips from friends are used to develop a potential list. Then, perhaps as many as 200 letters and resumes are sent out.

THE INTERVIEW STRATEGY

An outstanding cover letter, resume, and job-search strategy are not enough to get you the job you want. You must also perform well at the interview. The interview is an oral presentation with a representative of a company. A good recruiter is interested in how a job candidate expresses himself or herself. The interviewer is both an information source and an information prober. As an information source, the interviewer provides you with knowledge about careers in the organization and the company in general. As a prober, the interviewer wants to determine what makes you tick and what kind of person you are.

An Interview Plan

In searching for job openings, it is necessary to have a plan. This is also true of a successful interview. To do a good job at the interview, you must be thoroughly prepared. Of course, you must know yourself and what type of career you want. The interviewer will probe into the areas you covered in your self-assessment and in developing a career objective. During the interview, you must make it clear why the company should hire a person with your strengths and objectives.

Example of an Effective Resume

Jill M. Oganovich

4896 Creling Avenue • New York, NY 10011 • (212) 555-0019

OBJECTIVE		A challenging executive-level position in marketing, utilizing analytical and problem-solving skills.
EDUCATION	May 1990–Sept. 1985	New York University School of Business Administration Major: Marketing and Finance GPA 3.9; Phi Beta Kappa; Dean's List; NYU Tuition scholarship School of Social Sciences GPA 3.9; Dean's List; concentration in mathematics and psychology.
	June 1985–Sept. 1982	Notre Dame High School GPA 3.9 Class Honors; National Honor Society; State Champion, Women's Extemporaneous Speaking, 1979; Major Delegation Award at National Model United Nations in Washington, DC, 1978, 1979.
EXPERIENCE	January 2001–Present	Vice President – Europe, PepsiCo. Responsible for European markets and sales. Responsible for all planning, distribution, and joint ventures.
	May 1990–January 2001	**Assistant Marketing Manager,** PepsiCo. Responsibilities included the coordination of planning, implementing, and evaluating the Pepsi Challenge Program in New York City. This required close liaison with PepsiCo's marketing and sales activities as well as its advertising agency and the media. Achieved increase of over 100% in program participants, totaling over 60,000 people. Planned and implemented Mountain Dew sampling program. On own initiative, developed a Coordinator's Handbook, which PepsiCo plans to distribute nationwide.
	Sept. 1987–May 1988	**Vice President,** Alpha Kappa Gamma Sorority Responsible for housing policies, human resource planning, and discipline.
	Sept. 1986–Sept. 1987	**Assistant Treasurer,** Alpha Kappa Gamma Sorority Responsible for funds to finance all sorority events. Included collection, recording, and billing for 65 individual accounts.
	Summer 1986	**Salesperson,** Revlon, Inc.
	Summer 1895	**Information Manager,** Summer Concert Series at New York University
ACTIVITIES		Project Director, Marketing Club at New York University; Seminar for Republican Campaign Coordinators, Washington, DC; New York University Campus Orchestra; NYC Symphony Youth Orchestra.
REFERENCES		Available on request

EXHIBIT II-2   **Homework Information for the Interview**

- Location of headquarters, offices, plants
- Officers of the organization
- Future growth plans of the company
- Product lines
- Sales, profit, and dividend picture
- Price of stock (if available)
- Competitors of the company

- Organizational structure
- Kind on entry-level positions available
- Career paths followed by graduates
- Union situation
- Type of programs available for employees (stock option, medical, educational)

The preparation for answering the question "Why you?" involves some homework. You should gather facts about the employer. Annual reports, opinions from employees of the firm, brochures, up-to-date financial data from *The Wall Street Journal*, and recent newspaper articles can be used. Exhibit II-2 identifies some of the information that can be used to prepare for the interview. Whether the initial interview is on campus or in the office of the president of the company, preparation will impress the interviewer. This preparedness will allow you to explore other important areas about the company that you don't know about. It will also allow the interviewer to probe into such areas as your grades, motivations, maturity, ability to communicate, and work experience. This information is important for the company in deciding whether to have you visit for a second, more in-depth interview.

Preparation for the interview also involves your personal appearance and motivational state. There isn't enough space here to focus extensively on dress, hair, and value codes. The next best advice is to be yourself and to come prepared to meet with a representative of the organization. If you are to work as a financial analyst for some firm, then you must comply with standards of performance as well as dress and appearance codes. Use your own judgment, but be realistic: Employers don't like shoulder-length hair on a male salesperson or bare-footed production supervisors. These biases will not be

corrected in an interview, so don't be a crusader for a cause. The interview is not the best place to project a personal distaste for a discomfort with dress or hair-length standards.

Interviewing makes most people slightly nervous. But if you are well prepared and really motivated to talk to the representative, the interview will probably go well. Consider the interview as a challenge you can meet because you are interested in succeeding. An alert candidate with modest confidence has a good chance of impressing the interviewer.

The Actual Interview

The interview has been called a conversation with a purpose. During the interview, the company representative and the candidate both attempt to determine if a match exists. Are you the right person for the job? The attempt to match person and job follows a question-and-answer routine. The ability to answer questions quickly, honestly, and intelligently is important. The best way to provide a good set of answers is to be prepared.

Exhibit II-3 provides a list of some commonly asked questions. The way you answer these and similar questions is what the interviewer evaluates. Remember that the interviewer is trying to get to know you better by watching and listening.

EXHIBIT II-3   **Some Questions Frequently Asked by Interviewers**

- Why do you want to work for our company?
- What kind of career do you have planned?
- What have you learned in school to prepare for a career?
- What are some of the things you are looking for in a company?
- How has your previous job experience prepared you for a career?
- What are your strengths? Weaknesses?

- Why did you attend this school?
- What do you consider to be a worthwhile achievement of yours?
- Are you a leader? Explain.
- How do you plan to continue developing yourself?
- Why did you select your major?
- What can I tell you about my company?

| EXHIBIT II-4 | Some Questions Frequently Asked by Job Candidates |

- How is performance evaluated?
- How much transfer from one location to another is there?
- What is the company's promotion policy?
- Does the company have development programs?
- How much responsibility is a new employee given? Can you provide me with some examples?
- What preferences are given to applicants with graduate degrees?

- What type of image does the company have in the community?
- What schools provide the bulk of managerial talent in the company?
- What are the company's policies for paying for graduate study?
- What social obligations would I have?
- What community service obligations would I have?

One effective way to prepare for the interview session is to practice answering the questions in Exhibit II-3 before attending the actual interview. This does not mean developing "pat" or formal answers, but it does mean being ready to respond intelligently. The sincerity of the response and the intelligent organization of an answer must come through in the interview.

Most interviewers eventually get around to asking about career plans. Asking these kinds of questions helps interviewers determine your reasonableness, maturity, motivation, and goals. The important point is to illustrate by your response that you have given serious thought to your career plans. An unrealistic, disorganized, or unprepared career plan is one way to fail in the interview. Interviewers consider a candidate immature if he or she seems to be still searching and basically confused.

At various points in the interview, it may be appropriate to ask questions. These questions should be important and should not be asked just to appear intelligent. If something is important in evaluating the company, ask the question. It is also valuable if you can ask a question that displays meaningfulness. But don't ask so many questions that the interviewer is answering one after the other. Some frequently asked questions are summarized in Exhibit II-4.

The majority of interviews last between twenty and thirty minutes. It is best to close on a positive and concise note. Summarize your interests and express whether you are still interested in the company. The interviewer will close by stating that you will hear from the company. You may want to ask if he or she can give you an approximate idea of how long it will be before you hear from the company. Typically, an organization will contact a candidate within four or five weeks after the interview.

One valuable practice to follow after the actual interview is to write down some of the points covered. List the interviewer's name, when the company will contact you, and your overall impression of the company. These notes can be useful if you are called for a later interview. Any person talking to ten or more companies usually has some trouble recalling the conversation if no notes are available.

One issue that may not come up during the interview is salary. Most companies pay a competitive starting wage. Therefore, it is really not that important to ask what your starting salary will be. Individuals with similar education, experience, and background are normally paid the same. Instead of asking about salary in the initial interview, do some checking in the placement office at your school or with friends working in similar jobs.

Should you send a thank-you letter after the interview? This seems to be a good way to refresh the interviewer's memory. The follow-up handwritten letter should be short. Expressing your appreciation for the interview shows sincerity. It also provides an opportunity to state that you are still interested in the company.

Interviewers are important processors of information for the company, so it is important to impress them. Unfortunately, not every candidate can win (winning means that the candidate will be asked to visit the company or to undergo further interviewing). "Why was I rejected?" is a question everyone has to ask at some point. Exhibit II-5 lists some of the reasons why candidates are not successful in an interview.

VISITING THE COMPANY AND THE JOB OFFER

If you are fortunate enough to be invited for a company visit, consider yourself successful. The letter of invitation or telephone message will specify some available dates. If you are still interested in the company, you must send a formal acceptance. Even if you are not interested in visiting, a short note thanking the company demonstrates your courtesy.

Some Reasons for Not Winning

- Disorganized and not prepared
- Sloppy appearance
- Abrasive and overbearing
- Unrealistic goals or image of oneself
- Inability to communicate effectively

- No interest shown in the type of company interviewed
- Not alert
- Poor grades
- Interested only in money
- Provide contradictory answers to questions

In some cases, your visit will be coordinated by the interviewer you already met. However, it may be the personnel department or management development officer who handles the details. The important point is not who will be coordinating but that you must again prepare for a series of interviews. During this series, you should be asking specific questions about job duties, performance expectations, salary, fringe benefits, and career paths. It is at this phase of the career and employment decision process that you need this kind of information.

One of the main reasons for inviting candidates to visit the company is to introduce them to managers and the organization. These introductions will be brief, but they are important. It is reasonable to expect to meet five or more individuals during the company visit. In some cases, you will be given a tour of the plant, office, or laboratory. A wide array of people will be asked to comment on your employability after you leave. So consider every interview important, and remember to act alert, organized, and interested. You may be bored because many questions are repeated by different managers, but remember that sincerity and interest are variables that these managers will each be asked to comment on.

During the company visit, you will probably not be given a job offer. In most situations, a week to two weeks may pass before the company contacts you. If you are successful, you will receive a formal job offer. After receiving the offer, make an immediate acknowledgment. Thank the employer and indicate an approximate date when you will give your decision.

A CONCLUDING NOTE

This appendix has focused on planning. Self-assessment, seeking professional help, the job search, personalizing your job campaign, interviewing, and visiting companies all involve planning. The person who plans his or her campaign to find a worthwhile and satisfying job will be more successful than the disorganized person. Thus, the most important principle in finding the best job for you is to work hard at planning each stage. Good luck!

Glossary

A

Abilities   Innate or natural attributes a person has that can be developed into skills or knowledge.

Absolute Advantage   When a country can produce a product more efficiently than any other nation.

Acceptance   The ascent on the part of the receiving party to the terms of the offer.

Accounting   The process of identifying, measuring, and communicating economic information to permit informed decisions by users of the information.

Accounting Cycle   The steps—analyzing, recording, posting, and preparing reports—by which the results of business transactions are communicated.

Accounting Equation   Assets = Liabilities + Owners' Equity, indicating a company's financial position at any point in time.

Accounts   Record of all transactions affecting a particular financial statement element.

Accounts Receivable   The amount of money owed to a business from customers who purchased its goods or services.

Accounts Receivable Turnover   The number of times per year that the average accounts receivable is collected; computed by dividing net sales by average net accounts receivable.

Acquisition   The process in which one firm buys the assets and assumes the obligations of another company

Activity Ratios   Measure of how efficiently assets are being used to generate revenues.

Actuary   An insurance employee who predicts the likelihood of future events based on their occurrence in the past.

Adaptive Organization   An organization that is flexible enough to adjust or adapt to environmental changes, trends, and shifts.

Administered VMS   A marketing channel in which independent intermediaries use informal coordination; usually dominated by one channel organization.

Administrative Law   Regulations affecting business, passed by state and federal administrative agencies.

Advertising   A paid form of nonpersonal communication to a target audience through a mass medium such as television, newspapers, or magazines.

Advertising Media   Advertising outlets, including newspapers, television, direct mail, radio, magazines, and outdoor displays.

AFL-CIO   The merged body of the American Federation of Labor (craft union members) and the Congress of Industrial Organizations (industrial union members).

Agency   A legal relationship between two parties who agree that the agent will act on behalf of the principal.

Agency Shop   A workplace where all employees pay union dues, whether or not they are union members.

Agent   A person hired by a buyer or seller on a permanent basis and paid commissions.

American Federation of Labor   The voluntary federation of America's unions, representing more than 13 million working women and men nationwide. The AFL-CIO was formed in 1955 by the merger of the American Federation of Labor and the Congress of Industrial Organizations.

Americans with Disabilities Act (ADA)   Comprehensive antidiscrimination law, passed in 1990, aimed at integrating the disabled into the American workforce; prohibits all employers from discriminating against disabled employees or applicants.

Antitrust Improvement Act   An act that gives the FTC and the Justice Department a longer period of time to evaluate proposed mergers and allows state attorneys general to prosecute firms accused of price fixing.

Arbitrator   Third party to a labor dispute who makes the final, binding decision about some disputed issue.

Arithmetic-Logic Unit   The part of a computer's central processing unit that performs computations.

Artificial Intelligence   A technology that allows computers to solve problems involving imagination, abstract reasoning, and common sense.

Assembly Line   A production line made up of workers who each perform one specific task as the product moves past, toward completion.

Assets   Anything of value owned by the business and used in its operation.

Audit   An examination of a company's financial statements to determine the fairness of the statements in accordance with generally accepted accounting principles.

Authorized Stock   All the shares of a firm's stock that can be sold or issued.

Autocratic Leadership   A type of close supervision in which the manager delegates as little authority as possible.

Automated Clearinghouses (ACHs)   Allows payments or withdrawals to and from a bank account by magnetic computer tape.

Automated Teller Machines (ATMs)   Machine that dispenses cash from a customer's account, accepts deposits to the account, or performs other banking functions.

B

Balance of Payments   The total flow of money into and out of a country.

Balance of Trade   The difference (in dollars) between the amount a country exports and the amount it imports.

Balance Sheet   A financial statement that indicates a firm's financial position at a particular point in time; reflects a firm's solvency, or its ability to pay its debts as they come due. Also called the statement of financial position.

Bargaining in Good Faith   Both sides in labor-management relations must communicate and negotiate.

Bear Market   A market state in which stock values are generally declining and investors are generally pessimistic.

Behavior Modification   Application of learning principles called operant conditioning that is designed to modify behavior.

Benefits   Forms of indirect compensation that are financial in nature; examples include health insurance and pension fund contributions.

Bill of Rights of Union Members   Another name for the Labor-Management Reporting and Disclosure Act, which gave every union member the right to (1) nominate candidates for union office, (2) vote in union elections, and (3) attend union meetings.

Blank Endorsement   Accomplished when the payee signs the back of the instrument.

Blind Advertisement   A post office box number provided by a company which does not provide the company name to job applicants.

Blue-Chip Stocks   Stocks issued by large, well-capitalized companies that consistently pay dividends.

Blue-Sky Laws   State laws that prevent corporations from issuing worthless securities; also require stockbrokers to be licensed and securities to be registered.

Bond   An agreement between a firm and an investor with specific terms spelled out in an indenture.

Book Value   The value of common stock relative to the value of the company.

Boycott   A bargaining tactic in which the union refuses to do business with a firm or attempts to get people or other organizations to refuse to deal with the firm.

Brand   A name, sign, symbol, or design a company uses to distinguish its product from others.

Brand Name   The part of a product's brand that can be verbalized in the spoken or written word..

Breach of Contract   The failure of one party to live up to a contractual agreement.

Breakeven Analysis   A determination of how many product units must be sold at various prices for a firm to recover costs and begin making a profit.

Breakeven Quantity   The point at which the cost of making a product equals the revenue made from selling the product.

Broker   Wholesaler who brings together buyers and sellers on a temporary basis.

Brokerage Accounts   An account an investor holds with a brokerage firm (such as Charles Schwab or Fidelity) that allows the investor to trade in stocks, bonds, options, and other securities.

Bull Market   A market state in which stock values are generally rising and investors are generally optimistic.

Business   The exchange of goods, services, or money for mutual benefit or profit.

Business Ethics   The evaluation of business activities and behavior as right or wrong.

Business Plan   A formal document of what the entrepreneur intends to do to sell enough of the firm's product or service to make a satisfactory profit.

Business Representative   A union official who negotiates and administers the labor agreement and settles contract problems.

Business-to-Business   Commerce that involves all the steps in the buying process from product information to ordering, invoicing, fulfilling, paying, and providing customer service; also referred to as *B2B*.

Business Trust   A business used to hold securities for investors; allows the transfer of legal title to a property of one person for the use and benefit of another.

Buy Out   When a buyer and seller agree on terms involving the inventory, equipment, and price of an established business.

C

Call Option   An option to buy stock shares at a specified price and sell at market price.

Callable Bonds   Bonds that give a company the right to purchase back its bonds early.

Cancellation Provision   The contract provision giving a franchisor the power to cancel an arrangement with a franchisee.

Capital Budgeting   The budgeting of funds for future, generally major, investments of the firm's cash; investments are generally ranked on the basis of the return potential.

Capital Gains   Refers to the profit individuals make when they sell an investment for more than they paid for it.

Capital Resources   Goods produced for the purpose of making other types of goods and services; includes current assets (short-lived) and fixed capital (long-lived).

Capitalism   A type of economic system characterized by private ownership of capital, competition among businesses seeking a profit, and consumer's freedom of choice.

Cash Reserve   The inventory of uncommitted cash that a company has and can use for investing purposes.

Catalog Showroom   A form of warehouse showroom where customers select products from catalogs sent to customers' homes or available in the store.

Celler-Kefauver Act   An act that outlaws mergers through the purchase of assets, when the mergers tend to reduce competition.

Central Processing Unit (CPU)   The electronic hardware that performs the computer operations and controls the entire system.

Centralized Business   An organization in which all, or nearly all, authority to make decisions is retained by a small group of managers.

Certificates of Deposit (CDs)   Interest-bearing note issued by a commercial bank or brokerage firm.

Certified Management Accountants (CMAs)   Financial management professionals who combine accounting knowledge and professional management skills to provide employers with a variety of leadership and decision-making services.

Certified Public Accountants (CPAs)   Accountants who have their own businesses or who work for public accounting firms. They perform a broad range of accounting, auditing, tax, and consulting activities for their clients, who may be corporations, governments, nonprofit organizations, or individuals.

Chain of Command   A channel in which communication, coordination, and control flow through the various levels of management to subordinates.

Chapter 7 Bankruptcy   The business firm is dissolved and the assets are sold to pay off debt.

Chapter 11 Bankruptcy   Temporarily relieves a company from its debts while it reorganizes and works out a payment plan with its creditors.

Chapter 13 Bankruptcy   Allows an individual to establish a plan for repaying debts within three to five years.

Chief Financial Officer (CFO)   The title of the person in charge of a firm's financial affairs.

Civil Rights Act of 1964   An act that makes various forms of discrimination illegal. Title VII of the act spells out the forms of illegal discrimination.

Civil Rights Act of 1991   Increases the scope of Title VII of the Civil Rights Act of 1964. Victims are now entitled to jury trial and punitive damages.

Classroom Training   Training method used to help employees reach skill and knowledge objectives.

Clayton Act   An act that regulates general practices that potentially may be detrimental to fair competition. Some of these general practices regulated by the Clayton Act are price discrimination; exclusive dealing contracts, tying agreements, or requirement contracts; mergers and acquisitions; and interlocking directorates.

Closed Shop   A company that hires only workers who are members of the union; illegal under the Taft-Hartley Act.

Coaching/Mentoring   A method in which a supervisor teaches job knowledge and skills to a subordinate. The supervisor instructs, directs, corrects, and evaluates the subordinate.

Code of Ethics   A statement spelling out what an organization considers ethical behavior for its employees.

Collective Bargaining   Negotiation of a labor contract by union and management.

Commercial Bank   A profit-making institution that holds the deposits of individuals and businesses in checking and savings accounts and then uses these funds to make loans.

Commercial Paper   A short-term loan to a major corporation with a high credit standing.

Commission   Payment to an employee that is tied directly to performance standards.

Congress of Industrial Organizations (CIO)   Formed in 1935 to organize industrial and mass-production employees. The CIO merged with the American Federation of Labor (AFL) in 1955.

Commodities   Large-volume items, such as raw materials, precious metals, and agricultural products, in which individuals can invest.

Commodity Exchanges   Organizations that specialize in buying and selling commodities.

Common Law   The body of law created by judges through their court decisions.

Common Stock   Stock that confers voting rights but not preferential rights of dividends or claims against the assets of the firm.

Comparable Worth   The concept of equal pay for jobs that require similar levels of skills, training, and experience.

Comparative Advantage   When a country can produce one product more efficiently and at a lower cost than other products, in comparison to other nations.

Competition-Oriented Pricing   A method whereby a firm sets prices on the basis of its competitors' prices rather than its own costs and revenues.

Compounding   Refers to a type of ever-increasing interest payment; that is, money invested in interest-bearing accounts or other instruments earns a specific amount (interest). If that interest is reinvested rather than removed from the account, subsequent interest payments are higher.

Computer   An electronic device used to input, store, and process data and to output them as useful information.

Computer Network   A collection of computers connected so that they can function individually and communicate with one another.

Computer Program   A detailed set of instructions written in a computer language.

Computer-Aided Design (CAD)   The use of computers to draw plans for a product.

Computer-Aided Engineering (CAE)   The use of computers to plan engineering processes and test designs.

Computer-Aided Manufacturing (CAM)   The use of computers to guide or control the actual production of goods.

Concentration Approach   A marketing approach that allows a firm to use all its knowledge, experience, and resources to meet the needs of a distinct customer group.

Conceptual Skills   The ability to organize and integrate information to better understand the organization as a whole.

Conglomerate Merger   A merger involving firms selling goods in unrelated markets.

Congress of Industrial Organizations (CIO)   Formed in 1935 to organize industrial and mass-production employees. The CIO merged with the American Federation Congress of Industrial Organizations of Labor (AFL) in 1955.

Consideration   The item(s) of value that are exchanged between parties to a contract as payment for services rendered.

Consolidated Omnibus Budget Reconciliation Act (COBRA)   Law passed in 1985 ensures that terminated or laid-off employees have the option to maintain health care insurance by personally paying the premiums.

Consumer   A person who purchases a good or service for personal use.

Consumer Buying Behavior   The decisions and actions of individuals who purchase products for personal use.

Consumer Markets   People who purchase products for personal use.

Consumer Price Index (CPI)   A quarterly indicator of prices in the United States based on a standard "basket" of consumer goods.

Consumer Products   Goods or services used for personal or family consumption.

Consumer Sales Promotion   Activities—including coupons, rebates, samples, gifts, premiums, trading stamps, contests, and sweepstakes—directed to consumers to increase sales.

Consumerism   Activities of individuals, groups, and organizations aimed at protecting consumer rights.

Consumption Chain   An analysis of all of the steps involved in a consumer's purchasing decision.

Contest   A sales promotion method in which consumers compete for prizes on the basis of some skill.

Contract   A legally enforceable, voluntary agreement between two or more parties.

Contractual VMS   A marketing channel in which intermediaries are independent but have relationships formalized through legal agreements.

Control Unit   The part of a computer's central processing unit that guides the operations of the computer.

Controlling   The management function of checking to determine whether employees are following plans and progress is being made, and of taking action to reduce discrepancies.

Convenience Products   Frequently purchased, inexpensive items that buyers spend little effort to find and purchase.

Convenience Stores   Small retail stores with a convenient location and open for long hours.

Convertible Bonds   Bonds that may be paid off with the stock in the company.

Coordination   Procedures that link the different plans, units, and parts of an organization to help achieve a firm's mission.

Cooperative (Co-op)   An organization in which people collectively own and operate a business in order to compete with bigger competitors.

Copyright   Protection of an individual's exclusive right to publish and sell original written materials.

Corporate Charter   A state-issued document authorizing the formation of a corporation.

Corporate VMS   A marketing channel in which one organization owns successive stages of the channel.

Corporation   Legal entity separate from its owners.

Cost-Oriented Pricing   A method whereby a firm determines a product's total cost, then adds a markup to that cost to achieve the desired profit margin.

Countertrading   Bartering agreements between two or more countries.

Coupon   A sales promotion technique that reduces the price of a product by a stated amount at the time of purchase.

Craft Union   A union in which all members belong to one craft or to a closely related group of occupations.

Credits   Entries that record a decrease in an asset, an increase in a liability, or an increase in owners' equity; recorded on the right side of a journal or ledger entry.

Credit Unions   Member-owned savings cooperatives, normally sponsored by a union, company, or professional or religious group; typically concentrate on small, short-term consumer loans.

Cultural Diversity   Differences between and within cultures.

Cumulative Preferred Stock   Preferred stock that pays a dividend to the bearer, which will accumulate and be payable at a future date if the company is unable to pay at the regularly scheduled distribution date.

Currency   The coins and paper money spent to purchase things. Cashier's checks, money orders, and traveler's checks are also considered currency.

Current Assets   Cash plus items that can or will be converted to cash and used within one year.

Current Liabilities   Financial obligations of a firm that will be repaid within one year.

Current Ratio   The measure of a firm's ability to pay its current liabilities from its current assets; computed by dividing current assets by current liabilities.

D

Data   Facts, figures, and statistics concerning people, objects, events, and ideas.

Data Processing   Mechanically transferring raw data into some specific form of information.

Database   An integrated collection of data stored in one place for easy access and information processing.

Database Management Systems (DBMS)   Computer software that helps firms manage various data files.

Day Trading   The practice of trading in major securities markets during the day from a desktop computer or workstation in a day trading center.

Debenture Bonds   Unsecured bonds backed by the good name of the issuing company.

Debits   Entries that record an increase in assets, a decrease in liabilities, or a decrease in owners' equity; recorded on the left side of a journal or ledger entry.

Debit Card   A plastic card, similar to a credit card, that deducts funds directly from the customer's account rather than creating a loan.

Debt Capital   Funds obtained through borrowing.

Debt Ratios   Measure of a company's ability to pay its long-term debts.

Debt-to-Equity Ratio   A measure of a firm's leverage; computed by dividing total debt by owners' equity.

Decentralized Business   An organization in which a significant amount of the authority to make decisions is delegated to lower-level managers.

Decertification   The process, guided by the NLRB, that results in voting out a union that has been representing employees.

Decision Support System (DSS)   A system that enables managers to instantly access information on past and current performance.

Default   Failure to pay the interest on a debt instrument.

360-Degree Feedback   A performance appraisal approach that requests feedback on each employee from others who work for, with, and manage the individual

Delegation   Giving an employee at a lower level in the organization the responsibility for a given task as well as the authority to carry it out.

Demand   The quantity of a product that consumers will purchase at various prices.

Demand Deposits   Bank accounts against which an account holder can write checks, withdrawing money immediately and without prior notice.

Demand-Oriented Pricing   A method based on the level of demand for the product.

Democratic Leadership   A type of general supervision in which the manager consults with subordinates about job-related issues.

Department Stores   Large retailers offering a wide product mix, organized into separate departments and offering a full line of services.

Depreciation   Procedures for spreading the cost of a plant asset out over the course of its useful life.

Deregulation   The process of reducing government involvement in the regulation of business, by eliminating legal restraints on competition.

Derivatives   Financial securities whose value is derived from another "underlying" financial security.

Desktop Publishing   Producing printed materials using computer software that can do page layouts and formats, insert graphics, and print with high quality.

Direct Compensation   An employee's base pay (wages and salary) and performance-based pay (incentives).

Direct Marketing Nonstore retailing that uses nonpersonal media to introduce products to consumers, who then purchase the products by mail, telephone, or computer.

Direct Ownership The purchase of one or more business operations in a foreign country.

Directing The management function of initiating action; issuing directives, assignments, and instructions.

Discount Rate The rate of interest charged to member banks when they borrow money from the Fed.

Discount Stores Retailers offering a wide variety of general merchandise at low prices.

Dividends A distributed portion of the firm's earnings.

Division of Labor A principle of organization that a job can be performed more efficiently if the jobholder is allowed to specialize.

Doctrinaire Firm A firm that wants to continue to be nonunion.

Domestic Corporation An enterprise organized under the laws of one state or country and doing business within that state or country.

Double Taxation Taxing a corporate owner's money twice by taxing it as income of a corporation and as dividends of the individual owner.

Double-Entry Bookkeeping A method of recording business transactions in which offsetting debits and credits keep the accounting equation in balance.

Downsizing Cutting out entire layers of management in the organization.

Drug-Free Workplace Act of 1988 An act passed to help keep the problem of societal drug abuse from entering organizations.

Dumping Selling surplus products in a foreign country at a lower price than in the country of origin.

E

Economic Community An organization that facilitates the movement of products among member nations through the creation of common economic policies.

Economic Recovery Tax Act (ERTA) An act that was enacted in 1981 during the Reagan administration to reduce taxes on corporate profits in hopes of stimulating a lagging economy.

Economic System The accepted process by which labor, capital, and natural resources are organized to produce and distribute goods and services in a society.

Economics The study of how a society chooses to use scarce resources to produce goods and services and to distribute them to people for consumption.

Electronic Funds Transfer (EFT) The transfer of funds by means of an electronic terminal, telephone, computer, or magnetic tape that orders a bank or other financial institution to debit or credit an account.

Electronic Mail A computer network used to relay messages from one user to another instantly.

Embargo A total ban on specific imports and exports from and to a country.

Employee Assistance Programs (EAPs) A program created to provide counsel, support, and resources to employees who are going through stressful personal issues such as stress management, personal financial management, coping with alcohol or other addictions, and caregiving to elderly family members.

Employee Development Anything a company does to increase the effectiveness of employees to perform their jobs.

Employee Stock Option Plans (ESOPs) Plans in which employees are given an opportunity to purchase stocks and own a portion of the company at a fixed price.

Empowerment In a business environment, involves sharing information, providing the authority and power to make decisions, and encouraging people to go ahead and make the decision.

Endorsement A person's signature on the back of a negotiable instrument, making it transferable.

Enterprise Resource Planning (ERP) A program or system that attempts to integrate departments, tasks, and functions across a company into a single computer system that can satisfy the needs of those using the ERP.

Entrepreneurs People who take the risks necessary to organize and manage a business and receive the financial profits and nonmonetary rewards.

Equal Employment Opportunity Act of 1972 A law that has specific provisions about equal opportunities for employment; provided for the establishment of Equal Employment Opportunity Commission.

Equal Employment Opportunity Commission (EEOC) A federal agency whose purpose is to increase job opportunities for women and minorities.

Equal Pay Act of 1963 Designed to lessen the existing gap between male and female pay rates.

Equity Capital Funds provided in exchange for some ownership in the firm.

Esteem Needs The need for self-respect and respect from others.

E-tailing Companies sell goods and services to customers over the Internet.

Ethics The principles of behavior that distinguish between right and wrong.

Euro The new currency of the European Union (EU).

Exchange The process by which parties provide something of value to one another to satisfy the needs of each.

Exchange Controls Restrictions on the amount of a certain currency that can be bought or sold in a nation.

Exchange Rate The rate at which one country's currency can be exchanged for that of another country.

Excise Tax A tax on the manufacture or sale of a domestic product.

Exclusive Distribution Market coverage in which one outlet is used in a specific geographic area for distributing a product.

Exclusive Handling A form of control in which a franchisor requires the franchisee to purchase only supplies approved by the franchisor.

Executive Information System (EIS) A user-friendly decision support system designed for executives that requires little computer knowledge and provides instant high-quality displays.

Exercise Refers to when an investor cashes out a stock option; the transaction is said to be an "exercise" of that option.

Expenses Costs incurred to produce revenues.

Expert Systems Computer software that imitates human thinking.

Exporting Selling domestic-made goods in another country.

Express Contract   A contract that is put forth in writing, usually on paper.

Express Warranty   Oral or written assurances made by the seller regarding a product.

Extrinsic Rewards   Rewards external to the work itself and administered by someone else, such as a manager.

F

Factoring   The sale of accounts receivable to a bank or other lender, generally at a considerable discount.

Fair Credit and Reporting Act   Prospective employers must secure an applicant's permission before checking references.

Federal Reserve System   The twelve Federal Reserve Banks that serve as the central bank of the United States. Generally referred to as the Fed.

Federal Trade Commission Act   An act that established the Federal Trade Commission (FTC), a five-member committee empowered to investigate illegal trade practices.

Fee-for-Service Health Insurance   Reimbursement for physicians for the amount of services provided.

Finance   The study of money within the firm; the business function responsible for finding funds, managing them, and determining their best use.

Finance Companies   Institutions that offer short-term loans, typically at a higher rate, to businesses and individuals unable to obtain loans elsewhere.

Financial Accounting Standards Board (FASB)   An entity that consists of seven board members who issue statements and guidelines regarding accounting practices.

Financial Manager   The individual responsible for a firm's finance function.

Financial Statements   Documents presenting a company's financial position, results of operations, and cash flow during a stated period of time.

Financing Activities   Include issuing new stock, paying dividends to shareholders, borrowing from banks, and repaying amounts borrowed.

Fixed Exchange Rate   An unvarying exchange rate set by government policy.

Flexible Manufacturing Systems (FMS)   The use of computers to change from one production process to another in order to produce different goods.

Float   The amount of money not yet withdrawn from the company's checking account even though checks have been written.

Floating Exchange Rate   An exchange rate that fluctuates with market conditions.

Floor Planning   The term used to refer to financing a company receives that is secured by the work in process. For example, a car manufacturer may receive a loan from a bank that is secured against the inventory of cars currently under production.

Foreign Corporation   A business incorporated in one state or country and doing business in another state or country.

Form 10-K Reports   Annual registration statements filed by corporations, which are required by Section 10-K of the Securities Exchange Act of 1934.

Formal Authority   The right to give orders.

Formal Organization   The management-designed, official structure of the business.

403(b)   A retirement investment account that allows tax-free gains offered by not-for-profit organizations.

401(k)   A retirement investment account that allows tax-free gains offered by for-profit organizations.

Franchise   The right to use a specific business name (Pizza Hut, Subway, H&R Block, Blockbuster, Masterworks International) and sell its goods or services in a specific city, region, or country.

Franchise Agreement   Contractual agreement between franchise organization and franchisees. Usually outlines, among other things, amount of capital needed, training provided, managerial assistance available, and size of the franchise territory.

Free Enterprise   A system in which private businesses are able to start and do business competitively to earn profits, with a minimal degree of government regulation.

Free Sample   A free package or container of a product given as a sales promotion technique.

Functional Structure   A structure in which each unit or department has a different set of activities and responsibilities.

G

Gap Fillers   Reasonable provisions that are derived from the UCC to help complete a contract in case of a court-mediated dispute between contracting parties.

Generally Accepted Accounting Principles (GAAP)   Rules developed by the Financial Accounting Standards Board to which accounting practitioners adhere.

General Agreement on Tariffs and Trade (GATT)   An international organization formed to reduce or eliminate tariffs and other barriers to international trade.

General and Administrative Expenses   Costs incurred in the overall management of the business.

General Ledger   A book or computer file summarizing all accounts of the business.

General Partnership   A partnership in which at least one partner has unlimited liability; a general partner has authority to act and make binding decisions as an owner.

Global Business   The performance of business activities across national boundaries.

Global Market   The entire world is considered to be a potential consumer of a firm's products or services.

Goals   Broadly stated guidelines that an organization or an individual is attempting to achieve.

Goal Setting   The process of identifying specific levels of performance to be achieved in a certain time frame.

Graphic Rating Scale   Performance appraisal technique where supervisor is supplied with a printed form for each person to be rated and is asked to circle or check the phrase that best describes the individual on the particular trait.

Green Marketing Efforts by firms to move beyond the law to provide environmentally sound goods and services in areas ranging from conservation to pollution control.

Grievance Complaint made by an employee or the union about a job, person, or condition that creates dissatisfaction or discomfort.

Gross Domestic Product (GDP) A measure of the economic activity within the physical borders of a country.

H

Hardware The physical devices that make up a computer system.

Hawthorne Studies A series of experiments that found that work groups significantly affected the way workers behave and perform.

Hazard A condition that exists that either increases the chance for loss from particular perils or tends to make the loss more severe once the peril has occurred.

Health Maintenance Organizations (HMOs) Organizations that provide extensive medical care and services for members, based on a prepared monthly fee.

Hierarchy Refers to the authority and reporting lines within an organization.

Home-Based Business Business in which an individual works or conducts activities out of the home. About 22 percent of the total workforce now works out of the home.

Horizontal Merger A merger involving competitive firms in the same market.

Hostile Environment A situation in which an employee is subjected to unwelcome advances, requests for sexual favors, and other verbal or physical behavior that interferes with performance or creates an intimidating work environment.

Hot-Cargo Agreement A boycott agreement between management and union that workers may avoid working with materials that come from employers that have been struck by a union.

Human Relations Skills The ability to relate and interact with subordinates, peers, superiors, and customers or clients.

Human Resource Management (HRM) The process of acquiring, retaining, terminating, developing, and properly using the human resources in an organization.

Human Resource Planning The steps taken in estimating the size and makeup of the future workforce.

Humanistic Philosophy A set of moral principles focusing on individual rights and values.

Hygiene Factors External characteristics essential to avoiding job dissatisfaction.

I

Immigration Reform and Control Act (IRCA) A law, passed in 1986, that places a major responsibility on employers to stop the flow of illegal immigrants into the United States by not employing unauthorized aliens.

Implied Contract A contract that is assumed to exist by virtue of the way parties behave toward one another in the exchange of goods or services.

Implied Warranty Warranty legally imposed on the seller; ensures that the seller owns the products and that they will serve the purpose for which they are sold.

Import Tariff A duty, or tax, levied against goods brought into a country.

Importing Purchasing goods made in another country.

In-Home Selling Nonstore retailing activities that involve personal contacts with consumers in their homes.

Income Statement A financial statement showing a firm's revenues, expenses, and net income over a period of time; indicates profitability, the ability to generate income. Also called earnings statement or statement of profit and loss.

Indenture The agreement that spells out the maturity date and interest payments for a corporate bond.

Indirect Compensation Federally required and state-mandated protection programs, private protection programs, paid leave, and miscellaneous benefits.

Individual Incentive Plan The oldest type of compensation, which can take several forms: piecework, production bonuses, and commissions.

Individual Retirement Accounts (IRAs) Accounts that establish a trust or custodial account, which is a retirement savings plan; if you are under age 50 and have earned income, you can contribute up to $3,000 annually to an IRA; if you are under age 70.5 years old but over 50 and have earned income, you can contribute up to $3,500 annually.

Industrial Markets Those who purchase products to use in the production of other products or to resell.

Industrial Products Goods or services used by an organization in producing other goods or services or in carrying out its operations.

Industrial Union A union in which all members are employed in a company or industry, regardless of occupation.

Informal Organization The network of personal and social relationships that emerges when people work together.

Information Data with meaning attached.

Injunctions Court orders that prohibit defendants from engaging in certain activities, such as striking.

Input Device The hardware used to enter data into and make requests of the computer.

Insider Trading The practice of buying and selling stock on the basis of information gained through positions or contacts with others that is not available to other investors or the general public.

Institutional Advertising Advertising used to build goodwill and create a favorable public image.

Institutional Investors Professional investors who invest for large groups or organizations such as pension funds, insurance companies, mutual funds, and universities.

Intangible Personal Property Property represented by a document or other written statement.

Integrated Circuits Small silicon chips containing dozens of tiny transistors and connections; used in third-generation computers.

Intentional Torts Deliberate acts by a person or business firm.

Intensive Distribution Market coverage in which all available outlets are used for distributing a product.

Interest-Earning Checking Accounts Sometimes called NOW accounts (negotiable order of withdrawal), accounts that usually require a minimum balance. If the balance dips below this amount, you may not earn interest and will likely have to pay a fee.

International Monetary Fund (IMF) An international financial organization that lends money to countries to conduct international trade.

Intrapreneur An entrepreneurial person employed by a corporation and encouraged to be innovative and creative.

Intrinsic Rewards Rewards derived from a sense of gratification directly related to performing the job.

Inventory The term used to refer to finished goods that a firm has stored in preparation for distribution to a customer, or to supplies that will be used in product assembly.

Inventory Management The process of developing and maintaining stocks of products that customers need and want.

Investing Activities Activities that include buying fixed assets, buying stock in other companies, and selling stock held as an investment in another company.

Investment Bankers Financial specialists who handle the sale of new stock or bond offers.

Investment Company Act of 1940 The act that brought mutual funds under the jurisdiction of the SEC.

Issued Stock The term used to refer to shares of a company's stock to which another person or company has taken title.

J

Job Analysis The process of determining the tasks that make up a job and the skills, abilities, and responsibilities needed to perform the job.

Job Description A written statement that furnishes information about a job's duties, technology, conditions, and hazards; based on data from the job analysis.

Job Enrichment A motivational technique that involves incorporating variety, feedback, and autonomy in the job.

Job Evaluation Systems Processes by which the relative values of jobs within the organization are determined.

Job Rotation Method of transferring managers from job to job on a systematic basis with assignments lasting from two weeks to six months.

Job Security The relative comfort a person feels about whether his or her job will continue into the future.

Job Specification A written statement of the human qualifications, education, and experience needed to perform a job.

Joint Venture A special type of partnership established to carry out a special project or to operate for a specific time period.

Journal A book or computer file in which business transactions are recorded chronologically.

Junk Bond A low-grade bond that carries a very high risk.

Jurisdiction The right and power of a court to interpret and apply laws and make binding decisions.

Just-in-Time (JIT) A system for decreasing inventory by using suppliers who agree to deliver the fewest possible items at the latest possible moment to keep production moving smoothly.

K

Keogh Plans Self-employment retirement plans that allow the business owner to invest money and enjoy tax-free gains until retirement.

Knights of Labor The first union federation that attracted members from local unions from all crafts and occupational areas.

Knowledge Refers to the body of information in a subject area that is needed to adequately perform a job.

Knowledge Objectives Objectives that are concerned with understanding, attitudes, and concepts.

L

Labeling The display of important information on a product package.

Labor Resources The human talent, skills, and competence available in a nation.

Labor Unions Organizations of employees who join together to protect, maintain, and improve their economic, social, and political power and well-being.

Lagging Indicators Figures that tell where the economy has been and can be used to develop trend lines.

Laissez-Faire Leadership A type of supervision in which the manager avoids power and responsibility by giving assignments and support but staying out of the group's way.

Landrum-Griffin Act A 1959 labor law that requires unions and employees to file financial reports with the secretary of labor and that specifies certain activities to ensure democratic operation of the union.

Large-Scale Integrated (LSI) Circuits Superchips that contain thousands of small transistors; fourth-generation innovation that made personal computers possible.

Law A standard or rule established by a society to govern the behavior of its members.

Leadership The process of influencing the activities of an individual or group toward accomplishing objectives. Leadership may be autocratic, democratic, or laissez-faire.

Leading Indicators Figures that are tracked to determine where the economy is headed.

Leasing A cost-effective technique whereby companies pay monthly for assets used in business without taking ownership of those assets.

Leverage The use of long-term debt to raise needed cash.

Liabilities Debts owed by a business to its creditors.

Licensing An agreement in which one firm allows another firm to sell its product and use its brand name in return for a commission or royalty.

Limit Order An order to purchase stock only if the price is at or below a specified limit.

Limited Liability Company (LLC) A legal form that provides all the benefits of a partnership, but limits the liability exposure of each investor to the amount of his or her investment.

Limited Liability Partnership (LLP) Partnerships in which partners have the tax advantages of profit sharing and pension plans, not available to private persons and partnerships, as well as limited liability

Limited Partnership   A partnership with at least one general partner, and one or more limited partners who are liable for loss only up to the amount of their investment.

Lincoln Electric Plan   A plan which rewards good performance by issuing a bonus that an employee receives based on his (her) contributions..

Line Authority   Unquestioned, direct authority to make decisions and take action.

Line of Credit   A preapproved amount the holder may borrow in whole or in part, provided that the bank has sufficient funds.

Liquidity   A measure of how quickly an item can be converted to cash.

Liquidity Ratios   Measure of a firm's ability to pay its short-term debts as they come due.

Lockouts   Management pressure tactic that involves denying employees access to their jobs.

Long-Term Liabilities   Amounts owed by a business that must be repaid more than one year from the balance sheet date.

M

M1   The first level of money supply measurement; includes the most highly liquid forms of money; currency and demand deposits.

M2   The second level of money supply measurement; includes time deposits and money market accounts in addition to currency and demand deposits.

Macroeconomics   The study of inflation, unemployment, business cycles, and growth focusing on the aggregate relationships in a society.

Main Memory   The part of the computer central processing unit that stores data and instructions.

Mainframe   The largest and fastest type of computer, with the greatest storage capacity.

Maintenance of Membership Agreement   Agreement that, although employees do not have to join a union, union members must maintain membership in the union over the length of the contract.

Maloney Act   An amendment to the Securities Exchange Act that created the National Association of Securities Dealers (NASD) as a private trade organization to regulate the OTC market.

Managed Care Insurance   Provisions made to control costs of health care, making high-quality health care available at an affordable price.

Management   The application of planning, organizing, staffing, directing, and controlling functions in the most efficient manner possible to accomplish objectives.

Management Development   Programs and processes used to educate managerial personnel to prepare them for additional responsibilities.

Management Information System (MIS)   A combination of computers and procedures for providing information that managers use in making decisions.

Management Skill   The ability to use knowledge, behaviors, and aptitudes to perform a task.

Managerial Hierarchy   The levels of management in an organization, typically three distinct levels: executive, middle, and first-line.

Manufacturing   The actual processes of making products out of materials and parts. Literally, creating something by the work of one's hands.

Margin Call   A request from a broker to an investor to place additional funds into the brokerage account because the investor has insufficient funds to cover the money borrowed to invest in securities that have dropped in value.

Margin Trading   Purchasing more stock shares than a given amount of money would buy because a portion of the shares are bought on credit.

Market   People with the authority, financial ability, and willingness to purchase a product.

Market Coverage   The number of outlets in which a product is sold.

Market Niche   A small, somewhat unique part of a market segment.

Market Order   An order that authorizes a broker to purchase stock at the current market price.

Market Segments   Groups of individuals with one or more similar product needs.

Market Segmentation Approach   The division of the total market into segments, with a marketing mix directed to one of the segments.

Market Value   The price at which a share of common stock is currently selling.

Marketing   The process of planning and executing the conception, pricing, promotion, and distribution of ideas, goods, and services to create exchanges that satisfy individual and organizational objectives.

Marketing Channel (Channel of Distribution)   A group of interrelated organizations that directs the flow of products to ultimate consumers.

Marketing Concept   A managerial philosophy of customer orientation with the goal of achieving long-term success.

Marketing Environment   All the forces outside an organization that directly or indirectly influence its marketing activities.

Marketing Intermediary   An individual or organization in a marketing channel that provides a link between producers, other channel members, and final consumers of products.

Marketing Mix   The combination of four elements—product, price, promotion, and distribution—used to satisfy the needs of the target market.

Marketing Research   The systematic gathering, recording, and analyzing of information for guiding marketing decisions.

Marketing Research Process   Series of steps consisting of problem definition, research design, data collection, data analysis, interpretation, and conclusions.

Marketing Strategy   A plan for selecting and analyzing a target market and developing and maintaining a marketing mix that will satisfy this target market.

Markov Models   Models used to forecast human resource needs.

Markup   In cost-oriented pricing, a percentage added to the total cost of the product to cover marketing expenses and allow a profit.

Mass Production Rapid manufacture of large quantities of goods accomplished through division of labor, specialization, and standardization.

Master Limited Partnership (MLP) A partnership that sells units traded on a recognized stock exchange.

Materials Handling The physical handling of products during transportation and warehousing.

Materials Requirements Planning (MRP) A computerized forecasting system used to plan ordering of parts and materials for manufacturing.

Materials Resources Planning (MRPII) Developed around 1988 to enhance MRP.

Matrix Structure A functional structure combined with either a product or a project structural arrangement.

Media Plan Selection of specific media in which advertisements will be run and when they will be run to reach the target markets.

Mediator Third party to a labor dispute who tries to get union and management to reason and works at improving communication between them.

Merchant Wholesaler Marketing intermediary that takes ownership of goods and the risks associated with ownership.

Merger Combining two or more business enterprises into a single entity.

Microcomputers Personal computers, including a cathode ray tube and a keyboard.

Microeconomics Involves the study of household decision making on what to buy, business pricing decisions, and how markets allocate resources among alternatives.

Minicomputers Smaller, slower versions of the mainframe computer.

Minority-Enterprise Small-Business Investment Companies (MESBICs) Minority-enterprise small-business investment company. Such a company is owned and operated by established industrial or financial concerns, private investors, or business-oriented economic development organizations.

Mission Statement A statement of the purpose of an organization that expresses the vision of the leaders of the organization and gives focus to its members.

Mixed Economy An economy in which both the government and private business enterprises produce and distribute goods and services.

Molly Maguires An early militant union group from the Pennsylvania coal mines.

Money Anything commonly accepted as a means of paying for goods and services.

Money Market Accounts Deposits that pay interest rates very competitive with those paid on other short-term investments; some allow a limited number of checks to be written in amounts over $500.

Moral Philosophy The set of principles that dictate acceptable behavior.

Motivation The way drives or needs direct a person's behavior toward a specific goal; involves the level of effort put forth to pursue the goal.

Motivators Content-oriented characteristics that contribute to job satisfaction.

Multinational Corporations A firm that operates on a global basis, committing assets to operations or subsidiaries in foreign countries.

Multisegment Approach A marketing approach in which a firm directs its efforts at two or more groups by developing a marketing mix for each.

Municipal Bonds Bond issued by states, towns, and other municipalities to finance schools, hospitals, roads, and other civic projects.

Mutual Funds Funds formed by a group of individuals who pool their money to invest in securities, and usually handled by a professional investment manager.

N

Nationalism A sense of national awareness and consciousness that promotes the values, culture, and interests of one county over others.

National Labor Relations Board (NLRB) A group that investigates cases of alleged unfair labor practices by employers and unions and holds elections to determine whether groups of employees want to be unionized.

Natural Resources Resources that nature provides in limited amounts, including crude oil, natural gas, minerals, timber, and water.

Need for Achievement A strong desire to succeed, to grow, to accomplish challenging tasks.

Needs Hierarchy A motivational theory, offered by Maslow, that people have five needs arranged in a hierarchy from physiological to self-actualization.

Negative Reinforcer A consequence of behavior such as a reprimand that, when administered, encourages an employee to adapt more desirable behavior to avoid the unpleasant consequence.

Negligence Tort When one party fails to exercise reasonable care and causes injury to another.

Negotiable Instrument A written promise to pay a specified sum of money; it can be transferred from one person or firm to another.

Net Income The excess of revenues over expenses; also called the bottom line.

1986 Tax Reform Act Act passed during Ronald Reagan's second term as president that built on the corporate tax cuts from the 1981 Economic Recovery Tax Act.

Noncallable Bonds Bonds issued to holders that cannot be redeemed by the issuing company prior to their expiration date.

Nonprice Competition A policy of emphasizing aspects other than price, such as quality, service, or promotion, to sell products.

Nonprofit Corporation An enterprise (e.g., university, charity, church) that is not driven by a profit-seeking motive.

Nonstore Retailing Retailing that takes place outside of stores; includes in-store selling, direct marketing, and vending machines.

Norris-LaGuardia Act A 1932 law that limited the power of federal courts to stop union picketing, boycotts, and strikes; also made the yellow-dog contract unenforceable.

O

Objectives   Specific results or targets to be reached by a certain time.

Occupational Safety and Health Act (OSHA)   Law, passed in 1970, that mandates safety and health standards for U.S. business. Provided for the establishment of the Occupational Safety and Health Administration.

Occupational Safety and Health Administration (OSHA)   A federal agency with the primary purpose of ensuring safe working conditions.

Odd Lots   Stock purchases of less than 100 shares.

Offer   The exchange that will occur between the parties.

On-the-Job Training   A supervisor or other worker may show a new employee how to perform the job.

Open Shop   A company in which employees don't have to join a union or pay dues but can decide without pressure whether to become union members.

Operating Activities   A firm's primary revenue-generating activities.

Operating Agreement   An agreement that sets the rules for governing the company as well as the rights and responsibilities of the members toward the company and one another.

Operating Expenses   All costs of doing business except the cost of goods sold.

Operations   Any functions needed to carry out a strategic plan, to keep the company producing.

Order Getter   A salesperson who recruits new customers and increases sales to current customers.

Order Processing   The receipt and preparation of an order for shipment.

Order Taker   A salesperson who processes repeat sales and maintains positive relationships with customers.

Organizational Chart   A graphic blueprint, or map, of positions, people, and formal authority relationships in the organization.

Organizational Buying Behavior   The decisions and actions of buyers in organizations.

Organizational Structure   The arrangement of work to be done by a business.

Organizing   The management function of grouping people and assignments to carry out job tasks and the mission.

Orientation Programs   A series of activities (e.g., meetings, Q&A sessions, discussions) to bring new employees up to speed on the company, its cultures, policies, expectations, and programs.

Output Device   The hardware that displays the computer's requests or processed data.

Over-the-Counter (OTC) Market   An electronic network of several thousand brokers who communicate trades through NASDAQ.

Owners' Equity   Claims of owners, partners, and shareholders against the firm's assets; the excess of assets over liabilities.

P

Packaging   The development of a container and a graphic design for a product.

Partnership   A business owned by two or more people.

Partnership Agreement   A written or signed agreement between partners that can prevent or lessen misunderstandings at a later time.

Patent   The exclusive right of an inventor to make, use, or sell the registered product.

Perfomance Appraisals   Programs used to communicate expectations and to help subordinates improve personal deficiencies.

Peril   Describes a specific contingency that may cause a loss.

Personal Guarantee   Means that the owners of a company would be personally liable for a debt should the business fail to make scheduled interest payments.

Personal Selling   Person-to-person communication with one or more prospective customers in order to make a sale.

PERT Chart   Program evaluation and review technique that tracks a project's progress and enables management to make optimal allocation of resources.

Philosophy-Laden Firm   A firm that has no unions because its climate of labor-management relations is excellent.

Physical Distribution   Those activities that involve the movement of products through marketing channels from manufacturer to consumer.

Physiological Needs   Biological needs, such as for food, air, water.

Piecework   A plan in which the employee is paid a certain rate for each piece produced, with no other form of compensation.

Pioneer Pricing   New-product pricing strategy of charging the highest possible price to regain costs quickly (price skimming) or setting the price below competitors' prices to build sales quickly (penetration pricing).

Planned Economy   An economy in which the government owns the productive resources, financial enterprises, retail stores, and banks.

Planning   The management function of establishing objectives and developing plans to accomplish them.

Pledging   Using accounts receivable as collateral for a loan.

Plant Assets   Relatively permanent assets that a firm expects to use for more than one year.

Point-of-Purchase Displays   Promotional materials such as signs, posters, and freestanding shelves used in retail stores.

Point-of-Sale (POS) Systems   Systems, along with EFT, that allow merchants to draw money directly from a customer's bank account at the time a purchase is made.

Pollution   Contamination of air, water, and land.

Positive Feedback Loop   A systematic interaction that results in the amplification of a process.

Positive Reinforcer   A consequence of behavior such as praise or other rewards that, when administered, increases the chances that the behavior will be repeated.

Posted   Refers to transactions being recorded from the general journal or specialized journals to an account.

Power of Attorney   A legal document authorizing an agent to act on behalf of the principal.

Precedents   Standards established by judicial systems that later are used to help decide similar cases.

Preferred Provider Organization (PPO)   A form of health care coverage that offers employers reduced premiums; employees must choose physicians and hospitals from the PPO's fist of approved providers.

Preferred Stock   Stock that has preference over common stock in the payment of dividends and in claims against the assets of the firm but does not confer voting rights.

Premium   A fee paid to the insurance company for protection; also refers to a gift given to customers for purchasing a certain product.

Premium or Push Money   Additional compensation provided to salespeople to encourage them to sell a product.

Price   The value that buyers exchange for a product in the marketing transaction.

Price Competition   A policy of using price to differentiate a product in the marketplace.

Price Discounting   A policy of offering buyers deductions from the price of a product.

Price/Earnings Ratio (P/E)   The current market price of a stock divided by the annual earnings per share.

Pricing Method   A systematic procedure for determining prices on a regular basis; considers costs, product demand, or competitors' prices.

Primary-Demand Advertising   Advertising used to create demand for all products in a product group.

Principles   Guidelines that managers can use in making decisions.

Private Accountant   Accountant in any position not included in public accounting; may work in management accounting, government accounting, or academia.

Private Protection Programs   Provided by firms but not required by law including such benefits as health care, income after retirement, insurance against loss of life or limb, and, in some firms, guaranteed work and pay programs.

Producer Price Index (PPI)   An index that measures the average change over time in the selling prices received by domestic producers for their output. The prices included in the PPI are from the first commercial transaction for many products and some services.

Product   A good, service, or idea, including all the tangibles and intangibles provided in an exchange between buyer and seller.

Product Liability   Area of tort law that holds business firms responsible for negligence in design, manufacture, sale, and operation of their products.

Product Life Cycle   The theoretical life of a product, consisting of four stages: introduction, growth, maturity, and decline.

Product Line   A group of related products that are considered a unit because of marketing, technical, or use similarities.

Product Mix   The total group of products a firm offers for sale, or all of the firm's product lines.

Product Modification   The changing of one or more of a product's features as a strategy to extend its life cycle.

Product Structure   An organizational structure in which a manager is placed in charge of and has responsibility for a product or product line.

Production   The total process by which a company produces finished goods or services.

Production Bonus   A bonus or payment to employees based on a formula that encourages quantity and quality of output.

Productivity   A measure of output per unit of a particular input.

Professional Pricing   A policy—practiced by doctors, lawyers, and others with skills or experience in a particular field—of charging a standard fee for a particular service.

Professional Service Organization   An organization of professional people, organized under professional association laws and treated as a corporation for tax purposes.

Profit   The difference between business income (revenue) and business expenses (costs); the selling price of a product minus all costs of making and selling it, including taxes.

Profit-Sharing Plan   A plan in which an employer pays employees an amount based on profits earned plus regular salary.

Profitability Ratios   Ratios that measure a firm's financial performance by comparing earnings to sales or investment.

Progressive Tax   Form of taxation in which the percentage of income paid in taxes increases as income increases.

Promissory Note   A legally binding promise of payment that spells out the terms of the loan agreement.

Promotion   The communication of favorable, persuasive information about a firm or product in order to influence potential buyers.

Promotion Mix   The combination of advertising, personal selling, sales promotion, and publicity used to promote a specific product.

Property Tax   Taxes on residential and commercial property, such as houses, land, buildings, machinery, and automobiles to help local governments' operating revenues.

Prospectus   A statement used by potential investors that gives information about a firm, its management, its operations, the purpose for the stock issue, etc.

Protection Programs   Programs designed to assist employees and their families if direct compensation is terminated and to alleviate the burden of health care expenses.

Proxy   A written statement, signed by a shareholder of a corporation, allowing someone else to cast his or her number of votes.

Psychological Pricing   A policy that encourages purchase decisions based on emotion rather than reason; includes odd-even pricing, customary pricing, prestige pricing, and price lining.

Public Relations   A set of communications activities designed to create and maintain a favorable public image for a firm.

Publicity   A nonpersonal form of communication transmitted in news story form and not paid for directly by a sponsor.

Pull Strategy   Promotion of a product directly to consumers to stimulate strong consumer demand.

Punishment   An undesirable consequence of a particular behavior.

Purchasing Power Parity (PPP)   The adjustment of relative prices. A relative market basket of consumer goods is compared to the same market basket in terms of the currencies of the two countries.

Pure Risk   The threat of a loss with no chance of profit.

Push Strategy   Promotion of a product to wholesalers or retailers in the marketing channel, who in turn promote the product to consumers.

Put Option   An option to buy stock shares at market price and sell at a specified price.

Q

Qualified Endorsement   An endorsement in which the words *without recourse* are used—means the person who originally signed the instrument, not the endorser, is responsible for payment.

The endorser does not guarantee payment if the instrument is not backed by sufficient funds.

Quality   The totality of features and characteristics of a good or service that bear on the ability to satisfy stated or implied needs.

Quality Circles   Small groups of employees who meet regularly to identify, and sometimes solve, work- related problems.

Quid Pro Quo   A Latin term used to describe a contractual situation in which one party gives a valuable thing in exchange for another; in sexual harassment, the acceptance or rejection of a supervisors' sexual demands or advances in determining the terms of employment.

Quick Assets   Cash or those assets the firm expects to convert to cash in the near future.

Quick Ratio   The measure of a firm's immediate liquidity; computed by dividing quick assets by current liabilities. Also called acid-test ratio.

Quota   A limit on the amount of a product that can leave or enter a country.

R

Racketeer Influenced and Corrupt Organizations Act (RICO)   An act intended to be used to help keep organized crime out of labor-management business.

Railway Labor Act   A 1926 law that established collective bargaining as a means for resolving labor management disputes.

Rank and File   A term used to refer to union workers who vote on union matters but aren't otherwise involved in union administration.

Rate of Return   The dollar value of the interest earned or dividend received divided by the market value of the security.

Ratio Analysis   Method of analyzing financial information by comparing logical relationships between various financial statement items.

Real Property   Real estate and anything permanently attached to it, such as houses, buildings, and parking lots.

Reasonable Accommodations   Owners must make an attempt to provide accommodations for people with disabilities.

Rebate   An extra discount or refund given to consumers who buy a product and supply proofs of purchase.

Recruitment   Steps taken to staff an organization with the best-qualified people.

Recycling   Reusing materials such as paper, plastic, glass, and aluminum to make other products.

Reengineering   An organizational change strategy that involves removing layers of middle managers and generally flattening the organizational hierarchy.

Rehabilitation Act of 1973   A law that protects employees with AIDS.

Reinforcer   A consequence of behavior that improves the chances it will or will not reoccur.

Reserve   The percentage of money from deposits that a bank must keep on hand or on deposit in the Federal Reserve Bank. Funds above this amount can be loaned out.

Restrictive Endorsement   An endorsement that uses the words *for deposit only* along with the signature; it states what the instrument is for and is much safer than a blank endorsement.

Retailing   The marketing activities involved in selling products to final consumers for personal or household use.

Retained Earnings   A firm's accumulated net income minus dividends to shareholders.

Retention   Refers to efforts companies take to retain productive employees.

Return on Equity   Measure of the return the company earns on every dollar of owners' and shareholders' investments; computed by dividing net income by equity.

Return on Sales   Measure of a firm's profitability, or its ability to generate income; computed by dividing net income by net sales.

Revenues   Inflows of assets resulting from the ongoing operation of the business.

Revolving Credit Agreement   A line of credit guaranteed by the bank.

Right-to-Work Laws   State laws requiring that two people doing the same job be paid the same wages, whether or not they belong to the union.

Risk   The possibility of suffering an injury or loss.

Robinson-Patman Act   Passed in 1936, an act that outlaws price discrimination that substantially reduces competition.

Robots   Computerized, reprogrammable, and multifunctional machines that can manipulate materials and objects in the performance of particular tasks.

Round Lots   Stock purchases of 100 shares.

S

S Corporation   A corporation with 35 or fewer owners that files an income tax return as a partnership to take advantage of lower tax rates.

SA8000   Social accountability workplace standard that covers labor rights and certifies compliance through independent accredited auditors.

Safety Needs   Security needs, such as the need to be financially secure and protected against job loss.

Salaries   Compensation paid to employees on a weekly or longer schedule.

Sales Branch   Manufacturer-owned wholesaler that takes title to products, assumes the risks of ownership, and provides services.

Sales Contest   A competition designed to stimulate sales efforts by salespeople, distributors, or retailers.

Sales Law   Body of law involving the sale of products for money or on credit.

Sales Office   Manufacturer-owned sales force that sells products without maintaining an inventory.

Sales Promotion   An activity that offers customers or marketing intermediaries direct incentives for purchasing a product.

Sales Tax   Tax on the merchandise consumers buy.

Savings and Loan Association (S&Ls)   Institutions that now offer both checking and savings accounts and use the majority of their funds to finance home mortgages; sometimes called thrifts.

Savings Accounts   Accounts that are easy to open but low interest returns; money can be withdrawn easily and account holders receive a summary of transactions statement monthly or quarterly.

Savings Banks   Depositor-owned, banklike institutions that began in New England in the early nineteenth century with the purpose of paying interest on deposits.

Scalar Principle   The principle of organization that authority and responsibility should flow in a clear, unbroken line from the highest to the lowest manager.

Scanlon Plan   A plan in which each department of the firm has a production committee that receives and reviews employees' and managers' suggestions for improving work practices and procedures.

Scientific Management   The scientific study and breakdown of work into its smallest mechanical elements, and their rearrangement into the most efficient combination.

Secured Bond   A bond backed by some form of collateral—specific property such as real estate, inventory, or long-term assets that would pass to the bondholders should the company not live up to the terms of the agreement.

Secured Loans   Loans backed with some form of collateral.

Securities   Documents that can be bought or sold and that reflect ownership or debt.

Securities Act of 1933   The federal law that covers the new issue of securities. The Act also requires full disclosure of information relating to the new issues and contains many antifraud provisions. It regulates the primary market to prevent fraud on the sale of securities, and it provides purchasers of new issues information.

Securities and Exchange Commission (SEC)   The federal body that governs the issuance and sale of equity securities (stocks).

Securities Exchange Act of 1934   Another "full disclosure law" that requires public corporations to provide annual financial reports to shareholders.

Securities Investor Protection Act of 1970   The act that established the Securities Investor Protection Insurance Corporation.

Securities Investor Protection Insurance Corporation   The corporation that provides insurance protection for investors who suffer losses resulting from fraud or from a broker going out of business while still owing investors money.

Segmentation Base   The individual or group characteristics that marketing managers use to divide a total market into segments.

Selection   In employment, a series of steps that starts with the initial screening and ends with a hiring decision.

Selective (Brand) Advertising   Advertising used to sell a specific product or brand.

Selective Distribution   Market coverage in which only some of the available outlets are used for distributing a product.

Self-Actualization Needs   The need to use and display one's full range of skills and competence.

Selling Expenses   Costs incurred in marketing and distributing a firm's goods and services.

Selling Process   A series of steps salespeople perform, consisting of prospecting, preparing, approaching, presenting, answering objections, closing, and following up.

Serial Bonds   Bonds that mature at different intervals from the date of issue to enable a company to pay off debt in portions.

Service Standards   Specific, measurable goals relating to physical distribution activities.

Services   In business, intangible products that cannot be physically possessed and that involve performance or effort; examples include teaching, nursing, air travel, tailoring, accounting, and the opera. In employee compensation, indirect compensation in the form of programs, facilities, or activities supplied by employers for employees' use.

Sexual Harassment   Unwelcome advances and requests for sexual favors that affect a person's performance, and a hostile work environment in which employees are subjected to sexual comments, jokes, or materials.

Sherman Antitrust Act   One of the first laws passed to regulate competition, which declared that two or more business firms could not agree to the prices to be charged for goods; also prohibited business firms from dividing markets among themselves and from deciding not to sell or to buy from a particular company.

Shopping Products   Items that buyers will expend time and effort to find and purchase.

Sinking Fund   A fund that requires that the company set aside a certain sum of money each year to "sink" the bond debt, so that the company may pay off a portion of a bond each year or accumulate funds until the bond matures.

Skill-Based Pay   A form of competency-based rewards/skilled-based plan where employees earn higher rates of pay based on the number of skill modules they have mastered

Skill Objectives   Objectives that focus on developing physical abilities.

Skills   A term that describes observable capabilities to perform a learned behavior.

Small Business   One that is independently owned and operated and is not dominant in its field of operation.

Small Business Administration (SBA)   An independent agency of the federal government created in 1953 to protect the interests of small-business owners.

Small-Business Investment Companies (SBICs)   A privately owned and operated company licensed by the SBA to furnish loans to small firms.

Social Audit   A systematic review of an organization's performance of social responsibility activities.

Social Needs   The need to belong and to interact with other people.

Social Responsibility   The awareness that business activities have an impact on society, and the consideration of that impact by firms in decision making.

Social Security   A system in which funding is provided by equal contributions from the employer and employee under terms of the Federal Insurance Contribution Act (FICA).

Software   A sequence of instructions that a computer can carry out.

Sole Proprietorship   A business owned and managed by one individual.

Span of Control   The principle of organization that limits the number of subordinates reporting to a supervisor.

Special Endorsement   An endorsement that specifies to whom the instrument is payable by including the person's or firm's name on the back of the instrument along with the signature.

Specialty Products   Products with one or more unique features that a group of buyers will spend considerable time and effort to purchase.

Specialty Stores   Retailers that offer a narrow mix of products with deep product lines.

Spreadsheets   Electronic accounting ledgers generated by computer software.

Staff Authority   An advisory authority in which a person studies a situation and makes recommendations but has no authority to take action.

Staffing   The management function of selecting, placing, training, developing, and compensating subordinates.

Standard of Living   A measure of how well a person or family is doing in terms of satisfying needs and wants with goods and services.

Statement of Cash Flows   Financial statement showing the flow of cash into and out of a business during a period of time.

Statute   A law created by a federal, state, or local legislature, treaty, or constitution.

Statutory Law   As a body, the laws enacted by federal, state, and local governments, constitutions, or treaties.

Stock Exchange   An organization of individuals who buy and sell securities to the public.

Stock Option   The purchased right to buy or sell shares of stock at a predetermined price within a specified time period.

Stockbroker   An individual licensed to act on behalf of an investor in the buying and selling of securities.

Stop-Loss Order   An order that tells your broker to sell a stock when its price hits a price on the downside.

Strategic Alliance   An agreement in which two firms combine their resources in a partnership that goes beyond a joint venture.

Strict Product Liability   Legal concept that holds manufacturers responsible for injuries caused by products regardless of whether negligence was involved.

Strike   An effort to withhold employee services so that the employer will make greater concessions at the bargaining table.

Strike Price   Refers to the price at which the holder of a stock option is able to purchase the underlying security.

Succession   Passing a business on to children.

Supercomputers   Computers formed by connecting multiple mainframes.

Supermarkets   Large, self-service retailers that stock a wide variety of groceries and a limited assortment of nonfood products.

Superstore   A giant retail outlet that stocks food and nonfood items as well as most products purchased on a routine basis.

Supply   The quantity of a product that producers will sell at various prices.

Supply Chain Management (SCM)   The process of managing the flow of materials, parts, work in progress, finished goods, the return of goods, and information by coordinating activities of all the organizations in the chain.

Support Salespeople   Salespeople who assist in selling by locating potential customers, educating them about products, building goodwill, and providing after-sales service.

Sweepstakes   A sales promotion method in which consumers enter a drawing for prizes.

Sweetheart Contracts   Agreements between union leaders and management to terms that work to their mutual benefit but maintain poor working conditions for other employees.

Syndicate   Two or more businesses joined together to accomplish specific business goals; a popular form in underwriting large amounts of corporation stocks.

T

Taft-Hartley Act   A 1947 labor law that prohibits the closed shop, requires unions to bargain in good faith, and makes it illegal for a union to discriminate against employees who don't join the union.

Tangible Personal Property   Physical items, such as goods and equipment.

Target Market   A group to which a firm directs its marketing activities.

Tax   A payment for the support of government activities, required of organizations and individuals within the domain of the government.

Tax Reform Act of 1986   A law with provisions that affect indirect compensation.

Technical Skill   Skill involved in making a product or providing a service.

Term Insurance   Life insurance that covers an individual for a specified number of years but has no value when the term is over.

Term Loan Agreement   A promissory note that requires a borrower to repay a loan according to a schedule of specified installments at either a fixed or flexible rate of interest.

Territorial (Geographical) Structure   An organizational structure in which units are divided on the basis of territory or geographical region.

Theory X   Managerial assumptions that employees dislike work, responsibility, and accountability and must be closely directed and controlled to be motivated to perform.

Theory Y   Managerial assumptions that employees want to be challenged, like to display creativity, and can be highly motivated to perform well if given some freedom to direct or manage their own behavior.

Theory Z   Management theory that draws on the characteristics of successful Japanese and American managers; emphasizes consensus management practices.

Ticker Symbol   The symbol by which a company is represented on a stock exchange.

Time Deposits   Savings accounts that allow the financial institution to require notice before withdrawal or to assess a penalty for early withdrawal.

Times-Interest-Earned Ratio   The measure of how many times during the year a business earns the amount of interest it must pay; computed by dividing income before interest and taxes by interest expense.

Title VII   Part of the Civil Service Reform Act of 1978; outlawed certain unfair labor practices and created the Federal Labor Relations Authority (FLRA); granted covered employees the right to form, join, or assist any labor organization or to refrain from such activity freely and without reprisals.

Tort A noncriminal (civil) injury to other persons or their property or reputation; results from intentional acts or negligence.

Total Market Approach The tactic of developing one marketing mix for the total market for a product. Also called undifferentiated approach.

Trade Allowances Discounts a manufacturer gives for performing certain functions or making purchases during a specified time period.

Trade Credit Credit given by suppliers for the purchases the firm makes from these suppliers.

Trade Sales Promotion Activities a firm directs to wholesalers, retailers, or salespeople to encourage them to stock or sell its products.

Trade Shows Temporary exhibits where manufacturers display products to potential customers and gather names for a list of prospects.

Trademark A name or symbol, registered with the U.S. Patent and Trademark Office, that guarantees the owner exclusive rights to its use.

Trading Company A firm that buys products in one country and sells in another without being involved in manufacturing.

Trading Stamps Tokens given out by retailers based on the amount of purchase; redeemable for gifts.

Training A continual process of helping employees perform at a high level.

Transistor A small switch that controls electrical current; characterized second-generation computers.

Transportation Shipping goods to customers by railways, airlines, trucks, waterways, and pipelines.

Treasury Bill A loan to the U.S. Treasury that typically has a maturity date of three or six months; often called a T-bill.

U

Understudy Programs Programs in which a person works as a subordinate partner with a boss, with the goal of eventually assuming the full responsibilities and duties of the job.

Underwriting Includes all activities necessary to select risks offered to the insurer in such a manner that general company objectives are fulfilled; the main objective is to see that the applicant accepted will not have a loss experience that is very different from that assumed when the rates were formulated.

Undue Hardship Refers to provisions in the Americans with Disabilities Act that state that accommodations for people with disabilities should not require the business to experience excessive hardship.

Unemployment Compensation Benefits given when a person loses a job, to be jointly administered by the federal and state governments.

Uniform Commercial Code (UCC) Comprehensive statutory laws designed to eliminate differences between state laws governing business.

Union-Management Contract An agreement that designates the formal terms reached in collective bargaining

Union Racketeering Refers to illegal business activities such as loansharking, extortion, and bribery.

Union Shop A company that requires employees to join the union after being hired.

Union Steward A person who represents the interests of local union members in their on-the-job relations with managers.

Unissued Stock Shares that have been authorized by a company but that remain in its treasury to be issued at a future date.

Unity of Command The principle of organization that no employee should report to more than one superior.

Unlimited Liability Obligation of investors to use personal assets, when necessary, to pay off debts to business creditors; a disadvantage of sole proprietorships and partnerships.

Unsecured Loans Loans issued on the good credit of the borrower and requiring no collateral.

U.S. Savings Bonds Bonds issued by the U.S. government. The money paid for the bond helps pay to finance the United States borrowing needs.

Utilitarian Philosophy A set of moral principles focusing on the greatest good for the largest number of people.

Utility The ability of a product to satisfy consumers' needs.

V

Venture Capital Funds provided by individuals or organizations to new firms with high potential for growth; the investor receives a share of the ownership and frequently a share of control.

Vertical Integration The combining of two or more functions of a marketing channel under one management.

Vertical Marketing System (VMS) A marketing channel in which the different intermediaries are coordinated through management to improve distribution.

Vertical Merger A merger in which a firm joins with its supplier.

Very Large-Scale Integration (VLSI) Superchip circuitry, resulting from extremely compact transistors and circuits assembled on a single silicon chip; marked start of fifth generation of computers.

Vestibule Training Training in a mock-up or simulation of the actual work area.

Viral Marketing A concept that ranges from paying people to say positive things on the Internet to setting up multilevel selling approaches for directing people to specific websites.

Virtual Organization An organization that operates across space, time, and boundaries with members who communicate primarily through electronic technologies.

W

Wages A traditional payment method based on an hourly or daily rate.

Wagner Act A law that made collective bargaining legal and required employers to bargain with the representatives of the employees. The law is also referred to as the National Labor Relations Act.

Warehouse Clubs Large discount retail stores offering members a broad range of name-brand merchandise at low prices.

Warehouse Showrooms Retail stores carrying large inventories that deal in volume and provide limited services.

Warehousing   The physical distribution activities involved in receiving, storing, and shipping goods.

Wheel of Retailing   The idea that retailers enter the market as low-priced, low-status businesses, evolve into high-cost establishments, and become vulnerable to new competitors entering the market.

Wheeler-Lea Amendment   An amendment that expanded the FTC's power to eliminate deceptive business practices, including those affecting consumers as well as competitors.

Whistle-Blower   An employee who informs superiors, the media, or a government regulatory agency about unethical behavior within an organization.

Whole Life Insurance   Provides a combination of insurance and savings and stays in force for the life of the insured.

Wholesaling   The marketing activities of intermediaries who sell to retailers, industrial users, and other organizational customers.

Word Processing   Creating written documents with a computer.

Work Motivation Model   An explanation of motivation that defines hygiene factors and motivator factors, and how they affect job satisfaction and dissatisfaction.

Worker Adjustment and Retraining Notification Act (WARN)   Commonly referred to as the *Plant Closing Bill*, an act that requires employers with 100 or more full-time employees to give affected employees sixty days' written notice of plant or office closing or other mass layoffs.

Workers' Compensation   Benefits provided for temporary and permanent disability, disfigurement, medical expenses, and medical rehabilitation.

Working Capital   Measure of a firm's ability to meet short-term obligation; computed as current assets minus current liabilities.

World Bank   An international organization that lends money to underdeveloped and developing countries for development.

World Trade Organization (WTO)   Headquartered in Geneva, Switzerland, created by the GATT to mediate and resolve trade disputes.

Y

Yellow-Dog Contract   A statement signed by an employee promising not to form or join a union.

Company Index

Note: Page numbers in italics identify an illustration. An italic *t* next to a page number (e.g., 177*t*) indicates information that appears in a table.

Name Index

Subject Index

Note: Page numbers in italics identify information that appears in illustrations. An italic *t* next to a page number (e.g., 177*t*) indicates information that appears in a table.